THE DOW JONES

INVESTOR'S HANDBOOK

1990

THE DOW JONES

INVESTOR'S HANDBOOK

1990

Edited by PHYLLIS S. PIERCE

Dow Jones–Irwin
Homewood, Illinois 60430

ISBN 1-55623-309-4

Library of Congress Catalog Card No. 82-71541

Printed in the United States of Amercia

1 2 3 4 5 6 7 8 9 0 K 7 6 5 4 3 2 1 0

Contents

New Decade, Old Expansion

THE DECADE MAY BE spanking new, but when the 1990s dawned the economy's remarkable expansion since the near end of 1982 was already the second oldest upturn in the long history of the American business cycle—and it looked the part.

When it crossed the seven-year mark last November, the expansion was surpassed only by the 106-month upturn of the Soaring Sixties. But the feat was hardly effortless. There was much huffing and puffing along the way, and a good deal of speculation among economic forecasters about whether, at long last, a new recession might be imminent.

Still, as a new decade now begins to unfold, the consensus is that a bona fide recession is not about to set in—but please say a prayer for it may turn out to be a very near thing.

As late as the third quarter of 1989, the economy still was expanding at a perfectly respectable pace of about 3% annually, or close to its average yearly rate of gain over the full course of the 20th century. But in the closing few months 1989, as the old decade faded, the pace of overall business activity appeared to slacken to the point where talk of an approaching recession could no longer be dismissed as simply more lugubriousness from perennial mongers of doom-and-gloom.

However, as Alexander Pope long ago observed, hope springs eternal in the human breast, which may account in part for the fact that most forecasters anticipate a recession-free year. Besides hope, however, there appear to be a number of convincing economic reasons for the optimism.

Reasonably typical of the prevailing view is the assessment supplied by the group of prominent forecasters, 51 in all, who are polled regularly by Blue Chip Economic Indicator, a Sedona, Ariz., newsletter. These expert seers reckon, on the average, that economic growth—as reflected in the "real" or inflation-adjusted gross national product—will expand at a slowly accelerating rate as 1990 goes along. The pace will be snail-like for the first half, but will show modest improvement as 1991 draws near.

After a projected first-quarter gain of only 1.3% annually, the Blue Chip group anticipates growth of 1.7% in the second quarter, 2.0% in the third quarter and 2.4% in the fourth.

If the economy does in fact continue to expand in such a fashion in the year ahead, there should be varied accompanying developments, some beneficial and some unwelcome—though less so than if a recession were to intrude.

Among the major benefits anticipated is that a sluggish pace of business activity will serve to keep inflation in check. The Blue Chip consensus, for example, calls for inflation to hold steady at about 4% annually throughout 1990. This would mark a clear improvement over the recent pattern of price acceleration. Between early 1988 and mid-1989, consumer-price inflation accelerated from 3.9% annually to 6.4% and the rate of increase for the so-called GNP price deflator, a more comprehensive inflation gauge, accelerated from 2.0% to 4.6%.

With sluggish growth and inflation under control, most forecasters look for interest rates to be reasonably stable, more likely in fact to edge lower than higher. By and large, the guessing is that a sluggish economy, however unsettling it may be in some respects, will prompt the Federal Reserve Board to pursue a somewhat less restrictive monetary policy than if the expansion were to proceed brisky in coming months and in the process strain limited resources of labor and materials.

The Blue Chip consensus foresees rates on three-month Treasury bills, for example, declining modestly early in the new year and then remaining in the neighborhood of 7% or so, and the expected pattern for rates of top-graded corporate bonds is similar, with the level settling between 8.6% and 8.8%.

A sluggish economy, in addition, should bring with it at least a modest improvement in the sagging foreign-trade account. In the past, when economic activity has slowed at home, producers naturally have tried harder to take up the slack through greater efforts to sell abroad. By the same token, imports have naturally tended to diminish as domestic demand has slowed.

Richard B. Hoey, the chief economist of the New York-based securities firm of Drexel Burnham Lambert Inc., predicts that "the drop in imports should be quite substantial" in 1990. With the pronounced slowing of the economy that he expects, he foresees a 9% decline in import volume between the fourth quarter of 1989 and the fourth quarter of 1990.

The Blue Chip consensus reflects the widespread belief that the trade deficit will diminish appreciably in the new year, with the shortfall shrinking progressively from a projected level of nearly $58 billion in the first quarter to $56.1 billion in the second quarter, $55.2 billion in the third and $54.3 billion in the fourth. That would remain a lamentably large trade gap, but would nevertheless constitute a vast improvement over the quarterly deficits of close to $80 billion recorded during Ronald Reagan's final presidential year.

Unfortunately, a sluggish economy suggests to most forecasters, along with such benefits, developments that are a good deal less appetizing. For one thing, unemployment is likely to edge higher, which would mark an unhappy reversal of the remarkable shrinkage in the jobless level since the severe recession of 1981-82.

As low as 5.2% of the labor force in the third quarter of 1989, the unemployment rate, according to the Blue Chip consensus, will slowly rise in the first half of 1990, reaching perhaps 5.6% by mid-year, and then the rate will stick at the higher level until at least the start of 1991.

Still, this would be only about half as high as the jobless rate of 11% reached in late 1982, at the pit of the last recession. As recently as late 1986, after fully four years of brisk economic growth, more than 7% of the labor force remained unemployed.

In addition, corporate profits, which fell in 1989 despite the econony's persistent growth, will probably decline again in 1990. The Blue Chip group looks for a drop of 1% or so in the pretax profit total, for example, reflecting an anticipated speedup in the rise of labor costs, as well as the depressing effect of a sluggish economy on productivity, which the group expects will rise only six-tenths of a percent in 1990.

It is partly through productivity gains that corporations manage to offset their employees' yearly pay increases. The other approach, of course, is to raise prices, but this can be difficult when business is lackluster.

Troubles are also expected to continue plaguing such key industries as autos and housing, which already were experiencing difficulties in 1989.

The Blue Chip consensus expects sales of both domestic and imported cars to decline slightly in 1990 and housing starts to show little change for the year.

Weighing on both industries, analysts say, is a somewhat more restrained consumer mood after the freewheeling Reagan years. More emphasis is expected to be placed on saving, and less on spending. Indeed, most forecasters expect savings, in terms of after-tax income, to remain above the 5% mark through most of the new year. In Mr. Reagan's presidency, by comparison, this rate occasionally fell below 3%.

An additional weight on housing activity in particular, it should be added, will surely be the government's massive forced sales of real estate assumed as a part of the federal bailout of the tottering savings-and-loan industry. On Jan. 3, 1990, The Wall Street Journal reported that some 30,000 properties were owned as of Sept. 30, 1989, by the Resolution Trust Corp., the federal agency formed to sell insolvent S&Ls and their assets. This large number, the paper added, did not include "thousands more properties" seized after the September date, as well as others "still in foreclosure proceedings."

Economists who take a somewhat more sanguine view of the outlook for 1990 than the Blue Chip consensus tend to place a greater emphasis on such beneficial developments as the likelihood of stable-to-lower interest rates. This prospect suggests, in the optimists' view, a reinvigoration of economic activity in general, and especially of the troubled real-estate sector.

Conversely, economists who maintain a relatively pessimistic position are generally skeptical that the anticipated interest-rate stability will be sufficient to reverse the economy's increased sluggishness. They sense that the economic die is largely cast, so that even a pronounced monetary easing by a Federal Reserve wary of a new recession will be insufficient to the task. The Fed, they say, will be pushing on a string.

A proponent of the relatively optimistic view is Robert J. Genetski of the Chicago-based consulting firm of Stotler Economics. "Although the U.S. economy begins the 1990s on the verge of a recession," he says, "prospects for future growth are good." He attributes current weakness to "past monetary restraint" by the Fed. However, he adds that this restraint "has set the stage for lower inflation," and he is confident that in coming months, "as the Fed continues to relax its tight-money stance, economic growth will return." Indeed, he declares that "the march toward further economic prosperity is on track and set to continue."

A far less sanguine appraisal comes from Maury Harris, chief economist of the investment firm of Paine Webber Inc. in New York. He worries that the Fed may indeed be attempting to push with the use of only a string—an obviously impossible undertaking. He warns that the housing sector, for instance, is fundamentally "weak and won't respond much to lower rates." He points to high and rising home-vacancy rates and extensive "price weakness for existing homes" —developments likely to discourage further building.

A related concern is that price weakness in housing may also inhibit consumer spending, which accounts for roughly two-thirds of the gross national product. During the steep climb in housing prices in recent years, consumers came to regard their homes as nest eggs whose value would inexorably rise. In the process, many people were willing to save less income than in earlier post-World War II years.

Norman Robertson, the chief economist of Mellon Bank in Pittsburgh, attempts to balance the various pluses and minuses in the 1990 picture with this assessment:

"Notwithstanding all the uncertainties in the outlook, I remain cautiously optimistic about 1990. Not a banner year, perhaps, especially for real estate and a sizable part of the manufacturing sector, but the economy as a whole should continue to advance—albeit at a subpar rate—through the coming year. I expect that the current expansion will still be alive to celebrate its eighth birthday in November 1990."

Mr. Robertson adds that "consumers may be more cautious, increasingly selective and extremely price conscious," but this does not mandate the sort of "major retrenchment in outlays that might plunge the economy into a recession." Despite a "widely publicized slump in car sales," he says, "sales of department-store type merchandise—an important measure of discretionary outlays—have trended upward at a robust rate and spending on services has continued to climb briskly."

Lacy Hunt, the chief economist of the New York-based investment firm of Carroll McEntee & McGinley, shares the view that consumers will help fuel the expansion as the year goes along. He notes that after-tax income, adjusted for inflation and for so-called transfer payments, such as unemployment compensation and food stamps, has continued to climb briskly, for all the concern about consumers becoming strapped.

Normally, this key measure of consumer wherewithal has leveled off or begun to fall when an economic expansion is ending. But this was hardly the situation as the new year started. The income gauge was swiftly approaching $2.5 trillion, in terms of the dollar's 1982 buying power. This was a record, up sharply from $1.8 trillion a decade earlier.

Mr. Hunt also notes that various surveys show the general level of consumer confidence, while no longer rising sharply, to be holding at relatively high levels, which suggests sustained spending in coming months. Yet another precursor of persistent strength in the consumer sector, he adds, is the record percentage of the working-age population holding jobs. Much like the income gauge, this barometer—which economists call the employment ratio—usually wobbles

7

and falls near the end of an expansion. But lately it has increased steadily, reaching 64%, up from 57% early in the expansion.

With his scenario of a recession-free 1990, it is not surprising that Mr. Hunt is mildly optimistic about the stock market as an investment avenue.

For all its volatility from day to day and week to week, the stock market is still considered by most forecasters to be a usually reliable indicator of the economy's general course. Despite its woefully misleading performance when it crashed with no ensuing recession in October 1987, the stock market is still rated a key component of the Commerce Department's widely followed index of leading economic indicators.

Since a recession is still not in sight, in Mr. Hunt's view, share prices seem likelier to rise than fall in coming months. "In the very first week of the new year," he recalls, the Dow Jones Industrial Average reached a new high, which "hardly seems consistent with the notion that a recession may be at hand."

Tempering his optimism, however, is a suspicion that inflation may prove somewhat more intense than most forecasters anticipate. This, in turn, suggests to him modestly rising interest rates and slightly lower bond prices—a combination that eventually could drag down share prices as well.

Another potential depressant on share prices, of course, is the possibility that corporate profits will continue weak, as the Blue Chip consensus believes. After all, profits, and the dividends that they ultimately supply, are a crucial factor in the long-term price trend of a share of stock. Even so, the fact is that most share prices rose appreciably in 1989, while overall profits, as we have seen, edged down.

With the dawn of a new decade, it should be added, many forecasters are attempting gingerly to gauge the economy's longer-range prospects.

Risky at any time, efforts to peer much beyond the year ahead are doubly hazardous when, as now, enormous political and economic changes, such as are sweeping Eastern Europe and Russia, are under way around the world. Adding to the uncertainty is an awareness that the economy has expanded for well over seven years now, which is more than twice the average length for an upswing of the business cycle. By the law of averages, a recession is long overdue.

There is uncertainty as well about the impact of the unprecedented amounts of debt left over from the Reagan years.

Some economists maintain that the burden of servicing past borrowing will surely hobble business activity as the decade unfolds. David Bostian, the chief economist of the New York brokerage house of Jesup & Lamont, even suggests that the economy's vast debt overlay has somehow reduced the reliability of many statistical barometers that forecasters use in their crystal balls, making the indicators seem more favorable than conditions warrant.

Other analysts argue, however, that the debt buildup, as huge as it may be, poses no significant threat to the economy's continued growth. This contingent includes such respected economists as Robert Heilbroner of the New School in New York and Robert Eisner of Northwestern University in Evanston, Ill. Mr. Eisner claims, for example, that the way in which the federal government keeps its books makes federal debt seem unduly large.

Among the bold souls willing to look beyond the year ahead is Charles B. Reeder, a former chief economist of Du Pont Co. who now runs a consulting firm bearing his name in Wilmington, Del. In the new decade, he predicts, "economic growth will be significantly below the strong 4% average rate that prevailed" in recent years.

This anticipated slowing, he believes, will reflect several factors.

The economy has less slack in it now than in the early 1980s, when unemployment reached 11%. Further growth, accordingly, will come less easily. Demographics dictate, moreover, that the labor force will expand more slowly in the 1990s; there was a 16% drop in the number of births between 1965 and 1975. With the recent easing in East-West tensions, in addition, federal outlays for defense are likely to decline in the new decade. Also, the large amount of debt outstanding, particularly among households, seems bound to restrict new spending.

There is little doubt that debt has risen steeply. Total debt—of government, businesses and consumers—came to more than 180% of the gross national product at the start of 1990, up from about 140% a decade earlier.

On a somewhat happier note, Mr. Reeder expects that the dollar in the 1990s "will be more stable than it was in the 1980s." From mid-1980 to early 1985 the dollar soared over 50% in terms of a trade-weighted basket of other key currencies, and then, from early 1985 to the end of 1987, it plunged by more than one-third.

"The dollar appears to be in rough equilibrium today," the forecaster says, and its "fluctuations over the next several years should be in a fairly narrow range." Forces tending to lend support to the dollar's international worth, he says, include the prospect of a slowly narrowing trade deficit and the likelihood that inflation will "remain under control."

With defense spending declining and tax receipts rising along with the anticipated growth of income, Mr. Reeder also looks for a continuing, gradual reduction of the still-huge federal budget deficit. This, in turn, should bring somewhat lower interest rates, he says. And with lower interest rates, he predicts, "the Federal Reserve may be able to pursue a less restrictive monetary policy in the 1990s."

In all, he says, the new decade "looks pretty good," with the most "significant development" likely to be "the increasing extent to which the performance of the U.S. economy will be affected by policies and business decisions in the global marketplace."

First, of course, the economy must make its way safely through 1990, and in this regard it is encouraging to find that most forecasters believe the passage, though hazardous, will prove recession-free.

—ALFRED L. MALABRE JR.

Mr. Malabre is a Wall Street Journal editor and columnist, based in New York, as well as the author of five books on economics, including UNDERSTANDING THE NEW ECONOMY, published last year in hardcover by Dow Jones-Irwin and recently in paperback by New American Library.

Stock and Bond Yields

Monthly averages, in percent. ●Bonds ▬DJIA

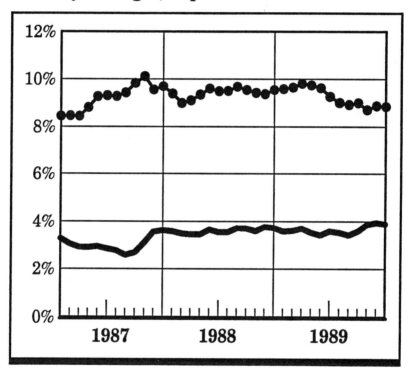

The Dow Jones Averages

The Dow Jones Stock Averages are compiled daily by using the New York Stock Exchange only closing prices and adjusting by the then current appropriate average divisor. The divisor for the Industrial Average is 0.586; Transportation, 0.703; Utilities, 1.988; 65 Stocks, 2.810. A list of the stocks on which these averages are based follows:

30 Industrial Stocks

Allied-Signal	Exxon	Philip Morris
Alcoa	General Electric	Primerica
American Express	General Motors	Procter & Gamble
AT&T	Goodyear	Sears Roebuck
Bethlehem Steel	IBM	Texaco
Boeing	Inter Paper	USX Corp.
Chevron	McDonald's	Union Carbide
Coca-Cola	Merck	United Technologies
Du Pont	Minnesota M&M	Westinghouse Electric
Eastman Kodak	Navistar Inter	Woolworth

20 Transportation Stocks

Airborn Freight	Consolidated Freight	Santa Fe So Pacific
Alaska Air	Consolidated Rail	Southwest Airl
AMR Corp.	Delta Air Lines	UAL
Amer President	Federal Express	Union Pac Corp.
Burlington North	Norfolk Southern	USAir Group
CSX Corp.	Pan Am Corp.	XTRA
Carolina Freight	Ryder System	

15 Utility Stocks

Amer. Elec. Power	Consol. Nat. Gas	Panhandle Eastern
Centerior Energy	Detroit Edison	Peoples Energy
Columbia Gas Sys.	Houston Indus.	Philadelphia Elec.
Com'wealth Edison	Niagara Mohawk Pr.	Pub. Ser. Enterp.
Consol. Edison	Pacific Gas & El.	SCE Corp.

The Dow Jones Averages

20 Bonds

The Dow Jones Bond Averages are a simple arithmetic average compiled daily by using the New York Exchange closing bond prices. A list of the bonds on which these averages are based follows:

10 PUBLIC UTILITIES

	Coupon	Age		Coupon	Age
Alabama Power	9¾s	2004	Detroit Edison	9s	1999
Am T&T deb.	8.8s	2005	Mich Bell	7s	2012
Commonwealth Edison	8¾s	2005	Pacific G&E	7¾s	2005
Consolidated Edison	7.9s	2001	Philadelphia Elec.	7⅜s	2001
Consumers Power	9¾s	2006	Public Service (Ind.)	9.6s	2005

10 INDUSTRIALS

	Coupon	Age		Coupon	Age
BankAmerica	7⅞s	2003	General Elec	8½s	2004
Beth Steel	6⅞s	1999	GM Acceptance	12s	2005
Eastman	8⅝s	2016	IBM	9⅜s	2004
Exxon	6s	1997	Socony Mobil	4¼s	1993
Ford Motor	8⅛s	1990	Weyerhaeuser	5.20s	1991

A list of Bonds on which the Confidence Index is based follows:

Barron's Best Grade Bonds

	Coupon	Age		Coupon	Age
Amer. Tel. & Tel.	8¾s	2000	Gen Elec	8½s	2004
Anheuser-Busch	8⅝s	2016	GMAC	8¼s	2006
Balt G&E	8⅜s	2006	IBM	9⅜s	2004
DuPont	8½s	2006	Ill Bell Tel	7⅝s	2006
Exxon Pipeline	8¼s	2001	Proc. & G	8¼s	2005

Barron's Intermediate Grade Bonds

	Coupon	Age		Coupon	Age
Alabama Power	9¾s	2004	GTE	9⅜s	1999
Beneficial Corp	9s	2005	Honeywell	9⅜s	2009
Cater Trac	8s	2001	Union Carbide	8½s	2005
Comwlth Edison	9⅛s	2008	USX Corp.	7¾s	2001
Firestone	9¼s	2004	Woolworth	9s	1999

Commodity Futures

The Dow Jones Commodity Futures Index is compiled daily by using the following commodities:

Cattle	Cotton	Silver
Coffee	Gold	Soybeans
Copper	Hogs	Sugar
Corn	Lumber	Wheat

Changes in Dow Jones Industrials

The present Dow Jones industrial average of 30 stocks began October 1, 1928, when the list was expanded to 30 from 20 and several substitutions were made. On October 1, 1928, the stocks making up the industrial average were:

Allied Chemical	General Railway Signal	Sears, Roebuck
American Can	Goodrich	Standard Oil (N.J.)
American Smelting	International Harvester	Texas Corp.
American Sugar	International Nickel	Texas Gulf Sulphur
American Tobacco B	Mack Truck	Union Carbide
Atlantic Refining	Nash Motors	U.S. Steel
Bethlehem Steel	North American	Victor Talking Machine
Chrysler	Paramount Publix	Westinghouse Electric
General Electric	Postum Inc.	Woolworth
General Motors	Radio Corp.	Wright Aeronautical

The divisor on October 1, 1928, was 16.67.

Subsequent changes in stocks making up the industrial average and changes in the divisor, together with the dates, were:

Date		Divisor	Explanation
1928 November	5	16.02	Atlantic Refining Split 4 for 1
December	13	14.65	General Motors split 2½ for 1
			International Harvester split 4 for 1
December	26	13.92	International Nickel reorganization
1929 January	8	12.11	American Smelting split 3 for 1
			Radio Corp. split 5 for 1
			National Cash Register replaced Victor Talking Machine
May	1	11.7	Wright-Aeronautical split 2 for 1
May	20	11.18	Union Carbide split 3 for 1
June	25	10.77	Woolworth split 2½ for 1
July	25	10.77	Postum name changed to General Foods
September	14	10.47	Curtiss-Wright replaced Wright Aeronautical
1930 January	29	9.85	General Electric split 4 for 1
			Johns-Manville replaced North American
July	18	10.38	Borden replaced American Sugar
			Eastman Kodak replaced American Tobacco B
			Goodyear replaced Atlantic Refining
			Liggett & Myers replaced General Railway Signal
			Standard Oil of California replaced Goodrich
			United Air Transport replaced Nash Motors
			Hudson Motor replaced Curtiss-Wright
1932 May	26	15.46	American Tobacco B replaced Liggett & Myers
			Drug Inc. replaced Mack Trucks
			Procter & Gamble replaced United Air Transport
			Loew's replaced Paramount Publix
			Nash Motors replaced Radio Corp.
			International Shoe replaced Texas Gulf Sulphur

Changes in Dow Jones Industrials

Date		Divisor	Explanation
1932 May	26	15.46	International Business Machines replaced National Cash Register
			Coca Cola replaced Hudson Motor
1933 August	15	15.71	Corn Products Refining replaced Drug Inc.
			United Aircraft replaced International Shoe
1934 August	13	15.74	National Distillers replaced United Aircraft
1935 November	20	15.1	DuPont replaced Borden
			National Steel replaced Coca Cola
1937 January	8	15.1	Nash Motors name changed to Nash Kelvinator
1939 March	14	15.1	United Aircraft replaced Nash Kelvinator
			American Tel. & Tel. replaced I.B.M.
1945 May	10	14.8	Loew's Inc. split 3 for 1
May	11	14.2	Westinghouse Mfg. split 4 for 1
October	23	13.6	Sears Roebuck split 4 for 1
1946 August	1	13.3	National Distillers split 3 for 1
1947 May	16	12.2	Eastman Kodak split 5 for 1
June	2	11.76	Johns-Manville split 3 for 1
July	14	11.44	Chrysler Corp. split 2 for 1
December	3	11.36	American Smelting 20% stock dividend
1948 January	19	10.98	Bethlehem Steel split 3 for 1
May	17	10.55	Union Carbide split 3 for 1
June	7	10.20	International Harvester split 3 for 1
November	26	10.14	National Steel 10% stock dividend
1949 June	3	9.88	U.S. Steel split 3 for 1
June	16	9.06	DuPont split 4 for 1
1950 March	22	8.92	Procter & Gamble split 1½ for 1
March	31	8.57	National Steel split 3 for 1
September	5	7.76	Allied Chemical split 4 for 1
October	3	7.54	General Motors split 2 for 1
1951 March	12	7.36	Standard Oil of California split 2 for 1
May	2	7.33	United Aircraft 20% stock dividend
June	12	7.14	Texas Corp. split 2 for 1
June	13	6.90	Standard Oil (N.J.) split 2 for 1
September	11	6.72	Goodyear split 2 for 1
December	3	6.53	American Smelting split 2 for 1
1952 May	2	6.16	American Can split 2 for 1; 100% stock dividend
1954 June	14	5.92	General Electric split 3 for 1
July	1	5.89	United Aircraft distributed 1 share of Chance-Vought for every 3 United Aircraft held
1955 January	24	5.76	Goodyear split 2 for 1
May	23	5.62	Corn Products Refining split 3 for 1
June	3	5.52	U.S. Steel split 2 for 1
September	26	5.46	United Aircraft 50% stock dividend (3 for 2)
November	10	5.26	General Motors split 3 for 1
December	19	5.11	Sears Roebuck split 3 for 1
1956 March	19	4.89	Standard Oil (N.J.) split 3 for 1
March	26	4.79	Johns-Manville split 2 for 1
June	8	4.69	General Foods split 2 for 1
June	11	4.56	Texas Co. split 2 for 1
June	18	4.452	Standard Oil (Calif.) split 2 for 1

Changes in Dow Jones Industrials

Date		Divisor	Explanation
1956 June	25	4.351	Procter & Gamble split 2 for 1
July	3	4.581	International Paper replaced Loew's Inc.
September	11	4.566	American Tel & Tel rights offering (1 share for each 10 held)
1957 February	7	4.283	Bethlehem Steel split 4 for 1
November	18	4.257	United Aircraft 20% stock dividend (6 for 5)
1959 April	14	4.13	Eastman Kodak split 2 for 1
June	1	3.964	American Tel & Tel split 3 for 1
			Anaconda replaced American Smelting
			Swift & Co. replaced Corn Products
			Aluminum Co. of America replaced National Steel
			Owens-Illinois Glass replaced National Distillers
December	29	3.824	Goodyear split 3 for 1
1960 January	25	3.739	Allied Chemical split 2 for 1
February	2	3.659	Westinghouse Electric split 2 for 1
May	3	3.569	American Tobacco split 2 for 1
May	31	3.48	International Nickel split 2 for 1
August	24	3.38	General Foods split 2 for 1
December	30	3.28	International Paper Co. split 3 for 1
1961 April	10	3.165	Procter & Gamble split 2 for 1
August	11	3.09	Texaco split 2 for 1
1962 May	1	3.03	American Tobacco split 2 for 1
June	5	2.988	DuPont distributed ½ share of General Motors
1963 May	13	2.914	Chrysler Corp. split 2 for 1
November	21	2.876	DuPont distributed 36-100 share General Motors stock for each share of DuPont common held
1964 January	13	2.822	Chrysler Corp. split 2 for 1
June	18	2.754	F. W. Woolworth split 3 for 1
June	23	2.670	American Tel & Tel split 2 for 1
November	19	2.615	DuPont distributed ½ share of General Motors
1965 March	23	2.543	Sears Roebuck split 2 for 1
April	12	2.499	International Harvester split 2 for 1
May	24	2.410	Eastman Kodak split 2 for 1
June	1	2.348	Owens-Illinois Glass split 2 for 1
June	16	2.278	Union Carbide split 2 for 1
November	1	2.245	United Aircraft split 3 for 2
1967 June	6	2.217	Swift split 2 for 1
June	12	2.163	Anaconda split 2 for 1
1968 May	27	2.078	Eastman Kodak split 2 for 1
August	19	2.011	International Nickel split 2½ for 1
1969 April	1	1.967	Johns-Manville split 2 for 1
May	7	1.934	Goodyear split 2 for 1
August	11	1.894	Texaco split 2 for 1
1970 May	19	1.826	Procter & Gamble split 2 for 1
1971 March	30	1.779	General Foods split 2 for 1
June	8	1.712	General Electric split 2 for 1
December	16	1.661	Westinghouse Electric split 2 for 1
1972 November	1	1.661	Standard Oil (N.J.) name changed to Exxon
1973 May	30	1.661	Swift name changed to Esmark
December	11	1.626	Standard Oil (Calif.) split 2 for 1
1974 February	4	1.598	Aluminum Co. of America split 3 for 2
1975 May	1	1.598	United Aircraft name changed to

Changes in Dow Jones Industrials

Date		Divisor	Explanation
1975 May	1	1.598	United Aircraft name changed to United Technologies
October	1	1.588	Esmark split 5 for 4
1976 April	21	1.588	International Nickel name changed to Inco
May	19	1.554	United Technologies split 2 for 1
June	2	1.527	U.S. Steel split 3 for 2
July	26	1.473	Exxon split 2 for 1
August	9	1.504	Minnesota Mining & Manufacturing replaced Anaconda
1977 April	11	1.474	Owens-Illinois split 2 for 1
July	18	1.443	Sears, Roebuck split 2 for 1
1979 June	29	1.465	International Business Machines replaced Chrysler
			Merck replaced Esmark
			DuPont split 3 for 1
1981 February	23	1.431	Aluminum Co. of America split 2 for 1
March	11	1.388	Standard Oil (Calif.) split 2 for 1
May	26	1.348	American Brands split 2 for 1
June	12	1.314	Exxon Corp. split 2 for 1
1982 August	30	1.359	American Express Co. replaced Manville Corp.
1983 February	11	1.344	American Express Co. split 4 for 3
February	22	1.292	Procter & Gamble split 2 for 1
June	2	1.248	General Electric split 2 for 1
August	11	1.230	American Express Co. split 3 for 2
1984 January	4	1.194	"New" AT&T replaced "Old" AT&T
May	30	1.160	Allied Corp. split 3 for 2
			Westinghouse Electric split 2 for 1
June	11	1.132	United Technologies split 2 for 1
July	2	1.132	Standard Oil (Calif.) name changed to Chevron
1985 May	20	1.116	Eastman Kodak split 3 for 2
September	19	1.116	Allied Corp. name changed to Allied-Signal Inc.
October	30	1.090	Philip Morris Cos. replaced General Foods Corp.
			McDonald's Corp. was substituted for American Brands Inc.
1986 February	20	1.090	International Harvester name changed to Navister International Corp.
March	4	1.044	Union Carbide split 3 for 1
April	11	1.008	Philip Morris split 2 for 1
May	27	0.956	Merck split 2 for 1
May	28	0.953	Distribution of one share of Henley Group Inc. common for each four shares of Allied-Signal common held.
May	30	0.929	F.W. Woolworth split 2 for 1
June	17	0.908	Owen-Illinois split 2 for 1
June	26	0.889	McDonald's split 3 for 2
July	8	0.889	U.S. Steel name changed to USX Corp.

Changes in Dow Jones Industrials

Date		Divisor	Explanation
1987 March	12	0.901	Coca-Cola Co. replaced Owens-Illinois Inc. Boeing Co. replaced Inco Ltd.
March	13	0.880	American Can Co. split 2 for 1
April	29	0.880	American Can Co. name changed to Primerica Corp.
May	11	0.866	American Express split 2 for 1
May	20	0.846	International Paper split 2 for 1
May	26	0.824	General Electric split 2 for 1
June	16	0.796	Minnesota Mining & Manufacturing split 2 for 1
June	23	0.784	McDonald's Corp. split 3 for 2
September	15	0.766	Exxon Corp. split 2 for 1
October	20	0.754	Eastman Kodak split 3 for 2
1988 May	26	0.703	Merck split 3 for 1
December	16	0.700	Primerica Corp. (old) merged into Commercial Credit Group Inc. which adopted Primerica Corp.'s name
1989 March	29	0.682	General Motors split 2 for 1
May	30	0.680	Texaco special dividend
June	12	0.670	Boeing split 3 for 2
June	19	0.659	McDonald's Corp. split 2 for 1
August	29	0.658	Texaco special dividend
October	11	0.610	Philip Morris split 4 for 1
November	20	0.586	Procter & Gamble split 2 for 1

Dow Jones Industrial Average
Earnings, Dividends and Price-Earnings Ratio

		Price	Earnings (by qtrs)	Preceding 12 mos. earnings	Price Earnings Ratio (col. 1 + col. 3)	Dividends
1989	December 29	2753.20	. . . .	. . . .	. . . .	23.50
	September 29	2692.82	56.23	225.48	11.9	28.70
	June 30	2440.06	56.97	226.52	10.8	28.14
	March 31	2293.62	61.32	229.75	10.0	22.66
			. . . .			103.00
1988	December 30	2168.57	50.96	215.46	10.1	20.79
	September 30	2112.91	57.27	181.04	11.7	20.54
	June 30	2141.71	60.20	168.54	12.7	20.18
	March 31	1988.06	47.03	144.45	13.8	18.02
			215.46			79.53
1987	December 31	1938.83	16.54	133.05	14.6	17.67
	September 30	2596.28	44.77	137.99	18.8	18.05
	June 30	2418.53	36.11	126.23	19.2	18.11
	March 31	2304.69	35.63	126.49	18.2	17.37
			133.05			71.20
1986	December 31	1895.95	21.48	115.59	16.4	17.09
	September 30	1767.58	33.01	118.80	14.9	16.79
	June 30	1892.72	36.37	103.39	18.3	16.94
	March 31	1818.61	24.73	96.43	18.9	16.22
			115.59			67.04
1985	December 31	1546.67	24.69	96.11	16.1	17.19
	September 30	1328.63	17.60	90.78	14.6	15.02
	June 28	1335.46	29.41	102.26	13.1	14.95
	March 29	1266.78	24.41	107.87	11.7	14.87
			96.11			62.03

Earnings and Price-Earnings Ratio

Earnings on the Dow Jones industrial average are computed by adding the per share results of the latest quarter of each of the 30 components. This total is then divided by the then-current divisor. Having obtained the figure for the quarter, the four most recent quarterly figures are totaled to give the 12-month figure.

The industrial average stood at 2692.82 on September 29, 1989, for instance (see above). The 12-month earnings for that date were 225.48, being the sum of the four previous quarters ended September.

To obtain the price-earnings ratio on the industrials, the industrial average on a given date is divided by the 12-month earnings of the same date.

Dow Jones Industrial Average
Earnings, Dividends and Price-Earnings Ratio

		Price	Earnings (by qtrs)	Preceding 12 mos. earnings	Price Earnings Ratio (col. 1 ÷ col. 3)	Dividends
1984	December 31	1211.57	19.36	113.58	10.7	16.99
	September 28	1206.71	29.08	108.11	11.2	14.72
	June 29	1132.40	35.02	102.07	11.1	14.98
	March 30	1164.89	30.12	87.38	13.3	13.94
			113.58			60.63
1983	December 30	1258.94	13.89	72.45	17.4	14.77
	September 30	1233.13	23.04	56.12	30.0	13.98
	June 30	1221.96	20.33	11.59	105.4	13.70
	March 31	1130.03	15.19	9.52	118.7	13.88
			72.45			56.33
1982	December 31	1046.54	d2.44	9.15	114.4	13.03
	September 30	896.25	d21.49	35.15	25.5	13.44
	June 30	811.93	18.26	79.90	10.2	13.75
	March 31	822.77	14.82	97.13	8.5	13.92
			9.15			54.14
1981	December 31	875.00	23.56	113.71	7.7	14.44
	September 30	849.98	23.26	123.32	6.9	13.73
	June 30	976.88	35.49	128.91	7.6	14.19
	March 31	1003.87	31.40	123.60	8.1	13.86
			113.71			56.22
1980	December 31	963.99	33.17	121.86	7.9	14.40
	September 30	932.42	28.85	111.58	8.4	13.53
	June 30	867.92	30.18	116.40	7.5	13.20
	March 31	785.75	29.66	120.77	6.5	13.23
			121.86			54.36
1979	December 31	838.74	22.89	124.46	6.7	13.87
	September 28	878.67	33.67	136.26	6.4	12.51
	June 29	841.98	34.55	128.99	6.5	12.49
	March 30	862.18	33.35	124.10	6.9	12.11
			124.46			50.98
1978	December 29	805.01	34.69	112.79	7.1	14.34
	September 29	865.82	26.40	101.59	8.5	11.41
	June 30	818.95	29.66	91.37	9.0	11.62
	March 31	757.36	22.04	89.23	8.5	11.15
			112.79			48.52
1977	December 30	831.17	23.49	89.10	9.3	13.24
	September 30	847.11	16.18	89.86	9.4	10.73
	June 30	916.30	27.52	97.18	9.4	11.41
	March 31	919.13	21.91	95.51	9.6	10.46
			89.10			45.84

Dow Jones Industrial Average
Earnings, Dividends and Price-Earnings Ratio

		Price	Earnings (by qtrs)	Preceding 12 mos. earnings	Price Earnings Ratio (col. 1 ÷ col. 3)	Dividends
1976	December 31	1004.65	24.25	96.72	10.4	12.13
	September 30	990.19	23.50	95.81	10.3	9.85
	June 30	1002.78	25.85	90.68	11.1	10.19
	March 31	999.45	23.12	81.87	12.2	9.23
			96.72			41.40
1975	December 31	852.41	23.34	75.66	11.3	9.63
	September 30	793.88	18.37	75.47	10.5	9.05
	June 30	878.99	17.04	83.83	10.5	8.97
	March 31	768.15	16.91	93.47	8.2	9.81
			75.66			37.46
1974	December 31	616.24	23.15	99.04	6.2	10.45
	September 30	607.87	26.73	99.73	6.1	9.43
	June 28	802.41	26.68	93.26	8.6	8.87
	March 29	846.68	22.48	89.46	9.5	8.97
			99.04			37.72
1973	December 31	850.86	23.84	86.17	9.9	10.62
	September 28	947.10	20.26	82.09	11.5	8.36
	June 29	891.71	22.88	77.56	11.5	8.27
	March 30	951.01	19.19	71.98	13.2	8.08
			86.17			35.33
1972	December 29	1020.02	19.76	67.11	15.2	8.99
	September 29	953.27	15.73	62.15	15.3	7.76
	June 30	929.03	17.30	58.87	15.8	7.87
	March 30	940.70	14.32	56.76	16.6	7.65
			67.11			32.27
1971	December 31	890.20	14.80	55.09	16.2	7.85
	September 30	887.19	12.45	53.43	16.6	7.51
	June 30	891.14	15.19	53.45	16.7	7.80
	March 31	904.37	12.65	52.36	17.3	7.70
			55.09			30.86
1970	December 31	838.92	13.14	51.02	16.4	8.25
	September 30	760.68	12.47	51.83	14.7	7.80
	June 30	683.53	14.10	53.18	12.8	7.80
	March 31	785.57	11.31	54.07	14.5	7.68
			51.02			31.53
1969	December 31	800.36	13.95	57.02	14.0	8.63
	September 30	813.09	13.82	59.60	13.6	7.82
	June 30	873.19	14.99	59.47	14.7	8.08
	March 28	935.48	14.26	59.34	15.8	9.37
			57.02			33.90

Dow Jones Industrial Average
Earnings, Dividends and Price-Earnings Ratio

	Price	Earnings (by qtrs)	Preceding 12 mos. earnings	Price Earnings Ratio (col. 1 ÷ col. 3)	Dividends
1968 December 31	943.75	16.53	57.89	16.3	8.59
September 30	935.79	13.69	57.05	16.4	7.73
June 28	897.80	14.86	55.71	16.1	7.73
March 29	840.67	12.81	53.98	15.6	7.29
		57.89			31.34
1967 December 29	905.11	15.69	53.87	16.8	8.03
September 29	926.66	12.35	52.73	17.6	7.25
June 30	860.26	13.13	54.27	15.8	7.36
March 31	865.98	12.70	56.67	15.3	7.55
		53.87			30.19
1966 December 30	785.69	14.55	57.68	13.6	10.01
September 30	774.22	13.89	57.36	13.5	7.18
June 30	870.10	15.53	56.23	15.5	7.26
March 31	924.77	13.71	55.05	16.8	7.44
		57.68			31.89
1965 December 31	969.26	14.23	53.67	18.1	8.54
September 30	930.58	12.76	52.74	17.6	6.58
June 30	868.03	14.35	50.84	17.1	6.79
March 31	889.05	12.33	48.55	18.3	6.70
		53.67			28.61
1964 December 31	874.13	13.30	46.43	18.8	10.46
September 30	875.37	10.86	45.88	19.1	5.79
June 30	831.50	12.06	44.46	18.7	7.16
March 31	813.29	10.21	42.60	19.1	7.83
		46.43			31.24
1963 December 31	762.95	12.75	41.21	18.5	7.39
September 30	732.79	9.44	40.18	18.2	5.35
June 28	706.68	10.20	38.71	18.3	5.52
March 29	682.52	8.82	37.35	18.3	5.15
		41.21			23.41
1962 December 31	652.10	11.72	36.43	17.9	7.66
September 28	578.98	7.97	35.52	16.3	5.26
June 29	561.28	8.84	34.74	16.2	5.23
March 30	706.95	7.90	34.11	20.7	5.15
		36.43			23.30
1961 December 29	731.13	10.81	31.91	22.9	7.57
September 29	701.21	7.19	29.03	24.2	5.09
June 30	683.96	8.21	29.29	23.4	5.05
March 30	676.63	5.70	29.53	22.9	5.00
		31.91			22.71

Dow Jones Industrial Average
Earnings, Dividends and Price-Earnings Ratio

	Price	Earnings (by qtrs)	Preceding 12 mos. earnings	Price Earnings Ratio (col. 1 ÷ col. 3)	Dividends
1960 December 31	615.89	7.93	32.21	19.1	6.55
September 30	580.14	7.45	31.64	18.3	4.86
June 30	640.62	8.45	31.26	20.5	4.83
March 31	610.59	8.38	33.82	18.2	5.12
		32.21			21.36
1959 December 31	679.36	7.36	34.31	19.8	6.73
September 30	631.68	7.07	35.70	17.7	4.53
June 30	643.60	11.01	35.71	18.0	4.59
March 31	601.71	8.87	31.04	19.4	4.89
		34.31			20.74
1958 December 31	583.65	8.75	27.95	20.9	5.83
September 30	532.09	7.08	27.97	19.0	4.59
June 30	478.18	6.34	29.41	16.3	4.62
March 31	446.76	5.78	32.56	13.7	4.96
		27.95			20.00
1957 December 31	435.69	8.78	36.08	12.1	6.91
September 30	456.30	8.51	36.70	12.4	4.91
June 28	503.29	9.49	34.82	14.4	4.79
March 29	474.81	9.30	34.30	13.8	5.00
		36.08			21.61
1956 December 31	499.47	9.40	33.34	15.0	8.17
September 28	475.25	6.63	33.65	14.1	4.83
June 29	492.78	8.97	35.51	13.9	4.98
March 29	511.79	8.34	36.02	14.2	5.01
		33.34			22.99
1955 December 30	488.40	9.71	35.78	13.7	8.13
September 30	466.62	8.49	34.41	13.6	4.25
June 30	451.38	9.48	32.11	14.1	4.24
March 31	409.70	8.10	29.65	13.8	4.96
		35.78			21.58
1954 December 31	404.39	8.34	28.18	14.4	5.76
September 30	360.46	6.19	26.99	13.4	3.75
June 30	333.53	7.02	27.52	12.1	3.92
March 31	303.51	6.63	27.20	11.2	4.04
		28.18			17.47

d-Deficit.

Dow Jones Transportation Average
Earnings, Dividends and Price-Earnings Ratio

		Price	Earnings (by qtrs)	Preceding 12 mos. earnings	Price Earnings Ratio (col. 1 + col. 3)	Dividends
1989	December 29	1177.81		. . . .	. . . .	4.98
	September 29	1450.04	24.30	98.38	14.7	5.45
	June 30	1148.77	34.39	121.22	9.5	4.30
	March 31	1060.16	16.52	114.12	9.3	4.24
			. . . .			18.97
1988	December 30	969.84	23.17	105.82	9.2	4.17
	September 30	906.96	47.14	98.17	9.2	4.14
	June 30	908.15	27.29	72.15	12.6	3.93
	March 31	863.05	8.22	66.44	13.0	39.75
			105.82			51.99
1987	December 31	748.86	15.52	61.78	12.1	4.00
	September 30	1047.68	21.12	57.23	18.3	3.93
	June 30	1026.08	21.58	56.03	18.3	3.58
	March 31	919.69	3.56	24.64	37.3	4.22
			61.78			15.73
1986	December 31	807.17	10.97	16.57	48.7	4.14
	September 30	800.38	19.92	14.09	56.8	4.05
	June 30	782.75	(d9.81)	9.99	78.3	4.15
	March 31	830.84	(d4.51)	35.65	23.3	4.02
			16.57			16.36
1985	December 31	708.21	8.49	47.27	15.0	3.93
	September 30	640.57	15.82	51.35	12.5	3.93
	June 28	664.09	15.85	55.31	12.0	3.88
	March 29	603.08	7.11	58.39	10.3	3.70
			47.27			15.44
1984	December 30	558.13	12.57	62.37	8.9	3.51
	September 28	517.61	19.78	62.22	8.3	3.71
	June 29	474.18	18.93	58.17	8.1	3.56
	March 30	510.19	11.09	52.93	9.6	3.51
			62.37			14.29
1983	December 30	598.59	12.42	38.84	15.4	3.06
	September 30	561.58	15.73	36.32	15.4	3.68
	June 30	585.92	13.69	31.12	18.8	3.85
	March 31	507.39	(d3.00)	28.91	17.5	3.54
			38.84			14.13
1982	December 31	448.38	9.90	29.46	15.2	3.53
	September 30	360.46	10.53	28.06	12.8	3.88
	June 30	320.59	11.48	35.69	9.0	3.54
	March 31	333.08	(d2.45)	35.34	9.4	3.93
			29.46			14.88

Dow Jones Transportation Average
Earnings, Dividends and Price-Earnings Ratio

	Price	Earnings (by qtrs)	Preceding 12 mos. earnings	Price Earnings Ratio (col. 1 ÷ col. 3)	Dividends
1981 December 31	380.30	8.50	46.17	8.2	4.27
September 30	350.03	18.16	51.40	6.8	3.56
June 30	415.18	11.14	45.35	9.1	4.26
March 31	437.62	8.37	44.14	9.9	3.95
		46.17			16.04
1980 December 31	398.10	13.73	43.14	9.2	3.42
September 30	333.86	12.11	39.99	8.3	3.55
June 30	273.50	9.93	37.95	7.2	3.54
March 31	246.30	7.37	42.99	5.7	3.11
		43.14			13.62
1979 December 31	252.39	10.58	42.77	5.9	3.37
September 28	260.47	10.07	42.17	6.2	2.95
June 29	242.26	14.97	45.87	5.3	3.22
March 30	225.17	7.15	45.31	5.0	2.83
		42.77			12.37
1978 December 29	206.56	9.98	41.42	5.0	3.01
September 29	244.11	13.77	39.98	6.1	2.73
June 30	219.86	14.41	36.48	6.0	2.87
March 31	207.15	3.26	32.59	6.4	2.59
		41.42			11.20
1977 December 30	217.18	8.54	34.44	6.3	2.71
September 30	215.48	10.27	33.36	6.5	2.46
June 30	238.80	10.52	31.76	7.5	2.59
March 31	222.97	5.11	29.31	7.6	2.34
		34.44			10.10
1976 December 31	237.03	7.46	27.47	8.6	2.45
September 30	217.34	8.67	25.10	8.7	2.21
June 30	224.77	8.07	22.83	9.8	2.26
March 31	207.97	3.27	17.63	11.8	2.09
		27.47			9.01
1975 December 31	172.65	5.09	13.68	12.6	2.10
September 30	155.97	6.40	12.46	12.5	1.96
June 30	171.13	2.87	14.03	12.2	2.23
March 31	165.48	(d0.68)	19.06	8.7	2.16
		13.68			8.45
1974 December 31	143.44	3.87	23.45	6.1	2.38
September 30	128.48	7.97	25.06	5.1	2.15
June 28	162.18	7.90	22.64	7.2	2.12
March 29	185.08	3.71	19.87	9.3	1.99
		23.45			8.64

Dow Jones Transportation Average
Earnings, Dividends and Price-Earnings Ratio

		Price	Earnings (by qtrs)	Preceding 12 mos. earnings	Price Earnings Ratio (col. 1 + col. 3)	Dividends
1973	December 31	196.19	5.48	19.22	10.2	1.97
	September 28	176.96	5.55	18.67	9.5	2.13
	June 29	156.18	5.13	18.64	8.4	2.03
	March 30	200.13	3.06	18.83	10.6	2.03
			19.22			8.16
1972	December 29	227.17	4.93	18.75	12.1	2.03
	September 29	217.70	5.52	18.36	11.8	1.89
	June 30	233.30	5.32	18.28	12.8	2.00
	March 30	258.93	2.98	17.23	15.0	1.88
			18.75			7.80
1971	December 31	243.72	4.54	15.25	16.0	1.77
	September 30	237.18	5.44	12.80	18.5	1.83
	June 30	215.60	4.27	10.56	20.4	2.31
	March 31	200.00	1.00	8.17	24.5	1.72
			15.25			7.63
1970	December 31	171.52	2.09	8.52	20.5	2.42
	September 30	153.45	3.20	10.74	14.3	1.86
	June 30	120.57	1.88	11.98	10.1	2.32
	March 31	173.06	1.35	13.89	12.5	1.92
			8.52			8.52
1969	December 31	176.34	4.31	15.39	11.5	3.14
	September 30	196.60	4.44	16.34	12.0	2.50
	June 30	211.99	3.79	15.60	13.6	2.85
	March 28	243.69	2.85	16.56	14.7	2.54
			15.39			11.03
1968	December 31	271.60	5.26	17.59	15.4	3.32
	September 30	267.69	3.70	16.61	16.1	2.53
	June 28	261.77	4.75	15.16	17.3	2.96
	March 29	218.99	3.88	13.86	15.8	2.66
			17.59			11.47
1967	December 29	233.24	4.29	12.79	18.2	3.28
	September 29	261.83	2.25	15.07	17.4	2.60
	June 30	254.84	3.45	17.84	14.3	2.86
	March 31	230.59	2.81	20.06	11.5	2.53
			12.80			11.27
1966	December 30	202.97	6.56	20.90	9.7	3.71
	September 30	193.49	5.02	20.75	9.3	2.53
	June 30	226.06	5.67	21.20	10.7	2.75
	March 31	249.17	3.65	20.68	12.0	2.39
			20.90			11.38

Dow Jones Transportation Average
Earnings, Dividends and Price-Earnings Ratio

		Price	Earnings (by qtrs)	Preceding 12 mos. earnings	Price Earnings Ratio (col. 1 + col. 3)	Dividends
1965	December 31	247.48	6.41	19.35	12.8	3.73
	September 30	222.91	5.47	16.89	13.2	1.93
	June 30	193.69	5.15	15.17	12.8	2.16
	March 31	210.77	2.32	14.16	14.9	2.26
			19.35			10.08
1964	December 31	205.34	3.95	14.49	14.2	2.92
	September 30	218.17	3.75	13.61	14.0	1.82
	June 30	213.56	4.14	14.82	14.4	1.86
	March 31	191.83	2.65	14.54	13.2	1.80
			14.49			8.40
1963	December 31	178.54	5.07	12.69	14.1	2.37
	September 30	170.53	2.96	12.33	13.8	1.60
	June 28	173.66	3.86	11.90	14.6	1.73
	March 29	152.92	0.80	9.86	15.5	1.72
			12.69			7.42
1962	December 31	141.04	4.71	9.38	15.0	2.12
	September 28	115.68	2.53	8.11	14.2	1.53
	June 29	118.63	1.83	8.67	13.7	1.69
	March 30	144.28	0.32	6.75	21.4	1.69
			9.38			7.03
1961	December 29	143.84	3.44	4.89	29.4	1.97
	September 29	143.96	3.09	4.28	33.6	1.60
	June 30	139.47	d.09	1.16	119.3	1.77
	March 30	146.20	(d1.54)	3.43	42.6	1.77
			4.89			7.11
1960	December 31	130.85	2.82	6.71	19.5	2.38
	September 30	125.42	(d.03)	7.31	17.2	1.79
	June 30	143.19	2.18	8.54	16.8	1.98
	March 31	143.74	1.73	10.71	13.4	1.93
			6.70			8.08
1959	December 31	154.05	3.42	11.11	13.9	2.26
	September 30	157.40	1.20	12.99	12.2	1.75
	June 30	167.62	4.36	16.36	10.2	1.87
	March 31	158.65	2.13	13.89	8.8	1.87
			11.11			7.75
1958	December 31	157.65	5.30	12.34	12.8	2.04
	September 30	144.61	4.58	10.91	13.2	1.71
	June 30	118.75	1.89	10.06	11.8	1.85
	March 31	103.88	0.58	12.25	8.5	1.89
			12.35			7.49

Dow Jones Transportation Average
Earnings, Dividends and Price-Earnings Ratio

		Price	Earnings (by qtrs)	Preceding 12 mos. earnings	Price Earnings Ratio (col. 1 ÷ col. 3)	Dividends
1957	December 31	96.96	3.87	15.55	6.2	2.19
	September 30	123.70	3.72	17.66	7.0	2.23
	June 28	146.46	4.08	18.55	7.9	2.25
	March 29	144.05	3.88	19.65	7.3	2.29
			15.55			8.96
1956	December 31	153.23	5.98	19.52	7.9	2.79
	September 28	154.01	4.61	16.76	8.2	1.86
	June 29	166.69	5.18	19.49	8.5	1.90
	March 29	171.82	3.75	19.32	8.9	2.23
			19.52			8.78
1955	December 30	163.29	5.22	19.79	8.2	2.82
	September 30	155.05	5.34	20.66	7.5	1.62
	June 30	160.95	5.01	18.88	8.5	1.69
	March 31	150.32	4.22	16.69	9.0	1.91
			19.79			8.04
1954	December 31	145.86	6.09	14.98	9.7	2.42
	September 30	115.18	3.57	14.19	8.1	1.44
	June 30	112.70	2.81	15.66	7.2	1.51
	March 31	101.42	2.51	17.65	5.7	1.55
			14.98			6.92
1953	December 31	94.03	5.30	19.65	4.8	2.38
	September 30	93.90	5.04	21.39	4.4	1.86
	June 30	104.77	4.80	20.81	5.0	1.46
	March 31	107.02	4.51	19.76	5.4	1.40
			19.65			7.10
1952	December 31	111.27	7.04	19.20	5.8	2.03
	September 30	100.35	4.45	18.44	5.4	1.31
	June 30	102.73	3.76	16.65	6.2	1.41
	March 31	94.36	3.95	16.13	5.8	1.30
			19.20			6.05
1951	December 31	81.70	6.28	14.87	5.5	1.62
	September 28	84.76	2.66	15.48	5.5	1.22
	June 29	72.39	3.24	17.53	4.1	1.07
	March 31	80.58	2.69	17.82	4.5	1.01
			14.87			4.92

d-Deficit.

Dow Jones Utility Average
Earnings, Dividends and Price-Earnings Ratio

	Price	Preceding 12 mos. earnings	Price Earnings Ratio (col. 1 ÷ col. 2)	Dividends
1989 December 29	235.04	. . . .	. . . .	3.64
September 29	216.17	13.14	16.4	3.64
June 30	209.70	10.44	20.1	3.75
March 31	184.03	11.38	16.2	3.76
				14.79
1988 December 30	186.28	12.17	15.3	3.70
September 30	181.54	16.49	11.0	3.72
June 30	181.07	18.96	9.6	3.74
March 31	171.47	18.91	9.1	3.98
				15.14
1987 December 31	175.08	18.55	9.4	3.93
September 30	196.95	18.12	10.9	3.97
June 30	205.90	18.13	11.4	4.02
March 31	212.69	13.85	15.4	4.01
				15.93
1986 December 31	206.01	14.01	14.7	3.94
September 30	199.71	14.91	13.4	3.79
June 30	200.10	13.95	14.3	3.92
March 31	193.73	19.40	10.0	3.64
				15.29
1985 December 31	174.81	18.27	9.6	3.56
September 30	150.29	17.60	8.5	3.55
June 28	164.85	18.74	8.8	3.54
March 29	153.01	19.15	8.0	3.49
				14.14
1984 December 31	149.52	21.02	7.1	3.46
September 28	139.16	21.49	6.5	3.63
June 29	124.28	21.18	5.9	3.38
March 30	126.83	20.75	6.1	3.34
				13.81
1983 December 30	131.84	19.79	6.7	3.27
September 30	134.68	18.90	7.4	3.26
June 30	127.63	16.78	7.6	3.24
March 31	124.54	17.77	7.0	3.19
				12.96
1982 December 31	119.46	18.34	6.5	3.15
September 30	115.36	18.86	6.1	3.12
June 30	107.70	19.31	5.6	3.21
March 31	108.25	18.09	6.0	2.96
				12.44

Dow Jones Utility Average
Earnings, Dividends and Price-Earnings Ratio

	Price	Preceding 12 mos. earnings	Price Earnings Ratio (col. 1 ÷ col. 2)	Dividends
1981 December 31	109.02	18.31	5.9	3.02
September 30	102.21	17.65	5.8	2.78
June 30	107.98	16.33	6.6	2.72
March 31	109.02	15.96	6.8	2.71
				11.23
1980 December 31	114.42	15.58	7.3	2.60
September 30	107.82	15.21	7.1	2.57
June 30	113.33	15.20	7.5	2.57
March 31	99.70	15.47	6.4	2.49
				10.23
1979 December 31	106.60	15.49	6.9	2.40
September 28	106.90	15.76	6.8	2.36
June 29	105.45	15.10	7.0	2.35
March 30	104.19	14.91	7.0	2.33
				9.44
1978 December 29	98.24	14.29	6.9	2.23
September 29	106.12	13.85	7.7	2.19
June 30	104.94	14.03	7.5	2.19
March 31	105.68	13.92	7.6	2.18
				8.79
1977 December 30	111.28	14.27	7.8	2.09
September 30	113.25	14.99	7.6	2.08
June 30	114.68	14.91	7.7	2.07
March 31	106.02	14.48	7.3	1.99
				8.23
1976 December 31	108.38	13.59	8.0	1.93
September 30	97.78	12.50	7.8	1.88
June 30	87.55	12.01	7.3	1.87
March 31	87.55	11.99	7.3	1.87
				7.55
1975 December 31	83.65	11.58	7.2	1.82
September 30	76.97	11.59	6.6	1.80
June 30	85.99	11.63	7.4	1.79
March 31	77.20	11.77	6.6	1.79
				7.20
1974 December 31	68.76	11.57	5.9	1.75
September 30	61.16	11.38	5.4	1.72
June 28	68.22	11.11	6.1	1.67
March 29	90.75	10.69	8.5	1.77
				6.91

Dow Jones Utility Average
Earnings, Dividends and Price-Earnings Ratio

	Price	Preceding 12 mos. earnings	Price Earnings Ratio (col. 1 ÷ col. 2)	Dividends
1973 December 31	89.37	10.79	8.3	1.75
September 28	103.40	10.83	9.5	1.73
June 29	102.12	10.79	9.5	1.72
March 30	108.00	10.99	9.8	1.72
				6.92
1972 December 29	119.50	10.94	10.9	1.70
September 29	110.56	10.65	10.4	1.68
June 30	106.63	10.42	10.2	1.68
March 30	112.47	10.17	11.1	1.67
				6.73
1971 December 31	117.75	10.12	11.6	1.65
September 30	109.31	10.09	10.8	1.64
June 30	118.45	9.92	11.9	1.64
March 31	122.83	9.79	12.5	1.63
				6.56
1970 December 31	121.84	9.69	12.6	1.61
September 30	108.19	9.64	11.2	1.60
June 30	95.86	9.70	9.9	1.58
March 31	117.75	9.68	12.2	1.58
				6.37
1969 December 31	110.08	9.54	11.5	1.56
September 30	111.16	9.44	11.8	1.55
June 30	122.09	9.39	13.0	1.55
March 28	129.67	9.32	13.9	1.55
				6.21
1968 December 31	137.17	9.23	14.9	1.54
September 30	130.37	9.32	14.0	1.53
June 28	132.60	9.15	14.5	1.53
March 29	121.58	9.46	12.8	1.51
				6.11
1967 December 29	127.91	9.24	13.8	1.50
September 29	130.34	9.03	14.4	1.49
June 30	131.39	8.96	14.7	1.46
March 31	138.55	8.95	15.5	1.44
				5.89
1966 December 30	136.18	8.75	15.6	1.69
September 30	124.72	8.80	14.2	1.41
June 30	131.60	8.76	15.0	1.38
March 31	141.24	8.66	16.3	1.36
				5.84

Dow Jones Utility Average
Earnings, Dividends and Price-Earnings Ratio

		Price	Preceding 12 mos. earnings	Price Earnings Ratio (col. 1 ÷ col. 2)	Dividends
1965	December 31	152.63	8.53	17.9	1.34
	September 30	157.60	8.38	18.8	1.31
	June 30	154.15	8.12	19.0	1.28
	March 31	162.36	7.88	20.6	1.26
					5.19
1964	December 31	155.17	7.88	20.3	1.24
	September 30	153.16	7.31	21.0	1.32
	June 30	143.40	7.25	19.8	1.19
	March 31	137.30	7.11	19.3	1.19
					4.94
1963	December 31	138.99	7.04	19.7	1.72
	September 30	139.95	7.06	18.8	1.31
	June 28	139.08	6.95	20.0	1.07
	March 29	136.19	6.68	20.4	1.04
					5.14
1962	December 31	129.23	6.48	19.9	1.04
	September 28	117.62	6.07	19.4	1.13
	June 29	108.28	6.05	17.9	.99
	March 30	130.01	6.02	21.6	.98
					4.14
1961	December 29	129.16	5.86	22.0	97
	September 29	122.44	5.78	21.2	1.17
	June 30	111.74	5.78	19.5	.93
	March 30	111.91	5.67	19.7	1.24
					4.31
1960	December 31	100.02	5.61	17.8	1.09
	September 30	91.29	5.54	16.5	1.09
	June 30	93.39	5.51	16.9	.90
	March 31	88.20	5.36	16.5	.90
					3.98
1959	December 31	87.83	5.31	16.5	.94
	September 30	87.91	5.27	16.7	.98
	June 30	87.30	5.23	16.7	.87
	March 31	99.43	5.16	18.1	.87
					3.66
1958	December 31	91.00	4.96	13.3	.85
	September 30	80.71	4.87	16.6	.97
	June 30	78.92	4.84	16.3	.84
	March 31	74.00	4.83	15.3	.83
					3.49

Dow Jones Utility Average
Earnings, Dividends and Price-Earnings Ratio

	Price	Preceding 12 mos. earnings	Price Earnings Ratio (col. 1 ÷ col. 2)	Dividends
1957 December 31	68.58	4.70	14.6	.94
September 30	66.67	4.63	14.4	.82
June 28	69.84	4.66	15.0	.82
March 29	71.47	4.28	16.7	.81
				3.39
1956 December 31	63.54	4.71	14.6	1.04
September 28	65.57	4.68	14.0	.76
June 29	67.38	4.73	14.2	.77
March 29	67.39	4.58	14.7	.76
				3.33
1955 December 30	64.16	4.34	14.8	.82
September 30	63.14	4.19	15.1	.70
June 30	64.34	4.08	15.8	.73
March 31	63.57	4.09	15.5	1.32
				3.57
1954 December 31	62.47	3.91	16.0	.67
September 30	61.04	3.68	16.6	.66
June 30	58.20	3.91	14.9	.70
March 31	55.99	3.85	14.5	.63
				2.66
1953 December 31	52.04	3.74	13.9	.64
September 30	49.48	3.75	13.2	.63
June 30	48.54	3.70	13.1	.62
March 31	52.25	3.69	14.5	.74
				2.63
1952 December 31	52.60	3.55	14.8	.79
September 30	50.17	3.61	13.9	.60
June 30	49.66	3.54	14.9	.64
March 31	50.21	3.50	14.3	.58
				2.61
1951 December 31	47.22	3.45	13.7	.61
September 28	45.67	3.47	13.2	75
June 29	42.08	3.51	12.0	.63
March 31	42.25	3.36	12.6	.52
				2.51
1950 December 30	40.98	3.52	11.6	.63
September 29	40.46	3.32	12.1	.49
June 30	40.64	3.33	12.2	.56
March 31	42.67	3.28	13.0	.48
				2.16

The Dow Jones Industrials—1988

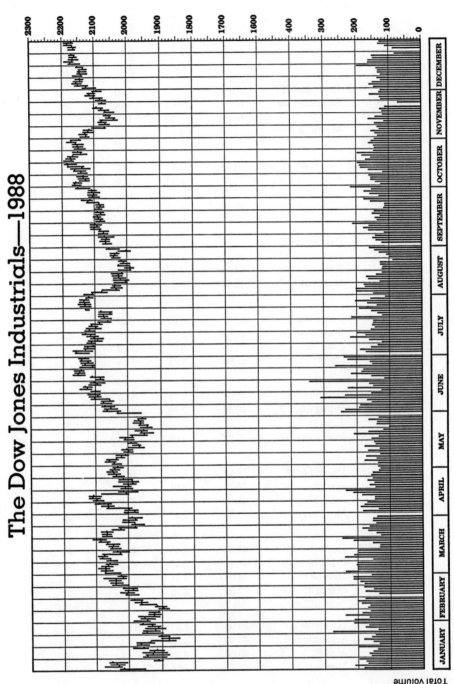

Sales in millions
Total volume

The Dow Jones Industrials—1989

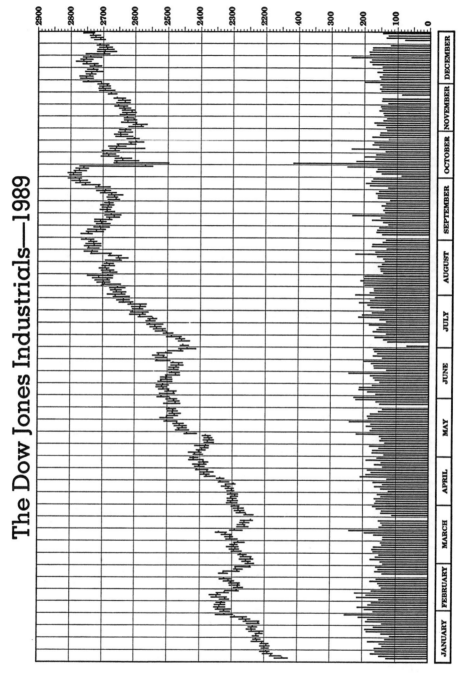

Sales in millions
Total volume

Daily Closing 1988 Dow Jones Averages

January

	-30 Industrials-			-20 Transport Cos.-			-15 Utilities-			Daily Sales -000-	20 Bonds	Commodity Futures
	High	Low	Close	High	Low	Close	High	Low	Close			
1						HOLIDAY						
4	2030.01	1950.76	2015.25	784.57	750.29	773.43	181.60	175.62	180.36	181,800	86.92	135.36
5	2075.27	2021.39	2031.50	795.29	774.71	780.29	184.68	181.07	183.56	209,520	87.17	136.16
6	2058.19	2012.77	2037.80	792.14	774.43	783.86	186.11	182.31	184.80	169,730	87.28	136.82
7	2061.51	2004.64	2051.89	795.71	771.14	789.43	188.89	183.85	188.42	175,360	87.30	136.84
8	2058.69	1898.04	1911.31	791.71	740.29	745.00	188.77	181.13	181.72	197,300	87.21	137.28
11	1985.25	1886.94	1945.13	763.43	735.14	756.43	183.80	178.76	182.31	158,980	87.02	137.10
12	1950.76	1877.98	1928.55	766.14	735.29	749.57	182.43	177.63	180.00	165,730	86.93	136.06
13	1959.55	1884.95	1924.73	756.43	732.14	746.29	182.49	177.39	180.06	154,020	87.03	135.75
14	1940.15	1894.06	1916.11	752.29	733.43	740.43	179.71	175.73	176.92	140,570	87.23	135.68
15	1988.40	1942.47	1956.07	767.43	749.29	756.00	181.66	175.73	178.40	197,940	87.30	135.00
18	1977.45	1938.99	1963.86	763.86	749.71	757.29	180.77	177.39	179.41	135,100	87.64	135.96
19	1977.29	1923.41	1936.34	768.14	748.29	755.00	182.08	175.51	180.06	153,550	88.14	136.31
20	1934.85	1858.59	1879.14	757.00	736.00	741.57	181.66	177.34	178.52	181,660	88.19	134.40
21	1903.35	1845.99	1879.31	748.71	728.71	737.57	180.18	177.10	178.64	158,080	88.49	135.30
22	1911.80	1876.16	1903.51	749.43	734.43	742.86	182.67	178.58	182.25	147,050	88.79	136.26
25	1960.54	1897.05	1946.45	758.14	738.29	749.29	184.80	181.19	184.15	275,250	89.17	134.05
26	1957.73	1906.50	1920.59	754.29	739.29	743.43	184.68	182.20	183.50	138,380	89.01	134.19
27	1951.76	1889.42	1911.14	758.14	739.14	746.00	185.87	182.43	183.97	176,360	89.35	133.73
28	1944.13	1904.34	1930.04	768.29	739.86	761.43	187.06	183.56	186.58	166,430	90.00	133.38
29	1967.67	1921.09	1958.22	773.29	749.71	764.29	190.14	185.34	190.02	211,880	90.61	131.86
High			2051.89			789.43			188.42		90.61	137.28
Low			1879.14			737.57			176.92		86.92	131.86

36

Daily Closing 1988 Dow Jones Averages

February

	–30 Industrials–			–20 Transport Cos.–			–15 Utilities–			Daily Sales –000–	20 Bonds	Commodity Futures
	High	Low	Close	High	Low	Close	High	Low	Close			
1	1985.41	1935.84	1944.63	773.86	756.86	765.00	190.67	187.17	188.42	210,660	90.84	132.16
2	1965.02	1921.09	1952.92	776.00	756.57	771.14	189.66	185.69	188.77	164,920	90.80	132.11
3	1971.98	1907.00	1924.57	778.14	754.43	759.14	189.37	184.63	186.17	237,270	90.75	131.91
4	1941.48	1902.85	1923.57	766.57	750.14	760.86	186.52	183.68	185.57	186,490	90.78	133.15
5	1940.32	1906.33	1910.48	770.00	753.00	758.57	187.65	184.92	186.28	161,310	90.71	132.69
8	1911.14	1878.15	1895.72	762.00	746.29	756.86	186.28	183.80	185.04	168,850	90.69	132.88
9	1921.58	1885.78	1914.46	764.00	749.14	760.43	185.93	183.14	184.86	162,350	90.47	133.19
10	1967.84	1916.78	1962.04	780.14	757.86	776.86	187.11	183.50	186.11	187,980	90.76	133.86
11	1982.43	1942.81	1961.54	785.14	767.00	774.14	186.94	182.79	184.33	200,760	90.65	133.87
12	1995.69	1958.06	1983.26	787.14	771.00	777.86	185.57	181.90	184.09	177,190	90.73	134.48
15						HOLIDAY						
16	2010.44	1969.83	2005.97	794.00	774.71	791.14	184.86	181.60	183.85	135,380	90.72	135.03
17	2026.19	1982.59	2000.99	808.42	787.81	795.67	185.34	182.25	183.68	176,830	90.57	136.01
18	2011.94	1972.81	1986.41	803.08	787.07	796.26	184.09	181.42	183.03	151,430	90.56	134.91
19	2018.90	1973.31	2014.59	819.69	792.26	815.54	184.74	181.07	184.57	180,300	90.41	135.17
22	2051.72	1998.67	2040.29	827.25	806.35	822.06	186.46	182.02	185.75	178,930	90.36	134.00
23	2057.03	2017.24	2039.12	826.36	810.13	819.69	186.52	183.26	185.34	192,260	90.55	132.71
24	2061.34	2022.88	2039.95	826.51	810.35	817.62	185.87	183.44	184.57	212,730	90.73	132.40
25	2078.08	2006.96	2017.57	844.60	812.28	822.66	186.28	181.37	182.49	213,490	90.80	131.99
26	2034.81	2005.14	2023.21	832.59	817.76	826.36	183.38	181.19	182.61	158,060	90.75	130.66
29	2074.60	2017.24	2071.62	837.49	821.03	834.96	184.51	181.13	183.74	236,050	90.97	130.36
High			2071.62			834.96			188.77		90.97	136.01
Low			1895.72			756.86			182.49		90.36	130.36

Daily Closing 1988 Dow Jones Averages

March

	-30 Industrials-			-20 Transport Cos.-			-15 Utilities-			Daily Sales -000-	20 Bonds	Commodity Futures
	High	Low	Close	High	Low	Close	High	Low	Close			
1	2086.87	2048.57	2070.46	841.34	824.29	832.59	183.50	179.88	181.72	199,990	90.82	130.75
2	2094.50	2058.19	2071.29	845.94	828.88	838.37	183.56	180.71	182.49	199,630	90.94	131.16
3	2085.38	2048.41	2063.49	858.54	834.82	849.94	183.80	180.77	182.73	203,310	91.25	130.46
4	2076.76	2033.44	2057.86	858.84	837.63	849.79	183.08	180.18	182.37	201,410	91.22	131.37
7	2069.30	2034.15	2056.37	856.32	839.71	850.68	182.20	179.05	179.94	152,980	91.00	131.31
8	2090.02	2055.04	2081.07	861.65	845.20	853.50	181.78	178.52	179.94	237,680	90.94	131.08
9	2094.16	2064.49	2074.27	868.48	848.90	858.24	180.06	177.22	178.11	210,900	90.60	131.32
10	2081.40	2020.72	2026.03	862.10	838.82	841.19	178.94	175.97	176.51	197,260	90.39	131.62
11	2049.07	1996.52	2034.98	853.05	828.59	847.12	178.22	175.50	177.34	200,020	90.50	131.71
14	2056.70	2023.04	2050.07	854.39	835.26	849.05	178.58	175.56	177.22	131,890	90.61	132.56
15	2062.17	2030.17	2047.41	862.90	847.82	854.09	179.23	176.68	178.70	133,170	90.71	132.30
16	2070.62	2027.02	2064.32	874.71	851.40	872.02	180.83	177.04	179.94	153,590	90.66	132.93
17	2093.17	2057.03	2086.04	884.41	864.40	876.94	181.42	178.28	180.30	211,920	90.82	132.44
18	2110.91	2067.14	2087.37	893.37	870.22	879.18	182.14	178.22	180.71	245,750	90.58	132.62
21	2081.23	2050.56	2067.14	886.50	868.13	880.08	180.12	177.04	178.17	128,830	90.40	132.72
22	2082.89	2052.06	2066.15	899.49	876.64	892.92	178.82	176.03	177.75	142,000	90.36	133.26
23	2085.05	2047.41	2067.64	916.97	890.53	904.12	178.11	175.56	176.51	167,370	90.07	133.97
24	2052.22	2011.44	2023.87	897.70	871.57	878.73	176.45	172.95	174.43	184,910	90.05	134.84
25	2031.00	1973.81	1978.95	883.66	854.69	860.96	175.14	171.82	173.07	163,170	89.88	134.53
28	1990.88	1951.26	1979.77	860.36	842.14	854.84	173.90	171.53	173.01	142,820	89.75	134.57
29	2018.57	1979.61	1998.34	872.76	854.69	863.80	174.43	172.24	172.95	152,690	89.76	135.02
30	2017.57	1973.81	1978.12	875.75	854.39	859.47	173.01	170.70	171.29	151,810	89.70	135.23
31	2000.66	1957.89	1988.06	867.08	847.82	863.05	172.18	169.81	171.47	139,870	89.76	134.74
High			2087.37			904.12			182.73		91.25	135.23
Low			1978.12			832.59			171.29		89.70	130.46

38

Daily Closing 1988 Dow Jones Averages

April

	− 30 Industrials −			− 20 Transport Cos. −			− 15 Utilities −			Daily Sales −000−	20 Bonds	Commodity Futures
	High	Low	Close	High	Low	Close	High	Low	Close			
1						HOLIDAY						
4	2013.26	1969.50	1980.60	870.07	847.82	856.78	171.76	169.45	170.52	182,240	89.52	135.10
5	2011.27	1969.99	1997.51	866.64	844.98	857.83	171.82	169.57	171.35	135,290	89.32	134.54
6	2067.47	1987.57	2061.67	880.08	852.75	875.15	175.08	170.28	174.55	189,760	89.16	133.98
7	2084.22	2042.94	2062.17	886.95	864.99	874.25	175.38	172.71	174.37	177,840	89.17	134.33
8	2103.78	2051.06	2090.19	887.99	867.08	883.66	177.04	173.13	176.56	169,300	89.51	134.46
11	2110.08	2075.27	2095.99	888.44	867.98	879.48	176.62	174.19	175.44	146,370	89.71	134.39
12	2120.69	2085.38	2110.08	889.19	873.66	884.56	176.27	173.72	175.44	146,400	89.70	133.46
13	2121.35	2082.56	2107.10	886.65	869.62	878.29	176.27	173.36	175.14	185,120	89.55	132.53
14	2083.22	1998.18	2005.64	869.77	838.11	841.85	174.13	169.22	170.16	211,810	89.53	133.33
15	2031.33	1969.99	2013.93	845.13	821.09	833.33	170.58	167.26	169.16	234,160	89.48	133.22
18	2023.04	1985.74	2008.12	841.70	823.03	836.17	170.34	167.20	168.56	144,650	89.33	132.71
19	2047.08	1990.55	1999.50	850.36	832.29	836.47	171.05	167.38	168.74	161,910	88.91	132.98
20	2015.42	1975.46	1985.41	846.33	823.33	827.36	169.69	166.25	167.26	147,590	88.72	132.72
21	2030.50	1968.00	1987.40	841.85	823.63	830.50	170.22	166.49	167.67	168,440	88.68	132.61
22	2029.01	1985.58	2015.09	853.05	835.72	847.67	171.47	167.02	169.87	152,520	88.87	132.61
25	2048.57	2011.60	2035.97	860.96	843.94	853.35	171.59	168.50	170.16	156,950	89.00	131.84
26	2062.83	2023.04	2044.76	860.22	843.94	850.81	172.36	169.27	171.17	152,300	88.83	132.02
27	2066.64	2033.16	2047.91	855.29	839.16	845.43	172.59	169.93	170.82	133,810	88.87	132.51
28	2057.53	2026.03	2041.28	848.72	833.33	840.20	171.65	169.16	170.40	128,680	88.90	132.00
29	2047.91	2014.09	2032.33	847.67	829.60	842.00	171.23	168.56	170.64	135,620	88.79	132.54
High			2110.08			884.56			176.56		89.71	135.10
Low			1980.60			827.36			167.26		88.68	131.84

Daily Closing 1988 Dow Jones Averages

May

	– 30 Industrials –			– 20 Transport Cos. –			– 15 Utilities –			Daily Sales –000–	20 Bonds	Commodity Futures
	High	Low	Close	High	Low	Close	High	Low	Close			
2	2050.40	2019.89	2043.27	858.27	839.76	853.79	170.99	168.15	169.69	136,470	88.65	131.90
3	2071.95	2036.64	2058.36	863.80	849.46	854.84	171.41	168.92	170.93	176,920	88.50	132.16
4	2067.14	2029.51	2036.31	868.13	844.53	856.78	171.23	168.21	168.80	141,320	88.53	132.44
5	2038.46	2008.95	2020.23	858.72	842.59	849.01	169.69	167.38	168.86	171,840	88.48	132.61
6	2038.13	1997.84	2007.46	857.23	837.96	843.04	170.58	168.21	169.04	129,080	88.29	132.80
9	2013.59	1984.08	1997.35	846.48	825.57	831.69	170.16	168.03	169.57	166,320	88.27	134.53
10	2020.23	1984.42	2003.65	841.40	826.16	835.13	170.76	168.27	169.51	131,200	88.24	134.39
11	1988.56	1950.27	1965.85	832.29	811.08	821.98	169.45	166.49	167.67	176,720	87.91	134.26
12	1986.07	1960.54	1968.00	826.46	816.31	818.40	169.39	166.43	167.79	143,880	88.01	134.62
13	2001.49	1971.65	1990.55	828.85	816.61	822.43	169.75	167.26	168.39	147,240	88.15	134.94
16	2012.60	1980.27	2007.63	832.29	817.05	829.30	169.81	167.61	169.22	155,010	88.42	135.29
17	2026.69	1982.10	1986.41	836.17	811.23	813.47	170.64	167.50	167.73	133,850	88.05	135.61
18	1992.87	1941.31	1951.09	815.56	793.76	796.74	169.22	166.19	167.08	209,420	87.85	136.15
19	1963.86	1921.58	1958.72	801.22	782.86	796.89	168.44	165.78	168.03	165,160	87.78	136.01
20	1978.78	1940.48	1952.59	804.51	787.19	796.59	169.22	166.90	168.74	120,600	87.69	136.68
23	1962.37	1927.22	1941.48	797.49	774.79	784.05	169.22	167.26	167.97	102,640	87.40	135.63
24	1967.67	1938.16	1962.53	798.39	782.11	794.95	169.39	167.56	169.16	139,930	87.42	135.81
25	1984.58	1952.42	1961.37	805.41	790.17	794.65	170.70	168.27	169.51	138,310	87.52	134.40
26	1981.15	1951.28	1966.75	808.39	791.22	800.33	171.17	169.04	170.34	164,260	87.31	134.13
27	1970.84	1944.35	1956.44	810.33	795.85	804.66	171.65	169.57	170.87	133,590	87.18	134.11
30						HOLIDAY						
31	2034.50	1959.38	2031.12	828.70	801.97	826.31	176.62	171.05	176.33	247,610	87.20	136.54
High			2058.36			856.78			176.33		88.65	136.68
Low			1941.48			784.05			167.08		87.18	131.90

Daily Closing 1988 Dow Jones Averages

June

	-30 Industrials-			-20 Transport Cos.-			-15 Utilities-			Daily Sales -000-	20 Bonds	Commodity Futures
	High	Low	Close	High	Low	Close	High	Low	Close			
1	2076.28	2021.34	2064.01	848.12	823.33	842.44	178.82	174.13	177.93	234,560	87.66	136.96
2	2073.26	2030.94	2052.45	857.23	833.63	847.67	178.22	175.20	177.45	193,540	87.58	139.75
3	2080.73	2040.01	2071.30	859.77	844.68	853.94	179.11	176.62	178.34	189,600	87.76	140.37
6	2083.93	2049.08	2075.21	862.31	847.67	857.97	178.76	176.27	177.99	152,460	87.65	142.44
7	2082.86	2042.85	2054.59	866.34	847.67	854.24	179.11	175.02	177.04	168,710	87.86	142.90
8	2113.62	2055.83	2102.95	877.39	852.45	873.06	181.01	177.10	180.30	310,030	87.83	140.73
9	2119.31	2081.79	2093.35	880.68	865.59	872.61	181.07	178.17	178.88	235,160	87.80	142.20
10	2123.58	2084.82	2101.71	886.95	869.47	877.39	180.65	178.28	179.11	155,710	88.00	141.62
13	2114.15	2084.64	2099.40	882.92	867.23	873.36	180.24	178.17	179.35	125,310	88.08	141.00
14	2148.12	2111.13	2124.47	891.88	875.45	881.12	182.79	179.82	181.37	227,150	88.42	140.89
15	2137.45	2109.53	2131.40	883.96	869.92	879.18	182.14	179.53	181.31	150,260	88.85	142.18
16	2120.73	2081.97	2094.24	876.34	859.62	865.89	181.90	178.22	179.47	161,550	88.58	142.68
17	2116.47	2070.06	2104.02	872.91	854.84	864.10	181.60	178.58	180.60	343,920	88.45	143.65
20	2100.11	2072.72	2083.93	866.79	851.85	856.93	180.89	178.94	180.24	116,750	88.33	144.54
21	2115.75	2072.55	2109.17	870.52	852.00	868.13	182.67	179.05	182.14	155,060	88.56	146.18
22	2169.10	2131.05	2152.20	890.08	874.55	882.77	185.34	182.31	183.68	217,510	88.59	145.53
23	2163.94	2131.58	2148.29	894.86	876.34	890.68	183.74	181.31	181.90	185,770	88.74	143.55
24	2165.36	2133.53	2142.96	906.51	890.83	898.89	183.14	180.24	181.66	179,880	88.85	141.89
27	2147.76	2101.17	2108.46	899.49	878.88	881.57	182.37	178.52	180.18	264,410	88.63	144.57
28	2139.94	2100.11	2130.87	894.71	875.45	890.23	181.72	178.94	180.83	152,370	88.73	142.68
29	2144.91	2106.15	2121.98	897.85	879.48	888.14	181.42	178.40	179.59	159,590	88.80	139.87
30	2147.23	2112.38	2141.71	911.44	888.14	908.15	181.48	178.70	181.07	227,410	88.87	141.23
High		2152.20			908.15			183.68			88.87	146.18
Low		2052.45			842.44			177.04			87.58	136.96

Daily Closing 1988 Dow Jones Averages

July

	-30 Industrials-			-20 Transport Cos.-			-15 Utilities-			Daily Sales -000-	20 Bonds	Commodity Futures
	High	Low	Close	High	Low	Close	High	Low	Close			
1	2151.14	2118.95	2131.58	912.93	895.46	899.34	182.14	179.17	180.42	238,330	89.00	141.76
4						HOLIDAY						
5	2162.52	2117.71	2158.61	912.49	891.58	908.45	182.73	178.99	182.14	171,790	89.19	141.05
6	2169.45	2107.40	2130.16	914.13	885.16	892.92	182.67	177.99	180.18	189,630	89.23	142.36
7	2136.02	2101.35	2122.69	899.79	880.53	894.41	180.24	177.87	179.59	156,100	89.27	141.08
8	2133.53	2099.40	2106.15	901.43	883.96	889.19	180.42	177.87	178.52	136,070	88.99	140.79
11	2126.07	2098.68	2111.31	897.10	883.21	890.83	179.82	177.63	178.64	123,300	89.05	139.08
12	2121.44	2077.52	2092.64	893.22	874.55	882.62	179.77	176.86	177.99	161,650	89.10	139.92
13	2114.15	2073.44	2104.37	892.17	874.55	887.69	179.41	176.80	178.82	218,930	88.94	141.04
14	2125.71	2089.26	2113.62	891.73	879.93	888.14	179.71	177.51	179.05	172,410	88.57	142.35
15	2140.11	2099.57	2129.45	898.00	883.96	892.77	180.42	177.28	179.65	199,710	88.58	142.54
18	2132.47	2099.40	2117.89	894.71	870.37	886.65	179.53	176.80	178.11	156,210	88.57	140.57
19	2127.67	2081.08	2097.26	889.78	874.85	877.09	179.11	176.51	178.05	144,110	88.38	141.91
20	2119.31	2091.39	2110.60	891.73	867.23	883.06	179.41	177.34	178.76	151,990	88.40	141.47
21	2113.62	2077.17	2086.59	882.92	851.11	869.47	178.88	176.92	177.45	149,460	88.23	141.79
22	2092.46	2050.32	2060.99	871.86	850.06	857.38	177.57	174.96	175.50	148,800	88.16	141.93
25	2082.68	2048.54	2071.83	865.29	854.24	858.27	176.92	174.61	175.85	215,140	88.25	138.98
26	2089.79	2059.57	2073.97	865.74	853.05	860.22	178.05	175.26	177.04	121,960	88.25	135.63
27	2089.97	2047.30	2053.70	870.82	849.61	855.73	178.64	175.56	176.08	135,890	88.29	135.00
28	2089.26	2047.30	2082.33	869.03		863.05	179.88	176.51	178.88	154,570	88.25	133.23
29	2133.00	2084.28	2128.73	888.89	863.20	886.20	183.26	178.52	182.85	192,340	88.33	134.61
High	2158.61			908.45			182.14				89.27	142.54
Low	2053.70			855.73			175.50				88.16	133.23

Daily Closing 1988 Dow Jones Averages

August

	-30 Industrials-			-20 Transport Cos.-			-15 Utilities-			Daily Sales -000-	20 Bonds	Commodity Futures
	High	Low	Close	High	Low	Close	High	Low	Close			
1	2146.16	2111.84	2130.51	898.87	880.53	891.28	183.74	181.42	182.43	138,170	88.50	134.53
2	2151.85	2112.20	2131.22	900.54	884.41	891.58	184.03	181.19	182.37	166,660	88.72	132.85
3	2147.94	2115.40	2134.07	897.85	880.82	887.84	184.09	181.90	183.44	203,590	88.64	134.24
4	2147.23	2117.71	2126.60	896.36	880.97	885.30	184.33	182.14	182.91	157,240	88.86	135.19
5	2128.73	2105.44	2119.13	886.65	874.55	881.27	183.14	181.60	182.67	113,400	88.77	135.39
8	2134.60	2103.13	2107.40	890.23	874.70	879.03	183.68	181.25	182.02	148,800	88.84	133.84
9	2110.95	2061.17	2079.13	880.68	861.86	867.53	182.08	178.22	178.99	200,710	88.68	134.31
10	2078.41	2023.65	2034.14	868.13	842.74	848.57	179.11	176.39	177.39	200,950	88.26	135.79
11	2050.68	2014.05	2039.30	857.23	837.81	849.01	178.52	175.79	177.45	173,000	88.18	135.50
12	2046.41	2019.38	2037.52	856.33	842.59	852.15	177.63	175.79	176.68	176,960	88.11	135.74
15	2040.72	1998.76	2004.27	856.03	838.11	842.44	176.39	173.13	173.60	128,560	88.05	135.29
16	2043.56	1993.78	2021.51	855.44	835.72	844.83	175.97	172.24	174.79	162,790	88.11	134.47
17	2042.50	2003.38	2025.96	853.49	837.22	846.33	176.39	173.66	175.62	169,500	88.05	135.01
18	2046.59	2014.22	2027.03	853.20	842.29	845.88	176.68	174.43	175.32	139,820	88.10	136.30
19	2048.90	2011.38	2016.00	853.05	840.20	844.83	177.75	174.96	177.34	122,370	88.10	136.31
22	2027.56	1987.02	1990.22	848.42	829.75	833.78	178.17	175.85	176.86	122,250	88.26	135.52
23	2008.36	1978.66	1989.33	840.80	825.27	831.54	178.17	175.91	176.62	119,540	88.05	134.54
24	2028.98	1990.04	2026.67	849.01	829.90	845.58	179.23	176.09	178.88	127,800	88.04	136.31
25	2022.05	1990.40	2010.85	844.38	831.24	838.56	178.82	176.51	177.81	127,640	87.90	136.12
26	2027.38	2002.13	2017.43	844.98	833.33	839.01	179.11	176.45	177.69	89,240	87.87	136.11
29	2047.48	2019.56	2041.43	853.35	839.16	849.91	179.59	177.57	178.58	99,280	88.00	135.70
30	2052.63	2028.63	2038.23	858.72	842.00	848.42	179.53	177.39	178.64	108,720	88.03	135.88
31	2052.45	2022.94	2031.65	856.18	839.61	846.62	180.00	177.69	178.70	130,480	87.99	136.57
High	2134.07			891.58			183.44				88.86	136.57
Low	1989.33			831.54			173.60				87.87	132.85

43

Daily Closing 1988 Dow Jones Averages

September

	– 30 Industrials –			– 20 Transport Cos. –			– 15 Utilities –			Daily Sales –000–	20 Bonds	Commodity Futures
	High	Low	Close	High	Low	Close	High	Low	Close			
1	2027.56	1988.44	2002.31	849.01	829.45	839.01	178.58	175.85	177.34	144,090	88.03	136.49
2	2064.72	2022.40	2054.59	863.35	842.29	857.23	181.37	178.17	180.65	159,840	88.30	136.71
5						HOLIDAY						
6	2074.68	2046.41	2065.26	873.21	853.35	869.18	181.60	179.17	180.54	122,250	88.18	137.33
7	2084.10	2052.99	2065.79	879.78	860.36	866.94	181.72	179.17	180.00	139,500	88.70	137.88
8	2079.30	2052.10	2063.12	872.01	859.32	866.64	180.71	178.76	180.06	149,380	88.71	137.76
9	2088.73	2038.94	2068.81	880.38	856.03	873.81	180.71	178.17	179.94	141,540	88.78	136.80
12	2088.55	2057.43	2072.37	878.43	865.59	867.68	180.42	177.93	178.52	114,880	88.94	136.48
13	2088.19	2055.30	2083.04	875.30	860.36	871.57	179.53	177.16	178.76	162,490	88.88	137.66
14	2111.66	2079.13	2100.64	880.68	866.94	875.30	180.30	178.11	179.82	177,220	88.87	137.96
15	2112.55	2084.28	2092.28	879.93	868.28	870.37	180.30	177.99	179.05	161,210	88.98	136.86
16	2113.26	2077.70	2098.15	879.63	864.10	876.94	180.42	178.17	180.24	211,110	89.15	135.25
19	2096.55	2066.86	2081.08	887.99	873.36	881.42	180.36	178.22	179.47	135,770	89.06	134.16
20	2097.26	2073.26	2087.48	892.77	877.24	886.80	180.71	178.64	180.18	142,220	88.95	134.65
21	2103.31	2078.77	2090.50	897.70	884.56	892.77	180.83	178.82	179.53	127,400	89.12	133.87
22	2097.08	2066.68	2080.01	897.55	879.03	888.29	180.30	178.40	179.53	150,670	89.05	134.67
23	2097.80	2070.41	2090.68	896.51	880.08	892.32	180.77	178.17	179.71	145,100	88.91	134.51
26	2098.33	2075.75	2085.17	898.30	884.56	891.73	180.30	178.28	179.35	116,420	88.88	133.99
27	2095.31	2069.88	2082.33	897.85	884.11	890.38	180.83	178.58	179.82	113,010	88.99	134.92
28	2096.37	2070.23	2085.53	897.10	884.56	894.41	180.95	178.94	180.77	113,720	89.00	134.82
29	2123.76	2084.46	2119.31	911.89	891.28	908.60	182.91	179.59	182.08	155,790	89.12	135.39
30	2140.29	2104.02	2112.91	921.30	901.28	906.96	183.56	180.42	181.54	175,750	89.16	135.64
High			2119.31			908.60			182.08		89.16	137.96
Low			2002.31			839.01			177.34		88.03	133.87

44

Daily Closing 1988 Dow Jones Averages

October

	–30 Industrials–			–20 Transport Cos.–			–15 Utilities–			Daily Sales –000–	20 Bonds	Commodity Futures
	High	Low	Close	High	Low	Close	High	Low	Close			
3	2116.82	2083.39	2105.26	917.11	898.89	911.14	183.03	180.24	181.72	130,380	89.51	135.78
4	2119.49	2090.68	2102.06	920.25	903.08	912.34	182.97	180.48	181.84	157,760	89.59	136.09
5	2119.84	2082.33	2106.51	923.39	907.71	918.01	183.38	181.13	183.20	175,130	89.73	135.91
6	2118.07	2092.64	2107.75	922.34	908.90	914.43	183.91	182.31	183.68	153,570	89.78	136.72
7	2157.72	2112.02	2150.25	932.80	909.65	929.06	187.83	183.56	187.47	216,390	89.94	136.56
10	2167.85	2139.05	2158.96	932.67	917.30	924.03	187.77	185.22	186.58	124,660	90.22	137.45
11	2164.83	2137.09	2156.47	929.01	917.30	924.47	186.82	184.57	185.75	140,900	90.07	137.43
12	2146.34	2113.44	2126.24	920.67	903.40	908.81	184.92	182.31	183.62	154,840	89.97	137.72
13	2149.54	2114.33	2133.36	919.06	903.54	912.76	185.16	182.55	184.39	154,530	90.09	138.51
14	2153.81	2118.78	2133.18	925.06	908.67	915.11	185.40	182.85	183.50	160,240	90.04	139.03
17	2150.60	2120.02	2140.47	922.42	910.28	916.42	184.68	182.49	183.97	119,290	89.91	139.28
18	2163.41	2124.29	2159.85	932.38	910.71	929.01	185.28	182.61	184.98	162,500	90.03	138.78
19	2173.01	2110.95	2137.27	938.67	911.01	918.91	185.57	182.14	183.74	186,350	89.96	139.57
20	2183.68	2129.80	2181.19	936.33	913.20	935.01	186.40	182.85	186.34	189,580	89.93	139.53
21	2193.28	2152.56	2183.50	942.48	925.20	937.50	187.41	184.45	186.70	195,410	90.03	139.23
24	2195.06	2162.16	2170.34	944.96	928.86	933.84	187.17	184.57	185.57	170,590	90.00	138.66
25	2188.66	2156.83	2173.36	943.15	927.02	938.33	186.94	184.86	186.05	155,190	89.96	138.78
26	2182.61	2148.47	2165.18	943.61	924.76	935.01	187.11	185.22	186.88	181,550	90.18	138.22
27	2165.54	2120.91	2140.83	939.54	913.30	921.59	187.06	184.51	185.87	196,540	90.22	137.90
28	2166.43	2135.67	2149.89	932.90	917.07	922.95	187.35	185.22	186.05	181,550	90.31	138.68
31	2161.63	2125.36	2148.65	929.43	914.81	926.72	187.59	185.28	187.23	143,460	90.53	139.13
High			2183.50			938.33			187.47		90.53	139.57
Low			2102.06			908.81			181.72		89.51	135.78

45

Daily Closing 1988 Dow Jones Averages

November

| | 30 Industrials | | | 20 Transport Cos. | | | 15 Utilities | | | Daily Sales | 20 | Commodity |
	High	Low	Close	High	Low	Close	High	Low	Close	–000–	Bonds	Futures
1	2165.36	2132.82	2150.96	936.52	921.59	931.09	188.12	186.34	187.59	161,250	90.58	139.22
2	2167.67	2131.40	2156.83	939.23	924.31	932.75	188.48	186.46	187.71	161,300	90.61	140.81
3	2185.99	2153.45	2170.34	945.87	930.34	936.67	189.19	187.11	188.30	152,980	90.62	139.62
4	2173.90	2139.58	2145.80	939.38	925.21	929.73	188.18	185.40	186.11	143,580	90.40	139.47
7	2143.14	2113.62	2124.64	930.04	916.16	921.14	186.70	184.45	184.92	133,870	90.46	139.20
8	2146.87	2119.67	2127.49	932.75	921.59	927.62	187.11	185.10	186.28	141,660	90.24	139.58
9	2134.25	2100.82	2118.24	932.30	916.62	925.36	185.51	183.44	184.03	153,140	90.01	140.27
10	2132.82	2103.31	2114.69	930.94	919.33	923.55	185.75	183.44	185.22	128,920	89.99	138.75
11	2107.04	2063.48	2067.03	923.40	907.12	909.38	185.04	181.96	182.55	135,500	89.94	138.65
14	2084.82	2050.85	2077.17	918.43	902.59	909.08	183.68	181.72	182.55	142,900	90.01	138.85
15	2088.02	2060.28	2065.08	914.66	902.44	906.51	183.91	181.96	183.08	115,170	89.93	137.84
16	2081.44	2026.67	2038.58	908.02	887.21	890.98	183.38	180.54	181.54	161,710	89.97	137.88
17	2064.19	2033.25	2052.45	900.78	885.40	890.98	183.08	180.89	182.31	141,280	89.79	136.53
18	2070.41	2047.12	2062.41	900.33	887.52	896.71	183.44	181.25	181.72	119,320	89.64	136.31
21	2070.06	2036.81	2065.97	903.20	886.46	897.32	182.49	180.42	182.25	120,430	89.41	136.14
22	2086.77	2052.63	2077.70	902.29	887.36	897.92	182.91	180.89	182.67	127,000	89.19	137.04
23	2103.49	2071.48	2092.28	922.20	897.17	919.48	183.38	181.90	182.67	112,010	89.26	138.68
24						HOLIDAY						
25	2085.53	2062.77	2074.68	914.51	900.93	907.72	182.91	180.95	182.37	72,090	89.05	139.23
28	2095.48	2062.23	2081.44	927.02	900.78	920.84	183.20	181.60	182.61	123,480	89.01	139.03
29	2112.73	2072.37	2101.53	933.96	911.64	928.98	184.92	182.25	184.45	127,420	89.10	139.12
30	2126.60	2095.48	2114.51	944.06	926.12	936.52	186.46	183.74	185.63	157,810	89.14	139.72
High			2170.34			936.67			188.30		90.62	140.81
Low			2038.58			890.98			181.54		89.01	136.14

46

Daily Closing 1988 Dow Jones Averages

December

	– 30 Industrials –			– 20 Transport Cos. –			– 15 Utilities –			Daily Sales –000–	20 Bonds	Commodity Futures
	High	Low	Close	High	Low	Close	High	Low	Close			
1	2120.02	2095.48	2101.88	941.50	927.02	935.77	185.81	183.85	184.39	129,380	89.32	139.82
2	2105.80	2075.39	2092.28	941.95	926.72	934.86	184.45	182.08	183.74	124,610	88.98	139.93
5	2135.49	2092.64	2123.76	951.00	933.96	946.17	185.16	182.79	184.57	144,660	89.02	139.89
6	2158.96	2117.18	2149.36	953.41	936.67	946.47	185.93	183.08	185.10	158,340	89.30	140.20
7	2167.50	2136.38	2153.63	954.31	940.89	947.98	186.52	184.45	185.87	148,360	89.41	140.74
8	2162.70	2133.18	2141.71	949.79	938.78	943.00	185.99	184.33	184.98	124,150	89.34	140.94
9	2157.01	2131.40	2143.49	954.92	938.33	951.30	185.75	184.27	185.04	133,770	89.31	141.79
12	2165.18	2133.89	2139.58	961.55	943.15	947.23	186.82	184.74	185.46	124,160	89.37	141.95
13	2151.14	2119.31	2143.49	950.69	936.52	946.17	185.99	184.33	184.98	132,340	89.27	140.67
14	2149.72	2121.44	2134.25	952.96	939.69	948.88	185.51	183.38	184.45	132,350	89.02	142.37
15	2146.87	2120.91	2133.00	962.45	943.31	954.76	184.80	182.31	183.38	136,820	88.59	141.69
16	2155.00	2131.25	2150.71	964.26	952.20	960.95	184.80	182.79	184.51	196,480	88.48	142.93
19	2179.64	2141.07	2172.68	975.12	956.27	970.90	185.99	183.20	184.98	162,250	88.44	144.58
20	2192.68	2161.25	2166.07	978.29	962.30	965.17	186.46	184.27	184.57	161,090	88.67	146.02
21	2178.57	2146.07	2164.64	970.30	955.52	962.91	185.87	183.50	184.57	147,250	88.71	146.32
22	2176.43	2151.43	2160.36	966.38	952.05	961.70	187.17	184.98	186.23	150,510	88.58	145.61
23	2176.79	2157.86	2168.93	970.45	957.93	965.32	187.41	185.16	186.52	81,760	88.55	146.36
26						HOLIDAY						
27	2179.29	2156.43	2162.68	971.20	959.29	964.57	187.47	185.34	185.75	87,490	88.57	145.67
28	2179.64	2153.57	2166.43	972.56	959.74	965.62	186.94	184.86	185.93	110,630	88.78	145.35
29	2193.04	2165.08	2182.68	977.53	963.81	973.61	187.23	185.28	186.82	131,290	88.53	145.35
30	2193.75	2162.50	2168.57	979.19	965.02	969.84	187.59	185.63	186.28	127,210	88.59	145.67
High			2182.68			973.61			186.82		89.41	146.36
Low			2092.28			934.86			183.38		88.44	139.82

47

Daily Closing 1989 Dow Jones Averages

January

	−30 Industrials−			−20 Transport Cos.−			−15 Utilities−			Daily Sales −000−	20 Bonds	Commodity Futures
	High	Low	Close	High	Low	Close	High	Low	Close			
2						HOLIDAY						
3	2168.39	2127.14	2144.64	970.01	951.36	959.95	186.58	183.44	184.15	128,500	88.47	145.96
4	2183.39	2146.61	2177.68	982.00	958.17	978.76	187.06	184.45	186.76	149,700	88.42	146.03
5	2205.18	2173.04	2190.54	985.89	972.92	978.11	187.71	185.46	186.34	174,040	88.35	146.71
6	2213.75	2182.32	2194.29	990.60	975.19	984.44	187.94	185.87	186.40	161,330	88.40	145.95
9	2209.11	2185.00	2199.46	992.87	978.60	986.54	188.42	186.17	187.23	163,180	88.35	144.97
10	2213.75	2182.32	2193.21	993.68	979.09	986.22	188.24	186.40	187.41	140,420	88.44	144.95
11	2211.96	2185.71	2206.43	996.60	981.52	992.70	189.25	186.82	188.95	148,950	88.40	143.57
12	2239.11	2200.71	2222.32	1003.89	985.89	996.11	190.26	187.89	188.95	183,000	88.53	143.95
13	2235.00	2210.54	2226.07	1002.27	989.95	996.76	189.54	187.53	188.54	132,320	88.71	144.17
16	2236.25	2215.36	2224.64	1005.35	990.60	996.60	189.60	187.89	188.66	117,380	88.97	143.96
17	2227.50	2203.75	2214.64	1012.32	990.60	1004.38	189.90	188.06	188.95	143,930	89.05	143.91
18	2247.32	2202.50	2238.75	1027.40	997.73	1021.89	191.20	188.24	190.73	187,540	89.18	143.60
19	2254.64	2225.71	2239.11	1032.59	1012.65	1020.91	191.09	189.19	190.37	192,030	89.24	143.49
20	2249.46	2221.25	2235.36	1024.48	1008.43	1014.27	190.61	188.77	190.02	166,100	89.24	143.70
23	2254.64	2214.29	2218.39	1027.08	1007.30	1012.48	191.20	188.72	189.31	141,640	89.12	143.60
24	2264.82	2214.82	2256.43	1031.61	1008.11	1023.83	191.80	188.83	191.15	189,620	89.22	142.48
25	2277.68	2242.32	2265.89	1031.61	1017.83	1024.81	191.56	189.25	190.49	183,610	89.34	141.98
26	2303.57	2252.86	2291.07	1044.10	1018.16	1039.23	191.56	189.19	190.43	212,250	89.39	142.25
27	2349.64	2295.18	2322.86	1063.55	1045.21	1051.72	192.09	189.60	189.96	254,870	89.52	141.78
30	2336.61	2304.82	2324.11	1062.91	1045.88	1054.31	191.20	189.07	190.73	167,830	89.40	141.41
31	2350.18	2302.68	2342.32	1075.88	1044.26	1071.50	191.56	189.43	190.97	194,050	89.34	141.11
High			2342.32			1071.50			191.15		89.52	146.71
Low			2144.64			959.95			184.15		88.35	141.11

48

Daily Closing 1989 Dow Jones Averages

February

	-30 Industrials-			-20 Transport Cos.-			-15 Utilities-			Daily Sales -000-	20 Bonds	Commodity Futures
	High	Low	Close	High	Low	Close	High	Low	Close			
1	2355.00	2319.29	2338.21	1081.23	1060.96	1070.69	191.09	188.72	189.54	215,640	89.49	140.48
2	2352.86	2319.64	2333.75	1083.66	1064.85	1076.85	190.85	188.83	189.96	183,430	89.49	139.91
3	2348.75	2319.29	2331.25	1091.85	1070.18	1083.44	190.67	189.01	189.54	172,980	89.37	139.70
6	2338.04	2307.68	2321.07	1095.73	1074.06	1084.73	190.02	187.94	189.19	150,980	89.32	139.27
7	2363.75	2314.64	2347.14	1099.61	1079.72	1087.97	191.26	188.60	190.85	217,260	89.46	139.87
8	2369.29	2332.86	2343.21	1094.44	1071.64	1076.16	191.62	189.31	190.08	189,420	89.62	139.67
9	2347.68	2308.39	2323.04	1082.63	1059.51	1068.89	189.90	187.59	188.00	224,220	89.56	139.04
10	2322.32	2278.93	2286.07	1071.47	1054.01	1059.99	188.18	187.59	188.00	173,560	89.13	137.87
13	2295.71	2266.07	2282.50	1071.96	1047.22	1068.08	187.53	185.63	187.11	143,520	89.11	137.06
14	2308.04	2274.82	2281.25	1079.24	1057.89	1062.10	187.89	185.63	186.05	149,560	89.02	136.76
15	2309.64	2275.71	2303.93	1079.40	1060.48	1075.36	187.17	185.10	186.52	154,220	88.94	137.55
16	2326.07	2293.04	2311.43	1086.03	1068.56	1079.24	187.47	185.69	186.17	177,450	88.80	137.08
17	2339.11	2301.96	2324.82	1089.26	1074.06	1082.79	187.41	185.51	186.46	159,520	88.83	137.37
20						HOLIDAY						
21	2340.89	2311.79	2326.43	1091.04	1072.77	1082.15	186.76	184.68	185.51	141,950	88.48	138.39
22	2327.50	2276.43	2283.93	1084.57	1057.89	1069.21	185.99	183.44	183.62	163,140	88.28	139.04
23	2295.71	2266.96	2289.46	1081.66	1059.83	1078.10	185.04	182.61	184.51	150,370	88.27	139.43
24	2291.79	2242.68	2245.54	1086.19	1060.16	1071.96	184.45	181.42	181.84	160,680	88.11	139.89
27	2260.18	2232.14	2250.36	1075.03	1053.20	1061.29	183.14	180.77	182.02	139,900	87.97	138.88
28	2269.82	2242.68	2258.39	1066.46	1046.57	1051.42	183.38	181.42	182.91	147,430	88.12	139.34
High			2347.14			1087.97			190.85		89.62	140.48
Low			2245.54			1051.42			181.84		87.97	136.76

Daily Closing 1989 Dow Jones Averages

March

	— 30 Industrials —			— 20 Transport Cos. —			— 15 Utilities —			Daily Sales –000–	20 Bonds	Commodity Futures
	High	Low	Close	High	Low	Close	High	Low	Close			
1	2277.50	2234.82	2243.04	1062.26	1036.38	1042.37	184.27	181.37	181.96	177,210	88.14	139.68
2	2274.82	2239.82	2265.71	1063.55	1036.71	1056.44	183.38	181.78	182.67	161,980	88.13	140.72
3	2281.79	2255.00	2274.29	1069.05	1048.57	1059.35	183.44	181.42	182.49	151,790	88.23	141.52
6	2302.50	2270.36	2294.82	1072.93	1053.20	1068.24	184.16	181.84	183.97	168,880	88.24	141.46
7	2308.57	2278.93	2290.71	1071.96	1053.04	1059.67	184.27	182.31	183.14	172,500	88.28	142.15
8	2316.79	2280.00	2295.54	1070.50	1050.13	1059.18	184.45	182.31	183.20	167,620	88.26	141.05
9	2306.61	2282.86	2291.43	1074.06	1055.30	1066.14	184.27	182.31	182.91	143,160	88.15	141.61
10	2295.54	2261.61	2282.14	1072.93	1054.33	1064.20	183.32	181.25	182.37	146,830	87.95	142.09
13	2319.64	2282.68	2306.25	1071.15	1056.27	1060.96	183.91	181.96	182.91	140,460	87.97	141.57
14	2322.68	2296.79	2306.25	1069.86	1053.20	1058.70	183.91	181.96	182.91	139,970	87.95	141.88
15	2332.86	2300.71	2320.54	1069.70	1053.20	1061.29	184.03	182.31	183.38	167,070	88.04	141.35
16	2351.07	2315.36	2340.71	1075.68	1054.01	1066.14	185.51	183.38	184.98	196,040	88.14	141.07
17	2307.68	2267.86	2292.14	1055.14	1028.95	1039.13	183.44	181.42	182.02	242,900	87.84	141.59
20	2286.25	2249.46	2262.50	1039.94	1019.08	1026.20	182.79	181.19	182.08	151,260	87.67	140.87
21	2284.82	2259.64	2266.25	1039.62	1023.45	1034.12	183.38	181.66	182.31	142,010	87.49	140.25
22	2276.61	2247.14	2263.21	1039.62	1019.08	1024.74	183.03	181.48	182.37	146,570	87.42	139.96
23	2274.82	2235.89	2243.04	1032.50	1000.16	1008.09	183.26	181.42	182.14	153,750	87.35	139.67
24						HOLIDAY						
27	2264.29	2234.46	2257.86	1018.60	1002.91	1011.80	183.03	181.01	182.43	112,960	87.48	139.12
28	2287.86	2258.93	2275.54	1043.98	1009.06	1032.18	183.85	181.42	182.91	146,420	87.43	138.24
29	2293.62	2262.65	2281.52	1041.56	1018.92	1032.02	184.09	182.02	182.73	144,240	87.39	138.19
30	2296.92	2264.30	2281.34	1035.74	1021.35	1027.98	182.97	181.31	181.84	159,950	87.44	136.72
31	2303.34	2277.49	2293.62	1069.37	1052.55	1060.16	184.21	181.54	184.03	170,960	87.59	137.28
High			2340.71			1068.24			184.98		88.28	142.15
Low			2243.04			1008.09			181.84		87.35	136.72

Daily Closing 1989 Dow Jones Averages

April

	-30 Industrials-			-20 Transport Cos.-			-15 Utilities-			Daily Sales -000-	20 Bonds	20 Commodity Futures
	High	Low	Close	High	Low	Close	High	Low	Close			
3	2317.45	2284.09	2304.80	1069.21	1053.36	1061.77	184.98	182.79	184.39	164,660	87.65	136.00
4	2314.88	2282.44	2298.20	1066.46	1050.78	1057.89	185.22	183.62	184.80	160,680	87.73	136.34
5	2315.80	2286.84	2304.80	1073.58	1054.01	1067.27	186.17	184.15	185.46	165,880	87.93	136.28
6	2305.72	2282.81	2291.97	1073.90	1055.63	1066.30	186.11	184.51	185.46	146,530	87.92	135.92
7	2314.88	2282.07	2304.80	1077.13	1057.24	1070.67	187.29	184.68	186.70	156,950	87.72	136.32
10	2316.35	2293.62	2301.87	1076.81	1062.90	1067.43	186.82	185.22	185.81	123,990	87.96	137.67
11	2321.48	2295.27	2311.58	1079.24	1061.61	1073.58	187.41	185.46	186.46	146,830	87.86	137.26
12	2332.84	2304.44	2319.65	1084.09	1066.62	1075.52	187.47	185.69	186.28	165,200	87.86	137.91
13	2321.85	2289.59	2296.00	1082.63	1066.95	1071.96	186.88	185.28	185.69	141,590	87.82	137.93
14	2342.93	2308.83	2337.06	1092.66	1071.64	1086.03	187.77	185.75	187.53	169,780	87.81	139.04
17	2348.42	2324.23	2337.79	1095.41	1080.21	1089.59	187.83	185.81	187.23	128,540	87.90	139.39
18	2386.00	2351.36	2379.40	1121.44	1100.42	1114.17	189.37	187.17	188.66	208,650	88.11	138.82
19	2398.46	2369.50	2386.91	1128.88	1104.30	1121.77	189.90	187.65	189.31	191,510	88.18	138.64
20	2399.19	2356.85	2377.38	1126.94	1104.46	1114.65	190.43	187.65	189.31	175,970	88.40	138.51
21	2412.57	2373.35	2409.46	1142.46	1112.87	1136.64	191.15	188.77	190.97	187,310	88.33	139.39
24	2416.06	2385.08	2402.68	1147.80	1127.59	1140.85	191.44	189.66	191.15	142,100	88.37	139.41
25	2421.55	2378.85	2386.91	1150.87	1125.97	1129.85	191.56	189.54	189.90	165,430	88.45	139.27
26	2404.14	2373.90	2389.11	1137.45	1120.63	1127.91	191.15	189.66	190.61	146,090	88.53	138.60
27	2433.10	2387.83	2418.99	1154.11	1123.87	1144.08	192.15	189.37	191.68	191,170	88.73	138.14
28	2430.17	2403.59	2418.80	1153.46	1133.25	1142.79	193.34	190.32	192.21	158,390	89.02	136.76
	High	2418.99			1144.08			192.21			89.02	139.41
	Low	2291.97			1057.89			184.39			87.65	135.92

Daily Closing 1989 Dow Jones Averages

May

	— 30 Industrials —			— 20 Transport Cos. —			— 15 Utilities —			Daily Sales —000—	20 Bonds	Commodity Futures
	High	Low	Close	High	Low	Close	High	Low	Close			
1	2420.45	2390.03	2414.96	1143.76	1128.40	1136.64	193.58	190.73	192.80	138,050	88.81	137.08
2	2434.38	2394.61	2402.86	1144.24	1127.26	1133.57	194.17	191.80	192.15	172,560	88.93	137.01
3	2410.56	2382.51	2393.70	1142.95	1122.25	1130.98	192.98	190.91	192.45	171,690	88.89	137.69
4	2399.01	2373.35	2384.90	1137.29	1120.63	1130.50	193.04	191.26	192.27	153,130	88.75	137.75
5	2415.69	2371.88	2381.96	1146.67	1123.38	1129.85	194.58	191.80	192.86	180,810	88.62	137.33
8	2387.28	2356.30	2376.47	1127.91	1110.28	1120.96	193.46	191.20	192.39	135,130	88.57	136.73
9	2390.03	2356.85	2371.33	1129.20	1109.15	1116.43	193.28	191.03	192.09	150,090	88.61	136.79
10	2387.83	2361.25	2374.45	1119.66	1104.79	1112.06	192.92	190.79	191.74	146,000	88.40	136.94
11	2393.51	2365.84	2382.88	1122.74	1107.70	1117.08	192.63	191.09	191.68	151,620	88.47	137.06
12	2447.95	2408.54	2439.70	1140.20	1118.86	1133.73	196.66	193.52	196.01	221,490	88.99	136.80
15	2474.89	2432.37	2463.89	1146.02	1128.72	1139.07	196.89	194.76	196.36	179,350	89.35	135.91
16	2469.76	2439.88	2453.45	1146.18	1131.31	1139.07	197.49	195.29	196.60	173,100	89.50	135.01
17	2478.74	2439.70	2462.43	1148.77	1131.47	1140.69	198.91	196.18	198.44	191,210	89.64	135.05
18	2482.77	2448.86	2470.12	1148.93	1133.09	1141.82	199.98	197.31	199.21	177,480	89.95	135.15
19	2509.35	2468.29	2501.10	1165.10	1141.49	1156.37	201.87	198.73	200.51	242,410	90.19	134.87
22	2521.63	2481.30	2502.02	1171.09	1151.52	1161.06	202.17	200.09	201.04	185,010	90.31	132.97
23	2501.83	2467.19	2478.01	1166.40	1149.09	1155.56	201.70	198.79	199.38	187,690	90.45	132.77
24	2494.68	2458.03	2483.87	1159.28	1145.38	1154.27	200.27	198.55	199.74	178,600	90.62	132.16
25	2498.72	2467.56	2482.59	1159.61	1147.32	1152.65	200.98	198.26	199.27	154,470	90.38	132.74
26	2501.83	2473.06	2493.77	1169.63	1151.84	1165.59	201.64	199.15	201.16	143,120	90.38	132.68
29						HOLIDAY						
30	2510.66	2459.74	2475.55	1176.75	1149.09	1156.05	202.41	199.03	199.80	151,780	90.69	132.38
31	2497.06	2462.68	2480.15	1160.25	1140.20	1152.33	201.16	199.09	200.39	162,530	90.52	131.50
High			2502.02			1165.59			201.16		90.69	137.75
Low			2371.33			1112.06			191.68		88.40	131.50

52

Daily Closing 1989 Dow Jones Averages

June

	-30 Industrials-			-20 Transport Cos.-			-15 Utilities-			Daily Sales -000-	20 Bonds	Commodity Futures
	High	Low	Close	High	Low	Close	High	Low	Close			
1	2504.23	2469.67	2490.63	1162.68	1146.51	1156.53	202.35	199.27	201.70	223,160	90.75	131.55
2	2530.88	2492.46	2517.83	1167.21	1152.33	1158.31	204.66	201.58	203.47	229,140	91.12	132.25
5	2523.71	2476.84	2480.70	1162.35	1143.60	1146.02	205.61	202.64	203.12	163,420	91.44	131.36
6	2507.54	2471.32	2496.32	1153.62	1132.60	1141.33	205.61	202.41	204.78	187,570	91.68	131.66
7	2526.65	2493.38	2512.32	1152.65	1137.45	1145.86	207.39	204.24	205.96	213,710	91.89	131.75
8	2534.38	2499.82	2516.91	1156.21	1136.64	1145.70	207.39	205.25	206.32	249,769	91.83	132.02
9	2533.64	2494.85	2513.42	1154.43	1132.12	1148.29	206.97	204.95	206.44	173,240	92.23	131.10
12	2528.17	2484.70	2518.84	1158.31	1137.29	1154.59	207.15	205.07	206.50	151,460	92.57	130.77
13	2520.71	2484.70	2503.54	1158.64	1142.30	1150.39	206.85	204.42	205.55	164,870	92.38	130.55
14	2520.71	2486.01	2503.36	1161.71	1138.75	1150.06	206.97	205.49	206.08	170,540	92.52	131.51
15	2505.97	2460.82	2475.00	1153.78	1134.54	1139.55	206.85	204.18	205.19	178,480	92.44	131.70
16	2495.52	2461.57	2486.38	1147.32	1130.50	1140.52	206.32	203.77	205.73	244,510	92.31	132.08
19	2497.15	2465.10	2479.89	1166.72	1142.63	1159.77	206.50	204.42	205.78	130,720	92.19	133.22
20	2496.02	2463.96	2472.88	1184.99	1157.66	1167.37	206.73	204.72	205.61	167,650	91.94	132.84
21	2489.38	2450.87	2464.91	1181.44	1157.50	1170.60	206.26	204.01	205.13	168,830	91.78	132.44
22	2489.76	2452.77	2482.17	1184.18	1164.46	1177.88	207.68	204.48	207.21	176,510	91.46	132.44
23	2536.04	2490.14	2531.87	1192.76	1175.29	1186.45	210.64	207.15	210.53	198,720	91.80	132.44
26	2536.99	2500.57	2511.38	1196.31	1177.39	1183.38	211.47	208.75	210.53	143,600	92.15	131.38
27	2544.95	2507.40	2526.37	1204.72	1180.47	1192.59	212.42	209.87	211.77	171,090	92.19	131.63
28	2531.87	2485.77	2504.74	1195.83	1172.06	1178.85	212.48	209.34	211.30	158,470	92.27	131.86
29	2500.00	2451.25	2458.27	1178.69	1149.74	1152.98	211.83	208.33	209.34	167,100	92.06	131.00
30	2466.05	2412.94	2440.06	1157.99	1130.34	1148.77	210.17	206.38	209.70	170,490	92.24	131.37
High			2531.87			1192.59			211.77		92.57	133.22
Low			2440.06			1139.55			201.70		90.75	130.55

53

Daily Closing 1989 Dow Jones Averages

July

	— 30 Industrials —			— 20 Transport Cos. —			— 15 Utilities —			Daily Sales —000—	20 Bonds	Commodity Futures
	High	Low	Close	High	Low	Close	High	Low	Close			
	2461.49	2434.37	2452.77	1168.18	1147.48	1164.46	210.89	208.25	210.07	68,870	92.37	130.61
3												
4						HOLIDAY						
5	2467.19	2431.53	2456.56	1175.94	1155.08	1170.44	210.58	207.94	209.95	127,700	92.26	132.03
6	2475.53	2446.51	2462.44	1188.23	1165.75	1179.82	211.08	208.38	210.32	140,450	92.54	130.83
7	2503.22	2456.56	2487.86	1217.98	1176.75	1200.84	212.84	209.19	212.02	166,430	92.63	129.95
10	2513.47	2482.74	2502.66	1220.41	1197.93	1208.93	213.66	210.89	212.97	131,870	92.75	128.97
11	2537.37	2503.41	2514.61	1225.74	1196.47	1203.43	216.30	213.09	215.73	171,590	92.67	128.46
12	2543.25	2504.93	2532.63	1206.50	1182.57	1196.31	216.55	214.03	215.73	160,550	92.80	128.23
13	2553.30	2517.83	2538.32	1202.94	1185.32	1194.70	216.49	214.41	215.61	153,800	92.91	129.04
14	2563.16	2512.52	2554.82	1216.04	1187.10	1210.54	217.49	214.22	216.86	183,480	93.02	129.46
17	2565.82	2535.85	2553.49	1234.64	1202.62	1229.30	217.30	215.23	216.74	131,960	92.91	128.86
18	2560.70	2531.68	2544.76	1245.47	1218.31	1232.05	216.74	214.41	215.61	152,350	92.84	129.50
19	2590.48	2546.47	2584.41	1248.54	1218.14	1233.34	217.87	215.17	217.68	215,740	92.85	129.04
20	2616.46	2566.58	2575.49	1250.16	1222.35	1232.37	219.44	215.17	216.55	204,590	92.92	129.55
21	2613.81	2558.23	2607.36	1240.78	1222.19	1231.40	217.68	214.73	217.05	174,880	92.93	129.48
24	2607.55	2574.36	2584.98	1250.32	1242.08	1240.30	217.24	214.91	215.92	136,260	92.75	129.15
25	2610.39	2565.63	2583.08	1264.72	1250.00	1253.07	217.12	214.29	215.42	179,270	92.79	129.05
26	2621.21	2563.73	2613.05	1280.08	1252.49	1266.66	217.24	213.91	217.18	188,270	92.93	129.42
27	2649.28	2604.70	2635.43	1283.61	1252.31	1266.18	218.75	215.67	217.93	213,680	93.08	129.07
28	2656.68	2615.71	2635.24	1279.16	1263.16	1269.20	221.08	217.62	219.82	180,610	93.42	127.93
31	2668.25	2615.52	2660.66	1281.83		1277.74	221.52	218.44	221.20	166,650	93.72	128.12
High			2660.66			1277.74			221.20		93.72	132.03
Low			2452.77			1164.46			209.95		92.26	127.93

54

Daily Closing 1989 Dow Jones Averages

August

	30 Industrials			20 Transport Cos.			15 Utilities			Daily Sales -000-	20 Bonds	Commodity Futures
	High	Low	Close	High	Low	Close	High	Low	Close			
1	2687.03	2628.98	2641.12	1298.36	1263.87	1278.98	222.40	218.88	220.45	225,280	93.91	128.47
2	2668.44	2626.33	2657.44	1284.85	1260.49	1273.47	220.51	217.74	219.19	181,760	94.15	128.70
3	2676.97	2640.74	2661.61	1283.96	1257.47	1266.89	219.76	217.68	218.81	168,690	94.13	129.00
4	2679.44	2629.17	2653.45	1271.69	1241.47	1250.00	219.38	216.86	218.18	169,750	93.83	128.93
7	2701.82	2643.59	2694.99	1348.86	1298.72	1344.06	221.64	217.87	221.52	197,580	93.84	128.57
8	2718.51	2676.97	2699.17	1373.76	1340.33	1355.80	222.52	219.88	221.64	200,340	93.62	128.62
9	2725.15	2678.11	2686.08	1421.94	1379.62	1406.29	223.53	218.50	220.32	209,900	93.34	128.41
10	2732.93	2669.58	2712.63	1438.48	1407.54	1419.63	221.27	217.56	220.20	198,660	93.39	128.41
11	2747.53	2668.06	2683.99	1447.72	1397.23	1413.23	221.83	217.05	217.56	197,550	93.44	129.23
14	2702.96	2654.97	2677.92	1432.08	1395.98	1413.94	219.00	215.29	216.23	142,010	93.35	128.45
15	2705.24	2665.02	2687.78	1417.32	1390.65	1404.69	218.56	215.10	217.74	148,770	93.30	129.27
16	2712.25	2680.58	2693.29	1413.05	1386.56	1401.67	220.20	216.68	218.31	150,060	93.30	129.25
17	2703.72	2663.13	2679.63	1437.59	1414.12	1428.34	218.81	215.54	216.55	157,560	93.11	129.82
18	2697.27	2665.97	2687.97	1453.24	1425.68	1442.39	217.74	215.10	216.93	145,810	92.99	129.97
21	2693.29	2640.74	2647.00	1458.04	1432.08	1438.12	217.37	213.03	213.91	136,800	93.10	130.44
22	2659.71	2619.88	2650.99	1440.97	1423.19	1433.50	214.54	211.90	213.34	141,930	93.04	131.12
23	2683.61	2641.12	2678.11	1445.41	1424.08	1437.77	216.68	212.78	216.30	159,640	93.02	131.68
24	2738.43	2672.23	2734.64	1458.21	1434.92	1448.79	219.82	215.54	219.32	225,520	93.04	131.30
25	2758.73	2715.48	2732.36	1476.17	1443.10	1467.99	220.70	217.43	218.37	165,930	93.01	131.48
28	2748.10	2710.74	2743.36	1499.64	1458.93	1492.89	219.19	216.55	218.94	131,180	93.00	131.09
29	2757.60	2704.98	2726.63	1525.60	1477.60	1506.58	219.82	216.80	217.74	175,210	93.16	130.54
30	2753.61	2705.36	2728.15	1547.30	1509.78	1529.52	218.81	215.92	217.05	174,350	93.12	130.70
31	2744.68	2717.90	2737.27	1522.94	1491.64	1509.42	218.37	215.92	217.30	143,420	93.05	131.34
High			2743.36			1529.52			221.64		94.15	131.68
Low			2641.12			1250.00			213.34		92.99	128.41

Daily Closing 1989 Dow Jones Averages

September

Date	30 Industrials High	Low	Close	20 Transport Cos. High	Low	Close	15 Utilities High	Low	Close	Daily Sales -000-	20 Bonds	Commodity Futures
1	2766.91	2726.82	2752.09	1535.38	1512.09	1526.32	219.25	216.11	218.62	133,300	93.18	130.58
4						HOLIDAY						
5	2768.24	2731.76	2744.68	1546.59	1524.18	1532.01	219.06	216.23	217.24	145,180	93.13	129.83
6	2752.09	2697.95	2719.79	1508.71	1526.67	1508.71	217.43	214.35	214.91	161,800	93.13	129.77
7	2748.10	2692.06	2706.88	1516.54	1474.93	1480.97	216.61	214.10	214.66	160,160	92.99	130.85
8	2728.72	2679.33	2709.54	1494.67	1456.97	1473.68	216.61	213.78	215.98	154,090	93.06	130.52
11	2720.74	2677.05	2704.41	1479.02	1458.75	1469.59	216.55	213.97	215.61	126,020	93.02	130.25
12	2726.06	2689.59	2707.26	1490.04	1464.08	1477.06	216.93	214.54	215.92	142,140	92.96	129.77
13	2725.87	2671.35	2679.52	1488.98	1459.99	1469.24	216.74	213.53	214.10	175,330	92.94	129.90
14	2690.16	2647.61	2664.89	1473.51	1437.23	1443.28	215.04	212.53	213.78	149,250	92.96	130.61
15	2695.67	2643.05	2674.58	1458.93	1428.70	1439.72	215.98	212.71	215.54	234,870	93.01	130.69
18	2694.91	2662.61	2687.50	1451.28	1431.01	1442.21	217.18	214.41	216.49	136,940	92.84	130.24
19	2709.35	2675.91	2687.31	1459.10	1438.48	1450.21	218.06	215.42	216.55	141,160	92.89	129.66
20	2703.46	2672.49	2683.89	1465.33	1443.63	1457.33	218.56	216.23	217.43	136,640	92.97	130.69
21	2707.83	2665.65	2680.28	1475.11	1448.08	1465.86	218.44	215.86	216.30	146,930	92.89	130.84
22	2696.62	2667.55	2681.61	1470.48	1442.57	1448.26	217.93	216.05	216.80	133,350	92.88	130.24
25	2685.41	2647.61	2659.19	1444.35	1423.19	1428.17	217.37	214.91	215.67	121,130	92.63	130.63
26	2688.64	2652.93	2663.94	1444.70	1419.45	1424.96	217.62	215.10	215.48	158,350	92.62	130.17
27	2685.03	2636.78	2673.06	1443.10	1410.74	1427.63	216.17	214.16	215.17	158,400	92.42	129.94
28	2709.16	2657.86	2694.91	1447.72	1419.63	1438.12	216.99	214.91	216.55	164,240	92.45	130.46
29	2721.12	2675.72	2692.82	1461.42	1433.85	1450.04	216.80	214.91	216.17	155,300	92.43	130.92
High			2752.09			1532.01			218.62		93.18	130.92
Low			2659.19			1424.96			213.78		92.42	129.66

56

Daily Closing 1989 Dow Jones Averages

October

	-30 Industrials-			-20 Transport Cos.-			-15 Utilities-			Daily Sales -000-	20 Bonds	Commodity Futures
	High	Low	Close	High	Low	Close	High	Low	Close			
2	2724.16	2677.05	2713.72	1466.39	1439.90	1455.19	216.86	214.85	216.49	127,410	92.36	131.95
3	2765.96	2708.97	2754.56	1469.77	1443.63	1459.28	217.87	215.92	217.56	182,550	92.45	131.48
4	2785.52	2738.79	2771.09	1474.57	1450.39	1467.11	218.69	215.98	217.68	194,590	92.59	131.26
5	2797.11	2747.15	2773.56	1519.74	1485.78	1498.76	218.81	216.74	218.37	177,890	92.51	130.98
6	2808.13	2765.58	2785.52	1518.49	1493.60	1504.62	219.82	217.74	218.69	172,520	92.59	130.68
9	2804.52	2766.34	2791.41	1523.83	1503.91	1518.49	219.69	217.81	219.13	86,810	92.62	129.77
10	2809.08	2766.53	2785.33	1524.00	1497.87	1505.87	220.13	218.18	219.50	147,560	93.01	129.15
11	2790.98	2750.82	2773.36	1503.91	1477.60	1484.53	219.94	218.00	219.00	164,070	92.89	129.25
12	2785.25	2744.06	2759.84	1496.27	1471.91	1484.35	219.88	217.87	219.25	160,120	92.94	129.86
13	2773.36	2545.49	2569.26	1490.04	1400.25	1406.29	219.82	211.08	211.96	251,170	93.06	129.87
16	2667.42	2496.93	2657.38	1335.53	1250.89	1304.23	215.92	207.05	214.73	416,290	93.00	129.72
17	2665.37	2588.73	2638.73	1288.41	1228.84	1254.27	215.92	211.83	214.54	224,070	92.74	129.72
18	2664.34	2610.66	2643.65	1270.80	1224.22	1247.87	215.61	212.90	213.97	166,900	92.70	129.90
19	2707.58	2650.61	2683.20	1279.52	1242.53	1263.51	216.68	213.66	215.42	198,120	92.68	130.13
20	2703.07	2660.25	2689.14	1253.02	1216.04	1230.80	216.68	214.03	215.48	164,830	92.76	129.62
23	2704.71	2648.77	2662.91	1258.89	1226.53	1236.66	216.42	214.22	215.35	135,860	92.73	129.49
24	2680.74	2570.29	2659.22	1223.33	1145.45	1210.70	216.11	211.33	215.04	237,960	92.83	129.24
25	2684.84	2627.66	2653.28	1223.51	1183.32	1199.32	217.05	214.29	216.49	155,650	93.09	129.48
26	2657.99	2597.75	2613.73	1222.44	1181.19	1205.19	217.62	214.79	215.67	175,240	93.13	129.22
27	2621.11	2573.57	2596.72	1209.99	1177.28	1190.43	217.24	214.60	215.86	170,330	93.15	129.49
30	2627.05	2588.11	2603.48	1207.86	1183.68	1191.86	218.00	215.17	216.74	126,630	93.11	129.38
31	2662.09	2606.97	2645.08	1214.08	1188.12	1205.01	219.82	216.36	219.19	176,100	93.15	129.63
High			2791.41			1518.49			219.50		93.15	131.95
Low			2569.26			1190.43			211.96		92.36	129.15

57

Daily Closing 1989 Dow Jones Averages

November

	– 30 Industrials –			– 20 Transport Cos. –			– 15 Utilities –			Daily Sales –000–	20 Bonds	Commodity Futures
	High	Low	Close	High	Low	Close	High	Low	Close			
1	2665.78	2622.95	2645.90	1219.24	1196.66	1206.26	221.01	215.17	220.45	154,250	93.19	129.91
2	2653.69	2607.58	2631.56	1216.75	1182.97	1192.92	221.27	218.81	220.07	152,440	93.12	130.50
3	2650.82	2612.91	2629.51	1220.31	1194.88	1211.77	221.01	218.31	219.69	131,500	93.05	130.14
6	2621.72	2574.59	2582.17	1212.84	1187.59	1192.57	219.76	217.18	218.06	135,480	92.83	130.06
7	2608.81	2563.11	2597.13	1197.72	1177.99	1188.30	220.01	217.24	219.63	163,000	92.89	130.72
8	2644.26	2594.67	2623.36	1208.93	1189.54	1199.15	221.52	218.88	220.95	170,150	93.00	131.35
9	2634.84	2595.90	2603.69	1209.82	1186.34	1192.39	221.01	218.88	219.50	143,390	93.18	131.57
10	2635.86	2603.07	2625.61	1211.06	1189.72	1203.41	221.58	218.88	220.95	131,800	93.32	131.13
13	2648.36	2602.05	2626.43	1221.91	1196.12	1210.53	221.71	219.44	220.82	140,750	93.33	131.79
14	2640.57	2597.13	2610.25	1217.82	1194.52	1201.46	221.96	219.06	219.88	143,170	93.16	131.65
15	2641.60	2600.00	2632.58	1214.62	1193.10	1205.19	221.89	219.06	221.58	155,130	93.35	131.97
16	2650.61	2613.52	2635.66	1210.53	1189.19	1197.72	223.28	220.70	222.40	148,370	93.50	131.49
17	2665.37	2623.16	2652.66	1201.10	1181.37	1191.15	222.59	220.38	221.08	151,020	93.52	131.81
20	2659.26	2615.40	2632.04	1195.95	1151.32	1163.23	221.71	218.75	220.01	128,170	93.52	131.11
21	2654.22	2614.97	2639.29	1175.32	1137.62	1158.25	221.20	218.62	220.01	147,900	93.61	131.39
22	2668.30	2629.91	2656.78	1173.54	1148.83	1166.43	221.77	219.25	221.33	145,730	93.57	131.75
23			HOLIDAY									
24	2686.01	2657.00	2675.55	1181.01	1161.45	1176.03	222.27	220.45	221.58	86,290	93.54	132.41
27	2713.95	2663.40	2694.97	1185.28	1167.32	1178.34	223.72	220.82	222.46	149,390	93.53	131.28
28	2715.02	2677.25	2702.01	1188.12	1168.92	1177.28	223.53	221.58	223.03	153,770	93.53	131.11
29	2713.10	2677.47	2688.78	1182.61	1162.34	1167.50	223.97	221.96	223.09	147,270	93.58	130.65
30	2718.22	2681.95	2706.27	1179.41	1159.32	1170.70	225.29	222.84	224.91	153,200	93.51	131.24
High			2706.27			1211.77			224.91		93.61	132.41
Low			2582.17			1158.25			218.06		92.83	129.91

58

Daily Closing 1989 Dow Jones Averages

December

	30 Industrials			20 Transport Cos.			15 Utilities			Daily Sales -000-	20 Bonds	Commodity Futures
	High	Low	Close	High	Low	Close	High	Low	Close			
1	2763.87	2705.42	2747.65	1210.35	1170.16	1202.35	228.56	224.47	227.80	199,200	93.49	130.77
4	2772.18	2731.02	2753.63	1226.71	1202.52	1217.64	229.25	226.86	228.24	150,360	93.59	128.89
5	2773.89	2731.23	2741.68	1237.73	1215.33	1220.84	229.56	227.05	228.06	154,640	93.57	129.15
6	2754.91	2722.70	2736.77	1231.69	1202.35	1213.73	229.63	226.92	227.68	145,850	93.64	129.79
7	2756.83	2702.01	2720.78	1223.15	1202.35	1211.06	229.38	226.36	227.55	161,980	93.44	129.58
8	2750.85	2716.51	2731.44	1219.95	1202.88	1209.46	229.56	227.55	228.75	144,910	93.41	129.39
11	2742.75	2705.63	2728.24	1213.55	1197.32	1201.10	229.44	226.99	228.81	147,130	93.47	130.33
12	2764.51	2716.51	2752.13	1221.73	1196.83	1212.13	231.95	228.18	231.64	176,820	93.40	130.02
13	2784.77	2737.20	2761.09	1221.37	1193.28	1203.41	235.04	230.45	233.46	184,660	93.45	130.26
14	2771.33	2732.08	2753.63	1204.66	1179.41	1185.63	235.35	232.58	234.66	178,700	93.45	129.94
15	2763.65	2703.92	2739.55	1190.61	1153.27	1170.70	236.54	233.15	235.98	240,390	93.37	130.74
18	2755.55	2679.82	2697.53	1176.56	1129.27	1140.83	236.73	232.58	233.65	184,750	93.47	130.05
19	2720.14	2658.70	2695.61	1152.20	1118.07	1139.22	235.04	231.70	233.65	186,060	93.43	129.83
20	2719.07	2667.02	2687.93	1149.72	1123.22	1136.74	235.29	231.83	233.84	176,520	93.48	129.67
21	2714.16	2671.72	2691.13	1157.18	1130.16	1143.67	235.98	231.39	233.40	175,150	93.42	129.96
22	2721.20	2682.59	2711.39	1163.76	1139.40	1158.78	235.54	232.39	234.53	120,980	93.43	130.37
25						HOLIDAY						
26	2728.88	2694.75	2709.26	1175.68	1154.87	1167.85	236.04	233.21	234.09	77,610	93.08	131.29
27	2739.12	2700.30	2724.40	1182.97	1157.18	1172.30	236.10	233.21	234.78	133,730	93.02	129.74
28	2742.53	2709.04	2732.30	1181.01	1158.96	1174.43	236.48	233.84	235.41	128,030	93.07	129.30
29	2763.01	2726.96	2753.20	1185.63	1164.47	1177.81	236.29	233.27	235.04	145,940	92.94	129.37
	High		2761.09			1220.84			235.98		93.64	131.29
	Low		2687.93			1136.74			227.55		92.94	128.89

59

DOW JONES INDUSTRIAL MONTHLY CLOSING AVERAGES

1989 Month ended		D-J Ind.	1988 Month ended		D-J Ind.	1987 Month ended		D-J Ind.
December	29	2753.20	December	30	2168.57	December	31	1938.83
November	30	2706.27	November	30	2114.51	November	30	1833.55
October	31	2645.08	October	31	2148.65	October	30	1993.53
September	29	2692.82	September	30	2112.91	September	30	2596.28
August	31	2737.27	August	31	2031.65	August	31	2662.95
July	31	2660.66	July	29	2128.73	July	31	2572.07
June	30	2440.06	June	30	2141.71	June	30	2418.53
May	31	2480.15	May	31	2031.12	May	29	2291.57
April	28	2418.80	April	29	2032.33	April	30	2286.36
March	31	2293.62	March	31	1988.06	March	31	2304.69
February	28	2258.39	February	29	2071.62	February	27	2223.99
January	31	2342.32	January	29	1958.22	January	30	2158.04

1986 Month ended		D-J Ind.	1985 Month ended		D-J Ind.	1984 Month ended		D-J Ind.
December	31	1895.95	December	31	1546.67	December	31	1211.57
November	28	1914.23	November	29	1472.13	November	30	1188.94
October	31	1877.81	October	31	1374.31	October	31	1207.38
September	30	1767.58	September	30	1328.63	September	28	1206.71
August	29	1898.34	August	30	1334.01	August	31	1224.38
July	31	1775.31	July	31	1347.45	July	31	1115.28
June	30	1892.72	June	28	1335.46	June	29	1132.40
May	30	1876.71	May	31	1315.41	May	31	1104.85
April	30	1783.98	April	30	1258.06	April	30	1170.75
March	31	1818.61	March	29	1266.78	March	30	1164.89
February	28	1709.06	February	28	1284.01	February	29	1154.63
January	31	1570.99	January	31	1286.77	January	31	1220.58

1983 Month ended		D-J Ind.	1982 Month ended		D-J Ind.	1981 Month ended		D-J Ind.
December	30	1258.64	December	31	1046.54	December	31	875.00
November	30	1276.02	November	30	1039.28	November	30	888.98
October	31	1225.20	October	29	991.72	October	30	852.55
September	30	1233.13	September	30	896.25	September	30	849.98
August	31	1216.16	August	31	901.31	August	31	881.47
July	29	1199.22	July	30	808.60	July	31	952.34
June	30	1221.96	June	30	811.93	June	30	976.88
May	31	1199.98	May	28	819.54	May	29	991.75
April	29	1226.20	April	30	848.36	April	30	997.75
March	31	1130.33	March	31	822.77	March	31	1003.87
February	28	1112.62	February	26	824.39	February	27	974.58
January	31	1075.70	January	29	871.10	January	30	947.27

1980 Month ended		D-J Ind.	Month ended		D-J Ind.	Month ended		D-J Ind.
December	31	963.99	August	29	932.59	April	30	817.06
November	28	993.34	July	31	935.32	March	31	785.75
October	31	924.49	June	30	867.92	February	29	863.14
September	30	932.42	May	30	850.85	January	31	875.85

DOW JONES INDUSTRIAL MONTHLY CLOSING AVERAGES

1979 Month ended		D-J Ind.	1978 Month ended		D-J Ind.	1977 Month ended		D-J Ind.
December	31	838.74	December	29	801.05	December	30	831.17
November	30	822.35	November	30	799.03	November	30	829.70
October	31	815.70	October	31	729.45	October	31	818.35
September	28	878.58	September	29	865.82	September	30	847.11
August	31	887.63	August	31	876.82	August	31	861.49
July	31	846.42	July	31	862.27	July	29	890.07
June	29	841.98	June	30	818.95	June	30	916.30
May	31	822.33	May	31	840.61	May	31	898.66
April	30	854.90	April	28	837.32	April	29	926.90
March	30	862.18	March	31	757.36	March	31	919.13
February	28	808.82	February	28	742.12	February	28	936.42
January	31	839.22	January	31	769.92	January	31	954.37

1976 Month ended		D-J Ind.	1975 Month ended		D-J Ind.	1974 Month ended		D-J Ind.
December	31	1004.65	December	31	852.41	December	31	616.24
November	30	947.22	November	28	860.67	November	29	618.66
October	29	964.93	October	31	836.04	October	31	665.52
September	30	990.19	September	30	793.88	September	30	607.87
August	31	973.74	August	29	835.34	August	30	678.58
July	30	984.64	July	31	831.51	July	31	757.43
June	30	1002.78	June	30	878.99	June	28	802.41
May	28	975.23	May	30	832.29	May	31	802.17
April	30	996.85	April	30	821.34	April	30	836.75
March	31	999.45	March	31	768.15	March	29	846.68
February	27	972.61	February	28	739.05	February	28	860.53
January	30	975.28	January	31	703.69	January	31	855.55

1973 Month ended		D-J Ind.	1972 Month ended		D-J Ind.	1971 Month ended		D-J Ind.
December	31	850.86	December	29	1020.02	December	31	890.20
November	30	822.25	November	30	1018.21	November	30	831.34
October	31	956.58	October	31	955.52	October	29	839.00
September	28	947.10	September	29	953.27	September	30	887.19
August	31	887.57	August	31	963.73	August	31	898.07
July	31	926.40	July	31	924.74	July	30	858.43
June	29	891.71	June	30	929.03	June	30	891.14
May	31	901.41	May	31	960.72	May	28	907.81
April	30	921.43	April	28	954.17	April	30	941.75
March	30	951.01	March	30	940.70	March	31	904.37
February	28	955.07	February	29	928.13	February	26	878.83
January	31	999.02	January	31	902.17	January	29	868.50

Month ended		D-J Ind.	1970 Month ended		D-J Ind.	Month ended		D-J Ind.
December	31	838.92	August	31	764.58	April	30	736.07
November	30	794.09	July	31	734.12	March	31	785.57
October	30	755.61	June	30	683.53	February	27	777.59
September	30	760.88	May	29	700.44	January	30	744.06

61

YEARLY HIGHS AND LOWS OF DOW JONES AVERAGES

	—Industrials—		—Transportation—		—Utilities—	
	Record High 2791.41		Record High 1532.01		Record High 235.98	
	Record Low 38.49		Record Low 13.23		Record Low 10.58	
	High	Low	High	Low	High	Low
1989	2791.41	2144.64	1532.01	959.95	235.98	181.84
1988	2183.50	1879.14	973.61	737.57	190.02	167.08
1987	2722.42	1738.74	1101.16	661.00	227.83	160.98
1986	1955.57	1502.29	866.74	686.97	219.15	169.47
1985	1553.10	1184.96	723.31	553.03	174.96	146.54
1984	1286.64	1086.57	612.63	444.03	149.93	122.25
1983	1287.20	1027.04	612.57	434.24	140.70	119.51
1982	1070.55	776.92	464.55	292.12	122.83	103.22
1981	1024.05	824.01	447.38	335.48	117.81	101.28
1980	1000.17	759.13	425.68	233.69	117.34	96.04
1979	897.61	796.67	271.77	205.78	109.74	98.24
1978	907.74	742.12	261.49	199.31	110.98	96.35
1977	999.75	800.85	246.64	199.60	118.67	104.97
1976	1014.79	858.71	237.03	175.69	108.38	84.52
1975	881.81	632.04	174.57	146.47	87.07	72.02
1974	891.66	577.60	202.45	125.93	95.09	57.93
1973	1051.70	788.31	228.10	151.97	120.72	84.42
1972	1036.27	889.15	275.71	212.24	124.14	105.06
1971	950.82	797.97	248.33	169.70	128.39	108.03
1970	842.00	631.16	183.31	116.69	121.84	95.86
1969	968.85	769.93	279.88	169.03	139.95	106.31
1968	985.21	825.13	279.48	214.58	141.30	119.79
1967	943.08	786.41	274.49	205.16	140.43	120.97
1966	995.15	744.32	271.72	184.34	152.39	118.96
1965	969.26	840.59	249.55	187.29	163.32	149.84
1964	891.71	766.08	224.91	178.81	155.71	137.30
1963	767.21	646.69	179.46	142.03	144.37	129.19
1962	726.01	535.76	149.83	114.86	130.85	103.11
1961	734.91	610.25	152.92	131.06	135.90	99.75
1960	685.47	566.05	160.43	123.37	100.07	85.02
1959	679.36	574.46	173.56	146.65	94.70	85.05
1958	583.65	436.89	157.91	99.89	91.00	68.94
1957	520.77	419.79	157.67	95.67	74.61	62.10
1956	521.05	462.35	181.23	150.44	71.77	63.03
1955	488.40	388.20	167.83	137.84	66.68	61.39
1954	404.39	279.87	146.23	94.84	62.47	52.22
1953	293.79	255.49	112.21	90.56	53.88	47.87
1952	292.00	256.35	112.53	82.03	52.64	47.53
1951	276.37	238.99	90.08	72.39	47.22	41.47
1950	235.47	196.81	77.89	51.24	44.26	37.40
1949	200.52	161.60	54.29	41.03	41.31	33.36

YEARLY HIGHS AND LOWS OF DOW JONES AVERAGES

	—Industrials—		—Transportation—		—Utilities—	
	High	Low	High	Low	High	Low
1948	193.16	165.39	64.95	48.13	36.04	31.65
1947	186.85	163.21	53.42	41.16	37.55	32.28
1946	212.50	163.12	63.31	44.69	43.74	33.20
1945	195.82	151.35	64.89	47.03	39.15	26.15
1944	152.53	134.22	48.40	33.45	26.37	21.74
1943	145.82	119.26	38.30	27.59	22.30	14.69
1942	119.71	92.92	29.28	23.31	14.94	10.58
1941	133.59	106.34	30.88	24.25	20.65	13.51
1940	152.80	111.84	32.67	22.14	26.45	18.03
1939	155.92	121.44	35.90	24.14	27.10	20.71
1938	158.41	98.95	33.98	19.00	c25.19	c15.14
1937	194.40	113.64	64.46	28.91	37.54	19.65
1936	184.90	143.11	59.89	40.66	36.08	28.63
1935	148.44	96.71	41.84	27.31	29.78	14.46
1934	110.74	85.51	52.97	33.19	31.03	16.83
1933	108.67	50.16	56.53	23.42	37.73	19.33
1932	88.78	41.22	41.20	13.23	36.11	16.53
1931	194.36	73.79	111.58	31.42	73.40	30.55
1930	294.07	157.51	157.94	91.65	108.62	55.14
1929	381.17	198.69	189.11	128.07	144.61	64.72
1928	300.00	191.33	b152.70	b132.60	....	....
1927	202.40	152.73	144.82	119.92	....	....
1926	166.64	135.20	123.23	102.41	....	....
1925	159.39	115.00	112.93	92.82	....	....
1924	120.51	88.33	99.50	80.23	....	....
1923	105.38	85.76	90.63	76.78	....	....
1922	103.43	78.59	93.99	74.43	....	....
1921	81.50	63.90	77.56	65.52	....	....
1920	109.88	66.75	85.37	67.83	....	....
1919	119.62	79.15	91.13	73.63	....	....
1918	89.07	73.38	92.91	77.21	....	....
1917	99.18	65.95	105.76	70.75	....	....
1916	110.15	84.96	112.28	99.11	....	....
1915	99.21	54.22	108.28	87.85	....	....
1914	a83.43	a71.42	a109.43	a89.41	....	....

a—The high and low figures for the industrials and transportation are for the period ended July 31, 1914. The industrial average was composed of 12 stocks when the New York Stock Exchange closed in July 1914 because of World War I. In September 1916, a new list of 20 stocks was adopted and computed back to the opening of the Exchange on December 12, 1914. On October 1, 1928, the stocks comprising the industrial average was increased to 30. The high and low for the industrial average for December 1914 was 56.76 and 53.17, respectively. The high and low for transportation for December 1914 was 92.29 and 86.40.

b—On March 7, 1928, transportation components were increased to 20 from 12.

c—Since June 2, 1938, the utility average has been based on 15 stocks instead of 20.

DOW JONES COMPOSITE AVERAGE—65 STOCKS

Record High 1115.15 October 9, 1989
Record Low 31.10 March 31, 1938

Year		High	Date		Low	Date	
1989	....	1115.15	October	9	816.95	January	3
1988	....	830.24	December	29	700.70	January	21
1987	....	992.21	August	25	653.76	December	4
1986	....	767.89	December	2	602.83	January	10
1985	....	619.41	December	16	480.93	January	4
1984	....	514.02	January	6	421.36	July	24
1983	....	515.11	November	29	401.03	January	3
1982	....	416.33	December	27	299.44	August	12
1981	....	394.56	April	20	320.59	September	25
1980	....	388.87	November	28	271.73	March	27
1979	....	315.05	August	15	274.27	February	28
1978	....	315.26	September	8	260.66	March	6
1977	....	324.86	January	3	274.31	October	25
1976	....	325.49	December	31	264.50	January	22
1975	....	268.20	July	15	205.32	January	2
1974	....	282.51	March	13	184.24	October	3
1973	....	334.08	January	3	247.67	December	5
1972	....	338.54	December	11	302.13	October	16
1971	....	318.44	April	28	270.18	January	4
1970	....	273.21	December	30	208.66	May	26
1969	....	346.23	February	7	252.99	December	17
1968	....	353.09	November	29	290.09	March	25
1967	....	337.32	August	4	282.69	January	3
1966	....	352.40	February	11	261.27	October	7
1965	....	340.88	December	31	290.37	June	28
1964	....	314.15	November	20	269.09	January	2
1963	....	269.08	December	18	228.67	January	2
1962	....	245.80	January	3	187.41	June	26

YEARLY HIGHS AND LOWS OF DOW JONES BOND AVERAGES

This table lists the yearly high and low range based upon the closing average for each day during the year.

20 Bonds	1989	1988	1987	1986	1985	1984
High	94.15	91.25	95.51	93.65	83.73	72.92
Low	87.35	86.92	81.26	83.73	72.27	64.81
10 Public Utilities						
High	95.26	91.88	98.23	95.79	82.88	70.31
Low	86.95	86.05	79.51	81.85	68.62	59.43
10 Industrials						
High	93.26	90.64	93.10	91.64	84.58	76.22
Low	87.60	86.96	83.00	84.82	75.61	69.61

NET ASSETS PER SHARE ON DOW JONES INDUSTRIAL STOCKS

Book value is total assets minus total liabilities, including the par value of the preferred stock, divided by the number of shares outstanding. The industrial average's book value is the total of the book values of each of its 30 components. This compilation has not been adjusted for stock splits.

As of 12/31	1988	1987	1986	1985	1984	1983	1982
Allied-Signal	12.72	10.48	9.49	25.09	23.93	31.52	52.14
Alum. Co. Am.	49.70	41.08	39.43	39.52	40.23	38.89	38.51
Amer. Brands	a	a	a	a	27.54	25.95	26.13
Amer Express	11.39	10.11	25.20	22.82	20.21	18.95	23.87
Amer. Tel.	10.65	13.43	12.64	13.68	13.26	62.41	68.55
Bethlehem Steel	19.55	14.30	11.55	15.13	20.02	23.53	28.32
Boeing	35.27	32.75	d	d	d	d	d
Chevron	43.23	46.13	45.29	45.47	43.15	41.23	38.72
Coca-Cola	8.42	8.46	e	e	e	e	e
duPont	61.01	55.30	51.04	51.62	48.88	45.76	44.87
Eastman Kodak	6.69	18.55	26.57	28.28	45.84	45.41	45.51
Exxon	24.64	24.38	44.58	39.80	36.85	34.80	32.84
General Electric	10.99	13.35	25.29	30.01	27.09	24.04	43.12
General Foods	b	b	b	b	40.92	39.15	36.06
General Motors	81.88	64.53	56.06	51.57	66.00	68.59	60.99
Goodyear	35.30	32.19	30.93	32.44	29.78	28.61	33.14
Inco	d	d	9.56	9.68	9.32	10.54	12.99
IBM	65.78	62.81	55.40	49.99	43.23	38.02	33.66
Int. Paper	38.40	36.35	67.07	66.60	66.04	65.30	63.36
Manville	c	c	c	c	c	c	c
McDonald's	16.50	14.06	17.51	23.59	a	a	a
Merck	6.69	14.48	17.83	36.15	35.29	32.59	29.49
Minnesota Mining	24.58	22.24	39.06	34.98	32.79	31.54	30.10
Navistar	2.41	1.50	d4.91	d22.02	d19.15	d28.96	nil
Owens-Illinois	e	e	27.77	51.03	47.07	46.86	50.22
Philip Morris	(d32.00)	11.71	23.77	39.69	b	b	b
Primerica	8.99	10.86	36.18	44.19	40.70	40.28	40.19
Proc. & Gamble	25.94	24.00	25.48	31.49	30.42	27.76	50.35
Sears Roebuck	36.09	34.74	32.94	30.61	28.39	26.51	25.08

NET ASSETS PER SHARE ON DOW JONES INDUSTRIAL STOCKS

As of 12/31	1988	1987	1986	1985	1984	1983	1982
Texaco	33.17	37.76	56.71	57.04	55.15	56.86	55.11
Union Carbide	12.97	8.89	7.87	59.46	69.89	69.95	73.54
USX	18.55	17.38	17.80	38.18	38.41	36.94	58.09
United Technologies	34.88	30.80	27.08	29.11	25.72	45.47	41.32
Westinghouse	22.24	21.58	19.30	17.22	18.06	32.08	30.12
Woolworth	26.20	26.55	22.49	37.60	32.67	31.92	31.58
Total	752.83	760.75	876.98	1,030.02	1,037.70	1,092.50	1,197.97
Divided (D-J Indus. Divisor)	0.700	0.754	0.889	1.090	1.132	1.230	1.359
DJI Book Value	1075.47	1008.95	986.48	944.97	916.70	888.21	881.51
Next year mkt low	2144.64	1879.14	1738.74	1502.29	1184.96	1086.57	1027.04
Ratio mkt to book value, %	199	186	176	159	129	122	116

d-Deficit.

Substitution in components: a-American Brands replaced by McDonald's Corp. b-General Foods replaced by Philip Morris. c-Manville replaced by American Express. d-Inco replaced by Boeing. e-Owens-Illinois replaced by Coca-Cola Company.

Stock splits: 1989: Boeing, June 3-for-2; General Motors, March 2-for-1; McDonald's, June 2-for-1. **1988:** Merck, May 3-for-1. **1987:** Eastman Kodak, October 3-for-2; Exxon, September 2-for-1; General Electric, May 2-for-1; Int'l. Paper, May 2-for-1; McDonald's, June 3-for-2; Minnesota Mining Manufacturing, June 2-for-1; Primerica, March 2-for-1. **1986:** McDonald's, June 3-for-2; Merck, May 2-for-1; Philip Morris, March 2-for-1; Owens Illinois, May 2-for-1; Union Carbide, March 3-for-1; Woolworth, May 2-for-1. **1985:** Eastman Kodak, May 3-for-2. **1984:** Allied Corp., May 3-for-2; United Technologies, June 2-for-1. **1983:** American Express, February 4-for-3 and August 3-for-2; General Electric, June 2-for-1; Procter & Gamble, February 2-for-1. **1982:** None. **1981:** Alcoa, February 2-for-1; American Brands, May 2-for-1; Chevron, March 2-for-1; Exxon, June 2-for-1.

Name changes: 1987: American Can name changed to Primerica Corp. **1986:** International Harvester name changed to Navistar International; U.S. Steel name changed to USX Corp. **1985:** Allied Corp. name changed to Allied-Signal. **1984:** Standard Oil (California) name changed to Chevron.

MAJOR INDEXES

| | ––––1989–––– | | | |
	High	Low	Close	% Chg.
Dow Jones Averages				
30 Industrials	2791.41	2144.64	2753.20	26.96
20 Transportation	1532.01	959.95	1177.81	21.44
15 Utilities	235.98	181.84	235.04	26.18
65 Composite	1115.15	816.95	1035.10	25.32
Equity Market Index*	337.63	258.45	329.85	26.50
New York Stock Exchange				
Composite	199.34	154.98	195.04	24.82
Industrials	237.76	187.87	232.76	22.88
Utilities	102.00	73.91	102.00	36.56
Transportation	212.37	145.54	178.33	21.64
Financial	173.29	127.46	156.15	21.81
Standard & Poor's Indexes				
500 Index	359.80	275.31	353.40	27.25
Industrial	410.49	318.66	403.49	25.60
Transportation	331.07	226.42	278.48	22.05
Utilities	156.04	111.15	156.04	38.53
Financial	35.24	24.30	31.30	27.81

*The Dow Jones Equity Market Index is a capitalization weighted index based on June 30, 1982=100. The index reflects 80% of the total market capitalization for nine specific economic sectors with a breakdown for eighty-two industry groups. Component issues include companies traded on the New York Stock Exchange and American Stock Exchange, as well as issues traded on the Nasdaq National Market System.

DOW JONES INDUSTRY GROUPS

BASIC MATERIALS

- **Aluminum:**
  Alcoa
  Amax Inc.
  Maxxam Inc.
  Reynolds Metals
- **Other Non-ferrous:**
  Asarco Inc.
  Brush Wellman Inc.
  Cyprus Minerals
  Magma Copper Co. "B"
  Phelps Dodge Corp.
- **Chemicals:**
  Air Prod & Chem.
  Amer Cyanamid
  Aristech Chemical
  Betz Labs
  Cabot Corp.
  Dow Chemical
  DuPont de Nemours
  Ethyl Corp.
  Georgia Gulf Corp.
  Goodrich (B.F.)
  Grace (W.R.) & Co.
  Great Lakes Chemical
  Hercules Inc.
  Int'l Minerals & Chem.
  Lubrizol Corp.
  Monsanto
  Morton Int'l.
  Nalco Chemical
  Olin Corp.
  Quantum Chemical
  Rohm & Haas Co.
  Sigma Aldrich Corp.
  Union Carbide
  Vista Chemical
- **Forest Products:**
  Boise Cascade
  Champion Int'l.
  Georgia Pacific
  Louisiana Pacific
  Potlatch Corp.
  Weyerhaeuser Co.
  Willamette Indus.
- **Diversified Mining:**
  Cleveland-Cliffs
  Freeport McMoRan
  Great Northern Iron
  Newmont Mining
  Nord Resources
- **Paper Products:**
  Bowater Inc.
  Consol. Papers
  Federal Paper Board
  Glatfelter (P.H.) Co.
  Gt. Northn Nekoosa
  Int'l. Paper Co.
  James River Corp.
  Kimberly-Clark
  Mead Corp.
  Scott Paper Co.
  Union Camp Corp.
  Westvaco Corp.
- **Precious Metals:**
  ASA Ltd.
  Battle Mountain Gold
  Handy & Harman
  Hecla Mining
  Homestake Mining
- **Steel:**

Allegheny Ludlum
Armco Inc.
Bethlehem Steel
Inland Steel Indus.
LTV Corp.
Nucor Corp.
Worthington Industries

ENERGY

- **Coal:**
  Addington Resources
  Ashland Coal
  Penn Virginia
  Pittston Co.
  Westmoreland Coal
- **Oil, Drilling:**
  Energy Service Co.
  Global Marine
  Helmerich & Payne
  Parker Drilling
  Rowan Cos.
- **Oil, Integrated Majors:**
  Amoco Corp.
  Atlantic Richfield
  Chevron Corp.
  Exxon Corp.
  Mobil Corp.
  Phillips Petroleum
  Sun Co.
  Texaco Inc.
  Unocal Corp.
- **Oil, Secondary:**
  Amerada Hess
  Anadarko Petroleum
  Ashland Oil
  Hamilton Oil
  Kerr-McGee Corp.
  Louisiana Land
  MAPCO Inc.
  Mesa L.P.
  Murphy Oil Corp.
  Noble Affiliates
  Occidental Petrol
  Oryx Energy
  Pennzoil
  Quaker State Corp.
  Union Texas Pet. Hldgs
  USX Corp.
- **Oilfield Equipment:**
  Baker Hughes
  Dresser Indus.
  Halliburton Co.
  McDermott Int'l.
  Schlumberger Ltd.
- **Pipelines:**
  Burlington Resources
  Coastal Corp.
  Enron Corp.
  Enserch Corp.
  Panhandle Eastern
  Sonat Inc.
  Transco Energy
  Williams Cos.

INDUSTRIAL

- **Air Freight/Couriers:**
  Air Express Intl.
  Airborne Freight
  Expiditers Int'l. Wash.
  Federal Express

Harper Group
- **Building Materials:**
  Armstrong World
  CalMat Co.
  Manville Corp.
  Masco Corp.
  Owens-Corning
  Sherwin-Williams
  USG Corp.
  Vulcan Materials
- **Containers &
  Packaging:**
  Ball Corp.
  Crown Cork & Seal
  Sonoco Products
  Stone Container
  Temple-Inland
- **Electrical Components:**
  AMP Inc.
  Emerson Electric
  Grainger (W.W.)
  Square D Co.
  Tecumseh Products
  Thomas & Betts
  Westinghouse
- **Factory Equipment:**
  Cincinnati Milacron
  Interlake Corp.
  Keystone Int'l
  Nordson Corp.
  Parker Hannifin
- **Heavy Construction:**
  Fluor Corp.
  Foster Wheeler Corp.
  Kasler Corp.
  Morrison Knudsen
  Stone & Webster
- **Heavy Machinery:**
  Caterpillar Inc.
  Clark Equipment
  Deere & Co.
  Harnischfeger Indus.
  Manitowoc Co.
  NACCO Indus. "A"
- **Industrial &
  Commercial Services:**
  Comdisco Inc.
  Commerce Clearing Hse.
  Deluxe Corp.
  Donnelley & Sons
  Dun & Bradstreet
  Ecolab Inc.
  Equifax Inc.
  Flightsafety Inc.
  Harland (John H.)
  Kelly Services "A"
  National Education Corp.
  National Service Ind.
  Ryder System Inc.
  Safety-Kleen
  ServiceMaster L.P.
  XTRA Corp.
- **Industrial Diversified:**
  Allied-Signal
  CBI Industries
  Asea Brown Boveri AB
  Cooper Industries
  Crane Co.
  Dexter Corp.
  Dover Corp.
  Engelhard Corp.

FMC Corp.
Harsco Corp.
Henley Group Inc.
Illinois Tool Wks.
Ingersoll-Rand Co.
Norton Co.
Penn Central Corp.
PPG Industries
Raychem Corp.
Stanley Works
Tenneco Inc.
Trinova Corp.
Tyco Labs Inc.
- **Marine Transportation:**
  Alexander & Baldwin
  American Pres. Cos.
  OMI Corp.
  Overseas Shipholding
  Sea Containers Ltd.
- **Pollution Waste Mgt.:**
  Browning-Ferris Indus.
  Ogden Corp.
  Rollins Environmental
  Waste Management Inc.
  Wheelabrator Tech.
- **Railroads:**
  Burlington Northern
  CSX Corp.
  Consolidated Rail
  Norfolk Southern
  Santa Fe Southern
  Union Pacific
- **Transportation Equip.:**
  Cummins Engine
  Eaton Corp.
  Navistar Int'l.
  Paccar Inc.
  Trinity Indus.
- **Trucking:**
  Carolina Freight
  Consol. Freightways
  Hunt (J.B.) Transpt.
  Roadway Services
  Yellow Freight Sys.

CONSUMER, CYCLICAL

- **Advertising:**
  Foote Cone Belding
  Grey Advertising
  Interpublic Group
  Mickelberry
  Omnicom Group
- **Airlines:**
  AMR Corp.
  Alaska Air Group
  Delta Air Lines
  Pan Am Corp.
  Southwest AirLines
  Texas Air Corp.
  UAL Corp.
  USAir Group
- **Automobile Mfg.:**
  Chrysler
  Ford Motor
  General Motors
- **Automobile Parts:**
  Dana Corp.
  Echlin Inc.
  Genuine Parts
  Goodyear Tire

Johnson Controls
Masco Industries
Snap-On Tools
Timken Co.
- **Casinos:**
Caesars World
Circus Circus
Golden Nugget
Aztar Corp.
Showboat
- **Home Construction:**
Centex Corp.
Kaufman & Broad
NV Ryan L.P.
PHM Corp.
U.S. Home Corp.
- **Home Furnishings/ Appliances:**
Black & Decker
Leggett & Platt
Maytag Corp.
Shaw Industries
Whirlpool Corp.
- **Lodging:**
Hilton Hotels
Holiday Corp.
La Quinta
Marriott Corp.
Prime Motor Inns
- **Media:**
Belo (A.H.) "A"
Cablevision Sys. "A"
CBS Inc.
Capital Cities/ABC
Dow Jones
Gannett Co.
Harcourt Brace J
Knight-Ridder
LIN Broadcasting
McGraw-Hill
Multimedia Inc.
New York Times "A"
Tele-Communications
Time Warner Inc.
Times Mirror "A"
Tribune Co.
Washington Post "B"
- **Recreation Products:**
Brunswick Corp.
Carnival Cruise Lines
Disney (Walt)
Eastman Kodak
Hasbro Inc.
MCA Inc.
Outboard Marine
Paramount Comm. Inc.
Polaroid
- **Restaurants:**
McDonald's Corp.
Shoney's Inc.
Sysco Corp.
TCBY Enterprises
Wendy's Int'l.
- **Retailers, Apparel:**
Gap Inc.
General Cinema
Limited Inc.
Mercantile Stores Inc.
Nordstrom Inc.
Petrie Stores Inc.
TJX Cos.
U.S. Shoe Corp.

- **Retailers, Broadline:**
Carter Hawley Hale
Dillard Dept. Stores "A"
Dayton Hudson
Penney (J.C.)
K mart
May Dept. Stores
Sears, Roebuck & Co.
Wal-Mart Stores
Woolworth Corp.
- **Retailers, Drug-Based:**
Longs Drug Stores
McKesson Corp.
Medco   Containment   Svcs
Rite Aid
Walgreen
- **Retailers, Specialty:**
Circuit City Stores
Home Depot Inc.
Jostens Inc.
Lowes Cos.
Melville Corp.
Pep Boys-Manny Moe
 & Jack
Pic 'N' Save
Price Co.
Tandy Corp.
Toys "R" Us
Waban Inc.
- **Textiles & Apparel:**
Brown Group
Hartmarx Corp.
Interco Inc.
Liz Claiborne
Nike Inc. "B"
Reebok Int'l
Russell Corp.
Spring Industries
VF Corp.

CONSUMER, NON-CYCLICAL

- **Beverages:**
A&W Brands Inc.
Anheuser-Busch
Brown-Forman "B"
Coca-Cola Bottling
Coca-Cola Co.
Coca-Cola Entrp.
Coors (Adolph) "B"
PepsiCo Inc.
- **Consumer Services:**
Block (H&R) Inc.
CPI Corp.
Fuqua Industries
Rollins Corp.
Service Corp. Int'l
- **Cosmetics/Personal Care:**
Avon Products
Gillette Co.
Int'l. Flavors & Frag.
Noxell Corp. "B"
Neutrogena
Tambrands
- **Food:**
Archer Daniels Midland
Borden Inc.
CPC International
Campbell Soup
Castle & Cooke Inc.

ConAgra Inc.
Dean Foods Co.
Flowers Industries
General Mills Inc.
Gerber Products
Heinz (H.J.)
Hormel (George A.)
Hershey Foods
Kellogg Co.
Lance Inc.
McCormick & Co.
Quaker Oats Co.
Ralston Purina
Sara Lee Corp.
Tyson Foods Inc. "A"
Whitman Corp.
Wrigley (Wm.) Jr. Co.
- **Food Retailers:**
Albertson's Inc.
American Stores
Bruno's Inc.
Circle K Corp.
Fleming Cos.
Food Lion "A"
Great Atlantic Pacific Tea
Giant Food "A"
Kroger Co.
Super Valu Stores
Vons Cos.
Winn-Dixie Stores
- **Health Care Providers:**
Community Psych. Ctrs.
Humana Inc.
Manor Care Inc.
National Medical Enterp.
U.S. Healthcare
- **Household Products:**
American Brands
Clorox Co.
Colgate-Palmolive
Johnson & Johnson
Philip Morris Cos.
Procter & Gamble
Rubbermaid Inc.
UST Inc.
Universal Corp.
- **Medical Supplies:**
Abbott Laboratories
Acuson Corp.
Bausch & Lomb
Baxter International Inc.
Bard (C.R.) Inc.
Becton, Dickinson Co.
- **Pharmaceuticals:**
American Home Products
Bristol-Myers Squibb
Lilly (Eli) & Co.
Merck & Co.
Pfizer Inc.
Rorer Group
Schering-Plough
Syntex Corp.
Upjohn Co.
Warner-Lambert

TECHNOLOGY

- **Aerospace & Defense:**
Boeing Co.
E-Systems Inc.
Gencorp Inc.
General Dynamics

Grumman Corp.
Lockheed Corp.
Loral Corp.
McDonnell Douglas
Martin Marietta
Northrop Corp.
Precision Castparts
Sundstrand Corp.
Thiokol Corp.
- **Communications:**
AT&T Co.
Communications Satellite
General Instruments
Harris Corp.
Motorola Inc.
- **Communications (Less AT&T):**
Communications Satellite
General Instruments
Harris Corp.
Motorola
- **Computers & Information:**
Amdahl Corp.
Apple Computer
Compaq Computer
Control Data
Cray Research
Data General
Digital Equipment
Hewlett-Packard
IBM
NCR
Seagate Technology
Sun Microsystems
Tandem Computers
Unisys Corp.
Wang Labs "B"
Zenith Electronics
- **Computers & Information (Less IBM):**
Amdahl Corp.
Apple Computer
Compaq Computer
Control Data
Cray Research
Data General
Digital Equipment
Hewlett-Packard
NCR
Prime Computer
Seagate Technology
Sun Microsystems
Tandem Computers
Unisys Corp.
Wang Labs "B"
Zenith Electronics
- **Diversified Technology:**
Corning Inc.
EG&G Inc.
Honeywell Inc.
Litton Industries
Minnesota Mining & Mfg.
Perkin-Elmer Corp.
Raytheon
Rockwell International
TRW Inc.
Tektronix Inc.
Texas Instruments
United Technologies

DOW JONES INDUSTRY GROUPS

Varian Associates
- **Industrial Technology:**
Ametek Inc.
General Signal
Intergraph Corp.
Millipore Corp.
Pall Corp.
- **Medical/Bio Technology:**
Amgen Inc.
Cetus Corp.
Genentech Inc.
Medtronic Inc.
Stryker Corp.
- **Office Equipment:**
AM International
Nashua Corp.
Pitney Bowes
Smith Corona
Xerox Corp.
- **Semiconductor & Related:**
Advanced Micro Devices
Analog Devices
Applied Materials Inc.
Avnet Inc.
Intel Corp.
Nat'l. Semiconductor
- **Software & Processing:**
Ashton-Tate
Autodesk Inc.
Automatic Data Process
Computer Associates Int'l
Computer Sciences Corp.
Lotus Development
Microsoft Corp.
Novell Inc.
Oracle Systems Corp.

FINANCIAL SERVICES

- **Banks, Money Center:**
Bankamerica
Bankers Trust N.Y.
Chase Manhattan
Chemical Banking Corp.
Citicorp
First Chicago Corp.
Manufacturers Hanover
Morgan (J.P.) & Co.
- **Banks, Central:**
Ameritrust Corp.
Banc One Corp.
Boatmen's Bankshares
Comerica Inc.
First Bank System
Fifth Third Bancorp
Huntington Bancshares
Manufacturers National
Michigan National Corp.
National City Corp.
NBD Bancorp
Northern Trust
Norwest Corp.
Society Corp.
Star Bank Corp.
- **Banks, Eastern:**
BayBanks Inc.
Bank of Boston
Bank of New England
Bank of New York
CoreStates Financial
First Fidelity Bancorp.

Fleet/Norstar Financial
Keycorp
Mellon Bank Corp.
Meridian Bancorp. Inc.
Midlantic Corp.
MNC Financial Inc.
PNC Financial Corp.
Republic New York
Shawmut National Corp.
State Street Boston
United Jersey Banks
- **Banks, Southern:**
Amsouth Bancorp
Barnett Banks Inc.
Citizens & Southern
Crestar Financial
Dominion Bankshares
First Union Corp.
First Wachovia
NCNB Corp.
Signet Banking Corp.
Southeast Banking Corp.
Sovran Financial
Suntrust Banks
- **Banks, Western:**
Bancorp Hawaii
First Interstate Bancorp.
Security Pacific Corp.
United Banks Colorado
U.S. Bancorp.
Wells Fargo & Co.
Zions Bancorp.
- **Financial Services, Diversified:**
Alexander & Alexander Svcs.
American Express
Beneficial Corp.
Dreyfus Corp.
FNMA
Household Int'l.
Marsh & McLennan Cos.
Primerica Corp.
Transamerica Corp.
- **Insurance, Full Line:**
Aetna Life & Casualty
American General
Aon Corp.
CIGNA Corp.
Kemper Corp.
Lincoln National
Travelers Corp.
- **Insurance, Life:**
American National Insurance
Broad Inc.
Capital Holding
Jefferson-Pilot
Provident Life & Accid. "B"
Torchmark Corp.
UNUM Corp.
USLIFE Corp.
- **Insurance, Property & Casualty:**
American International
Chubb Corp.
Cincinnati Financial
Continental Corp.
Fireman's Fund
GEICO Corp.
General RE Corp.
Loew's Corp.
Ohio Casualty Corp.

Progressive Corp.
Safeco Corp.
St. Paul Cos.
USF&G
- **Real Estate Investment:**
Federal Realty Invest Trust
First Union Real Estate Equity
Newhall Land
Rockefeller Center Properties
Rouse Co.
- **Savings & Loans:**
Ahmanson (H.F.) Co.
CalFed Inc.
Golden West Financial
Glenfed Inc.
Great Western Financial
Meritor Financial
- **Securities Brokers:**
Bear Stearns Cos.
Edwards (A.G.) Inc.
Merrill Lynch & Co.
Morgan Stanley Group
PaineWebber Group
Quick & Reilly Group
Salomon Inc.

UTILITIES

- **Telephone Systems:**
Alltel Corp.
Ameritech
Bell Atlantic Corp.
BellSouth Corp.
Centel Corp.
Cincinnati Bell
Contel Corp.
GTE Corp.
McCaw Cell Comm. "A"
MCI Communications
NYNEX Corp.
Pacific Telesis Group
So. New Eng. Telecom
Southwestern Bell
US West Inc.
Utd Telecommunications
- **Electric Utilities:**
Allegheny Power System
American Electric Power
Atlantic Energy
Baltimore Gas & Electric
Carolina Power & Light
Centerior Energy
Central Illinois Pub Svc.
Central & So. West Corp.
Cincinnati Gas & Elec.
CMS Energy
Commonwealth Edison
Consolidated Edison
DQE Inc.
Delmarva Power & Light
Detroit Edison
Dominion Resources
DPL Inc.
Duke Power
Entergy Corp.
Florida Progress
FPL Group Inc.
General Public Utils.

Gulf States Utilities
Houston Industries
Idaho Power Co.
Illinois Power Co.
Ipalco Enterprises
Kansas City P&L
Kansas Gas & Electric
Kentucky Utilities
Long Island Lighting
Louisville Gas & Elec.
Montana Power Co.
NIPSCO Industries
New England Elec. Sys.
New York State E&G
Niagara Mohawk Power
Northeast Utilities
Northern States Power
Ohio Edison
Oklahoma Gas & Elec.
PSI Holdings
Pacificorp
Pacific Gas & Electric
Pennsylvania Pwr & Lt
Philadelphia Electric
Pinnacle West Capital
Portland General
Potomac Electric
Public Service Colorado
Public Service Enterprise
Puget Sound P&L
San Diego Gas & Elec.
SCANA Corp.
SCEcorp
Southern Co.
Southwestern Pub. Svc.
TECO Energy
Texas Utilities
Tucson Elec. Power
Union Electric
Washington Water Power
Wisconsin Energy Corp.
- **Gas Companies:**
Arkla Inc.
Columbia Gas System
Consol. Natural Gas
Equitable Resources
Kansas Power & Light
Nicor Inc.
Oneok Inc.
Pacific Enterprises
Peoples Energy
Questar Corp.
- **Water Companies:**
American Water Works
California Water Service
Consumer Water
Hydraulic Co.
United Water Resources

CONGLOMERATES

General Electric
Greyhound Corp.
ITT Corp.
Teledyne Inc.
Textron Inc.

71

1989
DOW JONES INDUSTRY GROUP PERFORMANCE

(June 30, 1982=100)

Group	Close	---52 Week--- Change	% Change
BASIC MATERIALS	**344.39**	**+ 57.83**	**+ 20.18**
Aluminum	323.02	+ 49.48	+ 18.09
Other non-ferrous	215.69	+ 23.88	+ 12.45
Chemicals	397.55	+ 74.29	+ 22.98
Forest products	252.41	+ 36.15	+ 16.72
Mining, diversified	271.54	+ 61.57	+ 29.33
Paper products	409.53	+ 61.58	+ 17.70
Precious metals	299.61	+ 73.26	+ 32.37
Steel	129.50	− 3.43	− 2.58
CONGLOMERATE	**405.63**	**+109.34**	**+ 36.91**
CONSUMER, cyclical	**386.31**	**+ 63.57**	**+ 19.70**
Advertising	410.00	+133.77	+ 48.43
Airlines	360.08	+ 87.21	+ 31.96
Automobile manufacturers	319.26	− 28.58	− 8.22
Automobile parts & equip.	264.07	− 18.92	− 6.68
Casinos	575.09	+155.20	+ 36.96
Home construction	388.11	+ 27.31	+ 7.57
Home furnishings	252.40	+ 43.92	+ 21.07
Lodging	491.31	+119.50	+ 32.14
Media	534.38	+108.58	+ 25.50
Recreation products	272.35	+ 60.02	+ 28.27
Restaurants	463.15	+138.78	+ 42.78
Retailers, apparel	729.22	+ 93.03	+ 14.62
Retailers, broadline	436.36	+ 86.27	+ 24.64
Retailers, drug-based	313.46	+ 68.95	+ 28.20
Retailers, specialty	378.34	+ 78.77	+ 26.29
Textiles and apparel	532.58	+146.06	+ 37.79
CONSUMER, non-cyclical	**479.37**	**+141.56**	**+ 41.91**
Beverages	525.61	+180.75	+ 52.41
Consumer services	308.07	+ 18.24	+ 6.29
Cosmetics/personal care	391.15	+126.61	+ 47.86
Food	642.77	+161.44	+ 33.54
Food retailers	544.21	+105.38	+ 24.01
Health care providers	300.63	+115.12	+ 62.06
Household products	480.25	+161.85	+ 50.83
Medical supplies	329.49	+ 87.30	+ 36.04
Pharmaceuticals	436.78	+127.24	+ 41.10
ENERGY	**273.28**	**+ 69.58**	**+ 34.16**
Coal	260.86	+ 74.11	+ 39.68
Oil, drilling	126.91	+ 60.03	+ 89.75
Oil, integrated majors	318.45	+ 74.35	+ 30.46
Oil, secondary	240.98	+ 55.75	+ 30.10
Oilfield equip. & svcs	139.00	+ 49.34	+ 55.04
Pipelines	236.65	+ 81.76	+ 52.78
FINANCIAL	**309.26**	**+ 62.78**	**+ 25.47**
Banks, money center	213.48	+ 35.45	+ 19.92

DOW JONES INDUSTRY GROUP PERFORMANCE

Group	Close	---52 Week--- Change	% Change
BANKS, regional	**318.48**	**+ 34.66**	**+ 12.21**
Banks-Central	404.06	+ 73.99	+ 22.42
Banks-East	293.22	− 7.00	− 2.33
Banks-South	274.94	+ 43.65	+ 18.87
Banks-West	352.25	+ 56.50	+ 19.11
FINANCIAL SERVICES	**327.02**	**+ 77.94**	**+ 31.29**
INSURANCE, all	**349.59**	**+100.29**	**+ 40.23**
Ins.-Full line	242.00	+ 49.04	+ 25.42
Ins.-Life	470.34	+166.66	+ 54.88
Property/Casualty	429.42	+134.33	+ 45.52
Real estate	582.35	+188.54	+ 47.88
Savings & loans	485.45	+ 75.31	+ 18.36
Securities brokers	255.59	+ 19.83	+ 8.41
INDUSTRIAL	**331.55**	**+ 51.63**	**+ 18.45**
Air freight	197.38	+ 0.04	+ 0.02
Building materials	420.58	+ 25.56	+ 6.47
Containers/pkging	542.04	+ 31.21	+ 6.11
Elec comp/equip	336.65	+ 63.48	+ 23.24
Factory equipment	266.69	+ 8.77	+ 3.40
Heavy construction	255.68	+ 75.06	+ 41.56
Heavy machinery	185.18	+ 11.15	+ 6.41
Industrial services	331.58	+ 19.22	+ 6.16
Industrial, divers	292.17	+ 52.10	+ 21.70
Marine transport	557.92	+111.01	+ 24.84
Pollution control	873.13	+302.43	+ 52.99
Railroads	324.56	+ 61.27	+ 23.27
Transportation equip	233.27	− 19.94	− 7.87
Trucking	243.92	− 2.07	− 0.84
TECHNOLOGY	**252.67**	**+ 15.34**	**+ 6.46**
Aerospace/Defense	333.87	+ 38.99	+ 13.22
Commu-w/AT&T	412.81	+144.98	+ 54.13
Commu-wo/AT&T	231.21	+ 63.11	+ 37.54
Comptrs-w/IBM	183.02	− 41.43	− 18.46
Comptrs-wo/IBM	236.56	− 33.87	− 12.52
Diversified tech	236.83	+ 36.31	+ 18.11
Industrial tech	231.45	− 11.57	− 4.76
Medical/Bio tech	302.07	+ 97.67	+ 47.79
Office equipment	243.12	+ 1.47	+ 0.61
Semiconductor	220.98	+ 47.56	+ 27.43
Software	1,054.58	+256.91	+ 32.21
UTILITIES	**277.95**	**+ 73.89**	**+ 36.21**
Telephone	391.64	+136.41	+ 53.45
Electric	210.64	+ 37.42	+ 21.60
Gas	217.22	+ 53.49	+ 32.67
Water	383.25	− 1.85	− 0.48
DJ EQUITY MARKET	**329.85**	**+ 69.11**	**+ 26.51**

History compiled by Dow Jones and Shearson Lehman Hutton Inc.

Barron's Confidence Index

Barron's Confidence Index is the ratio of Barron's average of the yield on 10 best grade corporate bonds to the yield on 10 intermediate grade corporate bonds. The ratio is high when investors are confidently buying bonds below top grade. It is low when they take refuge in top grade issues.

(For bonds used in this tablulation, see page 13—the Dow Jones Averages.)

		Index col. 3 + col. 2	10 Intermediate Grade Bond Yield	10 Best Grade Bond Yield			Index col. 3 + col. 2	10 Intermediate Grade Bond Yield	10 Best Grade Bond Yield
1989						7	94.9	10.27	9.75
December	29	95.2	9.30	8.85	March	31	96.5	10.21	9.85
	22	95.7	9.26	8.86		23	96.8	10.21	9.88
	15	94.8	9.31	8.83		17	96.9	10.10	9.79
	8	95.3	9.29	8.85		10	97.4	10.01	9.75
	1	95.8	9.28	8.89		3	97.0	10.08	9.78
November	24	94.6	9.40	8.89	February	24	96.4	10.10	9.74
	17	94.3	9.35	8.82		17	96.3	10.01	9.64
	10	94.9	9.36	8.88		10	96.4	9.99	9.63
	3	94.4	9.40	8.87		3	95.6	10.02	9.58
October	27	94.4	9.42	8.89	January	27	95.0	10.04	9.54
	20	94.8	9.43	8.94		20	94.8	10.06	9.54
	13	94.6	9.47	8.96		13	95.8	10.08	9.66
	6	94.3	9.53	8.99		6	94.8	10.11	9.58
September	29	94.9	9.51	9.03					
	22	94.5	9.51	8.99	**1988**				
	15	94.5	9.47	8.95	December	30	94.4	10.12	9.55
	8	94.2	9.51	8.96		23	94.6	10.16	9.61
	1	93.7	9.67	9.06		16	96.0	10.00	9.61
August	25	93.4	9.65	9.01		9	95.1	9.97	9.48
	18	93.6	9.58	8.97		2	95.6	9.96	9.52
	11	93.2	9.56	8.91	November	25	95.2	9.99	9.51
	4	92.2	9.56	8.82		18	95.1	9.91	9.42
July	28	92.3	9.67	8.93		11	94.8	9.90	9.39
	21	94.2	9.56	9.01		4	92.7	9.87	9.15
	14	94.4	9.58	9.04	October	28	95.4	9.87	9.42
	7	93.4	9.65	9.07		21	95.1	9.86	9.38
June	30	94.3	9.72	9.17		14	94.6	9.92	9.38
	23	94.5	9.82	9.28		7	95.0	9.95	9.45
	16	93.9	9.80	9.20	September	30	94.8	9.97	9.45
	9	94.8	9.82	9.25		23	95.7	9.88	9.46
	2	94.8	9.92	9.41		16	95.9	9.86	9.46
May	26	95.2	9.94	9.46		9	96.2	9.93	9.55
	19	95.6	10.02	9.58		2	97.3	9.95	9.68
	12	96.0	10.15	9.74	August	26	97.7	9.98	9.75
	5	95.9	10.16	9.74		19	97.3	9.99	9.72
April	28	95.3	10.17	9.69		12	96.6	9.99	9.65
	21	95.7	10.17	9.73		5	96.7	9.91	9.58
	14	96.2	10.20	9.81	July	29	96.2	9.92	9.54

74

BARRON'S CONFIDENCE INDEX

Month	Day	Index col. 3 + col. 2	10 Intermediate Grade Bond Yield	10 Best Grade Bond Yield	Month	Day	Index col. 3 + col. 2	10 Intermediate Grade Bond Yield	10 Best Grade Bond Yield
	22	96.4	9.89	9.53		4	96.2	9.98	9.60
	15	95.7	9.99	9.56	August	28	96.2	9.82	9.45
	8	95.6	9.90	9.46		21	95.4	9.91	9.46
	1	94.9	9.95	9.44		14	94.9	9.89	9.39
June	24	94.1	10.01	9.42		7	95.1	9.87	9.39
	17	94.2	9.99	9.41	July	31	94.3	9.90	9.34
	10	93.9	10.10	9.48		24	94.1	9.90	9.32
	3	95.5	10.11	9.66		17	94.1	9.86	9.28
May	27	95.2	10.20	9.71		10	94.4	9.77	9.22
	20	96.2	10.09	9.71		2	94.8	9.76	9.25
	13	94.8	10.06	9.54	June	26	94.3	9.81	9.25
	6	94.5	10.00	9.45		19	94.5	9.81	9.27
April	29	94.5	9.96	9.41		12	94.3	9.92	9.36
	22	93.9	10.01	9.40		5	94.4	9.89	9.34
	15	93.5	9.90	9.26	May	29	93.1	10.00	9.31
	8	94.1	9.91	9.33		22	95.4	9.89	9.43
March	31	93.5	9.91	9.27		15	94.4	9.77	9.22
	25	93.5	9.79	9.15		8	95.0	9.72	9.23
	18	92.7	9.77	9.06		1	94.9	9.61	9.12
	11	92.7	9.75	9.04	Apr.	24	95.2	9.53	9.07
	4	92.5	9.69	8.96		16	95.9	9.32	8.94
February	26	92.1	9.75	8.98		10	94.1	9.21	8.67
	19	92.3	9.78	9.03		3	93.9	9.13	8.57
	12	91.9	9.76	8.97	Mar.	27	93.6	9.03	8.45
	5	92.2	9.83	9.02		20	93.1	9.05	8.43
January	29	91.5	9.92	9.08		13	92.8	9.09	8.44
	22	93.7	10.05	9.42		6	93.5	9.03	8.44
	15	92.8	10.25	9.51	Feb.	27	93.0	9.05	8.42
	8	92.7	10.27	9.52		20	93.1	9.14	8.51
1987						13	93.6	9.06	8.48
December	31	93.2	10.41	9.70		6	92.8	9.09	8.44
	24	92.9	10.43	9.69	Jan.	30	92.6	9.10	8.43
	18	93.5	10.37	9.70		23	92.1	9.13	8.41
	11	93.7	10.32	9.67		16	91.9	9.19	8.45
	4	92.9	10.27	9.54		9	91.7	9.20	8.44
November	27	93.1	10.23	9.52		2	91.3	9.27	8.46
	20	93.2	10.25	9.55	**1986**				
	13	92.8	10.27	9.53	December	26	92.1	9.26	8.53
	6	92.3	10.42	9.62		19	91.1	9.33	8.50
October	30	92.5	10.68	9.88		12	90.8	9.36	8.50
	23	93.9	10.75	10.10		5	90.5	9.41	8.52
	16	96.9	10.75	10.42	November	28	89.9	9.55	8.59
	9	95.2	10.62	10.11		21	91.9	9.42	8.66
	2	94.6	10.60	10.03		14	92.6	9.46	8.76
September	25	95.9	10.42	9.99		7	91.8	9.51	8.73
	18	95.2	10.46	9.96					
	11	96.5	10.13	9.78					

BARRON'S CONFIDENCE INDEX

		Index col. 3 + col. 2	10 Intermediate Grade Bond Yield	10 Best Grade Bond Yield
October	31	92.0	9.61	8.84
	24	92.0	9.64	8.87
	17	91.9	9.68	8.90
	10	92.2	9.65	8.90
	3	92.5	9.63	8.91
September	26	93.0	9.59	8.92
	19	93.4	9.55	8.92
	12	92.0	9.56	8.80
	5	92.1	9.51	8.76
August	29	92.2	9.50	8.76
	22	90.0	9.70	8.73
	15	91.6	9.74	8.92
	8	92.3	9.64	8.90
	1	92.7	9.65	8.95
July	25	92.4	9.60	8.87
	18	92.6	9.56	8.85
	11	92.2	9.58	8.83
	3	93.2	9.57	8.92
June	27	92.4	9.71	8.97
	20	93.5	9.71	9.08
	13	93.7	9.76	9.15
	6	93.3	9.74	9.09
May	30	93.4	9.70	8.98
	23	92.7	9.65	8.95
	16	92.1	9.60	8.84
	9	91.9	9.53	8.76
	2	93.0	9.52	8.85
April	25	92.1	9.62	8.86
	18	91.1	9.52	8.67
	11	90.4	9.75	8.81
	4	90.6	9.69	8.78
March	27	90.6	9.77	8.85
	21	92.5	9.71	8.98
	14	92.1	9.74	8.97
	7	91.6	9.88	9.05
February	28	90.4	10.08	9.11
	21	90.7	10.50	9.52
	14	91.8	10.59	9.72
	7	91.3	10.66	9.73
January	31	91.5	10.72	9.81
	24	91.9	10.80	9.93
	17	92.3	10.81	9.98
	10	90.9	10.84	9.85
	3	90.6	10.77	9.76

1985

		Index col. 3 + col. 2	10 Intermediate Grade Bond Yield	10 Best Grade Bond Yield
December	27	91.3	10.86	9.92
	20	92.1	10.79	9.94
	13	92.9	10.92	10.13
	6	93.7	11.01	10.32
November	29	93.3	11.09	10.35
	22	93.7	11.10	10.40
	15	92.5	11.30	10.45
	8	93.4	11.30	10.55
	1	94.1	11.39	10.72
October	25	95.4	11.39	10.87
	18	94.4	11.55	10.90
	11	94.9	11.56	10.97
	4	94.3	11.57	10.91
September	26	93.4	11.62	10.85
	20	93.9	11.62	10.91
	13	93.2	11.71	10.92
	6	92.9	11.56	10.74
August	30	92.1	11.60	10.68
	23	92.6	11.63	10.77
	16	92.3	11.87	10.96
	9	94.0	11.82	11.11
	2	94.5	11.70	11.07
July	26	94.6	11.60	10.97
	19	93.5	11.53	10.78
	12	92.6	11.58	10.72
	5	93.2	11.57	10.78
June	28	94.4	11.58	10.93
	21	93.9	11.38	10.69
	14	93.8	11.45	10.74
	7	93.9	11.42	10.72
May	31	92.4	11.85	10.95
	24	93.7	11.90	11.15
	17	92.8	12.17	11.30
	10	93.2	12.42	11.58
	3	92.6	12.54	11.61
April	26	92.4	12.59	11.63
	19	92.7	12.40	11.49
	12	93.3	12.63	11.78
	5	94.4	12.68	11.97
March	29	93.8	12.83	12.04
	22	93.9	12.89	12.11
	15	94.0	12.90	12.13
	8	95.7	12.80	12.25
	1	95.7	12.74	12.20

BARRON'S CONFIDENCE INDEX

Month	Day	Index col. 3 + col. 2	10 Intermediate Grade Bond Yield	10 Best Grade Bond Yield
February	22	95.6	12.50	11.95
	15	94.2	12.45	12.72
	8	94.7	12.41	11.75
	1	93.3	12.41	11.57
January	25	93.6	12.50	11.70
	18	93.8	12.69	11.90
	11	93.4	12.70	11.86
	4	93.0	12.77	11.87
1984				
December	28	92.7	12.76	11.83
	21	92.5	12.76	11.80
	14	93.7	12.96	11.96
	7	93.6	12.72	11.90
November	30	94.2	12.53	11.81
	23	94.1	12.78	12.02
	16	94.3	12.87	12.13
	9	94.6	12.80	12.11
	2	93.9	12.73	12.16
October	26	93.7	12.97	12.16
	19	94.8	13.18	12.49
	12	95.4	13.29	12.68
	5	92.6	13.73	12.71
September	28	92.1	13.74	12.65
	21	91.6	13.72	13.56
	14	91.6	13.90	12.72
	7	92.1	14.03	12.93
August	31	92.1	14.00	12.90
	24	92.1	13.97	12.87
	17	91.8	14.00	12.86
	10	92.3	13.91	12.85
	3	91.3	14.23	12.99
July	27	90.8	14.50	13.17
	20	91.2	14.51	13.22
	13	92.8	14.60	13.55
	6	93.5	14.65	13.70
June	29	93.7	14.66	13.73
	22	93.6	14.52	13.59
	15	92.9	14.55	13.51
	8	93.2	14.57	13.58
	1	95.0	14.58	13.85
May	25	93.2	14.58	13.59
	18	93.6	14.54	13.61
	11	94.6	14.19	13.43
	4	94.4	13.94	13.16
April	27	94.9	13.72	13.02

Month	Day	Index col. 3 + col. 2	10 Intermediate Grade Bond Yield	10 Best Grade Bond Yield
	19	95.6	13.67	13.07
	13	94.0	13.63	12.81
	6	95.2	13.62	12.97
March	30	94.5	13.55	12.80
	23	95.4	13.52	12.90
	16	95.3	13.47	12.83
	9	95.8	13.23	12.68
	2	96.3	12.99	12.51
February	24	95.5	12.92	12.33
	17	95.0	12.80	12.15
	10	94.9	12.72	12.07
	3	95.8	12.71	12.18
January	27	95.6	12.78	12.22
	20	95.3	12.85	12.24
	13	94.2	12.98	12.23
	6	94.3	13.08	12.34
1983				
December	30	91.0	12.92	11.76
	23	91.6	12.94	11.85
	16	90.3	13.17	11.89
	9	89.3	12.82	11.45
	2	91.3	12.60	11.50
November	25	90.7	12.61	11.44
	18	91.1	12.55	11.43
	11	91.8	12.50	11.47
	4	91.2	12.51	11.41
October	28	93.7	12.42	11.64
	21	93.3	12.37	11.54
	14	92.9	12.43	11.55
	7	91.6	12.36	11.32
September	30	89.4	12.58	11.25
	23	89.2	12.62	11.26
	16	90.4	12.67	11.46
	9	90.5	12.71	11.50
	2	89.9	12.72	11.44
August	26	89.6	12.64	11.32
	19	90.0	12.68	11.41
	12	90.3	12.85	11.60
	5	91.3	12.75	11.64
July	29	91.5	12.55	11.48
	22	91.2	12.50	11.40
	15	89.9	12.48	11.22
	8	91.3	12.36	11.28
	1	91.1	12.17	11.09
June	24	91.1	12.10	11.02

BARRON'S CONFIDENCE INDEX

		Index col. 3 + col. 2	10 Intermediate Grade Bond Yield	10 Best Grade Bond Yield			Index col. 3 + col. 2	10 Intermediate Grade Bond Yield	10 Best Grade Bond Yield
	17	90.1	12.17	10.97		13	90.5	14.70	13.31
	10	91.5	12.08	11.05		6	89.2	14.81	13.21
	3	89.9	11.99	10.78	July	30	89.3	15.00	13.39
May	27	90.2	11.89	10.72		23	90.9	14.77	13.42
	20	91.2	11.71	10.68		16	90.5	14.92	13.51
	13	90.7	11.53	10.46		9	91.7	14.93	13.69
	6	91.2	11.48	10.48		2	90.2	15.06	13.59
April	29	91.1	11.67	10.63	June	25	89.4	14.95	13.37
	22	91.6	11.73	10.74		18	90.5	14.71	13.31
	15	89.9	11.93	10.72		11	88.2	14.88	13.13
	8	89.6	12.12	10.86		4	87.5	14.82	12.97
March	31	89.5	12.03	10.77	May	28	88.6	14.60	12.94
	25	90.1	12.08	10.89		21	88.5	14.59	12.92
	18	88.7	12.26	10.87		14	88.8	14.59	12.96
	11	89.1	12.29	10.95		7	89.5	14.64	13.10
	4	87.0	12.35	10.75	April	30	89.2	14.70	13.11
February	25	88.3	12.55	11.08		23	88.4	14.91	13.18
	18	88.5	12.67	11.22		16	89.4	14.93	13.35
	11	88.7	12.81	11.36		9	89.3	15.07	13.45
	4	89.5	12.76	11.42		2	88.1	15.10	13.30
January	28	88.6	12.81	11.35	March	26	87.8	15.05	13.21
	21	89.3	12.63	11.28		19	88.0	15.12	13.30
	14	88.6	12.68	11.24		12	87.7	15.00	13.15
	7	87.4	12.80	11.19		5	88.5	14.94	13.23
1982					February	26	89.3	15.02	13.42
December	31	86.4	12.94	11.18		19	89.0	15.39	13.70
	24	87.9	12.77	11.22		12	90.6	15.19	13.77
	17	88.0	12.74	11.21		5	91.4	15.03	13.74
	10	87.3	12.89	11.25	January	29	90.5	15.27	13.82
	3	86.7	12.98	11.26		22	91.4	15.28	13.96
November	26	87.1	12.82	11.17		15	91.7	15.31	14.04
	19	86.5	12.89	11.15		8	89.5	15.25	13.65
	12	87.0	12.91	11.23					
	5	85.9	13.02	11.19					
October	29	85.2	13.35	11.38					
	22	87.4	13.13	11.47					
	15	88.2	13.18	11.62					
	8	88.9	13.67	12.16					
	1	88.6	13.77	12.20					
September	24	88.9	13.82	12.29					
	17	87.4	14.14	12.36					
	10	88.8	14.00	12.43					
	3	89.5	14.14	12.66					
August	27	88.3	14.16	12.50					
	20	87.9	14.28	12.56					

New York Stock Exchange

Composite Stock Index

Year	Open	High	Low	Close	Chg.
1989	156.26	199.34	154.98	195.04	+38.78
1988	138.23	159.42	136.72	156.26	+18.03
1987	138.58	187.99	125.91	138.23	− .35
1986	121.58	145.75	117.75	138.58	+17.00
1985	96.38	121.90	94.60	121.58	+25.20
1984	95.18	98.12	85.13	96.38	+ 1.3
1983	79.79	99.63	79.79	95.18	+14.15
1982	81.33	82.35	58.80	81.03	+ 9.92
1981	78.26	79.14	64.96	71.11	− 6.75
1980	60.69	81.02	55.30	77.86	+15.91
1979	53.93	63.39	53.88	61.95	+ 8.33
1978	51.82	60.38	48.37	53.62	+ 1.12
1977	57.69	57.69	49.78	52.50	− 5.38
1976	48.04	57.88	48.04	57.88	+10.24
1975	37.06	51.24	37.06	47.64	+11.51
1974	51.98	53.37	32.89	36.13	−15.69
1973	65.06	65.48	49.05	51.82	−12.66
1972	56.23	65.14	56.23	64.48	+ 8.05
1971	49.73	57.76	49.60	56.43	+ 6.20
1970	52.10	52.36	37.69	50.23	− 1.30
1969	58.94	59.32	49.31	51.53	− 7.37
1968	53.68	61.27	48.70	58.90	+ 5.07
1967	43.74	54.16	43.74	53.83	+10.11
1966	49.86	51.06	39.37	43.72	− 6.28
1965	45.37	50.00	43.64	50.00	+ 4.35
1964	40.47	46.49	40.47	45.65	+ 5.73
1963	34.41	39.92	34.41	39.92	+ 6.11
1962	37.34	38.02	28.20	33.81	− 4.58
1961	31.17	38.60	31.17	38.39	+ 7.45
1960	31.99	31.99	28.38	30.94	− 1.21
1959	29.54	32.39	28.94	32.15	+ 3.30
1958	21.71	28.85	21.45	28.85	+ 7.74
1957	24.43	26.30	20.92	21.11	− 3.24
1956	23.56	25.90	22.55	24.35	+ 0.64
1955	19.05	23.71	19.05	23.71	+ 4.31
1954	13.70	19.40	13.70	19.40	+ 5.80
1953	14.65	14.65	12.62	13.60	− 0.89
1952	13.70	14.49	13.31	14.49	+ 0.89

The New York Stock Exchange composite stock index has been computed on a daily basis since June 1, 1964. Prior to that date it was on a weekly basis. December 31, 1965, equals 50.

New York Stock Exchange

Volume, Shares and Turnover Rate

(Millions of Shares)

Year	Reported Stock Volume	Average of Shares Listed	Per Cent Turnover	Year	Reported Stock Volume	Average of Shares Listed	Per Cent Turnover
1989	41,698.5	82,797.7	52	1952	337.8	2,702.0	13
1988	40,849.5	76,093.0	56	1951	443.5	2,484.6	18
1987	47,801.3	65,711.4	73	1950	524.8	2,259.4	23
1986	35,680.0	56,023.8	64	1949	272.2	2,091.6	13
1985	27,510.7	50,759.4	54	1948	302.2	1,962.0	15
1984	23,071.0	47,104.8	49	1947	253.6	1,839.0	14
1983	21,589.6	42,316.9	51	1946	363.7	1,681.8	22
1982	16,458.0	38,907.0	42	1945	377.6	1,542.2	24
1981	11,853.7	36,003.5	33	1944	263.1	1,490.8	18
1980	11,352.3	31,871.0	36	1943	278.7	1,479.9	19
1979	8,155.9	28,803.0	28	1942	125.7	1,466.9	9
1978	7,205.1	26,833.2	27	1941	170.6	1,459.0	12
1977	5,273.8	25,296.5	21	1940	207.6	1,445.1	14
1976	5,360.1	23,489.0	23	1939	262.0	1,429.8	18
1975	4,693.4	22,108.0	21	1938	297.5	1,418.1	21
1974	3,517.7	21,351.8	16	1937	409.5	1,386.2	30
1973	4,053.2	20,062.6	20	1936	496.0	1,339.1	37
1972	4,138.2	18,329.4	23	1935	381.6	1,311.6	29
1971	3,891.3	16,782.1	23	1934	323.8	1,299.4	25
1970	2,937.4	15,573.6	19	1933	654.8	1,302.6	50
1969	2,850.8	14,139.1	20	1932	425.2	1,315.3	32
1968	2,931.5	12,410.0	24	1931	576.8	1,307.8	44
1967	2,529.9	10,079.5	22	1930	810.6	1,212.2	67
1966	1,899.5	10,495.0	18	1929	1,124.8	942.5	119
1965	1,556.3	9,641.0	16	1928	930.9	706.2	132
1964	1,236.6	8,668.8	14	1927	581.7	620.3	94
1963	1,146.3	7,883.7	15	1926	451.9	538.6	84
1962	962.2	7,373.6	13	1925	459.7	462.5	99
1961	1,021.3	6,773.2	15	1924	284.0	424.8	67
1960	766.7	6,152.8	12	1923	236.5	393.2	60
1959	820.3	5,432.0	15	1922	260.9	337.2	77
1958	747.1	4,910.2	15	1921	172.8	292.7	59
1957	559.9	4,632.9	12	1920	227.6	251.1	91
1956	556.3	4,149.2	13	1919	318.3	208.0	153
1955	649.6	3,505.3	19	1918	143.3	193.9	74
1954	573.4	3,050.4	19	1917	184.6	179.7	103
1953	354.9	2,857.4	12	1916	232.6	160.2	145

Source: NYSE Fact Book.

New York Stock Exchange

All Listed Stocks

End of Year	Number of Companies	Number of issues	Shares Listed (millions) Number	Market Value	a-Inst. Holdings
1989	1,721	2,246	82,797.0	$3,029,650.0	....
1988	1,681	2,234	76,093.0	2,457,461.8	....
1987	1,647	2,244	71,802.4	2,216,310.9	....
1986	1,575	2,257	59,620.0	2,199,258.0	....
1985	1,541	2,298	52,427.0	1,950,332.0	....
1984	1,543	2,319	49,092.0	1,586,098.0	....
1983	1,550	2,307	45,118.0	1,584,155.0	....
1982	1,526	2,225	39,516.0	1,305,355.0	....
1981	1,565	2,220	38,298.0	1,143,794.0	....
1980	1,570	2,228	33,709.0	1,242,803.0	....
1979	1,565	2,192	30,032.8	960,606.1	....
1978	1,581	2,194	27,573.1	822,735.9	....
1977	1,575	2,177	26,093.2	796,639.0	....
1976	1,576	2,158	24,499.8	858,299.2	....
1975	1,557	2,111	22,478.0	685,110.0	32.9%
1974	1,567	2,080	21,737.0	511,055.0	32.8
1973	1,560	2,058	20,967.0	721,012.0	31.8
1972	1,505	2,003	19,159.0	871,540.0	31.7
1971	1,426	1,927	17,500.0	741,827.0	30.1
1970	1,351	1,840	16,065.0	636,380.0	27.6
1969	1,311	1,789	15,082.0	629,453.0	26.0
1968	1,273	1,767	13,196.0	692,337.0	24.8
1967	1,274	1,700	11,622.5	605,816.8	24.0
1966	1,286	1,665	10,938.6	482,540.9	23.7
1965	1,273	1,627	10,057.7	537,480.6	22.7
1964	1,247	1,606	9,229.4	474,322.3	22.2
1963	1,214	1,572	8,108.2	411,318.0	21.3
1962	1,186	1,559	7,659.2	345,846.1	20.4
1961	1,163	1,541	7,088.0	387,841.2	19.4
1960	1,143	1,528	6,458.4	306,967.1	18.7
1959	1,116	1,507	5,847.3	307,707.7	18.1
1958	1,100	1,507	5,016.7	276,665.2	17.9
1957	1,107	1,522	4,803.8	195,570.2	17.8
1956	1,087	1,502	4,462.1	219,175.9	17.1
1955	1,087	1,508	3,836.3	207,699.2	16.2
1954	1,089	1,532	3,174.3	169,148.5	....
1953	1,084	1,530	2,926.6	117,257.2	....
1952	1,084	1,522	2,788.2	120,536.2	....
1951	1,075	1,495	2,615.1	109,483.6	....
1950	1,057	1,472	2,353.2	93,807.3	....
1949	1,043	1,457	2,165.7	76,292.0	14.5
1948	1,017	1,419	2,017.5	67,048.3	....
1947	996	1,379	1,906.5	68,312.5	....

a-Estimated holdings of New York Stock Exchange-listed stocks include insurance companies, investment companies, non-insured pension funds, non-profit institutions, common trust funds and mutual savings banks. The holdings do not include foreign institutions, mutual funds that aren't registered with the Securities and Exchange Commission, private hedge funds, non-bank trusts and bank-administered personal trusts.

Source: NYSE Fact Book.

New York Stock Exchange

Daily Reported Stock Volume: Average, High and Low Record Days

(Thousands of Shares)

Year	a-Average Daily Volume	High Day Volume	Date	b-Low Day Volume	Date	Year	a-Average Daily Volume	High Day Volume	Date	b-Low Day Volume	Date
1989	165,470	416,397	10-16	68,869	7- 3	1953	1,414	3,119	3-31	738	9- 8
1988	161,461	343,949	6-17	72,088	11-25	1952	1,297	2,352	11-19	780	5-19
1987	188,940	608,148	10-20	86,360	11-27	1951	1,674	3,877	1-17	973	7-11
1986	141,028	244,293	12-19	48,864	12-26	1950	1,980	4,859	6-27	1,061	3-13
1985	109,170	181,026	12- 5	62,054	12-26	1949	1,023	2,212	12-14	541	6-17
1984	91,190	236,565	8- 3	46,364	10- 8	1948	1,132	3,837	5-14	465	8-16
1983	85,334	129,411	1- 6	53,033	8-29	1947	952	2,197	4-14	476	8-27
1982	65,051	149,385	11- 4	36,760	1- 4	1946	1,370	3,624	9- 4	487	7- 5
1981	46,853	92,881	1- 7	23,945	12-24	1945	1,422	2,936	6-28	492	8- 6
1980	44,871	84,297	11- 5	16,132	12-26	1944	958	2,517	6-16	337	5-15
1979	32,237	81,619	10-10	18,346	1- 2	1943	1,012	2,805	5- 4	335	8-30
1978	28,591	66,370	8- 3	c7,580	1-20	1942	455	1,441	12-29	207	7- 1
1977	20,928	35,261	11-11	10,582	10-10	1941	619	2,925	12-29	224	5-19
1976	21,186	44,513	2-20	10,301	1- 2	1940	751	3,940	5-21	130	8-19
1975	18,551	35,158	2-13	8,670	9-15	1939	955	5,934	9- 5	235	7- 3
1974	13,904	26,365	10-10	7,402	7- 5	1938	1,080	3,100	11- 9	278	6- 8
1973	16,084	25,962	9-20	8,970	8-20	1937	1,492	7,288	10-19	424	6-21
1972	16,487	27,555	12-29	7,945	10- 9	1936	1,791	4,718	2-17	586	5-13
1971	15,381	31,731	8-16	7,349	10-25	1935	1,385	3,948	11-14	345	2- 4
1970	11,564	21,345	9-24	6,660	5-11	1934	1,178	4,940	2- 5	275	8-20
1969	11,403	19,950	10-14	6,758	12-26	1933	2,519	9,572	7-21	477	1-30
1968	12,971	21,351	6-13	6,707	3-25	1932	1,541	5,461	8- 8	385	10-31
1967	10,080	14,954	12-29	5,998	7- 3	1931	2,090	5,346	2-24	536	9- 1
1966	7,538	13,121	5- 6	4,268	6- 6	1930	2,959	8,279	5- 5	1,090	8- 1
1965	6,176	11,434	12- 6	3,028	7- 7	1929	4,277	16,410	10-29	1,996	12-24
1964	4,888	6,851	4- 2	3,051	8-10	1928	3,416	6,943	11-23	1,090	6-25
1963	4,567	9,324	11-26	2,513	7-26	1927	2,111	3,214	10- 4	1,219	1-28
1962	3,818	14,746	5-29	1,946	10- 8	1926	1,643	3,860	3- 3	607	5- 6
1961	4,085	7,077	4- 4	2,184	7- 3	1925	1,663	3,391	11-10	790	4-13
1960	3,042	5,303	12-30	1,894	10-12	1924	1,029	2,584	11-20	316	6- 2
1959	3,242	4,884	3-13	1,745	10-12	1923	863	1,559	11-22	283	7-16
1958	2,965	5,368	10-17	1,566	2-24	1922	950	2,008	4-17	236	7- 3
1957	2,222	5,093	10-22	1,256	9- 4	1921	632	1,290	3-23	280	8- 8
1956	2,216	3,921	2-29	1,233	10- 9	1920	828	2,008	4-21	227	6-29
1955	2,578	7,717	9-26	1,230	8-15	1919	1,179	2,697	11-12	299	2- 7
1954	2,275	4,433	12-29	1,215	1-11	1918	529	1,692	5-16	136	8- 2

a-A trading session of three hours or less is counted as one-half day.
b-Full days only.
c-Opened at noon due to snow storm.
Source: NYSE Fact Book.

New York Stock Exchange

Cash Dividends and Yields on Common Stocks

Calendar Year	Number of Issues Listed at Year End	Number Paying Cash Dividends During Year	Estimated Aggregate Cash Payments (Millions)	a-Median Yield (%) *Dividend Yield	Calendar Year	Number of Issues Listed at Year End	Number Paying Cash Dividends During Year	Estimated Aggregate Cash Payments (Millions)	a-Median Yield (%) *Dividend Yield
1989	1,683	1,303	101,778	*3.2	1965	1,254	1,111	15,300	a3.2
1988	1,641	1,270	102,190	*3.6	1964	1,227	1,066	13,555	a3.3
1987	1,606	1,219	84,377	*3.4	1963	1,194	1,032	12,096	a3.6
1986	1,536	1,180	76,161	*3.4	1962	1,168	994	11,203	a3.8
1985	1,503	1,206	74,237	*3.6	1961	1,145	981	10,430	a3.3
1984	1,511	1,243	68,215	a3.8	1960	1,126	981	9,872	a4.2
1983	1,518	1,259	67,102	a3.5	1959	1,092	953	9,337	a3.8
1982	1,499	1,287	62,224	a4.1	1958	1,086	961	8,711	a4.1
1981	1,534	1,337	60,628	a5.0	1957	1,098	991	8,807	a6.1
1980	1,540	1,361	53,072	a4.6	1956	1,077	975	8,341	a5.2
1979	1,536	1,359	46,937	a5.0	1955	1,076	982	7,488	a4.6
1978	1,552	1,373	41,151	a4.8	1954	1,076	968	6,439	a4.7
1977	1,549	1,360	36,270	a4.5	1953	1,069	964	5,874	a6.3
1976	1,550	1,340	30,608	a4.0	1952	1,067	975	5,595	a6.0
1975	1,531	1,273	26,901	a5.0	1951	1,054	961	5,467	a6.5
1974	1,543	1,308	25,662	a7.4	1950	1,039	930	5,404	a6.7
1973	1,536	1,276	23,627	a5.0	1949	1,017	887	4,235	a7.0
1972	1,478	1,195	21,490	a3.0	1948	986	883	3,806	a7.8
1971	1,399	1,132	20,256	a3.2	1947	964	851	3,255	a6.3
1970	1,330	1,120	19,781	a3.7	1946	933	798	2,669	a4.8
1969	1,290	1,121	19,404	a3.6	1945	881	746	2,275	a3.6
1968	1,253	1,104	18,124	a2.6	1944	864	717	2,223	a5.0
1967	1,255	1,116	16,866	a3.2	1943	845	687	2,063	a6.1
1966	1,267	1,127	16,151	a4.1	1942	834	648	1,997	a7.8

*Dividend yield based on common stocks of NYSE Composite Index.

a-Based on cash payments during the year and price at end of year for dividend-paying stocks only. N.A.-Not available.

Source: NYSE Fact Book.

Stock and Bond Trading for 1989

NEW YORK STOCK EXCHANGE COMPOSITE

The following tabulation gives the 1989 sales, high, low, last price and net change from the previous year in stocks listed on the New York Stock Exchange.

-A-

Stock	Symbol	Div	Yld	Sales 100s	Hi	Lo	Last	Net Chg
AAR	AIR	.48	22	91199	37½	24	36	+ 11¼
ACM OppFd	AOF	1.01	...	52868	9⅝	8½	9¼	+ ⅜
ACM Gvt Fd	ACG	1.26	...	132255	11⅝	10⅜	10⅞	+ ⅜
ACM MgdIncFd	AMF	1.01	...	82480	9⅞	8	8¾	...
ACM SecFd	GSF	1.26	...	251714	11½	10	10¾	+ ½
ACM SpctmFd	SI	1.01	...	128205	9⅜	8⅜	9⅛	+ ¼
AL Labs A	BMD	.16	19	31066	18½	11½	18¼	+ 4⅜
AMCA	AIL	.12e	9	25651	4⅛	3⅛	3½	+ ⅛
AM Int	AM		9	340282	6⅛	4	4⅛	− ⅞
AM Int pf		2.00	...	17645	23½	16⅝	17⅜	− 4⅛
AMR	AMR		7	f20073	107¼	52⅛	58	+ 4⅜
ANR pf		2.67	...	7749	27	25	25⅞	+ ⅜
ANR pf		2.12	...	9063	24⅞	23⅛	24⅛	+ ⅛
ARX	ARX		...	41086	6½	3⅛	3¼	− 3⅛
ASA	ASA	3.00a	...	185125	59¼	38	55½	+ 17½
AVX	AVX	.24	30	194227	31¼	16¼	30⅝	+ 13⅝
AbbotLab	ABT	1.40	18	977121	70⅜	46¼	68	+ 19⅞
Abitibi g	ABY	.50	...	27678	18¼	11⅜	11½	− 4¾
AcmeCleve	AMT	.40	14	33795	13	9¼	10⅞	+ 1⅜
AcmeElec	ACE	.32	12	7092	9¾	6	9⅛	+ 2⅞
Acuson	ACN		21	146028	38½	22	32	+ 5⅞
AdamsExp	ADX	2.06e	...	47324	15¾	12⅞	15⅝	+ 2¼
AdobeRes	ADB		...	74456	15⅜	6½	14⅝	+ 7⅞
AdobeRes pf		1.84	...	5200	20¼	16½	20	+ 3
AdobeRes pf		2.40	...	4690	21⅝	19⅞	21½	+ 1
AdvMicro	AMD		...	733539	10½	7⅛	7⅞	− ¾
AdvMicro pf		3.00	...	14515	35	28½	29½	− 1¼
Advest	ADV	.16	10	38455	10⅛	6⅝	7⅛	− ⅜
AetnaLife	AET	2.76	9	540064	62½	46⅝	56½	+ 9¼
AffilPub	AFP	.24	...	281040	14	11	12¼	...
Ahmanson	AHM	.88	10	852641	25	15¾	19	+ 2⅝
Aileen	AEE		...	15262	3⅞	2¼	2¼	− 1½
AirProduct	APD	1.32	12	405336	48¾	40	48	+ 6¾
AirbornFrght	ABF	.60	18	74803	39⅝	20⅞	35⅜	+ 13⅝
Airgas	ARG		13	43694	25⅛	14¾	23	+ 7⅞
Airlease	FLY	2.40	11	9116	20¾	18¼	19⅝	+ 1
AlaPwr pf		2.08e	...	18900	24¼	21¼	21¾	− 1⅝
AlaPwr pf		.87	...	26253	10¼	8½	9¾	+ ⅞
AlaPwr pf		9.00	...	1023	98⅝	88¼	97¼	+ 4¼
AlaPwr pf		11.00	...	z21900	107	102	105	+ 2
AlaPwr pf		9.44	...	1283	103½	93	101⅜	+ 8¼
AlaPwr pf		8.16	...	6946	93	80¼	90¾	+ 8½
AlaPwr pf		8.28	...	z54380	91	80⅞	88½	+ 7¼
AlaskaAir	ALK	.20	7	257759	30½	19⅞	20⅝	+ ⅝
AlbanyInt	AIN	.35	12	73862	23½	15¾	18⅞	+ 2
AlbertoCl	ACV	.36	20	22506	53⅜	32¾	44⅝	+ 7⅞
AlbertoCl A	ACVA	.36	16	23588	41½	25½	36⅞	+ 10⅝
Albertsons	ABS	.80	18	238199	60¼	36⅝	55½	+ 17⅝
Alcan	AL	1.12	6	f12917	25⅛	20⅛	22⅞	+ 1⅛
AlcoStd	ASN	.84	13	214594	36⅝	25⅜	34½	+ 6⅝
Alex&Alex	AAL	1.00	21	210982	34	22⅝	30⅝	+ 7⅛
Alexanders	ALX		29	5950	71¾	50¼	55½	− 12
AlleghanyCp	Y	1.63t	11	5608	103½	70½	91½	+ 20½
vjAllegInt	AG		...	65123	2⅜	⅛	9/32	− 1 11/32
vjAllegInt pr			...	9538	4⅞	5/32	3/16	− 2 15/16
vjAllegInt pf			...	12353	15⅛	7/16	¾	− 10⅛
AllegLud	ALS	1.20	7	79986	41⅝	29¼	40⅜	+ 10½
AllegPwr	AYP	3.16	11	253098	42½	35⅝	41⅞	+ 4½
AllenGp	ALN		16	45719	16⅞	9	10¾	− 2⅝
AllenGp pf		1.75	...	13236	19⅞	11½	15⅛	− ⅜
Allergan	AGN	.05e	...	679783	25½	15⅝	17⅜	...
AllncCapMgt	AC	1.48	20	46350	16	10½	15¼	+ 4¾
AlldIrishBk pf		.53e	...	13207	25⅜	23⅛	24	...
AlliedPdts	ADP		12	34191	27⅝	7⅛	9	− 6⅞
AlliedSgnl	ALD	1.80	10	809486	40⅜	31¾	34⅞	+ 2⅜
AllstMunTr	ALM	.78a	...	58455	10⅞	10	10½	+ ¼
AllstMunInII	ALT	.73	...	75400	10⅛	9¼	10	+ ¼
AllstMunInTr	AMO	.84	...	109149	11⅛	9¾	10¾	+ ¾
AllstMunOpp	AOT	.78	...	25384	10½	9⅛	9⅛	...
AllstMunInIII	ALL	.57	...	7035	10	8⅞	9⅜	...
AllstMunPrem	ALI	.69	...	62690	10	9	9⅜	...
ALLTEL	AT	1.28	19	176916	41⅞	23¼	38⅞	+ 14¾
ALLTEL pf		2.06	...	33	115½	71	114	+ 43¼
Alcoa	AA	1.60a	6	f11484	79⅝	55¼	75	+ 19
AmaxGold	AU	.08	33	61453	19½	10⅝	17½	+ 1¾
Amax	AMX	.80	3	f10942	29¾	20¾	23	+ ⅜
Amax pf		3.00	...	883	44⅞	39⅛	40¼	+ ¼
AmBas	ABC	.20	5	251416	16⅜	10¼	12¼	+ 1¼
AmcastInd	AIZ	.48	14	39469	13⅝	10⅞	12⅜	− ⅞
Amdura	ADU		7	84765	15⅝	5⅛	6	− 5½
Amdura pf		1.95	...	15222	27¼	10	12⅜	− 9⅝
AmerHess	AHC	.60	8	694742	51⅞	31	48¾	+ 17¼
AmBarrick	ABX	.15	54	295228	34⅜	16¼	31⅝	+ 15¼
AmBarrick wi			...	8	17⅛	8¼	16⅛	+ 7¾
AmBrand	AMB	2.72	12	650432	81⅞	61¼	71	+ 5½
AmBrand pf		2.75	...	8783	29⅞	26⅝	29⅝	+ 2¼
AmBrand pf		2.67	...	398	163¼	126	138	+ 5½
AmBldgMaint	ABM	.92	15	20589	39¾	27½	33⅛	+ 5½
AmBusnPdts	ABP	.80	12	9269	27	19½	21⅝	+ ⅝
AmCapBdFd	ACB	2.04e	...	19704	21¾	17⅛	17½	− 2⅝
AmCapCvSec	ACS	2.32e	...	6162	23⅛	19¾	20⅛	+ ¼
AmCapIncTr	ACD	1.10a	...	59711	9¾	7⅛	7½	− 1¾
AmCapMgt	ACA	.60	10	12759	11⅜	8¼	8½	− ⅜
vjAmCentury	ACT		...	11693	19/32	5/32	¼	+ 3/32
AmCyanmd	ACY	1.35	15	923225	60⅜	45⅝	53⅝	+ 6⅞
AmElecPwr	AEP	2.40	10	828077	33⅜	25¾	33	+ 5¾
AmExpress	AXP	.92	13	f23667	39⅜	26⅜	34⅞	+ 8¼
AmFamily	AFL	.32	18	694186	22½	13⅜	18	+ 4¼
AmGenerl	AGC	1.50	8	496749	38½	29½	31¼	+ 1⅝
AmGvIncFd	AGF	.84a	...	48228	8¼	7⅜	7⅝	− ⅜
AmGvIncoP	AAF	1.06a	...	43560	10⅛	8⅞	9⅝	− ⅛
AmGvTermTr	AGT	1.02	...	24025	10⅝	9¼	10	...
AmHlthProp	AHE	2.28	14	76505	24	17⅞	22¾	+ 4⅞
AmHeritgLf	AHL	1.20	11	1565	29	25	28⅛	+ 2⅜
AmHomePdts	AHP	3.90	16	490366	109⅜	79¾	107½	+ 24¼
AmHomePdts pf		2.00	...	14	441½	369½	441½	+ 94
Ameritech	AIT	3.16	15	742114	68¼	47⅜	68	+ 20⅛
AmIntGroup	AIG	.48	13	696959	112	66¼	103½	+ 35¾
AmMedInt	AMI	.72	18	f11516	26¾	5½	7⅛	− 8½
AmMedInt wd			...	18501	8	6	6⅝	...
AmOpIncoFd	OIF	.18e	...	7442	10⅛	9¾	9¾	...
AmPresidnt	APS	.60	23	133837	40⅞	26¾	28⅛	− 5⅞
AmRE Ptnrs	ACP	2.00	6	29700	16	10¼	10½	− 4⅝
AmRltyTr	ARB	1.52	2	57451	9¾	5¼	6½	− 2½
AmSvgBk	ASB	.80	5	71991	18¾	5	7½	− 5⅜
AmSvgBk pf		1.81	...	18015	19½	7⅞	9¾	− 6¾
AmShipBldg	ABG		...	27558	5⅛	2	2⅜	− 2¼
AmStores	ASC	1.00	24	170999	72½	53	56½	− 1⅜
AmT&T	T	1.20	23	f46206	47	28⅛	45½	+ 16¾
AmWaterWks	AWK	.74	11	83719	21½	16¾	18⅛	+ 1
AmWaterWks pf		1.25	...	z45140	15⅜	13¼	14⅞	+ ⅞
AmWater pf		1.25	...	z16190	17	13¼	15	+ ⅝
AmHotel	AHR	8.00c	...	12777	15	6¼	6⅝	− 6½
Ameron	AMN	1.28	14	6215	46¼	30¾	45½	+ 14⅜
AmesDeptStr	ADD	.10	...	466584	20	8¾	10⅜	− 3⅝
Ametek	AME	.64	18	158526	15⅞	12	13½	+ ½
AMEV Sec	AMV	1.08a	...	11528	11	9¾	10¾	+ ½
Amoco	AN	1.90	17	f15237	55¾	36¾	54⅝	+ 17⅛
AMP	AMP	1.20	16	632905	49⅜	40	44½	...
AmpcoPgh	AP	.30	...	11925	15⅞	11½	11½	− 2
AMRE	AMM	.08	...	117861	13¼	6¼	7¾	− 4½
AMREP	AXR		59	22459	9¾	5¾	5⅞	− 1⅞
AmSouthBcp	ASO	1.40	7	40726	29⅛	22¾	23¾	+ 1
Anacomp	AAC		15	479131	7½	3⅝	4¼	− 2½
AnadrkPete	APC	.30	40	364592	38½	24½	37	+ 11⅜
AnalogDevcs	ADI		17	292987	12⅞	8⅛	9¾	− 2½
Angelica	AGL	.80	15	38461	30⅜	22	30⅜	+ 8⅛
AngellRE	ACR	1.52	...	16554	11⅝	6¼	6¾	− 1⅜
AnheuserB	BUD	.88	14	f14954	46	30⅝	38½	+ 7
AnthemElec	ATM		15	82290	17¾	8⅞	17½	+ 7⅛
AnthonyInd	ANT	.44b	10	61677	20⅝	11¼	17	+ 5⅜
AonCp	AOC	1.40	13	173425	43¼	27	42¼	+ 14¼
ApacheCp	APA	.28	36	382790	18⅜	7⅞	18⅜	+ 10½
ApexMunFd	APX	.88	...	25223	12⅜	10¾	10⅞	...

NEW YORK STOCK EXCHANGE COMPOSITE

Stock	Symbol	Div	Yld	Sales 100s	Hi	Lo	Last	Net Chg
AppalchPwr pf		8.12	...	4404	92½	80¼	90⅛	+ 6⅛
AppalchPwr pf		7.40	...	2920	83¾	73¼	82⅞	+ 5⅞
AppalchPwr pf		2.65	...	2721	27	25½	26½	− 1⅜
AppleBcp	APK		7	22675	38⅞	30	31⅝	+ ⅞
AppliedMagn	APM		129	103967	15½	8¼	9	− 5¾
ArcherDan	ADM	.10	14	f12815	23½	13⅝	23⅛	+ 9¼
ARCO Chm	RCM	2.50	8	233326	40⅜	28¾	36¼	+ 7⅛
AristChm	ARS	1.00	7	759941	27⅝	17¼	20⅜	...
ArizPubSvc pf		6.95e	...	z31060	72½	65	65	− 7
ArklaExpl	ARK		...	33551	23¼	21½	22⅞	...
Arkla	ALG	1.08	...	498669	27¾	20	27¼	+ 7⅛
Arkla pf		3.00	...	19066	51	40	50⅜	+ 10¼
Armco	AS	.20e	5	765007	13½	9½	10¾	+ ¾
Armco pf		2.10	...	2499	24¾	21⅝	22¾	− ⅞
Armco pf		4.50	...	2953	48⅜	41¾	43¾	+ ½
ArmstrngWld	ACK	1.06	11	514198	50⅞	33⅜	37¼	+ 2¼
ArrowElec	ARW		...	66238	6¾	3⅛	3⅞	− 2¾
ArrowElect pf		1.94	...	19704	14⅝	8¼	10⅜	− 3½
ArtraGp	ATA		...	71116	36¼	9½	10⅜	− 18⅞
ArvinInd	ARV	.68	16	102792	26¾	14½	15¾	− 3⅝
ArvinInd pf		3.75	...	9877	49¾	39¼	40	...
Asarco	AR	1.60	5	343092	35⅞	26⅛	29⅞	+ 2½
AshlandCoal	ACI	.32	13	49374	17¼	11½	17⅛	+ 5⅝
AshlandOil	ASH	1.00	36	375135	43	33⅛	40	+ 6½
AsiaPacFnd	APB	.18e	...	125366	18⅝	6¼	17¾	+ 11⅜
AssetInvest	AIC	1.56e	5	95539	12¼	5⅜	8⅝	− 2⅝
AssocNG	NGA		...	7027	21	9	20⅝	+ 9⅜
AtalantaSos	ATL	.30e	7	3804	7⅜	3⅝	4½	...
AthloneInd	ATH	1.00	8	51387	23⅛	11½	13⅞	− 2⅛
AtlaGasLt	ATG	1.96	16	72833	30¾	23⅞	30⅜	+ 5⅛
AtlanEngy	ATE	2.88	10	94889	39¾	32½	38½	+ 5¾
AtlanRich	ARC	4.50	12	807965	114⅜	80⅜	111⅜	+ 30¾
AtlanRich pf		3.00	...	40	751	576½	751	+ 214
AtlanRich pf		2.80	...	509	271¼	192⅝	267	+ 74
AtlasCp	AZ		17	24760	18½	10¾	16¼	+ 2¼
ATMOS En	ATO	1.16	...	19057	18	14⅝	17⅞	+ 1⅝
AudioVideo	AVA		...	50243	7¼	3	3⅝	− 2⅛
Augat	AUG	.40	22	81500	15⅜	11½	13½	+ 1⅝
Ausimont	AUS	1.20	14	104256	36¼	33⅜	34¾	+ ¾
AustriaFd	OST	.07e	...	94102	21	10¾	20½	...
AutoDataProc	AUD	.60	19	497437	50¾	35¾	49	+ 10¼
Avalon	AVL	1.01e	...	14472	7⅛	4⅝	6	+ 1¼
AVEMCO	AVE	.40	14	19780	27½	20⅜	24	− 1⅞
AveryInt	AVY	.56	17	189526	33¼	21	32⅜	+ 9⅝
Avnet	AVT	.60	19	211446	32¾	20⅝	31	+ 8¾
AvonPdts	AVP	1.00	...	f16365	41¼	19½	36⅞	+ 17⅜
AvonPdts pf		2.00	...	196562	33½	21⅛	28	+ 6⅞
Aydin	AYD	1.00e	9	19501	21⅜	13⅝	16½	+ 1⅛
-B-								
BellCda g	BCE	2.52	...	304159	39⅜	30½	39¼	+ 8
BET	BEP	.90e	10	10755	20½	15⅝	17	+ 1
BMC	BMC		8	27425	10½	6¾	7⅝	+ ⅝
BP Prudhoe	BPT	1.05e	...	38159	29	25½	27¾	...
BRE Prop	BRE	2.40	7	11293	31⅞	27⅛	28	− 2¾
BRT RltyTr	BRT	2.24e	5	28664	19¼	10¾	11⅞	− 6⅞
Bairnco	BZ	1.00	21	61655	25¼	17½	17⅞	− 6⅞
BakrFentrs	BKF	3.56e	...	19239	24⅞	19¼	21½	+ 1⅝
BakrHughs	BHI	.46	40	f11190	27⅝	13⅝	25½	+ 11½
BakrHughs pf		3.50	...	20882	60	41¼	56¼	+ 14¾
BaldorElec	BEZ	.44	16	16589	24½	15¼	21⅛	+ 5⅝
Ball Cp	BLL	1.12	34	91433	34⅜	25¼	33⅝	+ 5¾
BallyMfg	BLY	.30	17	683928	29¾	13½	15⅛	− 7
BaltimrBcp	BBB	.55	8	83115	15¾	11⅞	13⅛	+ ½
BaltimrGE	BGE	2.10	11	407436	34⅞	28½	34½	+ 3⅜
BaltimrGE pf		4.50	...	z26680	53	48½	51½	+ 1
BancOne	ONE	1.04	12	541719	37	22¼	32⅜	+ 10⅛
BancFla	BFL	.44	25	19674	12	6⅝	7	− 2¼
BancoBilV	BBV	.91e	...	59133	35⅞	29⅞	34½	− ½
BancoCentrl	BCM	.59e	9	11741	22½	19⅜	21¼	...
BancoSantdr	STD	1.18e	13	3660	61½	48¾	54	− 6
BancTexas	BTX		...	115984	13/16	3/16	5/16	− 7/16
Bandag	BDG	1.00	17	37992	89¼	64¼	84¼	+ 19⅛
BankBost	BKB	1.24	10	721989	30⅝	15¾	19	− 4⅝
BankBost pf		3.48e	...	2750	40⅝	29¼	32¼	− 7¾
BankBost pf		3.62e	...	5710	39¼	28⅝	31½	− 6¾
BankBost pf		6.54e	...	3122	74	50	57	− 10½
BankNewEng	NEB	1.36j	3	675835	24⅞	7¼	9⅜	− 12⅝
BankNY	BK	2.12	006	514200	55	36¾	40¼	+ 3¼
BankNY adj		8.89e	...	3859	102	98¾	99	− 1

Stock	Symbol	Div	Yld	Sales 100s	Hi	Lo	Last	Net Chg
BankNY adA		3.39e	...	3829	39⅝	36½	36½	...
BankAmer	BAC	.60	6	f22578	36⅜	17	26¾	+ 9⅛
BankAmer pf		3.48e	...	22546	38⅛	33	34¾	+ 1⅛
BankAmer pf		6.00e	...	13589	65⅞	54⅝	61⅝	+ 6⅝
BankAmer pf		2.25	...	40065	7¼	5	5⅛	− 1½
BankTrst	BT	2.33	...	662193	58¼	34½	41⅜	+ 6⅜
BannerInd	BNR		4	58299	17⅛	8⅛	15⅛	+ 7
Barclays	BCS	1.80e	6	34674	37	26¾	37	+ 7¾
Barclays pr		1.18e	...	32962	26⅛	24	24⅞	...
Barclays prB		.09e	...	22365	26⅝	23⅝	24⅝	...
Bard CR	BCR	.40	17	589339	26½	18¾	22⅛	− ⅞
BarnesGp	B	1.40	11	9547	38¾	29	29	− 6⅝
BarnettBks	BBI	1.20	9	295095	40	32¼	36⅛	+ 2⅛
BaroidCp	BRC	.20	56	418850	11¼	4⅜	11¼	+ 6¾
BattleMtn	BMG	.10	34	631977	18¼	13	16⅝	+ 2⅝
BauschLomb	BOL	1.16	18	220253	65⅞	40¾	65	+ 21⅝
BaxterInt	BAX	.56	17	f18238	25⅞	17½	25	+ 7⅜
BaxterInt pf		3.21e	...	34978	40	35	35⅞	− 2¾
BaxterInt pf		3.50	...	75207	78⅜	58½	75	+ 16¼
vjBayFnl	BAY		...	18063	14	⅞	1	− 10⅝
BayStGas	BGC	1.20	13	15629	22⅞	16¾	22¾	+ 5⅞
BearStearns	BSC	.56b	7	560009	17⅞	12⅛	13⅜	+ ¾
BearStearns pf		3.71e	...	8172	42	37½	37½	− ½
BearingsInc	BER	.64	11	42853	32⅞	24½	27⅞	+ 2⅝
Beazer	BZR	.61e	7	13225	15½	8⅜	11⅝	− 1
BeckmanInstr	BEC	.28e	11	263006	22¾	17⅛	17¾	+ ⅛
BeckmanInstr wi			...	29137	18⅝	17	18¼	...
BectonDksn	BDX	1.08	14	352858	62¼	48⅜	61⅞	+ 9⅞
BeldenHem	BHY	.64	10	3740	39	26¾	32⅜	+ 2⅞
BellAtlantic	BEL	4.40	16	595513	112¼	69⅜	111¼	+ 40⅛
BellIndus	BI	.40	16	26286	17¾	14⅝	15⅛	+ ½
BellSouth	BLS	2.52	16	f12137	58⅛	39	57⅞	+ 18
Belo AH	BLC	.44	44	52570	41	23	38	+ 14⅞
Bemis	BMS	.60	20	64810	37½	22½	34⅜	+ 11⅛
Beneficial	BNL	2.20	11	150525	56⅝	42⅝	49	+ 5⅝
Beneficial pf		4.30	...	3471	46¾	39½	44¾	+ 4¾
Beneficial pf		4.50	...	z10740	48	41½	45½	+ 4
Beneficial pf		5.50	...	z2330	252	198½	218⅜	+ 16⅛
Beneficial pf		2.50	...	z40440	26¾	23½	26	+ 2¾
Benguet	BE	.02i	3	129457	3⅜	1⅝	2½	...
Bennetton	BNG		...	68497	14⅞	12¾	13½	...
vjBerkey	BKY		...	21975	7/16	1/256	7/256	− 73/256
BerkHathwy	BRK		22	z4971	08900	4625	8675	+ 3975
Berlitz	BTZ		...	27025	16¾	15	16⅝	...
BerryPete	BRY	.55a	26	22894	15⅞	11¾	15⅝	+ 2⅛
BestBuy	BBY		100	35593	11½	5⅝	6	− 2⅜
BethSteel	BS	.10e	6	943651	28½	15¼	18½	− 4¾
BethSteel pf		5.00	...	23032	56¼	46½	49¾	− 1¾
BethSteel pf		2.50	...	29357	27⅝	23⅛	25	− ¾
BeverlyEnt	BEV		...	901950	10	5	6	− ¼
BiocraftLabs	BCL	.10e	16	117965	23½	8⅞	16¾	+ 7¼
BirmghamStl	BIR	.50	10	187117	29⅞	20¾	28	+ 4⅛
BlackDeck	BDK	.40	38	715210	25¼	18⅛	19½	− 3⅝
BlackHills	BKH	1.52	12	20258	29⅞	24⅞	28⅝	+ 3⅜
BlackstnIncTr	BKT	1.10	...	210787	9⅝	8¼	8⅝	− ⅞
BlackstnTgt	BTT	1.00	...	431331	11	8¾	10⅛	+ ½
BlockHR	HRB	1.28	19	346066	37⅜	26⅛	36	+ 7⅝
BlockbstrE	BV		36	975218	21⅝	9¾	17	+ 7⅛
BlueArrow	BAW	.34e	13	591188	18¾	13⅛	14⅝	− ⅜
BluChipValFd	BLU	.78e	...	58148	8⅛	5⅞	7	+ 1
Boeing	BA	1.20	18	f16419	61⅞	38½	59⅜	+ 19
BoiseCasc	BCC	1.52	7	382477	48	39¾	44⅜	+ 3⅛
BoltBerNew	BBN	.06	...	105948	11¼	6	7	− 3½
BondIntGold	BIG		...	142203	11	6⅜	10¼	+ 3
BondIntGold wt			...	32593	2	⅜	11/16	− 11/16
BordChm un	BCP	3.02e	4	410924	24	10	11	− 7¼
BordChm	BCU	3.02e	4	151925	24	9⅞	10¾	− 7⅜
BordenInc	BN	.96	...	556351	38⅝	27⅝	34⅜	+ 4¾
BostCelts	BOS	1.40e	10	11919	19½	13½	18⅛	+ 4⅜
BostEdsn	BSE	1.52	11	299389	22⅛	15⅜	20	+ 3½
BostEdsn pf		8.88	...	z53720	93	82½	92½	+ 8
BostEdsn pf		1.46	...	7715	15⅞	14	15¼	+ 1
Bowater	BOW	1.20	7	557544	34⅛	25¾	27⅝	+ ¼
BrazilFd	BZF	.80e	...	211787	14⅜	7⅛	12⅞	+ 5
BriggsStrat	BGG	1.60	...	115958	31⅛	24⅛	26⅝	− 2⅛
BrisMyrsSqb	BMY	2.12	...	f22452	58	44	56	+ 10¾
BrisMyrsSqb pf		2.00	...	36	238	190	235	+ 45
BritAir	BAB	1.46e	7	267905	37¾	27⅞	37⅝	+ 8¼
BritGas	BRG	1.67e	11	131621	39½	27⅝	39¼	+ 10⅜
BritPetrol	BP	4.24e	11	498301	65⅞	53⅝	65⅜	+ 11⅝
BritPetrol wt			...	66194	9⅜	5½	6¾	− ¾

NEW YORK STOCK EXCHANGE COMPOSITE

Stock	Symbol	Div	Yld	Sales 100s	Hi	Lo	Last	Net Chg
BritSteel	BST	1.38e	5	138392	23⅞	18⅞	21⅞	...
BritTelcom	BTY	1.90e	12	276096	52	39¼	50½	+ 4⅝
BroadInc	BRO	.20	15	377040	12¾	6⅞	11¾	+ 3
BrokenHill	BHP	1.08r	13	33910	32⅜	22⅜	29⅜	+ 7½
BklynUnGas	BU	1.84	13	62039	32¼	23	32⅛	+ 8½
BklynUnGas pf		2.47	...	3184	29	26¾	28¼	+ 1⅛
BrownShrp	BNS	.32	13	17199	18½	11¼	13⅞	− 2⅞
BrownGp	BG	1.60	62	79462	35½	26¾	27⅛	− 4¼
BrownFer	BFI	.64	22	930689	42¾	26⅞	38¾	+ 11⅜
Brunswick	BC	.44	...	868742	21½	13	14⅛	− 2¾
BrushWell	BW	.68	11	111814	30¼	20¼	20⅞	− 5⅝
BuckeyePtr	BPL	2.60	10	35659	28⅜	21⅛	28¼	+ 7
BunkerHill	BHL	1.76a	...	5372	17⅞	15½	17¼	+ 1⅜
BurgerKgInv	BKP	1.72a	11	17711	15⅝	12	12½	− ¾
BurlgtnCoat	BCF		12	19711	24⅝	17	24⅝	+ 7½
BurlgtnNthn	BNI	1.20	10	751042	32⅜	21⅜	31½	+ 8⅜
BurlgtnNthn pf		.55	...	3270	9¾	7⅝	9⅛	+ ⅞
BurlgtnRes	BR	.61e	73	f18367	53⅝	32⅛	48½	+ 15⅞
BusinssId	BLI		10	326091	15¼	7¾	9⅜	− 5½

-C-

Stock	Symbol	Div	Yld	Sales 100s	Hi	Lo	Last	Net Chg
CBI Ind	CBH	.60	33	103246	33⅞	25¼	32⅜	+ 7
CBS	CBS	4.40	17	128610	221	166	188	+ 17½
CBS pr		1.00	...	13	146⅝	115½	125½	− 23½
CCX	CCX		...	10131	4⅛	2¾	3	− ⅝
CCX pf		1.25	...	z13250	11⅛	9¼	10¾	− ⅛
CDI	CDI		14	39400	18½	9⅞	14½	+ 4½
CIGNA	CI	2.96	9	345870	66¾	45⅞	59½	+ 12⅜
CIGNA High	HIS	1.20	...	134338	10⅛	7⅛	7¾	− 1⅝
CML	CML		...	88527	28½	15	20½	+ 2⅞
CMS Engy	CMS	.10e	10	541473	39⅝	22½	38	+ 13⅝
CMS Enhanc	CME		6	239791	17½	9½	10	− 4
CNA Fnl	CNA		9	99191	108¾	57⅝	98	+ 37½
CNA IncShrs	CNN	1.24a	9	10806	12⅜	10⅞	11¾	+ ⅝
CPCInt	CPC	1.80	18	487733	73¾	49⅜	73¾	+ 21⅞
CPI Cp	CPY	.48	17	101391	33⅞	19¾	33⅝	+ 13¾
CRIIMI	CMM	.13e	...	10045	9⅞	7⅞	8⅞	...
CRI Liq	CFR	.24e	...	6037	13⅛	11½	12⅝	...
CRS Sirr	CRX	.12	13	62935	21⅞	12⅜	17	+ 3¾
CSX	CSX	1.40	9	545813	38⅝	29¾	35⅞	+ 4⅛
CSX pf		7.00	...	8	222	196	222	+ 42
CTS	CTS	.75	...	13056	25⅝	22¼	23	+ ¾
CUC Int	CU		...	524581	15⅜	9⅝	14½	+ 2
CablWirels	CWP	.19e	...	128503	28½	21¾	27⅝	...
CabltrnSys	CS		...	116960	16¾	9¼	9⅜	...
Cabot Cp	CBT	1.04	66	124853	45⅛	32⅞	36⅜	− 1⅝
CaesarWld	CAW		12	474415	43¼	27	30¾	− ¼
CalFedInco	CFI	1.00	...	39563	8	5⅛	5¾	− ⅞
CalFed	CAL	1.40	7	285979	28½	18	20⅜	− 1⅝
CalifREIT	CT	.40e	...	6626	5⅞	2½	2¾	− 3
CalifREIT wt			...	1656	3½	3/256	1/64	...
CallahnMng	CMN		...	41575	16⅜	12¾	14½	− ¼
CalMat	CZM	.56	16	72364	30⅝	24¾	30⅛	+ 2
Calton Inc	CN		4	153700	3⅜	13/16	1	− 2
CampblRes g	CCH			71284	1 5/16	½	13/16	+ ⅛
CampblSoup	CPB	1.00	293	581244	60⅚	30½	58⅝	+ 27⅛
CdnPac g	CP	.92	...	f13566	24⅜	18	22¼	+ 3¾
Canal Cap	COW		...	8536	6¼	2⅛	2⅜	− 3⅝
Canal Cap pf		1.30	...	1127	9⅜	5¾	5⅞	− 2¾
CapCities	CCB	.20	23	58535	568	353	564⅛	+ 201
CapHldg	CPH	1.08	9	191293	52¼	31¼	52	+ 19¼
CapHldg pf		6.75	...	3654	87	81	82	− 6
CapstdMtg	CMO	2.16	7	40164	20¼	14⅛	15⅝	− ⅞
CapstdMtg pf		1.60	...	3931	14½	12⅜	13	...
Careercom	PTA		...	196476	10¾	4⅝	5½	− 3⅞
Carlisle	CSL	1.20	13	35748	44⅜	31⅞	33	− 2
CarolcoPic	CRC		15	97451	12⅝	6⅝	12⅛	+ 4⅞
CarolcoPic wt			...	11144	4¼	15/16	3½	+ 2⅜
CarolFrght	CAO	.60	13	39212	27¼	18	18¾	− 5⅞
CarolPwr	CPL	2.92	11	365153	48	35	46⅜	+ 9
CarpTech	CRS	2.40	14	42628	54⅝	44⅞	47⅝	+ 1¼
Carriage	CGE	.10	28	15907	6½	3½	3⅞	− 1⅜
CarterHaw	CHH		...	145908	14⅝	7	8¼	− ⅛
CarterWal	CAR	.82	18	56011	60½	39⅛	57⅝	+ 18⅜
CascadeNG	CGC	1.28	10	10618	20⅝	14⅛	18½	+ 3½
CastlCook	CKE		23	293657	45¼	25⅜	34¾	+ 6½
Caterpillar	CAT	1.20	11	f10539	69	52⅞	57⅞	− 5¾
CedarFair	FUN	1.25	9	44430	13⅞	9½	13⅜	+ 3⅜
Centel	CNT	1.28	104	247835	67½	32⅞	64½	+ 31
CentrEngy	CX	1.60	...	733958	20⅞	13⅜	20⅝	+ 7⅛

Stock	Symbol	Div	Yld	Sales 100s	Hi	Lo	Last	Net Chg
Centex	CTX	.40	9	103757	41⅞	27¼	30⅞	+ 1⅝
CentlSoWest	CSR	2.60	13	453726	40¼	29¾	40⅛	+ 8⅛
CentlHudGE	CNH	1.76	10	52513	24⅛	20⅜	23½	+ 2
CentlHudGE		1.98e	...	4068	23	20	20	− 2½
CentlIllLt pf		4.50	...	z11920	52	44½	51½	+ 5½
CentlIllPS	CIP	1.80	10	225915	24⅛	20⅛	22⅞	+ ⅝
CentlLaElec	CNL	2.44	10	35682	36	31⅛	36	+ 4⅛
CentlMePwr	CTP	1.56	14	146279	20⅝	16⅞	20⅝	+ 2
CentlNews	ECP	.09e	18	43159	25¾	21½	22¾	...
CentlVtPS	CV	2.04	14	17156	29	22⅛	28½	+ 4⅝
CenturyTel	CTL	.41	43	138564	36	20	36	+ 15
CenvillInv	CVI	1.60e	7	19332	16⅜	8⅝	9⅛	− 6½
ChampInt	CHA	1.10	7	776430	37¾	28⅞	32	− ⅛
ChaparlStl	CSM	.10	8	59581	15¼	8½	9½	− 2⅜
ChartHousEnt	CHT		...	45241	15½	12⅝	12⅞	...
Charter	CHR	.05e	16	114920	5¾	4	4½	+ ⅜
ChaseManh	CMB	2.36	...	f14783	44⅞	28	34¾	+ 6⅛
ChaseManh pf		6.75	...	278	78	67	76	+ 7¼
ChaseManh pf		7.60	...	343	86	76	83½	+ 6¾
ChaseManh pf		5.25	...	7223	53½	48⅞	50⅝	+ 1⅛
ChaseManh pf		4.66e	...	34858	48¼	40¼	41¼	− 3¾
ChaseManh pf		4.22e	...	25224	43½	35½	36	− 4⅛
ChaseManh pf		2.62	...	30946	28½	24⅛	26⅜	+ 2⅛
ChaseManh pf		2.44	...	6873	26½	24½	25⅛	...
Chaus	CHS		26	91999	9⅜	3½	4½	+ ⅛
Chemed	CHE	1.84	14	33273	38¾	32½	35½	+ 3
ChemBank	CHL	2.72	...	776853	41⅛	28½	29⅞	− 1⅛
ChemBank B	CHLB	.76	...	303340	5	2½	2⅝	− 1½
ChemBank pf		.92e	...	260662	9½	7¼	7⅜	− 1½
ChemBank pf		4.72e	...	23917	47½	37	38½	− 4⅛
ChemBank pf		4.15e	...	17765	42¼	35⅜	36¼	− 2⅜
ChemBank dpf		2.69	...	56654	28	24⅛	25⅝	...
ChemWaste	CHW	.12	31	359262	23⅝	12¼	21½	+ 8⅞
Chesapke Cp	CSK	.72	8	49725	24⅛	17⅞	19⅞	− ⅛
Chevron	CHV	2.80	18	f20306	73½	45⅜	67¾	+ 22
ChiMilw	CHG	6.00e	19	3881	149	131	143¼	+ 11½
ChiMilw pf		5.00	...	766	72	54	56	− 11½
ChileFd	CH	.34e	...	57546	19⅝	13	15⅝	...
Chilis	EAT		22	102064	34½	20½	32⅞	+ 11⅞
ChockFull	CHF	.31t	16	47508	9½	5¾	6⅝	− 1¼
ChrisCrft	CCN	1.56t	52	170060	44⅛	21⅜	36⅜	+ 14½
ChrisCrft pf		1.00	...	42	16	11	14¼	+ 3½
ChrisCrft pf		1.40	...	48	971	560	971	+ 411
Christiana	CST		28	6049	10⅝	5¾	9⅜	+ 3⅛
Chrysler	C	1.20	3	f17050	29⅝	18⅛	19	− 6¾
Chrysler pf		2.37	...	320	35	26¾	26¾	− 3½
Chubb	CB	2.32	10	287020	99½	57⅝	95¼	+ 37¼
Chyron	CHY	.11r	...	29193	4⅝	2⅛	2¼	− 1¾
Cilcorp Inc	CER	2.46	11	23723	39⅜	31¾	38¼	+ 5¾
CincBell	CSN	.68	19	102203	35	20	27¼	+ 5⅜
CincGE	CIN	2.32	8	288614	32⅜	24⅜	31½	+ 5¼
CincGE pf		4.00	...	z28970	46	39	45¼	+ 5¼
CincGE pf		4.75	...	z36690	52	45	52	+ 4½
CincGE pf		9.30	...	z39960	99	88	97½	+ 8½
CincGE pf		7.44	...	z74630	80¾	71	80	+ 8¾
CincGE pf		9.28	...	1934	98	87½	97¼	+ 8¼
CincGE pf		9.52	...	z41510	100	90	98⅞	+ 7⅞
CincGE pf		10.20	...	z27340	105⅝	103½	103½	− 1⅜
CincMilacron	CMZ	.72	22	107804	25⅛	15	17½	− 4½
CineplxOde	CPX		...	703885	16⅜	6⅜	6¾	− 5
CircleK	CKP	.14j	...	984208	16⅝	3¼	3⅜	− 8
CircuitCty	CC	.08	14	305007	27	17⅝	21¾	...
Circus	CIR		22	192834	57	28¾	56	+ 26⅞
Citicorp	CCI	1.62	5	f23882	35½	24⅝	28⅞	+ 3
Citicorp pf		6.00e	...	25937	70	62⅜	64¼	...
Citicorp pfA		7.00e	...	13799	81⅝	73	74	− 2½
Citicorp pfB		9.41e	...	5407	102½	99½	101⅜	+ 1⅛
Citicorp pfC			...	13673	25½	24	24½	...
Citz&SoCp	CTZ	1.40	9	586346	36	24⅜	30¾	+ 6
CityTrBcp	CYT	1.12	...	26458	47⅜	9¼	13¼	− 24⅞
Clabir	CLG		...	37866	1¼	9/256	7/128	− 1 25/128
ClairStrs	CLE	.10	17	239237	14⅜	4⅝	13⅝	+ 8¾
ClarkEquip	CKL		11	111185	44	30⅛	36⅝	+ 5⅞
ClayHomes	CMH		8	43653	10¼	7⅝	8¾	+ ¼
ClemteGlob	CLM	.16e	...	29056	10⅛	7⅛	10⅛	+ 2¾
CleveCliff	CLF	.80	6	81282	34	25¾	29	+ 2⅜
CleveElec pf		7.40	...	1306	78½	65½	77	+ 11⅞
CleveElec pf		7.56	...	3592	80½	67¼	78½	+ 12¼
CleveElec pf		8.40e	...	1174	83⅜	77⅜	81	+ 3½
Clorox	CLX	1.24	16	253178	44½	30⅛	42	+ 11

NEW YORK STOCK EXCHANGE COMPOSITE

Stock	Symbol	Div	Yld	Sales 100s	Hi	Lo	Last	Net Chg
ClubMed	CMI	.27e	9	24891	21⅞	13⅛	19⅛	+ 6
Coachmen	COA	.40	...	45539	11	6⅜	6⅝	− 2¼
CoastSvg	CSA	.40	...	131931	20⅜	9⅜	11¾	− 3
Coastal	CGP	.40	17	373922	49⅝	33	49⅝	+ 15⅜
Coastal wi			...	32	32½	22	32	+ 9¼
Coastal pfA		1.19	...	14	121	104	121	...
Coastal pfB		1.83	...	74	119	80	119	+ 41
CocaCola	KO	1.36	23	f15461	81	43⅜	77¼	+ 32⅝
CocaColaEnt	CCE	.05	20	516500	18¾	14¾	16	+ 1
ColesMyer	CM	.48e	...	4135	24¾	18⅛	19⅞	− 2⅛
ColgatePalm	CL	1.80	13	531966	64⅞	44⅛	63½	+ 16½
ColgatePalm pf		4.25	...	z17080	67½	55¾	60½	+ 2¾
CollinsFds	CF	.20	15	114282	22¾	16¼	19⅞	+ 3¼
ColonlHiIncо	CXE	.80	...	67067	10	8⅝	9⅜	...
ColonlIntmk	CMK	.24e	9	14629	12	10¾	10¾	...
ColonlHigh	CIF	1.20	...	55434	9⅝	7⅛	7¼	− 2
ColonlInvMn	CXH	.24e	...	21993	12⅛	11¼	11⅞	...
ColonlMuni	CMU	.72	12	86325	10¼	9⅛	9⅜	− ¼
ColumGas	CG	2.00	21	390438	52¾	33¾	52	+ 17½
ColumSL	CSV	.28	...	237370	11¾	1½	2¾	− 4⅜
ColumSL pf		.01	...	14639	11⅝	1¾	2½	− 4⅝
ColumSoPwr pf		3.45	...	2864	29	27¼	27⅞	− ¾
ColumSoPwr pf		2.42	...	252	27	24⅛	26¾	+ 2¼
ColumSoPwr pf		15.25	...	z18250	114⅞	105	111	+ ¼
ColumSoPwr pr		15.25	...	z26860	115½	106	113	− 1½
CombustEngr	CSP	1.00	...	492136	40	24¼	39¾	+ 11⅞
Comdisco	CDO	.24	10	236073	34	20⅞	24¾	+ 3¾
CommerclMtls	CMC	.52	9	29911	23⅞	19¾	21⅞	+ ¾
CommodoreInt	CBU		10	457526	19¾	7⅛	10¾	− 3¼
ComwEd	CWE	3.00	13	f11863	40¾	32⅛	37⅝	+ 4⅝
ComwEd wtA			...	5	12¾	10⅞	12¾	+ 2¼
ComwEd wtB			...	3	12¾	11½	12¾	+ 2⅛
ComwEd pf		1.42	...	338	40⅜	32⅞	37⅛	+ 3⅞
ComwEd pr		1.90	...	8235	21½	18¼	20⅝	+ 2
ComwEd pr		2.00	...	4802	22½	19⅜	22	+ 2¼
ComwEd pf		12.75	...	z28510	111	102¾	108½	+ 1½
ComwEd pf		11.70	...	1862	108	102	108	+ 3½
ComwEd pfB		8.40	...	1207	100	89	100	+ 10½
ComwEd pf		8.38	...	3825	92	79	89	+ 10
ComwEd pr		2.37	...	4850	26¼	24¾	25⅜	+ ¼
ComwEd pf		2.87	...	5574	28¾	25½	27⅜	+ 1¼
ComwEd pf		8.40	...	4851	92	79	87½	+ 7½
ComwEd pr		7.24	...	1672	80½	68½	80	+ 11¼
ComwEngy	CES	2.80	10	15510	38½	29⅝	38⅜	+ 6⅞
ComwMtg	CMA	.27j	...	71126	3	11/64	3/16	− 1 13/16
Comsat	CQ	1.32	10	191619	40⅝	26	35¾	+ 8¾
CmuntyPsych	CMY	.36b	17	410257	34	20⅜	29¾	+ 8¼
Compaq	CPQ		9	f15304	112½	59¼	79½	+ 19⅞
ComprehnCr	CMP	.10j	...	217906	13	2⅝	2⅞	− 5⅝
CptrAssoc	CA		13	f17041	21⅝	10½	12½	− 3⅜
CptrFactry	CFA		18	144004	13½	5⅞	6¼	− 5½
CptrSci	CSC		17	115887	58½	46¼	57¾	+ 10¼
CptrTask	TSK	.05	20	37944	15⅝	8½	9⅛	− 4½
ComstockPtr	CPF	1.03e	...	724446	10⅞	8⅝	10⅜	+ 1¼
ConAgra	CAG	.60	16	429116	30¼	19¼	28½	+ 9¼
ConnEngy	CNE	1.23	14	7514	18⅞	14	17⅝	+ 3⅛
ConnNatGas	CTG	1.36	14	14040	19	15⅛	18	+ 1⅝
Conseco	CNC	.20	6	60514	28	11¼	26⅞	+ 15¾
ConEdison	ED	1.72	12	428715	29⅞	22⅛	29⅛	+ 5⅞
ConEdison pf		6.00	...	13	338	290	333	+ 39½
ConEdison pf		4.65	...	1061	57	47½	56	+ 7
ConEdison pf		5.00	...	1937	58	51	57	+ 3¼
ConFrgt	CNF	1.06	13	566912	37¾	25¼	26½	− 6½
ConsNatGas	CNG	1.84	27	221342	51½	37⅛	50⅜	+ 10
Conrail	CRR	1.40	11	589196	49⅜	32	47⅞	+ 14⅛
ConStore	CNS		15	463037	8⅜	3⅜	3⅞	− 2⅝
ConstarInt	CTR	.64	11	61962	33⅞	20¼	33⅞	+ 13⅞
ConsPwr pf		4.16	...	z21340	61	41½	61	+ 19¾
ConsPwr pf		4.50	...	z78180	67½	44⅜	61	+ 16⅝
ConsPwr pf		7.45	...	1314	87	72⅝	84	+ 11¼
ConsPwr pf		7.72	...	1972	88½	74½	86¾	+ 12
ConsPwr pf		7.76	...	2469	90	74¾	88½	+ 13
ConsPwr pf		7.68	...	2154	88	74	86½	+ 12¼
Contel	CTC	1.10	21	713670	36¾	19⅞	34⅛	+ 14
ContlCp	CIC	2.60	...	362081	38⅝	30	31⅛	− 1¼
ContlBkCp	CBK	1.00	4	284350	26⅝	18½	19⅞	− ⅞
ContlBkCp pf		3.00e	...	11379	43¼	38¼	39⅛	+ ⅝
ContlBkCp pfA			...	24698	25½	24	24¾	...
vjContl Info	CNY		...	125269	2¼	3/16	7/32	− 1 29/32
ControlData	CDA		...	531124	24	16¼	18⅛	− 1½
ControlData pf		4.50	...	z21860	45½	38½	39	− 6
ConvtHldg	CNV		...	60970	6	4⅛	5½	+ 1¼
ConvtHldg pf		1.41e	...	26008	12¼	11	11½	...
ConvexCptr	CNX		29	233177	16	9⅜	15⅜	+ 5⅜
CooperCo	COO		...	258432	5⅜	2⅛	3¼	− 2⅛
CooperInd	CBE	1.00	16	470049	40	26⅞	40	+ 13
CooperInd pf		8.00	...	8448	128	123½	127½	...
CooperT&R	CTB	.36	12	273138	39	22½	32⅜	+ 8⅜
Copperwld	COS	.40	7	21707	16	11½	12¼	+ ⅝
CoreInd	CRI	.72	16	27432	14⅞	10¼	11¾	− ¾
Corning	GLW	.90a	17	478339	43⅜	32	43	+ 8⅜
CorroonBlk	CBL	1.24	17	112489	41	30¾	36⅛	+ 5
CounselTndm	CTF	.10a	...	33479	11½	6¼	11½	+ 5¼
CounselTndm pf		3.63	...	3891	48¼	43¾	47½	+ 2
CntrywdCrd	CCR	.27r	13	118930	10¼	6¼	8¼	+ 1⅞
CntrywdMtg	CWM	.56	5	66970	5¾	3½	3¾	− 1⅝
Craig	CRA		9	36050	26⅝	8¼	17¾	+ 9½
Crane	CR	.75	14	39587	25	15	23¼	+ 7¾
Crawfrd	CFD	.54	24	27570	36¼	14¾	33¾	+ 19
CrayResrch	CYR		10	495467	65⅞	30½	39	− 21¾
CrompKnls	CNK	.62	18	35300	31½	14⅞	30¾	+ 15½
CrossldSvg	CRL	.80j	...	241518	19¼	2⅞	3⅜	− 14
CrossldSvg pf		1.81j	...	31280	21	4⅝	6	− 14⅜
CrossldSvg pf		12.75j	...	19361	93⅜	28¼	31¼	− 62
CrownCork	CCK		15	159190	57	43⅞	53⅛	+ 6⅞
CrysBrnds	CBR	.20	10	64925	37⅞	21¾	28½	+ 6¼
Culbro	CUC	.80	...	4837	48	33⅜	36¼	+ ¾
CumnEng	CUM	2.20	...	166776	72¼	48	50¾	− 13½
CumnEng pr		3.50	...	22693	51	39¼	40	− 7⅛
CurIncoShrs	CUR	1.10a	...	6689	12⅝	10⅞	12¼	+ 1¼
CurtWrght	CW	1.60	10	7586	62	52⅜	59	+ 5¼
CyCareSys	CYS		325	14118	9⅞	5½	9¾	+ 2⅞
CyclopInd	CYC		6	15566	37¼	23⅜	32	+ 8⅝
CypressSemi	CY		14	352666	14½	9¼	9⅞	− 1
CyprusMinl	CYM	.80	4	399775	33	21¼	26½	+ 4⅞
CyprusMinl pf		3.75	...	51027	68¼	50½	57½	+ 3¾

-D-

Stock	Symbol	Div	Yld	Sales 100s	Hi	Lo	Last	Net Chg
DCNY	DCY	.40	...	32948	22	12½	14⅛	− 6⅝
DPL Inc	DPL	2.24	10	273000	30⅞	24⅛	30⅜	+ 5⅛
DQE Inc	DQE	1.36	12	266285	23⅞	17⅜	23⅞	+ 5⅛
Dallas Cp	DLS	.66	98	45005	23⅞	13½	23⅝	+ 8½
Dana Cp	DCN	1.60	9	213212	42⅞	33	34⅝	− 4¼
Danaher	DHR		9	81165	18⅜	12⅞	15¼	+ 1⅛
DanielInd	DAN	.18	26	50739	16½	8⅝	15⅝	+ 7
DataGen	DGN		...	305013	19½	11¾	12½	− 6
Datapoint	DPT		...	123786	6¼	3	3⅜	− 1⅛
Datapoint pf		4.94	...	10982	25	6¾	7¼	− 14⅞
DataDsgn	DDL	.12j	...	83561	8⅛	3⅜	5⅜	− 2½
DavisW&W	DWW	.28	30	14765	17¼	12½	13	− 1¾
DaytnHud	DH	1.12	15	719875	67	38¾	63⅝	+ 24
DaytnPL pf		7.48	...	z58000	84½	73¼	81¾	+ 7½
DaytnPL pf		7.70	...	z84650	86½	74⅛	83½	+ 7⅜
DaytnPL pf		7.37	...	z30750	83	72	81½	+ 6¼
DeanFood	DF	.66	14	72970	37⅞	28⅞	33¼	+ 3⅜
DeanWtGvTr	GVT	.88	...	251133	9½	8½	8¾	− ¼
Deere	DE	2.00	12	764085	64¼	44	61½	+ 13½
DelValFnl	DVL	1.86	10	11135	18⅞	15⅞	18¼	+ 1⅝
DelmarPL	DEW	1.54	13	162207	21¼	17	20⅞	+ 3⅛
DeltaAir	DAL	1.20a	7	860972	85¾	48¾	68¼	+ 18⅛
DeltaWdsde	DLW	.30	7	37732	18	10¼	11⅛	+ ⅝
Deltona	DLT		...	16027	6⅜	4	4⅞	− ⅛
DeluxeCp	DLX	1.04	20	300757	35¾	24	34⅜	+ 9⅜
DenisnMfg	DSN	1.32	10	58878	32⅞	22⅜	23½	− 1⅜
DeSoto	DSO	.40	...	106251	52½	32⅜	46	+ 11½
DetEd	DTE	1.68	...	787644	25⅞	17⅛	25⅜	+ 8
DetEd pf		5.50	...	132	140	98	140	+ 43⅛
DetEd pfA		9.32	...	1049	98	84	96	+ 11
DetEd pf		7.68	...	1315	82½	70	81	+ 10¼
DetEd pf		7.45	...	1362	81	68½	78	+ 9
DetEd pf		7.36	...	3218	81	67⅛	77½	+ 9
DetEd prF		2.75	...	2069	27⅞	24¾	26⅝	+ ⅞
DetEd prB		2.75	...	2150	27¾	24⅞	26⅜	+ 1⅜
DetEd pf		9.72	...	z2870	100¼	94½	100	− ⅝
DetEd pr		2.28	...	4224	25⅛	21¾	24¾	+ 2⅜
Dexter	DEX	.88	13	528514	34¾	20⅛	21⅞	− ⅜
DiagnstPdt	DP	.24	29	18056	38	19¼	33¾	+ 14¼
DiGiorgio	DIG	.64	16	68068	35¾	23½	27⅜	+ 2½
DiaShamOff	DSP	2.80	19	82530	13⅛	5½	6⅛	− 4¾
DiaShamRM	DRM	.44	8	231496	28½	14⅞	25	+ 9¾

NEW YORK STOCK EXCHANGE COMPOSITE

Stock	Symbol	Div	Yld	Sales 100s	Hi	Lo	Last	Net Chg
DiaShamRM pf		2.00	...	40234	39½	26½	36	+ 9¾
DianaCp	DNA		...	18519	8⅞	4	4¼	− ¾
Diebold	DBD	1.50	15	161721	47¾	36⅜	38½	− ⅜
DigitalComm	DCA		16	469471	25½	16⅝	19¾	+ 1¼
DigitalEqp	DEC		10	f17084	122⅜	79¾	82	− 16⅜
DillardStrs	DDS	.20	18	131217	74¼	41	71	+ 28⅝
DimeSvgNY	DME	.60	14	141575	17¾	8¾	10¼	− 3¾
Disney	DIS	.48	22	f11988	136¼	64⅞	112	+ 46¼
DivrsEngies	DEI	1.56	24	114595	39	23½	37½	+ 12¾
DivrsInd	DMC		15	11635	6¼	4⅜	4⅞	− ¼
DixonGp	DXN	.26e	11	1158	8½	5⅛	6¾	− 1⅛
DominRes	D	3.32	12	499326	47⅞	40⅜	47½	+ 5⅜
Domtar	DTC	.50	...	107052	15⅜	11	11¼	− 1
Donaldson	DCI	.38	14	35399	24¼	16½	22¼	+ 1½
Donelley	DNY	.88	18	272768	51¼	34¼	51¼	+ 16⅝
Dover	DOV	.72	16	300993	39½	27¼	36	+ 7⅛
DowChem	DOW	2.60	7	f17288	72¼	55½	71⅜	+ 12⅞
DowJones	DJ	.72	10	220835	42½	29¼	33¼	+ 3¾
DowneySL	DSL		8	67910	24	10¼	17¾	+ 7½
Dravo	DRV		17	144836	22¾	13	16¼	+ ⅛
DresserInd	DI	1.00	19	623214	48	29	44⅞	+ 15½
Dresher	DSR	.12j	...	17826	6⅛	2¼	2⅝	− 2⅝
Dreyfus	DRY	.52	17	248120	37⅞	25⅛	35⅝	+ 10⅝
DreyfusMuni	LEO	.81	...	110082	11⅛	10⅛	10¾	+ ¼
DreyfStrGvFd	DSI	1.08	...	46256	11⅝	10	10⅜	− ⅜
DreyfStrMuni	DSM	.78	...	12800	10⅛	10	10	...
DuPont	DD	4.80	12	f12897	126½	86⅛	123	+ 34¾
DuPont wi			...	1244	42⅛	28⅝	41½	+ 12⅛
DuPont pf		3.50	...	1172	45½	38⅞	44¾	+ 4¼
DuPont pf		4.50	...	5974	58¼	49⅝	58	+ 7
DuffPhelps	DNP	.76e	...	656808	8⅞	7⅝	8⅝	+ ¾
DukePwr	DUK	3.12	13	346402	56½	42¾	56⅛	+ 9⅞
DukePwr pf		6.75	...	14	220	180	220	+ 35
DukePwr pf		8.70	...	1263	99¾	88	97¼	+ 7¾
DukePwr pf		8.20	...	2987	96	83	93⅛	+ 9⅛
DukePwr pf		7.80	...	5642	91½	79½	89⅞	+ 8
DukePwr pfN		8.84	...	1708	104¾	99½	102	+ 2¼
DukePwr pfM		8.84	...	1723	100	90	98	+ 6
DukePwr pf		8.28	...	5954	97	84½	94½	+ 8½
DukeRltyInv	DRE	.68	...	21076	6¼	4¼	4¾	− ⅞
DunBradst	DNB	2.00	15	f13821	60¼	41¼	46	− 7⅝
DuqLght pfA		2.10	...	z61780	24¼	20¼	22⅜	− ⅛
DuqLght pf		1.87	...	z63760	21¾	18	20	+ 1
DuqLght pf		2.00	...	z83780	22	18½	20⅝	+ ¾
DuqLght pf		2.05	...	z49520	23	19½	21¼	+ ¾
DuqLght pf		2.07	...	z65120	23¼	19¼	21¾	+ 1¼
DuqLght pfG		2.10	...	z30750	23	20	22⅜	+ 2⅝
DuqLght pfK		2.10	...	1554	23½	19¼	22⅛	+ 1⅜
DuqLght pr		2.31	...	7109	25¼	21½	24½	+ 2
DuqLght pf		7.20	...	1176	79½	68	79	+ 9
DynaAmer	DYA	.20	288	7580	25⅜	21⅝	23	+ ⅛

-E-

Stock	Symbol	Div	Yld	Sales 100s	Hi	Lo	Last	Net Chg
ECC Int	ECC	.20	...	20902	8¼	5¼	5½	− 1⅛
EMC Cp	EMC		...	100830	6⅛	2¾	3¼	− 2⅛
EG&G	EGG	.76	14	134642	36½	28⅜	34	+ 5¼
EQK Green	EGA	1.30	27	27007	13⅝	11¼	12	− ⅝
EQK Rlty	EKR		...	25904	14¾	6	6⅛	− 4⅝
ERC Int	ERC		12	43261	12⅞	7¼	12¾	+ 2⅜
E Systems	ESY	.50	12	189562	37⅞	27¼	30⅞	+ 1⅝
EaglePich	EPI		...	98617	17½	8⅛	9¼	− 6⅜
EasternEnt	EFU	1.40	14	150966	35¼	22¾	34⅞	+ 11¾
EastUtil	EUA	2.50	15	159217	41¾	30⅜	41¾	+ 10¼
EKodak	EK	2.00	15	f28186	52⅜	40	41⅛	− 4
Eaton	ETN	2.00	10	180711	67½	53	57	+ 1¼
Echlin	ECH	.70	20	342039	18⅜	13¼	15⅝	− ⅞
Ecolab	ECL	.66	21	271061	35¾	24⅞	28½	+ 2
EdisonBros	EBS	2.08	11	58115	70¼	32	63½	+ 31¼
EdisonBros wi			...	118	35⅛	16	32	+ 15⅞
EDO	EDO	.28	10	18859	11⅞	6⅞	7⅛	− 4¼
EdwardsAG	AGE	.68b	9	121155	28⅜	17	22¾	+ 5⅜
1838BondFd	BDF	1.82	...	4804	22¼	17¾	21⅞	+ 4¼
EkcoGp	EKO		24	96725	3⅝	2⅜	2⅝	− ¼
ElPasoRefin	ELP	.50e	...	8519	25¼	23⅜	24½	...
Elcor	ELK	.22	...	13682	12	8⅛	12	+ 3¼
EldonInd	ELD	.24	19	17514	17½	12⅜	16¼	+ 3¼
ElectAssoc	EA		22	12053	4⅛	2	2⅞	+ ⅝
EljerInd	ELJ	.28	...	91524	34¾	19	19⅜	...
Elscint	ELT		56	77766	2½	⅞	2¼	+ 1¼
EmerldHom	EHP	.94j	7	19362	8⅞	1⅝	1⅞	− 6⅝
EmerldMtg	EIC	.50e	...	50455	8	2⅜	3¼	− 4⅝
EmersElec	EMR	1.26	15	868566	39⅞	29½	39	+ 8⅝
EmersRadio	EME		18	239054	7	4	5⅞	+ 2
EmpDistElec	EDE	2.32	11	8124	32⅛	26½	31	+ 3¼
EmpDistElec pf		.47	...	z55570	6¼	4¾	5⅞	+ ½
EmpDistElec pf		.50	...	z36320	6⅜	5¼	5¾	− ⅛
ENDESA	ELE	.43e	8	383611	23⅜	14⅛	21	+ 6¾
Energen	EGN	.88	22	63197	24⅜	15⅜	20⅛	+ 3⅛
Engelhard	EC	.56	10	167993	25⅞	17¼	19¼	+ 2
EnnisBsFrm	EBF	.64	17	23046	27½	17¾	25½	+ 7½
EnronCp	ENE	2.48	25	239309	61	35½	57⅝	+ 21
EnronOG	EOG	.05e	...	77327	25¼	19	25¼	...
Enron pfJ		10.50	...	2854	208½	125	201	+ 61
Enserch	ENS	.80	40	481478	27½	18⅝	26⅝	+ 7¾
Enserch pf		4.35e	...	12165	45¼	39	41	− 3¾
Enserch pf		7.79e	...	5637	79⅝	72½	72½	− 7¼
EnserchExp	EP	.30	23	120575	13⅝	8½	9⅝	+ ¼
Entergy	ETR	1.00	...	864821	23¼	15½	23¼	+ 7¼
Enterra	EN		...	43099	14⅜	5⅞	14⅜	+ 8⅜
EnviroSys	ESC		...	147212	14½	7¼	11¾	− 2⅜
EnviroSys pf		1.75	...	18858	15⅝	9	12⅜	− 2⅛
Equifax	EFX		20	84601	20	13	16	+ 2½
Equimark	EQK	.16	5	86520	16⅞	10⅝	12	− ⅞
Equimark pf		2.31	...	1152	24¼	21½	23	+ 1½
EquitRE	EQM	1.04	22	25078	9⅜	7	7¼	− 1⅝
EquitRes	EQT	1.34	19	61621	44	32	41½	+ 7⅝
Equitec	EFG		...	8736	3⅛	1¼	1½	− 1⅛
EsselteBusn	ESB	.96	16	39611	46¼	29⅞	45⅞	+ 15¾
Esterline	ESL		12	45717	15½	9⅞	11¼	− 1⅜
EthylCp	EY	.48b	15	423852	29	21	27½	+ 5⅞
EthylCp pf		2.40	...	8	533	436	533	+ 92
Excelsior	EIS	1.35e	...	5243	16½	14⅝	16⅛	+ 1⅛
Exxon	XON	2.40	16	f33619	51⅝	41½	50	+ 6

-F-

Stock	Symbol	Div	Yld	Sales 100s	Hi	Lo	Last	Net Chg
FAI Insur	FAI	.52e	11	16073	12⅝	8¾	11⅛	− ⅛
FMC Cp	FMC		8	149855	49	31⅝	35¼	+ 3¼
FMC Gold	FGL	.05e	14	42322	14¼	8½	11⅜	+ ⅛
FPL Gp	FPL	2.28	11	733841	36¾	29	36⅝	+ 5¼
FabriCtrs	FCA		12	13184	14⅝	11	13¾	+ 1¾
Fairchild pf		3.60	...	3098	40⅛	32	38½	− 1⅝
Fairfield	FCI		30	66077	7¾	3½	3⅞	− 2¼
FamDollr	FDO	.36	14	163160	14⅛	9¾	10⅝	− 3⅛
Fansteel	FNL	.40a	188	25344	13½	6¾	7½	− 2⅞
FarWestFnl	FWF	.10i	...	19926	14⅛	5¼	6½	− 1⅜
Farah Inc	FRA		...	55073	12⅝	5¼	6¾	− 1¾
FaysInc	FAY	.20b	14	51290	15	9⅛	10⅝	− ¾
Fedders	FJQ	.40	11	235785	18⅜	11⅞	13½	+ ⅞
FedlExp	FDX		18	493450	57⅞	42⅛	45¾	− 4⅞
FedlHmLoan	FRE	1.60	11	f12640	104¾	48¾	67⅛	+ 16⅝
FedlMogul	FMO	.92	13	148340	29½	18⅝	21	− 2¾
FedlNMtg	FNM	.56	13	f17313	46⅜	16⅝	33⅞	+ 17
FedlNMtg wt			...	897250	32⅝	18⅛	21	...
FedPapBd	FBO	1.00	5	451867	29⅞	19⅝	25¾	+ 5½
FedlPapBd pf		1.20	...	46	144½	99¼	118	+ 23
FedlPapBd pf		2.87	...	42184	55	41¾	48¾	+ 6⅛
FedlRlty	FRT	1.40	20	37940	26	20¾	22	+ ⅞
FedlSgnl	FSS	.84b	15	42737	32⅛	17⅛	32⅛	+ 12¾
Ferro	FOE	.64	11	468071	40	22¼	25¾	+ 3½
Fiat	FIA	.78i	21	8670	44¼	31	44¼	...
Fiat pf		.78i	...	359	27¾	20¾	25⅜	...
Fiat pfA		1.07e	...	163	27¾	20¾	26	...
Fieldcrst	FLD	.80	11	89753	30¼	18⅝	22½	+ 2⅝
Filtertek	FTK	.44	12	23629	10⅛	6⅞	8	− 1¾
FniCpSBar	FSB		...	51199	3¾	⅝	13/16	− 2 7/16
FinevstFd	FVF	.12	...	44478	10⅞	6¾	8¾	+ ⅜
FstBkSys	FBS	.82	...	759582	26⅞	15⅝	16¾	− 4⅜
FstBkSys pf			...	43320	27½	24½	25⅝	...
FstBosInco	FBF	.90	...	69005	9	7⅞	7⅞	− ½
FstBosStrg	FBI	1.20	...	28624	11½	8⅞	9¼	− 1⅞
FstBrands	FBR		...	18402	19	18	18¾	...
FstCapHldgs	FCH		4	465809	14⅝	6⅛	8⅞	+ 2⅜
FstChicago	FNB	1.80	7	453733	49⅝	29¼	37⅛	+ 7½
FstChicago pf		3.97e	...	18750	46	39½	39⅞	− 3⅝
FstChicago pfB		6.00e	...	9845	69	63	63¼	− 2¾
FstChicago pfC		7.23e	...	5733	82	73	73	− 7¼
FstChicago pf		3.75	...	5132	70¾	50	55	+ 4¼
FstCityTex	FBT	1.48	8	143153	39½	26	36⅞	+ 10⅝
FstCityTex pf		5.50	...	17024	76	56	70⅜	+ 14⅜
FstFidlty	FFB	2.00	...	385167	34	21⅜	23¼	− 3⅝
FstFidlty pfB		2.15	...	25919	28½	21¼	22¼	− 1⅝

NEW YORK STOCK EXCHANGE COMPOSITE

Stock	Symbol	Div	Yld	Sales 100s	Hi	Lo	Last	Net Chg
FstFidlty pfD		8.27e	...	z63410	90	84	84	− 12½
FstFnlFd	FF	.22a	...	71051	11⅝	6⅞	8	+ 1
FstInterste	I	3.00	6	746425	70⅜	40¾	41⅞	− 1½
FstInterst pf		2.37	...	472	25	22⅛	23½	− ½
FstInterst A	I.A		...	412503	2⅛	3/16	1½	+ 1 5/16
FstInterst pf			...	24105	35¾	27⅛	28¼	− 4½
FstMiss	FRM	.30	25	218891	20½	13⅛	16	− 1¾
FstPenna	FPA		14	355798	17⅛	12⅜	16⅛	+ 3⅝
FstPhilpnFd	FPF	.08e	...	128483	18	12¼	13¾	...
FstUnionCp	FTU	1.00	8	421184	27	19⅝	20⅝	− 1½
FstUnionRE	FUR	1.50	10	68465	21¼	15½	16⅜	− 1⅞
FstVaBks	FVB	1.24	9	58474	35⅝	23¾	30	+ 5¼
FstWachva	FW	1.52	11	153606	45⅜	31	40⅞	+ 9⅜
Firstar	FSR	1.12	9	34746	35	25⅝	32½	+ 6⅛
Firstar pf		8.29e	...	3196	92½	84¼	84¼	− 7¼
FstFedFnl	FED		9	40198	27¼	13⅛	21	+ 7⅛
Fischbach	FIS		...	72531	27½	8⅛	12⅛	− 3½
FleetNorstr	FNG	1.40	8	375453	30⅞	23¾	26⅛	+ ⅝
FleetNorstr pf		3.01e	...	4318	37¼	32½	32½	− 3½
FleetNorstr pfA		2.97e	...	5437	37¼	32¾	33⅛	− 3¼
FleetwdEnt	FLE	.76	9	185361	30⅝	22	24	− 1⅛
Fleming	FLM	1.00	11	302451	40	27½	30⅛	− 4⅞
Flghtsfty	FSI	.20	27	118965	51	24⅛	47⅞	+ 23⅛
FloatPtSys	FLP		...	53580	3¾	1⅜	1⅝	− 1¼
FlaECstInd	FLA	.40a	14	9563	73½	56	62¾	+ 6⅜
FlaProgrss	FPC	2.64	11	233185	40¼	33¼	40	+ 5
FlowGen	FGN		...	63164	6⅝	3½	4¾	− ½
FlowersInd	FLO	.56	25	155675	21⅛	16¼	19	− ¼
FluorCp	FLR	.24	27	748342	37¾	21⅝	36¾	+ 13⅜
FooteCone	FCB	1.20	20	41926	32	22½	29¼	+ 6⅜
FoothillGp	FGI	.28b	6	25809	9¾	6¼	7	− ⅛
FordMotor	F	3.00	4	f26388	56⅝	41⅜	43⅝	− 6⅞
FtDearborn	FTD	1.36	...	8735	15½	13⅜	14¾	+ ⅜
FostrWheelr	FWC	.44	23	286247	22	14¼	20¾	+ 6¼
Foxboro	FOX	.40	19	42864	35½	21	22⅞	− 8⅛
FrankMulln	FMI	.14e	...	4749	10⅛	8½	9⅝	...
FrankPrnTr	FPT	1.05	...	65321	10⅜	9⅜	9¾	...
FranklnRes	BEN	.60	14	67282	45⅛	22½	42⅞	+ 20⅜
FrankUnivTr	FT	1.12	...	74977	9⅞	8	8¼	− 1
FrptMcEngy	FMP	2.20e	22	122536	14½	8⅝	10⅛	− 2¾
FrptMcGold	FAU	.05a	64	74339	14½	9⅛	12⅞	− 1½
FrptMcOil	FMR	1.59e	5	56263	6	4⅛	5¾	+ 1⅜
FrptMcCopr	FCX	2.22e	8	91749	23	14¼	21½	+ 5⅞
FrptMcInc	FTX	1.50a	13	567939	38	27⅛	32	+ 4⅝
FrptMcInc pf		1.87	...	194616	38	29⅝	33½	+ 4¼
FrptMcRes	FRP	3.03e	10	366072	31¼	18⅛	20	− 8½
FundAm	FFC	.60	12	267420	40¾	29	34¾	+ 5½
Fuqua	FQA	.32	...	215519	33⅜	24½	25	− 5⅛
Furr/Bish	CAF	1.30	31	47667	9⅛	6⅝	7½	− ⅜

-G-

Stock	Symbol	Div	Yld	Sales 100s	Hi	Lo	Last	Net Chg
GATX	GMT	2.00	11	96115	75¾	53½	68	+ 11½
GATX pf		2.50	...	97	89⅝	71	83½	+ 16½
GATX pfA		3.87	...	13030	51¾	47	51	...
GEICO	GEC	1.80	14	11556	156	122¾	152½	+ 28½
GEO Int	GX		...	85462	5½	3⅜	3⅞	− ⅛
GF Cp	GFB		...	6707	5⅜	1⅜	1¾	− ⅜
GTE	GTE	2.92	18	f14239	71⅛	42⅞	70	+ 25½
GTE pf		2.50	...	154	92½	57½	92¼	+ 33⅝
GTE pf		2.00	...	3540	54¾	33⅝	54¼	+ 19¼
GTE pf		2.48	...	13942	28½	25½	28⅜	+ 2¼
GTE Fla pf		1.25	...	z70620	15	13	14½	+ 1
GTE Fla pf		1.30	...	z98730	16¼	13¾	15½	+ 1½
GTE Fla pf		8.16	...	1432	95	83⅜	94⅜	+ 8⅞
GabelliTr	GAB	1.31e	...	289400	14¾	9⅝	14	+ 4⅛
Gallaghr AJ	AJG	.52	17	27514	26½	16⅛	24⅝	+ 7⅞
GaloobToys	GAL		6	266369	14¾	6⅜	11⅞	+ 5⅜
GaloobToys pf		1.70	...	7239	20⅜	17¾	18⅛	...
GalvstnHou	GHX		53	98725	6	1⅞	5⅞	+ 3½
Gannett	GCI	1.20	18	741920	49⅞	34½	43½	+ 7⅞
Gap Inc	GPS	.76	19	335793	61½	35¼	51⅜	+ 9⅝
GeminiII	GMI	.19	3	48743	18⅛	12⅝	15⅝	+ 2¾
GeminiII pf		1.59e	...	23716	13¾	12⅜	13⅛	+ ⅜
GenCorp	GY	.60	11	344082	19⅛	10⅞	12	− 4¾
Genentech	GNE		138	858396	23⅜	16	20¾	+ 4¾
GenAmInv	GAM	1.73e	...	33095	19⅞	13½	18⅛	+ 4¾
GenCinema	GCN	.44	17	325263	28½	23⅛	25¾	+ ¼
GenCinema pf		.47e	...	961	27¾	22¾	25⅜	...
GenData	GDC		...	68784	6⅝	4	4½	− ⅛
GenDevlpmt	GDV		6	104481	18⅞	9⅜	9¾	− 2⅞
GenDynam	GD	1.00	5	213565	60½	42½	44⅞	− 5⅞
GenElec	GE	1.88	15	f35762	64¾	43½	64½	+ 19¾
GenHomes	GHO		...	18257	2	9/32	9/32	− 7/32
GenHost	GH	.30	...	91373	10	5½	6⅛	− 3
GenHouse	GHW	.24	15	32829	15	6⅞	10⅜	+ 3½
GenInstr	GRL	.50	13	897336	41¾	25¼	39¾	+ 13⅜
GenMills	GIS	2.20	18	408776	76⅞	50⅜	72⅜	+ 20½
GenMotor	GM	3.00	6	f25227	50½	39⅛	42¼	+ ½
GenMotor pf		3.75	...	1835	46⅜	41	44¼	+ 1
GenMotor pf		5.00	...	4138	62¼	55⅜	60	+ 2⅝
GenMotor E	GME	.96	16	243607	57⅝	42½	54⅝	+ 9¾
GenMotor H	GMH	.72	13	46248	32⅛	23½	25½	+ ⅛
GenPubUtil	GPU	2.20	10	397677	47¼	36¼	47¼	+ 9¼
GenRe	GRN	1.36	13	537871	96¼	54⅜	87⅛	+ 31⅝
GenSignl	GSX	1.80	13	136448	57⅞	45¾	48¼	+ ¾
Genesco	GCO		8	210351	9¼	4¾	7½	+ 2½
GenRad	GEN		...	171308	8¾	4	5⅛	− 2¼
GenuinePart	GPC	1.20	17	331286	43½	34⅞	42	+ 6½
GeorgiaGulf	GGC	1.00	6	606620	59⅞	36	44¾	+ 6
GaPacific	GP	1.60	7	636717	62	36⅝	48½	+ 11⅝
GaPwr pf		2.50	...	7989	27½	24⅝	26⅛	+ 1¼
GaPwr pf		2.43	...	21342	27	24	25⅝	+ 1¼
GaPwr pf		2.30	...	8569	25¾	21½	24⅝	+ 2¼
GaPwr pf		2.47	...	7139	26⅜	23⅛	25⅝	+ 1⅝
GaPwr pf		2.03e	...	18369	21⅞	20½	20¾	− ⅛
GaPwr pf		1.95e	...	14175	21	19	19	− ¾
GaPwr pf		3.00	...	3864	29¼	26⅞	29	+ 2⅛
GaPwr pf		1.71e	...	17773	23⅞	21⅜	21⅜	− ½
GaPwr pf		2.56	...	6469	26⅝	24¼	25⅞	+ 1½
GaPwr pf		2.52	...	3300	26½	24	25¾	+ 1⅛
GaPwr pf		2.75	...	3764	27⅛	25⅝	26⅜	+ ⅛
GaPwr pf		7.80	...	2316	85½	73⅛	81⅞	+ 8¾
GaPwr pf		7.72	...	z67190	82	73	81½	+ 8½
GerbPdts	GEB	.96	19	193447	52¼	28¾	47½	+ 18¼
GerbSci	GRB	.20	12	154477	21	14⅛	16⅛	− 3⅛
GermanyFd	GER	.25e	...	215355	19½	6⅝	19¼	+ 11¾
GettyPete	GTY	.28	9	24219	23¼	17	19½	+ 2¾
GIANT	GPO		12	31072	20⅞	10¼	15⅞	+ 4⅝
GiantInd	GI		...	7660	15	13½	14½	...
GibraltrFnl	GFC		...	208874	1⅜	1/16	15/128	− 1 17/128
Gillette	GS	.96	19	f10486	49¾	33	49⅛	+ 15⅞
GitanoGp	GIT		15	51660	40	20	29¾	+ 8¾
GlaxoHldg	GLX	1.02e	18	813962	26⅞	18½	26	+ 6¾
Gleason	GLE		14	31763	19½	12⅛	16½	+ 4⅛
GlenFed Inc	GLN	1.20	5	253685	26¼	14¾	16	− 3⅝
GloblGvtFd	GOV	.80	...	274965	9½	7	7½	− 1⅝
GloblInPlFd	GLI	.88e	...	116220	10⅜	7¾	8½	− 1¾
GlobMar	GLM		...	568255	3¾	1⅛	3⅝	...
GlobMar wt			...	49901	1¾	½	1⅜	...
GloblUtilFd	GL		...	579	12⅛	12	12	...
GloblYldFd	PGY	1.08	...	257859	9⅞	7	7¾	− 1⅝
GoldNug	GNG		...	187715	34	16⅜	27⅜	+ 9⅝
GldVlyMicrw	GVF		20	142639	38⅞	20¼	30	+ 4¾
GoldWstFnl	GDW	.16	11	347371	33¾	15⅜	26⅞	+ 11⅛
Goldome	GDM		...	121885	4½	2	2¼	+ ⅛
Goodrich	GR	2.00	6	552658	69	38½	41½	− 10¼
Goodrich pf		7.85	...	z1340	94½	90	93½	− 1¼
Goodrich pf		3.50	...	24390	63¾	41¼	43¾	− 9¼
Goodyear	GT	1.80	10	769826	59¾	42⅛	43½	− 7⅝
Gottschks	GOT		27	30628	13⅜	8	8¾	− 3
GraceWR	GRA	1.40	11	933142	39⅛	25⅛	32¾	+ 6¾
GraceEngy	GEG		...	37059	24½	20¾	24½	...
Graco	GGG	.60	9	17045	20¾	15⅜	17⅞	− 1¼
Grainger	GWW	1.04	16	119620	66¼	52½	64½	+ 10⅝
GtAmBk	GTA	.20	...	181356	14⅞	5¾	6⅞	− 4⅜
GtAtlPac	GAP	.70	16	145579	65⅜	44¼	58⅞	+ 14¼
GtLakesChm	GLK	.40	14	144229	48	28⅛	47¼	+ 18⅛
GtNorIron	GNI	7.80e	12	8460	76¼	32½	73	+ 40½
GtNorNek	GNN	1.32	10	845203	63⅜	35⅝	61½	+ 22¼
GtWestFnl	GWF	.80	10	f13183	25⅛	14⅝	17½	+ 2½
GreenMtPwr	GMP	1.98	11	8034	27⅞	22⅛	26	+ 3¼
GreenTree	GNT	.60	10	192218	18½	5⅜	14½	+ 4⅛
Greyhound	G	1.32	12	599557	37¾	28¾	32	+ 2
Greyhound pf		4.75	...	z18680	58	51½	52	− 1
GrowGp	GRO		...	149445	14⅞	6⅝	7⅝	− 4⅛
GrowthStkTr	GSO	.43e	...	69882	10¼	8⅞	9⅞	+ ⅝
Grubb/Ellis	GBE		75	76934	6¾	3½	4½	+ ½
Grumman	GQ	1.00	7	156652	23	14¾	15⅜	− 4⅜
Grumman pf		2.80	...	9334	26⅞	25¼	25½	− ¾
GuardsmnPdt	GPI	.50	16	18552	16⅛	10	15¾	+ 3¾
Guilford	GFD	.80	9	39995	34¼	23¼	23¾	− 3

NEW YORK STOCK EXCHANGE COMPOSITE

Stock	Symbol	Div	Yld	Sales 100s	Hi	Lo	Last	Net Chg
GulfRes	GRE		...	46562	14¼	9½	9¾	−3⅛
GulfRes pf		1.30	...	1093	20¼	15¼	15¾	−3¼
GulfStUtil	GSU		...	942582	14⅜	7⅝	11⅞	+4
GulfStUtil pfB			...	z15780	47½	35½	45½	+9
GulfStUtil pfG			...	z7690	48	36¼	46	+11
GulfStUtil pfE			...	z22120	54½	39⅛	51½	+11⅝
GulfStUtil pfD			...	5299	50½	39¼	49	+9⅝
GulfStUtil prN			...	8742	35⅞	27⅜	32¾	+5
GulfStUtil prM			...	12300	38½	29¼	35¼	+5¾
GulfStUtil pfK			...	1836	98½	70½	94⅜	+24⅛
-H-								
HQHealth	HQH		...	30907	10	6⅛	9¾	+3⅜
HREProp	HRE	1.80	500	13614	26⅜	21½	22¼	+¾
HadsonCp	HAD		...	246689	4½	2⅜	2⅝	−1
Hall FB	FBH		...	80372	4⅝	2½	2¾	−⅛
Hall FB pfB			...	331	65	40½	45¼	+1¼
Hallibrtn	HAL	1.00	46	926584	44½	27½	42¾	+14¾
Hallwood	HWG		...	15307	7⅝	3½	5⅛	...
HancockFab	HKF	.48	17	51344	34¼	18	34	+15½
HancockJS	JHS	1.47	...	11789	16⅛	14⅛	15½	+1
HancockJI	JHI	1.84a	...	7992	22¼	19¼	21	+1¼
Handleman	HDL	.40	16	85729	22⅛	17¾	21	...
HandyHar	HNH	.66	23	109407	21½	15	16⅛	−1⅛
Hanna	MAH	.50	8	159563	29¾	19¼	27	+7¾
Hannaford	HRD	.36	17	38845	40¾	21¼	33	+10⅝
Hanson	HAN	.85e	12	f12951	19⅞	14	18½	+4⅜
Hanson wt			...	212640	8¼	2½	6	+3¼
HarBrJ	HBJ		...	f10016	18⅝	3¾	4¾	−4⅝
HarBrJ pf		1.62t	...	756121	12¼	3⅝	4⅝	−4⅞
HarkenEngy	HEC		122	71905	6	4¼	4⅞	−¾
Harland	JH	.68	15	221476	25	19½	22⅛	−⅛
HarleyDav	HDI		11	100962	43	24⅜	39¼	+13⅞
HarmanInt	HAR		11	58591	24	15⅞	20¼	+3⅜
Harnisch	HPH	.20	13	563692	22⅜	15	20¾	+3⅜
Harris	HRS	.96	49	272151	39½	26⅜	33⅛	+6⅛
Harsco	HSC	1.20	...	158993	31⅛	22½	25½	−2⅜
HartfdFire pf		3.90e	...	14865	50⅛	47	47¾	−1¼
Hartmarx	HMX	1.20	13	144567	28⅛	18¾	19¾	−4½
HattersSec	HAT	1.56a	10	4498	16⅞	14⅞	15¼	+¼
HawaiiElec	HE	2.16	13	49928	40¼	29⅜	40¼	+10⅝
HlthRehab	HRP	1.16	13	60998	10½	7½	9⅝	+1⅛
HlthCareProp	HCP	2.84e	21	49235	32	24⅝	31⅝	+5¾
Hlthsouth	HRC		24	196295	19⅛	9¼	17¼	+7⅞
HeclaMin	HL	.05e	...	246973	16⅛	11½	14	+1⅜
HeiligMyrs	HMY	.40	13	101621	26	15⅞	20⅝	+2¾
Heinz	HNZ	.84	20	552765	35⅞	22½	35	+11⅝
Heinz pf		1.70	...	15	306	210	306	+96
HeleneCur	HC	.20	15	25806	35⅛	19¼	24⅞	+5⅜
HelmPayne	HP	.44	37	126213	34½	20⅜	34⅜	+14
HelvetiaFd	SWZ		...	73900	15⅞	8⅞	15⅛	+5⅝
Hercules	HPC	2.24	13	300144	52¼	38⅜	39	−5½
Hershey	HSY	.78	20	418703	36⅞	24¾	35⅞	+9⅞
HewlettPk	HWP	.42	13	f14630	61½	40¼	47¼	−6
Hexcel	HXL	.44	12	88304	35⅝	18⅜	19⅛	−13⅜
Hibernia A	HIB	.92	10	111699	26	17⅜	22	+4⅝
HiShearInd	HSI	.44	59	6684	17½	14⅞	15¼	−1
HighIncoTr	YLD	1.20	...	190188	9¾	5¾	6¾	−2½
HiIncoTrII	YLT	1.20	...	225677	9¾	6¼	7	−2⅛
HiIncoAdvIII	YLH	1.20	...	63688	10	7⅞	8½	...
HighYldFd	HYI	1.14	...	51594	9⅜	7	7⅜	−1½
HighYldPlsFd	HYP	1.14	...	52084	9	7⅛	7½	−1⅛
Hillenbrnd	HB	.50	23	55820	45⅛	26⅜	43¾	+13⅛
HillDeptStr	HDS		...	36520	9⅞	5	5¼	−2⅞
Hilton	HLT	1.00	34	851422	115½	48⅜	82½	+29⅛
Himont	HMT	1.60	13	197980	51	36¾	51	+13¾
Hitachi	HIT	.54e	25	33315	133¾	100	105½	−23½
Holiday	HIA		22	709798	89	26⅜	71¾	+44¾
HomeDepot	HD	.12	28	415699	38⅜	19⅛	36⅝	+15⅝
HomeIns pf		2.95	...	62127	22¼	19¼	19⅞	−⅞
HomeOwnrSvg	HFS		...	85342	10½	½	1⅛	−7¼
HomeFed	HFD	.20	6	289400	47½	24½	31⅞	+7
Homestake	HM	.20	41	723657	20⅝	12⅜	19⅛	+6½
HomestdFnl	HFL	.19j	...	22086	5⅜	1½	1¾	−2⅝
HomestdFnlB	HFLB	.11j	...	972	5	1⅜	1⅝	−2½
HondaMotor	HMC	.08i	16	58649	34⅞	24½	25⅛	−8⅛
Honeywell	HON	2.75	...	755420	91¾	59½	86¾	+27
HongKongTelcm	HKT	.86e	...	219022	22⅛	16⅝	20	+1½
HopperSol	HS		...	20724	11⅜	5½	6	−¾
HorizonCp	HZN		...	8213	2½	1¾	2⅜	+¼
HorizonHlth	HHC		...	10343	2¼	1⅛	1¾	−⅜
HotelInvTr	HOT	1.00	...	74768	10¼	6⅛	6¾	−2½
HougtnMif	HTN	.70	21	158162	50¼	28⅛	30⅞	−3½
HouseFab	HF	.48	12	93214	25	15½	17⅜	−4⅛
HouseInt	HI	2.14b	8	253291	61¾	46⅜	51⅞	+3¾
HouseInt pf		6.25	...	7618	143	110¼	118⅜	+6⅜
HouseInt pfA			...	1015	25¼	24⅝	24¾	...
HoustnInd	HOU	2.96	13	953603	35⅞	26¾	35	+7
HoustnOilR	RTH	.08e	...	8789	1⅞	⅞	15/16	−7/16
HowellCp	HWL	.07e	...	4057	10	7¼	9½	+1⅜
HudsonFood	HFI	.12	6	58943	16⅞	9¼	10½	−⅛
Huffy	HUF	.40	11	83477	23	13	19	+5
HughsSply	HUG	.36	10	17333	21⅞	17½	18½	+⅞
Humana	HUM	1.04	16	563255	44	24⅜	44	+18⅝
HuntMfg	HUN	.31	21	27003	24¾	16½	24⅝	+5⅝
HuntgInt	HTD	.22i	22	57683	27½	13⅛	24	+10⅛
Huntway	HWY	1.38	...	31454	13⅞	10½	11⅛	−½
Hydraulic	THC	1.58	13	12945	29⅝	24⅜	24⅝	−4⅛
HyperionFd	HTR	1.26	...	35253	12⅛	10¼	10⅜	...
-I-								
IBP Inc	IBP	.60	16	236560	17¾	13½	15⅜	−¼
ICM Prop	ICM	.92e	...	24236	10½	6½	6¾	−2¾
ICN Pharm	ICN		...	130774	6⅞	5	5⅛	−1⅞
IE Ind	IEL	2.06	12	32505	28	21⅝	27⅝	+5
IMC Fertlzr	IFL	1.08	7	353708	49¾	31¼	33¾	−10⅜
INA Invest	IIS	1.68a	...	6198	18¼	15⅞	17	+⅛
IP Timber	IPT	2.88	7	36076	22⅜	19	19⅞	−¼
IRT Prop	IRT	1.16	18	25931	15⅝	12⅛	12½	−2¼
ITT Cp	ITT	1.60	10	406290	64½	49¾	58⅞	+8½
ITT Cp pfK		4.00	...	17586	104	84⅝	95½	+10½
ITT Cp pfO		5.00	...	3660	95⅞	81	87¾	+5¾
ITT Cp pfN		2.25	...	955	79⅞	64	75	+9½
IdahoPwr	IDA	1.86	13	144647	30	22	29⅜	+6⅛
IdealBasic	IDL		...	154305	3	1½	1½	−½
IdexCp	IEX		12	34954	16⅞	13⅞	16⅞	...
IllPwr	IPC	1.32j	...	969415	21¾	13⅜	18¾	−1⅛
IllPwr pf		2.04	...	1777	21½	17¾	21½	+2
IllPwr pf		2.10	...	z89560	23¼	18¾	22¾	+3
IllPwr pf		2.13	...	z65150	22¾	17¾	21½	+1½
IllPwr pf		2.21	...	z59310	24	18½	22¼	+1¼
IllPwr pf		2.35	...	z87520	24½	19½	23½	+1¼
IllPwr pf		4.12	...	2586	42½	36	42	+3¼
IllPwr pf		3.78	...	1198	39¾	32½	38	+1⅞
IllPwr pfP		8.00	...	876	93	87	93	+8
IllPwr pf		4.26	...	1612	48	44⅞	47	−¾
IllPwr pf		3.71e	...	4942	38	34⅞	35⅞	−2⅜
IllPwr pf		5.75	...	1990	54½	50¼	54½	+2⅛
IllPwr pf		3.00e	...	3772	31⅝	27⅝	30½	−½
IllPwr pf		4.47	...	1363	44½	38⅜	43½	+1½
IllPwr pf		4.00	...	1622	40¾	34¾	40	+2¾
Ill Tool	ITW	.60	15	214883	47½	33	44⅞	+10⅛
ImoInd	IMD	.44	9	122058	22¾	13⅞	15⅞	−4
ICI	ICI	4.68e	8	241845	87¼	68⅛	74¼	+1⅜
ImperialCpAm	ICA		...	105907	9⅛	⅞	15/16	−8 3/16
Inco Ltd	N	1.00	4	843935	37⅝	25⅝	26⅞	+1
IndiaGrFd	IGF	1.10e	...	55403	19¾	8⅞	19½	+10¼
IndiMich pf		7.08	...	1540	77⅝	66½	76½	+9¼
IndiMich pf		7.76	...	1911	85¼	74	83⅛	+8⅞
IndiMich pf		8.68	...	z18910	92	81½	90½	+7¼
IndiMich pf		12.00	...	z4050	108	101	105	+2
IndiMich pf		2.15	...	4913	24⅜	20¾	23⅜	+1⅝
IndiMich pf		2.25	...	2655	25⅛	21½	24⅜	+2¼
IndiMich pf		2.75	...	557	27½	25½	26½	−1
IndiEngy	IEI	1.28	11	17456	21⅞	15¾	21⅜	+5¼
IngersolRand	IR	1.20	14	349505	50¼	33⅝	50¼	+16
InlandStl	IAD	1.40	7	502621	48½	31⅜	33¾	−7¾
InspirRsc	IRC	.12	14	432511	9¼	6	6⅛	−¾
Integra	ITG		...	39008	3	¼	½	−1½
Integra pf		.04	...	9778	7/16	1/16	⅛	−¼
IntegrRes	IRE			303543	18	7/64	3/16	−13 11/16
IntegrRes pfC		2.48j	...	30503	33	⅛	13/64	−32 51/64
IntegrRes pfD		2.48j	...	28064	29½	⅛	5/32	−27 11/32
IntegrRes pf			...	30336	13⅛	3/32	3/32	−12 5/32
IntlogcTra	IT		...	73321	5¼	2	2½	−1¾
IntrRgnlFnl	IFG		...	14936	10⅝	7	8½	−1⅛
IntcapSec	ICB	2.10	...	12701	23	19⅜	21	+⅞
Interco	ISS		...	695845	3⅞	½	9/16	−3 1/16
Intlake	IK		11	104553	17½	9⅝	13½	+3
IntAlum	IAL	1.00	9	9825	30¾	25	25¾	−⅞
IBM	IBM	4.84	10	f40233	130⅞	93⅜	94⅛	−27¾

NEW YORK STOCK EXCHANGE COMPOSITE

Stock	Symbol	Div	Yld	Sales 100s	Hi	Lo	Last	Net Chg
IntFlavor	IFF	2.16	19	257252	77½	48¼	67¾	+ 18⅜
IntMinl	IGL	1.00	14	304674	55½	38	52⅛	+ 13⅞
IntMinl pf		4.00	...	370	51	39	43	+ 1
IntMinl pfB		3.25	...	17653	69¼	52	67	+ 13½
IntMultfood	IMC	1.18	13	57197	33⅜	27¼	29	+ 1¼
IntPaper	IP	1.68	7	f12740	58¾	45⅛	56½	+ 10⅛
IntRect	IRF		...	50695	6½	3⅜	5¾	+ 1⅛
IntTech	ITX		23	217953	7⅜	4⅝	6⅞	+ 1⅝
IntpubGp	IPG	.68	16	131033	37⅞	24¼	32⅝	+ 8⅛
IntstPwr	IPW	2.00	10	17725	25¾	21¼	25¼	+ 2⅞
IntstPwr pr		2.28	...	z93120	26	22½	26	+ 2¾
IntertanInc	ITN		13	58723	62¾	35⅛	55⅞	+ 20⅝
IntstJhnsn	IS		...	17246	8¼	4⅞	5¼	− ⅞
IowaIllGas	IWG	3.26	11	26295	46¼	37⅛	46⅛	+ 7⅞
IowaRes	IOR	1.70	12	59428	22	17	21⅝	+ 4⅛
Ipalco Ent	IPL	1.72	10	146756	26⅝	21¾	26⅜	+ 3⅝
IpcoCorp	IHS		...	40137	13⅝	7¼	8	− ½
Italy Fd	ITA	.15e	...	78961	17⅜	7¾	17	+ 8⅞
ItelCp	ITL		96	228600	28⅞	18	22	+ 3⅝
ItelCp pf		3.37	...	5838	65½	48	55½	+ 7
-J-								
JHM Mtg	JHM	.92e	...	23421	9¾	5¼	6½	− 3⅛
JP Ind	JPI		10	77986	18¼	12⅛	12½	− 1⅛
JWP	JWP		17	111161	31½	16⅛	30	+ 12½
Jackpot	J	.28b	11	50207	17¼	8⅞	9⅜	− 5⅝
JacobEngrg	JEC		14	18442	28⅞	22¼	27¼	+ 4¼
JamesRiver	JR	.60	10	447372	34⅜	25¾	28⅜	− ¼
JamesRiver pf		3.37	...	11485	50	42¼	44	− ¼
JamesRiver pf		3.50	...	8879	50½	43½	44¾	− 1⅝
Jamesway	JMY	.08	18	165191	12¼	6⅛	6⅜	− 2¼
JeffPilot	JP	1.36	13	165379	45½	29¾	42½	+ 12½
JerCentl pf		4.00	...	z13910	43½	38	42½	+ 2½
JerCentl pf		8.12	...	z98060	91¼	78¼	91¼	+ 9¾
JerCentl pf		8.00	...	1568	90	78¼	89⅛	+ 9⅝
JerCentl pf		7.88	...	2959	89½	77	88	+ 9½
JerCentl pf		2.18	...	9299	24½	21⅜	24¼	+ 2⅛
JohnsJohns	JNJ	1.16	19	f14587	59½	41½	59⅜	+ 16⅞
JohnsContrl	JCI	1.20	13	367251	46¾	27⅞	32¼	− 4⅜
JohnstnInd	JII	.50i	9	4656	14⅝	10⅛	10¾	− ⅛
Jorgensen	JOR	1.00	13	5845	32¼	27⅜	32¼	+ 4⅛
Jostens	JOS	.72	20	152235	30⅜	18⅛	27⅞	+ 9⅜
-K-								
KLM	KLM	.81e	8	134291	26½	19⅞	25⅜	+ 4⅜
K mart	KM	1.64	10	f16694	44⅞	32½	35	− ⅛
KN Engy	KNE	1.00	...	30089	25⅝	17⅝	25¼	+ 7⅛
KanebPipe	KPP		...	9490	22⅛	19⅛	21⅜	...
KanebSvcs	KAB		...	414460	6½	2⅛	5	+ 2⅞
KanebSvcs pf			...	1160	94½	62	82	+ 17⅞
KanCityPL	KLT	2.56	12	176629	36⅛	28⅛	34⅞	+ 3½
KanCityPL pf		3.80	...	z11900	42½	36½	41	+ 2¾
KanCityPL pf		4.35	...	z31830	48¾	42	47¼	+ 4¼
KanCityPL pf		4.50	...	z40150	52	44	50	+ 6
KanCityPL pf		2.20	...	1951	25	22⅜	25	+ 2⅛
KanCityPL pf		2.33	...	2375	26½	23¼	25⅞	+ 1⅜
KanCitySou	KSU	1.08	...	66308	54¾	31½	45¼	+ 11⅜
KanCitySou pf		1.00	...	z48980	16½	11	15½	+ 3¼
KansasGE	KGE	1.72	13	231287	24¼	19	23⅜	+ 2⅝
KansasPL	KAN	1.76	12	142614	25⅜	21⅝	24¾	+ 1⅞
KatyInd	KT		16	38586	26⅛	18¼	24⅜	+ 6
KatyInd pf		1.46	...	956	66¾	48	62½	+ 16½
KaufBrdHome	KBH	.30a	6	309696	21¾	9⅞	13⅝	+ 3½
KayJewlrs	KJI	.40	26	106981	24⅜	10⅜	13¾	+ 1½
Kellogg	K	1.72	18	395104	81⅝	57¾	67⅝	+ 3⅜
Kellwood	KWD	.80	8	72525	35⅜	20½	22¼	− 4⅜
KemperCp	KEM	.84	8	278304	51⅞	22¾	47	+ 23
KemperHigh	KHI	1.20	...	79010	12¼	8½	8⅝	− 2¾
KemperGvt	KGT	1.00	...	89229	10	8⅞	9⅞	+ ⅝
KemperMulti	KMM	1.40	...	70717	12⅛	9¼	9⅝	...
KemperMuni	KTF	.87	...	69404	12⅛	10⅞	11⅝	− ⅜
KemperStrat	KSM	.90	...	36786	12⅜	11⅛	11⅝	...
Kennmetl	KMT	1.16	10	64041	37⅝	27¼	30	− ½
KyUtil	KU	1.40	10	141494	20⅞	17⅞	20⅞	+ 2½
KerrGlass	KGM	.44	...	12509	14⅞	8⅝	10	+ 1⅜
KerrGlass pf		1.70	...	1800	22⅛	17⅛	19¾	+ 2⅞
KerrMcGee	KMG	1.32	17	447743	52	37⅜	50¾	+ 12⅞
KeyCorp	KEY	1.28	8	116249	29¾	19⅝	26⅜	+ 6½
KeystnCon	KES		...	11211	24¾	11⅛	22¼	+ 8¾
KeystnInt	KII	.56	21	118815	21¼	14½	21¼	+ 6⅛
KimbClark	KMB	2.60	14	514781	75⅜	57⅜	73½	+ 15¼
KingWorld	KWP		13	241261	40⅝	22⅞	38⅛	+ 14⅜
KleinBenAus	KBA	1.75e	...	32120	11¼	8¾	9⅜	− 1¾
KnghtRidder	KRI	1.32	13	233194	58⅜	42⅞	58⅜	+ 13
Knogo	KNO	.30	78	26866	17½	12¼	12½	− ⅜
KogerProp	KOG	2.80	170	49219	28⅛	22¼	23¾	− 1⅛
Kollmrgn	KOL	.32	88	203194	25⅞	11⅜	12¼	− 9½
KoreaFd	KF	1.96e	...	190914	43⅛	25¼	34⅜	+ 8⅛
Kroger	KR		...	731122	19¾	8⅜	14¾	+ 5⅞
Kubota	KUB	.67e	97	317	195	143	178½	+ 35½
Kuhlman	KUH	.03e	11	30360	16½	9	11⅛	+ 1⅜
Kyocera	KYO	.54r	28	11101	97½	70¼	75	− 8½
KysorIndl	KZ	.60	36	25916	21⅛	12⅜	12¾	− 8¼
-L-								
LAGear	LA		11	921266	46¾	10¾	31⅛	+ 20¼
LAC Min	LAC	.14	...	199711	12⅝	8⅞	12	+ 2
LN House	LHC	1.61e	7	5695	16¼	10⅛	10¾	− 3⅞
LLE RoyalTr	LRT	.61e	...	79291	4⅞	2⅝	2⅞	− 1½
LSI Logic	LSI		...	586505	12⅜	6¼	7⅛	− 3⅝
viLTV	LTV		...	326621	2½	1⅛	1⅛	− 1⅛
viLTV pf			...	544	16⅜	14⅛	14⅛	− ⅞
viLTV pfB			...	12814	4¾	2¼	2¼	− 1⅜
viLTV pfC			...	2870	12¼	6⅛	6⅜	− 4
viLTV pfD			...	10280	3⅛	1⅞	2	− ½
LVIGp	LVI		...	76859	3	9/16	11/16	− 2 1/16
LVIGp pf			...	11548	17⅞	4¾	5¼	− 10¼
LaQuinta	LQM		...	59072	18½	13	16½	+ 3⅛
LaQuintaPtr	LQP	2.00	...	21614	13	6½	6⅝	− 4¾
LaZ Boy	LZB	.56	118	22087	23¼	16⅞	17¾	− 1¼
LacledeGas	LG	2.36	12	10618	34	28	34	+ 3
Lafarge	LAF	.40	9	74914	20½	15½	17¼	+ ½
LamsonSes	LMS		9	169556	17½	8	9½	− 3⅜
LandBanc	LBC	.80	7	22820	18⅛	14⅛	16	+ 1⅞
LandsEnd	LE	.20e	14	166958	35¾	19	20¼	− 7¾
LawterInt	LAW	.52	16	87730	13⅞	11⅜	12⅞	+ 1⅛
LeaRonal	LRI	.48	13	14004	19⅛	14	16	− ½
Lee Ent	LEE	.72	18	25349	34¾	24¾	30⅝	+ 3⅝
LeggMason	LM	.28	10	31783	16¼	10⅜	12⅜	+ 1¼
LeggetPlat	LEG	.76	11	48792	34⅞	23⅝	30	+ 6¼
Lehman	LEM	1.63e	...	143715	14¼	11½	13	+ 1⅜
LeisrTech	LVX		...	49812	6½	2	2⅝	− 1¼
LeisrTech pf		2.25	...	7520	25¾	11	12⅝	− 4¼
Lennar	LEN	.24	7	24386	23⅞	17¾	19½	+ 1⅞
LeslieFay	LES		7	72704	16½	8⅞	10	+ ¾
LeucdaNat	LUK		11	15285	21⅞	14½	21⅜	+ 7
LibtyAS	USA	.96e	...	301759	8⅝	6⅞	8¼	+ 1
LibtyCp	LC	.80	23	13551	45	32½	43⅜	+ 7⅜
LifetimeCp	LFT		19	46682	24¾	15¾	24¾	+ 6¾
Liggett	LIG	.56	9	42496	11⅞	8⅞	10⅜	− ⅛
LillyEli	LLY	1.64	22	f10049	68½	42⅜	68½	+ 25¾
LillyEli wt			...	321080	63	24¼	62⅜	+ 37⅝
Limited Inc	LTD	.32	20	f10440	39⅞	25¼	34⅞	+ 7⅝
LincNatSec	LNV	.96a	...	27875	14¼	11½	13⅜	+ 1⅞
LincNatCp	LNC	2.60	12	111735	62⅞	42¾	60⅞	+ 17⅜
LincNatCp pf		3.00	...	79	228¾	190	228¾	+ 47¾
LincNatInco	LND	2.28a	...	3812	26½	23⅝	25⅞	+ 2⅛
Litton	LIT		11	155048	98	71½	77¼	+ 5⅜
Litton pf		2.00	...	242	25	21⅝	24½	+ 1½
Lockheed	LK	1.80	14	719416	54¾	35¾	39	− 2¼
Loctite	LOC	1.12	15	87587	51	32¾	46¾	+ 14
Loews Cp	LTR	1.00	10	372561	135	77	124¼	+ 45⅜
Logicon	LGN	.36	9	23994	24⅜	18⅝	19	− 2¼
viLomasFnl	LFC	.53j	...	404149	13¾	7/16	1	− 11⅝
LomasNetMtg	LOM	2.16	98	81820	19⅜	5	5⅞	− 12⅛
LomasNetMtg wt			...	11427	⅜	1/256	1/256	− 35/256
LomasMtgFd	LSF	1.26	...	100899	12⅛	10	10¾	− 1¼
LoneStar	LCE	1.90	9	181666	37	16¼	17½	− 10
LILCo	LIL	1.00	...	980444	20¼	12⅝	20¼	+ 7½
LILCo pfB		5.00	...	z34600	74½	46½	51	− ½
LILCo pfE		4.35	...	z88480	64	41	44	− ¼
LILCo pfI		5.75	...	203	134⅞	100	117	+ 18
LILCo pfJ		8.12	...	1493	112½	75¼	81½	+ ½
LILCo pfK		8.30	...	2941	118½	76	84	− 1
LILCo pfY		2.65	...	34313	26½	25	26⅛	...
LILCo pfT		3.31	...	38128	42¼	25⅝	26¼	− 6⅛
LILCo pfS		9.80	...	3296	142	92½	96	− 10½
LILCo pfP		2.43	...	23350	35	22½	24⅞	− ⅞
LILCo pfO		2.47	...	15048	36⅛	23⅜	25	− 1½
LongsDrg	LDG	.96	15	48915	48½	34½	44⅝	+ 9⅛

NEW YORK STOCK EXCHANGE COMPOSITE

Stock	Symbol	Div	Yld	Sales 100s	Hi	Lo	Last	Net Chg
LongvwFibr	LFB	2.40	11	95910	82¼	62	63⅞	– ⅞
Loral	LOR	.80	9	194175	37⅞	27½	29⅝	– 2⅝
LaGenlSvcs	LGS	.74	...	9873	17⅞	12¼	17⅝	+ 5
LaLandExpl	LLX	1.00	35	178011	45½	31⅛	44¼	+ 12¼
LaPacific	LPX	1.00	10	265902	43⅜	28	43¼	+ 15
LaP&L pf		3.16	...	11610	27¾	25¾	27¾	+ 1¾
LouvlG&E	LOU	2.78	11	99506	41¾	32	41¼	+ 7¼
Lowes Cos	LOW	.52	14	151626	32⅛	20¾	29½	+ 8½
Lubrizol	LZ	1.44	9	367274	45⅜	33¾	37½	+ 2
LubysCafe	LUB	.64	16	53418	28⅜	23⅛	26⅞	+ 3⅛
Lukens Inc	LUC	1.20	9	51390	38⅞	24½	38¼	+ 11¼
Lydall	LDL		13	11265	36⅝	14⅞	31⅜	+ 16⅛
Lyondell	LYO	1.60	...	667248	33½	16¾	21½	...

-M-

Stock	Symbol	Div	Yld	Sales 100s	Hi	Lo	Last	Net Chg
M/A Com	MAI	.24j	475	111247	9¼	4⅝	4¾	– 3¾
MAIBasic	MBF		...	69614	11	2¾	2⅞	– 5⅝
MBIA	MBI	.40	12	41271	32¾	20	32¼	+ 12½
MCA	MCA	.68	23	823515	71⅜	45⅜	62¼	+ 16⅞
MCN	MCN	1.57	10	102213	23⅞	16⅞	23⅜	+ 4⅞
MDC Cp	MDC		...	38848	3¾	1	1⅜	– 1⅜
MDU Res	MDU	1.42a	12	40514	23	17⅞	22⅝	+ 3⅝
MEI Divrs	MEI		...	54997	7⅛	4	4½	– 1¼
MFS Charter	MCR	1.51	...	124010	12⅛	10¼	10¼	...
MFS Intermd	MIN	1.05	...	687599	9½	8⅛	8¼	– ⅝
MFS MultInco	MMT	1.23	...	558195	10⅛	8½	8¾	– 1⅛
MFS MuniTr	MFM	.76	...	74878	10½	9½	9⅞	+ ⅛
MFS MultTot	MFT	.84a	...	64420	9¼	8	8½	+ ⅛
MFS GvMkTr	MGF	1.18	...	387546	10⅜	9⅜	9⅞	+ ⅛
MFS Inco	MFO	1.20	...	28962	10⅜	8½	8⅝	– 1¼
MFS SpcVal	MFV	.14e	...	7606	15⅛	14½	14½	...
MGI Prop	MGI	1.12	9	39811	18⅜	11¾	12⅛	– 5½
MGM/UA	MGM		...	168039	23⅛	13⅛	17½	+ 4⅜
MGMGrand	MGG		...	6194	15¾	15	15⅝	...
MHI Gp	MH		...	42718	1⅜	½	11/16	– 5/16
MNC Fnl	MNC	1.16	7	213575	29¼	20	22⅛	+ ⅛
MagneTek	MAG		9	52179	14¼	7⅞	8¼	...
MalaysaFd	MF	.11e	...	103967	20⅜	7	18¾	+ 11¼
ManhattnNat	MLC		...	7248	6⅜	4⅞	5½	– ½
ManorCare	MNR	.13	25	141118	17⅛	12⅜	16¾	+ 4¼
MfrsHan	MHC	3.28	...	699580	44¾	27¾	33⅛	+ 4¾
MfrsHan pf		4.71e	...	26177	45	37¾	40¼	+ 2¼
MfrsHan pf		4.19e	...	28325	40¾	34½	38	+ 3½
Manville	MVL		...	185359	10½	7	9⅛	+ 2
Manville pf			...	67408	12¾	9½	9⅞	+ ⅜
Manville wt			...	52315	4⅝	2⅛	3⅜	+ 1⅛
MAPCO	MDA	1.00	14	410255	42¾	27⅛	40	+ 12¾
Marcade	MAR		14	60958	2½	1½	1⅝	– ⅜
MarineMid pf		3.40e	...	7094	40½	35	35	– 4⅛
MarionMDow	MKC	.36	56	f16523	29⅝	16	27	+ 10¾
Maritrans	TUG	1.15	8	37635	10¼	8¼	9	– ⅝
MarkIV	IV		8	78279	15⅞	12⅝	14	+ 6¾
Marriott	MHS	.28	16	698156	41¼	29¾	33⅜	+ 1¾
MarshMcL	MMC	2.50	20	309129	89¾	55⅛	78	+ 21¾
Marshl Ind	MI		9	60373	19⅜	14	18⅞	+ 2¾
MartinMar	ML	1.35	9	305377	53½	37¾	44⅜	+ 3⅞
Masco	MAS	.52	14	850806	31⅛	23¾	24⅜	– 1
MassMuInv	MCI	2.80	...	17296	37⅞	24¼	25⅛	– 7⅞
MassMuPrtInv	MPV	.88a	...	37127	10	8	8¼	– 1⅝
MatsuElec	MC	.74r	25	10484	208	153¾	164	– 43½
Mattel	MAT		14	543504	20⅞	9⅜	19¾	+ 10¼
MaunaLoa	NUT	1.14e	13	18143	11⅜	9¾	10⅞	+ 1
MaxusEngy	MXS		...	644269	11⅛	6⅝	11	+ 4⅛
MaxusEngy pf		4.00	...	11870	40⅞	33¾	40	+ 5¾
MayDeptStrs	MA	1.42	14	635576	52⅝	34⅝	47⅞	+ 11⅝
Maytag	MYG	.90a	12	f12660	26¾	18⅞	19½	+ ⅛
McClatchy A	MNI	.12	18	67932	30⅞	14¾	20½	+ 5¾
McDerm pf		2.20	...	11258	31	21½	27¼	+ 5½
McDerm pf		2.60	...	14303	27½	22	24⅛	+ 2⅛
McDermInt	MDR	1.00	...	414406	26¼	14⅝	23⅛	+ 8⅜
McDermInt wt			...	65850	3½	½	¾	...
McDnInvst	MDD	.20	11	8819	8½	6⅛	6⅛	– ⅜
McDonalds	MCD	.31	18	f21225	34⅞	23	34½	+ 10½
McDonDoug	MD	2.82	19	222196	94½	59⅝	61¼	– 14
McGrawH	MHP	2.00e	14	622344	86⅛	53½	56¾	– 5½
McKesson	MCK	1.44	14	203089	39¾	29⅝	35⅝	+ 4½
McKesson pf		1.80	...	83	125	99⅛	112	+ 10½
Mead	MEA	.88	10	793622	46⅝	34¼	36¾	– 2¼
Measurx	MX	.40	12	190055	32	23	25⅛	– 4¼
Meditrust	MT	2.19	15	77345	21½	15¾	20⅛	+ 3⅛
Medtronic	MDT	.70	18	132895	71	38½	65⅝	+ 26⅞
MedusaCp	MSA		21	53131	15⅜	11⅜	14	+ 1
Mellon Bk	MEL	1.40	6	361439	38⅛	25	28⅝	+ 3⅝
Mellon Bk pf		2.80	...	11809	28¼	25⅝	26¾	+ ⅛
Mellon Bk pf		1.69	...	2705	21⅝	17¼	18⅝	+ ⅛
Melville	MES	1.30	14	497238	53⅝	36⅞	44⅝	+ 7½
MercStrs	MST	.92	10	106196	50½	37½	39⅛	– 3⅝
Merck	MRK	1.80	21	f19385	80¾	56¼	77½	+ 19¾
MercurySL	MSL	.10j	...	31590	7¾	1⅛	1½	– 5⅜
MercuryFin wi		.48	19	40548	26¾	15	23¾	...
MercuryFin	MFN	.42	20	40593	19¾	11¼	18¼	...
Meredith	MDP	.64	21	93449	39¼	29⅞	34⅞	+ 4½
MerrillLynch	MER	1.00	14	695087	36¾	23½	26¼	+ 2¼
MesaLP	MLP	1.50	...	572415	13½	6⅞	8½	– 5¼
MesaLP pf		1.50	...	378442	12⅜	8	9⅞	– 2⅝
MesaOffsh	MOS	.16e	...	321644	1⅝	7/16	½	– 1⅛
MesaRoyTr	MTR	1.90e	36	2364	48¾	37	44½	+ 6½
MesabiTr	MSB		...	52939	4⅜	2¼	3¼	+ ¾
Mestek	MCC		9	8040	9¾	6	8½	+ 2½
MetroEd pfC		3.90	...	z23370	42	37	41	+ 1½
MetroEd pfF		8.12	...	z36270	91	78	88	+ 7¾
MetroEd pfG		7.68	...	1829	86⅝	75	83½	+ 8⅜
MetroEd pfJ		8.32	...	1259	91½	80¼	90⅞	+ 9¾
MetroEd pfI		8.12	...	2480	90¾	79	89⅝	+ 10½
MetroEd pfH		8.32	...	3268	92¾	79¼	90	+ 8¼
MetroFnl	MFC	.44b	5	33742	19⅜	12¼	15¼	+ 1½
MetroFnl pf		2.00	...	6304	26⅜	22	22½	...
MexicoFd	MXF	.62e	...	277287	12¾	5¼	11⅜	+ 5⅞
MichConGas pf		2.05	...	4858	25½	24⅛	25	+ ⅜
Mickelby	MBC	.06	...	11195	8½	3⅞	4⅛	– ⅝
MidwayAir	MDW		27	353175	21¾	12⅛	12½	+ ¼
MidwayAir pfD		1.87	...	3658	23¼	19¼	20¼	...
MidwEngy	MWE	1.60	10	25308	22¼	18	22	+ 2⅞
Millipore	MIL	.40	14	263759	37⅜	25¼	26⅝	– 8⅛
MiltonRoy	MRC	.48	13	58985	21⅜	12¼	18	+ 5⅝
MinnMngMfg	MMM	2.60	14	f11923	81⅞	60⅝	79⅝	+ 17⅝
Minn P&L	MPL	1.78	9	97288	27⅝	22⅞	27¼	+ 3⅝
Mitel	MLT		...	135180	3⅝	2⅜	2½	...
MitsubBk	MBK	.23e	...	6838	23	21½	22⅝	...
Mobil Cp	MOB	2.60	14	f17479	63¼	45¼	62⅝	+ 17⅛
MonarchCap	MON		9	58504	47¾	15½	17⅛	– 26⅜
MonarchCap pf		5.00	...	308	49	37	41	– 6
MonarchM	MMO	.80	23	10267	21	13⅝	14	– 5
Monsanto	MTC	3.40	12	536493	124¼	80½	115⅜	+ 33⅝
MontPwr	MTP	2.84	14	239572	42¼	34	42¼	+ 6½
Montedisn	MNT	.24e	9	12566	18⅝	13⅝	15⅝	– ⅛
Montedisn pr		.43e	...	63	9	8	9	+ 2
MontgSt	MTS	1.80	...	13669	20⅛	17⅛	18¾	+ ⅞
MONY	MYM	.29c	11	33275	9⅛	7½	7¾	– ½
Moore Cp	MCL	.88	13	120188	33¾	24⅞	28⅞	+ 3⅝
Morgan JP	JPM	1.82	...	f14890	48⅛	34	44	+ 9⅛
Morgan JP pf		5.00e	...	2927	64	56¼	59	– 1¾
MorganGren	MGC	.25e	...	23474	10⅛	7¼	9⅝	+ 2¼
MorganKeg	MOR	.20	26	9038	12	7½	9⅛	+ 1⅜
MorganPdts	MGN		205	54177	18⅜	9¾	10¼	– 4½
MorganStan	MS	1.10	6	145635	79½	54¾	64⅝	+ 9⅜
MorrKndsn	MRN	1.48	...	96560	48½	36¾	46⅝	+ 7¼
MtgRlty	MRT	2.00	8	49261	18½	13	13⅞	– 3⅛
Morton	MII	.88	19	151941	41⅞	31½	35⅞	...
Motel 6	SIX	1.22	126	101955	18¾	11½	15⅛	+ 3
Motorola	MOT	.76	15	f13888	62½	39½	58⅝	+ 16⅜
MunHiIncFd	MHF	.78	...	49772	10¼	9	9½	– ⅛
MuniFd	MEN	.78	...	61228	12	10	10⅞	...
Munsngwear	MUN		...	44710	5⅜	2	2⅛	– 1⅛
MurphyOil	MUR	1.00	27	152009	44¼	29⅝	41⅜	+ 11¾
MutOmaha	MUO	1.26e	...	8740	14⅞	13½	13¾	+ ¼
MyersLE	MYR	.03e	8	23520	7⅜	2⅞	6¾	+ 3⅜
MylanLabs	MYL	.10	56	623464	25⅜	7½	24¼	+ 15⅜

-N-

Stock	Symbol	Div	Yld	Sales 100s	Hi	Lo	Last	Net Chg
NBB Bcp	NBB	.92	9	25865	17⅛	14¼	14⅜	– ⅜
NBD Bcp	NBD	1.28	9	195516	35⅜	24⅛	32	+ 7
NBI	NBI		...	102778	2¾	¼	5/16	– 2 1/16
NCH	NCH	.88	13	27137	60½	40½	59½	+ 18⅛
NCNB	NCB	1.20	12	765185	55	27	46¼	+ 19
NCR	NCR	1.32	11	701788	66⅝	52½	58⅞	+ 5½
NIPSCO	NI	1.04	12	541966	19⅝	13⅛	19⅜	+ 5½
NL Ind	NL	.60	8	142648	28	18½	24⅜	+ 5½
NUI	NUI	1.56	13	10482	19⅛	16⅞	18¾	+ ⅞
NACCO	NC	.58	11	26293	56	31¼	55½	+ 24

NEW YORK STOCK EXCHANGE COMPOSITE

Stock	Symbol	Div	Yld	Sales 100s	Hi	Lo	Last	Net Chg
Nalco	NLC	1.32	17	250056	49 7/8	34 1/2	49 1/2	+ 14 1/4
Nashua	NSH	.60	15	246241	42 7/8	28 3/4	35 1/4	− 1 3/8
NtlAustrlBk	NAB	2.32e	...	39112	28 5/8	22 3/8	25 3/4	− 5/8
NtlCity	NCC	1.68	9	128144	41 1/2	30 3/4	39 1/8	+ 6 1/4
NtlConvStr	NCS	.36	...	73644	9 7/8	6 7/8	7 1/4	− 5/8
NtlEducat	NEC		11	502064	27 1/2	5 3/4	6 7/8	− 16 3/8
NtlEnt	NEI		...	17562	1 3/8	1/4	5/16	− 13/16
NtlFuelG	NFG	1.34	14	96264	27 7/8	17 7/8	27 5/8	+ 8 5/8
NtlHeritg	NHR	.14j	19	76533	5 7/8	11/16	1 1/2	− 2 7/8
NtlIntgp	NII		...	280455	20 7/8	12 1/8	14 3/8	− 3
NtlIntgp pf		5.00	...	2500	49 1/2	41	44 1/2	+ 4
NtlMedEnt	NME	.72	19	733190	39	21 3/8	38 3/4	+ 17 1/4
NtlMineSvc	NMS		8	7352	6 1/8	2 5/8	5 1/2	+ 2 1/2
NtlPresto	NPK	1.40a	12	39907	40 5/8	32 1/2	37 7/8	+ 4 5/8
NtlSemi	NSM		...	f11274	10	6 3/8	7 1/4	− 2 1/2
NtlSemi pf		4.00	...	21804	44 3/4	33 3/8	33 1/2	− 11
NtlSemi wt			...	69171	1 7/8	3/16	5/16	− 1 5/16
NtlSvcInd	NSI	.92	14	118992	30 3/8	21 3/8	27 7/8	+ 6 3/8
NtlStand	NSD		...	8975	10 1/8	5 5/8	5 7/8	− 3 1/4
NtlWestmin	NW	1.00e	5	70427	35 3/8	26 1/4	33	+ 4 3/4
NatwdHlth	NHP	.90e	10	63616	15 1/2	10 1/4	13 5/8	+ 1 7/8
Navistar	NAV		17	f20950	6 3/4	3 5/8	3 7/8	− 1 1/2
Navistar wtA			...	38839	3 3/4	1 1/4	1 3/8	− 1 3/8
Navistar wtB			...	41327	1 3/8	1/16	3/32	− 23/32
Navistar wtC			...	21590	2 5/8	5/8	3/4	− 1
Navistar pfD			...	7245	20 7/8	11 1/4	11 1/2	− 5 1/4
Navistar pfG		6.00	...	9212	51 7/8	45 1/2	48 1/4	− 3 1/4
NeimanMarc	NMG	.20	50	84942	23 1/4	15	16 1/8	− 5/8
NERCO	NER	.64	12	42846	22 7/8	13 7/8	22 1/4	+ 8 3/8
NetwkEqpt	NWK		24	188413	31 7/8	16 1/2	31 1/2	+ 13 1/2
NevPwr	NVP	1.56	14	68885	25 7/8	19 1/4	25 5/8	+ 5 1/4
NewAmFd	HYB	1.35e	...	193529	10 1/8	5 1/4	6	− 4
vjNewAmShoe	NSO		...	33090	1 3/4	1/32	1/16	− 15/16
NewEngElec	NES	2.04	14	210555	28 7/8	22 1/4	28 3/4	+ 4 3/4
NewJerRes	NJR	1.40	14	35595	21 1/2	17 1/8	21	+ 3 1/4
NewPlnRlty	NPR	1.04	19	57875	18 3/4	15 1/4	18 3/4	+ 2 7/8
NYSE&G	NGE	2.04	11	281792	29	21 7/8	28 7/8	+ 6 1/8
NYSE&G pf		3.75	...	z15140	40	35	39	+ 3
NYSE&G pf		8.80	...	z21150	93	81	90	+ 8 1/2
NYSE&G pfA		2.11e	...	6388	23 3/4	20 3/4	21 1/2	− 1 7/8
NYSE&G pf		2.12	...	1922	23 3/4	20 1/2	23	+ 2 5/8
Newell	NWL	.50	17	173560	25 1/4	12 3/4	22 1/8	+ 8
NewhallLd	NHL	1.60a	24	32874	71 1/2	50 1/8	60 1/4	+ 3 5/8
NewmtGold	NGC	.05	45	167260	52	29 1/4	49 1/8	+ 14 5/8
NewmtMin	NEM	.60	33	518582	49 3/4	31 5/8	47 1/2	+ 14 3/8
NewsCorp	NWS	.13e	10	288010	27 1/8	16 5/8	22 1/4	+ 5 3/4
NewsCorp pf		3.50	...	34456	63	49 7/8	60	...
NiaMoPwr	NMK	.60j	21	f10467	14 3/4	10 3/4	14 3/8	+ 1 3/8
NiaMoPwr pf		3.40	...	z41620	36 1/2	31 1/2	34 1/4	+ 1 3/4
NiaMoPwr pf		3.60	...	z74250	37 1/4	33 1/2	36	+ 1 3/4
NiaMoPwr pf		3.90	...	z44420	40 1/2	35 1/4	40	+ 3
NiaMoPwr pf		4.10	...	z48970	44	39 1/2	41 3/4	+ 2
NiaMoPwr pf		4.85	...	z47230	51 5/8	43 3/4	49 1/2	+ 2 1/2
NiaMoPwr pf		5.25	...	z82040	55	49 1/4	52	+ 1
NiaMoPwr pf		6.10	...	z26680	62 7/8	56 1/4	61 3/4	+ 2 7/8
NiaMoPwr pf		2.30e	...	20009	25 1/8	20 3/4	21 1/4	− 3 3/8
NiaMoPwr pf			...	16810	26	23 1/2	24 3/4	− 1/4
NiaMoPwr pf		1.80e	...	7750	21	17 1/4	17 1/4	− 2 1/2
NiaMoPwr pf		10.60	...	z65300	106	100	101	− 2 1/2
NiaMoPwr pf		7.72	...	z69590	80	72 1/4	79	+ 4
NiaShare	NGS	1.50e	...	27648	15	11 7/8	14 1/4	+ 2 1/4
NichAplgte	GEF	.27e	...	58819	10 1/4	7	10 1/4	+ 3
Nicolet	NIC		...	61321	14 3/8	8 3/4	13 3/4	+ 4 7/8
NICOR	GAS	2.00	13	138877	46	29 5/8	46	+ 14 3/4
NICOR pf		1.90	...	108	42 3/8	30 1/8	42 1/8	+ 11 5/8
NobleAffil	NBL	.16	24	230765	17	10 5/8	16 3/4	+ 4 3/8
NordRes	NRD		16	85704	14 3/8	9 1/8	13 1/2	+ 4 1/8
NorflkSo	NSC	1.44	11	822672	41 1/4	30 1/4	40 1/2	+ 9 1/8
Norsk	NHY	.44e	9	335327	27 3/4	18 1/2	25 1/4	+ 7 1/4
Nortek	NTK	.10	...	64618	9 3/4	4 3/4	5 1/2	− 3 5/8
NoEuroOil	NET	1.03e	16	22401	17	11 3/8	17	+ 5 1/4
NoeastSvg	NSB		...	27795	7 7/8	2 5/8	3 1/8	− 3 1/4
NoeastSvg pf		2.25	...	13508	17 1/8	7	9 1/8	− 5 3/8
NoeastUtil	NU	1.76b	11	392557	23	18 1/2	22 1/2	+ 2 5/8
NoIndPS pf		3.13e	...	2181	37 1/2	34 1/2	34 3/4	− 2 1/2
NoStPwr	NSP	2.22	14	279047	40	30 1/4	39 3/4	+ 7
NoStPwr pf		3.60	...	z33041	44	36	42 1/4	+ 6 1/4
NoStPwr pf		4.08	...	z21300	48 1/2	42 1/4	48	+ 5 3/8
NoStPwr pf		4.10	...	z29500	49 3/4	42	49 3/8	+ 5 3/8
NoStPwr pf		4.11	...	z31590	49	43 1/8	47 7/8	+ 5
NoStPwr pf		4.16	...	z22620	51 1/2	43 1/2	48 1/4	+ 4 3/4
NoStPwr pf		4.56	...	z9800	55 1/2	48	55 1/2	+ 4 1/4
NoStPwr pf		6.80	...	z53350	82	70	78 3/4	+ 6 3/4
NoStPwr pf		7.84	...	6296	93 1/4	80 1/4	92 1/2	+ 10 1/4
NoStPwr pf		8.80	...	z66360	101 3/4	87 3/4	100 1/4	+ 10 1/4
NoStPwr pf		7.00	...	1636	83	72	82 3/8	+ 9 1/2
NoTelecm	NT	.28	33	548083	24 1/8	14 1/4	23 1/8	+ 6 1/2
NogateExp g	NGX		...	47984	7 1/4	4 7/8	6 3/8	+ 1 1/8
Northrop	NOC	1.20	...	375297	29 3/4	16	17 1/2	− 10 1/4
NowstPL pf		2.50	...	822	26	25	25 7/8	+ 7/8
NowstPL pf		2.36	...	1253	26 1/4	25	25 1/4	+ 1/4
Norton	NRT	2.00	13	163195	61 1/4	44 3/4	58 7/8	+ 10 7/8
Norwest	NOB	.82	9	294764	24 1/8	15 7/8	22 1/2	+ 6 1/2
NovaAlberta g	NVA	.52	...	f10044	11 7/8	7 1/8	7 1/2	− 2 5/8
NovaAlberta rt			...	160360	3/16	1/32	1/8	...
NovoNord	NVO	.46e	11	57278	52	38 3/4	50 1/8	+ 11 3/8
Nucor	NUE	.44	23	95937	67 1/2	44 7/8	60 1/4	+ 12 1/2
NuveenCalIn	NCM	.82a	...	15954	12 5/8	11	12 1/4	+ 7/8
NuveenCalPP	NCP		...	2937	15 1/4	14 5/8	14 7/8	...
NuveenMnAdv	NMA		...	3409	15 1/8	15	15 1/8	...
NuveenCal	NCA	.67a	...	39813	10 5/8	9 5/8	10 1/8	+ 1/4
NuveenNY	NNY	.68a	...	34368	11 3/8	9 7/8	10 3/4	+ 3/4
NuveenNYPP	NNP		...	4660	15 1/4	14 3/4	14 7/8	...
NuveenMun	NMI	.84	...	16567	12 3/8	11 1/8	12 1/8	+ 1
NuveenVal	NUV	.71a	...	354148	10 5/8	9 5/8	10 1/8	+ 3/8
NuveenPerf	NPP	1.05	...	70606	15 1/8	13 3/4	14	...
NuveenPrInc	NPI	1.08	...	106749	15 3/8	13 7/8	15	+ 1
Nynex	NYN	4.36	15	775184	92	65 1/4	91 3/8	+ 25 3/8

-O-

Stock	Symbol	Div	Yld	Sales 100s	Hi	Lo	Last	Net Chg
OHM Cp	OHM		45	74503	14 7/8	10 1/8	10 3/4	− 2 1/2
OakInd	OAK		...	361053	1 5/8	3/4	1	...
OakwdHome	OH	.08	12	11785	9	6 1/8	6 5/8	− 1/4
OcciPete	OXY	2.50	35	f17626	31	25 1/8	29 5/8	+ 4 1/4
OcciPete pf		14.00	...	z22180	141	124	140	+ 13
OceanDrill	ODR	.30e	...	208709	25 1/8	14 7/8	24 1/2	+ 9 3/8
Ogden	OG	1.25b	17	284336	34 3/4	25 1/2	31 7/8	+ 2 1/2
Ogden pf		1.87	...	14	200	161	193	+ 20
OgdenProj	OPI		...	68963	31	16 3/8	25 3/8	...
OhioEd	OEC	1.96	16	651770	24	18 5/8	23 3/4	+ 4 7/8
OhioEd pf		3.90	...	z15860	43	36 1/4	41 1/2	+ 3 1/2
OhioEd pf		4.40	...	z15890	48	41	47	+ 5
OhioEd pf		4.44	...	z42430	49 3/4	41 1/2	47	+ 4 1/2
OhioEd pf		4.56	...	z38610	50	42 1/2	48	+ 4 1/2
OhioEd pf		7.24	...	1073	78	67 3/4	75 1/2	+ 6 7/8
OhioEd pf		7.36	...	1282	80	69 7/8	77 1/2	+ 7 1/2
OhioEd pf		2.42e	...	15737	25 3/8	23 3/4	24 1/4	− 1/2
OhioEd pf		8.20	...	z95780	88 1/8	77 1/4	86	+ 8 1/4
OhioEd pf		9.12	...	1003	97 3/8	86	94 1/2	+ 9
OhioEd pf		8.64	...	z46820	91	80 1/8	90	+ 8 3/8
OhioPwr pf		8.04	...	z12640	87	75	83 3/4	+ 4 3/4
OhioPwr pfB		7.60	...	2128	86 1/8	75	84 3/8	+ 8 7/8
OhioPwr pfC		7.60	...	5608	86 1/2	74 1/4	84 1/2	+ 7 3/4
OhioPwr pfG		2.27	...	4118	25 1/2	23 3/8	24 7/8	+ 1 1/8
OhioPwr pfE		8.48	...	3197	93 5/8	82 1/2	91 3/4	+ 7 1/4
OhioPwr pfD		7.76	...	3235	88	75 5/8	86 1/4	+ 9 5/8
OklaGE	OGE	2.48	13	171372	39	32	39	+ 6 1/4
OklaGE pf		.80	...	z62560	10 3/4	8 3/4	9 5/8	+ 5/8
Olin	OLN	2.00	11	142803	68 1/4	49 3/8	60	+ 9
Omnicare	OCR	.08	19	27353	9 3/8	7 3/4	8 1/2	+ 3/8
OnLineSftwr	OSI		...	38683	9 3/4	4 1/2	9 3/4	+ 4 3/4
Oneida	OCQ	.48b	9	42037	19 1/4	13 3/4	14 5/8	− 1/8
ONEOK	OKE	1.40	12	71080	34	18 1/2	31 7/8	+ 13
OppenCap	OCC	1.60	11	34805	17 5/8	11 3/8	16 1/8	+ 4 5/8
OppenGvt	OGT	.99	...	24384	9 7/8	8 3/8	8 5/8	− 1 1/8
OppenMlti	OMS	1.11	...	109881	11	9 1/2	9 7/8	− 7/8
OrangeCo	OJ		42	16867	10 7/8	7 1/4	7 1/2	− 3
OrangeRkl	ORU	2.30	11	28070	32	27 1/4	31 7/8	+ 2 5/8
OregSteel	OS	.80	9	59867	28 1/4	17 3/4	24 1/4	+ 6
OrientExpr	OEH		2	26687	6 1/2	2	5 1/8	+ 3
OrionCap	OC	.84	6	41359	28 1/2	15 3/8	22 5/8	+ 7 1/4
OrionCap pf		2.12	...	6268	25	17 1/2	22	+ 4 3/4
OrionCap pf		4.50e	...	2484	40	35 3/8	36 1/2	...
OrionCap pf		1.90	...	20226	30 3/8	19 1/4	25 1/8	+ 5 7/8
OrionPic	OPC		25	95582	27	14	20 1/2	+ 6 3/8
OryxEngy	ORX	1.20	...	393886	46 1/4	25 1/2	44 3/8	+ 18 1/2
OutbrdMar	OM	.80	7	405739	46	25	26	− 5
OverShip	OSG	.50	16	81310	25 3/4	18	22 1/2	+ 3 3/8
OwenMinor	OMI	.26	24	53353	15 7/8	11 1/4	12 3/4	− 1 5/8
OwenCorn	OCF		6	312148	36 7/8	22 1/4	25 1/8	+ 2 7/8
OxfordInd	OXM	.50	12	18972	13 3/8	10 1/2	12 5/8	+ 2 1/8

NEW YORK STOCK EXCHANGE COMPOSITE

-P-Q-

Stock	Symbol	Div	Yld	Sales 100s	Hi	Lo	Last	Net Chg
PHH Cp	PHH	1.16	11	66956	38⅞	31⅝	33⅜	– 1½
PHM	PHM	.12	4	128407	18⅞	9½	11⅛	...
PNC Fnl	PNC	2.12	8	408084	49	38½	41⅝	+ 1⅞
PNC Fnl pfC		1.60	...	243	39½	32½	33½	+ ½
PNC Fnl pfD		1.80	...	1661	39½	32½	33½	...
PNC Fnl pfE		2.60	...	193	29	25½	27	– 1½
PPGInd	PPG	1.52	9	431255	46	37	39¾	– ⅝
PS Gp	PSG	.60	37	14483	37¼	31⅞	34½	+ 2⅝
PSI Hldng	PIN	.60e	10	453621	18	13⅛	18	+ 4⅛
PacAmShrs	PAI	1.48	...	8095	16¼	14⅛	15⅜	+ ⅜
PacEnt	PET	3.48	16	196760	53¾	37⅛	50½	+ 13
PacGE	PCG	1.40	11	f12660	22	17¼	22	+ 4½
PacScientif	PSX		...	31479	18½	9¾	15⅛	+ 5⅜
PacTelesis	PAC	1.88	18	f16500	51⅛	30⅜	50⅜	+ 19½
PacifiCp	PPW	2.76	10	450034	46¼	33⅛	45¾	+ 10¾
PaineWebber	PWJ	.52	20	205716	23⅝	15⅝	16⅞	+ ¾
PaineWebber pf		1.37	...	7299	18⅛	14	15⅛	+ ⅞
PanAm	PN		...	f20429	5⅛	2¼	2⅝	+ ⅜
PanAm wt			...	56558	1¼	11/32	13/32	+ 1/16
PanhdlEast	PEL	2.00	272	f11674	30¾	20½	29⅞	+ 4¼
PansophSys	PNS	.20	18	123507	18½	12⅛	18½	+ 4½
ParPharma	PRX	.04j	17	119000	11⅞	3⅞	6	– 3⅛
ParTech	PTC		24	6475	8⅞	4½	5⅛	– 1¾
ParCom	PCI	.70	16	f18172	66⅜	39½	50½	+ 9⅞
ParkElchm	PKE	.32	12	13174	17⅝	12¼	12⅞	– 4½
ParkerDrl	PKD		...	291139	10⅛	4⅛	10	+ 5½
ParkerHan	PH	.84	12	338521	32⅛	24	25¼	– 2⅞
PatheComm	PCC		...	34235	5½	2⅝	3¼	– 1
PatrickPete	PPC		61	100650	7 11/16	3¾	6⅛	+ 2⅛
PatrDivFd	PDF	1.20a	...	101843	11	9	10⅞	+ 1½
PatrDivFdII	PDT		...	1905	12⅛	12	12⅛	...
Patten	PAT	.12j	8	87391	4¼	2⅜	2½	– 1¼
PennCentral	PC	.48	12	298157	28⅜	22⅞	27½	+ 3¼
Penney JC	JCP	2.24	11	642734	73¼	50⅜	72¾	+ 22⅛
PennP&L	PPL	2.86	12	235038	42⅞	34¼	42⅞	+ 6¾
PennP&L pf		4.40	...	z15410	51½	44	50½	+ 5
PennP&L pf		4.50	...	z43210	51½	45	50	+ 3½
PennP&L pf		8.60	...	z78670	94½	84¾	92¾	+ 6¼
PennP&L pr		8.40	...	z54630	93	81	91¼	+ 5¾
PennP&L pf		9.24	...	z80420	104	100	100⅝	– 1⅛
PennP&L pr		8.00	...	z42700	90½	80	88½	+ 8
PennP&L pr		8.70	...	z32440	95¼	85⅛	94	+ 8½
Pennzoil	PZL	3.00	14	219227	88⅞	71⅝	88⅝	+ 16⅞
PeopEngy	PGL	1.60	11	95576	26¾	18⅞	25¾	+ 6½
PepBoys	PBY	.11	18	327151	17¼	10½	11⅞	– ¼
PepsiCo	PEP	1.00	19	f15618	65⅞	37¾	64	+ 24½
PerkFamR	PFR	1.20e	14	27793	16	9⅝	16	+ 6⅛
PerkElmer	PKN	.68	...	440931	28¾	20¾	22⅝	– 2
PermRltyTr	PBT	.46e	16	61170	6½	5	6⅜	– ⅛
PermPtnrs pr		1.15	...	82726	7	2⅞	3⅜	– 1⅜
PerryDrug	PDS		12	143789	13½	6¾	8⅝	+ 1⅞
PetrieStrs	PST	.20	32	195573	26¾	16⅜	21⅜	+ 4⅞
PeteRes	PEO	2.40e	...	21128	27¾	21⅛	27	+ 6
PeteRes pf		1.57	...	4043	17	15⅜	16⅝	+ ⅞
PeteInv	PIL	.09j	...	26495	1¼	9/16	11/16	– ¼
Pfizer	PFE	2.20	16	f10854	75¾	54	69½	+ 11½
PhelpsD	PD	3.00a	4	780902	75⅜	45⅜	59⅛	+ 12¼
PhilaElec	PE	2.20	10	f10222	24½	19⅛	23⅛	+ 3⅛
PhilaElec pfA		3.80	...	z38520	40½	33⅝	39	+ 5
PhilaElec pfB		4.30	...	z48510	46	37½	44⅜	+ 6⅞
PhilaElec pfC		4.40	...	z20590	48	39	45½	+ 4½
PhilaElec pfD		4.68	...	z35200	50	41	50	+ 8
PhilaElec pfE		7.00	...	z73120	75	66¼	74	+ 9
PhilaElec pfG		8.75	...	2031	89⅛	76	86	+ 9
PhilaElec pfS		9.50	...	5171	100½	85¾	100½	+ 14¾
PhilaElec pfT		9.87	...	7092	103⅜	94	103⅜	+ 9⅜
PhilaElec pfR		1.41	...	7413	13⅜	11¾	12⅞	+ ⅞
PhilaElec pfQ		14.62	...	1507	114½	109½	112½	– 2
PhilaElec pfP		1.33	...	11665	12½	10⅞	12⅛	+ 1
PhilaElec pfH		7.85	...	1659	82	68¼	78¼	+ 8¾
PhilaElec pfO		1.28	...	13501	12⅛	10⅝	11¾	+ ¾
PhilaElec pfM		15.25	...	1333	118½	106⅞	115⅛	+ 6⅞
PhilaElec pfL		9.52	...	z41390	99¾	90½	97	+ 7½
PhilaElec pfK		9.50	...	1454	97	82	93	+ 11
PhilaElec pfJ		7.80	...	1086	82⅛	67¼	78	+ 10¾
PhilaElec pfI		7.75	...	z26300	80½	67	80	+ 13½
PhilaSub	PSC	.94	12	17461	14½	12¾	13⅞	+ ¾
PhilipMor	MO	1.37	16	f28034	45½	25	41⅝	+ 16¼
PhilipsInd	PHL	.60	15	216193	25¼	18⅛	23⅜	+ 4⅛
PhilipsNV	PHG	.86e	10	387846	25¼	16⅜	25	+ 7⅞
PhillipsPete	P	1.00	10	f21391	30⅛	19⅛	25¼	+ 5¾
PhillipsVanH	PVH	.28	9	60754	25	13⅝	16⅛	+ 2
PHLCorp	PHX		7	27044	17½	10¾	15⅞	+ 4¼
PiedmontNG	PNY	1.60	12	31842	29⅝	23	28⅛	+ 3¾
Pier 1	PIR	.16	15	294388	14¼	9½	10⅜	– 1¼
PilgrimBkShrs	PBS	1.08e	...	54720	10¾	7½	9⅛	+ 1⅜
PilgrimsPr	CHX	.06	8	60649	11¼	5¾	6⅞	+ ⅞
PinWstCap	PNW	1.20j	...	f11873	16⅜	5	11⅛	– 4⅝
PioneerElec	PIO	.24e	...	3908	86⅝	46½	86	+ 28
PitneyBws	PBI	1.04	15	451021	54¾	40⅞	47½	+ 4¾
PitneyBws pr		2.12	...	154	216	166	206	+ 36
Pittston	PCO	.20	28	287919	22¼	16⅞	21⅜	+ 3⅞
PlacrDome g	PDG	.30	...	963491	19¾	12⅛	18¼	+ 5⅛
PlainsPete	PLP	.10e	27	43930	40½	26⅛	33¾	+ 6½
Playboy	PLA		...	5011	18⅜	12⅛	15⅛	+ 3
PlumCreek	PCL	2.40	...	143145	24½	20¼	24¼	...
PogoProdcg	PPP		103	97938	10¼	4	10¼	+ 6⅛
Polaroid	PRD	.60	38	996827	50⅜	35⅛	45¾	+ 8⅞
Polygram	PLG		...	90794	18⅛	16¼	17¾	...
PopeTalbot	POP	.60	7	65815	29¾	17⅞	25⅞	+ 7⅞
Portec	POR		88	12000	8⅞	4⅞	5¼	– ⅞
PortlndGen	PGN	1.96	12	325959	25½	20⅞	21⅜	+ ⅜
PortlndGen pf		2.60	...	1962	29⅛	25¾	27⅞	+ 1⅝
PortugalFd	PGF	.08e	...	40617	17½	15⅛	17	...
PotashCp	POT		...	17000	15¼	12⅜	13½	...
Potlatch	PCH	1.20	8	95009	38⅝	30¾	36¾	+ 5¾
PotmElec	POM	1.46	11	451818	24¼	19¼	23⅞	+ 3⅝
PotmElec pf		2.44	...	37	133⅝	113⅛	129	+ 1
PotmElec pf		3.37	...	3672	44¼	38¼	42¾	+ 3½
PrecisnCast	PCP	.08	18	233226	38¾	26½	31	+ 3¼
PremarkInt	PMI	.84	12	199451	42	29⅜	30¾	– ¾
PremierInd	PRE	.60	20	40096	38¼	25⅜	37¾	+ 9¾
PremierInd wi			...	nt	25½	16⅞	18⅝	...
Primark	PMK		...	89808	10¼	6½	9½	+ 2⅞
PrimeCptr	PRM		...	973269	21	6	6⅜	– 11⅛
PrimeMotr	PDQ	.08	10	428225	37½	21⅝	23¾	– 8¼
PrimeMotrLP	PMP	2.08	10	22960	18⅜	9	10	– 6
Primerica	PA	.32	8	913885	30	20¼	28½	+ 6¾
ProctGamb	PG	1.80	18	991504	70⅜	42⅛	70¼	+ 26¾
ProgrsvCp	PGR	.44	10	129400	43⅜	22½	38½	+ 15½
ProlerInt	PS	.56	8	19656	29⅞	18⅞	23¼	+ 4⅜
PropTrAm	PTR	.84	21	20656	10¾	9	9¼	– ½
ProspctSt	PHY	1.08	...	79619	10⅛	5⅛	5⅞	– 4⅛
PruInterm	PIF	.96	...	199936	9½	7⅞	8⅛	– ¾
PruRlty	PRT		2	18900	1⅜	3/16	¾	– ½
PruRltyInco pf		.68	...	18200	6¾	5⅜	5½	– ¾
PruStratg	PSF	1.05a	...	293182	9	7⅛	7½	– 1⅛
PubSvcCol	PSR	2.00	10	373833	27	20	26¼	+ 4¾
PubSvcCol pf		7.15	...	z10570	78¾	68¾	78¾	+ 9¾
PubSvcCol pf		2.10	...	2360	24	20½	23⅜	+ 2⅛
PubSvcInd pf		1.04	...	z39450	13¾	10½	11¾	+ ¾
PubSvcInd pf		1.08	...	z43130	13⅞	10⅜	11½	+ ⅛
PubSvcInd pf		7.15	...	z65540	80½	68	78¼	+ 11
PubSvcInd pf		8.52	...	2420	93¾	81½	91	+ 7½
PubSvcInd pf		8.38	...	3004	93½	81	88	+ 5¾
PubSvcInd pf		8.96	...	1370	98⅛	87½	96	+ 8
vjPubSvcNH	PNH		69	328609	6⅜	2¾	2¾	– 2
vjPubSvcNH pf			...	2329	21⅛	7	20	+ 8
vjPubSvcNH pfB			...	8402	20⅞	7½	20⅛	+ 9⅜
vjPubSvcNH pfC			...	5847	22	9⅜	21⅜	+ 6⅝
vjPubSvcNH pfD			...	7304	21	8¼	20⅜	+ 7⅛
vjPubSvcNH pfE			...	12179	21⅜	8¼	20¼	+ 6¾
vjPubSvcNH pfF			...	9038	21¼	8⅛	20⅜	+ 8⅞
vjPubSvcNH pfG			...	13915	21	8¼	20¼	+ 8¼
PubSvcNM	PNM	.38j	...	416606	15⅞	10¾	14⅝	+ 2⅛
PubSvcEnt	PEG	2.08	11	720681	29⅜	23	29¼	+ 4¾
PubSvcEG pf		4.08	...	z90470	48¼	40¼	46½	+ 5¾
PubSvcEG pf		4.18	...	z69210	49½	41¼	48	+ 5⅜
PubSvcEG pf		4.30	...	z37670	50¾	42	49¾	+ 5½
PubSvcEG pf		5.05	...	1017	59¼	50¼	57⅝	+ 6⅛
PubSvcEG pf		5.28	...	1210	62	52	60	+ 7½
PubSvcEG pf		8.16	...	z19120	94	80⅜	90¼	+ 9⅝
PubSvcEG pf		6.80	...	1288	77¾	66½	77	+ 9½
PubSvcEG pf		7.70	...	5947	89	75⅝	87½	+ 10⅞
PubSvcEG pf		7.80	...	3434	90¼	76¾	87⅞	+ 9⅞
PubSvcEG pf		8.08	...	z14830	88	78	85	+ 6½
PubSvcEG pf		7.52	...	3817	86⅞	73¾	84⅝	+ 9⅝
PubSvcEG pf		7.40	...	3888	85½	72¼	83⅞	+ 9⅞

NEW YORK STOCK EXCHANGE COMPOSITE

Stock	Symbol	Div	Yld	Sales 100s	Hi	Lo	Last	Net Chg
Publicker	PUL		...	50052	3⅝	1⅞	2⅜	– ⅞
PR Cement	PRN	.80a	7	10607	59½	41⅛	49¾	– ½
PugetP&L	PSD	1.76	10	222223	22½	18	22⅛	+ 3⅝
PutnmDivrPrem	PDN	.10e	...	13516	12⅛	9¾	10⅜	...
PutnmDivInco	PDI	.46a	...	10376	12⅝	12⅛	12¼	...
PutnmHiInco	PCF	.85	...	46411	8⅛	6½	6⅝	– 1⅛
PutnmHiMun	PYM	.78	...	55842	10⅜	9⅛	9¼	...
PutnmIntmGv	PGT	1.01	...	272628	9½	8⅝	9	+ ¼
PutnmInvMun	PGM	.07e	...	16766	12⅛	10½	10⅝	...
PutnmMgdMun	PMM	.75a	...	127401	10¼	9⅜	9½	...
PutnmMstIntm	PIM	1.03a	...	186997	9⅜	7⅜	7⅝	– 1⅛
PutnmMstInco	PMT	1.10a	...	221741	9⅝	7⅞	8	– 1
PutnmPrem	PPT	1.14	...	632922	9¾	7⅝	8	– 1
QMS	AQM		7	97420	12	7¼	11¼	+ 3⅞
Qantel	BQC		...	66928	1	5/32	3/16	– ⅜
QuakerOats	OAT	1.40	21	529753	68⅞	49⅝	57¾	+ 4⅝
QuakerState	KSF	.80	26	293327	19⅜	13⅝	14⅜	– 2½
Quanex	NX	.40	7	113558	19	13⅛	15	+ 1⅝
Quanex pf		2.28	...	9631	31¾	25	26	– ⅝
QuantumChm	CUE	3.00a	2	425215	59½	28½	29¾	– 25⅞
QuestValuInc		1.20a	...	77906	13½	10⅜	13	+ 2½
QuestValuCap	KFV		...	92180	14¼	8½	14⅛	+ 5½
Questar	STR	1.92	16	39882	39⅝	31½	38⅜	+ 6⅛
QuikReily	BQR	.28a	12	41882	18¼	10⅞	13⅝	+ 2¾

-R-

Stock	Symbol	Div	Yld	Sales 100s	Hi	Lo	Last	Net Chg
RAC IncoFd	RMF	1.20a	...	38406	12	9⅞	10⅜	– 1⅝
RAC MtgInv	RMR	.53e	...	95893	8⅜	1⅞	3⅛	– 5
RLC Cp	RLC	.20b	10	62948	10½	7⅜	8¾	...
RLI Cp	RLI	.40	8	14909	9½	6⅞	8½	+ ⅞
ROC TaiwanFd	ROC	.38e	...	78642	19¼	11¼	13⅛	...
RPC Engy	RES		18	18551	8¼	5¼	6½	+ ¼
RPS RltyTr	RPS	.81e	6	56349	6⅝	5⅜	5⅝	– ⅞
RacalTelcom	RTG	1.21e	60	462087	85¾	33⅝	63½	+ 29¾
Radice	RI		...	16980	5⅝	2½	2¾	...
RalstonPur	RAL	1.65	13	276323	101½	78¾	83	+ 1⅛
RangerOil	RGO		28	212925	6⅝	5	5⅞	+ ⅞
Raychem	RYC	.32	31	324971	39¼	29¼	31¾	– 3¼
RayJamFnl	RJF	.24	7	11086	19⅛	10½	15⅜	+ 4⅜
Rayonier	LOG	2.80	5	25700	21	18	20⅛	+ 2
vjRaytech	RAY			11603	3¾	½	1⅝	– 1¼
Raytheon	RTN	2.20	9	377915	85	64⅝	69½	+ 2½
ReadBates	RB		...	53275	5	15/16	2⅞	...
REIT Cal	RCT	1.38	10	15900	17	15	15⅛	– ¾
RltyRef	RRF	1.72	8	1220	16⅛	13½	14½	+ ¼
RecogEqpt	REC		...	119520	12⅜	5½	7¼	– 4¾
Reebok	RBK	.30	15	f11663	19⅝	11⅛	19	+ 6¾
ReeceCp	RCE	.15e	53	2885	16	10⅜	10½	– 1⅜
RegalInt	RGL		...	34599	½	7/64	3/16	– 1/32
RegionFnl	BNC	.29e	...	64981	9¾	6	8¾	+ 2¾
ReichTang	RTP	1.76a	9	8947	15⅝	12½	14⅛	+ 1
RelianceGp	REL	.32	...	87963	8⅝	4¼	5⅛	+ ½
Repsol	REP	.35e	...	481886	24⅞	16¼	23	...
RepGypsum	RGC	.20	24	15736	5¾	4⅜	5	+ ¼
RepNY	RNB	1.28	...	77308	51⅝	42⅝	51⅜	+ 8½
RepNY pfB		3.76e	...	2379	44½	40⅝	41½	– 2¼
RexeneCp	RXN	7.80j	2	224151	15⅛	3⅜	3½	– 11⅜
Reyn&Reyn	REY	.80	10	89313	33⅞	23¼	24⅛	+ ¼
ReynMetl	RLM	1.80	6	785674	62¾	49	53⅝	– ⅛
RhonPoulnc pfC			...	9606	48½	35	39¾	– 2⅞
RhonPoulnc pfA			...	2139	19	17⅝	18⅜	...
RhonPoulnc wt			...	4415	3	1⅞	2⅝	...
RhonPoulnc	RPU		...	25635	21	18⅝	20¾	...
RiteAid	RAD	.82	13	268546	41⅛	29½	33⅜	+ ¾
RiverOaks	ROI		...	22589	7/16	⅛	3/16	– 5/32
RobrtsonHH	RHH		...	33837	12¾	8⅞	11	+ 2⅛
RochG&E	RGS	1.56	12	130512	22⅛	17	21½	+ 4¼
RochTele	RTC	1.46	18	81422	45¾	25⅝	40½	+ 14⅞
RockeCtr	RCP	1.88	19	104766	22⅛	18½	20⅝	+ 1
Rockwell	ROK	.78	8	779536	27⅛	19¾	23¾	+ 2
Rockwell pf		4.75	...	52	495	413	460	+ 30
Rockwell pf		1.35	...	39	181	150	153	– 3
RodmanRen	RR		...	9886	8	4⅞	5⅝	– 1⅝
RohmHaas	ROH	1.20	12	218865	37½	31	34¾	+ ⅜
RohrInd	RHR		25	277642	37⅞	18⅞	20⅜	– 7½
RollinsEnv	REN	.08	...	544119	14⅛	9⅝	14	+ 3⅛
Rollins	ROL	.54	19	41866	21	16⅞	18⅜	+ ⅝
RorerGp	ROR	.84	22	543566	48	36⅛	46⅞	+ 4¼
RowanCos	RDC		...	639113	11⅞	5⅝	11¼	+ 5½
RBSct pr			...	16586	25⅝	23¼	24⅞	...
RoylDutchP	RD	3.36e	7	f12574	77⅝	56⅞	77½	+ 20½
RoyalOptical	RIO	.20a	11	69702	16	8½	9⅛	– ⅝
RoyceValTr	RVT	.51e	...	49541	10	8	9½	+ 1⅜
Rubbermaid	RBD	.52	25	252440	37¾	25	36¾	+ 11⅝
RussBerr	RUS	.40	18	42282	21¼	14⅛	15	– 4⅜
RussTogs	RTS	.20	210	40924	15	10⅜	10½	– 2½
Russell	RML	.28	18	95467	26½	15⅝	26⅛	+ 10
RyderSys	R	.60	22	946853	31⅛	19¾	20⅜	– 5⅝
Rykoff	RYK	.60	15	70881	29½	19⅞	23¼	+ 5¼
RylandGp	RYL	.60	7	99293	25¾	18¼	18⅞	– 1¾
Rymer	RYR		...	14379	14¾	8⅞	11¾	+ 3
Rymer pf		1.17	...	5719	10⅝	8¼	10	+ 1⅜

-S-

Stock	Symbol	Div	Yld	Sales 100s	Hi	Lo	Last	Net Chg
SCEcorp	SCE	2.56	11	801171	41	31	39⅜	+ 7
SCOR US	SUR	.20e	14	38161	14½	7½	14⅛	+ 5
SL Ind	SL	.17b	13	8833	9½	7¾	8⅛	– ¼
SPS Tech	ST	1.28	11	18854	60⅛	41	41½	– 1½
SPX Cp	SPW	1.00	6	203220	36⅝	26⅞	28¾	– ⅝
SSMC	SSM		98	90731	36⅝	21⅞	33¼	+ 11¼
Saatchi	SAA	.48e	...	317122	22½	11¼	12¾	– 5⅛
SabineRTr	SBR	1.38e	10	13940	14⅝	12¼	13⅛	– ⅜
SafecardSvc	SSI	.10	7	46246	7	4¼	5¾	– ¼
SafegrdSci	SFE		11	22900	19	12¾	13⅝	– 2⅞
SafetyKln	SK	.36	23	250473	38¾	23¾	30½	+ 6¼
SaharaCas	SAH	1.12	20	22156	9¼	8⅛	8⅝	+ ⅛
StJoeL&P	SAJ	1.52	10	7922	24⅝	20	23⅞	+ 3⅝
Salant	SLT		13	20231	28⅞	11⅝	11¾	– 7⅝
SallieM	SLM	.52	20	455428	53½	33¼	48	+ 14¼
SallieM pf		2.50e	...	3227	38½	31½	32⅛	– 4⅞
Salomon	SB	.64	9	979870	29⅜	20½	23⅜	– ¾
SanDieGE	SDO	2.70	15	216944	45⅝	36⅜	45⅛	+ 6⅞
SanJuanBsn	SJT	.17e	49	89193	9⅞	7¼	8¼	+ ⅜
SaAnitRlty	SAR	2.08	19	38011	35	27¾	29¼	– 3¼
SaFeEPtrs	SFP	2.88	...	38380	14⅝	6⅜	6⅝	– 5¼
SaFePacPipe	SFL	2.40	...	86861	27¾	20½	27	+ 6¼
SantaFePac	SFX	.10e	17	907190	25¾	16¾	18½	+ 1¼
SaraLee	SLE	.84	19	468355	33¾	21⅜	33½	+ 12½
SaraLee pf		3.97e	...	3393	52½	49	50	+ 1
SavnhEP pfA		2.37	...	14583	27¼	23⅝	25¾	...
Savin	SVB		...	f12031	9/16	⅛	9/32	– 5/32
Savin pfA			...	823	14¾	10¾	13¾	+ 1¾
Savin pfB		.80t	...	14076	9⅜	5⅜	5⅞	– 2½
Savin pfD		.10t	...	1903	9⅛	5⅞	6⅛	– 2⅛
SCANA	SCG	2.46	12	132414	35¾	29⅝	35¾	+ 3½
SchaferTr	SAT	.55e	...	59446	11⅜	7⅝	10⅜	+ 2⅜
ScheringPl	SGP	1.80	21	628471	86	55⅜	85½	+ 28¾
Schlumbgr	SLB	1.20	29	f11504	50½	32	49⅛	+ 16½
SchwabC	SCH	.12	29	108233	17	6¾	13⅞	+ 7⅛
Schwitzer	SCZ		...	57148	17	5	6⅞	...
SciAtlanta	SFA	.16	15	310681	25⅛	12⅝	23¾	+ 10⅝
Scotsman	SCT	.24	...	51354	15	8⅞	10¼	...
ScottPaper	SPP	.80	9	447455	52½	38⅜	48⅛	+ 8⅞
ScudAsiaFd	SAF	1.38e	...	51680	16⅞	8⅞	15⅞	+ 7
SeaCont	SCR	.45e	13	515017	74¼	29⅞	68	+ 37⅞
SeaCont pf		1.46	...	2435	14½	12¾	13½	+ ¼
SeaCont pfB		2.10	...	3534	17	14½	15⅞	– 1
SeaCont pfC		2.10	...	4468	17	15	15⅞	– 1⅛
SeaCont pfD		4.12	...	25498	119⅜	52	108½	+ 55½
Seagram	VO	1.40	13	305208	91½	60¼	91½	+ 30⅛
SeagullEngy	SGO		17	55137	23	14¾	22¾	+ 7⅜
SealedAir	SEE		14	115958	23⅝	10¾	20⅜	...
Sears	S	2.00	12	f18492	48⅛	36½	38⅛	– 2¾
SecPacific	SPC	2.28	7	f11916	54⅞	35½	40⅝	+ 4½
SequaA	SQAA	.60	12	25439	77½	56⅝	72⅛	+ 15⅜
SequaB	SQAB	.50	12	5647	80½	61	75	+ 14
Sequa pf		5.00	...	3650	106	86	101	+ 14½
ServiceCp	SRV	.56	...	486956	22	12¾	15⅝	– 1⅞
SvcMdse	SME	.06a	6	917047	15⅛	7⅝	9⅜	+ 1⅜
SvcRes	SRC		136	20927	9¾	1⅞	9½	+ 3¾
SvcMastr	SVM	1.78e	10	118513	24¼	20⅞	21½	– 1⅛
ShawInd	SHX		18	130799	32⅛	11⅛	31	+ 19¼
ShawmutNtl	SNC	1.44	6	555312	29¾	17½	20¼	– 3¼
ShearsonLeh	SLH	.75	15	222132	24	12½	12¾	– 5⅜
ShelbyWill	SY	.24	16	22250	12¼	8¾	9⅞	+ ¼
ShellTrans	– SC	2.25e	12	245671	48½	35¾	48½	+ 12¾
SherwinWill	SHW	.70	14	246056	35¾	25	34⅜	+ 9
Shoneys	SHN		27	201870	13¼	7¾	11⅞	+ 3¾
Showboat	SBO	.10	12	84292	15⅝	8½	9¼	+ ½
SierraPac	SRP	1.84	12	60934	25⅞	22⅜	25⅛	+ 1⅝
SignlAprl	SIA		...	12838	8¼	4	4¼	– ½
SignlAprl pf		1.60	...	304	32½	19	19	– 4½

NEW YORK STOCK EXCHANGE COMPOSITE

Stock	Symbol	Div	Yld	Sales 100s	Hi	Lo	Last	Net Chg
SignetBk	SBK	1.56	7	187819	43¼	28¾	32⅛	+ 2⅜
SizelerProp	SIZ	1.56	14	11430	16¾	12⅞	13¾	– 1
Skyline	SKY	.48	14	94484	20¼	13⅞	14¾	– ¾
SmithCorona	SCO	.60	7	233654	23⅜	13	14	...
SmithInt	SII		...	157907	14⅛	8½	12½	+ 4
SmithklBeech	SBH	.17e	...	114060	49	40⅛	48⅞	...
SmithklBeech eq	SBE	.17e	...	913949	44¾	35½	43⅛	...
SmithFood	SFD	.20	21	99095	25	20½	24	...
Smucker	SJM	1.04	18	14693	78	57¾	72⅞	+ 13⅛
SnapOnTools	SNA	1.08	12	305329	41⅞	28⅞	32½	– 2½
SnyderOil	SOI	.60	...	66698	4½	3⅛	3⅝	– ¼
SnyderOil pf		2.09	...	9169	12⅜	8¼	8¾	– 2¼
Solitron	SOD		...	22933	3¾	1	1½	– 2¼
Sonat	SNT	2.00	20	244872	50⅜	28⅝	48¾	+ 19¾
Sony Cp	SNE	.27e	29	95738	65¾	49¾	60½	+ 2⅝
SooLine	SOO		76	51986	25½	16¾	21¼	+ ½
SourceCap	SOR	3.60	...	9217	43⅞	36⅜	42½	+ 5½
SourceCap pf		2.40	...	1880	26½	23½	26	+ 1¾
SoCarEG pf		2.50	...	211	29	26	28⅛	+ ⅞
SoJerseyInd	SJI	1.40	13	15793	23⅜	18	20¾	+ 2⅜
Southdown	SDW	.50	13	101630	29¼	19¼	27⅝	+ 7¼
SoeastBk	STB	1.12	5	356057	29⅛	18⅛	19⅝	– 2⅞
SouthernCo	SO	2.14	10	f12438	29¾	22	29⅛	+ 6¾
SoIndGE	SIG	1.80	11	33767	32⅛	27½	31⅝	+ 2¾
SoNE Tel	SNG	3.52	15	133079	93	53⅜	89¾	+ 35½
SoNE Tel wi			...	95	45	42¼	45	...
SoRlwy pf		2.60	...	1678	32¾	28⅛	32⅝	+ 3¾
SoUnion	SUG	.20	...	93214	13½	8⅛	13½	+ 5¼
vjSouthmark	SM		...	405923	2⅜	3/64	7/64	– 1 33/64
vjSouthmark pf			...	38207	10¼	⅛	7/16	– 6 5/16
vjSouthmark pfH			...	39514	6⅜	7/32	7/32	– 4 13/32
SowestAir	LUV	.14	9	420509	30¾	19⅝	24	+ 3¾
SowestGas	SWX	1.40	9	82906	20⅜	16⅝	17¼	– ¼
SowestBell	SBC	2.60	17	f10832	64⅜	38⅞	63⅞	+ 23½
SowestEngy	SWN	.56	22	41336	33¼	17¼	32¼	+ 14¼
SowestPS	SPS	2.20	12	263271	31⅜	25¼	30⅛	+ 3⅜
SovranFnl	SOV	1.80	9	161640	43¼	33	38	+ 3¾
SpainFd	SNF	.98e	...	223876	39	10⅜	31¾	+ 21⅛
SpartonCp	SPA	.52	...	14939	12⅝	5⅞	6¼	– 4⅜
SpragueTech	SPG	.05e	...	68627	12⅞	6½	7¼	– 4¼
SpringsInd	SMI	1.20	10	106232	45¼	30½	38¼	+ 6¾
Square D	SQD	2.00	12	158037	62¾	47½	53⅜	+ 5⅜
StdBPaint	SBP		30	75562	19⅜	12⅛	15	+ ⅛
StdCommrcl	STW	.52	...	8490	18⅜	13	13⅛	– 4¼
StdFedBk	SFB	.40	6	122131	12¾	8⅝	9½	+ ⅝
StdMotor	SMP	.32	13	28361	20	13¾	15⅛	+ 1⅛
StdPacific	SPF	1.95e	4	275262	19⅞	11⅞	14⅜	+ 2⅜
StdProducts	SPD	.92	9	27338	34½	21¾	22⅛	– 7¼
StandexInt	SXI	.68	11	24524	26½	20½	23⅝	+ 2⅞
Stanhome	STH	.80	12	224438	35½	18⅜	25⅞	+ 7½
StanleyWks	SWK	1.08	15	226368	39¼	27½	39	+ 10½
Starrett	SCX	.64	9	5678	26⅛	20⅝	21	– 4½
StateMSec	SMS	1.08a	...	11696	11⅛	9¾	10⅞	...
SteegoCp	STG		95	2801	5⅜	3⅞	4¾	...
SterlBcp	STL	.20	...	27708	11¼	7¼	7½	– 2⅞
SterlingChm	STX	1.00	4	223005	18¾	6⅞	7¾	– 8⅜
StoklyVC pf		1.00	...	z70050	12¾	10½	12	+ 1¼
Stifel Fnl	SF		26	10566	7⅞	5¾	5⅞	– ⅜
StoneWeb	SW	1.20	19	16886	45¾	34⅛	38	+ 3⅛
StoneCont	STO	.72	4	778258	36⅜	22⅛	23⅞	– 8⅛
StonrdgRes	SRE		...	32934	10⅝	6⅜	8⅛	+ ⅞
StorEqui	SEQ	1.40	10	34437	14½	10½	10⅞	– ⅜
StorTech	STK		12	121823	17⅝	9¼	11¾	...
StratusCptr	SRA		14	644331	35¼	19¼	23	– 4¼
StrideRite	SRR	.40	18	288639	30¼	13	28⅞	+ 15½
SuaveShoe	SWV		23	3064	7⅝	5	5⅜	– 1
SunDstrib	SDP	1.10e	8	65690	12⅞	9⅜	12⅛	+ 2⅝
SunElec	SE		...	205913	24¾	13⅛	16¼	+ 1¾
SunEngy	SLP	1.16e	68	31460	14	10⅞	11⅝	...
SunCo	SUN	1.80	13	395454	43¼	31⅜	40⅞	+ 8¾
Sundstrand	SNS	1.80	18	133894	83½	50⅛	64⅞	+ 14⅞
SunshMin	SSC		...	421618	4¼	2⅞	3¼	...
SunshMin pf		1.19	...	15111	9⅜	8⅜	9	+ ¼
SunTrustBk	STI	.84	9	303072	26⅞	19¾	22⅞	+ 3
SuprFoodSvc	SFS		16	22663	22	17	20⅛	+ 2⅜
SuperValu	SVU	.60	15	316656	30⅛	22⅝	29	+ 4½
SuprInd	SUP	.28	10	32863	26⅞	15⅜	19¼	+ 3½
SymbolTech	SBL		18	252339	25⅝	15⅛	16¼	– 1⅞
SymsCp	SYM		11	7761	14	10¼	11⅞	+ 1½
SynovusFnl	SNV	.34	17	25464	19½	11¼	16⅜	+ 4⅜
SyntexCp	SYN	1.50	18	f17726	54½	36½	50⅜	+ 9¾
SyscoCp	SYY	.20	25	264447	32	18¼	31⅝	+ 12⅜
SystemCtr	SMX		21	56797	25⅝	16¾	20⅞	+ 3⅝

-T-

Stock	Symbol	Div	Yld	Sales 100s	Hi	Lo	Last	Net Chg
TCBY Ent	TBY	.08	18	364618	29	11⅛	19¼	+ 8
TCF Fnl	TCB	.40	8	59085	17⅜	8⅞	13½	+ 4⅝
TCW Fd	CVT	.84	...	84025	8½	7⅛	8	+ ⅝
TDK Cp	TDK	.12i	...	9338	46¼	29⅜	40⅜	+ 2⅞
TECO Engy	TE	1.52	13	242532	29½	22	29½	+ 5¾
TGIF	TGI		19	30094	15½	10¾	14¼	+ 1⅜
TIS MtgInv	TIS	1.22e	...	56445	9⅛	5½	7⅝	– ⅜
TJX Cos	TJX	.40a	103	874229	21¼	13⅞	15⅜	– 2⅝
TNP Ent	TNP	1.55	8	16937	22⅜	19	21¼	+ 1⅝
TRW	TRW	1.72a	12	294260	49⅞	41¼	49⅜	+ 7¾
TRW pf		4.40	...	33	210	180	205	+ 20
TRW pr		4.50	...	57	181	158	166	+ 11
TW Serv	TW	.05j	38	697073	39	26	34¼	+ 8
TacomaBt	TBO		31	202413	1	9/64	5/16	– 7/16
TaiwanFd	TWN	14.75e	...	66264	49⅞	27¾	49¾	+ 21⅜
TalleyInd	TAL	.50	5	90149	16¼	9½	10¾	– 3⅛
TalleyInd pf		1.00	...	5317	21⅜	14⅛	15⅜	– 3½
Tambrands	TMB	2.08	21	321571	76½	52⅝	70	+ 10⅞
Tandem	TDM		20	f12375	26⅜	14¾	23	+ 6⅛
TandyCp	TAN	.60	11	722829	48¾	37	39⅛	– 1⅞
Tandycrfts	TAC		13	4202	17¼	12⅝	17	+ 4⅜
TechSym	TSY		14	62827	14¼	9	9⅝	– 1⅞
Tektronix	TEK	.60	46	161899	24¼	16⅛	17⅞	– 2½
TelCom	TEL		44	7685	2⅛	1⅛	1¾	+ ½
TelcmUSA	TTT		24	261618	40	17½	23⅜	+ 4⅝
Teledyne	TDY	4.00	13	36927	380¾	317½	343¼	+ 11
TeleEspana	TEF	1.08e	14	733278	27⅞	22⅝	24⅝	+ 1
Telerate	TLR	.32	23	395627	21⅛	13¼	20¾	+ 5⅛
TempInland	TIN	1.16	9	185379	71	46¾	69½	+ 21⅞
TemplMktFd	EMF	.33e	...	61289	15½	8	15¼	+ 7⅜
TemplGlbGvt	TGG	1.02	...	76793	10⅛	8¼	8½	– 1½
TemplGlob	GIM	1.02	...	512411	9⅝	8⅛	8½	– ⅝
TemplValFd	TVF	.43e	...	74457	10¼	8¼	9⅞	+ 1⅜
Tenneco	TGT	3.04	18	727789	64¼	46⅞	62¼	+ 13⅜
Tenneco pr		7.40	...	6959	97⅜	93	95	+ ⅛
Teradyne	TER		122	194180	14¾	9⅞	11	– ¾
Tesoro	TSO		...	83857	14⅛	8¾	9¼	– 2⅝
Tesoro pf		2.16	...	7154	25½	17	17½	– 2⅞
Texaco	TX	3.00a	13	f29726	59	48½	58⅞	+ 7¾
Texaco pfC			...	63279	50½	47⅜	47½	...
TexInd	TXI	.80b	...	26383	36⅞	22	22⅞	– 10⅝
TexInstr	TXN	.72	10	f10671	46¾	28⅛	35⅞	– 5⅛
TexPacTr	TPL	.40	52	8477	54	30⅛	34¼	+ 3¼
TexUtil	TXU	2.92	9	f23079	37⅝	27¾	35⅛	+ 7
TexfiInd	TXF		6	90411	12⅛	5¼	7½	+ 1⅝
TexfiInd pf		1.00	...	1619	10½	9½	9⅞	– ⅛
TexfiInd pfB			...	6006	10⅛	9⅛	9¾	+ ⅜
Textron	TXT	1.00	8	463711	29⅜	22⅝	24⅝	+ ⅞
Textron pf		2.08	...	428	63⅞	50	52¼	+ 2¼
Textron pf		1.40	...	126	51¾	41	43½	+ 1
Thackeray	THK		22	6314	9¾	6⅜	6⅜	– 1⅛
ThaiFd	TTF	2.45e	...	161281	33⅜	11⅝	32¼	+ 20½
ThermoElec	TMO		24	121055	37⅞	19⅛	30⅝	+ 10⅜
Thiokol	TKC	.30	...	166557	16	12⅛	13⅛	...
ThomBetts	TNB	2.00	15	75091	55¾	46	49⅞	+ 2⅝
ThomInd	TII	.76	12	23445	20⅝	17⅝	20¼	+ 1¾
ThomsMcK	TMA	1.31e	6	56515	16	6⅝	7⅞	– 2½
ThorInd	THO	.12	15	6195	14	9½	10¼	– 3
ThortecInt	THT		...	53869	4⅛	⅜	9/16	– 3 3/16
Tidewtr	TDW		...	217932	14⅞	7¼	14⅜	+ 7
Tidewtr pf		6.64k	...	16	98	92	98	+ 6¼
Tiffany	TIF	.20	24	93352	61¼	26	46¾	+ 18¾
TimeWarner	TWX	1.00	198	f11605	182¾	103⅝	120⅝	+ 13⅝
TimeWarner pfC			...	40080	45¾	43½	45½	...
TimeWarner pfD			...	33527	44¾	41½	43¾	...
TimesMir	TMC	1.08	14	389749	45	32⅜	35¾	+ 2⅞
Timken	TKR	.92	9	138709	39¼	25½	27¾	– 7¾
Titan	TTN		...	34293	3⅜	1¾	2⅜	+ ⅛
Titan pf		1.00	...	1101	10	8⅛	9⅝	+ 1⅝
vjToddShip	TOD		...	51271	8⅛	1⅞	4	+ 2
vjToddShip pf			...	6113	25⅝	10⅛	17¼	+ 7½
Tokheim	TOK	.56	26	39758	26	17⅛	21	+ 1⅜
ToledoEd pf		2.50e	...	10356	24½	21¾	22¼	+ ⅝
ToledoEd pf		2.81	...	16561	28	24⅞	26½	+ 1⅝
ToledoEd pf		2.36	...	1593	24⅞	21⅞	24¾	+ 3
ToledoEd pf		2.21	...	1302	23½	20⅛	23¼	+ 3¼
ToledoEd pf		2.29e	...	4102	23	20⅝	20⅝	– ½

NEW YORK STOCK EXCHANGE COMPOSITE

Stock	Symbol	Div	Yld	Sales 100s	Hi	Lo	Last	Net Chg
Toll Bros	TOL		7	56953	5 7/8	2 7/8	3 1/4	- 1 1/2
Tonka	TKA		8	212780	22 7/8	8 1/2	11 1/8	+ 2 3/8
TootsieRoll	TR	.23b	17	18468	38 1/2	25	36 1/2	+ 6 1/2
Torchmark	TMK	1.40	16	167360	58 3/4	30	55 3/4	+ 25 1/4
Torchmark pf		7.80e	...	5732	91 3/8	82	82	- 8 1/2
Toro	TTC	.48	13	58025	26	18 5/8	25 1/4	+ 6 1/8
Tosco	TOS	.60	16	875859	26 1/4	15 5/8	22 3/4	+ 7 1/8
Tosco pf		2.37	...	56985	67	41 1/8	59 1/4	+ 17 7/8
TotlSysSvc	TSS	.07e	40	6201	29 1/8	17 1/4	27	+ 5 1/4
ToysRUs	TOY		26	f11324	40 1/4	24	35 7/8	+ 11 1/8
TrammellRE	TCR	.98e	...	38966	8	4 1/4	4 5/8	- 2 5/8
TWA pf		2.25	...	19252	17 3/4	15 1/8	15 5/8	+ 3/8
TransamCp	TA	1.92	10	368439	48	32 3/4	44 1/4	+ 10 3/8
TransamInco	TAI	2.16	11	6912	24 1/2	20 1/4	23 3/4	+ 2 1/8
TransCda g	TRP	.68	...	51215	15 1/4	10 1/2	14 1/2	+ 3 7/16
Transcap	TFC	1.69e	...	7629	8	4 1/4	4 3/8	- 2 5/8
Transco	E	1.36	...	265315	50 1/4	33 7/8	48 1/8	+ 13
Transco pf		4.75	...	12665	54 3/4	47	54 1/2	+ 7 1/4
TranscoExpl	EXP	9.85c	4	296392	13 1/2	3 1/4	3 1/2	- 2 1/4
Transcon	TCL		...	41894	3 1/2	7/8	1 7/8	- 5/8
TransGas pf		6.65	...	z3630	94	90	93	+ 2 3/4
TransGas pf		8.64	...	z11910	102	97	101 3/8	+ 3 3/4
TransGas pf		2.50	...	1371	26 3/4	25	26 1/2	+ 3/8
TrancntlRlty	TCI	.40	...	35347	7 7/8	2 1/2	3 1/4	- 2
TransTech	TT	.96	21	22156	20	10 7/8	11 1/2	- 6 1/4
Travelers	TIC	2.40	9	545441	45	34 1/2	36 7/8	+ 2 1/8
TredegarInd	TG	.24	...	68033	17 5/8	12 7/8	15 7/8	...
TriContl	TY	3.39e	...	91888	23 1/4	22 1/4	23	+ 5 1/2
TriContl pf		2.50	...	1220	30 3/4	26 3/4	28 3/4	+ 1 3/4
Tribune	TRB	.88	16	516157	63 1/8	36 3/8	47 3/8	+ 8 1/2
TrinityInd	TRN	.80	12	290469	46	28 5/8	30	- 4
Trinova	TNV	.68	23	257732	30 3/8	21	24 1/2	- 3
TritonGp	TGL		...	28884	16 3/4	10 5/8	11 1/4	- 4 3/4
TritonEngy	OIL	.10b	12	120077	18	12 3/8	15 1/2	+ 2 5/8
TritonEngy pf		2.00	...	16836	25 3/8	19 3/4	23 1/4	+ 3
TucsonElec	TEP	1.60	...	417370	50 1/4	16 1/8	18	- 31 1/2
Tultex	TTX	.36	17	121448	14 5/8	7 3/4	10	+ 1 3/4
TurkishFd	TKF	.03e	...	38555	12 1/4	9 5/8	12	...
TwinDisc	TDI	.90	8	6598	35	21 1/2	23 3/8	- 3 5/8
TycoLabs	TYC	.32	21	298232	53 3/4	32 1/4	50 3/8	+ 14 5/8
TylerCp	TYL	.08	...	16144	9	4 7/8	8 5/8	...

-U-

UAL Cp	UAL		8	f12364	294	105 1/4	171 1/4	+ 61 3/4
UDC pf		3.75	...	7113	28 5/8	22 1/2	24 1/4	- 1 5/8
UDC	UDC	2.40a	5	40770	27	17 3/4	21 3/8	+ 2 5/8
UDC pfB			...	8254	25 3/4	20 3/4	21 3/8	...
UGI	UGI	2.25	12	94579	40 1/8	28 3/4	38 3/8	+ 8 1/2
UJB Fnl	UJB	1.16	7	217802	28 7/8	18	18 7/8	- 1 7/8
UJB Fnl pf		3.55e	...	11900	44	37 1/2	42 1/8	- 1 3/8
UNC	UNC		6	256995	9 3/8	4 7/8	5 1/4	- 3 5/8
UNUM	UNM	.60	13	218326	49	26 5/8	48	+ 21
USF&G	FG	2.80	26	686920	34	28 1/4	29	+ 1/2
USF&G pf		4.10	...	18379	46 1/2	40 1/4	42 1/8	+ 1 5/8
USG	USG		4	348179	7 3/8	2 7/8	4 1/2	- 1 1/8
USLICO	USC	1.00	8	26499	25 3/8	21 7/8	23 5/8	+ 1 5/8
UST Inc	UST	.92	20	594198	30 3/4	19 3/4	30 5/8	+ 9 5/8
USX	X	1.40	11	f28664	39 1/2	28 7/8	35 3/4	+ 6 1/2
USX pf		4.65e	...	20109	49 1/8	44 1/2	45 1/2	- 1 3/8
Ultimate	ULT		10	71380	12 1/4	7 1/8	7 5/8	- 1 3/4
Unifirst	UNF	.12	21	4612	24	12 3/4	23 7/8	+ 11
Unilvr plc	UL	1.21e	14	56181	47 3/4	33	47 3/4	+ 14 3/4
Unilvr NV	UN	2.00e	15	345839	84 3/4	57 3/4	84 3/4	+ 26 1/2
UnCamp	UCC	1.48	8	430083	41 3/8	33 1/2	36 7/8	+ 2 1/2
UnCarbide	UK	1.00	5	f31685	33 1/4	22 3/4	23 1/4	- 2 3/8
UnionCp	UCO		13	60076	21 3/8	12 3/8	20 3/8	+ 7 3/4
UnElec	UEP	2.08	12	396147	28 5/8	23	28 5/8	+ 4 1/2
UnElec pf		3.50	...	z8740	41	34	38 1/2	...
UnElec pf		4.00	...	z73920	48	40	46	+ 5 3/4
UnElec pf		4.50	...	z16060	50 1/2	44 3/8	50 1/2	+ 5
UnElec pf		4.56	...	z57000	53 1/2	45	52 1/4	+ 6 1/4
UnElec pf		6.40	...	1274	74 7/8	63 1/2	74 7/8	+ 10
UnElec pf		8.00	...	z28020	92	84 1/2	91	+ 5
UnElec pf		7.44	...	4938	87	74	85 3/8	+ 10 3/8
UnElec pfH		8.00	...	z58380	92	81	90 1/4	+ 7 3/4
UnExplor	UXP	1.82e	18	38779	19 1/4	13 1/8	17 1/4	+ 4
UnPacific	UNP	2.32	14	567200	81	63 1/4	76 5/8	+ 12 3/8
UnionPlantr	UPC	.48	22	42466	15 3/4	10 5/8	11 1/4	- 1 3/8
UnTexas	UTH	.20	12	166291	18 3/4	10 3/8	18 1/8	+ 7 3/4
UnFedFnl	UFF	.44	5	64009	24 1/8	13 3/8	17 7/8	+ 4 3/8

Stock	Symbol	Div	Yld	Sales 100s	Hi	Lo	Last	Net Chg
Unisys	UIS	1.00	...	f20333	30 1/2	12 3/8	14 3/4	- 13 3/8
Unisys pf		3.75	...	339736	54 1/2	31	33 7/8	- 18 1/8
UnitCp	UNT		...	75743	3 5/8	1 7/8	3 1/2	+ 1 1/2
Utd AssetMgt	UAM	.36	20	33550	21 1/8	13 1/2	18 3/8	+ 4 5/8
Utd Brands	UB	.20	9	23388	17 5/8	12 7/8	17 3/8	+ 1
Utd Illum	UIL	2.32	5	73071	34 1/4	24 5/8	34 1/4	+ 7 3/8
Utd Illum pr		2.20	...	z72790	23 3/4	20	23	+ 2 1/4
Utd Industrl	UIC	.64	13	31384	15 5/8	10 5/8	10 7/8	- 2 1/2
Utd Inns	UI		...	4086	31 7/8	22	22	- 3/4
Utd KingFd	UKM	.50e	...	28561	11 1/2	8 1/2	10 3/4	+ 1 3/8
Utd MerMfg	UMM		...	82712	5 1/8	1 5/8	2 1/8	- 1 1/8
Utd ParkMin	UPK		...	18710	2 1/8	1 1/8	1 1/2	+ 1/4
USAirGp	U	.12a	25	805612	54 3/4	30 5/8	33 3/8	- 1 1/8
US Home	UH		...	216357	2 1/4	1	1 1/2	- 5/8
US Shoe	USR	.46	18	669026	27 1/2	16 3/8	20 1/8	- 4 5/8
US Surg	USS	.80	22	66577	61 1/4	30 3/4	54 3/4	+ 22 3/8
US West	USW	3.76	14	563578	80 5/8	56 3/4	80 1/8	+ 22 3/8
Utd Tech	UTX	1.60	11	825608	57 3/8	39 7/8	54 1/4	+ 13 1/8
Utd Telecm		2.00	29	821768	87 1/2	44	75	+ 28 5/8
Utd Telecm	UT	1.00	29	824229	43 3/4	22	38	+ 14 7/8
Utd Telecm pf		1.50	...	39	124	69	114 3/8	+ 44 1/8
Utd Telecm 2pf		1.50	...	205	103	55 7/8	93	+ 36 5/8
Utd WaterRes	UWR	.88	21	26677	17 7/8	15 3/4	16 1/8	- 1 1/4
Unitrode	UTR		59	50939	8 3/8	4 1/8	4 3/4	- 2 5/8
UnivarCp	UVX	.30	11	8801	17 7/8	12 1/8	13 3/8	+ 1 1/8
UnivCp	UVV	1.48	11	68518	39	33	35 1/2	+ 2 1/2
UnivFoods	UFC		15	207222	26 1/4	21 3/8	23 7/8	+ 3/4
UnivHlth	UHT	1.48	11	24604	14 7/8	11 1/2	12 5/8	+ 3/4
UnivMatch	UMG		...	28766	8 1/8	4 3/4	5 1/8	- 1 7/8
UnivMed	UMB	.06e	...	87276	4 3/4	1 7/8	2	- 1 7/8
UnivMed pf			...	301	9	5 7/8	7 7/8	+ 1/2
UnocalCp	UCL	.70	...	969882	31 1/4	18 5/8	29 3/4	+ 10 7/8
Upjohn	UPJ	1.00	19	f20483	42 1/8	27 5/8	38 1/2	+ 9 3/4
USLIFE	USH	1.48	11	116001	48 1/8	34 1/8	45	+ 10 1/8
USLIFE pr		3.33	...	157	37	34 3/4	36 5/8	+ 7/8
USLIFE Fd	UIF	.92	...	10437	9 3/4	8 1/2	9 1/8	+ 3/8
UtiliCorp	UCU	1.44	11	79872	22 1/4	17 1/2	22	+ 2 3/4
UtiliCorp pf		2.44	...	667	26 1/4	23 3/4	26	+ 2
UtiliCorp pr		2.61	...	743	28 1/8	25 1/2	27 1/8	+ 1 1/4
UtiliCorp pr		1.77	...	11494	23 1/4	19 1/4	23 1/8	...

-V-

VF Cp	VFC	1.00	12	355185	38 3/8	27 3/4	31 7/8	+ 3 1/8
VMS MtgInv	VMG	1.20	...	98401	8 3/4	4 1/4	4 7/8	...
Valhi	VHI	.20	16	70857	18 1/4	11 3/4	18 1/4	+ 6
ValeroEngy	VLO	.10e	14	844599	19 5/8	8 7/8	15 1/8	+ 6 1/4
ValeroEngy pf		3.44	...	6399	28 1/8	25 7/8	26 7/8	+ 1 1/8
ValeroNGas	VLP	2.50	79	73119	22 1/8	14 7/8	16 1/2	+ 1 1/8
ValleyInd	VI		...	13079	2 1/2	13/16	15/16	- 11/16
VanDorn	VDC	.60	16	25943	19 3/8	13 5/8	14 3/4	- 1 5/8
VanKampMun	VMT	.68	...	61946	10 1/2	8 3/4	9 1/8	- 1
VanKampHiInco	VIT	.92e	...	60295	10 1/8	7 1/4	7 3/8	...
VanKampInv	VIG		...	978	12 1/8	12	12 1/8	...
VanKampLtd	VLT	.74e	...	25349	12 1/8	8 7/8	9	...
VanKampLtd pf			...	14593	26	24	25	...
VarcoInt	VRC		104	207624	7 1/2	2 7/8	7 1/4	+ 4 1/4
Varian	VAR	.26	14	217064	30 5/8	19 7/8	21 5/8	- 6 3/8
VarityCp	VAT		8	f11951	3 3/8	2	2 1/2	- 3/8
VarityCp wi			...	886	2 5/8	2 1/8	2 1/2	...
VarityCp pf		1.30	...	76292	22 3/4	16 3/8	18 5/8	- 1 7/8
VestaurSec	VES	1.20a	11	8320	14	12	13 3/8	+ 1
Vestron	VV		...	69362	6 1/4	1	1 1/8	- 2 1/2
VirgE&P pf		5.00	...	z6630	57	51	55 1/2	+ 3 1/2
VirgE&P pf		7.72	...	2933	90 1/4	76 1/2	87 3/8	+ 8 3/8
VirgE&P pf		8.60	...	48	97	91	96	+ 1/2
VirgE&P pf		8.60	...	z59400	102 3/8	95	100	+ 3
VirgE&P pfJ		7.72	...	2485	90 7/8	76	88	+ 10
VirgE&P pf		7.20	...	2491	84 3/8	71 1/4	81 5/8	+ 6 5/8
VirgE&P pf		7.45	...	1113	87	74	84 3/4	+ 7 1/4
Vishay	VSH		12	49100	20 3/4	13 3/4	17	- 1 3/4
VistaChm	VC	1.80	5	322185	56 3/8	36 1/8	38 7/8	- 5 1/4
Vivra	V		...	42996	32	23	26 5/8	...
VolCap	VCC		...	21736	3 3/8	1 1/8	1 5/8	- 1/2
VonsCos	VON		...	196978	23 3/4	11 3/8	19 1/2	+ 8
Vornado	VNO		28	2319	126 1/2	113	114 1/2	- 8
VulcanMat	VMC	1.12	13	59217	48 1/2	40 1/2	44 1/2	+ 3

-W-

WICOR	WIC	1.40	11	23847	25 1/2	19 3/8	24 7/8	+ 5 3/8
WMS Ind	WMS		29	75958	15	5 3/8	9 3/4	+ 4

NEW YORK STOCK EXCHANGE COMPOSITE

Stock	Symbol	Div	Yld	Sales 100s	Hi	Lo	Last	Net Chg
WPL Hldg	WPH	1.68	14	49686	24½	21⅞	24⅜	+ 1⅜
WabanInc	WBN		...	351761	20	10	12	...
WabashRR pf		4.50	...	1172	72	57½	62⅛	− 1⅜
Wackenhut	WAK	.60	18	6126	24¾	17	24½	+ 7½
WainocoOil	WOL		52	138389	11	6¼	11	+ 4½
WalMart	WMT	.22	26	f15513	44⅞	30	44⅞	+ 13½
Walgreen	WAG	.80	19	441096	50¼	30	46¾	+ 16½
WallaceCS	WCS	.46	17	52496	31½	21	31⅛	+ 9⅜
WarnerComm	WCI	.68	66	f25612	67⅞	35⅝	63¾	+ 27⅛
WarnerCptr	WCP	.32t	17	27674	7½	4⅛	5⅞	+ 1½
WarnerLamb	WLA	3.04	20	467291	118¾	74½	115½	+ 37⅛
WashGasLt	WGL	1.96	13	49248	31¾	23⅝	31½	+ 6¾
WashNtl	WNT	1.08	...	31155	29⅛	24	27⅞	+ ⅞
WashNtl pf		2.50	...	79	52½	46	51	+ 2¾
WashWater	WWP	2.48	11	67755	31⅜	26	30⅝	+ 3⅛
WasteMgt	WMX	.32	30	f13171	35⅞	20⅜	35	+ 14⅜
WatkinsJohn	WJ	.48	7	45286	27¼	19	21	− 5¾
WaxmanInd	WAX	.12	10	62032	11	6⅞	8¼	− ¾
WeanUtd	WID		...	7682	5⅛	1½	4¼	+ 2⅜
WeanUtd pf			...	448	10¼	6¾	9	+ 1¼
WebbDel	WBB		...	143731	15¾	7⅛	8⅜	− 7
Wedgestone	WDG		...	20690	3¾	¾	1¼	− 1½
WeingtnRlty	WRI	1.76	31	37133	32½	25⅛	31⅝	+ 6
WeirtnStl n	WS	.32e	...	47335	15⅜	10⅜	11⅛	...
WeisMkts	WMK	.56	16	34405	37½	28⅛	30	+ 1¾
Wellman	WLM	.12	21	320743	43	18⅜	35⅛	+ 16⅜
WellsF	WFC	3.60	7	313991	87½	59	74⅛	+ 13¾
WellsF pf		3.15e	...	14356	39	33¾	34¼	− 1¾
WellsF pf		3.32e	...	6557	39¾	35¼	35¼	− 4⅛
Wendys	WEN	.24	14	653526	7	4½	4⅝	− 1⅛
WestCo	WST	.40	15	31336	22⅝	14⅞	19	+ 4
WestPennP pf		4.50	...	z24430	51½	45½	50½	+ 2⅞
WestPtPeprl	WPM	.32e	18	299155	58¾	41⅝	42	− 1⅞
WestcstEngy g	WE	.80	17	6179	18⅝	13¼	17⅞	+ 4⅜
WestnCoNA	WSN		...	127715	15	5⅜	13¾	...
WestnGas pf		1.80	...	3794	16¾	12⅝	16	+ 3⅝
WestnGasRes	WGR		...	18864	13⅜	11½	13⅜	...
WestnUnion	WU		...	586577	2⅞	¼	13/32	− 31/32
WestnUnion pfA			...	9955	43¾	5⅝	6⅝	− 13⅞
WestnUnion pfB			...	94228	16	2¼	3⅛	− 3⅞
Westnghse	WX	2.40	12	777061	76¼	51¼	74	+ 21⅜
WestpacBk	WBK	2.02e	...	53916	22⅜	17⅞	21⅝	...
WestpacBk pf		.70e	...	3824	26⅜	25¼	25⅞	...
Westvaco	W	1.00	9	186530	33⅜	26⅞	30¼	+ 1¼
Weyerhsr	WY	1.20	9	f11258	32¾	24½	27⅝	+ 2½
Weyerhsr pf		2.62	...	33830	40¾	33½	37	+ 3⅛

Stock	Symbol	Div	Yld	Sales 100s	Hi	Lo	Last	Net Chg
WheelbrTch	WTI		...	85776	42⅝	33⅜	35⅛	...
vjWheelPit	WHX			51789	16¾	7⅝	11⅛	+ 2⅜
vjWheelPit pfB			...	z42160	36¼	26	29¼	− ¾
vjWheelPit pf			...	z47490	30	20	20¼	− ¾
Whirlpool	WHR	1.10	18	413933	33¼	24¼	33	+ 8¼
Whitehall	WHT		...	19353	17¼	10⅞	14	+ 2⅝
WhitmanCp	WH	1.02	20	f10816	38¼	27½	28¾	− 4⅜
Whittaker	WKR		2	36912	13½	7⅝	7¾	...
Wilfred	WAE		...	10828	3¼	⅝	⅞	− 2¼
WillcoxGbs	WG	.10	13	54747	20½	15½	16¼	+ 3⅝
WilliamsCos	WMB	1.40	...	481687	44¾	29¾	38⅝	+ 8⅛
WilliamsCos pf		3.87	...	31157	61¾	49¾	56⅞	...
WilliamsNG pf		3.64e	...	874	43	40	40¼	− 5¾
WilshireOil	WOC	.20t	88	13207	7⅛	5	6⅛	+ ⅜
Windmere	WND		7	539148	29	7¾	9	− 8¾
WinnDixie	WIN	1.98	19	63699	65	42⅞	65	+ 21
Winnebago	WGO	.20	...	86857	9⅜	4½	5	− 4¼
WiscEngy	WEC	1.66	13	308199	32⅛	25⅛	32	+ 5
WiscPS	WPS	1.62	12	79203	24⅞	20½	23¾	+ 2⅛
WitcoCp	WIT	1.72	11	97425	45⅛	34⅝	38½	+ 3½
WolverineWW	WWW	.16	10	61850	15⅝	10⅝	11¼	+ ⅜
Woolworth	Z	1.88	14	791354	72¼	48⅜	63⅞	+ 12⅛
Woolworth pf		2.20	...	108	200	140	177	+ 31½
WorldCp	WOA		9	40462	15	5⅜	13¼	+ 7⅜
WorldValFd	VLU	1.61e	...	14412	19¾	15¾	19	+ 2⅞
Wrigley	WWY	.80a	20	72975	53¾	35½	53⅝	+ 17½
WyleLabs	WYL	.28	18	51388	11⅜	7¾	11⅜	+ 1⅜
WynnsInt	WN	.60	11	14485	28	21	23½	+ 2¾
WyseTech	WYS		...	469643	12¼	4½	9¾	+ 2½

-X-Y-Z-

Stock	Symbol	Div	Yld	Sales 100s	Hi	Lo	Last	Net Chg
Xerox	XRX	3.00	15	984286	69	54⅜	57¼	− 1⅛
Xerox pf			...	11262	47⅝	43⅝	46¾	...
Xerox pf		4.12	...	6494	49	44½	47¼	+ ½
XTRA	XTR	.72	19	69541	44¼	23½	24	− 13½
XTRA pf		1.94	...	20610	33	21⅜	22	− 6⅝
Zapata	ZOS		...	186701	4¼	2	3½	+ 1⅜
ZemexCp	ZMX	.20	...	1721	13¼	7⅞	8⅜	− 4½
ZenithElec	ZE		...	498434	21½	11½	12¾	− 6¼
ZenithNtl	ZNT	.84	8	38458	21½	16¾	18	+ ½
ZenixFd	ZIF	1.20	...	48357	10	6½	6⅞	− 2¼
ZeroCp	ZRO	.40	14	53077	18½	13⅞	14⅞	+ ⅞
ZurnInd	ZRN	.76	19	100004	44¼	25¾	40⅜	+ 13⅛
ZweigFd	ZF	1.12e	...	105741	12⅜	10	12⅜	+ 2
ZweigTotlFd	ZTR	.96	...	306170	9⅞	8¾	9¾	+ ⅝

Sales figures are unofficial.

f-Add 0000. g-Dividend or earnings in Canadian money. Stock trades in U.S. dollars. No yield or PE shown unless stated in U.S. money. n-New issue in the past year. The range begins with the start of trading in the new issue and does not cover the entire year. s-Split or stock dividend of 25 per cent or more in the past year. The high-low range is adjusted from the old stock. Dividend begins with the date of split or stock dividend. The net change is from an adjusted previous year's closing price. v-Trading halted on primary market.

Unless otherwise noted, rates of dividends in the foregoing table are annual disbursements based on the last quarterly or semi-annual declaration. Special or extra dividends or payments not designated as regular are identified in the following footnotes.

a-Also extra or extras. b-Annual rate plus stock dividend. c-Liquidating dividend. e-Declared or paid in preceding 12 months. i-Declared or paid after stock dividend or split-up. j-Paid this year, dividend omitted, deferred or no action taken at last dividend meeting. k-Declared or paid this year, an accumulative issue with dividends in arrears. r-Declared or paid in preceding 12 months plus stock dividend. t-Paid in stock in preceding 12 months, estimated cash value on ex-dividend or ex-distribution date. z-Sales in full.

pf-Preferred. pp-Holder owes 2 instalments of purchase price. rt-Rights. un-Units. wd-When distributed. wi-When issued. ww-With warrants. wt-Warrants. xw-Without warrants.

vj-In bankruptcy or receivership or being reorganized under the Bankruptcy Act, or securities assumed by such companies.

NEW YORK BONDS

The following tabulation gives the 1989 sales, high, low, last price and net change from the previous year in bonds listed on the New York Stock Exchange.

		Sales $1,000	High	Low	Last	Net Chg.
-A-						
AL Lb 7¾14	cv	1389	106	99½	105½	...
AMR 9s16	9.8	85	92	88½	92	...
ANR 8⅝93	8.8	211	100	97	98¼	+ ½
ANR 9⅝94	9.7	143	99¾	97	99⅝	+ 1⅝
ANR 10⅝95	10.5	423	101½	99¾	100¾	+ ½
ANR 13¼97	13.1	50	104	101	101½	− 4⅞
ANR 11¾97	11.4	253	103½	99	103½	+ 3⅜
AVX 13½00	12.7	740	109½	100½	106	+ ½
AVX 8¼12	cv	1773	140⅞	99	140⅞	+ 39⅞
AbbtL 6¼93	6.7	106	94½	89¾	93	+ 1⅝
AbbtL 7⅝96	8.2	57	93½	87	93⅛	+ 2
AbbtL 9.2s99	9.2	489	101½	95½	100	− 1
AbbtL 11s93	11.0	5598	104⅜	100	100	− 1⅞
Advst 9s08	cv	3965	93	80½	85	+ 4
AetnLf 8⅛07	8.5	1125	95⅝	83⅜	95½	+ 8½
AirPr 12¾94	12.2	115	110	104½	104½	− 2½
AirPr 11½95	10.7	25	107¼	105	107¼	− 6¾
AirPr 11⅜15	...	71	107¾	105	107¾	+ ¼
AirbF 7½11	cv	1484	140	94	126	+ 30½
AlaBn 9s99t	9.3	154	100	97¼	97¼	− 2½
AlaP 9s2000	9.0	1533	100¾	91⅝	99⅝	+ 5¾
AlaP 8½s01	8.8	1428	97	87⅛	96¼	+ 7¼
AlaP 7⅞s02	8.6	818	92⅜	83	91⅜	+ 6⅛
AlaP 7¾s02	8.5	1312	92¼	82⅛	91⅛	+ 7⅝
AlaP 8⅞s03	9.1	2406	99	89	97¾	+ 6½
AlaP 8¼s03	8.9	923	95	84⅜	93	+ 5
AlaP 9¾s04	9.5	2055	103	95¾	103	+ 5⅜
AlaP 10⅞05	10.4	1088	106	101	104¼	+ 1
AlaP 10½05	10.1	2383	106	99⅛	103½	+ 2
AlaP 8⅞06	9.1	881	100	88⅜	97⅛	+ 6¼
AlaP 8¾07	9.2	2099	97⅜	87¼	95½	+ 6¾
AlaP 9¼07	9.3	1869	100	92⅛	99⅝	+ 7¼
AlaP 9½08	9.3	1517	102	92	101¾	+ 7¼
AlaP 9⅝08	9.6	2139	102¾	94	100⅝	+ 5⅜
AlaP 12⅝10	11.9	4521	108	104	105¾	− ¾
AlaP 9⅜16	9.4	144	100¼	97	99¼	+ 3¾
AlaP 10⅝17	10.0	35	105¾	101½	105¾	+ 2½
AlaP 10s18	9.7	878	104	97½	103	+ 3¾
AlskAr 6⅞14	cv	2468	107	88¾	89	...
AlskH 17¾91	16.1	2296	115	107½	110	− 5
AlskH 11¾92	11.6	91	109	100¾	101	− 1
AlskH 11½93	11.4	25	107	101	101⅛	− 1⅞
AlskH 11⅜93	11.0	332	105⅞	100½	103½	− 2⅜
AlskH 10¾93	10.5	225	103¼	99⅞	102	+ ⅝
AlskH 11½93l	11.4	116	104	100⅜	101	− ½
AlskH 12⅞93	12.3	340	108⅜	102½	105	− 3½
AllgWt 4s98	5.6	50	73	67½	72	− 1
AlegCp 6½14	cv	324	111	99	104	...
vjAlgl 10¾99f	...	5011	95½	14	21	− 71
vjAlgl 10.4s02f	...	8313	69¾	10⅞	16⅞	− 48⅝
vjAlgl 9s89mf	...	3327	93	17	17¾	− 70¼
AlldC zr92	...	4242	79	69¼	78¼	+ 8¾
AlldC zr96	...	944	60½	49½	58	+ 6⅞
AlldC zr98	...	2793	49	38½	47¾	+ 8¾
AlldC zr2000	...	6483	40¼	31¾	39	+ 7¾
AldC dc6s90	6.2	1661	98	92¾	97½	+ 4
AlldC zr91	...	960	87	78⅜	86½	+ 8⅛
AlldC zr9	...	725	73¾	62½	73	+ 10¼
AlldC zr95	...	2880	63	52⅛	61⅝	+ 8⅜
AlldC zr97	...	2335	51¾	42¾	50⅞	+ 5⅞
AlldC zr99	...	2655	44¼	36	42	+ 4¾
AlldC zr01	...	2850	36¾	28⅝	36	+ 6½
AlldC zr03	...	2420	31	24⅞	29⅝	+ 5⅝
AlldC zr05	...	2615	27	19⅝	25	+ 3⅝
AlldC zr07	...	4565	22½	16¼	21½	+ 4¾
AlldC zr09	...	20895	18½	13⅛	16¾	+ 3
AldSig 9⅞97	9.7	593	103	98	101⅜	+ 2⅜
AldSig 9½16	9.9	130	97	95¾	96	...
AldSig 9⅞02	9.5	432	104	98	104	+ 3
Alcoa 6s92	6.4	365	95	88⅝	94	+ 2¼
Alcoa 9s95	9.0	1658	101	96⅛	100	+ 2⅝
Alcoa 7.45s96	7.9	536	97	88⅜	94¼	+ 1¼
Alcoa 9.45s00	9.5	587	100¼	96⅞	100	+ 1⅜
AMAX 8½96	9.0	453	95½	89½	94¼	+ 3⅞
AMAX 9⅜00	9.5	772	100	90	98½	+ 7⅝
AMAX 8⅝01	9.5	487	92	84	91⅛	+ 7⅛
AMAX 14¼90	14.0	2485	107	101	102	− 3⅛
AMAX 14½94	12.3	3931	119	113⅝	118	+ 2½
AmBas 11¾08	12.0	152	100	93¼	98	...
AmBas 14⅞98	16.3	36815	108	89	91¼	− 14¾
Amdur 5½93	cv	880	92	68	68	− 17
AForP 5s30	9.4	2137	55½	50⅝	53⅜	+ ⅜
AForP 5s30r	9.5	559	55	51	52⅝	...
AAirl 4¼92	4.8	1310	90	83	89	+ 5
AAir dc6¼96	7.2	1847	98⅛	85⅝	86⅝	+ 1
AAirl 5¼98	6.9	169	76	70⅝	76	+ 2
ABrnd 4⅝90	4.8	37	97½	91	97 5/32	+ 2 29/32
ABrnd 8⅝90	8.6	4016	100 3/32	96⅝	99 31/32	+ 2 19/32
ABrnd 9⅛16	9.7	3273	95⅜	85	94⅛	+ 11⅛
vjACM 6¾91f	cv	1401	34	8	27½	+ 21½
ACyan 7⅜01	8.1	196	93⅝	90⅛	91⅜	− ⅝
ACyan 8⅜06	8.9	405	94¼	85¼	94¼	+ 6½
AExC 7.8s92	7.9	210	98¼	95⅛	98¼	+ 1¼
AExC 11¼00	10.9	993	106	100⅛	103	− ¾
AExC 11¾12	10.7	231	111¼	104¼	109½	+ 5½
AExC 10⅞13	10.0	70	108⅞	104	108⅞	...
AmGn 9⅜08	9.3	795	101	90¼	101	+ 4
AmGnFn 8s92	8.2	209	99	93½	98⅛	+ ⅜
AmGnFn 9⅜92	9.5	25	99¾	97¼	99⅛	− ½
AmGnFn 10½94	10.3	28	102	100	102	− ¼
AmGnFn zr90s	...	1556	92¼	83⅛	91 17/32	+ 8 25/32
AmGnFn 12⅜94	12.0	20	103½	101½	102¾	+ ¾
AmGnFn 12¼95	11.6	30	106	103⅜	106	− 2½
AmGnFn 10¾93	10.6	2	101	101	101	− ¼
AmGnFn 9s93	9.0	25	99¾	99¾	99¾	+ 2¾
AHosp 7⅞07	9.4	343	87	74⅛	84	+ 8½
AmMed 9½01	cv	11615	106¼	59	62	− 32½
AmMed 8¼08	cv	7258	76½	49¼	51½	− 20½
AmMed 11s98	12.5	606	100⅜	85⅜	88	− 11⅝
AmMed 11¾99	11.6	743	101⅜	88½	101	+ 1
ATT 3⅞s90	4.0	7030	98	93⅝	98	+ 4½
ATT 3⅞90r	4.0	678	97 27/32	93½	97 25/32	...
ATT 5⅝95	6.4	4732	88⅝	79⅜	87¾	+ 6⅞
ATT 5½97	6.5	3421	85⅛	76	84¼	+ 6¾
ATT 6s00	7.2	9598	83¾	73⅞	83¼	+ 8⅞
ATT 5⅛01	6.8	4346	78¼	66¾	75½	+ 7⅛
ATT 8¾00	8.8	62985	101⅛	91½	99⅝	+ 7
ATT 7s01	7.9	20293	89½	79¾	88⅛	+ 8
ATT 7⅛03	8.1	20015	89½	78⅜	87⅝	+ 6⅞
ATT 8.80s05	8.9	33942	100⅜	90⅛	99⅛	+ 7¾
ATT 8⅝s07	8.8	22534	98¾	88¼	98½	+ 9¼
ATT 8⅝26	9.0	27405	98½	86	95⅜	+ 7⅜
Ames 10s95	10.1	246	100	95	99½	− ½
Ames 7½14	cv	1867	100	73½	74	...
Amoco 6s91	6.2	1892	98⅜	91½	96¼	+ 3¾
Amoco 6s98	6.9	1960	88½	80½	87	+ 1¼
Amoco 9.2s04	9.0	3534	102½	94½	101¾	+ 4¾
Amoco 8⅜05	8.7	2365	98½	88	96⅝	+ 6⅝
Amoco 7⅞07	8.5	2127	94⅝	82½	93	+ 8
Amoco 7⅞96	8.2	1250	98	89⅛	96	+ 5¼
Amoco 8⅝16	8.9	1575	102	87½	96¾	+ 6⅛
AmocoCda 7⅜13	6.1	27169	122	95½	120	+ 23⅝
AmocoCd na13½03	...	64	132	110	130	+ 10
Ancp 13⅞02f	cv	3284	104½	89	91	− 10½
Andarko 5¾12	cv	3026	117½	94½	116½	+ 16½
Andarko 6¼14	5.3	310	118	110¾	118	...
Anhr 8s96	8.4	1384	98⅞	89¼	95¼	+ 5⅛
Anhr 8⅝16	9.2	991	95	87	93⅝	+ 5⅝
Anhr 5.45s91	5.7	77	96¼	92¾	95⅞	+ 2¾
Anhr 6s92	6.4	409	94½	91⅝	93½	+ 1⅛
Anhr 7.95s99	8.2	159	97½	91½	97½	+ 3½
Anhr 9.20s05	9.2	451	101	93¼	99¾	+ 5½
Anhr 8.55s08	8.8	50	97¼	92	97¼	+ 5¼
Apch 7½12	cv	3901	128½	75¾	128½	+ 52¾
Aristr 8½90	8.6	156	99	97	99	+ 2⅛
Aristr 14¼94	12.3	111	116¾	111	115½	− 1¼
ArizP 7.45s02	8.8	1170	86⅞	76	84¼	+ 2½
ArizP 10⅝00	10.4	2630	104	98¼	102½	+ ⅜
Arml 5.9s92	6.6	136	98	89⅝	89⅝	+ 1⅝
Arml 13½94	12.6	1704	110⅜	104¾	107⅜	+ 1¾

NEW YORK BONDS

		Sales $1,000	High	Low	Last	Net Chg.
Arml 8.7s95	9.4	484	94¼	87½	93	+ 5½
Arml 9.2s00	10.0	2111	93¼	84	91¾	+ 7¾
Arml 8½01	10.0	919	88½	79⅞	85⅛	+ 4¾
ArCk 8s96	8.4	243	95	90¼	95	+ 3
ArRub 11½95	11.5	80	100	99⅝	100	− 6
ArmWld 9¾08	9.9	30	98¾	38	98¾	...
Asar 9¾2000	9.8	427	100½	95⅜	99¾	+ 3¼
AshO 6.15s92	6.5	534	94¾	90½	94¾	+ 2⅜
AshO 8.8s00	8.9	492	98⅝	91¾	98⅝	+ 6¼
AshO 8.2s02	8.9	210	93	86	92¼	+ 6¼
AshO 11.1s04	10.7	371	105	100	104	+ 2¼
AshO 6¾14	cv	863	100¾	92½	97½	...
AsCp 12⅛00	11.7	395	105	103	103½	− 6⅜
AsCp 13⅛00	12.5	168	110	105	105	− 2½
AsCp dc6s01	7.7	50	78	73	78	+ 4½
AsCp 11½90	11.4	60	102⅛	100¾	100¾	− 1¾
AscCp 11s90	10.9	188	102	100	101	...
AsCp 10½91	10.4	361	102½	100¾	101	− 3
AtalSos 7½01	cv	34	79¼	77	79¼	+ 1¼
Atchn 4s95st	5.3	81	78	70	75	+ 1
Atchn 4s95st r	5.2	91	77	71	77	...
Atchsn 4s95	5.1	1067	78⅞	70	78	+ 7½
Atchn 4s95r	5.2	524	78	70⅜	77	...
Athlne 11s93	11.1	175	101¼	96⅛	99½	+ 4⅞
Athlne 15⅝91	15.3	414	107	100	102	− 4
ARich 5⅝97	6.8	206	88	82⅛	82⅛	− 2⅞
ARich 8⅝00	8.7	758	99⅜	91	98⅞	+ 6⅛
ARich 7.7s00	8.4	455	95	84⅛	91¼	+ 3⅜
ARich 7¾03	8.3	529	94¾	82½	93	+ 7½
ARch dc7s91	7.2	2857	98	90¼	97¼	+ 4⅛
ARch 11s13	10.3	179	107¼	103⅛	107¼	+ 3
ARch 11⅛15	10.0	255	110⅞	104¼	110⅞	+ 5⅞
ARch 10⅜95	9.7	4664	108⅞	101	107½	+ 4½
ARch 10⅞05	9.5	1170	117	103⅝	114¾	+ 7½
ARch 10½95	9.9	4758	106¾	100½	106½	+ 4½
ARch 9½96	9.3	7074	103½	96¾	102⅜	+ 2⅝
ARch 9¼93	9.1	3992	105	96½	101⅜	+ 3
ARch 9⅞16	8.9	736	113⅜	99	111	+ 11¼
ARch 9⅛11	8.8	970	105	92⅛	103⅝	+ 8⅛
Avaln 7s92f	cv	58	88½	87	88½	+ 2½
AvcoF 7⅝97	8.1	300	100	87½	94¼	+ 4¼
AvcoF 8.35s	8.8	220	98	88¾	95	+ 4½
AvcoF 9⅜93	9.4	11	100½	96½	99⅜	− ⅛
AvcoF 9⅛98	9.4	314	100	93½	97⅜	+ 2
AvcoF 9⅜98	9.4	115	99⅝	92⅜	99⅝	+ 5⅜
AvcoF 9¾99	9.8	75	101⅞	97½	100	+ 2
Avnet 8s13	cv	6056	95½	81	95	+ 13¾
Avnet 6s12	cv	3698	92¼	75	90	+ 13
-B-						
BPNA 9¼16	9.5	166	102	90	97⅝	+ 7½
BPNA 10s00	9.9	333	103⅞	97⅛	101	+ 1½
BPNA 9¼01	9.2	810	100½	95	100½	+ 2⅜
BRE 9½00	cv	5	165	165	165	− 1
BRE 9½08	cv	4900	105½	96¾	99	− 1½
BakrHgh 9s08	9.4	870	97	87¼	95½	+ 8¼
BakrHgh 9½06	cv	4862	104	91	104	+ 11½
Bally 6s98	cv	10021	105	59½	66⅜	− 26⅛
Bally 10s06	cv	17901	105	80	84	− 10⅝
B O 4¼95	5.4	123	79	74	79	+ 5
B O 4¼95r	5.5	11	76¾	73½	76¾	...
BalGE 3¼90	3.4	113	95 21/32	90	95 21/32	+3 29/32
BalGE 3¼90r	3.6	20	90⅛	90⅛	90⅛	...
BalGE 4s93	4.7	78	87	80⅜	85½	+ 3⅞
BalGE 8⅜06	8.9	531	96	84⅞	94	+ 4
BalGE 8¼07	8.7	682	95⅝	84½	94¾	+ 9½
BalGE 9⅜08	9.2	1607	103⅞	94⅝	102	+ 6⅞
BalGE 9⅛16	9.2	154	99½	90½	99	+ 5¼
BncFla 9s03	cv	1744	84	73½	75	− 4¾
BkNE 8.85s99	10.9	1698	99¾	70⅛	81	− 12
Banka 7⅞03	9.2	2477	89½	78½	85¼	+ 5¼
Banka 8⅞05	9.3	4645	97¼	85¼	95⅛	+ 8⅝
Banka 8¾01	9.5	3457	97	86⅝	91⅞	+ 4⅞
Bkam 8.35s07	9.2	3672	92⅝	81⅛	91	+ 9⅝
Bkam zr90s	...	4540	94	84⅜	93 29/32	+9 25/32
Bkam zr92s	...	14373	78½	67⅝	77⅞	+ 9⅜
Bkam zr91s	...	1700	91	80¾	90⅝	+ 10¼
Bkam zr93s	...	11596	74¼	63¾	73½	+ 9¼
BkAm 8½95t	8.7	165	99¼	95⅝	97½	− 1⅛

		Sales $1,000	High	Low	Last	Net Chg.
BkAm 8⅛96t	8.3	143	99⅜	94	97½	+ 1⅛
BkAm 9.6s94	9.6	220	99¾	97⅜	99¾	+ 4¾
BnkTr 8⅛99	8.7	1783	95½	85½	93½	+ 3½
BnkTr 8⅝02	9.0	1485	97¼	86¼	95⅞	+ 6⅛
Baner 12¼96	13.3	241	99	92	92	− 4⅛
Baner 13⅛06	13.8	321	97	93½	95	...
Baner 12s01	13.3	50	95	90¼	90¼	− 1¾
Baner 13s07	14.0	230	94¼	91½	93	...
BarcA 7.95s92	8.1	176	100	93¼	98	+ 3
BarcA 8¾97	8.9	173	100	90½	98¼	+ 6¼
BarcA zr90s	...	2401	93 9/16	84⅜	93½	+ 9
BarcNA 11⅝03	10.3	32	113	105¼	113	+ 7¾
Barnt 8½99	8.9	485	96⅞	87½	95	+ 6⅜
BaxL 4⅜s91	cv	32	250	240	250	− 10
BaxL 4¾s01	cv	15	215	160	215	+ 64⅜
BearStr 8⅛97	9.1	127	93¼	89½	89½	− 2¼
BellCn 8¾06	9.0	1449	98	88⅛	97½	+ 5¾
BellCn 9s08	8.9	1187	100¾	90⅛	100¾	+ 6¾
BellCn 13⅜10	10.7	122	124¾	118	124¾	+ 1¼
BellPa 8⅝06	8.8	3199	99¾	88½	98	+ 7
BellPa 7⅛12	8.5	2484	86½	72½	84¼	+ 9⅛
BellPa 7½13	8.6	1776	88½	76⅛	87	+ 8¼
BellPa 9⅝14	9.3	5192	105½	92⅝	103	+ 4⅛
BellPa 8¾15	9.0	1582	100½	87⅞	97⅝	+ 6⅞
BellPa 8⅛17	8.7	1641	95⅜	83⅛	93½	+ 8⅝
BellPa 9¼19	9.2	2248	101½	92½	101	+ 6¾
BenCp 7½96	8.3	510	92¾	83½	90	+ 4½
BenCp 7.45s00	8.6	236	88	78	87⅛	+ 5½
BenCp 7½02	8.6	55	87	78	87	+ 7¼
BenCp 7½98	8.2	249	91¼	80¼	91¼	+ 7
BenCp 8s01	8.1	10	99	99	99	− ⅜
BenCp 8.3s03	9.0	176	92½	84	92½	+ 8¼
BenCp 8.4s07	9.3	479	92⅝	80¼	90¼	+ 6¼
BenCp 8.4s08	8.5	370	100¼	98	99	− ⅛
BenCp 9s05	9.5	98	95	86½	95	+ 7
BenCp 12⅞13	10.7	156	121⅝	116	120	− 2
BenCp 12¾13	11.1	192	115	110	114⅜	+ 2⅞
BenCp 12½93	11.5	15	108⅝	108⅛	108⅝	+ ⅞
BenCp 12.45s94	11.4	90	109½	109	109	+ ⅞
BenCp 12.60s94	11.4	50	111	108	111	+ 1½
BenCp 9⅜90	9.4	21	99⅜	98¾	99⅜	+ ¼
BrkHa zr04	...	9254	45	41½	44½	...
BstBy 10s97	11.2	273	93	86	89	− 6
BestPr 12⅝96	13.0	11497	103½	88	97	− ⅞
BethSt 4½90	4.5	3526	100	94⅝	99⅜	+ 4⅝
BethSt 5.4s92	5.8	1918	92½	86½	92½	+ 6¼
BethSt 6⅞99	8.8	1949	79½	72	77¾	+ 5⅝
BethSt 9s00	10.1	5209	93	83½	89	+ 4
BethSt 8.45s05	10.6	12262	85½	75⅜	80	+ 3¼
BethSt 8⅜01	10.1	2264	88	78	83	+ 5
Bevrly 7⅝03	cv	11104	66	53¾	55½	+ 2
Beverly zr03	...	2292	32⅞	28	32⅞	+ 5
BlkD 8⅜97	9.1	200	97¼	87⅛	92½	+ 3½
BlkBst zr04	...	416	31⅝	27½	27¾	...
Boeing 8⅜96	8.4	1332	101½	92½	99⅛	+ 5⅜
BoisC 13⅛94	12.4	40	106	106	106	+ 4⅞
BoisC 11⅞93	11.0	4	108	108	108	− ¼
BoisC 7s16	cv	2977	111	100½	107½	+ 3½
BoltBer 6s12	cv	7749	64⅛	45½	48	− 10½
Bordn 10¼95	9.6	1497	106⅝	100	106⅝	+ 2⅜
Bordn 8⅜16	9.3	202	91	83	90⅛	+ 7½
BorW 7⅞s91	8.0	177	98⅞	96⅛	98⅛	− ⅜
BorW 7½s93	7.9	96	96½	93⅜	95½	+ 1⅞
BorgW dc6s01	8.0	150	76½	68	74¾	+ 5
BorW 5½s92	6.2	350	92½	87¼	88⅝	+ 2⅛
BosE 9¼07	9.6	283	98¾	89	96⅝	+ 5⅛
Bowatr 12⅜15	11.1	20	111	111	111	− 2
BrkUn 4⅝90	4.8	20	96 13/16	94⅞	96 13/16	+3 11/16
BrkUn 6¼92	6.6	222	95¼	90½	95	+ 4⅝
BrkUn 9⅛95	9.1	625	102	95½	100	+ 3½
BrkUn 7⅞97	8.3	303	94¾	87¾	94½	+ 5
BrkUn 8¾99	8.8	317	99½	92¼	99½	+ 4
BrkUn 9⅝96	9.5	332	103½	98	101	+ 1
BwnSh 9¼05	cv	2072	99	86¼	91½	− 1
BrnGp 7⅜98	7.6	32	100½	97½	97½	...
BrnGp 9⅞00	10.0	291	101	97	99	+ ⅞
BwnFer 6¼12	cv	24702	115	90¾	108½	+ 17¼
Bulova 6s90	cv	125	100	95	97	+ 3
BurNo 8½96	8.7	722	98⅞	93	98	+ 3⅛
BurNo 8.6s99	8.8	406	98¾	92	98⅛	+ 5⅛

		Sales $1,000	High	Low	Last	Net Chg.
BurNo 11⅝15	10.9	140	108⅞	100⅛	107	+ 3
BurNo 9⅝96	9.5	2079	102	96	101⅝	+ 4⅛
BurNo 9s16	9.6	565	95	89¾	93¾	– ¼
BurNo 9¼06	9.3	275	100	91	100	+ 6
BurNo 10s97	9.8	377	103¼	98½	102¼	+ 2⅜
BusInd 5½07	cv	1835	89	65½	66½	– 15½
-C-						
CBI 7s11	...	2717	107	93	100	+ 6½
CBS 10⅞95	10.5	9453	105⅞	100¾	103⅞	+ 1¼
CIGNA 8.2s10	cv	10262	107	91¾	101	+ 8¼
CIT 9½95	9.5	2565	101⅝	94⅝	100⅛	+ 1⅞
CIT 8⅜s01	9.3	342	94	82	90½	+ 4½
CIT 9s91	9.0	798	101⅛	94¾	100	+ 2¼
CIT 8.8s93	8.9	975	100	94	98⅝	+ 2⅜
CIT 8¾08	9.5	580	97	84⅝	92	+ 7
CIT 9.85s04	9.8	1187	101¾	93	100¼	+ 5¾
CIT 9⅝09	9.6	826	100½	89½	100	+ 7
CIT 11½05	11.2	1808	103⅝	101	102⅝	– ⅞
CNA 8½95	8.7	648	99¾	89	97¾	+ 4¾
CSX 9½16	9.6	678	99	88½	98⅞	+ 7⅜
CUC zr96	cv	2828	53	46¼	48	...
CamrIr 7s12	cv	124	103	100	102	...
CPc4s perp	8.3	3374	50¼	40⅜	48¼	+ 6¼
CPC 4sr	8.3	1605	50	40⅜	48⅜	...
CapHd 12¾06	11.8	405	111	107½	107⅞	– 2⅛
Carolco 14s93	14.9	2305	98	88½	93¾	+ 64¼
CaroCl 4½90	4.6	2	97 15/16	97 15/16	97 15/16	...
CaroFrt 6¼11	cv	3247	84½	68	72¼	– 1¾
CarPL 7¾02	8.6	1024	93½	81⅝	90⅛	+ 7⅛
CaroT 9⅛00	9.2	468	101	91¾	99½	+ 6
CaroT 7¾01	8.2	371	94⅞	83	94⅞	+ 9⅜
CaroT 8.1s03	8.9	728	93½	83⅜	91⅜	+ 3⅜
CaroT 9s08	9.1	225	99	91	99	+ 5½
CartHaw 12¼96	13.6	6690	99⅜	88½	89⅞	– 7⅝
CartHaw 12½02	14.5	8928	97⅜	84¼	86⅜	– 7⅝
CastlC 8½97	8.8	42	96¾	96½	96½	+ 4½
CatTr 5.3s92	5.7	119	93⅛	88¾	93⅛	+ 3⅝
Caterp 6⅞92	7.3	15	94⅝	93⅞	94¼	+ 1⅛
Caterp 8.6s99	8.7	229	98½	90	98½	+ 5⅞
Caterp 8¾99	9.1	154	97¾	93	96¼	+ 2½
Caterp 8s01	8.3	237	96¾	84	96¾	+ 9⅝
Cenco 5s96	cv	102	69½	69	69½	+ ½
Cenco 4¾97	cv	99	59	57	57	+ ½
Centel 8.1s96	8.4	400	100	88	95⅞	+ 6⅞
CtrlTel 8s96	8.3	414	100	87½	96⅞	+ 7⅞
CATS zr11-91	...	138	83½	76⅛	83½	+ 7¼
CATS zr05-92	...	33	72½	71	72½	+ 1⅝
CATS zr11-94	...	87	65⅝	59	65⅝	+ 10⅝
CATS zr05-95	...	109	67½	56⅝	67½	+ 11½
CATS zr11-96	...	92	55⅛	50½	54	+ 6
CATS zr05-97	...	19	49	44	49	+ 4
CATS zr05-98	...	116	48	40	44¼	– ¾
CATS zr11-99	...	140	43⅞	36⅛	40⅜	+ 2⅜
CATS zr11-01	...	84	37	29¼	33¼	+ ¼
CATS zr11-02	...	22	30	27	30	...
CATS zr11-03	...	96	29	27¼	28⅛	+ ⅛
CATS zr2006-11	...	4220	25⅝	19¾	25½	+ 5⅛
ChSp 5⅞s92	6.0	54	98¼	96¼	97⅝	– 2¼
Champ 6½11	cv	5405	111½	96½	100	– 5½
ChartC 12s99	12.7	3585	94⅞	91	94¼	+ 1½
ChsCp 8.90s99t	9.2	1261	101⅞	96½	96½	– 2
ChsCp 9.65s09t	10.6	966	93	88	91	+ 3
ChsCp 7⅜94	7.8	1926	96	87⅝	94½	+ 5⅞
vjChmtrn 9s94f	...	4414	95½	68	68½	– 23½
ChNY 8.4s99	9.5	645	95	88	88	+ ⅞
ChNY 8¼02	9.3	818	92⅞	83¼	88⅞	+ 3⅞
ChNY 9.9s04t	10.5	361	97	93½	94	+ 3
C&O 4½92	4.9	318	91½	85⅜	91⅛	+ 5
C O 4½92r	5.0	111	91	88	90⅞	...
CPoM 7¼12	8.6	1071	85⅝	74¾	84¾	+ 5¾
CPoM 8⅞09	9.1	1590	99⅝	88	97¼	+ 6¼
CPoM 9s18	9.0	924	99⅝	88⅛	99⅝	+ 9¼
CPom 11¼25	10.4	45	108¾	107⅛	108⅛	...
CPoV 7¼12	8.7	568	85½	76⅝	83¾	+ 5¾
CPoV 8⅝09	9.0	1829	100	87⅛	96¼	+ 7¾
CPoV 9¼15	9.2	1223	102	91	101	+ 7¾
CPoV 9½19	9.4	812	104	94¼	101	+ 6
CPoWas 7¾	9.1	871	89	79	85½	+ 5½

		Sales $1,000	High	Low	Last	Net Chg.
CPWV 7¼13	8.7	316	85	76¼	83⅛	+ 5⅛
CPoWV 9s15	9.4	907	99¼	87¾	96⅛	+ 6
CPWV 9¼19	9.3	626	104	92	100	+ 7
ChvrnC 12s94	11.4	2294	108½	103¼	105	– ⅝
ChvrnC 10¾95	10.3	5396	106	101	104	+ 1⅝
ChvrnC 7⅞97	8.4	2189	96¼	86½	93⅜	+ 3⅜
ChvrnC 9¾17	9.6	440	104⅞	98	102	+ 4
Chvrn 5¾92	6.2	2108	93⅞	87⅜	93¼	+ 3½
Chvrn 7s96	7.6	2115	93⅛	86⅞	91⅞	+ 4⅛
Chvrn 8¾05	9.0	3237	99¾	88¾	97⅝	+ 5⅞
Chvrn 8½95	8.6	3303	100	93	98⅞	+ 3⅞
Chvrn 8¾96	8.8	7250	101½	93	99½	+ 4½
Chvrn 9⅜16	9.3	2845	103⅝	92	100½	+ 5¾
ChiBQ 3s90	3.1	139	96 9/16	93	96	+ 2⅜
CGtW 4½38f	...	66	50	45	46	– 8
ChckFul 7s12	cv	3134	95	68	69½	– 15¾
ChCft 13s99	12.7	270	104	100¼	102	+ 2
Chrysl 8⅞95	8.9	3020	100⅞	97	99½	+ ½
Chryslr 8s98	8.6	3159	96	87¼	92⅞	+ 3⅜
Chryslr 12¾92	12.0	3204	109⅜	104¾	106¼	– 1¾
Chryslr 13s97	11.6	1659	116¾	109½	112	+ ½
Chryslr 12s15	11.3	4379	110	104	106¼	– ⅛
Chryslr 9.6s94	9.6	2565	102⅞	96⅜	99⅞	+ 1⅛
Chryslr 10.95s17	10.9	1616	108½	99	100¼	– ¼
Chryslr 10.4s99	10.1	623	105	98⅛	103	+ 1
ChryF 8.35s91	8.6	1096	101	96½	97	– 2⅝
ChryF 7.7s92	7.9	675	100	94⅛	97⅞	+ ⅞
ChryF 8.95s97t	9.1	60	99	92¾	98	+ 3
ChryF zr90	...	1122	91¾	82¾	91½	+ 7⅞
ChryF 13¼99	11.7	10	113½	113½	113½	– 4½
ChryF 12¾99	10.0	42	128	106	128	+ 13⅝
ChryF 11¾90	11.7	2220	102	100⅛	100⅛	– 1½
ChryF 12s92	11.3	1044	107½	104	106	...
ChryF 12⅛90	12.1	2165	102⅞	99 17/32	99 31/32	– 2 29/32
ChryF flt95	8.8	10	99¾	99	99¾	+ ¾
ChryF 10.6s90	10.5	4199	102¾	99½	100⅝	– ¼
ChryF 9¾90D	9.7	8368	102	98½	100½	+ ⅝
ChryF 9¾90F	9.7	3722	100¾	98 19/32	100⅛	+ ⅛
ChryF 9⅜91	9.4	2702	101⅛	96¼	100	+ ½
ChryF 9¼91	9.4	2577	101¾	97	98⅞	– ⅛
ChryF 7¼89	7.3	1058	99½	98¼	99⅜	+ 1/32
ChryF 9.30s94	9.5	745	100½	95	98¼	+ 1
ChryF 8⅜97	9.4	310	97½	86⅜	89¼	– 2½
ChryF 7⅞91	8.0	1441	98¼	93⅛	98	+ 3¾
ChryF 8⅛94	8.6	3787	97½	90	95	+ 3⅛
ChryF 7⅝92	7.9	1008	98¼	92	96¼	+ 2¼
ChryF 9½92	9.4	316	101½	96	101½	+ ½
ChryF 8¾92	8.8	416	100	97½	99¾	+ 1
ChryF 8½18	8.7	35	98½	98	98	...
CirclK 8¼05	cv	13059	122	34	36¾	– 63½
CirclK 12¾97	22.2	4310	105½	44	57½	– 48
CirclK 7¼06	cv	12162	96	39	42	– 52¾
CirclK 13s97	29.9	13605	102	40⅛	43½	– 57⅛
Citicp 5¾00	cv	41	155	125	153¼	+ 31¼
Citicp 8.45s07	9.2	6328	96½	84⅛	92	+ 5
Citicp 8.80s07	9.8	2305	93	82⅛	89⅝	+ 6½
Citicp 8.80s98t	9.0	1779	99	93	98	+ 2⅜
Citicp 8.8s04t	9.2	1791	98	94	96	+ 1¾
Citicp 11⅞95	11.8	9557	103¾	100¼	100½	– 4
CitiPP 12½96	cv	308	106	101¾	102¾	– 4¾
Clmt zrD89	...	28	98	91⅛	98	+ 8
Clmt zrD90	...	110	91¼	80¾	91¼	+ 10⅛
Clmt zrD91	...	267	83¼	74⅛	82¾	+ 9⅛
Clmt zrD92	...	311	77	66⅛	76¾	+ 10⅛
Clmt zrD93	...	391	70	59½	70	+ 9½
Clmt zr94	...	134	64	55¼	63⅜	...
Clmt zrD95	...	24	57½	49	57½	...
Clmt zrD96	...	114	53½	42⅝	52¾	+ 6⅞
Clmt zrD97	...	264	50	40½	50	+ 10
Clmt zrD98	...	256	44½	34¾	44½	+ 8½
Clmt zrD99	...	242	41	32¾	39⅝	+ 6⅜
Clmt zrD00	...	141	37¾	28⅛	36⅞	+ 8⅞
Clmt zrD01	...	163	36	26	33	+ 5¼
Clmt zrD02	...	408	31	23	30¼	+ 7⅞
Clmt zrD03	...	248	28	21½	28	+ 7¾
Clmt zrD04	...	393	27	20⅛	25¼	+ 4¾
Clmt zrD05	...	278	23½	18¼	22½	+ 4¾
Clmt zrD06	...	374	22	15½	20	+ 6
Clmt zrD07	...	119	20¾	14½	20¾	+ 7½
ClkEq 9⅝99	9.7	89	99⅞	93	99½	+ 4⅜

NEW YORK BONDS

		Sales $1,000	High	Low	Last	Net Chg.
ClkEq 7.85s91	8.0	541	98⅝	93	98⅝	+ 5½
Claytn 7¾01	cv	1553	105	94¼	98	+ 4
Claytn 6s07	cv	1034	86	75	83	+ 5½
ClevEl 7⅛90	7.2	760	99 23/32	96½	99 17/32	+2 17/32
ClevEl 3⅞93	4.5	267	86	77⅝	86	+ 6
ClevEl 4⅜94	5.5	41	80⅜	77	80¼	+ 3⅞
ClevEl 8⅜91	8.5	1384	99½	94½	99	+ 3½
ClevEl 8¾05	9.3	1297	95¾	84⅜	94¼	+ 8¼
ClevEl 9¼09	9.6	1536	97⅞	86¾	96¼	+ 7¾
ClevEl 9.85s10	9.8	2258	101½	92⅜	100⅜	+ 7¼
ClevEl 8⅜11	9.4	1963	90⅞	80½	89	+ 7¾
ClevEl 8⅜12	9.4	1184	91¼	80¼	89	+ 6⅜
Coastl 11¼96	10.7	20898	105½	96	105	+ 5
Coastl 11¾06	11.2	16726	107⅜	96½	104¾	+ 3½
Coastl 8.48s91	8.6	26486	98½	93	98⅛	+ 2⅞
Coastl 11⅛98	10.9	15208	104	95⅜	102	+ 4⅛
Coastl 10¼04	10.0	165	102¾	101¾	102½	...
Collnt 8½91	8.7	75	97⅜	96⅜	97⅜	+ ⅜
ColUte 13s02	11.8	20	110	110	110	− 5
ColuG 9s94	9.0	1100	101⅛	93	100	+ 2⅛
ColuG 8¾95	8.9	671	99½	92¼	98½	+ 1½
ColuG 9⅛95	9.2	854	102	95⅝	99½	+ 1⅜
ColuG 8⅜96	8.7	579	98½	93	96⅛	+ 2⅞
ColuG 8¼96	8.7	379	97⅛	92⅛	95¼	+ ⅝
ColuG 7½97M	8.2	257	93	86⅜	91⅞	+ ⅞
ColuG 7½97J	8.2	228	93	87⅝	91¾	+ 1¼
ColuG 7½97O	8.2	145	93	88¼	91⅜	+ 1⅛
ColuG 7½98	8.3	305	97	90	90½	+ ⅛
ColuG 9⅞99	9.8	101	101¾	96⅞	101¼	+ 1¾
ColuG 10⅛95	9.9	457	103	96⅝	102	+ 2
ColuG 9⅛96	9.1	275	100¼	97½	100	+ 1⅛
ColuG 10¼99	10.1	138	102⅞	98½	101¼	+ 1¼
ColuG 9s93	8.9	289	101	94	101	+ 4⅞
ColuG 10½12	10.1	126	104½	98	104⅛	+ 4⅛
ColPic 9¾98	9.5	132	103	95	103	+ 6
ColPic 10⅝18	10.0	269	106	95	106	+ 9
CEn 7.45s96	8.2	125	92⅜	89⅜	90¾	+ 6⅝
Cmdis 9.65s02	9.9	2758	98¾	87⅛	97¼	+ 10
Cmdis 10s94	9.9	565	101½	94½	101½	+ 7½
CmlCr 8¾91	8.8	1131	101	95¾	99½	+ 3⅝
CmlCr 7¾92	7.9	1069	98⅛	92½	97⅞	+ 3⅞
CmlCr 7¾93	8.0	661	97¼	89⅝	96½	+ 4⅜
CmlSo 4½91	cv	137	92⅛	86¾	92⅛	+ 5⅞
CmwE 2¾99	4.1	5	67¾	66⅜	67¾	+ 3¼
CmwE 2⅞01	4.2	17	69⅛	68¼	69⅛	...
CmwE 7⅝03F	8.8	1390	89⅝	80	87⅛	+ 6⅛
CmwE 7⅝03J	8.9	591	87⅝	80	86⅛	+ 5⅝
CmwE 8s03	9.0	2277	93	82	89	+ 4⅞
CmwE 8¾05	9.3	2479	96⅜	86	94⅛	+ 5½
CmwE 9⅜04	9.4	3682	102¾	92	100	+ 7
CmwE 8⅛07J	9.3	1724	92	81¼	87½	+ 5¼
CmwE 8⅛07D	9.2	1431	91¼	80¾	88¾	+ 5¼
CmwE 8¼07	9.0	3190	92¾	81⅜	91⅞	+ 9⅝
CmwE 9⅛08	9.4	4723	100¼	88	97	+ 7⅜
CmwE 15⅜00	13.8	600	118	106½	111⅝	+ 3⅝
CmwE 11⅛10	10.4	1503	107½	101½	106¾	+ 3¾
CmwE 10⅝95	10.2	749	105⅜	100	104	+ 1¼
CmwE 11¾15	10.8	998	110½	104⅝	109	+ 3⅝
Compq 6½13	cv	15956	171¾	112⅛	131	+ 19
Conoco 9⅜09	9.4	535	101¾	94⅜	100¼	+ 4⅝
Consec 12½96	14.7	709	85½	81	85	...
Consec 12¾97	15.0	2236	86	79	85	...
ConEd 4¾90	4.8	90	98	93⅛	98	+ 5
ConEd 4¾90r	4.9	10	97	97	97	...
ConEd 5s90	5.2	634	97½	91½	96 23/32	+ 3 7/32
ConEd 5s90r	5.2	90	96¾	92⅜	96¾	...
ConEd 4¾91	5.0	413	95½	88⅝	95½	+ 5
ConEd 4¾91r	5.1	30	92¼	91¾	92¼	...
ConEd 4⅝91	4.9	630	94⅛	88¼	94⅛	+ 5⅝
ConEd 4⅝91r	5.0	52	91⅝	88¼	91⅝	...
ConEd 4⅜92V	4.8	756	91¾	85⅞	91½	+ 5¾
ConEd 4⅜92v r	4.8	115	90½	85⅜	90½	...
ConEd 4⅜92W	4.8	721	90⅝	84¾	90⅝	+ 6
ConEd 4⅜92w r	4.9	58	89¾	84⅛	89¾	+ 5⅜
ConEd 4⅝93	5.3	1319	90	81⅝	87¼	+ 5¼
ConEd 9⅜00	9.2	5457	102⅝	94⅛	101⅝	+ 5⅛
ConEd 7.9s01	8.5	3055	95½	83¾	92⅝	+ 6⅝
ConEd 7.9s02	8.5	2457	94½	83½	93	+ 7⅞
ConEd 7¾03	8.4	2435	93	82¾	92¼	+ 8¾
ConEd 8.4s03	8.8	2868	98½	86½	96	+ 7
ConEd 9⅛04	9.1	4777	101¾	92⅛	100¼	+ 6⅝
CnNG 4¾90	5.1	35	94	92⅜	92⅞	+ ¾
CnNG 6⅛92	6.6	292	95⅞	89¾	93	+ 2⅜
CnNG 7¾94	8.1	375	97⅜	91¾	96⅛	+ 1⅜
CnNG 8¼94	8.4	465	99	94	98⅛	+ 2⅞
CnNG 9s95	9.0	705	101½	95	100	+ 3¼
CnNG 7⅞95	8.2	378	97	90½	96¼	+ 3⅝
CnNG M 8⅜96	8.6	310	99	90½	97⅝	+ 3¼
CnNG 7¾96	8.1	143	96	90⅞	95½	+ 3¼
CnNG 7⅝97	8.0	83	98	90⅛	95⅞	+ 5⅞
CnNG 9⅜97	9.1	65	105	102⅛	103	...
CnNG 7¾98	8.2	124	94⅞	89⅜	94⅞	+ 5¾
CnNG 8⅝99	8.8	127	100	92	98⅛	+ 4⅜
CnNG 9¼95	9.2	864	103	95¼	100½	+ 1½
CnNGS 8⅜96	8.5	247	98⅛	92½	98⅛	+ 2¼
CnNG 8⅛97	8.4	373	100	90	97	+ 5½
CnNG 7⅝96	8.0	267	95	88	94¾	+ 4⅛
ConNG 9⅛92	9.0	455	101½	96½	101⅜	+ 2⅜
ConNG 8¾99	8.7	89	101	99⅜	101	...
ConNG 8¾19	8.9	5	98¾	98¾	98¾	...
CnPw 4⅝90	4.8	157	95½	90⅛	95½	+ 4
CnPw 4⅝90r	4.9	35	95¼	91¼	95¼	...
CnPw 4⅝91	5.0	316	92¾	87⅝	92¾	+ 6⅝
CnPw 5⅞96	7.0	1191	85	75¾	83⅜	+ 6¼
CnPw 6⅞98	7.9	1214	86⅝	78⅝	86⅝	+ 7⅝
CnPw 6⅝98	7.8	622	85¼	76	84¾	+ 6
CnPw 7⅝99	8.5	1887	91¼	81½	90	+ 7⅜
CnPw 8⅝00	9.2	1155	96	86	94¼	+ 6¼
CnPw 8⅛01	9.0	1034	91⅞	84½	90½	+ 5
CnPw 7½01	8.5	1108	88½	80	88⅛	+ 7⅜
CnPw 7½02J	8.7	1043	88⅝	78⅝	86⅜	+ 6⅜
CnPw 7½02O	8.5	923	88½	78½	87⅞	+ 6½
CnPw 8⅝03	9.2	1304	95⅝	85½	93⅞	+ 6¾
CnPw 9¾06	9.8	2377	103½	92⅝	99½	+ 3½
CnPw 9s06	9.5	1199	98	87⅛	95⅛	+ 5⅞
CnPw 8⅞07	9.3	885	96⅛	87	95¾	+ 7⅜
CnPw 8⅝07	9.1	1193	94½	84¼	94½	+ 7¼
CnPw 9s08	9.3	1618	97⅝	88	96⅝	+ 8⅛
Contel 9⅞11	10.9	10	90¼	89¼	90¼	...
viCtlInf 9s06f	cv	10739	36	5¼	5¾	− 28¾
CtlOil 4½91	4.8	105	93⅝	90¼	93⅝	+ 3⅝
CtlOil 7½99	8.1	345	93¼	85⅝	92⅞	+ 5½
CtlOil 9⅛s99	9.1	496	101	95	99⅞	+ 3⅞
CtlOil 8⅞01	9.0	265	99½	93	99⅛	+ 4⅞
CtlDat 12¾91	12.7	15640	103	95½	100½	− 1
CtlDat 8½11	cv	4292	98	84½	85	− 11
CoopCo 10⅝05	cv	14541	75½	57	67	+ 4
Copwld 7⅞01	8.8	74	92¼	89⅝	89¾	+ 1⅝
Copwld 9.92s08	cv	1990	109	97⅜	100	...
CrnPd 5¾92	6.2	499	93⅛	86¾	92⅛	+ 4⅝
Cornl 7¾98	8.6	152	94	84¼	90	+ 1
CntryCr 7s11	cv	1141	92½	74	84	+ 9
Crane 6½92	6.9	249	96	91½	94⅝	+ 1½
Crane 7s93	7.6	577	94	86⅜	92⅛	+ 5
Crane 7s94	7.7	3462	94	84½	91¼	+ 4¼
CrayRs 6⅛11	cv	9285	99½	63	72	− 23
Crestr 7¾97	8.3	347	94	85¼	93⅛	+ 6⅝
Crstwd 6¼91	cv	597	94¼	90¾	93⅛	+ 1⅛
Crstwd 7s00	cv	72	94⅜	93¾	94¼	+ ⅜
CritAc 12.3s13	11.9	211	105	100⅜	103	− ½
CritAc 12s13	11.8	82	103⅜	100	101⅜	− 1⅛
CritAc 12.15s13	12.1	105	103½	99¾	100¾	− 1⅜
CritAc 11⅞14	...	92	107	100⅛	107	+ 5
CritAc 12¼14	11.7	110	105	100⅛	105	+ 1½
CritAc 12.35s14	12.1	271	104½	100	101⅞	− 1⅛
CritAc 13.30s14	12.8	278	108¾	100	104	+ ⅜
CritAc 13.10s14	12.7	93	105½	103	103⅛	− 1⅛
CritAc 13⅛14	12.7	133	105½	102⅛	103⅛	− ⅞
CritAc 11½15	11.3	235	105⅞	100½	102⅛	+ ⅛
CritAc 11¼15	10.8	240	104¼	100	104¼	+ 1⅞
CritAc 11.85s15	11.3	196	106	100	104¾	+ 1¾
CrocN 8.6s02	9.1	570	97	86	94	+ 3
Culb 11½05	11.5	234	100⅝	99	100⅜	− 3⅝
CumE 8⅞95	9.2	258	98¼	94	96½	+ 1½
CumE zr05	...	5427	35	28	29	− 3
-D-						
DCS 12.20s94	11.9	232	109¾	101¼	102½	− ⅛
Dana 9s2000	9.4	400	96⅝	90½	96	+ 4
Dana 8⅞08	9.8	350	91⅞	87	90¼	− ½

NEW YORK BONDS

		Sales $1,000	High	Low	Last	Net Chg.
Dana dc5⅞06	cv	10111	91¾	76	79	− 11¼
DataDes 8½08	cv	1645	92½	59¾	70½	− 23½
DatGen 8⅜02	10.2	205	87¾	82	82	− 2⅛
Datpnt 8⅞06	cv	8768	58	30⅛	32¾	− 19¾
DaytH 10¾13	10.2	2625	107	99	105⅜	+ 5⅛
DaytP 8⅛01	8.8	328	92¼	82⅝	92¼	+ 6⅝
DaytP 8s03	8.7	304	93¼	81⅛	92	+ 7½
DaytP 10.7s05	10.3	219	103⅞	100	103⅞	+ 4⅞
DaytP 8¾06	9.2	153	95⅝	86⅞	95⅝	+ 6⅛
DaytP 8½07	9.2	155	93	84⅝	92½	+ 7
DaytP 9s16	10.2	62	93	88	88	− 2
DaytP 8⅞16	9.4	57	94⅞	82⅜	94⅞	+ 4⅜
Deere 8.45s	8.9	249	97½	88¼	94⅞	+ 3⅛
Deere 5½01	cv	143	183	139	183	+ 39
Deere 8s02	8.5	92	98	92¼	94⅝	− 2¾
DeereCa 9.35s03	9.6	309	99¾	93⅛	97¾	+ 3
DelPw 6⅜97	7.3	183	87	75¼	87	+ 7¼
DelPw 6⅜97r	7.6	28	84	81	84	...
DlmP 4⅝94	6.1	15	77	76	76	− 2¾
Denn 8¼96	8.5	143	97	92⅝	97	+ 4
DetEd 6s96	7.2	1024	85	75⅜	83⅝	+ 7⅞
DetEd 6.4s98	7.6	579	83¾	75½	83¾	+ 8⅜
DetEd 9s99	9.1	2092	100	89¾	99	+ 7¼
DetEd 9.15s00	9.2	1913	99½	91	99½	+ 7⅝
DetEd 8.15s00	8.7	1203	93¾	84	93¼	+ 8
DetEd 8⅛01	8.8	1777	92½	82¼	92½	+ 8½
DetEd 7⅜01	8.5	1017	87½	78⅛	87	+ 8¾
DetEd 7½03	8.6	1288	87⅛	78	87	+ 7¼
DetEd 9⅞04	9.9	3200	102⅞	94⅛	100⅛	+ 4⅞
DetEd 11⅞00	11.3	1120	108	100½	105	+ 2
DetEd 10⅝06	10.3	979	106	98⅞	103¼	+ 1½
DiaSTel 7s08	8.9	85	80	74	79	+ 3⅜
Divers 10½91	10.8	125	99⅜	96½	97½	− ½
DmBk 7¾96	8.4	197	92⅛	83	92⅛	+ 4⅛
Dow 6.70s98	7.4	725	95	83½	90¼	+ 6¼
Dow 7.75s99	8.1	791	95⅞	87½	95⅝	+ 5⅞
Dow 8⅞2000	8.8	1203	100⅝	93⅛	100⅜	+ 5⅜
Dow 8.92000	8.9	1508	100½	93	99⅞	+ 4⅞
Dow 7.4s02	8.1	580	93½	82⅝	91¼	+ 3⅜
Dow 7⅝s03	8.1	438	94	84	94	+ 8
Dow 8½s05	8.8	1778	97⅛	87	97⅛	+ 8⅞
Dow 8½s06	8.9	2745	96	86	95⅝	+ 7½
Dow 7⅞07	8.6	1669	91⅝	80½	91⅝	+ 6⅝
Dow 8⅝08	9.0	2208	97¼	87	95⅝	+ 6½
DwCrn 9⅝05	9.5	131	101	94	101	− ½
Dresr 9⅜95	9.3	441	100½	96⅝	100½	+ 2⅛
Dresr 9⅜00	9.4	26	99½	95¼	99½	+ 2¾
Dresr 11¾07	11.3	69	105	104⅜	104⅜	+ 2⅛
duPnt 8.45s04	8.8	5972	99½	87¾	96	+ 5½
duPnt 8½06	8.8	5281	98	87½	96¾	+ 6⅜
duPnt dc6s01	7.5	25090	81¾	71⅛	80½	+ 7½
duPnt 8½16	8.9	1675	99⅜	87¼	95	+ 3½
duPnt 7½93	7.7	8379	98⅜	90⅝	97¼	+ 4¼
DukeP 7⅜01	8.3	896	91	80¾	88¾	+ 6¼
DukeP 7¾02	8.4	1182	93¾	83⅛	92	+ 8⅜
DukeP 7⅜02	8.3	1178	90	78⅜	88¾	+ 8
DukeP 7¾03	8.2	1332	95	82½	95	+ 11
DukeP 8⅛03	8.7	1976	95½	85	93¾	+ 7
DukeP 9¾04	9.4	2673	105	97⅛	103½	+ 3¼
DukeP 9½05	9.3	2021	104	95½	101⅝	+ 4⅝
DukeP 8⅜06	8.7	1583	97	84⅝	96⅜	+ 7⅜
DukeP 8⅛07	8.8	601	94	83⅛	92½	+ 8⅛
DukeP 9⅜08	9.2	1279	102½	93⅜	101½	+ 6½
DukeP 10⅛09	9.6	1893	105⅝	99¼	105⅜	+ 4⅜
DuqL 5s2010	6.9	34	72¾	62⅞	72¾	+ 10⅛
DuqL 8¾00	9.1	1134	97	86⅝	95⅞	+ 7⅜
DuqL 9s06	9.5	1412	99	87	94¾	+ 4⅞
DuqL 8⅜07	9.2	400	90⅞	83⅜	90⅞	+ 5⅞
DuqL 10⅛09	10.0	1224	104	96⅛	101½	+ 1½
-E-						
ECL 9s89f	...	2922	98	40	98	+ 15
EKod 8⅝16	9.6	33381	94⅛	83⅜	90	+ 4⅛
Eaton 7⅞03	8.8	425	91	81	89⅛	+ 6⅞
Eaton 8¾01	9.4	78	95	86	93¼	+ 1¼
Eatn dc7s11	8.8	165	79½	73½	79½	+ 5½
Eaton 9s16	9.6	121	95	90½	94	+ 3
EdisEll 5s95	6.1	15	82½	80	82½	+ 4½
ElPaso 12⅞02	12.0	36	107	103	107	+ 4
ElPaso 9⅝11	9.8	477	101	93¼	98	+ 3
ElPaso 8⅝12	9.1	134	95	83	95	...
Enron 10¾98	10.3	2463	106	99⅝	104½	+ 4⅜
Ens 7.65s98	8.5	297	90⅜	87¾	90	+ 2¼
Ens 8.95s99	9.2	144	97½	89⅛	97¼	+ 5½
Ens 8¾01	9.2	125	96	90⅞	94⅝	+ 2⅝
Ens 8½02	9.3	34	91½	89¾	91½	+ 4
Ens 10⅞05	10.6	283	103	99½	102¾	+ 2¾
Ens 10s01	cv	6574	109½	98½	107	+ 8½
Ens 11⅜95	10.9	205	104⅛	100	104	...
Entex 8⅞01	9.2	392	96¾	89½	96¾	+ 7¼
EnvSys 6¾11	cv	8908	65¼	42¾	57	− 9¼
EqutR 9s96	9.1	242	100	93¾	99	+ 1⅞
EqutR 7½99	8.6	59	88½	85	87	+ 3½
Equitc 10s04	cv	3217	68½	24½	26	− 34⅛
Exxon 6s97	6.9	11272	87⅛	78⅛	86⅝	+ 5⅜
Exxon 6½98	7.3	7175	89½	79¾	88⅞	+ 5½
Exxon 6½89	6.5	465	99¾	97¾	99¾	+ 15/16
Exxon 8¼94	8.2	320	100⅝	100⅛	100⅝	...
ExxP 8¼01	8.5	1055	98¾	89	97	+ 1½
ExxP 5⅝97	6.7	25	84¼	81	84¼	+ 3¼
ExxP 6⅝98	7.0	46	94	90	94	+ 3¾
ExxSh 7½11	7.8	35	96¼	95	96¼	+ 2¾
-F-						
FMC 7½01	8.7	273	88¾	82	86	+ 4¼
FMC 9½2000	9.8	1495	97½	90⅛	97	+ 6½
Frch 9¾98	11.3	210	89	75	86	− 2
Fairfd 14¼89	15.4	2051	101	82	92½	− 4½
Fairfd 13¼92	19.3	4620	90	65⅝	68½	− 18½
Famly 4¾90	4.9	142	97	91⅜	96 11/32	+ 5 23/32
Farah 5s94	cv	662	72	64	67½	− ½
FdHL zr92	...	106	81 5/32	70	81 5/32	+ 12 21/32
FdHL zr94	...	63	65	65	65	+ 12
FdHL zr19	...	202	8	7	8	+ 1½
FdMog 7½98	8.8	30	87	84¼	85¼	− ⅜
FdMog 8⅜93	8.5	18	98⅞	92	98⅞	+ 5¾
FedN zr14s	...	7645	14	9	13⅝	+ 4⅛
FedN zr19s	...	13215	9½	6½	8⅞	+ 1⅞
FdPapr 7.85s97	8.1	70	97⅜	90½	97⅜	+ 7
FdRty 8¾10	cv	42	150	130¾	150	+ 16
Ferro 5⅞92	6.4	7	92⅛	88½	92⅛	+ 2⅛
Fldcst 6s12	cv	5722	83	65	69½	+ 1¾
Fireman 9⅝16	9.6	438	101	91½	100⅜	+ 4⅞
FtAtl 11¾93	11.6	386	102	100	101¼	− 1¾
FtPenn 5½93	cv	1357	89	81	87⅛	+ 2⅝
FtSec 9¼99t	9.3	446	102	99	99⅝	+ ⅝
FUnRE 10¼09	cv	2407	110	103	105	+ 2
FUnRE 8⅜94	8.8	55	95½	94¼	95½	...
Firstar 10s96	10.5	65	101½	95	95	− 5
FisbM 4¾97	cv	397	51	35	40¾	+ 2¼
FisbCp 8½05	cv	1156	73½	39¾	43½	− 11½
FleetF 11¼93	10.6	110	106½	103¼	106½	− 5⅛
FleetFn 8½10	cv	995	151½	124⅝	129½	+ 3½
Flemg 9½16	10.0	148	97½	91¾	94⅝	− 3⅜
Flemg 96	...	2378	102½	88	89¾	...
FlaECs 5s01	7.1	42	71	69	70⅛	+ ⅛
FlowGn 14.30s04	14.4	5532	101½	90	99⅜	− ¼
Flwr 8¼05	cv	3652	127¼	110	119	− 4
Ford 8⅛90	8.1	667	100½	98 9/32	100	+ ½
FrdC 7½91	7.7	1281	98¾	94⅛	97½	+ 2¼
FrdC 4⅞98	cv	1	434	434	434	+ 124
FrdC 7½92	7.7	1678	99	92½	97¾	+ 4¼
FrdC 8.7s99	8.7	2550	101	91⅛	99⅝	+ 4⅛
FrdC 7½93	7.7	484	97¾	88⅛	97⅝	+ 4⅝
FrdC 7⅞93	8.1	1246	99	92¼	97¾	+ 2⅞
FrdC 8⅜01	8.8	1417	98	86	95	+ 6¾
FrdC 8⅜02	8.9	1709	97	85⅛	94¼	+ 3½
FrdC 8½02	8.9	500	97¼	87½	96	+ 5⅞
FreptM 10⅞01	10.7	474	102¼	97½	101⅞	+ 3⅛
FreptM 8¾13	cv	4891	125	106½	118½	+ 12
FrufF 12½93	12.3	116	104	100	101¼	− 2¾
Fuqua 9½98	10.4	2631	95	86	91½	+ 4½
Fuqua 9⅞97	10.5	837	98½	86	94	+ 4¼
-G-						
GTE 12¼94	11.6	802	108	102	103½	− 1½
GTE 10⅝95	9.9	191	107	100¼	107	+ 3½
GTE 10s2000	9.8	172	105	99	102	+ 3
GardD 9¼05	9.6	60	96⅝	93⅛	96⅝	+ 2⅜
GnCorp 11⅞93	11.9	10	100	100	100	− 2⅝

NEW YORK BONDS

		Sales $1,000	High	Low	Last	Net Chg.
GnCorp 12⅜03	12.1	340	102⅝	98½	102⅝	+ 2⅜
GnDev 12⅞95	15.5	5960	101	81½	83	− 12¼
GnDev 12⅝05	18.3	22452	91	58½	69	− 18½
GdDyn 5¾11	...	2664	100½	84½	92	− 2
GnDyn 7⅞93	8.1	545	98	91	97	+ 4⅛
GnDyn 9s16	9.6	1703	96⅞	85½	93¾	− 3¼
GnDyn 9.95s18	9.7	361	105	99	103	...
GnDyn 9⅜95	9.4	283	102	94½	100	+ 1¾
GnEl 5.3s92	5.4	1575	97⅞	89½	97⅞	+ 6⅜
GnEl 7½96	7.9	4290	96⅞	88¼	95¼	+ 4⅛
GnEl 8½04	8.6	7938	99⅞	89½	98½	+ 5⅝
GElCr 8¼97	8.4	2936	99¾	89	98½	+ 6¾
GElCr 11¾05	11.3	1782	107⅛	102¾	104⅜	− ½
GElCr 8s11	8.1	1145	101	97½	99	+ ¾
GElCr 8¼11	8.4	1662	100¼	92	98¼	+ 3⅜
GElCr 6¾11	6.9	90	97¼	91¾	97¼	+ 3¼
GnHme 15½95f	...	9450	28½	10	13½	− 1½
GnHme 12¾98f	...	9291	26	8	14	− 2½
GHost 6s90f	6.4	47	97	89½	94	+ 4
GHost 7s94	9.2	701	82	72½	76	− 2
GnInst 7¼12	cv	12817	111½	88	108	+ 20
GMills 8⅞95	8.9	1565	101	95⅞	100⅛	+ 3⅞
GMills 8s99	8.5	88	95	93¾	94⅛	+ ⅝
GMills 9⅜09	9.3	1260	102	91½	100⅜	+ 6⅝
GMA 7⅛90	7.2	4271	98⅞	94⅛	98¾	+ 2⅞
GMA 8s93M	8.2	7598	99	91¼	97¾	+ 3¾
GMA 7¾94	8.0	12335	97⅝	89	96½	+ 5⅛
GMA 7¼95	7.8	6623	95½	86⅝	93½	+ 5
GMA 7⅛92	7.4	9778	96⅞	90¼	96⅝	+ 4⅝
GMA 7.85s98	8.4	4706	95	84¾	93¼	+ 6¼
GMA 8⅞99	8.9	17514	100	90⅝	99¾	+ 6¼
GMA 8¾s00	8.9	8253	99⅞	89¼	98½	+ 6¾
GMA 8¾s01	8.8	6366	99¾	89½	99¼	+ 7⅛
GMA 8⅛96	8.5	6734	98½	88⅞	95¾	+ 5¾
GMA 8s02	8.6	2180	94	84	93¼	+ 7⅝
GMA 8s07	8.8	2178	92½	81	91⅛	+ 6¾
GMA 8¼06	8.9	2255	94	83⅛	92⅝	+ 6⅜
GMA 8.65s08	9.4	1678	97⅞	87⅛	92¼	+ 2¼
GMA 12s05fb	11.7	2568	105	101¼	102⅝	− ⅞
GMA 12s05	11.7	2589	105¼	102⅛	102½	− 1⅞
GMA 11¾00	11.4	3386	105½	102¼	103¼	− ⅝
GMA dc6s11	8.3	24454	74⅜	63⅞	72	+ 5⅞
GMA zr12	...	22737	155¼	119¾	153⅝	+ 32⅜
GMA zr15	...	35402	132⅝	97	125⅞	+ 26⅞
GMA 10½89	10.5	384	100 7/32	99⅞	99⅞	− 5/16
GMA 10⅜95	10.0	28040	106	99⅞	103⅜	+ 2⅛
GMA 9¼93	9.2	50558	101⅞	96½	100⅞	+ 2¼
GMA 8½91	8.5	6947	101⅞	95¾	100	+ 2
GMA 8⅞96	8.9	20794	101⅜	93	99⅝	+ 4⅝
GMA 8s96	8.3	6696	97⅛	88½	96⅛	+ 6
GMA 8¼16	9.0	1191	94⅞	82	91⅞	+ 6½
GMA 8s90	8.0	3847	100¼	97	99 13/16	+ 2 1/16
GMA 8⅛92	8.2	8164	100⅛	93⅞	99	+ 3¾
GMA 8s93J	8.2	13167	99⅜	91⅞	97¾	+ 3⅞
GMA 7.80s93	8.1	1606	99	90½	96⅝	+ 4¾
GMA 8s93O	8.2	8176	99⅜	91⅝	97⅞	+ 3⅝
GMA 7¼90	7.3	5603	99⅛	95	99	+ 3
GMA 8s94	8.2	5095	98⅞	90⅜	97½	+ 5⅜
GMA 7⅛92j	7.3	4737	97⅝	91¾	97½	+ 4⅜
GMA 7⅞97	8.2	5192	96⅝	87	95⅝	+ 6⅛
GMA 7.45s94	7.8	2322	97	89	95⅝	+ 5¼
GMA 8⅜97	8.5	418	100½	94	98⅝	+ 1⅛
GM 8⅝s05	9.0	2947	97⅞	88½	95¾	+ 5¾
GM 8⅛91	8.1	3714	100⅜	95⅛	99⅞	+ 3⅝
GSignl 8⅞99	9.0	218	99	98	99	+ 2
GTE 6⅝91	6.9	777	97¼	90⅝	96	+ 2½
GTE 9⅜99	9.2	1086	103	91	102	+ 3⅞
GTCal 8⅞96	9.0	212	100	91	98½	+ 2½
GWat 8¾s96	9.1	154	99¼	93⅝	96⅛	+ 1⅛
Gene 14¼94	14.0	527	104	100	102⅛	+ ⅞
Gene 15¼94	14.5	481	108	102½	105⅜	+ 2⅞
Gene dc9¾93	10.1	1195	98	90	96⅜	+ 5⅞
Genrad 7¼11	cv	4493	76⅞	57	58	− 11
GaPac zr15	11.6	55	97	91	97	...
GaPw 8⅞00	9.2	3253	98	88¼	96½	+ 6⅛
GaPw 7⅜01	8.4	1203	87¾	79¼	87¾	+ 8½
GaPw 8⅛01	8.9	1598	93¼	83¼	91¼	+ 6¼
GaPw 7⅝01	8.5	1017	90	79¼	89¼	+ 8¼
GaPw 7½02J	8.6	990	88¼	79⅛	87½	+ 8¼
GaPw 7½02D	8.6	814	88¾	76⅝	87½	+ 8
GaPw 7⅞03	8.8	910	91½	80¾	89¼	+ 8½
GaPw 8⅝04	9.2	2410	95	84¾	93½	+ 6¾
GaPw 11⅝00	11.2	2262	106	101¼	104	+ 1
GaPw 11¾05	11.3	5325	105	101	103⅝	+ 1
GaPw 9⅞06	9.8	2783	102	93¾	101	+ 4½
GaPw 9⅝08	9.6	2131	101	91⅝	99⅞	+ 7
GaPw 9¾08	9.8	2060	101⅛	92⅝	99⅞	+ 5⅜
GaPw 10½09	10.2	3090	104¾	97½	102¾	+ 2¾
GaPw 11s09	10.7	2447	105½	100	103¼	+ 2⅝
GaPw 13⅛12	12.4	7221	106	103⅛	105½	+ 2
GaPw 10s16J	9.9	2863	102½	93	101¼	+ 6
GaPw 10s16A	9.9	3792	102	93⅞	101¼	+ 5¾
GaPw 10¾17	10.4	1289	105½	98¼	103⅜	+ 3⅝
GaPw 10⅛97	10.1	185	104	97½	100⅛	+ 2
GaPw 10¾18	10.3	131	104	98⅝	104	+ 2¼
Getty 14s00	13.1	750	110	104½	107	...
GibFn 9¼08f	cv	13552	32	¾	1	− 27¼
GlbeUn 8s97	8.6	20	92¾	91½	92¾	...
GldNug 8⅜92	9.8	1460	92⅞	85⅛	85¾	− 5¼
GdNgF 13¼95	14.8	26218	102¾	75¾	89⅝	− 9⅜
Gdrch 8¼94	8.6	429	96½	92	96	+ 2
Gdrch 7s97	8.1	224	88½	78⅜	86⅛	+ 5⅛
Gdyr 8.6s95	8.8	786	98⅛	94¼	97⅜	+ 1⅞
Gdyr 7.35s97	8.4	931	88⅞	83	87¾	+ 2½
Grace 4¼90	cv	773	129	100⅜	109	+ 8½
Grace 6½96	cv	47	234½	181¼	228½	+ 58½
Grace 11¾08	11.1	30	106	103	106	+ 2
Grace 10⅜97	10.3	263	104½	99	101	+ 1
GranC 4⅝94	cv	278	68¼	61	68	...
GranC 4⅝94r	6.8	5	68	68	68	...
GtNoN 7⅞98	8.2	5	96½	96½	96½	+ 2¼
GtNoN 8.7s08	9.7	223	96½	87	90	− ¾
GtNoR 3⅛00	4.9	184	64	55	64	+ 10¾
GtNoR 3⅛00r	5.3	13	59½	56	59½	...
GtNoR 2⅝10	6.3	667	43¼	35½	41¾	+ 2⅛
GtNor 2⅝10r	6.3	75	42	36½	41½	...
GtNoR 3⅛90	3.2	192	99 5/32	93⅝	99 5/32	+ 6 9/32
GtNor 3⅛90r	25.3	62	98⅜	12⅜	12⅜	...
GrnTr dc8¼95	10.6	2954	83⅞	66	78	− 2
Greyh 6½90	cv	108	188	159½	164	+ 1½
GreyF zr94	...	10411	65½	53¼	63⅞	+ 8⅞
GreyF 13⅝94	13.0	71	108½	102⅝	104¾	− 2¼
GrowGp 12½94	13.5	1055	101½	91½	92½	− 3
GrowGp 8½06	cv	3333	118	80	84	− 18
Grumn 13⅜94	12.7	17	107½	105⅜	105⅜	...
Grumn 9¼09	cv	5547	97½	82½	83½	− 11½
Grumn 9½96	9.7	351	99¼	96½	98⅜	+ ⅜
Grumn 10½11	10.8	50	97	97	97	− 3⅛
Gulfrd 6s12	cv	3074	89¾	73	76	+ 1½
GulfMo 5s56f	11.1	309	50	43⅛	45	− 5
GlfMo 5s56f rg	11.5	48	48	41⅛	43½	...
GlfRes 10⅞97	13.1	1161	91⅞	79⅛	83	− 8½
GlfRes 12½04	13.9	2105	94	89	90⅛	− 3⅞
GlfStU 7¼92	cv	373	108	89½	100	+ 8
-H-						
Hall 8.7s91	11.8	2469	75	63	74	− 6
Hallb 7.95s95	8.0	235	99	91¼	99	+ 7⅜
Hallb 9¼00	9.3	372	100¾	94	99¾	− ¼
HallB 10.20s05	9.8	139	104	98⅛	104	+ 3¾
HalwdGp 13½09	...	8113	90	71	76	...
Harns 15s94	13.9	451	110	106	108	− 3¾
Harris 7¾01	9.4	34	82½	82½	82½	+ 5½
Harsc 5½92	6.0	6	91	89⅞	91	+ ½
Harsc 9⅞00	10.1	41	99¼	97⅞	98	− 2
Hartfd 8½96	9.1	261	97¾	90⅛	93¼	+ 3
Hartmx 8½96	8.8	222	97	93½	97	+ 1½
Hawn 9s2000	9.0	512	100¾	91	100	+ 7¾
Hawn 8.2s01	8.9	225	93½	85⅜	91¾	+ 4⅜
Hawn 7⅝02	8.7	105	88	80¾	88	+ 3
Hawn 8.35s03	8.9	169	94⅛	86⅛	93⅞	+ 7⅞
HltCrPr 9½96	9.8	41	97	97	97	+ 9⅞
Hltsou 7¾14	cv	307	125⅜	114	117	...
HeclMn zr04	...	3388	36½	30⅞	34	...
Heinz 7¼97	7.8	65	93¼	83¾	93¼	+ 9¼
Hellr 7¾92	8.0	437	98	93	97⅛	+ 3½
Hellr 8s93	8.5	39	95⅜	93½	94⅛	+ ⅛
Hellr 7¾93	8.1	464	96½	91	95⅝	+ 3⅜
Hellr 8½93	8.6	53	99¾	93½	98⅜	+ 3¼
Hellr 8¾02	9.3	190	96½	88¾	94⅜	+ 1⅞

		Sales $1,000	High	Low	Last	Net Chg.
Hercul 6½99	cv	282	142	128	141⅞	+ 12⅞
Hercul 8s10	cv	3309	117	98	99	− 9
Hercul 9⅞93	10.1	5	97½	97½	97½	...
Hersh 7¼97	8.1	26	90	87⅛	90	...
Hersh 9½09	9.4	837	101¼	98	101	+ 1
Hertz 8⅞s01	9.1	96	97⅜	95¼	97⅛	+ 3¼
Hills 11s02	cv	485	101	84	84	− 9
HltNJ 11⅜92	11.4	743	102	99½	100	− 1¾
HltNJ 10⅝94	10.6	1497	102⅝	99	100½	− ¼
HockV 4½99	6.4	95	70½	63	70½	+ 5⅞
HockV 4½99r	6.7	4	67⅛	67⅛	67⅛	...
Holidy 8⅜96	9.1	1045	93	78	92¼	+ 2½
Holidy 10½94	10.6	62861	101½	92⅝	99⅛	+ 1⅝
Holidy 11s99	10.7	58214	102½	91½	102½	+ 6
Holidy 9⅜93	9.7	956	100	90	97	+ 3
Holidy 15s92	14.7	241	106	102	102	− 1½
HmeDep 6¾14	cv	5062	127¾	101	126½	...
HomFSD 6½11	cv	4209	114	77½	90⅜	+ 12⅜
HmGrp 14⅞99	15.2	1501	100	94	98	...
HonyF 8.2s98	9.0	780	95	85½	91¼	+ 4⅜
Honey 9⅜09	9.7	420	98	90¾	96⅝	+ 8⅝
HousF 7½95	8.1	654	95	87¼	93	+ 5¾
HousF 7¾99	8.6	807	93½	82	90	+ 5
HousF 8½01	8.9	263	96½	86	95⅜	+ 4⅞
HouF 10½94	10.4	918	103	99½	101	− ¾
HousF 9s00	9.1	732	99¾	90¾	99⅜	+ 7¼
HousF 8⅜03	8.8	273	94¾	84¼	94¾	+ 7½
HouF 8.45s97	8.8	602	97	89½	95⅞	+ 4⅞
HousF 8.2s07	9.1	667	92	81	90	+ 6
HousNG 8.7s01	9.4	7	92⅜	92⅜	92⅜	...
HudFd 8s06	cv	4247	90⅞	66¼	72	+ 3
HudFd 14s08	cv	3469	138½	106	110	− 3
Huffy 7¼14	cv	217	111	101	102½	...
Humn 9½98	9.8	116	99½	91	97⅛	+ 7⅛
Humn 13¾13	12.7	1982	114	108½	108½	− 1⅛
Humn 8½09	cv	18199	118	93⅞	118	+ 24⅛
Humn 10⅛91	10.0	214	101½	98⅛	101½	+ 1⅝
viHuntIR 9⅞04f	...	2539	12½	4¾	6¾	+ 2
-I-						
IBM Cr 8s90	8.0	8874	101	97⅛	99 25/32	+ 1 9/32
IBM Cr 8⅜90	8.4	5289	101¾	96⅞	99 25/32	+ 1 17/32
IBM Cr 9⅝92	9.3	4784	104⅜	99	103⅞	...
ICN 12⅞98	18.1	14277	92⅞	69⅛	71	− 15½
ICI 9.05s95	9.1	148	100	95⅛	100	+ 1⅛
ICI 8⅞03	9.0	146	98¼	92¼	98¼	+ 4¼
ITTF 8.1s92	8.2	155	99¼	94½	99	+ 1¾
ITTF 8½02	8.9	363	97½	85	95⅝	+ 8½
ITTF 8⅞03	8.9	245	100½	94½	100	+ 2¾
ITTF 11¼90	11.2	145	102	100 1/32	100 1/32	− 2 7/32
ITTR 8s96	8.5	20	94⅛	92⅜	94⅛	+ 1½
IdealB 9¼00	11.0	1148	86	75⅞	83⅞	+ 5
IllBel 7⅝06	8.3	2607	93	80¾	91½	+ 9¾
IllBel 8s04	8.4	2603	96¾	84⅝	95	+ 8¾
IllBel 8¼16	8.8	1356	96½	83½	93½	+ 6⅝
IlCnt 11¼99	11.3	1651	101⅞	99	99¼	− ¾
IlCnt 15½94	14.5	33	109⅞	105	107	− 2⅞
IllPw 10s98	9.7	229	103	97½	103	...
IllPw 7.6s01	8.7	478	88	78	87⅛	+ 6⅛
IllPw 7⅝03	8.9	275	86⅞	78½	85¼	+ 6¼
IllPw 10½04	10.1	2577	104	97¼	103¾	+ 4¾
IllPw 8⅝06	9.2	1358	94	83	93¼	+ 6¾
IllPw 8¼07	8.9	1043	92⅞	78½	92⅞	+ 8⅛
IllPw 8⅞08	9.4	719	94⅞	85⅛	94	+ 4
IllPw 10⅛16	10.0	895	102½	92	101	+ 5
IllPw 9⅞16	9.9	926	101¼	93⅝	100	+ 3⅝
IllPw 9⅜16	9.6	1958	100	86⅛	97⅜	+ 5⅞
Inco 6.85s93	7.5	154	91¾	88⅝	91¾	+ 3
Inco 12⅜10	11.8	335	110	100	105¼	+ 5¾
IndBel 8⅛11	8.7	2124	95	83½	93¾	+ 8⅜
IndBel 10s14	9.5	676	107¾	99⅛	105¼	+ 4¼
IndBel 8⅛17	9.0	1325	96	82½	90½	+ 6½
IndBel 8s14	8.9	805	92⅝	82	89⅞	+ 6⅞
IngR 8.05s04	8.8	217	92	83	91⅝	+ 7¾
InldStl 6½92	7.1	120	92⅛	88½	92⅛	+ 2⅝
InldStl 8¾95	8.9	279	99¼	97⅜	98⅜	− ¼
InldStl 8⅞99	9.5	150	94	89¼	93¾	+ 2¼
InldStl 9½00	9.9	118	95⅝	93	95½	...
InldStl 7.9s07	9.5	1731	84¼	72	83⅛	+ 7⅛
InspRs 8½12	cv	2837	127	92	94	− 10
ItgRs dc8⅝97f	...	4331	74½	2	2⅞	− 76⅛
ItgRs 13⅛95f	...	45031	97⅞	3	3⅜	− 94½
ItgRs 10¾96f	...	33776	87⅛	3	3⅜	− 81⅜
ItgRs 10s90f	...	12438	99⅞	16⅜	18	− 81½
ItgRs 10¾92f	...	5144	98	18⅛	18½	− 79½
ItgRs 11⅛94f	...	7981	92⅞	18	20	− 81
ItgRs 12¼98f	...	13394	99	3¼	4	− 96
Intlgc 11.99s96	21.8	1720	85¾	47	55	− 28
IBM 9⅜04	9.2	21894	103	96⅝	101⅞	+ 2¾
IBM 7⅞04	cv	1245	102¾	95½	97⅛	− 4⅛
IBM 10¼95	9.8	25422	108	100¾	104¾	+ 1¾
IBM 9s98	8.8	22491	103¼	96	102⅝	+ 4¼
InMin 4s91	cv	5	184	184	184	...
InMin 9.35s00	9.7	100	97⅜	92⅛	96¼	− ⅛
InMin zr05	...	2716	30¾	24⅝	26⅝	− 2⅜
IPap 8.85s95	8.9	3108	100½	95¼	99½	+ 1½
IPap 8.85s00	9.0	330	99⅞	92⅝	98	+ 2
IPap dc5⅛12	...	6518	63⅜	54⅛	61⅛	+ 6⅛
IPap 10⅞95	10.5	495	105	100½	103¼	− ⅜
IPap 8¼91	8.4	190	99½	97	98⅝	...
IntRec 9s10	cv	12733	57¾	40⅛	53½	+ 6½
IntTch 9⅜96	12.0	260	79	76½	78¼	...
IntTT 8⅝00	cv	5	200¾	200¾	200¾	+ 5¾
Intnr 11s93	10.8	489	102¾	99	101⅝	− ⅜
Intnr 11½94	10.9	535	105½	101⅛	105½	+ ½
Intnr 11s95	10.8	494	104¾	99½	102	...
IntJh 7¾11	cv	1003	71	58	59½	− 3
-J-						
JPInd 7¼13	cv	1657	95½	76¾	81	− 4
Jamswy 8s05	cv	5204	97½	70	72¼	− 11½
JCP 9⅝06	9.4	549	102	91⅜	102	+ 7½
JCP 9¾06	9.5	895	102⅛	93⅜	102⅛	+ 6⅞
JCP 8¾07	9.3	146	101	84⅛	94	+ 5¼
JCP 9s08	9.2	59	97⅞	90½	97¾	+ 8⅛
JCP 10⅜18	10.1	80	102½	102⅜	102⅜	...
viJonsLI 6¾94f	...	6198	29⅞	9¼	15½	− 11¼
viJonsLI 6½88f	...	1386	29½	12	12½	− 14⅜
viJoneL 6¾94f	...	2191	32⅞	13¼	15½	− 11¼
viJoneL 9⅞95f	...	2730	77	69⅜	69½	− 4½
viJoneL 8s98f	...	1231	75½	69¼	69¼	− 3½
viJoneL 9¾96f	...	2068	76⅞	69¾	70	− 4
-K-						
KFW Int 9⅜98	9.1	218	104	97⅞	103	+ 1⅜
K mart 12½95	...	188	113	104¾	113	+ 3
K mart 8⅛97	8.5	1402	97½	87	96	+ 5⅛
K Mart 8⅜17	9.4	2608	92	82⅛	88¾	+ 5½
KCSo 12s10	12.0	10	100	100	100	...
KaufBd zr04	...	1708	34	28¼	30¼	...
Kellwd 9s99	cv	15	326	220	220	− 60
Kenn 7⅞01	8.3	430	97⅛	87½	94½	+ 3½
KerrGl 13s96	12.7	3430	103⅞	98	102¼	+ 1¾
KerrMc 8½06	9.3	111	94	85⅝	91¾	+ 2¾
KerrMc 7¼12	cv	2849	120½	102½	119½	+ 16
Keycrp 7¾02	8.9	636	89½	80¼	87	+ 4
KimCl 5⅞91	6.1	426	96⅜	91½	95¾	+ 4
KimCl 5⅞92	6.3	339	93½	88¼	93½	+ 4½
KimCl 11½13	10.8	20	107	106	106	− 1¼
KingCt 6s97	7.5	35	82⅞	74⅛	80¼	+ 4¾
Koger 8s00	6.5	172	138	122½	122½	− 11
KogerP 9¼03	cv	3304	95	86	86	− 3
Kolmrg 8¾09	cv	5929	80½	62	64	− 13¼
Kraft 6⅞96	7.6	151	91	83	91	+ 7
Kraft 8⅜04	8.8	763	96	87⅜	95	+ 6½
Kraft 7.6s07	8.6	566	88½	77½	88½	+ 6½
Krogr 8s93	7.9	50	101¾	101¾	101¾	+ ¾
-L-						
viLTV 5s88mf	...	22081	31	12½	15	− 14⅞
viLTV 9¼97f	...	4796	46	20	26	− 12⅜
viLTV 11s07f	...	11502	32⅞	12	14	− 16
viLTV 13⅞02f	...	6416	46½	24⅜	25¼	− 13¾
viLTV 95t f	...	5585	35	11½	13⅞	− 24⅛
viLTV 14s04f	...	33222	47	25	26½	− 13
viLTV 10¼95f	cv	405	37	20	21½	− 5¼
viLTV 11½97f	...	9878	29½	9¾	13½	− 16
viLTV 7⅞98f	...	5823	27¾	10	12½	− 13¾
viLTV 8¾98f	...	12333	27⅝	10⅝	12	− 15½
viLTV Int 5s88f	cv	253	30	14¾	22	− 9

		Sales $1,000	High	Low	Last	Net Chg.
viLTV 10⅜99f	...	1693	37	18	19	− 11¾
viLTV 15s00f	...	9986	45½	20⅛	24	− 14½
LaFrg 7s13	cv	1356	104	93¼	98¾	+ 1¾
LaQuin 10s02	cv	2631	106¾	95¾	103	+ 7
Leget 6½06	cv	3950	103	84½	96	+ 11½
Leucd 14s93	13.7	10	102	102	102	− 6⅝
LincFt 8½96	8.8	327	96¾	88	96¼	+ 5¼
Litton 11½95	11.1	1939	106	102⅛	103¾	...
Litton flt00	...	600	101	95	95¼	− 3¾
Litton 12⅝05	11.3	715	116½	104	111⅝	+ ⅝
LoewCp zr04	...	3020	42	38¾	39½	...
LomF zr01f	...	8244	31½	5¾	8	− 22
viLomF 9s10f	cv	14465	86	14	21	− 64
LomF 7s11f	cv	8837	73½	15	21	− 52½
LomF 10¾93f	...	15562	98½	20	26	...
LomF 11⅜95f	...	4886	94	20	25½	...
LomNM 10½93	12.7	1280	89	79	83	...
LglsLt 10¼94	9.9	2290	104	99¼	103⅛	...
LglsLt 12⅝92	12.2	1355	105	100	103⅛	+ 3⅛
LglsLt 10⅞99	10.4	2059	105½	99⅜	104¾	...
LglsLt 13¼95	12.4	1552	110	102	106⅝	+ 3⅝
LglsLt 11¼96	10.6	2484	106¾	95⅝	106¼	+ 9
LglsLt 11⅞15	11.1	2519	108½	96¾	107	+ 10⅛
LglsLt 11.7s93	11.0	3363	106¾	96½	106	+ 10⅜
LslsLt 11⅜93	10.9	2478	105½	102½	104½	...
LglsLt 11¾94	11.0	2161	107⅞	96	106½	+ 9
LglsLt 11½14	11.0	15078	104⅝	91½	104⅛	+ 12⅜
LglsLt 11⅜19	10.4	1935	105¾	99½	105⅝	...
Loral 10¾97	10.4	365	104¾	99	103¼	+ 3¼
Loral 7¼10	cv	7185	100	88	88¾	− 4½
Lorilld 6⅝93	7.0	200	97¼	92⅞	94½	+ ⅝
Lorilld 6⅞93	7.4	7851	94	86⅝	93⅛	+ 4¼
LouLE 8½00	cv	1875	92½	82¾	89½	+ 4½
LouN 2⅞03	5.5	89	52¾	47½	52⅝	+ 7⅞
LouN 3⅜03F	6.0	159	56	47	56	+ 8¾
LouN 3⅜03fr	...	10	56½	56½	56½	...
LouN 7⅜93	7.9	257	94¾	89¼	93¼	+ 1⅜
LouGs 4⅞90	5.1	28	95¾	95	95¾	+ 3¼
LouGs 9¼00	9.2	371	102	93¼	101	+ 6½
LouGs 8¼01	8.9	166	94½	86⅛	93	+ ¼
LouGs 7½02	8.5	80	91½	80½	88½	+ 5½
viLykes 7½94N f	...	1441	31⅜	10	11½	− 15
viLykes 7½94f	...	9279	29⅞	10⅛	13¾	− 13
viLykes 11s00f	...	3414	29¼	11⅛	13⅛	− 14¼

-M-

		Sales $1,000	High	Low	Last	Net Chg.
MACOM 9¼06	cv	6021	82	64	65	− 8
MGMUA 12⅝93	13.0	4181	101½	88¾	97¼	− ¼
MGMUA 13s96	15.7	21658	97½	75	82⅝	− 9⅞
MckTr 7⅞97	9.1	485	95	81⅝	86½	+ 1½
MeYk 9.1s02	9.2	856	99	91¼	99	+ 6⅝
MeYk 8½02	8.7	221	97½	91½	97½	+ 6½
MeYk 7⅝02	8.8	103	88	82⅝	86⅞	+ 3⅞
MfrH 8⅛04	9.6	2969	91¾	79⅝	85	+ 4¾
MfrH 8⅛07	9.7	3706	89	78½	83½	+ 4¾
Manvl 12s92	11.9	12351	102½	99¼	100⅝	− ⅛
Manvl zr03	...	6642	51⅝	42⅝	45¼	− 1¾
Mapco 10¾99	10.6	607	103⅜	97	101⅛	+ 1
Mapco 11¾03	11.4	100	105	100	103½	− 1
MarO 8½00	9.3	925	94½	85⅜	91	+ 2¼
MarO 8.5s06	9.8	3834	91	82⅜	86⅞	+ ¾
MarO 9½94	9.5	62372	101¾	95½	100⅛	+ 2⅜
MarM 7⅝03	8.5	342	90	80¼	89¼	+ 6¼
MarkIV 13⅜99	13.4	427	100½	98	99½	...
MarkIV 12⅜03	12.3	995	101	87½	101	+ 3¾
MrtM d7s11	10.0	11	70	70	70	+ 5
Masco 5¼12	6.7	8802	92	76¼	78	− 1¼
Mattel 11⅝03	11.6	3058	100	87	100	+ 10
Mattel 14¾00	13.9	478	108⅞	104⅝	106	+ 2⅛
Maxus 8½08	10.2	544	85	71½	83½	+ 6⅞
Maxus zr04	...	1817	40⅞	29	40⅞	...
McCro 6½92	cv	202	74	65	69½	...
McCro 7½94	13.6	1037	63⅞	55	55	− 4⅜
McCro 7½94N	12.1	184	66¼	59	61¾	+ 1
McCro 7⅝97	11.2	147	68	55½	68	+ 12
McCro 7¾95	13.7	849	67	56¾	56¾	− ¾
McDe 10.20s99	10.1	363	100⅞	96¼	100½	+ 4⅜
McDe 10s03	11.0	3978	97	84⅝	90¾	+ 4¾
McDe 9⅝04	10.4	60	94⅛	92¾	92¾	...
McDInv 8s11	cv	955	80½	71¼	71½	− 4
McDnl zr94	...	8783	72¾	62	72⅝	+ 10⅛
McDnl 11⅝95	11.3	729	104	101⅜	102⅝	− ⅜
McDnl 8⅞16	9.2	60	96	93	96	− 1
Mcdnl 9¾17	9.6	884	105	94	102	...
McDnl 7¼91	7.4	505	98½	92¼	98½	+ 3½
McDnl 9¾99	9.5	296	106½	98¼	103	...
McDnl 9¾19	9.5	105	103	100½	102½	...
McDD 4¾91	cv	11	271½	271½	271½	+ 20½
McGE 7½96	8.1	187	94	83½	92⅝	+ 5¾
McKes 6s94	cv	1	218	218	218	− 2
McKes 9¾06	cv	766	177	138	163	+ 17½
Mead 8½95	8.6	215	99	90	98¾	+ 7
Mead 9⅞00	9.9	172	100	95⅜	100	+ 2½
Mead 15⅞92	14.8	92	126	107½	107½	− 22
Mead 6¾12	cv	4336	104	90	91½	− 4½
Melln 8.6s09	9.3	3052	95½	83	92½	+ 8¼
Melln 7¼99	7.7	4085	95¾	81¾	94½	+ 12
Melln 8⅞98	9.2	1771	97¼	88½	96¼	...
Memx 5¼90	cv	347	100	93¼	100	+ 5⅞
MerSt 8.7s95	8.8	53	98¾	93⅝	98¾	− 1¼
MLCPS 15¾06	13.8	1034	120	111	114	+ 1
MerLy zr06	...	15900	27⅞	24⅞	27½	+ 2⅜
MerLy zr91	...	3961	86¼	76⅛	85½	+ 8⅜
MesaCap 12s96	12.4	8445	100½	92	96¾	− 1⅛
MesaCap 13½99	13.2	2330	107⅜	97	102	...
MichB 4⅜91	4.6	478	94⅛	86⅞	94⅛	+ 3⅞
MichB 7¾11	8.4	2932	91¾	79½	91¾	+ 9⅝
MichB 7s12	8.4	1218	85¾	73½	83¾	+ 7¾
MichB 9.6s08	9.3	5355	104	96¼	103¼	+ 5
MichB 8⅛15	8.9	1855	95	83½	91	+ 6¾
MichB 9⅛18	9.0	3013	101¼	91	101⅛	+ 7⅛
MCGC 8⅛98	8.6	204	95	87⅞	95	+ 6
MichG 13½03	13.1	72	103	100⅞	103	− 2⅛
Mickl dc11½98	13.7	135	89	84	84⅛	− 4⅞
Midcon 13⅜94	12.8	186	104¼	101	104⅛	+ 1⅛
Midcon 13s93	12.8	15	101⅝	100⅝	101⅝	− 3¼
MdlndAm 12¾03	10.5	164	121½	113½	121½	+ 7⅜
MidlBk 11.35s93	10.9	239	107	103½	104½	− 1¾
MMM 8.85s	8.9	886	102	93	99¾	+ 3¾
MKT 4s90	4.1	1042	97⅝	92	97⅝	+ 5⅞
MKT 5½33f	...	1278	71	51⅜	51⅞	− 16⅛
MKT 5½33fr	...	408	67⅛	50	53⅞	...
MPac 4¼90	4.3	400	99 17/32	94¾	99 17/32	+ 4 29/32
MPac 4¼90r	4.3	12	100	12	100	...
MPac 4¼05	6.9	1335	64	54	61⅝	+ 5⅛
MPac 4¼05r	6.9	658	62⅞	53½	61¾	...
MPac 4¾20f	...	954	55	47	54¼	+ 5
MPac 4¾30f	...	1473	54	46¼	52⅜	+ 4⅜
MPac 5s45f	...	4287	56	47⅛	54½	+ 3
MoAl 8.4505	8.9	894	96¼	86½	95	+ 6⅜
Mobil 8½01	8.7	17109	99⅝	90⅝	97⅞	+ 5¼
Mobil 14.4s04	14.2	16564	103½	100 5/32	101½	− 1
Mobil 7⅝91	7.7	3320	99½	93⅝	98½	+ 2⅞
MobO 7⅜01	8.3	844	91	80	89	+ 6¼
Mobil 7¼91	7.4	1190	98½	93⅛	98⅜	+ 4
Mobil 7⅛92	7.3	2036	98	92⅛	97¾	+ 4¾
Mobil 8¼92	8.3	1490	100½	93¾	99¾	+ 3½
Mobil 8⅝94	8.5	8864	104	94⅜	101⅛	+ 4½
Mobil 8¾90	8.8	2036	100½	97⅜	100	+ ⅞
Mobil 8¾91	8.7	2643	102½	96⅝	100¾	+ 2¾
Mobil 8.7s91	8.7	1125	101½	96¼	100⅜	+ 2½
MoblCda 8⅜93	8.5	1394	100⅛	94	99	+ 3¼
MohD 5½94	cv	1246	44½	19½	35	− 10½
Monog 10s99	13.3	335	82⅞	74	75⅛	− 3⅞
Monog 11s04	14.0	575	94	70	78⅝	− 2⅝
Monon 6s07f	...	214	64½	58⅛	64	− ⅛
Monon 6s07f r	...	20	64¼	62	64¼	...
Mons 9⅛00	9.3	354	101	96½	98⅛	+ 1⅛
Mons 8½00	8.8	1016	97	87	96⅛	+ 6⅜
Mons 8¾08	9.1	846	96⅜	86⅜	96	+ 8¾
MonyM 7s90	cv	223	99	95⅝	98¾	+ 3
Moran 8¾08f	cv	4969	82½	56	68¾	− 2⅞
Morgn 4¾98	cv	18	204	187	204	+ 14
Motrla 8s07	8.9	207	91¾	86¾	89½	+ 4½
Motrla zr09	...	4985	34	30½	31¾	...
MtSTI 7⅜11	8.6	2045	86½	76¾	85⅝	+ 7⅜
MtSTI 7¾13	8.8	1980	89½	78¼	88	+ 7⅞
MtSTI 9¾12	9.6	2423	104¼	96	102	+ 3½
MtSTI 9⅝15	9.4	3570	103	94	102½	+ 6

		Sales $1,000	High	Low	Last	Net Chg.
MtSTI 7⅞16	8.8	1450	92¼	79⅜	90	+ 9¾
MtSTI 8s17	8.9	2544	92⅜	80¼	89¾	+ 7⅞
MtSTI 8⅝18	9.0	3891	97⅞	85¼	95½	+ 8½
MtStTI 9¼14	9.1	2728	101¾	91	101¼	+ 7¼
MtStTI 12¼25	11.1	343	112½	109⅛	110¾	+ ¼

-N-

		Sales $1,000	High	Low	Last	Net Chg.
NBD 8¼10	cv	387	175	126	165	+ 35¼
NBI 8¼07	cv	9344	43½	20¼	25	− 11
NCNB 8⅜99	8.8	964	96½	86	95⅜	+ 4⅜
NCNB 11⅛97	10.6	37	105	104½	104¾	+ 1¼
NCNB 8½96	8.8	369	99	89½	97	+ 2¾
NCNB 12⅝96	12.0	240	106	102⅛	105⅛	+ 1
NLInd 7½95	9.1	376	87	82½	82½	− 3⅛
NLInd 9⅜00	9.5	554	100	88½	99	+ 8¾
Nabis 7¾s01	9.4	1012	88⅜	77¾	82¾	+ 7⅝
Nabis 7¾s03	9.7	648	85	75	80	+ 5
Naco 12s94	18.2	7995	68	47⅛	66	+ 15⅞
NCash 5.6s91	5.9	259	96	90	95½	+ 3⅞
NCash 7.7s94	7.9	623	97½	91	97⅛	+ 3⅝
NConv 9s08	cv	5234	79	65	66¼	− 7
NDair 4⅜92	4.8	32	91½	85¼	91½	+ 6
NtEdu 6½11	cv	9154	114	41	43¼	− 61¾
NEnt 4¾96	cv	299	44	20	20	− 24½
NtGyp zr04	...	58625	67	36⅛	43	− 22½
NInd 10s99	11.2	270	93	83½	89	+ 4
NMed 99s	...	157	100	93¼	96¼	+ 3
NMed 12¾99A	12.4	1959	105	100¼	102⅝	+ 2⅜
NMed 12⅛99B	11.9	1017	104¾	99	101½	+ 1⅜
NMEd 12s00	11.7	1382	103⅜	100	103	+ 2⅞
NMed 12½00	12.2	1007	105	100½	102⅝	+ ⅝
NMed 12⅛95	11.1	195	110	103½	108¾	+ 8¾
NMed zr04	...	15877	43	29⅞	41	+ 11
NRUt 7.40s07	8.9	140	83	77	83	+ 4
NRUt A9¾09	9.8	90	100½	96	99½	+ 1½
NRUt 13½10	12.7	40	106⅝	105	106⅝	+ 2⅓
NRUt S9¾09	9.7	28	100¼	98½	100¼	− 1¾
NRUt 14¾11	14.0	235	111⅜	104	105¼	− 7⅞
NRUt 10½95	10.2	231	105	99⅛	102½	+ ½
NRUt 9¼92	9.0	96	102½	99	102½	...
NRUt 9⅜95	9.3	670	102¾	96	100¾	+ 1¾
NRUt 9⅝96	9.5	41	101½	98	101	...
NStl 8s95	8.8	264	95	89¾	91	− 1
NStl 8⅜06	10.0	1060	84	74⅛	83⅞	+ 8⅞
Navstr 4.8s91	4.9	328	99⅛	89¾	98⅞	+ 9⅛
Navstr 6¼98	7.6	1161	84	74⅝	82	+ 5⅞
Navstr 8⅝95	9.0	2120	98	90½	96	+ 2⅝
Navstr 9s04	9.8	7070	96½	85¼	91½	+ 1¾
NavFin 8⅝91	8.7	1502	100½	94⅛	99	+ 3⅛
NavFin 7⅝93	8.0	1056	96	88⅞	95	+ 3⅝
NavFin ⅞½94	8.0	1276	94½	86⅜	93½	+ 5¼
NavFin 11.95s95	12.0	3437	103	99¼	99½	− 4
NEMtl 7⅜97	8.1	384	94⅜	85¾	91	+ 3¼
NJBTI 7¼11	8.5	2100	87¼	76	85⅛	+ 7⅛
NJBTI 7⅜12	8.6	1165	88	76½	86	+ 8¼
NJBTI 7¾13	8.6	1902	91	80¼	89¾	+ 7⅝
NJBTI 8¼16	8.7	882	97	84	95	+ 8½
NJBTI 8s16	8.7	1096	94½	81⅞	91¾	+ 7¾
NJBTI 8¾18	8.9	1468	100	88⅜	98¾	+ 7¾
NYEG 7⅝01	8.8	391	88	77¼	87	+ 5¾
NYEG 9⅜05	9.4	1156	100	91⅛	99¼	+ 6¾
NYEG 9⅜06	9.4	337	99¾	91	99¾	+ 6⅞
NYEG 8⅝07	9.1	193	95	83	95	+ 8⅞
NwZeal 10⅝05	...	100	114	114	114	...
NiMP 10.2s05	10.2	931	104	96½	100¼	+ ¾
NiMP 8.35s07	9.3	522	91⅝	83	90⅛	+ 6¼
NblAfl 7¼12	cv	1576	103	86	103	+ 14¼
NorfW 4s96	5.2	270	77	68¼	76⅞	+ 8⅝
NorfW 4s96r	5.3	150	75½	68	75⅛	...
NorfW 4.85s15	8.6	97	57	49½	56½	+ ½
NoAPh 4s92	cv	49	89	83⅝	87⅛	+ 3½
NoAPh 9¾00	9.7	253	100½	97	100½	+ 2¼
NoIllG 8¾01	9.1	104	98	90⅞	96½	+ 3½
NoNG 8s91	8.1	275	98⅜	94⅜	98⅜	+ 1⅜
NoNG 7⅜92	7.8	200	94½	91	94	+ 2¼
NoNG 9s95	9.4	59	95½	93	95½	− ½
NoPac 4s97	4.7	147	91	79	85	+ 5
NoPac 4s97r	4.4	101	91	80¼	91	+ 10¾
NoPac 4s97st	5.5	1163	73¾	57½	73	+ 7
NoPac 4s97tr	5.4	499	74	66	74	+ 9
NoPac 3s47	3.8	167	83	77	79¾	+ 2⅝
NoPac 3s47r	3.6	298	83¾	77	82¾	...
NoPac 3s47st	8.5	1815	35¾	25	35⅛	+ 2⅞
NoPac 3s47str	8.6	1009	35¼	32	34⅞	...
NoSP 5s90	5.2	162	96 17/32	91⅜	96 17/32	+4 13/32
NoSP 4⅞s91	5.2	32	94⅛	90	94⅛	+ 3½
NoSP 4⅞91	5.5	5	89⅛	89⅛	89⅛	...
NoSP 4⅜s92	5.0	67	88½	84¼	87⅜	+ 3⅛
NoSP 4⅜s93	5.0	97	87½	80½	87½	+ 7½
NoSP 4⅜93r	5.5	10	80¼	80¼	80¼	...
Norwst 6¾03	cv	3	218	218	218	+ 59
Norwst 8¼89t	9.4	5	88	88	88	− 2
NwPipl 9½98	9.6	35	99	97	99	+ 1⅛
NwnBl 3¼96	4.3	147	75½	68⅛	75½	+ 5½
NwnBl 3¼96r	4.7	2	69⅛	69⅛	69⅛	...
NwnBl 7⅞11	8.7	2225	94	81½	91	+ 9
NwnBl 7½05	8.4	1306	89⅞	79½	89⅛	+ 7⅞
NwnBl 10s14	9.6	2205	105½	99	103¾	+ 2⅝
NwnBl 8⅝12	9.1	1733	97¾	87	94½	+ 4⅞
NwnBl 8⅛17	8.8	1570	93½	81⅝	92	+ 8½
NwnBl 9½16	9.4	4686	102	93	101½	+ 5½
Norton 7¾12	cv	3377	118	102	114½	+ 7
NortS 6s98	7.5	455	87	78	80	+ 2
NortS 7.7s96	9.0	267	85⅜	79¾	85⅜	+ 5½
NortS 9½s99	10.3	393	92	89⅛	92	+ 4

-O-

		Sales $1,000	High	Low	Last	Net Chg.
OakIn 10½02	cv	353	83½	74½	76	+ 1¾
Oakwd 6½12	cv	2466	64	56½	61½	+ 4
OccP dc9.65s94	9.9	1040	100	94⅝	97½	+ 1½
OcciP d8.95s94	9.4	16962	98	91¾	95¼	+ 1¼
OcciP 10s91	9.9	30279	101½	98	100¾	+ 1
OcciP 9.64s92	9.6	1116	101½	95	100	+ 1
OcciP 10½93	10.4	23081	103	98⅛	101	+ 1
OcciP 10⅞96	10.6	27978	105½	99½	102⅜	+ 1⅛
OcciP 11¾11	11.2	25380	108	102⅜	104¾	+ ⅞
OcciP 10¾98	10.4	89	103	102⅛	103	...
OcciP 10½93	10.1	5020	105	99¼	104	+ 3¾
OcciP 11⅛19	10.9	9035	105⅜	101½	101¾	...
OcciP 9⅝99	10.1	13240	100⅛	95½	95¾	...
OcciP 9¼19	9.9	493	95¼	92¾	93	...
OcciP 10⅛09	10.3	4887	101⅝	97⅝	98¼	...
OcciP 10⅛01	10.2	1241	99¾	98¾	99¼	...
OceanSh 11⅜02	13.2	354	95½	85⅛	86⅛	− ⅜
Ogden 5s93	cv	57	208	184	198	+ 12
OhBIT 7½11	8.5	2000	89½	78⅜	88¾	+ 7½
OhBIT 7⅞13	8.7	2971	94	80⅝	90¾	+ 8
OhBIT 9s18	8.9	2605	101⅝	89⅞	101	+ 8¼
OhBIT 8¾26	9.0	11	97¼	92	97¼	+ 9¼
OhEd 9½06	9.6	2525	101	92	99⅛	+ 7⅜
OhEd 8½06	9.2	722	93⅜	83¼	92¼	+ 8¼
OhEd 8⅜07	9.0	1722	93	82	93	+ 11
OhEd 9½08	9.5	2810	101	90	100	+ 7⅞
OhEd 15½10	14.0	472	114	109	110⅝	− ⅞
OkIGE 4¼93	4.8	44	88⅝	82½	88⅝	+ 8⅝
OkIGE 4¼93r	5.0	10	85½	85½	85½	...
OkIGE 4½95	5.5	66	82½	75½	82½	+ 6
OkIGE 4½95r	6.0	5	75	75	75	...
Orient 10¼98	12.3	1333	92	81¼	83⅛	− 2⅜
OriCap 12½97	12.1	678	104⅛	100	103	+ 2⅜
Orion 11s98	12.2	2304	93	86	90	+ 3½
Orion 10s99	12.2	433	87⅜	78¼	82⅛	+ 1¼
Orion dc10s94	11.4	2752	91	80¾	88	+ 4
Orion 12½98	12.6	173	99⅞	94	99	− 1⅞
Oryx 9¾98	9.5	35	102½	99	102½	+ 2⅛
Oryx 10⅜18	10.2	65	102	98½	102	+ 3¾
Oryx 7½14	cv	2815	129	100¼	123	...
OutbM 7¾96	8.5	337	93½	86¾	91½	+ 5
OwCor 9½00	9.6	457	99¼	90⅜	99¼	+ 7¼
OwCor 12s10	11.7	3237	105¾	99¾	103	+ 2
OxyOG 6⅛97	7.7	606	81½	75¾	80	+ 4¾
OxyOG 6⅝99	8.5	926	81½	74	78	+ 1⅞
OxyOG 7.65s01	9.0	776	88	80	85	+ 4
OxyOG 9¾00	10.0	585	100	93½	97⅜	+ 3
OxyOG zr89	...	5249	99 21/32	91 17/32	99⅝	+ 8

-P-Q-

		Sales $1,000	High	Low	Last	Net Chg.
PPG 9s95	8.9	2537	100⅞	96⅜	100⅞	+ 2⅝
PPG 8½2000	8.7	62	98	93	98	+ 3
PPG 9½91	9.5	160	101	98¼	100⅛	− ⅞

NEW YORK BONDS

		Sales $1,000	High	Low	Last	Net Chg.
PPG 10⅛95	10.0	173	103	100	101	− 1
PS Grp 14s93	13.5	2415	107⅝	103¾	103⅞	− 3⅛
PGE 4½s90	4.6	285	97 21/32	93	97 21/32	+ 4 25/32
PGE 4½90r	4.6	25	97⅞	92⅞	97⅞	+ 5
PGE 5s91	5.3	799	94¾	87⅝	94⅝	+ 5
PGE 5s91r	5.4	210	94½	88½	92¼	...
PGE 4⅝s92	5.2	260	91	83½	89¼	+ 3⅜
PGE 4⅝92r	5.2	79	89⅝	83	89½	...
PGE 4½s93	5.1	340	88½	79	88½	+ 8¼
PGE 4½93r	5.1	67	87½	79½	87½	...
PGE 4⅜s94	5.1	79	85	77	85	+ 7⅞
PGE 4⅜94r	5.2	26	83½	77	83½	...
PGE 4¼s95	5.5	106	79¾	73½	77⅛	+ ⅝
PGE 4¼95r	5.7	22	74	73⅝	74	...
PGE 4½96JJ	5.7	67	80⅝	72	78½	+ 3½
PGE 4½96JJr	6.1	2	74⅛	74⅛	74⅛	...
PGE 4½96KK	5.6	127	80	70	80	+ 10
PGE 8⅞s02	8.9	2647	99⅞	90⅛	99⅜	+ 7⅜
PGE 8s2003	8.6	2161	92¾	82⅞	92½	+ 8¼
PGE 7½s03	8.4	2510	89⅜	78¾	89	+ 8⅞
PGE 7½s04	8.5	1922	88⅝	78¼	88⅛	+ 7⅝
PGE 7¾05ZZ	8.7	1088	90⅛	79⅝	89¼	+ 7⅞
PGE 7¾05A	8.7	1043	90½	79¼	89½	+ 8¼
PGE 9⅛s06	9.2	5414	100½	90⅛	99⅜	+ 8
PGE 9⅝s06	9.5	6305	102	93⅜	101	+ 4¼
PGE 8¼08	8.9	2493	96¼	82⅝	93	+ 9¾
PGE 8½09	9.1	3514	95	83¾	93	+ 7¼
PGE 9⅜11	9.4	4828	101⅛	91	100	+ 6½
PGE 10⅛12	9.8	7513	104¼	97½	103¾	+ 4
PGE 12¼18	11.1	209	114⅜	109	109⅞	− 5⅝
PcLumb 12s96	14.8	3595	86	78⅛	81	− 3
PcLumb 12.20s96B	15.4	104	84⅜	79⅜	79⅜	...
PcLumb 12½98	15.6	429	88	77¼	80	− 2
PcLumb 12.2s96	14.4	50	84⅝	80⅜	84⅝	+ 12¼
PNwT 8⅝10	9.0	2750	97½	87	96	+ 7½
PNwT 8¾08	9.0	2246	98¾	88½	96¾	+ 6¾
PNwT 9s12	9.0	2057	100	90	100	+ 7¼
PNwt 8¾18	9.1	1000	97½	88¼	96¼	+ 7⅞
PacSci 7¾03	cv	2837	71½	65	70¾	+ 5¼
PacTT 3⅝91	3.9	600	93⅝	87¾	93	+ 5¼
PacTT 3⅝91r	4.0	58	91	87	91	...
PacTT 8.65s05	8.9	7978	98½	87¾	97	+ 7⅞
PacTT 8¾06	9.0	8716	99	88⅛	97⅛	+ 6⅝
PacTT 7.8s07	8.5	3200	92	80½	91⅝	+ 8½
PacTT 7¼08	8.3	4080	88	76⅛	87⅝	+ 9
PacTT 7⅝09	8.7	3143	90	78½	88	+ 7
PacTT 9½11	9.4	7084	102¾	93¾	100¾	+ 4
PacTT 8⅞15	9.1	5468	98⅞	88⅛	97½	+ 7⅞
PacTT 8⅜17	9.0	5464	96	83¼	93⅜	+ 7⅞
PacTT 9⅝14	9.5	10724	102¼	94	101¼	+ 4⅞
PacTT 9s18	9.1	10877	100¼	88¼	98¾	+ 7⅞
PacTT 9⅝18	9.5	6755	102	93¾	101	+ 5½
PacTT 9⅞16	9.6	10637	103⅝	96	102½	+ 4¼
PacTT 9¾19	9.6	12571	103	94⅝	101½	+ 4½
Paine 13⅜94	12.7	25	107½	103	105½	− 3½
PAA 11½94B	11.4	987	101½	99⅝	100½	+ ½
PAA dc13½03	26.9	54962	76⅞	46	50⅛	− 7⅞
PAA 15s04	27.9	1034	81	50½	53¾	− 8⅛
PAA 9s10	cv	62273	68½	38½	39	− 6½
PanEP 9.15s92	9.4	95	97½	94	97½	...
ParCm 7s03A	9.1	6762	79¼	71¾	77⅛	+ 1
ParCm 7s03B	9.1	3243	78½	72	77¼	+ 1¾
ParkrH 4s92	cv	11	200	180	180	− 84
Paten 8¼12	cv	4655	60	41¼	44¾	− 15
PennC 11s97	10.7	2357	104½	100	102⅝	+ ⅝
PenyF 7⅞91	8.0	462	99⅛	94¼	98¾	+ 4
PenyF 10.2s94	10.0	287	103¾	98	101½	+ 1½
Penny 8⅞95	8.9	1591	100⅞	95	100¼	+ 4
Penny 9s99	9.0	1525	101	94	100	+ 3¾
Pennzl 8⅜96	8.7	264	98	93	96½	+ 3¾
Pennzl 8¾01	9.0	98	98	90	97	+ 9
Pennzl 12⅛07	11.1	65	109	106½	109	+ ⅞
Pennzl 8⅝96	8.8	303	98½	95	98	+ ½
Pennzl 9s01	9.1	249	100	95⅛	99¼	+ 3⅝
Pennzl 12¼07	11.2	64	110½	109	109¼	+ ¼
PepBoy 6s11	cv	5332	105	81	85	− 3½
Pepsic 7⅝98	8.0	2072	94⅞	83⅜	94¾	+ 7¾
PeryDr 8½10	cv	9721	88¼	68	81½	+ 13
Petrie 8s10	cv	7487	119	95	107¼	+ 12¼
Pfizer 8½99	8.5	905	99¾	91	99¾	+ 7¼
Pfizer 8¾06	cv	350	260	193	257½	+ 52½
Phelp 8.1s96	8.3	299	97⅞	94	97⅜	+ 1⅛
PhilEl 6½93	7.0	1111	93	86⅜	92¼	+ 3½
PhilEl 4½94	5.5	315	84	75⅜	82½	+ 8⅜
PhilEl 6⅛97	7.4	1671	83⅛	75	83	+ 6
PhilEl 9s95	9.1	2335	101	92⅛	99	+ 4⅝
PhilEl 7¾00	8.7	1404	90	78⅞	88⅝	+ 5⅝
PhilEl 8¼96	8.7	1835	96	87½	94⅞	+ 5⅜
PhilEl 7⅜01	8.6	1576	86⅞	78	85½	+ 6½
PhilEl 7½98	8.4	1126	93	81¾	89½	+ 6⅝
PhilEl 7½99	8.4	782	90½	80½	89⅜	+ 7⅝
PhilEl 8½04	9.2	3395	93¾	84	92½	+ 7¾
PhilEl 11⅝00	11.0	2807	107¼	100½	105⅜	+ 2⅝
PhilEl 11s00	10.6	2620	105	99½	104	+ 3½
PhilEl 9⅛06	9.4	2353	97⅛	87½	96⅞	+ 8
PhilEl 9⅝02	9.5	1915	102½	92	101⅛	+ 6⅜
PhilEl 8⅝07	9.2	1533	93⅞	82½	93¾	+ 9¾
PhilEl 8⅝03	9.3	1096	94	84⅛	93⅛	+ 7⅛
PhilEl 9⅛08	9.5	2668	97½	87½	96½	+ 8
PhilEl 12½05	11.6	2134	108¾	106	108	+ 1
PhilEl 14¾05	13.3	1547	114½	107⅝	110½	− 4¼
PhilEl 10⅞95	10.6	282	104	100	102⅛	− ⅛
PhilEl 11¾14	10.7	778	109½	102	109½	+ 6½
PhilEl 11s11	10.6	18674	106	97	104¼	+ 5⅞
PhilEl 10⅜96	10.1	2071	104	95¾	102¼	+ 2⅛
PhilEl 8¾94	8.9	184	98½	93⅝	98½	+ 2½
PhilEl 10¼16	10.0	2375	104	93¾	102⅛	+ 6¾
PhilEl 9⅜17	9.7	1231	99¼	88	97	+ 7¾
PhilEl 10s97	9.8	1255	104⅝	97	102½	+ 3
PhilEl 11s16	10.2	1550	108¼	98¾	107⅝	+ 7⅝
PhilEl 11s97	10.4	101	106	102	106	+ 3
PhilEl 12⅛16	11.1	297	109½	102	109	+ ⅝
PhilM 9⅛03	9.1	590	102	89½	100	+ 6
PhilIP 7⅝01	8.8	1244	89	81	87⅛	+ 6
PhilIP 8⅞00	9.1	929	97½	87¼	97½	+ 8½
PhilIP 12¼12	11.4	797	109¾	103⅝	107	+ ¼
PhilIP 11¼13	10.5	2059	107½	98⅛	106⅞	+ 4⅞
PhilIP 13⅞97	11.7	14820	114¾	109	111¼	+ ¾
PhilP 14¾00	13.4	15471	115½	110	112¼	...
PiedNG 8⅝97	8.8	197	98½	92¼	97⅞	+ 3⅛
PierOn dc11½03	11.8	652	99½	90½	97¾	+ 7¼
Pittstn 4s97	cv	828	67	61⅛	64	+ ¼
Pittstn 9.2s04	cv	2575	96	87	91¼	− 1¾
Pneum 9⅝98	10.9	132	92⅝	83¾	88	− 6
PogoP 8s05	cv	5249	76	61½	75	+ 12¼
PopeTl 6s12	cv	4488	115½	82	105½	+ 21½
PorG 9½s06	9.6	605	102½	91⅝	98½	+ 1
PorG 8¾07	9.1	471	97½	87	95⅞	+ 7
Potltch 5¾12	cv	3736	96¼	84	95⅜	+ 10⅝
PotEl 9½s05	9.3	3859	103	96⅜	102	+ 3¾
PotEl 7¾s07	8.5	565	92	80¾	91	+ 8½
PotEl 8⅜09	9.0	1754	96⅛	85	93½	+ 6⅜
PotEl 9¼16	10.1	10	92	92	92	...
PotEl 8¾16	9.3	10	94	90½	94	+ 7
PotEl 8¼17	9.1	149	90⅝	83½	90⅝	+ 3⅝
PotEl 7s18	cv	5318	95	85	94½	+ 8½
PrmCpt 5¾12	cv	8191	76½	37½	37½	− 33¾
PrmeM 6⅝11	cv	6209	101½	73	74	− 21
PrmeM 7s13	cv	2762	101	71	72½	− 22¾
Primca 6s93	7.4	1226	86	76	81⅜	+ 3⅜
Primca 7¾01	8.8	354	88	82	88	+ 7
Primca 13¼93	13.2	602	104	100½	100½	− 3
ProcG 7s02	8.0	1019	88½	79⅜	87⅛	+ 4⅛
ProcG 8¼05	8.7	6538	97½	85⅞	95¼	+ 7⅛
PrudRt zr90s	...	171	97¼	89½	97	+ 9
PrudRt zr91s	...	43	89	81	89	+ 9½
PrudRt zr92s	...	57	81¼	77¼	81¼	+ 9⅛
PrudRt zr93s	...	8	73	66¼	73	+ 7⅞
PrudRt zr94	...	30	66½	61	66½	...
PrudRt zr95s	...	106	62¼	53	62¼	+ 7¼
PrudRt zr96s	...	45	57½	51	57½	+ 7½
PrudRt zr97s	...	27	52	42⅛	52	+ 8
PSCol 8¾00	9.1	822	97¼	89⅛	96⅛	+ 7
PSCol 7¼01	8.4	150	86⅛	76⅝	86	+ 4½
PSCol 7½02	8.7	249	86⅛	77⅛	86⅛	+ 5⅞
PSInd 7⅝01	8.6	360	88½	79¼	88¼	+ 6
PSInd 7s02	8.6	332	83	75½	81	+ 3¾
PSInd 8s04	8.9	350	89¾	80¾	89¾	+ 6⅛
PSInd 9.6s05	9.7	948	102½	91⅜	98¾	+ 3¾
PSInd 7⅝07	8.9	362	85¼	77	85¼	+ 8⅝

		Sales $1,000	High	Low	Last	Net Chg.
PSInd 8⅛07	9.4	480	89¼	80⅜	86⅜	+ 5⅛
PSInd 8⅞08	9.3	1024	95½	85	95	+ 6¾
viPNH 12s99f	...	1589	105	97¾	103¾	+ 1½
viPSNH 14½00f	...	1774	109	101⅝	106	+ ½
viPSNH 18s89f	...	4868	110	100½	108¼	+ 5
viPSNH 15¾88f m	...	36162	103½	55¼	99	+33 9/16
viPSNH 14⅜91f	...	33996	105	56	103¼	+ 37¾
viPSNH 15s03f	...	33212	105½	56	104½	+ 39½
viPSNH 17½04f	...	1744	100	55¾	100	+ 34
viPSNH 13¾96f	...	7854	134¼	104	134	+ 28½
PSEG 8s37	9.4	134	85	81	84¾	+ 2¾
PSEG 8s37r	9.5	31	84⅝	81	84⅝	...
PSEG 5s37	9.4	244	59⅝	53	53¼	− 3¼
PSEG 5s37r	8.8	51	57	51½	57	...
PSEG 9s95	8.9	1679	103	96¼	101	+ 3⅞
PSEG 8½04	9.0	851	97	87½	94⅜	+ 6⅜
PSEG 12s04	11.3	454	107⅜	103	105⅞	+ ⅝
PSEG 8¾06	9.1	597	98¾	88⅛	96½	+ 8½
PSEG 8.45s06	9.2	553	95	84	92¼	+ 4¾
PSEG 8¼07	8.9	883	94	84	93	+ 7¾
PSEG 9⅜08	9.4	1380	102¾	93	99½	+ 6½
PSEG 9¾09J	9.6	412	102	95	101⅞	+ 3⅛
PSEG 8¾15	8.8	285	100⅜	97⅛	99¾	− ¼
PSEG 9⅛16	9.3	363	98½	89½	98¼	+ 7¼
PSEG 7½96	8.0	324	93⅞	87⅛	93⅞	+ 5⅞
PSEG 8¾16	9.1	333	96½	86¾	96½	+ 9¾
PSEG 8¾94	8.7	598	101¼	93⅞	101	+ 5
PSEG 8¾92	8.7	531	101⅜	96	101	+ 3⅞
PSEG 9⅛93	9.2	236	101⅞	96½	99¼	+ ½
PSEG 8¾99	...	7	102	95	102	...
PullL 7¾s92	8.0	75	98½	97	97	+ 3¾
Quak 7.7s01	8.4	1424	96⅜	84½	91⅞	+ 6¾
QuaStC 9s95	9.1	252	100	96¼	99⅜	+ 3⅜
-R-						
RJR 13.85s99	13.6	463	104	99	101¾	...
RJR Hd zr01	...	4409	54⅝	44	47¾	...
RJR Hd 13⅛01	12.9	14433	104	99	102	...
RJR Hd 13½01	13.0	69382	108½	99	103½	...
RJR Hd 15s01	16.9	56279	107	82	89	...
RJR Hd na14.7s07	...	6279	99	72¾	80	...
RJR Hd zr09	...	4091	102¼	83¼	91¾	...
RJR 7⅜01	9.9	5100	83	72	74¼	+ 1⅝
RJR 8s07	8.2	360	98¼	78	98	+ 25
RalsP 7.7s96	8.0	125	97	85	96⅜	+ 9⅛
RalsP 9½16	9.9	12111	98⅝	88⅛	96	+ 3¼
RalsP 9s96	9.0	4636	101¾	93⅛	100	+ 4¾
RalsP 9⅜16	9.8	5883	98½	87⅛	95¼	+ 5½
RalsP 10.45s18	10.0	415	104⅜	97⅞	104⅜	+ 6½
RapA72 7s94	13.0	2874	62	52½	53⅞	− 4¼
RapA69 7s94	12.9	2773	62	53¾	54⅛	− 8¼
RapA 10¾03	19.2	14814	65¾	51	56	− 4⅝
RapA 12s99	18.5	1126	81	65	65	− 14¾
RapA 10¾04	15.6	459	71⅜	60	69	+ 7⅞
RapA 11s05	17.7	500	69⅞	62	62	− 3
RayJm 7½06	cv	474	115	78½	100	+ 20
RelFncl 8½92	9.0	44	96	94½	94½	...
RelFncl 9⅝97	10.1	250	97⅝	94	95	− 1
RelFncl 11⅜08	13.2	378	99	83¼	86	− 14
RelGp 14s96	14.9	6342	102	92	94	− 3
RelGp 11s96	14.0	5635	86	75	78½	− 6½
RelGp 9⅞98	12.8	1061	82	76	77⅜	− 4½
RelGp 14¼98t	14.0	30	102	102	102	...
RelGp 9⅞99	12.6	625	81	75	78⅛	− 2⅛
RelGp 11½01	16.9	298	70⅛	68	68	...
RepSt 11½95	cv	50	61½	55	55	− 6½
RepNY 9s01	9.0	778	101⅝	93⅛	99⅞	+ 6⅞
RepNY 8¾02	9.4	257	98½	91¾	93¼	...
RepNY 13¾05	13.0	50	106	102⅝	106	− 7
RepNY 15¾91	14.3	125	111⅞	108	110	− 2
RepNY 16s07	13.6	186	122½	110¾	117½	− 18
RepNY 8⅜96	9.0	143	98	83	93¼	+ 1¼
viRepStl 8.9s95f	...	7412	53	40	41	− 1⅜
viRepStl 12⅛03f	...	26918	32	15	17⅜	− 11⅛
Revl 10⅞10	13.4	10105	83½	78	81	+ 2
Revln 11¾95	12.7	20393	97¼	89⅜	92⅜	+ 2¾
ReyTb 7⅞94	8.7	1186	95	85¼	90⅛	+ 3⅝
RochG 9¼06	9.2	830	100⅛	88¾	100⅛	+ 9⅜
RochG 8⅜07	9.4	277	91	83½	89⅜	+ 3⅞

		Sales $1,000	High	Low	Last	Net Chg.
RockIn 4¼91	1.2	10	424	353	353	...
RocInt 7½97	8.1	135	93	85¾	93	+ 6½
RocInt 8⅞99	8.8	384	100⅞	98⅛	100¾	...
RohmH 9⅞00	9.7	65	101¾	98½	101¾	+ 2
Rohr 7s12	cv	3442	100½	77	80½	− 9¼
Rorer 7¾13	cv	2269	126	110	124	+ 5
Rotorx 5s96	cv	1210	72¾	61¼	70¼	+ 7¾
Rotorx 8⅞94	10.3	219	87⅞	80⅛	86	+ 2⅜
Rowan 13¾96	13.1	8307	106⅛	103½	105	+ ½
Ryder 8⅛92	8.3	13	98	97	98	+ ¾
Ryder 10s94	10.3	1	97½	97½	97½	− 2½
Ryder 9¼98	9.6	4	96½	96½	96½	...
Ryder 11⅝93	11.5	465	103	100	101	+ ⅞
Ryder 14s94	13.0	26	108⅝	107	108	− 9⅝
Ryder 13⅜94	12.8	41	104¼	102	104¼	− 6¾
Ryder 12½95	11.9	156	107	103½	105	− 5
Ryder 10⅞95	10.6	224	104	100⅝	102¾	+ 2⅜
Ryder 7¾94	8.0	110	97	89½	97	+ 4⅝
Ryder 8¾17	10.4	45	84½	78	84¼	− 2⅜
Ryder 8⅜17	9.7	92	87	85	86	...
Ryder 9⅜98	9.3	636	101⅞	94⅜	100½	+ 4¼
-S-						
StLSaF 4s97	5.4	605	76	67	74½	+ 7½
StLSaF 4s97r	5.4	30	74½	69½	74½	...
StLSaF 5s06f	...	978	64	54½	63½	+ 5½
StReg 10⅝10	10.4	625	102½	94⅜	102	+ 2
SallM zr14	...	14055	12	8 15/16	11	+ 1¾
SallM zr22	...	4820	8	5⅝	7 25/32	+ 1 9/32
SalmnIn 90	...	2717	125	101	121¾	+ 19¾
SalmnIn 11¾05	11.3	328	106	103¾	104	− 1
SalmnIn 8s96	8.5	683	94½	87⅛	94	+ 7
SalmIn 8s97	8.3	376	96	87	96	+ 11
SanD 8¾07	9.0	1071	98½	87¼	97	+ 6½
SanD 9¾08	9.6	881	103	95¼	101¼	+ 2½
SFeR 8.35s02	9.1	109	92¼	85¼	91⅞	− 1⅛
SFeSP na16s03	...	49464	114⅞	104¼	108½	− 3⅛
SaraL 7⅜96	7.9	409	93⅞	86	93¾	+ 3¾
Savin 11⅜98f	...	1701	77	64⅛	71	...
Savin 14s00f	...	1294	89	75⅛	84	− 1
Scot 8⅞2000	9.0	403	100½	92	99⅛	+ 4⅝
Scot 8¾2000	8.9	637	99⅝	92⅜	98	+ 4½
SeaCst 8.35s96	8.5	354	98½	93½	97¾	+ 3¼
SeaCst 7¾98	8.1	66	95⅜	94⅛	95⅜	+ 4⅝
Seafst 9¼01	9.8	757	100	88⅝	94	+ 3¾
Seagrm zr06	...	10289	41⅜	30¼	41⅜	+ 11⅛
Sears 13¼92	12.0	2441	113½	107⅜	110½	− ½
Sears 12s94	10.8	3858	112⅝	105⅛	111½	+ 3
Sears 7½99t	7.8	132	97	90⅛	96½	+ 4½
SecP 11¾93	11.6	1175	104	101	101½	− 1¼
Sequa 10½98	10.4	5	100½	100½	100½	...
SvceCp 6½11	cv	6234	101¼	77½	82	− 6
ShrLehm 10¾96	10.2	4197	108½	100½	105	+ 2½
ShrLR 10¾03	10.7	1745	102	98⅝	100¼	+ ⅛
ShellO 5.3s92	5.7	339	93¼	87⅝	93¼	+ 6¼
ShellO 8½00	8.6	2127	99	89⅝	98½	+ 5⅞
ShellO 7¼02	8.0	851	90⅞	81⅛	90½	+ 8⅜
ShellO 8¾05	8.8	1707	100	90½	99⅜	+ 5⅞
ShellO 8s07	8.4	1120	95	83⅞	95	+ 8½
ShllPL 7½99	8.5	136	90	87¾	88⅛	− ⅞
ShWi 5.45s92	5.9	669	93⅜	87¼	92⅞	+ 5⅝
ShWi 6¼95	cv	4	487	487	487	+ 70
ShWi 9.45s99	9.5	110	101	95	100	+ 3½
Shoney zr04	...	521	38	28⅝	38	...
Showbt dc13s04	13.4	766	103¼	97	97	− ½
Signl 5⅞97	7.1	235	83½	76⅜	83¼	+ 1⅛
Signl 8s09	cv	1220	85	76	81½	+ 4¾
SkilCp 5s92	cv	4	237½	232	232	+ 39
Socny 4¼93	4.8	375	90¼	81	87⅞	+ 4¾
Socny 4¼93r	5.0	2	84⅜	84⅜	84⅜	...
SohioP 8¾01	8.9	666	99¼	91¼	98½	+ 5
SooLne 10¾95	10.3	67	104	98	104	− 3⅝
SoestB 4¾97	cv	740	104½	77	77	− 15
SoestB 6½99	cv	2082	99	84	87½	+ 3½
SoCG 8.85s95	8.8	822	100½	92¼	100½	+ 4¾
SoCG 7⅝97	8.3	99	91¾	85¾	91¾	+ 6⅝
SoCG 8¾s96	9.0	110	99⅞	92⅛	97¼	− 2¼
SoCG 8½97	8.7	84	98½	92⅝	98	+ 2⅛
SoCG 9⅜16	9.4	22	100	93½	100	+ 7
SoCG 8¼96	8.9	100	93	93	93	+ 3

NEW YORK BONDS

		Sales $1,000	High	Low	Last	Net Chg.
SooCG 8⅞93	9.0	12	99	99	99	+ 2
SoCG 9⅜98	9.2	40	102	101	102	...
SCouG 9½95	9.5	438	101¼	96⅝	100½	+ 1½
SoNG 7.7s91	7.8	418	99⅜	97½	98¼	− ⅝
SoNG 11⅜94	11.2	456	103½	101	102	+ ⅝
SNET 8⅛08	8.7	2595	98	83¾	93½	+ 8¼
SNET 9⅝10	9.2	1000	104⅞	96¼	104⅞	+ 5⅞
SPac 10.35s94	10.2	1807	102½	97⅛	101½	+ 1⅞
SPac 2¾s96	3.8	384	72	62¾	71½	+ 8½
SPac 2¾96r	4.0	18	68	68	68	...
SPacTr 8.2s01	9.0	189	93	85⅞	90⅞	+ 4½
SouRy 5s94	5.8	277	87¼	80	86⅛	+ 4⅛
SouRy 5s94r	5.8	230	87	80¼	86⅛	...
SouRy 8½01	8.8	36	96⅛	92¼	96⅛	+ 2⅛
SRyM 5s96	6.3	26	78⅞	75½	78⅞	+ 2⅜
vjSomk 15¼91f	...	35880	65	2	2¾	− 44¾
vjSomk 13¼94f	...	79679	55	2	3¼	− 41
vjSomk 8½98f	cv	21780	37½	2	2¾	− 27¼
vjSomk 10⅞89f	...	90537	84¼	12¾	17 27/32	− 62 21/32
vjSomk 11491f	...	23463	67¾	3⅞	18	− 42
vjSomk 11⅞93f	...	48100	67¾	13	18⅛	− 38⅜
SwstFrst 12⅛01	12.2	1386	103¾	99	99	− 3¾
SwEng 8½10	cv	2052	110	89	108	+ 18
Sprague 14s98	13.9	4118	108¾	98½	101	− 2
StBrn 6¾93	7.6	337	91⅞	87	88¼	− 1⅛
StBrn 7¾01	10.2	260	83	73	76⅛	+ 2
StBrn 9½04	10.6	286	93	77	90	+ 2
StdOil 7.6s99	8.0	861	99	93⅝	95⅜	+ 1¼
StdOil 8½00	8.9	1260	98¼	90⅛	96	+ 4
StdOil 8⅜07	8.9	502	95¼	86¼	94¼	+ 4¼
StdOh 7⅝91	7.7	1281	99⅜	93¾	98⅝	+ 3⅜
StdOh zr90	...	110	96¾	92	96¾	+ 6⅝
StdOh dc6.3s01	8.5	15	76	74½	74½	+ 1
StdOil 8s93	8.1	1268	100	91¾	98½	+ 4½
StdPac 12¾99	12.8	113	103½	99½	100	+ ½
StdPac 13⅞04	13.6	1377	108	99¾	101⅞	− 1⅛
Stauf 8⅛96	8.4	156	98	93	97⅛	+ 4
Stauf 8.85s01	9.1	131	97	93¾	96⅞	+ 2⅜
Stego 14¾01	18.4	873	100	80	80	− 16
SterlBn 6½90	cv	100	98⅞	87	98¼	+ ¼
SterlBn na92s	...	46	115	100¼	100¼	...
StrlBn na94s	...	256	106⅜	95¼	96	− 10⅜
StrlBn na96s	...	329	101½	95	95	− 5½
StrlBn 98	...	173	101	96	96	− 4⅜
Stokly 8s98	8.5	72	94	90¾	94	+ 2½
StoneCn 13⅝95	13.0	15834	107⅝	101	104½	− 1½
StoneCn 11½99	11.6	4160	100¾	96¾	98¾	...
StrEq dc9⅞90	9.9	262	100	99 5/32	100	+ ⅞
StrTch 13½96	...	11648	111	93⅛	95⅛	− 11½
Suave 5s97	cv	195	85	70	76	− 2⅛
SunCo 7⅛02	8.4	45	86	84⅛	85	− 1
SunCo 6¾12	cv	1105	110	94	110	+ 10¼
SunCo 9⅜16	9.5	128	101⅞	95	99	+ 5⅜
SunOil 4⅝90	5.0	35	94½	91⅛	91¾	+ ¾
SunOil 8½00	8.9	320	95⅞	85¼	95⅞	+ 5¾
vjSunbe 5½92f	...	1468	97	84	87	− 9⅞
Sunsh 8½95	9.4	190	94⅜	84	90½	− 4½
SunsS 8½95	9.4	230	95	86½	90⅞	− 1⅛
Sunsh 8s95	8.9	522	92½	81	90	+ 6¾
Sunsh 9¾04	10.8	94	102	90½	90½	− 4½
Sunsh 9s94	10.8	2867	85	72	83¼	+ 13
Sunsh 9½94	11.4	1859	90	72½	83	+ 11½
Sunsh 9½95	...	1746	85	70	80½	+ 12½
Sunsh 10¾95	12.3	1166	89	82	87¾	+ 5¾
Sunsh 8⅞08	cv	3540	92½	79	82⅞	− 7⅛
SupOil 9⅝99	9.6	161	100½	95⅛	100	+ 1
Sysco zr04	...	2775	44	39¼	43	...

-T-

		Sales $1,000	High	Low	Last	Net Chg.
TJX 7¼10	cv	7743	100¼	84	88	+ 2
TJX 9½16	10.0	293	95	89	95	+ 4½
TRW 5½92	6.0	186	93¼	88	92⅛	+ 1¼
TRW 8¼96	...	332	96	86½	92⅝	+ 1⅝
TRW 8¾91	8.8	264	100	95¼	99¾	+ 1⅝
TRW 8⅛04	9.0	321	91¾	82¼	90	+ 5½
TRW 9⅞s	9.9	185	100⅛	95	100⅛	+ ⅛
TRW 8¾96	8.8	107	99	93	98⅞	+ 7⅛
Tandy 10s94	10.0	1653	102¾	99½	100½	− 1½
Teledy 6½92	6.8	179	95⅞	93⅜	95⅛	+ 1⅛
Teledy 7⅞94	8.3	120	94¾	93	94¾	+ ⅝
Teledy 7s99	8.3	2069	86¼	79¾	84⅜	+ 4⅝
Teledy 10s04A	10.0	6762	100⅞	94⅛	100¼	+ 3
Teledy 10s04C	10.0	8768	100½	95	99⅞	+ 3
TencCr 8⅜97	9.0	230	95	89⅝	93⅜	+ 2
TencCr 9¾94	9.6	718	103	96⅝	101½	+ 1¾
Tenco 9⅜93	9.4	2131	104	94¼	100	+ 2¼
Tenco 10s08	10.0	320	100¼	97⅛	100¼	− ⅝
TencoCr 9s95	9.0	192	100	97½	100	...
TennGas 8⅜02	9.2	592	95½	85¼	91⅛	+ 6
TennGas 8⅞03	9.1	397	97⅜	89⅜	97	+ 4
TennGas 9½04	9.7	262	100	96¾	98⅜	+ ⅛
TennGas dc6s11	9.0	17059	69⅛	59½	66⅜	+ 4⅞
TennGas 13.7s92	12.3	921	112	106⅜	111½	+ 3⅜
TennGas 11⅛13	10.5	959	107½	100	105¾	+ 1¼
TennGas 9¼96	9.3	1581	101	92⅛	99½	+ 4⅜
TennGas 10¼16	10.1	2650	104⅜	95½	101⅞	+ 5⅜
TennGas 9s97	9.1	966	100¾	90½	98½	+ 6½
TennGas 9⅜17	9.9	1093	98⅝	88	95	+ 3⅝
TVA 7s97	7.7	2146	93½	84	91½	+ 6⅝
TVA 7s97r	7.7	681	94⅜	83⅞	91½	...
TV 7.35s97B	7.9	1369	94⅞	85	93	+ 6½
TV 7.3597Br	8.0	502	95⅝	85⅜	92¼	...
TV 7.35s97C	7.8	1598	95	84½	93¾	+ 8¾
TV 7.3597Cr	7.8	854	94⅝	85	93⅞	...
TVA 7.4s97	8.0	1869	94¾	85⅛	92⅞	+ 6½
TVA 7.4s97r	8.0	591	94¾	84	93	...
TV 7.35s98A	7.9	1125	94	84¾	92⅞	+ 5⅜
TV 7.3598Ar	7.9	356	93¾	84⅜	93½	...
TV 7.35s98B	7.9	1500	94⅝	84⅜	92⅝	+ 7
TV 7.3598Br	7.8	1007	94½	84½	93⅞	...
TV 7¾s98C	8.1	1692	96⅜	86¾	95⅜	+ 7½
TV 7¾98Cr	8.1	830	96⅝	86	95⅝	...
TVA 7.7s98	8.1	1235	96⅜	86⅛	95	+ 8
TVA 7.7s98r	8.1	583	96½	85½	95	...
TerR 4s19	8.4	92	48	39	47½	− 2
TerR 4s19r	8.8	5	45¼	45¼	45¼	...
Tesoro 5¼89	cv	3	100½	100½	100½	+ 2⅝
Tesor dc12¾01	15.3	5586	93	75	83⅜	− 9⅝
Texco 9s99	9.0	447	100½	95½	100½	+ ½
Texco 13⅝94	12.7	14071	109¼	105⅛	107¼	+ ¾
Texco 10¾00t	10.8	1365	101	99⅜	100	+ ¼
Texaco zr00	...	4386	105	99⅛	100	− ¼
Texco 9s96	8.9	95	101	100⅞	101	...
Texco 5¾97	7.0	7162	82⅝	72	82¼	+ 9¾
Texco 7¾01	8.6	6680	91	77⅝	90¼	+ 11¼
Texco 8⅞05	9.1	13382	98½	83	97⅛	+ 13⅜
Texco 8½06	9.1	11558	95¼	79	93½	+ 13⅝
TxNO 3⅜90	3.6	37	95	91	95	+ 3½
TxNO 3⅜90r	3.6	2	92¾	92¾	92¾	...
TxPac 5s00	6.9	246	73½	64	72	+ 2
TxInd 7¾92	8.3	57	97⅛	93⅝	93⅞	− ⅜
TxInd 9s08	cv	1768	110½	91½	94	− 9½
TxIns 4.8s90	5.2	4	92	92	92	+ ¼
TxIns 8⅞93	9.0	520	100¼	94⅝	99⅛	+ 3⅞
TxOG 7½92	7.8	20	95⅞	95⅞	95⅞	+ 2¼
TxOG 7⅜92	7.9	25	92⅞	90⅜	92⅞	+ ½
TxOG 8¼94	8.7	52	94⅞	93	94⅞	− ⅛
TxOG 10¼95	10.3	417	102	98¼	100	− ½
TxOG 8¼97	8.9	205	93	90	92⅞	+ 2
TxOG 9s98	9.3	52	98½	94	97⅛	+ 3⅛
TxOG 11½02	11.4	25	101¼	100¾	101⅛	+ 1⅝
Texfi 4¾96	cv	166	65⅛	62	65	+ 3
Texfi 11¼91	cv	101	100	96¼	100	+ 2
Textrn 7½97	8.2	575	92	90	91	+ 5⅞
Textrn 11¾95	11.6	10	101⅜	101⅜	101⅜	− 1⅞
Textrn 11s95	10.6	202	105	102	104¼	− 1⅛
Textrn 9¼16	9.9	453	95	83	93½	+ 4⅛
Textrn 9½16	10.0	30	95	88¾	95	+ 5
Textrn 9¼17	10.1	224	98¼	85	91⅝	+ 8
Thckry 9s90f	cv	18	106	105	106	+ 3
Thermo 5¾12	cv	10787	124½	81	106	+ 22¼
Thortc 6½12	cv	2399	40¾	14	14	− 26
Thortc 8⅝04	53.1	5561	45	14	16¼	...
Tidwtr 7¾05	cv	304	67	55	67	+ 11
Tidwtr 7s10	cv	10217	74⅜	52	74⅜	+ 19⅜
Tiger 11½95	11.5	453	101⅞	96⅝	100¼	+ 2⅝
Tiger 8⅝05	cv	145	83½	80½	81½	− 2
Time 9⅞09	10.2	715	98½	89⅛	97	− 1½
Time 8¾17	10.2	6906	89	79¾	86	...

NEW YORK BONDS

		Sales $1,000	High	Low	Last	Net Chg.
viTodSh 14s96f	...	13964	96¾	80	93⅜	+ 12⅜
TolEd 9s00	9.4	817	98⅜	88⅛	95⅝	+ 5⅞
TolEd 7½02	9.0	601	86	76	83⅝	+ 6
TolEd 8s03	9.0	490	89½	77¾	88½	+ 10½
TolEd 9.65s06	9.8	1429	99¾	90½	98½	+ 7
TolEd 9⅝08	9.7	454	99¾	91	99	+ 7
Tosco 12½91	12.2	5676	105	99	102½	− 2
Toyota 8¾91	8.7	849	101	96⅛	100½	+ 1½
TrailF 8½96	9.5	175	89½	85½	89½	− 4
TrailF 7⅞93	8.0	335	98¼	95⅞	98¼	− ¼
TranF 7⅞91	8.0	686	99½	94¼	99	+ 2⅜
TranF 8½01	8.5	61	100	99¼	99¾	+ ¼
TranF 9⅞99	9.9	102	104	99⅛	99⅝	+ ⅝
Trvlr 8.7s95	8.8	2195	100	92½	99¼	+ 4¼
Trvlr 7⅝97	8.0	495	95	86⅜	94⅞	+ 5⅞
Trvlr 8.32s15	cv	12631	104	93¼	98½	+ 4⅝
Trinty zr01	...	428	61	45	49	+ 2
TrinLs 6¾12	cv	2054	137½	102	102	− 13
Triton zr05	...	598	32	25	30⅝	+ 5⅛
TucEP 8⅛01	9.2	1079	93	84⅛	88	+ 1⅜
TucEP 7.55s02	8.9	740	86	80	84⅞	+ 3⅜
TucEP 7.65s03	9.2	936	86¼	79	83½	− ½
TucEP 10½05	10.2	2983	105	99	102½	− ½
TCFox 10¼98	11.4	1203	91½	83½	89⅞	+ 2⅞
TCFox 13¼00	13.1	4136	101	96	100⅞	+ 4
-U-						
UCCEL 7¼95	cv	506	83½	79	82	+ ½
UNC 7½06	cv	4121	80½	57	59⅜	− 18⅞
UNC 11½96	12.2	349	99¼	91	94⅛	− 4¾
USG na16s08	...	40448	105¼	36	51½	− 49⅛
USLICO 8s11	cv	1510	97	90	93¼	+ 1¼
USLICO 8½14	cv	12	105	101	104½	...
USX 4⅝96	5.6	7647	82⅝	72½	82	+ 8¼
USX 7¾01	8.3	1548	93¾	81½	93½	+ 8⅝
USX 5¾01	cv	17735	78½	70	74¾	+ 4⅜
USX 9s92	9.0	21415	101½	95½	99¾	+ 1⅝
USX 7s17	cv	102	105	102½	104½	...
UT Crd 8¼02	8.9	50	94¼	89½	92½	+ 10¾
UT Crd 8.85s03	9.5	47	95	88½	93	− 2
UT Crd 9s03	9.2	14	98	92½	98	...
UT Crd 11¼93	11.2	363	102	100¼	100¼	− 1¾
UBk 7.35s01	8.4	524	90	80	88	+ 6
UnCa 7½96	8.2	100	95	86⅛	91¼	+ ¼
UnCa 10⅞10	10.7	20	103	101½	101½	− ½
UnCa 12¾12	11.8	626	109	108¼	108¼	...
UCarb 5.3s97	6.7	1643	79¼	73	78⅞	+ 5½
UCarb 8½05	9.3	6403	92¼	81	91	+ 10
UCarb 7½06	8.3	400	95	81¼	90⅝	+ 9⅜
UCarb 9.35s09	9.7	6806	97⅜	85⅞	96⅝	+ 9⅝
UCarb 13¼93	13.2	5672	105½	100⅛	100½	− 3
UCarb 14¼96	13.8	642	114½	103⅝	103⅝	− 3⅜
UCarb 15s06	13.0	889	119	110	115	+ 1⅝
UCarb 7½12	cv	31744	106½	87	88¼	− 5¼
UCarb 9¾94	9.6	31999	102	94⅜	101⅜	+ 5⅝
UnEl 10½05	10.2	1760	107	99¼	103¼	+ 1¾
UnEl 8⅞06	9.2	514	100	88	96¼	+ 6⅛
UnEl 8⅝07	9.1	385	96⅝	84½	95	+ 8⅜
UnEl 9⅜16	9.4	55	100	92	100	+ 6½
UnEl 8⅞96	9.0	174	102⅜	94	99⅛	+ 5⅛
UOilC 6⅝98	7.8	740	89	81	84⅞	+ ¼
UOilC 8⅝06	9.2	375	97¾	91¼	94¼	− 1¼
UPac 4¾99	cv	58	532	438	504	+ 74
UPac 8.4s01	8.7	575	96¾	88	96¾	+ 4
UPac 11⅞10	11.1	314	111	103	107	+ ⅞
UTexP 13s95	12.4	307	107⅝	100	104½	− ⅝
Unisy 8.55s95	8.8	10	97⅝	97⅝	97⅝	− 2⅜
Unisys 8.2s96	8.6	473	97	91	95	+ 2½
Unisys 13⅞92	12.7	994	117	107⅝	109	− 3¾
Unisys 10¾95	10.6	1629	104¼	100	101	− 1½
UnAL 5s91	5.4	1313	92⅝	86½	91¾	+ 3⅞
UnAL 4¼92	4.8	1656	90	80⅛	89⅛	+ 5
UBrnd 5½94	cv	4624	100	85½	100	+ 4
UBrnd 9⅛98	10.3	426	88½	80½	88¼	+ 7¾
UBrnd 10½04	11.5	6067	93	86⅛	91⅝	+ 2⅝
UBrnd 10¼05	11.6	1642	91⅞	84⅛	88⅛	− ⅛
UBrnd 11⅞03	12.2	1153	101	95⅝	97½	− 3½
UJer 7¾97	8.5	411	94	87½	90⅞	+ 2¼
UnMM 13¾00	38.3	7760	72	29½	35⅞	− 35⅝

		Sales $1,000	High	Low	Last	Net Chg.
USAir 12⅞00	11.3	17	115¾	109	114	+ 2
US Bnc 12.50s10	11.4	25	109½	109½	109½	+ 28½
USGy 4⅞91	5.5	60	90½	87	88¼	+ ½
USGy 7⅞04	10.9	15	85	70	80	...
USHo 5½96	cv	344	55	46	46	− 4½
USHo 13¼94	17.8	10057	82⅝	44	74¼	+ 1¾
USHo 11¼00	12.2	152	92	73¼	92	...
USHo na10s95B	...	1	86	86	86	...
USBO 7¾02	9.0	314	87½	82	86⅜	+ 3⅝
USPIC 8s96	8.4	380	97	94⅝	95⅝	+ ⅜
USTNY 8½01	9.1	88	93⅞	86⅞	93⅞	+ 4⅞
UnTec 5⅜91	5.8	190	93¼	89	92½	+ 3
UnTec 4½92	5.1	92	94	82⅛	88	+ 4⅞
UnTec 9⅜04	9.4	150	100	91	100	+ 2½
UnTec 7¾98	8.3	70	93¾	86	93¾	+ 4⅝
UnTec 8⅛96	8.4	369	100	91¼	97¼	+ ½
UnTel 9.4s99	9.4	233	100	96	100	+ 2
UnTel 11s00	10.8	112	102½	99½	101½	+ 1½
UnTel 9¾10	5.4	1814	179½	116	179½	+ 62¾
UTelO 7.6s02	8.8	48	87⅝	81⅝	86⅝	+ 4⅜
UTelO 9s08	9.3	73	96¾	89½	96¾	+ 3⅝
UnUtil 5s93	cv	1	159	159	159	− 2¾
Univar 9¾99	9.8	106	100¾	96¼	99½	+ 2¾
Utilicp 6⅝11	cv	2676	92½	87½	91¾	+ 1¼
-V-						
VerP 9⅝98	9.6	802	101½	92	100	+ 4
VerY 8½98	9.3	69	91½	88⅝	91½	+ ⅞
VerY 10⅛07	10.1	347	101	94⅝	100⅝	+ 5
VerY 9⅜07	9.4	190	99½	88¼	99½	+ 11⅛
VerY 9⅞07	10.0	77	99	94	98⅞	+ 5⅜
Vestrn 9s11	cv	24827	65	19¾	21	− 34
VaSw 5s2003	7.6	86	66	61	66	+ ½
VaRy 6s2008	8.4	117	71½	65¾	71½	+ 5¼
viVough 6¾88f	...	1228	70	62½	63	− 2
Vul 10¼2000	10.4	46	103	99	99	− ⅝
-W-						
WMS 12¾96	cv	2406	103	91	99	+ 3
WaRR 4¼91	4.5	38	95	90⅝	93½	+ 2⅞
WaRR 4¼91r	4.4	2	95⅝	92⅝	95⅝	
WarC 9⅛96	9.6	1826	98	87	95⅛	+ ⅛
WarC 10⅞95	10.6	4474	104	99	102½	+ 1
WarC 11¼13	11.2	3759	106	100	102½	− 1½
WarL 8⅞00	9.2	201	100	93	96¾	+ 2¼
WasteM 01s	...	2059	116	71½	116	+ 43¾
WasteM 8¾18	9.1	35	97¼	96½	96½	− ½
WasteM zr12	...	45260	40½	25⅜	37½	+ 11¾
Wean 5½93n	cv	443	62½	44¼	62½	+ 18¼
Wean 5½93	cv	527	62½	44	62	+ 17¾
Wean 12s99	19.0	259	75	51¼	63	+ 10
Webb 10⅜09	cv	1959	98½	82¼	88	...
Weingrt 8s09	cv	1587	105	99½	102	...
WellF 7⅞97	8.6	753	95	84	91⅞	+ 5⅝
WellF 8.6s02	8.8	250	97⅜	85	97⅜	+ 7⅜
Wendys 7¼10	cv	5083	74½	66½	72¼	+ 5¾
WElec 8⅜95	8.5	1854	99⅝	92⅝	98½	+ 4½
WElec 7½96	7.9	303	95¼	89	95¼	+ 4¾
WPI 10s01	11.8	1399	89⅞	80	85	+ 3
WUC 5¼97	cv	3748	42½	13	20	− 10½
WUC 10¾97	43.0	3871	59½	15½	25	− 22
WUC 19¼92	50.3	21847	96	35¼	38¼	− 50¾
WUTI 5s92	23.5	2000	65	20⅛	21¼	− 19¾
WUTI 8.45s96	40.2	360	50	18⅛	21	− 25
WUTI 7.9s97f	...	222	38	15⅛	17	− 17⅜
WUTI 8.1s98	47.6	71	43½	17	17	− 13
WUTI 9¼97f	...	143	49½	22	22	− 28
WUTI 16s91f	...	5812	95¾	31¼	34¼	− 44¾
WUTI 13¼08	55.2	6121	67¼	18	24	− 32⅞
WUTI 13⅝94	47.4	501	75½	20½	28¾	− 42¼
WstC 8½91	8.5	220	99½	95	99½	+ 2½
WstC 7.6s97	8.2	515	94⅛	84⅜	92⅜	+ 5⅞
WstC 7s96	7.1	50	99¼	97⅛	99¼	...
WstC 8⅜96	8.5	340	98½	89⅜	98	+ 5⅛
WstgE 5⅜92	5.8	702	93	88	92¾	+ 2¾
WstgE 9s09	cv	730	242	165¾	234	+ 68
Wstv 9¾2000	9.8	93	101	98⅝	99⅜	+ ⅜
Wstvco 12⅛12	11.1	50	108¾	108¾	108¾	+ 3¾
Wstvco 12.3s15	11.4	50	107¾	107¾	107¾	+ ⅝
Wstvco 10¼18	10.3	5	100	100	100	...

	Sales $1,000	High	Low	Last	Net Chg.			Sales $1,000	High	Low	Last	Net Chg.
Weyh 5.2s91	5.5	409	96	91⅞	95⅜ + 3⅜		Woolw 7⅜96	7.5	865	99	94⅜	98⅜ + 4
Weyh 7.65s94	7.9	604	98⅝	91⅝	97 + 3⅞		Woolw 9s99	9.1	4829	100	93⅛	99⅜ + 4⅜
Weyh 8⅝00	8.8	550	98⅞	92½	98⅛ + 5⅛							
Weyh 8.9s04	9.1	372	98½	92	98 + 4½		**-X-Y-Z-**					
Weyh 7.95s06	8.8	544	93	82¼	90⅛ + ¾		Xerox 6s95	cv	9566	96	89	92 + 3
Whirl 9⅝00	9.4	2	102½	102	102½ + 4		Xerox 8⅝99	8.7	1149	98¾	91	98¾ + 6⅛
Whitkr 9⅝93	10.4	26	92½	92	92½ + 3		Xerox 10⅝93	10.5	11080	102½	100	101¼ − ⅜
Whitkr 10s96	11.0	1356	94½	83	91 + 6		Xerox 13¼14	11.5	25	117	115	115 − 5½
WilcxGb 7s14	cv	1286	100	90	92 ...		Xerox 8⅛96	8.5	2026	97	88½	95½ + 5⅞
Wms 9.40s96	9.4	259	100	96½	100 + 2⅛		viYngS 4½90f	...	344	96½	92⅜	94 + ⅝
WisBl 7¼07	8.4	1118	88	77½	86⅛ + 7⅝		viYngS 10½00f	...	3939	118	106¼	116½ + 8¾
WisBl 8s14	8.8	2127	95	82	91⅜ + 7¾		viYngS 9⅞91f	...	1403	118	105⅞	116 + 10⅜
WisBl 8¼16	8.8	716	95¾	84	93½ + 6½		Zapt 10⅞01f	...	9528	91⅞	30	40⅝ − 41⅜
WisG 10⅝95	9.8	120	108	101⅛	108 + 6		Zapt 10¼97f	...	12069	95	30	41⅞ − 42⅛
Witco 4½93	cv	20	260	260	260 − 8		ZapOff 8⅝96	8.6	282	100	94½	99¾ + ⅝
Witco 7.45s97	8.1	25	92½	92½	92½ ...		Zenith 6¼11	cv	11092	84½	60½	62½ − 15
Witco 5½12	cv	6751	94	79	81 + 2		ZenNt 10¼94	9.9	961	103⅛	97	103⅛ + 3⅛
							Zurn 5¾94	cv	23	289	194	289 + 96

Sales figures are unofficial.

cv-Convertible bond. ct-Certificates. dc-Deep discount. ec-European currency units. f-Dealt in flat. m-Matured bonds, negotiability impaired by maturity. NA-No accrual. pr-Exchangeable into debentures. r-Registered. rp-Reduced principal amount. st-Stamped. t-Floating rate. wd-When distributed. ww-With warrants. xw-Without warrants. zr-Zero coupon. kd-Danish Krone. il-Italian Lira.

vi-In bankruptcy or receivership or being reorganized under the Bankruptcy Act, or securities assumed by such companies.

AMERICAN STOCK EXCHANGE

The following tabulation gives the 1989 sales, high, low, last price and net change from the previous year in stocks listed on the American Stock Exchange.

Stock	Symbol	Div	Yld	Sales 100s	Hi	Lo	Last	Net Chg
-A-								
ABM Gold	AGO		...	64724	3⅜	2½	3⅛	– ⅛
AIFS	AIF		14	6641	5½	2¾	4¾	– ½
AIM StratFd	AST	1.14	...	25084	10⅛	9⅝	9¾	...
AIM Tel	AIM		16	9515	5	2⅝	2¾	– 1¼
AMC Entn	AEN		10	25008	12⅜	3¾	8⅝	+ 4½
AM Int wt			...	4533	2¾	1	1⅛	– ⅝
AOI Coal	AOI	.05e	60	16214	3	2½	3	+ ¼
ARC Int	ATV		...	24379	4¾	1⅞	2⅛	– 1⅜
AT&E	ATW		...	118113	19¼	7⅞	15	+ 6½
AT&T Crd wt			...	20726	1½	⅝	⅝	
ATI Med	ATI		16	56070	11	3¾	8⅜	+ 4⅝
AT&T Fund	ATF	2.30e	...	23842	61⅝	40⅛	61⅝	+ 20⅞
Abiomed	ABD		...	11153	16⅞	10⅛	11	+ ⅞
AckrlyComm	AK		...	21506	12	8½	9	...
AcmeUtd	ACU		...	5231	6½	4	4⅛	– 1⅞
ActionInd	ACX		9	13512	5	2¾	3	– 1
ActonCp	ATN		3	16871	24⅛	11	14	+ 2¼
Acton pf		3.75	...	1055	30	24	26½	+ 1½
AdamsRes	AE		8	7396	2⅛	1⅜	1⅝	+ ⅛
AdvMedTech	AMA		...	62225	11⅞	4⅝	11	...
AdvMedTech pf		1.00	...	11639	7⅝	5⅝	7½	...
AirWaterTech	AWT		...	60141	21½	15¼	21½	...
AirExprss	AEX		10	15048	19½	14	14¾	– 2¾
AircoaHotel	AHT	2.28	...	10459	13	8⅞	9⅛	– 1
Alamco wi			...	179	5⅜	4¼	5	...
AlbaWaldn	AWS		...	2236	9⅛	6¼	6⅝	– ⅝
Alfin	AFN		...	30600	4⅝	1½	1⅞	– ½
AllncBcp	ABK		...	1019	1⅜	¼	¼	– ⅝
AllouHlth	ALU		...	3853	3	1⅞	1⅞	...
AllouHlth wt			...	2326	11/16	5/16	5/16	...
AllstarIns	SAI	1.00i	...	34021	7⅞	1⅜	1⅞	– 3⅞
AlphaInd	AHA		48	27189	5½	3¼	3⅜	– ½
AlpineGp	AGI		...	16125	6½	1⅜	2	– 4⅛
Alcoa pf		3.75	...	2720	45	38¼	44½	+ 4¼
Alza	AZA		84	261997	45⅞	22⅜	43⅞	+ 21½
Alza un			...	28950	34⅞	13⅛	32¾	+ 19¼
AmBrit	ABI	.04i	...	3732	4¾	1½	1¾	– 2¾
Amdahl	AMH	.10	9	989666	23⅜	10¾	14⅜	– 5⅞
AmFPrepFd2	PF	1.83e	...	5325	17	12⅜	13¾	– 2⅛
AmBiltrite	ABL	.15	13	2383	19½	15¾	16½	– 2¾
AmBkCT	BKC	1.20	7	837	20⅝	18⅝	18⅞	– 1⅜
AmCapital	ACC		...	5593	3½	5/16	⅝	– 2¼
AmCapital pf		3.75	...	2740	20¾	4⅜	5⅜	– 14¾
AmExplor	AX		41	68983	4⅜	2½	4⅛	+ 1½
AmExplor wt			...	13055	2⅛	11/16	1 7/16	+ 11/16
AmFructse A	AFCA		10	89041	24½	8¼	22¾	+ 13¼
AmFructse B	AFCB		10	13256	23¼	8⅜	21½	+ 12⅝
viAmHlthCare	AHI		...	12690	13/16	1/16	⅛	– ⅜
AmIsraelPapr	AIP	.24e	10	1753	19¼	12	17⅝	+ 5½
AmList	AMZ	1.70e	19	4128	17⅜	10	16⅝	+ 6⅝
AmMaize A	AZEA	.52	28	14716	24¾	15½	19⅝	+ 3¾
AmMaize B	AZEB	.52	30	4384	24⅞	15⅛	20⅝	+ 5⅛
AmMedBldgs	A		...	20991	1⅛	¼	⅜	– ⅜
AmOil&Gas	AOG		...	7580	8¾	5¼	7⅜	+ 2¼
AmPetrfina A	APIA	3.20	8	3617	90	67¼	74⅝	+ 5¾
AmPrecInd	APR	.20	26	8803	20¼	12⅜	19½	+ 3⅝
AmRestrtPtrs	RMC	1.40	8	2439	10½	8⅛	10¼	+ 1¼
AmSciEngrg	ASE		...	24198	10⅜	4½	7⅝	+ 2½
AmSciEngrg wt			...	6153	3⅜	9/16	1¾	+ 13/16
AmShrdHosp	AMS		...	11417	7⅝	3	3⅜	– 4¼
AmSowestMtg	ASR	.72e	...	82407	8⅜	3	3⅞	– 4⅜
AmTechCeram	AMK		13	5324	3¼	2⅛	2½	– ¼
A-TrAmExp un	XPU	.87	...	2914	38	28½	35	+ 8
A-TrAmExp	XPP	.87	...	23089	32	23⅞	29⅝	+ 5½
A-TrAmExp sc	XPS		...	93194	10⅝	2⅞	6½	+ 3¼
A-TrAmHom un	HPU	3.85	...	562	109	80½	105½	+ 23½
A-TrAmHom	HPP	3.85	...	4527	81¼	70½	80½	+ 9
A-TrAmHom sc	HPS		...	23785	32½	10¼	27	+ 16
A-TrATT un	ATU	1.15	...	11157	44¼	28	43½	+ 13¾
A-TrATT	ATP	1.15	...	49049	27⅛	22⅝	26⅜	+ 3⅝
A-TrATT sc	ATS		...	240601	21	5⅞	19½	+ 13⅜
A-TrAmoco un	AOU	1.88	...	595	54¾	37⅛	54¾	+ 17¼
A-TrAmoco	AOP	1.88	...	2735	45¼	35	45¼	+ 10⅛
A-TrAmoco sc	AOS		...	27816	12⅞	2¼	11⅝	+ 9¼
A-TrArco un	RFU	4.45	...	1161	112	84½	112	+ 35¼
A-TrArco	RFP	4.45	...	3710	92¾	74¾	91¼	+ 16⅞
A-TrArco sc	RFS		...	16891	22½	6	21¼	+ 15⅛
A-TrBriMyr un	BYU	2.09	...	777	60½	44¾	60½	+ 13½
A-TrBriMyr	BYP	2.09	...	23036	47½	39⅛	47⅜	+ 6⅜
A-TrBriMyr sc	BYS		...	78412	15⅞	5¼	14	+ 8¼
A-TrChevrn un	CVU	2.75	...	1015	71	46¼	67	+ 22⅛
A-TrChevrn	CVP	2.75	...	18387	59½	43½	57½	+ 13¼
A-TrChevrn sc	CVS		...	76781	17⅜	3	10⅞	+ 7⅞
A-TrCoke un	KKU	1.31	...	1725	78¾	46	76¾	+ 32⅜
A-TrCoke	KKP	1.31	...	13266	48½	37¼	47⅞	+ 9⅝
A-TrCoke sc	KKS		...	53689	32⅛	6¼	29	+ 22¾
A-TrDowChm un	DOU	2.57	...	2214	77	58¼	77	+ 19¾
A-TrDowChm	DOP	2.57	...	11144	60½	47¼	60½	+ 11¼
A-TrDowChm sc	DOS		...	62802	20¾	8¾	16	+ 6¾
A-TrDupont un	DPU	4.75	...	1538	125	86½	124	+ 43⅛
A-TrDupont	DPP	4.15	...	5983	96	78	95½	+ 15¾
A-TrDupont sc	DPS		...	65255	33¼	9	28¾	+ 19⅜
A-TrExxon un	XNU	4.75	...	320	97½	86¾	96¾	+ 12¾
A-TrExxon	XNP	4.75	...	4674	60½	56½	60	+ ¼
A-TrExxon sc	XNS		...	17470	42½	26	39¾	+ 9¾
A-TrGTE un	LDU	2.87	...	81	66⅛	45	66⅛	+ 21⅝
A-TrGTE	LDP	2.87	...	16904	42½	35⅝	42¼	+ 6⅜
A-TrGTE sc	LDS		...	79775	29	7½	28	+ 19⅞
A-TrGE un	GNU	1.86	...	3855	64½	44¾	64½	+ 19⅛
A-TrGE	GNP	1.86	...	16238	52⅞	41¼	52⅝	+ 10⅝
A-TrGE sc	GNS		...	79153	14⅛	3½	13⅛	+ 9½
A-TrGM un	GCU	2.97	...	2028	50¼	40⅞	43	+ ⅛
A-TrGM	GCP	2.97	...	12159	42	35⅜	38½	+ ¼
A-TrGM sc	GCS		...	50324	8¾	3⅞	4⅝	+ ⅝
A-TrKodak un	KDU	1.95	...	3858	54⅝	43	43	– 3¾
A-TrKodak	KDP	1.95	...	16291	42¾	36⅜	37⅜	– 3⅞
A-TrKodak sc	KDS		...	79812	13	3⅝	6⅞	+ 2¾
A-TrFord un	FCU	2.98	...	1203	52½	46⅞	52½	+ 2½
A-TrFord	FCP	2.98	...	14000	43⅝	37⅜	39¼	– 1⅝
A-TrFord sc	FCS		...	35192	13	5½	6¼	– 4¼
A-TrHewltP un	HLU	.37	...	1195	58	42¾	46⅛	– 4⅞
A-TrHewltP	HLP	.37	...	12337	51¼	36⅝	43½	– 2¾
A-TrHewltP sc	HLS		...	44520	10¾	5	5⅞	– ⅞
A-TrIBM un	BZU	4.79	...	3049	129½	97¾	98	– 24
A-TrIBM	BZP	4.79	...	26869	117½	88⅞	91⅛	– 21⅞
A-TrIBM sc	BZS		...	221259	15¾	7⅜	7⅝	– 2¼
A-TrJ&J un	JNU	1.14	...	499	54	42½	53½	+ 11⅛
A-TrJ&J	JNP	1.14	...	8093	46¾	37	46	+ 8⅛
A-TrJ&J sc	JNS		...	34289	14¾	4½	14½	+ 9⅝
A-TrMerck un	MKU	1.78	...	3714	79¾	57⅝	77⅛	+ 19⅜
A-TrMerck	MKP	1.78	...	6054	56¼	47⅛	55	+ 7⅜
A-TrMerck sc	MKS		...	22166	26⅜	10	22½	+ 12⅜
A-TrPhMor un	HMU	1.36	...	7294	45	25⅛	45	+ 19⅝
A-TrPhMor	HMP	1.36	...	19611	25	20⅛	24⅝	+ 4¼
A-TrPhMor sc	HMS		...	135021	22	5	19¼	+ 14
A-TrMobil un	MBU	2.55	...	309	61	46¾	61	+ 15½
A-TrMobil	MBP	2.55	...	11013	51	40½	50	+ 8¾
A-TrMobil sc	MBS		...	64323	15	3⅞	12⅞	+ 8¾
A-TrPrctrG un	OGU	1.75	...	209	62	44½	59¾	+ 18¼
A-TrPrctrG	OGP	1.75	...	4343	47¼	37½	46¾	+ 8¾
A-TrPrctrG sc	OGS		...	26221	24⅜	5¼	23¼	+ 17¾
A-TrSears un	RSU	1.95	...	495	47⅛	37¼	37¼	– 1¾
A-TrSears	RSP	1.95	...	10182	41½	33¾	34⅝	– 2⅝
A-TrSears sc	RSS		...	47592	7½	3¼	3⅜	– ⅞
A-TrUnPac un	UPU	2.27	...	90	78	66¾	78	+ 16¼
A-TrUnPac	UPP	2.27	...	4482	65	54¾	64⅞	+ 7⅞
A-TrUnPac sc	UPS		...	11877	18	7¾	13½	+ 5⅝
A-TrXerox un	XXU	2.95	...	778	68½	55	55	– 3¾
A-TrXerox	XXP	2.95	...	6437	61	51¾	53¼	– 1⅛
A-TrXerox sc	XXS		...	37697	9¾	4	4¼	– ¼
Amerhlth	AHH		...	3590	1⅜	¼	5/16	– 7/16
AmpalAm A	AISA	.07e	16	29151	2⅛	1½	1⅞	+ ¼
Amwest	AMW	.20	8	9048	12⅜	9¾	10⅞	– 1
Andal	ADL		134	3075	6⅝	3⅛	5⅜	– ½
AndreaRadio	AND	.52	20	1591	16⅛	9½	10	+ ¼
Angeles	ANG		...	4073	9¼	5½	7	+ 1¼
Angeles wt			...	939	5/16	1/16	3/16	+ ⅛
AngelesFnl	ANF	1.80	6	2274	16¼	12¼	12¾	...

AngelesMtg	ANM	2.16	...	2937	17⅝	13⅝	15		...
AngelesPtMtg	APT	2.09	...	589	20⅛	18	19¼		...
ArcAlaska	ICE		12	89521	12⅛	6⅝	12⅛	+	3⅞
ArizComBk	AZB		...	4612	2½	½	9/16	–	1 13/16
ArizLand	AZL	.81e	...	3777	9¾	5¼	5⅜	–	3⅞
ArkRestr	RK		53	8881	3¼	1⅞	2⅛	–	⅜
Armatron	ART		7	2182	4	2⅛	3⅛	+	⅞
ArrowAuto	AI		...	2744	5⅞	3½	3⅝	–	1¼
Astrex	ASI		...	1427	2¼	9/16	¾	–	1¼
Astrotech	AIX		...	7225	2⅜	⅞	1⅛	–	¾
Astrotech pf		1.20	...	2247	12¾	7¾	8¼	–	3⅛
Astrotech wt			...	984	½	⅛	⅛	–	⅛
Atari	ATC		...	344818	12¾	4¾	8⅝	+	3
AtlantisGp	AGH	.23t	...	7597	5⅝	2⅞	3	–	1⅛
AtlasMin	ACMB		1	124042	3	1½	2⅛	+	½
AtlasCp wt			...	13742	7⅜	3¾	6⅛	+	1¾
Audiotronics	ADO		...	2520	1	5/16	⅜	–	⅜
Audiovox	VOX		...	20664	5	2⅛	2½	–	2⅛

-B-

B&H Maritime	BHM	.85e	...	24662	17½	12¼	13¾		...
B&H Ocean	BHO	3.20e	6	28525	20¼	14¾	15⅜	–	1⅛
BAT Ind	BTI	.53e	12	f17368	15	8	13 5/16	+	5¼
BB REIT wt			...	2015	3/32	1/64	1/64		...
BHC Comm wi			...	20371	54	48¾	51½		...
BSD Bcp	BSD	.10e	8	9542	10⅛	3⅞	8⅝	+	4¾
BSN	BSN		28	25610	8¼	5¼	5⅞	–	⅜
BSN wt			...	177	1	⅝	⅝		...
BadgerMeter	BMI	.60	13	2313	22⅞	16	19⅝	+	1½
BakerMicheal	BKR		18	26325	17½	8⅛	17½	+	9⅜
BaldwinSec	BAL	.32	...	1322	8⅜	2⅞	3¼	–	3¼
BaldwinTech	BLD	.10	17	58305	15⅜	6½	12⅛	+	5⅜
BalfourMac	BML	.16	22	6802	9	5¾	7⅛	–	1¾
BambPolym	BPI		...	14517	9	4½	5	–	2⅞
BancroftFd	BCV	1.79e	...	8670	19⅜	17½	18⅛	+	½
BanstrContl g	BAN		...	8958	14⅛	6⅛	10½	+	4¼
BankBldg	BB	.20j	...	6160	5¾	1¼	1¾	–	3⅝
BkSanFran	BOF		9	3092	11	4⅝	9	+	4⅜
BkSanFran 8%B		.56	...	48	10¼	7¼	10	+	2⅝
BankAtlFnl	BFC		...	4709	8⅛	4⅜	5½	+	¾
Barnwell	BRN	.33e	9	4648	37½	14¼	34⅝	+	20
BarristerInfo	BIS		...	11188	2½	1⅛	1¼	–	1
BarrLabs	BRL		...	9362	6⅜	4	4⅞	–	⅜
BarryRG	RGB		12	31935	13	5¼	10¾	+	5¼
BaruchFostr	BFO		...	3168	6	4	5½	+	1½
BayMeadws	CJ	.25e	50	11899	26½	15½	17⅞	+	2⅛
BayouStl	BYX		7	32887	7⅞	4	4¼	–	3¼
BeardOil	BOC		...	8084	8½	3⅝	8	+	4½
BeldenBlake	BBE		...	6888	3⅜	1¾	2¾	+	½
Belvedere	BLV	.04	16	7750	6½	4¼	5¼	+	¾
BergnBruns	BBC	.32	14	149097	27¼	18	24⅜	+	6⅛
BergstrmCap	BEM	6.40e	...	3088	66¾	47⅝	65⅛	+	16⅞
BethlehemCp	BET		5	1337	1⅞	1⅛	1⅛	–	¼
BIC Cp	BIC	1.12	16	11919	31⅜	22½	31⅛	+	4¼
BinksMfg	BIN	1.00	12	4508	39⅛	25⅞	34¾	+	8⅝
BioRadLab B	BIOB		12	509	19¾	14¼	15½	–	1¼
BioRadLab A	BIOA		13	17797	20	14⅛	16	–	1
BiomagTecg	BMT		...	11367	9⅛	5¼	7⅜		...
Biopharm	BPH		...	21467	1⅞	⅝	13/16	–	3/16
BiscayHldg	BHA	1.60e	4	8309	4⅝	2	3⅞	–	⅝
BlairCp	BL	2.15e	9	20197	41¾	28⅞	30⅜	–	10½
Blessings	BCO	.56a	15	10997	16½	10⅝	15¾	+	4¼
Blount A	BLTA	.45	8	22087	14	9¼	10¾	–	2⅛
Blount B	BLTB	.40a	8	1029	13⅝	9¼	10⅜	–	2⅞
BoddieNoell	BNP	1.36	10	6144	13⅞	10¼	10¾	–	2½
BolarPharm	BLR	.04	11	435436	32¼	12¾	18¼	–	3¼
BowValley	BVI	.24	...	7836	13⅜	10¼	12¼	+	1½
BowlAmerica	BWLA	.56	15	3587	21⅜	14¼	21⅛	+	6⅝
Bowmar	BOM		...	15742	2¾	1	1¼	+	¼
Bowne	BNE	.25	24	94852	14⅝	10½	11¼	–	1
BradlyREIT	BTR	.68	56	10799	15¼	9½	9½	–	4
Brascan A g	BRSA	1.04	...	29791	27½	22⅛	23¼	+	¾
BrwnForm A	BF.A	2.08	22	5167	81¾	54	81¾	+	27⅛
BrwnForm B	BF.B	2.08	24	57544	88¼	56¼	88¼	+	30⅝
BrwnFormn pf		.40	...	1329	5½	4¼	5	+	¼
Buell	BUE	.20	...	2617	23¾	13¾	15¼	–	6⅝
BufftonCp	BFX		...	22294	8	2⅞	3⅜	–	2¾
BurnhmPac	BPP	1.36	17	14975	21	18	19⅜	+	⅝
BushInd	BSH		9	14291	13¾	7½	7¾	–	2¾

-C-

CIM HiYld	CIM	1.20e	...	17488	9⅞	6¾	7	–	2½
CMI Cp	CMX		...	40761	3⅞	2⅛	2⅜	–	⅞
CSS Ind	CSS		7	13384	24½	13⅜	22⅜	+	9
CVB Fnl	CVB		20	2557	28	10⅜	22⅜	+	11⅝
CXR Telcm	CXR		10	32934	6⅝	3⅜	3¾	–	1¼
CablvisnSys	CVC		...	31903	47¼	29¾	37⅛	+	5¼
CaesarsNJ	CJN		9	8571	28⅜	18⅛	18¼	–	2¾
Cagles A	CGLA		5	13171	14	6⅜	6⅝	–	¼
CalEngy	CE		32	129591	17⅛	7½	12½	+	1⅜
Calprop	CPP	.65t	7	9435	8½	6¼	6½	–	⅜
CdnMarc g	CMW	.28	40	7801	16¼	12¼	12¼	–	1⅞
CdnOcci	CXY	.40	28	2779	18⅝	13½	17¼	+	3½
CanWine A	CDGA		19	4538	12½	7½	9⅞	+	2⅜
CanWine B	CDGB		19	2964	12⅝	7½	9⅞	+	2⅝
CapHousing	CAP	.42e	...	8104	8⅝	7	7¼		...
Carmel	KML		...	3238	4½	1¾	1⅞	–	2
CarnivlCru	CCL	.40	13	315588	26⅜	14⅞	19⅞	+	4⅜
CaroP&L pf		5.00	...	z19610	59	50	56¼	+	5¼
CashAmInv	PWN	.08	29	44915	22⅝	9⅝	22⅝	+	11¾
CaspenOil	CNO		...	12125	⅞	⅛	7/16	–	¼
CaspenOil pf			...	324	8	5⅜	7	–	⅝
CastleAM	CAS	.68	10	7812	16¾	12½	12⅞	–	⅜
CastleFd	CVF	1.79e	...	5568	19⅞	17⅞	18¾	–	¼
CatalinaLt	LTG		18	55723	15¼	8¾	10	+	1
CavlrHomes	CXV	.08	14	6464	5⅝	3⅛	3⅞	–	1
CentenGp	CEQ		15	33281	3½	1⅜	1½	–	1⅞
CentlFdCda	CEF	.01e	...	87232	6	4 3/16	5½	+	¾
CentlMePwr pf		3.50	...	z45400	38¾	33¾	38¾	+	2⅞
CentlPac	CTA	.01e	20	47239	27	7½	26⅞	+	19⅜
CentlSec	CET	1.00e	...	7109	10	8⅜	9⅝	+	1⅜
CentlSec pfD		2.00	...	58	28	25	27½	+	1½
CentrustSvg	DLP		...	20339	6¾	½	9/16	–	5 3/16
CentrustSvg pf		.64e	...	1393	6½	¾	¾	–	5¼
CenturyComm	CTY		...	51493	16⅝	8	13	+	4⅝
CenvillDev	CVL		10	7211	9¾	5	6⅛	+	1⅛
ChamDev B	CDVB		34	10938	38	21	33¾	+	11¼
ChamDev A	CDVA		34	84619	38	20½	34	+	12⅛
ChampEnt	CHB		...	32858	4⅞	2¼	2½	–	1¼
ChariotGp	CGR	.74j	18	2789	5¼	2⅝	2¾	–	2⅛
ChartPwr	CHP	.11	...	7597	7	4⅝	5½	–	¼
ChiRivet	CVR	1.20a	11	1150	26¼	21⅛	21⅝	+	⅝
Chieftain	CID		...	47795	20⅜	11½	20¼		...
Citadel	CDL		15	5632	55⅜	34⅝	43¾	+	9
Citicp wtM			...	16443	4	1⅛	1 5/16	–	9/16
Citicp wtY			...	11619	1⅞	15/16	1⅛	+	⅛
Citicp wtY93			...	27199	5⅞	2 9/16	4	+	1 7/16
CitiznFst	CFB	.72	7	41366	15⅝	10¼	11	–	2½
CitiznFst pf		2.50	...	35	92	83	91	+	3½
Clabir pf			...	11139	10¼	1	1	–	9¼
ClearChanl	CCU	3.00e	60	6245	16⅜	10	14½	+	1⅜
CoastDistr	CRV		8	8607	8¾	6⅛	6⅜	–	⅜
Coeur dAMn	CDE	.15e	26	45954	24⅛	15½	21⅝	+	5⅜
Cognitron	CGN		29	8649	8	2¼	6	+	3¾
Cohu	COH	.28	7	7530	14¾	9	9¾	–	1⅞
CollinsInd	GO		28	8891	3⅞	2½	3⅜	+	¾
ColorSys	CLR		...	28359	2¾	11/16	1¾		...
ColumREI	CIV	.90e	7	13935	8	6⅜	6⅞	+	¼
ColumbLabs	COB		...	12890	17⅞	12¾	15⅛		...
ComSys	CTM		...	24706	6½	2¼	3⅛	–	¼
ComFedBcp	CFK	.06j	...	32565	5¼	1	1⅜	–	3⅞
Cominco	CLT	.50e	18	31683	27¼	20⅜	23⅝	+	2¾
Commtron	CMR		10	18182	10⅜	4⅜	8⅛	+	3½
CompuDyne	CDC		...	2314	8¼	1¾	2⅜	–	6⅛
Comptek	CTK	.16	15	3171	8	4¾	4⅞	–	1¼
Compumat	CPT		7	14542	7	2⅜	2¾	–	⅞
Computrac	LLB		11	14268	5¾	2⅞	3⅜	–	1⅛
ConcordFab	CIS		5	5927	5⅝	2½	4⅞	+	1¾
ConcordFab B	CISB		5	2219	5⅜	2½	4⅝	+	1½
ConquestExpl	CQX		...	112493	2¾	1⅝	2⅛	+	⅛
Conston	KCS		...	16147	4½	2⅛	2½	–	1
ContlMatrl	CUO		...	6861	21⅝	12	16⅜	+	3¾
Continuum	CNU		93	23994	25⅛	12⅜	23⅛	+	9⅞
ConversnInd	CVD		4	59857	7⅜	3	5	+	1⅝
Convest	CEP		9	6325	3½	1¼	2¾	+	1⅝
CopleyProp	COP	1.44	15	15232	18¼	10	11¼	–	6⅛
CorcapInc	CCP		...	6921	5	1⅝	2¼	–	2
Corona A	ICRA	.05e	...	213704	9¾	6	9	+	2¾
Courtaulds	COU	.23e	8	6287	6⅞	4¾	6⅛	+	1⅜

AMERICAN STOCK EXCHANGE COMPOSITE

Stock	Symbol	Div	Yld	Sales 100s	Hi	Lo	Last	Net Chg
CrossAT A	ATXA	1.24	17	71067	41	32	36¼	+ 1
CrowleyMil	COM	1.00	135	538	32½	19⅞	23	− 1¾
CrwnCentl A	CNPA	1.10e	8	27938	41¾	20⅝	31⅛	+ 9¾
CrwnCentl B	CNPB	1.10e	7	43049	36¾	19¾	29⅛	+ 8¼
CrwnCrfts	CRW	.20b	15	16931	30	16⅛	28	+ 10
CrwnCrfts wi			...	nt	15	8	9	...
CruiseAm	RVR		...	26112	8⅜	4¼	5⅜	+ ⅛
CrystalOil	COR		...	104563	3⅜	1⅝	3	+ 1¼
CubicCp	CUB	.42	6	20100	19⅝	14⅛	16½	+ ½
CurticeBrns	CBI		14	16383	27	17¼	25½	+ 8
Customedix	CUS		...	53228	⅞	3/16	11/16	+ 1/16
CypressFd	WJR		...	68210	12¼	6⅞	10⅞	+ 3⅞

-D-

Stock	Symbol	Div	Yld	Sales 100s	Hi	Lo	Last	Net Chg
DI Ind	DRL		...	5463	2½	1	2¼	+ 1¼
DWG Cp	DWG		...	644282	16	5⅜	12	+ 5
DamsonE A	DEPA		...	29148	¾	¼	½	+ 3/16
DamsonE B	DEPB		...	24202	1	¼	9/16	+ ¼
Datametrics	DC		...	8979	2⅞	⅞	⅞	− 1⅜
Datapdts	DPC	.16	...	276249	17½	7½	9	− 4½
DataramCp	DTM		11	11136	11⅝	7¼	9⅝	+ 2⅜
DaxorCp	DXR		...	14932	6¾	2¾	3	− 2½
DeRoseInd	DRI		...	1365	1⅛	¼	⅜	− 1/16
DecoratorInd	DII		103	849	7	3⅞	4⅛	+ ⅛
DelLabs	DLI	.40	27	1477	34	30	32⅝	+ 2⅝
Delmed	DMD		...	105126	1	¼	½	− 5/16
Desgntrnic	DSG		...	3086	3⅝	2	2	− 1½
Desgncraft	DJI		...	12971	7½	2⅜	2¾	− 1¾
DevonEngy	DVN		...	46520	14¾	4⅝	13½	+ 8¾
DevonEngy pf		1.94	...	6421	35	25⅛	32½	...
DiagRetr A	DRSA		...	12389	9	3⅞	4	− 3
DiagRetr B	DRSB		...	6617	8⅛	3¼	3½	− 2⅞
Diasonic	DIA		68	503066	4½	1 15/16	4 1/16	+ 1 13/16
DicknMn A g	DMLA		...	5117	6½	3¾	5¼	+ 1
DicknMn B g	DMLB		...	970	7⅜	4¼	5⅛	+ ¼
Diodes	DIO		188	3137	2⅞	1½	1⅞	− ¼
DiviHotels	DVH		...	34603	11⅛	2¾	3⅝	− 5⅛
DixonTi	DXT	.10i	...	22190	18⅝	8⅜	9	− 4
Donnelly	DON	.28	13	9588	15⅜	8½	9	− 3⅝
DowChem rt			...	48622	9	7⅞	8¼	...
DreyfMunIn	DMF	.72	...	46496	10¼	8¾	10	...
DreyfCalMn	DCM	.66	...	12874	10⅜	8¾	9¾	− ⅜
DreyfNYMn	DNM	.66	...	8906	10¼	8½	9½	− ½
DriverHar	DRH		8	7915	11½	8⅛	9½	+ 1
Ducommun	DCO		...	24086	5⅞	1⅜	3¾	+ 1⅞
DuplexPdts	DPX	.72	11	23981	23⅝	18¼	20	+ 1½

-E-

Stock	Symbol	Div	Yld	Sales 100s	Hi	Lo	Last	Net Chg
EAC Ind	EAC		...	11526	8¼	2	2⅞	− 5⅜
ECI Envr	ECI		...	7719	9	7½	7¾	...
EECO	EEC		...	13745	7⅜	3⅜	3⅞	− 3¼
ENSR	ENX		...	33449	10⅜	4⅛	4⅜	− 4½
ESI Ind	ESI		7	7341	3	1⅝	1⅝	− 1⅛
ESI Ind wt			...	216	¼	1/32	1/16	− 3/16
EagleFnl	EAG	.50	7	7529	11¾	8⅛	8⅝	+ ½
vjEastnAir pfD		2.84	...	75734	18	13½	15	+ ½
vjEastnAir pfE		1.37t	...	16532	13	5	8	+ 1
vjEastnAir pfF		1.48t	...	56869	13⅞	5⅞	9⅝	+ 2¼
vjEastnAir pfG		1.44t	...	18219	14¼	5⅞	8⅞	+ 1⅞
EasternCo	EML	.56	18	3066	20½	13	17½	+ 4¼
Eastgroup	EGP	2.90e	6	6334	25	19¾	20⅜	− 1⅛
EchoBayM	ECO	.07	40	844343	20⅛	12¾	18⅜	+ 4⅜
EcolgyEnv	EEI	.14	15	9179	13⅝	9⅛	11⅛	+ ⅛
EdistoRes	EDS		...	8770	17¾	14½	17¼	...
EdistoRes pf		2.60	...	378	18¾	15¾	18⅛	...
EhrlBober	EB		...	8414	3⅞	1¾	2⅛	− 1½
EldoradoBcp	ELB	.28	11	3756	17⅝	12	16⅞	+ 3⅞
ElecChmInd	EIF		...	22	3½	3¼	3½	...
ElecSound	ESG		...	12007	3	9/16	1⅛	− 1⅞
Elsinore	ELS		...	444482	⅞	¼	⅝	+ 5/16
ElsworthFd	ECF	.81e	...	21146	8	7	7½	+ ⅜
EmElec wt			...	9967	3⅝	1¼	1¼	− ⅜
EmpireAmBk	EOA		...	61202	1¾	⅛	¼	− 1⅛
EmpireCar	EMP	.05	...	5082	10⅛	4	6	+ 1¾
Endevco	EI		...	14777	7¼	4⅛	5⅝	− 1⅜
EnergyDev	EDP		5	40055	4⅝	2½	4¼	+ 1¼
EnergySvc	ESV		23	569146	4⅜	1⅞	4⅜	+ 2⅜
EnergySvc pf		1.50	...	38475	32¾	17	31⅝	+ 14⅜
Engex	EGX	1.36	...	2084	11⅛	8	9½	+ 1¼
Enstar pf		.30e	...	2473	1⅝	1⅛	1⅛	− ⅜
EntertnMkt	EM		...	68326	2⅞	1⅜	2¼	+ ⅛
EntnPub			...	11643	19⅜	8¼	17⅜	+ 8¾
Enviropact	ENV		...	11995	6⅜	1½	1¾	− 4⅜
EnzoBiochm	ENZ		...	21784	5	2⅝	3⅝	+ ⅜
EqptGrthFd	GFX	2.20	20	5348	19¾	17⅝	17⅞	...
Escagen	ESN		...	7155	6⅜	2⅞	2⅞	− 2¼
Espey	ESP	.60	9	2771	27⅜	18	18⅜	+ ¼
EsqRadio	EE	.90	17	511	39¼	31½	31½	− 5½
EtzLavud	ETZ		...	3697	7⅝	3⅞	7½	+ 3½
EverstJ B	EJ.B	.05i	...	813	12	8⅜	8½	− 1¾
EverstJ A	EJ.A	.10i	...	10351	11⅜	7⅜	8	− 1
Excel Ind	EXC	.40	8	12294	13	9½	9⅞	− 2⅛

-F-

Stock	Symbol	Div	Yld	Sales 100s	Hi	Lo	Last	Net Chg
FFP Ptnrs	FFP	1.50	125	11272	11	4½	5	− 4¾
FPA Cp	FPO		...	2903	5	1	1¼	− 2⅝
FabInd	FIT	.80	11	2974	37¾	27⅝	35	+ 7¼
FalconCbl	FAL	2.16	...	16613	22⅛	17⅜	18	− 1⅜
Fibreboard	FBD		58	27067	19¼	12	13¼	− 6
FideltyFnl	FNF	.40	7	6388	10¼	6	9¼	+ 1¾
FstAustFd	IAF	.61e	...	53730	10¾	7¼	8¾	+ ⅝
FstAustPr	FAX	1.08a	...	332518	9⅞	8¼	8 15/16	− 3/16
FstCentFnl	FCC	.08e	14	10011	8⅛	4⅝	8	+ 2⅝
FstConn	FCO	2.00e	9	1451	17¾	12⅛	15⅝	− 1½
FstFedAm	FFA		14	33960	36½	15¼	33¼	+ 17¾
FstEmpire	FES	1.20	10	10910	72½	51⅜	65¾	+ 13½
FstFedBcp	FFS		9	10353	7⅜	3¾	6⅛	+ 2
FstIberFd	IBF	.30e	...	131208	17	7¾	13⅜	+ 5⅝
FstNtlCal	FN	.20b	10	8583	23⅛	9	15½	+ 6½
FstRepBcp	FRC		19	7107	9	5½	6¾	− 1¾
Firstcorp	FCR		...	8565	7¾	2¼	2½	− 4⅞
FischPort	FP	.70t	...	8087	14⅝	11¼	13½	− ¼
FitchbrgGE	FGE	2.00	18	1981	35	27⅛	32¾	+ 2⅝
Flanigans	BDL		...	2804	3¼	11/16	1⅛	− ⅞
FlexibleBd	FLX	.97e	...	41506	10⅛	8⅛	8¼	− 1¾
FlaRockInd	FRK	.50	13	11544	41¾	29¾	31¾	+ 1½
FlukeJohn	FKM	.32	9	34498	27¾	17⅞	25	+ 7⅛
Foodarama	FSM		70	2313	38⅝	27¼	29⅜	− 1¾
FordCda g	FC	11.00e	...	z87790	168	114	161	+ 47½
Ford wt91			...	32977	3⅝	1	2	+ ⅝
FordCrd wt92			...	19447	2	11/16	1⅛	− 1/16
FordCrd wt93			...	38580	5½	2¾	3½	+ ¾
ForestCtyA	FCEA	.42	39	5990	56¾	35⅛	39½	− ⅝
ForestCtyB	FCEB	.36	39	812	58½	39⅝	39⅝	− 1¾
ForestLabs	FRX		32	166938	44½	24⅛	41⅞	+ 17⅛
ForumRetir	FRL	1.35	...	23925	6⅝	2⅜	2½	− 3⅝
FountnPwrbt	FPI		...	16406	5⅞	2⅝	3	...
Franklin	FKL		...	1984	10⅝	7¾	8	− ⅝
FredHollywd	FHO	.10	15	14526	16	4⅝	12⅜	+ 7⅝
FreqElec	FEI		23	23892	12⅜	8⅞	9	− 1⅜
FriedmanInd	FRD	.24r	8	8414	5½	3⅛	3⅜	− 2
FriesEnt	FE		...	8270	3⅜	1⅝	2¼	...
Frischs	FRS	.24b	57	15675	30⅛	17	26⅜	+ 1¼
FrozenFood	JIT	.20	7	13884	11⅜	6⅞	7⅛	...
FruitLoom	FTL		10	823193	16	6¼	14⅞	+ 8½
FurVault	FRV		...	144701	4⅝	2⅛	2⅜	− ⅛

-G-

Stock	Symbol	Div	Yld	Sales 100s	Hi	Lo	Last	Net Chg
GRI Cp	GRR		...	7409	9⅝	3½	4⅞	− 4¾
GTI Cp	GTI		9	10221	6¼	2¾	3	− ½
GW Util	GWT		...	2002	21½	19	20⅝	+ 1¼
Gainsco	GNA	.59t	11	12859	8½	4¾	7¾	+ 2½
GalacRes g	GLC		...	98876	4 5/16	2½	3⅜	− 9/16
GalaxyCbl	GTV	1.40	...	9349	26	18¼	19⅜	+ ⅜
Garan	GAN	1.00a	9	5387	38½	25⅞	31¾	+ 4
GaylrdContr	GCR		3	62046	15¾	7¼	8	− 6⅝
GelmanSci	GSC		21	14242	20⅞	10⅝	14	+ 3¼
GemcoNtl	GNL		...	5479	2¼	1	1⅜	− ⅝
GenAutom	GA		...	21919	1 5/16	7/16	11/16	+ 3/16
GECap wtY			...	12884	2 7/16	1	1 3/16	...
GECap wtM			...	14492	3½	1 3/16	1¼	− 1
GenEmploy	JOB	.20r	6	6783	4½	2	2⅜	+ ⅜
GenMicro	GMW		...	3955	8¾	5	5⅜	− ⅜
GeniscoTech	GES		...	7123	2⅜	¾	13/16	− 11/16
GenovDrg A	GDXA	.24b	14	9040	12⅞	8¾	10⅛	+ 1¼
GeoRes	GEO		...	13276	4¼	⅛	⅜	− 3¾
GeoRes pf			...	4600	4⅝	½	⅝	− 3⅝
GiantFood A	GFSA	.50	17	194538	36¼	22⅛	28½	+ 4¼

AMERICAN STOCK EXCHANGE COMPOSITE

Stock	Symbol	Div	Yld	Sales 100s	Hi	Lo	Last	Net Chg
GiantYel g	GYK		...	18669	11¾	8⅛	9⅞ –	⅝
GibsonCR	GIB	.20	19	3186	12⅞	8¾	12⅝ +	3½
Glatfelter	GLT	1.00	11	28994	49	37	43¾ +	5⅝
Glenmore B	GDSB	1.00	14	4365	27⅝	22½	24 –	1⅝
GloblNRes	GNR		...	88621	8	4⅞	7⅞ +	2½
GloblOcean	GLO	1.30e	...	28243	15½	11⅞	13¼ –	¾
Goldfield	GV		3	52664	¾	¼	7/16 +	1/16
GormanRupp	GRC	.96	14	4369	26½	21½	21⅝ –	3⅞
GouldInvLP	GLP		...	655	62½	48¾	54 +	5
Graham	GHM	.05e	8	21473	41	7	24½ +	17⅜
GrahamFld	GFI		...	16053	2⅞	1¾	2 –	⅛
Granges g	GXL		...	35219	3¼	1⅞	2⅜ –	9/16
Granges wt			...	4909	11/16	⅛	¼ –	3/16
GrtWashInv	GWA		...	4917	4⅝	3¼	3½ –	⅝
Greenman	GMN		16	47752	8⅜	4⅜	5¾ +	1⅜
GreinerEngrg	GII	.20	16	11783	23⅝	11¼	21⅝ +	10⅝
GuardnBcp	GB		12	7830	24⅝	13¼	17⅞ +	4⅛
GulfCdaR	GOU	.40	...	102988	14½	11⅝	13½ +	1⅜
GulfCdaR pf		.47e	...	4978	4¼	3⅞	4⅛ +	3/16
GundleEnvr	GUN		29	114135	25	11½	13⅞ –	5¼
-H-								
HAL	HA		...	22017	40¼	20⅛	20⅝ –	2⅝
HMG Prop	HMG	.60a	...	1554	12¼	9⅛	12⅛ –	⅜
HUBCO	HCO	.40	9	3191	13⅝	8¾	9⅛ –	3¾
HalifaxEng	HX	.14	16	3207	7	5⅛	5½ –	½
HallwdEngy	HEP	.08	...	16766	13/16	½	13/16 +	3/16
HalseyDrug	HDG	o	20	58969	7⅜	2¾	5⅞ +	2 15/16
HalseyDrug wt			...	17365	5⅜	1¼	4⅝ +	3½
HampInd	HAI	1.27t	7	7198	15	6⅞	11 +	3¾
HampUtil	HU	.44e	...	3475	11⅛	8⅜	11⅛ +	2¼
HampUtil pf		4.00	...	323	48⅝	44¼	47⅛ +	¼
HarlynPdt	HRN		11	5522	5⅞	3¼	4⅜	...
HarveyGp	HRA		9	11663	3¾	2⅛	2¾ –	⅛
Hasbro	HAS	.16	12	399864	24⅜	15¼	18¾ +	3⅛
HastingMfg	HMF	.40a	23	1589	41½	31½	32½ +	1
HealthInt	HII		...	28959	5⅝	⅜	9/16 –	2 5/16
HealthCrREIT	HCN	1.68	8	16942	16	11⅜	14⅝ +	2¾
HealthChm	HCH		13	12164	4⅛	1⅞	2⅛ –	⅞
HlthCncpt	HCF		18	2509	4½	3⅝	4	...
HealthMor	HMI	.68	19	1372	11¼	9⅝	10	...
Healthvest	HVT	2.00j	3	113923	18	3⅝	4¼ –	13¼
Heico	HEI	.10	15	15087	14¼	8⅝	9⅞ –	2¼
HeinWerner	HNW		8	14304	18⅛	10⅝	12⅛ –	2⅜
HeldorInd	HDR		...	7206	3⅛	1⅛	1¼ –	⅝
HelmRes	H		...	54120	9/16	¼	⅜ –	3/16
HeritageE	HHH		...	40074	2⅝	1⅛	1½ –	⅜
HeritageE wt			...	535	3/16	1/16	1/16 –	1/16
HeritgMedia	HTG		...	95333	5¾	2½	3⅛ –	1⅜
HersheyOil	HSO		135	11700	7	4	6¾ +	2⅝
Hinderliter	HND		...	8299	2¼	11/16	⅞ –	1⅜
Hipotronics	HIP	.26	12	7742	18⅝	12½	17⅞ +	3⅝
HofmannInd	HOF		48	7482	8⅛	4¼	8⅛ +	2½
HolcoMtg A	HOLA	.90e	...	952	4½	3¼	3⅜ –	½
HollyCp	HOC	.40a	8	38356	34½	15	25⅞ +	10½
HomeShop	HSN		...	350983	7⅝	3	7¼ +	2¾
HooprHolm	HH	.30	17	9339	10⅞	8⅛	9½ +	⅝
HormelGeo	HRL	.52	18	67933	33⅞	20⅛	33¾ +	11¾
HornHardt	HOR		...	123939	8½	6	6¾ –	1⅛
HotlInv wtB			...	6529	1¼	1/32	3/32 –	1 1/32
HousOilTr	HO	.01e	38	122706	2	⅞	1⅞ +	1
HovnanEnt	HOV		6	40270	12¼	7⅛	8 +	⅜
HoweRichrd	HRI		140	2066	8⅜	6⅜	7 –	1⅜
HowellInd	HOW	1.00	6	1158	30¼	20⅛	20¼ –	2½
Howtek	HTK		...	51236	21	9⅛	9⅞ –	5⅞
HubbellA	HUBA	1.36b	16	5039	46	35⅜	44½ +	7⅜
HubbellB	HUBB	1.36b	16	40385	48⅜	33¼	45¾ +	10
HudsGen	HGC	.40	...	3515	21¾	13⅛	14¾ –	1⅛
-I-								
ICH	ICH		13	243557	6⅞	3⅜	5⅞ +	1⅛
ICH pf		1.75	...	54360	10⅞	8¾	10⅜ +	¾
ICN Biomed	BIM	.14	28	20093	12½	7½	10⅝ –	1
IGI Inc	IG		...	139037	18	7	7⅝ –	⅛
IRT Cp	IX		...	10784	2⅜	1	1⅝ +	¼
ISI Sys	SYS	.28	19	27637	20	11½	19⅞ +	7⅛
ISS Int	ISI	.24	17	4446	9⅞	5¾	9⅞ +	3¼
ImperlHly	IHK	.48	6	23894	31½	11½	27½ +	15⅞
ImperOil A g	IMOA	1.80	...	165034	55⅜	40⅝	55⅛ +	13¼
IncoOpRlty	IOT	.55e	...	12075	9½	4⅛	5½ –	2⅜
IncstarCp	ISR		...	43870	11⅛	5⅜	10¾ +	3¼
IncstarCp wi			...	4549	3½	2⅛	3½	...
InsteelInd	III	.24	7	14670	13¼	8⅛	10⅞ +	2⅝
InstronCp	ISN	.12	25	11093	13¼	9⅛	9⅞ –	1½
InstrSys	ISY		11	78764	2	1	1¾ +	¾
InstrSys pf		.25e	...	2740	2⅝	1⅞	2¼ +	¼
IntellgSys	INP		1	37908	3⅛	1⅞	2¼	...
IntCtyGas g	ICG	.72	...	72173	21⅜	17½	20⅛ +	1½
Intmark	IMI	.12b	...	20456	14½	9½	9⅞ –	3¾
Intmark pf		.11	...	2980	11½	9	9 –	¾
IntBknte	IBK		11	184008	5⅞	3	4⅜ +	1
IntIncoProp	IIP	1.08	50	5588	15⅝	13⅛	13½ +	¼
IntPwrMach	PWR		9	1176	4½	1⅞	1⅞ –	2⅜
IntProtein	PRO		10	2565	16	10⅝	11⅛ –	2¼
IntRecvry	INT		24	43334	16⅞	9⅝	16⅝ +	6⅜
IntTelchrg	ITI		...	310746	12¾	2⅝	3½ –	3
IntThrgbrd	ITB		...	137627	11/16	¼	5/16 –	¼
IntThrgbrd pf			...	9944	½	¼	¼ –	3/16
IntstGen	IGC	.80	6	11346	9⅛	6⅝	7¼ +	¾
Ionics	ION		30	16441	26⅝	15⅜	24 +	8
IroquoisBrd	IBL		...	8927	19½	2⅞	5⅛ –	9¾
IvaxCp	IVX		...	45117	14½	10	11⅞ +	1¼
IversonTech	IVT		15	16675	10¼	3⅛	3⅝ –	6⅛
-J-								
Jaclyn	JLN	.50b	15	5888	12	7⅞	10¾ +	⅜
JamesMadsn	JML	.30	27	12581	7⅝	5½	5⅞ –	⅛
JanBellMkt	JBM		35	219490	34	12⅛	25⅛ +	11⅞
Jetronic	JET		...	9337	3⅞	1½	2¾ +	⅝
Jewlmstrs	JEM	.10e	...	7708	5½	1⅝	2⅛ –	2¼
JohnsPdt	JPC		27	6369	3¾	1⅝	3¼ +	1⅜
JonesIntcbl	JTV	1.60	...	24954	15⅝	12¾	13¼ –	1⅛
JonesPlumbg	JPS		7	3312	4¼	2	2⅝ –	⅜
Joules	JOL		6	2962	3⅛	1½	1⅞ –	⅞
JumpJkShoe	JJS		...	4853	3⅛	1	1⅜ +	¼
-K-								
KMW Sys	KMW		50	6868	6	3	5 +	1¼
KV Pharm	KV		...	15304	16	10⅝	13⅜ +	¾
KanGE pf		4.50	...	z7900	48¼	42	47¾ +	4⅛
KappaNtwks	KPA		...	3967	1½	7/16	½ –	1
Kear.eInc	KEA		16	2201	21⅞	6¾	21½ +	14¾
KeithlyInstr	KEI	.18	10	4598	16⅞	11¾	12⅛ –	3¾
KelleyOG	KLY	1.28	70	26086	24	13¾	23¾ +	10
KentElec	KEC		11	21365	9⅜	5⅝	8⅜ +	2¼
Kenwin	KWN		...	842	10¼	6⅞	7¼ –	2⅝
Kerkhoff	KIX		...	7231	2¾	1⅜	2 +	½
Ketchum	KCH		...	2677	7⅝	1⅝	2 –	5
Ketema	KTM		...	29329	18¾	12¼	13⅞ +	⅞
KeystnCam	KYC		...	123113	2¼	⅞	1¼ –	½
KeystnCam wtA			...	3969	¼	1/16	3/16	...
KeystnCam wtB			...	3600	7/16	¼	5/16	...
KillernProp	KPI		5	2598	9	5⅜	5½ –	⅜
KinarkCp	KIN		9	11818	5½	3⅞	4¾ +	⅝
KirbyExpl	KEX	.10e	19	189771	9¾	4⅜	9⅜ +	5
Kit Mfg	KIT		8	837	7⅞	5⅜	5½ –	1⅝
KleerVuInd	KVU		...	31807	1⅝	¼	11/16 +	1/16
KoalaTech	KOA		...	23923	⅜	1/16	3/16 –	⅛
KogerEqty	KE	1.80	184	46358	20¾	16⅞	18⅜ –	⅜
-L-								
LSB Ind	LSB		6	15170	3¼	1½	1¾ +	⅜
LSB Ind pfC		2.20	...	4114	24	14⅛	16 +	2⅛
LaBarge	LB		...	6255	1⅛	9/16	11/16 +	1/16
LaJollaBcp	LJC	.10b	24	8766	13⅝	7⅛	13⅜ +	6¼
LancerCp	LAN		11	6458	6	3¾	4⅜ –	⅝
LandmkSvg	LSA	.30	6	11176	9⅜	6½	7¼ +	¼
LandmkLand	LML	.40j	6	20336	22⅝	9¾	12 –	8⅛
LandsgPac	LPF	.80	...	11023	9⅝	7⅛	9⅜ +	⅞
LarizzaInd	LII		...	17653	7½	1¾	1¾ –	5⅜
LaserInd	LAS		...	23336	4¾	2⅛	4⅛ +	⅜
LatshawEnt	LAT	.40a	8	625	20¼	16½	16¾ –	2⅛
LaurenCap	LQ		24	5012	3⅛	2¼	2⅝ –	¼
LawrInsGp	LWR	.28	13	1578	8½	6½	6¾ –	1⅛
LawsonMaGp	LMG	.40	...	5711	11	9	9¼ –	1⅜
LazareKap	LKI		10	2778	10¾	4¼	8 +	3½
LeePharm	LPH		...	18747	5⅜	1⅞	2 –	1⅞
Leiner	PLI		12	6614	14¼	8¾	10 +	1¼
LeosInd	LI		..	7740	19⅝	9⅞	13	...

AMERICAN STOCK EXCHANGE COMPOSITE

Stock	Symbol	Div	Yld	Sales 100s	Hi	Lo	Last	Net Chg
LilVernon	LVC		15	24695	25 1/2	12 1/8	23 5/8	+ 11 1/2
LillyEli un			...	19215	1/2	3/16	3/16	− 1/16
LinProProp	LPO		28	4769	2 3/4	1 1/4	1 3/8	− 1 1/4
LincolnNC	LRF	.84	18	8510	10 3/4	6 1/2	7	− 2
LionelCp	LIO		23	308532	8 1/2	4 1/2	5	+ 1/8
LittlefldAd	LFA		...	2242	2	15/16	1 1/2	+ 5/8
LoriCp	LRC		...	5280	8 7/8	2 3/4	3 5/8	− 2 3/4
Lumex	LUM	.08	20	16088	12 7/8	8 3/4	10 5/8	− 2 1/8
Luria	LUR		27	20067	11 5/8	9	9 1/2	− 1 5/8
LynchCp	LGL	.05i	20	4154	31 3/8	13 1/8	26 1/4	+ 13 1/8
-M-								
MC Shipping	MCX	.60e	...	30057	15 3/8	12 1/2	14 1/8	...
MSA Rlty	SSS	.60	...	30715	10 7/8	6 1/2	9 1/2	+ 1 5/8
MSR Expl	MSR		...	22225	2 1/4	1 1/4	2 1/4	+ 7/8
MacNealSch	MNS	.32	13	59513	13 3/8	8 3/8	10 1/2	+ 1/4
MagmaCopper	MCU		2	334708	8 7/8	4 5/8	5 1/8	− 1 7/8
MagmaCopper wt			...	58683	4 5/8	1 5/8	2 1/8	− 1/4
MainePS	MAP	1.60	10	4687	24 7/8	20 1/4	22 3/8	+ 1 7/8
Malartic g	MHG	.20	...	9782	8 5/8	4 5/8	7 1/2	+ 2 3/4
ManfHome	MNH		...	23558	7 3/8	1/4	9/16	− 5 11/16
MarltonTech	MTY		...	6171	1 1/8	7/16	1/2	...
MarsGrphic	WMD		12	2902	6 1/8	2 3/4	5 1/4	...
MatecCp	MXC	.05e	19	2868	6 5/8	5 1/4	6 3/8	+ 7/8
MatlackSys	MLK		...	28991	10 1/4	4 1/2	8 1/4	...
MaterlSci	MSC		82	16089	17 1/2	14 3/8	15 5/8	+ 5/8
MattWrigt	MW		...	8397	1 1/2	3/8	3/4	+ 7/16
Maxxam	MXM		6	92131	51	23 3/8	47	+ 22 5/8
McRaeInd A	MRIA	.48	7	2189	6 3/8	4 5/8	4 7/8	− 5/8
McRaeInd B	MRIB		7	499	6 1/8	4 3/4	4 7/8	− 3/8
MedChmPrd	MCH		6	34338	11 3/8	4 3/4	4 7/8	− 4 7/8
MediaGen A	MEGA	.44	...	99063	40 1/2	29 7/8	31 3/8	− 3
MedMgtAmer	MMA	.09	...	5267	4 3/4	1	1 3/8	− 2 1/8
MedProp	MPP	1.20	8	10790	9 1/8	7 1/8	7 1/8	− 1/2
Medicore	MDK		...	11278	3 3/8	1 7/8	2 5/8	− 1/8
Mediq	MED	.12	10	29079	6 1/8	3 1/8	4 1/4	+ 3/4
Mediq pf		.07	...	1228	6	2 7/8	4 1/8	+ 3/4
MEMCo	MEM	.40	33	1961	15 3/8	9 1/2	10 1/4	− 2 3/8
MerchGp	MGP		4	6838	11 1/2	8	10 3/4	+ 2 5/8
MercuryAir	MAX		...	11708	6 1/8	3 1/8	6	+ 1 7/8
Merimac	MRM	.10a	14	3445	7 1/16	5 1/4	6	− 1
MetPro	MPR	.20	18	12233	24 5/8	11 1/2	20 1/8	+ 8 1/8
MetroMob A	MMZA		...	28876	79	41 1/2	71 1/2	+ 28
MetroMob B	MMZB		...	71423	78 7/8	39 3/4	72 1/2	+ 30 1/2
Metrobank	MBN	.12e	10	4454	16	10 1/8	13 1/8	+ 2 7/8
MetroCircuit	MPB		...	2679	1 1/8	5/16	5/16	...
MetroRlty	MET	.75e	...	450	9 3/4	6 5/8	7 1/8	− 2
MichaelStr	MKE		12	107646	10 1/4	4 7/8	5 1/8	− 1 3/4
MicronPdt	PMR		...	7491	3	1 1/8	1 3/8	− 3/8
Middleby	MBY	.08e	10	30583	10	5 3/8	5 3/4	...
Midland	MLA	.38	10	2664	36	23 3/8	28 3/4	+ 3 3/8
MinnPL pf		5.00	...	z9250	59	51	58 1/2	+ 5 3/4
MinnPL pf		7.36	...	z26310	84 3/4	75	84 1/2	+ 8 1/2
MinvenGld	MVG		...	2369	3 5/8	3 1/8	3 3/8	...
MissionRes	MRP	.60	21	33695	20 1/4	3 3/8	12 3/4	+ 9
MissionWest	MSW	.36	16	928	9 3/4	7 1/8	7 3/8	− 2 1/4
MitchlEngy	MND	.32	42	87301	21 7/8	11 3/8	21 7/8	+ 10 1/2
MongPwr pf		4.40	...	z6610	52	44	50 7/8	+ 5 5/8
MongPwr pf		4.50	...	z5190	54 1/4	46	52	+ 4
Moog B	MOGB		20	1608	15 1/4	11 1/2	12 1/8	− 1 3/8
Moog A	MOGA		13	23874	11 1/8	7 1/4	7 7/8	− 1/4
MooreMed	MMD		...	19810	15 1/8	8 1/4	9 3/8	− 1 1/4
Morgan JP wtM			...	19463	3 7/8	1 1/8	1 3/8	− 1/8
MorgnFoods	MR		...	20136	1 5/8	3/4	1 5/8	+ 7/8
MtgRlty wt			...	4969	7/8	1/16	1/8	− 9/16
MtgInvPls	MIP	.80e	12	20401	8 3/8	6 3/4	6 7/8	− 3/8
MottsHldg	MSM		...	2673	8 1/8	6 3/8	7	− 3/4
MountnMed	MTN		17	38004	21 5/8	8	8 7/8	− 2
MuniInsFd	MIF	.88e	...	36983	12	9 5/8	9 5/8	− 3/8
MunivestFd	MVF	.75e	...	126656	10 3/8	8 3/4	9 5/8	...
MyersInd	MYE	.20b	12	7115	19 1/8	15	16 5/8	+ 1 1/8
-N-								
NoCaroFed	NFC		...	4824	4 1/4	1	1	− 2 1/2
NECO Ent	NPT	1.50	...	5533	20 1/2	14 1/2	19 1/4	− 3/4
NHI Nelson	NNH		...	186137	16 1/4	3 3/4	11	+ 6 5/8
NS Gp	NSS	.10	12	36538	11 1/2	7	11 1/2	+ 4 1/8
NVR	NVR	.92e	4	87611	8 1/4	4 3/4	5	− 7/8
NantuckInd	NAN		13	15766	10 1/4	4 5/8	8 5/8	+ 3 7/8
NastaInt	NAS		3	16824	5 1/4	3 1/8	3 3/4	+ 1/4
NaborsInd	NBR		32	19697	4	1 1/2	3 1/2	+ 1 5/8
NaborsInd wt			...	7010	13/16	1/8	5/8	+ 1/2
NtlEnvrGp	NEG		...	8139	2 7/8	5/16	1/2	− 3/4
NtlGasOil	NLG	.40b	14	1664	13 3/4	11 3/8	12 3/4	+ 1
NtlHlth	NHC	1.00e	8	10454	16 1/8	9 3/8	15 1/4	+ 5 7/8
NtlPatent	NPD	.02i	16	96789	8 7/8	6 1/8	7 1/4	+ 3/4
NtlRlty	NLP	.80	...	30443	12 3/4	2 1/4	2 3/8	− 8 1/4
NewLine	NLN		16	22395	9 1/4	5	6	+ 7/8
NewMexAriz	NZ		...	7538	20	8 1/4	9 3/8	− 4 7/8
NYTaExFd	XTX	.66e	...	4788	10	8 3/4	9 3/8	− 1/8
NYTimes A	NYTA	.52	14	358630	34 3/4	24 1/2	26 1/2	− 3/8
Newcor	NEW		10	8634	13 3/8	8 1/8	10 1/8	+ 1 1/4
NewmkLewis	NLI		16	21213	7 1/2	3 1/2	3 3/4	...
NicholsInst	LAB		29	25037	13 1/4	6	12 1/2	+ 6 3/8
NicholsSE	NCL		...	12467	4 1/4	7/8	1	− 2 5/8
NorcenEngy g	NCN	.50	...	3095	23 1/4	18 5/8	21 3/4	...
NorcenEngy A g	NCNA	.50	...	785	21 1/4	17 1/4	20 5/8	...
NorexAm	NXA		22	13053	8 1/4	2 1/4	5 3/4	+ 3 1/8
Nortankers	VLC	.20e	...	41378	18 3/8	14	15 5/8	...
NorthbayFnl	NBF		...	3637	20	11	16 7/8	...
NoCdaOil g	NCD	.20	...	13020	21 1/8	15 1/4	20	+ 4 1/4
NoIndPS pf		4.25	...	z27440	46 3/4	40 1/4	46	+ 5
NuHorzElec	NUH		12	8532	3	1 7/8	2	− 1/2
NuHorzElec wt			...	1982	3/4	7/16	7/16	− 7/16
NumacOG	NMC		...	6507	9 5/8	7 1/8	8 3/8	+ 1 3/8
NuvnNYM	NNM	.81a	...	7549	12 3/4	10 5/8	12	+ 1 1/2
-O-								
OEA Inc	OEA		13	3639	35 1/4	27 3/8	30 1/4	+ 2 3/8
OMI Cp	OMM		11	319521	11	7 1/4	9 7/8	+ 2 1/2
OBrienEngy	OBS		...	90478	7 7/8	3 5/8	6 5/8	+ 2 7/8
Odetics A	O.A		29	4019	6 1/2	3 3/4	4	− 1 5/8
Odetics B	O.B		39	625	6 5/8	5 1/2	5 1/2	− 5/8
OhioArt	OAR	.24a	...	1047	48 3/8	28 3/4	28 7/8	− 12 7/8
OldSpagWareh	OSW		17	40590	20 1/2	5 7/8	17 7/8	+ 11 7/8
OlstenCp	OLS	.24	14	44664	23 3/8	16	16 3/4	− 1 1/4
OneLiberty	OLP	.40i	...	4860	16	10 5/8	10 5/8	− 3 5/8
OneLiberty pf		1.60	...	1033	15 1/2	13 3/8	13 3/4	...
OneitaInd	ONA		11	28955	14 5/8	4 7/8	12 1/4	+ 7 1/4
OOkiepCop	OKP	1.76e	3	6636	14 1/4	8 3/4	10 1/8	+ 1/8
OppenhmrInd	OPP		...	26346	7 3/8	1 3/4	2	− 3 1/8
Organogene	ORG		...	76327	17 3/4	9 1/2	12 5/8	− 3 1/2
OrioleHoA	OHCA	.40a	4	2196	12 1/2	8 3/8	8 5/8	− 1 1/2
OrioleHoB	OHCB	.45a	4	1821	11 3/4	8 5/8	8 5/8	− 1 1/4
OrmandInd	OMD		...	4041	1 7/8	9/16	5/8	− 1/4
OSullivan	OSL	.28	11	7324	16 1/8	10	10 3/8	− 5 3/8
OxfrdEngy	OEN		425	13770	6 1/2	3 1/2	4 1/4	− 1/4
-P-Q-								
PLM Int	PLM	.76	7	11840	11 3/8	7 1/4	8 3/8	+ 5/8
PSE	POW		22	12558	12 1/4	5	12	+ 6 1/4
PacEnt pf		4.36	...	z85710	47 1/4	40 3/4	45 1/8	+ 2 5/8
PacEnt pf		4.40	...	z21290	50	42	45 1/8	+ 1 1/8
PacEnt pf		4.50	...	z70270	49 1/2	42	46 7/8	+ 4 3/8
PacEnt pf		4.75	...	z49370	52	12 1/4	48 1/4	+ 3 1/4
PacEnt pf		7.64	...	z36750	81 1/4	71	80	+ 5 7/8
PacGE pfA		1.50	...	5447	17 3/4	14 7/8	17 1/8	+ 2
PacGE pfB		1.37	...	1585	16	13 3/8	15 1/8	+ 1 1/4
PacGE pfC		1.25	...	787	14 3/8	12 1/4	13 7/8	+ 1 3/8
PacGE pfD		1.25	...	3009	14 1/2	12 1/4	14	+ 1 1/4
PacGE pfE		1.25	...	2282	14 7/8	12 1/8	14 3/8	+ 1
PacGE pfG		1.20	...	1826	14	11 5/8	13 3/4	+ 7/8
PacGE pfW		2.57	...	9652	28 1/4	24 5/8	27 5/8	+ 2 1/4
PacGE pfV		2.32	...	22406	26	22 5/8	25 1/2	+ 2 3/8
PacGE pfT		2.54	...	7267	27 7/8	24 3/4	27 3/8	+ 2 1/4
PacGE pfS		2.62	...	10295	27 7/8	25 1/4	27 5/8	+ 2
PacGE pfH		1.12	...	2119	13 1/2	11	13 1/2	+ 2 1/8
PacGE pfR		2.37	...	9455	26 3/4	23 1/4	26 1/4	+ 2 5/8
PacGE pfP		2.05	...	7159	30 1/2	20	23 1/4	+ 2 1/2
PacGE pfO		2.00	...	10038	23 1/8	19 1/8	22 1/2	+ 2 1/4
PacGE pfM		1.96	...	10877	23	19 1/4	22 3/8	+ 2 3/8
PacGE pfL		2.25	...	1183	25	21 3/4	24 3/8	+ 2 3/8
PacGE pfK		2.04	...	18261	23 5/8	19 3/4	23	+ 2 3/8
PacGE pfJ		2.32	...	812	25 3/4	22 1/8	25 1/2	+ 2 1/2
PacGE pfI		1.09	...	1202	12 1/2	10 7/8	12 1/2	+ 1 1/8
PacWstBcshr	PWB	.24	13	46191	13 1/2	5 1/4	11 3/4	+ 6 3/8
Pacificp pf		5.00	...	z16425	59	52 1/8	57 1/2	+ 2 7/8
Pall Cp	PLL	.48	23	190373	36 3/8	27 1/8	34 1/4	+ 6 3/8
ParkParsl	PDP	2.40	14	19332	16 1/2	11 5/8	16	+ 4 1/8
PauleyPete	PP		256	6701	15 3/8	10	10 1/4	− 3

AMERICAN STOCK EXCHANGE COMPOSITE

Stock	Symbol	Div	Yld	Sales 100s	Hi	Lo	Last	Net Chg
PaxarCp	PXR		13	4593	13	5⅝	9⅞	+ 2⅞
PayFoneSys	PYF		...	1836	4¾	2⅛	2⅞	− ¾
PEC Israel	IEC		7	295	12⅛	8⅝	12	+ 2⅞
PeerTube	PLS	.30i	...	4592	7	4¼	6½	+ ½
PegasusGld	PGU	.10e	31	216100	15⅜	8⅞	13½	+ 2
PennEngrg	PNN	.80	10	1110	37	25⅛	26½	− 3½
PennTraf	PNF		...	16209	27⅞	12½	18	+ 4⅝
PennRE Tr	PEI	1.68	21	10614	27⅛	21⅛	27⅛	+ 4⅜
Penobscot	PSO	.20	22	2539	6¾	5	5⅛	− ⅝
Penril Cp	PNL	†	6	18531	8⅝	3¼	6⅝	+ 3⅜
PeoplesBcpNC	PBK	.56	9	6042	16¾	12¼	15⅝	+ 1¼
PeriniCp	PCR	.80	57	10579	39⅝	30¾	34¾	+ 2¾
PeriniCp pf		2.12	...	8445	28⅛	23⅞	25⅝	+ 1⅞
PeriniInv	PNV	.60	...	8568	18¾	15	15	− 1⅜
PetersJM	JMP		4	38334	14⅞	7⅝	9¼	+ ⅝
PeteHeatPwr	PHP	1.83	...	6330	17½	14	16	− ⅛
PhilLongD	PHI	.15e	10	127174	25	10¼	17½	+ 7⅛
PicoPdts	PPI		...	8003	2¾	⅝	1¼	− 1
PioneerSys	PAE		...	7019	5/16	⅛	⅛	...
PittsWVaRR	PW	.56	10	2508	6⅜	5½	5¾	− ½
PittDesMoin	PDM	.80	12	3152	29¼	22½	27½	+ 4¼
PittwayCp	PRY	1.80	15	5253	110	95⅝	109½	+ 14½
PlyGem	PGI	.12	11	55122	15	10⅞	11¼	− ⅝
PlymRub A	PLRA		...	1112	2¾	1⅜	1¾	− ⅛
PlymRub B	PLRB		...	1236	2⅞	1⅝	1¾	− ¼
PolarisInd	SNO	2.40a	6	39397	27¼	15⅛	24½	+ 9⅛
PortaSys	PSI		13	58335	15¾	9⅝	13¾	+ 3⅝
PortageInd	PTG		...	8427	2⅞	1½	2⅝	+ ⅜
PraireOil	POY		19	2028	8⅜	5⅜	8⅛	+ 2¾
PrattHotl	PHC		...	11911	1⅝	7/16	9/16	− 9/16
PrattLamb	PM	.52	15	12900	18	13¼	16¼	− ⅛
PrecisnAero	PAR		...	4586	3¾	2⅛	2¼	− ⅜
PfdHlthCr	PY	.10r	22	11419	9½	5	8¼	+ 2¼
PrepdLegal	PPD		56	17774	2¼	⅜	9/16	− 1 5/16
PresRlty A	PDLA	1.66	4	749	14¼	8⅛	8⅛	− 5¾
PresRlty B	PDLB	1.66	4	4970	14¼	7⅞	8½	− 5½
Presidio B	PRSB		194	4287	8⅜	4⅜	7¾	+ 2⅞
Presidio A	PRSA	.10	...	32467	9⅛	4¼	9	+ 3¾
Presidio pf		.48	...	18285	11¼	4½	11⅛	+ 4¾
PriceComm	PR		...	52031	7⅜	4⅜	6	+ 1
PrimeFnl	PFP	.40e	...	3898	4	2	2	− 2
PrimFnl pf			...	141	7⅜	6½	6¾	− ⅞
PrismEntn	PRZ		13	7876	4¼	2¼	3¾	+ ¾
PrncDiagLab	PDA		238	4220	3⅞	2¼	2⅜	+ ⅛
PrncDiagLab wt			...	2596	¼	1/128	1/128	− 15/128
PrncDiagLab un			213	1683	3¾	2⅛	2⅛	− ⅜
ProMedCap	PMC	.42	14	5020	5⅞	3	5½	+ 1⅝
ProfCare	PCE		13	23175	7¼	2¼	5¼	+ 3
PropCapTr	PCT	2.61c	9	33262	21⅜	11	12⅛	− 8⅝
ProviEngy	PVY	1.40	...	5839	19⅛	16⅜	18⅜	− ⅝
PubSvcColo pf		4.25	...	z11400	46	40½	45½	+ 4
PugetPL pfD		2.34	...	2991	26½	25	25¾	+ ⅜
PuntaGorda	PGA		...	4333	2½	5/16	⅜	− 2¼
Quebecor g	PQB	.48	...	4487	18¼	12⅜	13	− 3¾

-R-

Stock	Symbol	Div	Yld	Sales 100s	Hi	Lo	Last	Net Chg
RB&W Cp	RBW		10	7849	8¼	5½	5⅝	− ½
RMS Int	RMS		...	2905	2½	⅜	⅜	− 1⅝
RaganBrad	BRD	.12	...	1310	25½	20½	20½	− ¼
RavenInd	RAV	.30	11	11942	15	7¾	13¼	+ 5⅜
ReCapCp	RCC		12	10625	14⅞	9⅛	14¼	+ 5⅛
RE SecFd	RIF	1.00	...	12329	9¼	6⅝	6¾	− 1⅝
RltySouth	RSI	.68	9	9219	10⅞	5¾	6⅛	− 4⅜
RltySouth wt			...	1652	¼	1/16	1/16	− ⅛
RedLionInn	RED	2.10	29	27960	21⅛	14⅜	17¾	+ 3
RedlawInd g	RDL		...	9121	4	2⅛	2⅜	− ⅜
RedlawInd rt			...	4044	5/16	3/16	7/32	...
RedlawInd wtA			...	1556	3	⅝	¾	...
RegalBeloit	RBC	.48	14	40852	19	13	16⅜	− ½
RelEl pf		1.50	...	6442	10⅛	10	10⅛	...
ResidnMtg	RMI	.08e	...	17240	3¼	1⅛	1⅝	− 1½
RsrtIncoInv	RII	1.60	...	16748	12⅛	9⅛	9⅝	− 2½
ResrcRecyc	RRT	.20r	...	600	10	8⅛	8¾	+ ⅜
ResponsTch	RTK		...	15238	4⅜	3/16	⅝	− 3¼
RichtonInt	RHT		...	10638	4⅜	2⅜	3⅛	+ ⅝
RiedelEnvr	RIE		21	13541	20⅜	10⅝	11⅜	− 4⅜
RioAlgom g	ROM	.85	...	3128	23⅛	19	19½	− ⅞
RiserFoods	RSR		...	12619	9¼	5¾	7⅛	+ ⅛
Riverbend	RIV		12	5648	6⅛	4⅜	4¾	− ⅛
RobtMark A	RMKA		24	2061	3⅞	1⅝	3⅞	+ 2¼
RobtMark wt			...	731	½	⅜	7/16	+ 1/16
RogersCp	ROG	.12	...	10537	27⅝	20	23⅜	− ⅛
RoweFurn	ROW	.16a	7	2584	8⅞	5⅞	6	− ½
RoyalPalm	RPB	2.25c	3	3538	6⅝	3⅝	4	− 1¼
Ruddick	RDK	.40a	14	18268	29⅜	20⅝	28⅞	+ 7⅝
Ruddick pf		.56	...	113	53¾	42	53¾	+ 10¾
RymacMtg	RM	1.60	...	23231	9	6⅜	6⅞	− 1⅝
Rymer wt			...	4595	3⅞	1¾	2¾	+ 1
Rymer wt wd			...	4	3¼	3⅛	3⅛	...

-S-

Stock	Symbol	Div	Yld	Sales 100s	Hi	Lo	Last	Net Chg
SFM Cp	SFM		...	1159	3⅞	2⅞	3	+ ⅛
SJW Cp	SJW	1.82	18	1911	29½	25⅝	27¼	− 2⅛
SPI Hldg pf		2.14t	...	10267	15⅛	4⅜	4⅝	− 5⅜
SPI Pharm	SPI	.08b	8	7979	11⅞	7⅜	8	+ ¼
SalemCp	SBS		2	2919	15⅞	7¾	7⅞	− 6
SamsonEngy	SAM	1.60	...	7275	16⅞	13⅞	16¾	+ 2½
SanCarlos	SAN	.14e	17	6324	4¼	2⅛	3⅛	+ ⅞
SanDgoGE pf		.88	...	1024	11	9¼	10⅝	+ ½
SanDgoGE pf		.90	...	986	11⅜	9⅝	10¾	+ ½
SanDgoGE pf		1.00	...	739	12¼	10⅝	11½	+ ⅛
SanDgoGE pr		7.80	...	z65400	91¾	78½	88¾	+ 3
SanDgoGE pr		7.20	...	z33850	84½	72½	82	+ 3
SanDgoGE pr		2.47	...	2386	29	24¾	27¾	+ 1⅞
SandyCp	SDY		...	5010	5½	2¼	3⅛	+ ¾
SanmrkStar	SMK		12	11653	4¾	3½	3¾	...
Sbarro	SBA		24	32597	24¼	13¾	24	+ 9¼
ScandnvaCo	SCF		...	18311	7½	4⅞	6⅜	...
SceptreRes	SRL		86	6411	4 11/16	2⅝	4 5/16	+ 1 11/16
ScheibEarl	ESH	.36	66	9841	17⅝	12	13¼	+ 1⅜
SciMgt	SMG	.10	...	13168	6⅞	3	3½	− 3⅜
ScopeInd	SCP	.60	15	849	41¾	32⅜	40	+ 6⅛
ScurryRain	SRB	.50	...	1910	21¾	14¾	21⅝	+ 6⅞
SeabrdCp	SEB	.50	...	300	181	113	116	+ 1
Seaport	SEO		...	2044	1¾	⅜	½	− 7/16
Seaport pf			...	z2800	6¾	3½	3½	− 2⅜
Seitel	SEI	†	12	36527	10⅞	3⅞	8⅜	...
SelasCp	SLS		11	5948	18⅞	7⅞	17	+ 8¾
Semtech	SMH		7	7400	3⅞	1½	1⅞	− 1⅞
Servotrnics	SVT	†	9	2545	4⅛	2¼	2½	− 1¾
ShaerShoe	SHS	.48e	101	2159	14⅛	10⅛	10⅛	− 2⅝
SheltrCmpnt	SST		6	10172	7¼	3½	4	− ½
Sherwood	SHD		...	37056	2	1⅛	1½	+ ⅜
ShopcoLau	LSC	1.10e	...	11791	10½	8⅛	8⅜	− 1¼
Sierra VI	SZF	.28	...	3744	7¼	4⅛	4⅞	− 2½
Sierra VIpf		.33	...	2879	8¼	5	7¼	− 1¼
SierraCap IV	SZD	.30	63	7804	6	4	4⅜	− 1¼
Sierra VII	SZG	.43	...	3425	9⅛	5⅝	6⅛	− 1⅝
Sierra VIIpf		.50	...	4985	9⅝	7⅛	8	− 1⅝
SierraHlth	SIE		...	67660	9⅝	1½	8⅝	+ 7
Sierracin	SER		19	9080	14⅝	5⅞	13⅞	+ 7⅜
SifcoInd	SIF	.20	10	10252	15⅞	7⅝	13⅞	+ 5⅞
SikesCp A	SK.A	.24	13	44205	16¾	9¼	15	+ 5⅝
Silvercrest	SLV		...	8894	2⅝	⅛	½	− 1⅝
Skolniks	SKN		100	7325	3¼	1⅞	2	− ¾
Skolniks wt			...	2169	⅜	⅛	¼	...
SmithAO A	SMCA	.80	10	4893	22⅜	13¼	13¾	− 2¾
SmithAO B	SMCB	.80	10	12123	18½	12½	13	− 2⅜
SmithAO pf		2.12	...	5428	25¾	19⅞	20¼	− 2⅛
Sorg Inc	SRG		...	8765	9	1	1¾	− 4½
Sothebys	BID	.20	16	297507	37	9¾	23½	+ 13½
SoCalEd pf		1.02	...	5204	12¾	10½	12¼	+ 1⅛
SoCalEd pf		1.06	...	15636	13¼	10¾	12⅝	+ ⅞
SoCalEd pf		1.08	...	3285	13⅜	11⅛	12½	+ 1
SoCalEd pf		1.19	...	2666	14¾	12¼	13⅞	+ ⅞
SoCalEd pf		1.45	...	14130	17¾	15¼	17¼	+ 1¾
SoCalEd pf		8.54	...	2218	102⅝	95	101¾	+ 5⅜
SoCalEd pf		7.58	...	9276	90	77¼	89⅛	+ 9
SoCalEd pf		8.70	...	1153	99	88	96½	+ 7⅞
SoCalEd pf		8.96	...	1094	99¾	89½	98½	+ 5½
SowestRlty	SWL		...	6440	1¾	½	1⅛	+ 5/16
Spartech	SEH		16	7831	6½	2⅞	3	− 3⅛
SpeedPrint	SBM		3	2695	4⅜	2⅛	3½	+ 1⅛
SpellingA	SP		31	53624	12¼	6¼	12¼	+ 5⅞
SalMae wtY93			...	27506	8⅛	6¾	7½	+ ¾
SumitTE Fd	SUA	1.40	...	20364	15⅞	9⅜	9¾	− 3⅜
SunCityInd	SNI		...	1360	6	4⅜	4¾	− ¼
SunbeltNur	SBN		...	6035	7	3⅝	6½	+ 2⅝

AMERICAN STOCK EXCHANGE COMPOSITE

Stock	Symbol	Div	Yld	Sales 100s	Hi	Lo	Last	Net Chg
SunshJr	SJS	.12j	34	1182	14⅝	10⅜	11⅜	– 2½
SuprSurg	SGC	.60	10	4367	40⅛	29¼	30¾	+ ¼
SupTeltec	STT		8	5207	3⅜	2⅜	2¾	...
SwiftEngy	SFY		8	26317	13½	7	11½	+ 4⅝
Synalloy	SYO	.40	6	43565	10⅞	5½	10⅛	+ 4¼
SystemInd	SYI		...	20105	4½	1	2⅝	– 1
-T-								
T2 Med	TSQ		28	45923	23⅞	9⅝	22⅛	+ 11⅛
TCS Ent	TCS		...	1526	4⅝	2⅜	2⅜	...
TIE Comm	TIE		...	238174	2½	1	1	– ⅝
TII Ind	TI		...	15692	4⅜	⅞	1½	– 2
TRC Cos	TRR		13	91974	16¾	6¾	8⅛	+ 1
TSF Comm	TCM		...	19723	12⅜	7	8½	...
Tab Pdts	TBP	.20	18	14468	14½	10⅝	13⅝	+ ⅝
TandyBrnd	TAB		15	58013	27⅝	11	19¾	+ 8¾
TastyBak	TBC	.70	12	12518	25⅛	17⅞	19⅛	– 2⅞
Team	TMI	.12e	10	18678	11⅜	6⅜	11¼	+ 3¾
TechOpsL	TO	1.00e	18	21257	34¼	18⅛	27¾	+ 9⅜
TechOpsS	TOC	.37e	9	9424	8½	4⅝	6⅜	+ 1⅞
Technitrol	TNL	1.12	11	4101	42¾	29	40¼	+ 10¾
TejonRnch	TRC	.05e	259	29055	56	29⅝	44	+ 8½
TeleConcpts	TCC		...	4432	1½	½	9/16	– 3/16
Teleflex	TFX	.48	13	37431	38¾	28⅛	31⅜	+ 1⅞
TeleData	TDS	.26	133	144736	46½	26⅞	46⅜	+ 19
Telesphere	TSP		...	235086	4⅝	1¼	3⅛	+ 1½
TemcoNtl	TEM		...	7229	2¾	1	1¼	...
TemcoNtl wt			...	506	9/16	¼	¼	...
Tenera	TLP	.80	7	4391	6¾	5⅞	6¼	...
TenneyEngrg	TNY		...	4572	1½	½	⅝	– ½
TexasAir	TEX		...	f11912	23⅜	11⅛	11½	– ⅜
TexMeridnRs	TMR		...	23894	¾	¼	½	+ ¼
Thermed	TMD		158	93975	19¾	9¾	14¼	+ 1⅞
ThermEnvr	TEV		81	25334	10⅛	6¾	8⅛	+ ½
ThermCardio	TCA		...	26607	14⅝	7⅜	13½	...
ThermInst	THI		23	52466	20⅝	10⅝	16⅜	+ 5⅜
ThermPrc	TPI		91	23620	15	2⅞	12¾	+ 9⅝
Thermwood	THM		...	7538	3⅜	½	2¼	+ 1⅜
ThorEngy	THR		18	5398	2⅜	7/16	1⅝	+ 1 11/16
ThreeD B	TDDB	.06	41	2111	5⅜	3½	4½	+ ⅞
ThreeD A	TDDA	.10	42	2761	5¼	3½	4⅝	+ 1
TimberInd	TBL		30	56047	15½	8¾	11½	– 3¾
Tofutti	TOF		...	13211	4⅜	1⅜	1⅝	– ¼
ToledoEd pf		8.32	...	437	83¾	70	83	+ 11¾
ToledoEd pf		4.25	...	z17650	44¼	36¼	41¾	+ 6
ToledoEd pf		7.76	...	z31550	79	67¾	79	+ 12¼
ToledoEd pf		10.00	...	z27930	99½	84	96	+ 11½
Torotel	TTL		...	4201	3⅛	¾	2	+ ⅝
TotalPete	TPN	.80	11	140555	30½	20⅛	28	+ 7⅝
TotalPete pf		2.88	...	5612	45⅛	33⅞	42¾	+ 8⅞
TownCnty	TNC		21	48046	10	5½	6¼	– 3¾
TransLux	TLX	.08b	...	3242	8½	6⅝	7¼	– ½
TransicoA	TNIA	.30	24	16457	8¼	5	6⅝	+ ¾
TransicoB	TNIB	.10	23	2289	7⅞	5⅛	6½	+ ⅝
Tranzonic	TNZ	.16	9	1519	15⅞	10⅞	12⅛	+ 1⅛
Tranzonic B	TNZB	.28	9	1103	14	9½	12⅛	+ 2¾
TriStMotr	TSM		22	5163	19½	15⅛	18½	+ ¾
TrianglCp	TRG	.20	...	7036	7¾	4¼	5⅛	– 1½
TrianglHme	THP		11	2078	2⅞	1¾	1¾	– ⅜
TridexCp	TDX		12	8451	6⅞	3⅛	4¼	+ ¼
TrustAm	TRS		...	3617	8⅛	1⅞	2½	– 5⅝
TubosMex	TAM		...	100508	7⅞	3⅝	5⅞	+ 1⅜
TurnBdcst A	TBSA		...	25631	64	17	50½	+ 33⅝
TurnBdcst B	TBSB		...	32618	59⅞	14⅜	50	+ 35⅜
TurnerCp	TUR	1.00	76	5181	19⅜	13⅛	13⅝	– 3⅛
TwoPesos	TWP		...	13887	3	1	1⅜	– ⅜
-U-								
USFG Pachldr	PHF	2.10	...	8530	19¾	14⅞	15½	– 1⅞
USP REIT	URT	1.00	...	5885	8	4⅜	4⅝	– 3¼
UniCareFnl	UFN		10	1562	20	11	16¼	+ 4⅞
Unicorp	UAC	.22j	...	22313	7⅝	1⅞	2	– 3¾
Unimar	UMR	.76e	...	23338	6¼	4⅝	5½	...
UnionVally	UVC		...	698	7¼	3½	3½	– 3⅛
UnionValley wt			...	409	2	⅞	1⅛	...
UtdCapital	ICU		13	9355	8⅞	3½	3⅝	– 3⅝
UtdFoodsA	UFDA		8	27278	3¾	1⅜	2⅝	+ 1¼
UtdFoodsB	UFDB		8	11906	3⅝	1⅜	2¾	+ 1¼
UtdMed	UM		10	8884	7¼	5⅛	6	+ ¾
US Biosci	UBS		...	18954	14	6½	12⅜	...
US Cellu	USM		...	48262	41⅜	20¼	31⅛	+ 10⅝
UnitelVid	UNV		22	3594	14⅜	11¾	13½	+ ⅞
UNITIL	UTL	2.08	12	659	38⅞	30	37	+ 6⅞
UniversityBk	UBN	.20	...	4821	3¾	1⅝	1¾	– 1¼
UnivPatnt	UPT		...	28939	9	3¾	5⅞	+ 2
Uno Restr	UNO		29	23381	16⅜	8	14½	+ 6
-V-								
VMS Hotel	VHT	.90	4	28282	7	2¾	3	– 3½
VMS Hotel wt			...	12803	9/16	3/16	3/16	– 5/16
VMS IncoTr	VST	1.04	5	19711	8⅛	4⅜	5	– 2¾
VTX Elec	VTX		5	3813	4⅛	1⅝	1⅞	– 2⅛
VaderGp	VDR		...	2289	5¾	3⅛	3⅜	– 1¼
ValleyForg	VF	.26	11	3836	16½	8⅞	9	– 1⅛
ValleyRes	VR	.56	16	2004	15¾	12¼	12¾	– ⅜
Valspar	VAL	.56	17	13977	36½	23¾	35¾	+ 11¾
VanKamMerCal	VKC	.65	...	9069	10	8⅞	9¼	– ¾
VeritInd	VER		...	2425	6¾	2½	3⅛	– 1¾
VtAmer A	VACA	.40b	24	27359	41	21	40	+ 17⅞
VtResrch	VRE		4	4379	3	1⅜	1¾	+ ⅜
Versar	VSR		...	9556	9⅜	4½	7	+ 2⅜
Viacom	VIA		...	57554	65¼	30½	57½	+ 26⅜
Viatech	VTK		16	6542	19¾	7⅞	17⅞	+ 7⅜
ViconInd	VII		105	8466	6⅜	4⅛	5¼	+ ⅝
VircoMfg	VIR	.04b	10	2802	11⅛	7	7⅜	– 2¾
Vitronic	VTC		18	11172	3¼	1½	1¾	– 15/16
VoplexCp	VOT	.40	115	6312	9⅝	5⅝	5¾	– ⅝
VulcanCp	VUL	1.00e	14	2136	20⅞	15¼	17¾	+ 1⅜
Vyquest	VY		...	3591	1¾	⅛	⅛	– 1½
-W-								
WCI pf		.94t	...	20565	15⅛	5¼	6	...
WangLab B	WANB	.12j	...	f12362	10⅞	4⅝	5⅛	– 3⅝
WangLab C	WANC	.08j	...	4881	13	5⅝	7⅜	– 1½
WashPost B	WPOB	1.84	20	19525	311	204	281½	+ 70¾
WashRITr	WRE	1.08	20	19971	21½	18⅜	19	– 2
Watsco A	WSOA	.20a	11	3207	10¼	6½	9	+ 2⅝
Watsco B	WSOB	.16b	11	2047	10¾	6½	9⅜	+ 2¾
Weathfrd	WII		...	78608	5⅛	1¾	5	+ 3⅛
Weathfrd pf			...	2680	26¾	11	25½	+ 14⅝
WedcoTech	WED	.08e	12	1047	8⅞	7¼	7¼	– 1¼
Weiman	WC		...	2094	4⅛	1⅞	2¾	– 1
Weldotron	WLD		...	4132	7⅜	2⅞	3⅛	– 4⅛
WellcoEnt	WLC	.25	5	1409	17¾	13⅛	13⅛	– 2⅛
WellsAm	WAC		...	7649	1⅞	5/16	⅜	– 1⅛
WellsGrdnr	WGA		...	8472	6¼	3	3¾	– 1⅜
WescoFnl	WSC	.78	15	3725	77¼	40⅝	62¼	+ 21¼
WstTexUtil pf		4.40	...	z8270	50¼	44⅛	50	+ 5½
Westair	WAH		11	21788	10⅞	5¾	6⅛	– 3¼
WstamBcp	WAB	.40	20	7413	25⅛	16⅜	23¼	+ 6¾
WstbrdgeCap	WBC		...	3906	2¾	1⅞	2	– ½
Westcorp	WES	.10e	13	20465	11⅛	6⅛	8½	+ 2
WestDigital	WDC		13	341147	15¼	5¾	8⅜	– 6⅜
WestRETr	WIR	1.40	18	35060	21	17⅛	19¼	+ 1½
WichitaRiv	WRO		...	9981	6¾	1⅞	6⅛	+ 1⅛
Wickes pf		2.50	...	7386	15¼	10¼	10⅜	...
Wickes wt			...	8409	9/16	1/16	1/16	– 3/16
WienerEnt	WPB	.18j	...	1184	9¼	4⅛	4⅜	– 4¾
WinstonRes	WRS		...	6314	3⅛	1⅜	1½	– 1⅛
WinthrpInv	WMI	1.49e	10	5371	13½	11½	12¾	+ ¾
WiscPL pf		4.50	...	z9680	55	46⅞	53	+ 4¼
WolfHB	HBW	.20e	8	3119	5¼	2⅜	3⅞	+ 1⅜
WorldIncoFd	WOI	1.04	...	107963	10¼	7¾	9	– ⅝
WorthenBk	WOR		15	13340	12⅛	7¼	12	+ 3⅞
-X-Y-Z-								
Xerox wt			...	10786	1⅞	11/16	13/16	+ ⅛

Footnotes on Page 98

AMERICAN BONDS

The following tabulation gives the 1989 sales, high, low, last price and net change from the previous year in bonds listed on the American Stock Exchange.

		Sales $1,000	High	Low	Last	Net Chg.
-A-						
AMC 13.6s00	15.3	288	98	86	89	– 6½
AMC 11⅞01	...	272	86	78	80¾	– 5¼
APL 10s92	12.0	42	83	70⅜	83	+ 13
Action 11¼92	12.3	88	92	89	91⅜	+ 3⅜
Alpine 13½96f	...	1689	84	39	55	– 29
AmFruc 9.4s00	10.7	160	88	82½	88	+ 4¼
AmShrd 16½96	14.6	28	100	96	96	...
Andal 5½97	cv	64	67	50	52	– 13
Angles 12½95	15.2	4431	85⅝	80	82	– 2½
Anth 11¼00	cv	725	237	137	210	+ 71
Arrow 12s98	15.2	415	91½	78	79	– 10
Arrow 9s03	cv	1234	74	62	68	– 6
Arrow 13¾04	18.0	2369	98	74	76½	– 18⅜
Atari 5¼02	cv	1291	85	56	67⅞	+ 16⅞
Atlant 14½97	...	356	100	80	87	– 11
Audiot 10¼02	cv	609	38	21	21¼	– 13¾
-B-						
BSN 7¾01	cv	1659	74	55	62	– 4
Balfor 13½98	15.2	1164	94¼	83	89	– 5
vjBayCol 6¾91	cv	4	92	90	92	...
BergBr 6⅞11	8.6	587	83	66¼	80	+ 15½
Bless 10s92	10.1	195	100	98¼	99	...
Bowmr 13½95	cv	651	85	71	72	...
BrnhP 8½12	cv	758	117	101	106	+ 1
-C-						
Candg 7s11	cv	2802	64	56½	60	+ 3
ChmbDv 6¾04	cv	1437	107¼	101	102½	...
ChtMd 15.85s08f	...	5060	110	89½	97	– 9¾
ChtMd 15.85s08n	...	118	104	90	98	...
ChckFul 8s06	10.1	7515	98	75½	79	– 11½
CircE 13½97	43.5	4083	67½	25	31	– 27
Clabr 14½04f	...	1034	70	39¼	45⅞	+ 5⅞
ColnInd 10½94	12.6	356	88	81½	83½	+ 2
Conair zr91	...	90	80⅜	72	73	– 3¾
ConqEx 9½14	cv	1027	110	98	109	...
ContAir 11s96	13.7	1782	85	76¼	80½	+ ½
ContHlt 14⅛96	17.7	317	97¼	80	80	– 10
Curtis 13⅛02	14.1	5	93	93	93	+ 2½
CustE 15s97f	cv	127	98	85	87	– 10
-D-						
DamsO 13.2s00f	...	840	37	19	25	– ¼
DamsO 12s03f	...	2371	40	18½	20	– 3
DamsO 14s93f	cv	1402	25½	16¾	25½	+ 8⅝
DamsO 12⅞93f	cv	1389	23	18	22½	+ 4½
DamsO 14⅝93f	cv	99	25	17½	19	– 13⅛
DiagR 8½98	cv	2818	88	72½	73½	– 9½
DorchG 8½05f	cv	211	65	52	60⅝	– ⅜
Ducom 7¾11	14.1	6743	66½	35	55	+ 18½
-E-						
vjEAL 5s92f	cv	10975	74	40	63	+ 16
vjEAL 4¾93f	cv	8187	68	37½	58	+ 18
vjEAL 11½99f	cv	41569	82½	49	62½	+ 5½
vjEAL 11¾05f	cv	10651	82	51⅞	68	+ 7
vjEAL 11¾93f	...	3425	98½	90	93	...
vjEAL 12¾96f	...	1424	96	84½	94	...
vjEAL 13¾01f	...	2508	97	78	92	...
Eckerd 11⅛01	12.8	6941	95	82	87	– 6
Eckerd 13s06f	...	752	79	70	72½	+ ½
EntM 8½06	cv	4181	51½	37¼	43	+ 3½
-F-						
FPA 14½00	16.1	15	90	90	90	– 6
FarWst zr95	...	37	56	51	56	+ 21
FtCtrl 9s00	cv	105	120	95	120	...
Fthill 12½98	13.3	79	97	94	94	– 3
Fthill 9½03	cv	1150	115	97¼	100¼	+ ¼
FruitL 7s11	11.2	2557	67	57⅛	62½	+ 4½
FruitL 12⅜03	13.0	3715	99⅛	91	95	– 2

		Sales $1,000	High	Low	Last	Net Chg.
-G-						
GTE Sou 7½02	8.8	105	87	79	85	+ 4½
GTE Sou 7¾03	9.2	63	86½	80	84½	+ 1¼
GECa 8⅛90	8.6	5	95	95	95	– 4⅞
GECa 8s90	8.1	15	99	98	99	...
GTFla 7½02	8.8	117	88	79	85½	+ 5½
GTFla 8⅛03	...	96	89	83	89	+ 1
GTFla 9⅜05	9.4	197	102¾	93	99¾	+ 3⅛
GeoRs 13s91f	...	3273	66	21	21	– 44
GeoRs 13¾96f	...	6205	65	21	21	– 44
GrfRst 13⅞98f	...	5478	101	44	48¼	– 51¾
GrfRst 13½95f	...	1723	101	43⅛	49	...
-H-						
HarteH 04f	...	3114	99½	86	99¼	+ 9¾
HarteH 11⅞00	12.0	30	100	99	99	...
HlthCr 14⅜95	151.3	2336	96¾	5	9½	– 87¾
HlthCh 10⅜99	cv	2923	69½	60	68½	+ 7½
Heldr 9s91t	cv	228	91	85	91	+ 1⅛
HomShp 11¾96	12.8	9894	94⅞	80	91½	+ 4¼
HudGn 7s11	cv	2996	79	60	65	+ 5
-I-						
InstSy 7s91	cv	67	86⅝	79	82	– 1½
InstSy 12½97	15.9	1091	84	76¾	78½	+ 1½
Intmk 11⅞99	13.8	855	98	86	86	– 5
Intmk 13.20s98	13.3	88	100	95	99	– 2
Intmk 13.2s98	14.2	18	93	93	93	– 5
Intmk 7⅜07	8.6	2388	105	82	86	– 8½
IntBkn 10s98	13.3	736	88	72	75	– 8
IntCtr 14½06f	...	3905	62	31	32½	– 24
IroBr 12s99	19.4	332	82	62	62	– 17½
-J-						
JonesIn 13s00	14.1	30	100⅝	92½	92½	...
-K-						
Kane 12¾01	13.9	2	92	92	92	– 11
Katem 8s03	cv	474	120	107	110	...
Kogr 8.4s96	9.3	60	93	90	90	+ 2
Koor 12s96f	...	6185	74	38	40	– 19
-L-						
LSB 13¾95	14.5	353	98	87	95	+ 8
LeisT 6¾s96	cv	50	63¼	60	60	– ½
LeisT 15¾99	17.5	864	100	90	90	– 5½
LeisT 13⅝96	21.0	1695	95½	64	65	– 16¾
Lynch 8s06	cv	5007	106	67½	94	+ 27
-M-						
MSA Rty 9¼93	15.4	40	81½	60	60	...
MagCop 18s98f	...	8934	107	96	99⅜	– 5⅝
MagCop 14½01	16.1	234	107½	88½	90	...
MarkIV 7s11	cv	4529	115½	72	107¾	+ 37¾
MarkIV 12¾01	14.7	20	87	87	87	– 17½
Maxam 13⅝92	14.4	2632	98	93⅛	94½	...
Maxam 12½99	15.0	1132	87½	78¼	81	– 2
Maxam 14¼92	15.3	3	93¼	93¼	93¼	...
Maxam 16s00	17.1	11183	99	81	93⅝	– ⅜
Mediq 7¼06	cv	3547	72⅞	55	64	+ 4
Moog 9⅞06	cv	4391	85½	72½	73½	– 4
MtgRty 6¾91	cv	66	98⅛	93	95⅝	– 2⅞
Multm 16s05A f	...	78	96	85	96	+ 13
Multm 16s05B f	...	2935	96	84¼	96	+ 11
-N-						
NCNB 7¾02	8.8	17	88	78	88	+ 8
NRM 13⅞99	...	15	105	101½	105	...
NVR LP 10s02	cv	4821	89	25½	72	– 7
NVR LP 13¾97	cv	1035	100	91¾	91¾	– 6¼
Nasta 02	cv	829	92½	77	83	...
Nich 15s00	30.0	879	89½	48	50	– 40
Nich 14⅞99	25.2	2318	95	50	59	– 26

		Sales $1,000	High	Low	Last	Net Chg.
-O-						
Oakwd 7½01	cv	3707	83½	67	72¼	+ 5¼
OBrien 7¾02	cv	6340	164	85	137	+ 52
Olsten 7s13	cv	3929	104½	89	89½	− ½
Openh 12¾03	14.0	3205	95½	88	91	− ¼
Openh 12¾02	14.0	3323	94⅞	88½	90⅞	− 1⅛
-P-Q-						
PeopBc 8¾05	cv	303	105	99	101	...
PlyGm 10s08f	cv	987	85	74	78	...
PrceC 13s96	21.0	1184	90	57	62	− 30
PSvEG 6s98	7.3	273	83⅛	75	82¾	+ 6¾
Pulte 8½08	cv	7276	94	69	74	+ 6
PuntGl 6s92f	cv	280	72½	60	65¼	− 5¾
-R-						
RMS 9¾95	cv	124	82½	70	70½	− 7½
RsrtInt 16⅝04f	...	38600	96¼	23½	27½	− 69
RsrtInt 10s99f	...	14193	74	18	21½	− 42⅞
RsrtInt 10s98f	...	13746	75	18¼	21¾	− 44½
RsrtInt 11⅜13f	...	38710	65½	19	22⅞	− 41⅛
Rudick 8s11	cv	4647	147½	112	145½	+ 31½
RyanM 16s12A	14.3	173	112	108	112	+ 2½
RyanM 14s12B	13.1	90	107	103½	107	+ 1
RyanM 13¾12C	13.1	62	106	103⅛	104¾	+ ¼
RyanM 12s12D	11.7	234	104	101	102½	+ ⅜
RyanM 12¾12E	12.4	230	105¼	102½	102⅞	− ¾
RyanMtg 12½12	12.0	194	105¼	101½	104	+ 1½
RyanM 12s13G	11.7	264	104	101	102¾	...
RyanM 12s13H	11.7	156	106	101½	102¾	− 1¼
RyanM 11¾13I	11.5	412	105	100½	102	− 1
RyanM 11½13J	11.3	521	106	100¾	101½	− 1
RyanM 11⅜13K	11.2	299	103¼	100½	102	− ⅜
RyanMtg 12s13I	11.5	302	104½	102	104	+ 1¾
RyanM 12⅜13M	12.0	290	106	101	103	...
RyanM 12⅞14	12.3	280	106	103	105	− ¾
RyanM 12¾14o	12.1	328	106	102½	105	+ 1½
RyanM 12½14P	11.9	150	105⅛	102½	105	+ 2
RyanM 12s14	11.5	136	105	101½	104	+ 1½
RyanM 11⅞14	11.7	180	103½	100	101¾	...
RyanMt 11.4s15	11.0	166	103½	100½	103½	+ 1¾
RyanM 11¼15	10.9	136	103½	101¼	103	+ 1
RyanM 12⅛13BB	11.9	1	102	102	102	...
RyanM 12¾13CC	12.1	188	106	102½	105½	+ ½
RyanMtg 12½14	12.0	68	105	101½	104½	...
RyanM 12½15	12.1	116	103	100½	103	...
-S-						
SCIHld 15s97	13.8	368	113	106	109	− 1½
SCIHld 1zr90	...	49	89¼	80⅛	89¼	+ 12¾
SCIHld 2zr91	...	97	80	70	80	+ 22
SCIHld 3zr92	...	210	71	66¼	71	+ 14
SCIHld 4zr93	...	72	60	56⅝	59	+ 21½
SCIHld 5zr94	...	376	56	44	53⅜	+ 8⅜
SCIHld 6zr95	...	110	49	39¾	49	+ 3¼
Sage 8½05	cv	4437	65½	57	62⅞	− ⅛
Sanmk 12⅞01	...	36	90	79⅞	82	− 15
SvceCp 10s00	10.8	186	100	92	92¼	− 2¾
SvcMer 11¾96	13.1	16986	96	86½	89¾	+ ¾
ShlrG 13¾01f	...	3438	83	64	81½	+ 12⅝
SCE 4½s90S	4.6	118	98¼	94	98	+ 3½
SCE8⅛94 Y	8.3	1343	99	90	98	+ 4⅞
SCE7⅞s95 Z	8.2	881	97½	88½	95¾	+ 6½
SCE8s96 AA	8.3	930	97⅞	88¾	96	+ 5¾
SC7⅜s97 BB	7.8	725	94¼	84½	94¼	+ 9¼
SC8¼s99 CC	8.7	585	99	88⅜	95¼	+ 6⅛
SCE 8⅞00	8.9	1089	101	90⅛	99¼	+ 5¾

		Sales $1,000	High	Low	Last	Net Chg.
SCE 8⅞01	9.0	704	99½	91	98½	+ 6
SCE 8¼02	8.6	1094	96½	85¼	96	+ 9⅛
SCE 9⅝03	9.4	2414	103	87⅛	102⅜	+ 4⅝
SCE 13s15	11.9	80	113⅛	109	109	− 1⅝
SCE 7¾96	8.2	417	95	88⅛	95	+ 2½
SCE 9s95	9.1	58	101	94¾	98½	...
SwBell 8¾07	9.0	5455	99	89¼	97⅝	+ 7⅞
SwBell 6⅞11	8.4	2666	83	72⅛	81½	+ 7½
SwBell 7¾09	8.8	1429	90½	79½	88¼	+ 6¾
SwBell 7⅜12	8.6	1940	87½	76⅛	86¼	+ 7¾
SwBell 7⅝13	8.6	2456	89⅝	78	88½	+ 9
SwBell 8¼14	9.0	3298	94	83	92	+ 8¼
SwBell 9¼15	9.3	4487	103	86	100	+ 7½
SwBell 8½16	9.0	2650	95½	85½	94¼	+ 8
SwBell 8¼17	8.9	2501	93½	83¼	93	+ 7¾
SwBell 8¾18	9.1	1170	97⅝	86½	96	+ 7⅝
SwBell 9⅝19	9.5	12980	103⅛	94½	101	+ 4
Spartc 9s99	15.3	1558	96	56	59	− 36
SpellA 12¼93	12.3	356	100	96	100	+ 2
StrlEl 10¾09	12.6	459	101½	85	85	...
StrlSft 8s01	cv	2543	70½	60	70⅛	+ 6⅝
Storer 10s03	12.8	3856	84	77	78	− 3½
-T-						
TeamI 13s04	cv	1104	148	15	147	+ 35
TxAir 15¾92	16.4	6452	102	94½	96	− 3
TxAir 15¾92b	16.3	6443	102	93	96½	− 1½
TxAr 14⅜90	14.7	7269	101¼	93¼	98	− 1½
TxAr 14.9s95	16.0	3189	102	91	93	− 3
TxAr 14¼93	16.0	3845	101	89	89	− 6
TrnLux 9s05	cv	1240	85	79	81	+ 1
Tridx 10¼96f	cv	623	81	65⅛	70	+ 3⅞
TCastl 13¾97	14.9	1237	106¾	92	92	− 10½
TCastl 7s99	11.1	2202	70¼	60½	63	− 2½
TmpTaj 14s98	16.3	18347	102	84⅛	86	− 13¾
TurnBd 12s01	11.8	552	102	100½	102	...
TurnBd zr04	...	1124	31	28	29¾	...
-U-						
Ultrs 7¾06	cv	3162	93	66	66	− 20
Unimx 7½92	cv	123	82	74	82	+ 8¾
Unimx 10¾97	cv	194	80	60	69	− 1⅛
UnValy 14¼01	21.8	246	97	65	65½	− 31½
USAir 6s93	cv	103	101	87	95	+ 7½
-V-						
ViacmI 15½06f	...	10128	105	100	101½	...
Viacm 14¾02	16.5	83	91	78	89½	...
Viacm 11½91	11.4	30	101	99	101	+ 1
Viacm 11.8s98	11.7	311	103	97	100½	+ 1⅝
Vyqst 13¾01	...	707	65	25	25	− 74
-W-						
Wainoc 10¾98	11.0	2643	98	88⅛	97⅝	+ 10⅝
Wang 7¾08	cv	12869	77¾	41½	44	− 31¼
Wang 9s09	cv	18034	87½	47½	50½	− 36
WarC 7⅝s94	8.8	219	90	81	87	− 2⅛
Watsc 10s96	cv	66	105	100	105	+ 5
Westbr 11.7s96	25.2	329	67½	45	46½	− 18½
WstDig 9s14	cv	5792	101¼	81	83½	...
WstInv 8s08	cv	5589	101	91½	96	+ 4½
Wherhse 6¼06	cv	1364	50¾	48	48¾	− 2
Wickes 12s94	14.9	4772	94⅞	79¼	80½	− 9
Wickes 7½-10s05	16.5	9554	65	43½	45½	− 14¾
Wickes 15s95	22.1	3831	103	67	68	− 31½
Wickes 11⅜97	21.3	1373	80½	51	53½	− 23⅝
Wickes 11⅞01	20.7	7339	86	53½	57½	− 23½

Footnotes on Page 112

GOVERNMENT NOTES AND BONDS

Over the counter U.S. Government Treasury Bonds and notes 1989 price range.

Rate	Mat.		High	Low	Last	Net Chg.
7.88	Dec 1989	p	99-29	98-09	99-29+	1-04
8.38	Dec 1989	p	100-01	98-22	99-28+	17
7.38	Jan 1990	p	99-31	97-24	99-31+	1-26
10.50	Jan 1990	n	101-08	100-02	100-02-	1-05
3.50	Feb 1990		98-21	94-05	98-21+	4-06
6.50	Feb 1990	p	99-25	96-30	99-25+	2-21
7.13	Feb 1990	p	99-27	97-12	99-27+	2-05
11.00	Feb 1990	p	101-26	100-09	100-09-	1-17
7.25	Mar 1990	p	99-24	97-07	99-24+	2-02
7.38	Mar 1990	p	99-24	97-11	99-24+	1-31
10.50	Apr 1990	n	101-21	100-10	100-19-	30
7.63	Apr 1990	p	99-28	97-13	99-25+	1-23
7.88	May 1990	p	99-31	97-19	99-29+	1-21
8.25	May 1990		100-11	98-03	100 +	31
8.13	May 1990	p	100-05	97-26	100 +	1-13
11.38	May 1990	p	102-20	101-04	101-04-	1-17
7.25	Jun 1990	p	99-20	96-16	99-18+	2-08
8.00	Jun 1990	p	100-03	97-15	99-31+	1-20
10.75	Jul 1990	n	102-18	100-21	101-11-	26
8.38	Jul 1990	p	100-17	97-24	100-06+	1-12
7.88	Aug 1990	p	100-30	97-04	99-28+	1-29
9.88	Aug 1990	p	102-02	99-22	101-01+	04
10.75	Aug 1990	n	102-26	100-23	101-18-	24
8.63	Aug 1990	p	100-25	98-02	100-11+	1-08
6.75	Sep 1990	p	99-05	95-10	99-01+	2-23
8.50	Sep 1990	p	100-23	97-23	100-08+	1-15
11.50	Oct 1990	n	104-06	101-30	102-18-	31
8.25	Oct 1990	p	100-17	97-08	100-05+	1-24
8.00	Nov 1990	p	100-08	96-28	100 +	2-02
9.63	Nov 1990	n	102-05	99-09	101-10+	20
13.00	Nov 1990	n	106-12	104-02	104-02-	2-09
8.88	Nov 1990	p	101-12	98-05	100-24+	1-08
6.63	Dec 1990	p	98-29	94-18	98-24+	3-10
9.13	Dec 1990	p	101-26	98-19	101-02	......
11.75	Jan 1991	n	105-15	102-25	103-20-	1-00
9.00	Jan 1991	p	101-26	98-09	100-31	......
7.38	Feb 1991	p	99-18	95-15	99-09+	2-22
9.13	Feb 1991	p	102-02	98-16	101-04+	1-08
9.38	Feb 1991	p	102-15	98-31	101-14	......
6.75	Mar 1991	p	98-23	94-05	98-16+	3-14
9.75	Mar 1991	p	103-04	100-04	102	......
12.38	Apr 1991	n	107-13	104-09	105-04-	1-08
9.25	Apr 1991	p	101-25	97-05	101-15	......
8.13	May 1991	p	100-27	96-14	100-05+	2-13
14.50	May 1991	n	112-11	108-24	108-24-	3-04
8.75	May 1991	p	101-29	99-22	100-30	......
7.88	Jun 1991	n	100-17	95-20	99-23+	2-20
8.25	Jun 1991	p	100-06	99-15	100-11	......
7.75	Jul 1991	p	100-06	98-21	99-20	......
13.75	Jul 1991	p	110-30	107-16	108-04-	1-31
7.50	Aug 1991	p	99-29	94-25	99-07+	3-05
8.75	Aug 1991	p	102-04	97-10	101-03+	2-06
14.88	Aug 1991	n	114-10	110-29	111-03-	2-17
8.25	Aug 1991	p	100-26	99-15	100-11	......
8.38	Sep 1991	p	101-10	99-26	100-19	......
9.13	Sep 1991	p	103	98-04	101-25+	1-31
7.63	Oct 1991	p	99-30	99-07	99-14	......
12.25	Oct 1991	p	109-09	104-29	106-29-	16
6.50	Nov 1991	p	97-27	91-31	97-17+	4-07
8.50	Nov 1991	p	101-27	96-20	100-27+	2-18
14.25	Nov 1991	n	114-17	110-19	111-29-	1-12
7.75	Nov 1991	p	100-01	99-17	99-21	......
7.63	Dec 1991	p	99-18	99-15	99-18	......
8.25	Dec 1991	p	101-11	95-27	100-19+	3-01
11.63	Jan 1992	p	108-24	103-27	106-20+	13
6.63	Feb 1992	p	97-25	91-23	97-12+	4-10
9.13	Feb 1992	p	103-18	98-03	102-06	......
14.63	Feb 1992	n	116-23	112-03	113-16-	1-11
7.88	Mar 1992	p	100-23	94-22	99-28+	3-16
11.75	Apr 1992	k	109-27	104-18	107-21+	22
6.63	May 1992	p	97-20	91-02	97-04+	4-15
9.00	May 1992	p	103-18	99-22	102-05	......
13.75	May 1992	n	115-02	109-31	112-08-	18
8.25	Jun 1992	p	101-23	95-08	100-21+	3-14
10.38	Jul 1992	p	107-05	101-06	105-12+	1-30
4.25	Aug 1987-92		96-28	91-02	91-28-	2-21
7.25	Aug 1992		99-03	92-15	98-09+	4-04
8.25	Aug 1992	p	101-24	95-03	100-20+	3-18
7.88	Aug 1992	p	100-24	98-16	99-26	......
8.75	Sep 1992	p	103-05	96-18	101-28+	3-09
9.75	Oct 1992	p	106	99-14	104-11+	2-21
7.75	Nov 1992	p	100-09	99-17	99-21	......
8.38	Nov 1992	p	102-04	95-07	101 +	3-22
10.50	Nov 1992	n	108-10	101-20	106-10+	2-05
9.13	Dec 1992	p	104-17	97-24	103-01	......
8.75	Jan 1993	p	103-15	96-11	102-01+	3-16
4.00	Feb 1988-93		97-02	90-23	92-08-	2-09
6.75	Feb 1993		97-18	89-23	96-17+	4-23
7.88	Feb 1993		100-29	93-29	99-27+	4-02
8.25	Feb 1993	p	102-02	94-23	100-24+	4-00
10.88	Feb 1993	n	110-02	103-02	107-28+	2-12
9.63	Mar 1993	p	106-15	100-04	104-21	......
7.38	Apr 1993	p	99-13	91-22	98-08+	4-21
7.63	May 1993	p	100-05	92-13	98-29+	4-19
10.13	May 1993	n	108-07	100-24	106-07+	3-03
8.13	Jun 1993	p	102-02	98-29	100-15	......
7.25	Jul 1993	p	98-31	90-25	97-25+	4-29
7.50	Aug 1988-93		99-26	91-13	98-09+	4-22
8.63	Aug 1993		103-18	95-29	101-30+	3-30
8.75	Aug 1993	p	104-03	96-03	102-12+	3-31
11.88	Aug 1993	n	114-19	106-27	111-29+	2-00
8.25	Sep 1993	p	101-28	100-16	100-31	......
7.13	Oct 1993	p	98-13	90-02	97-09+	5-10
8.63	Nov 1993		104-02	95-21	102-01+	3-22
11.75	Nov 1993	n	114-29	106-26	112-05+	2-14
9.00	Nov 1993	b	105-04	97-02	103-11+	3-30
7.63	Dec 1993	p	99-06	99-03	99-04	......
7.00	Jan 1994	p	97-29	89-10	96-23+	5-19
9.00	Feb 1994		105-31	97-20	103-18+	3-30
8.88	Feb 1994	p	105-02	96-15	103-05+	4-11
7.00	Apr 1994	p	97-27	88-30	96-22+	5-27
4.13	May 1989-94		97-20	90-19	91-24-	2-27
13.13	May 1994	p	121-25	112-31	118-28+	2-24
9.50	May 1994	p	107-21	98-30	105-18	......
8.00	Jul 1994	p	101-25	92-21	100-13+	4-31
8.63	Aug 1994	p	104-17	99-25	102-24	......
8.75	Aug 1994		104-21	96-09	103-05+	4-04
12.63	Aug 1994	p	120-21	111-16	117-23+	3-04
9.50	Oct 1994	p	108-01	98-28	106-03+	4-31
10.13	Nov 1994		110-21	101-15	108-21+	4-21
11.63	Nov 1994	p	117-07	107-27	114-20+	4-00
8.25	Nov 1994	p	102-06	99-16	101-13	......
8.63	Jan 1995	p	104-13	95-03	102-25+	5-18
3.00	Feb 1995		98-06	90-23	91-31-	2-20
10.50	Feb 1995		112-15	103-12	110-12+	4-16
11.25	Feb 1995	p	116-01	106-15	113-15+	4-10
7.75	Feb 1995	p	100-09	99-10	99-18	......
8.38	Apr 1995	p	103-17	93-29	101-26+	5-28
10.38	May 1995		112-11	102-28	110-08+	4-25
11.25	May 1995	p	116-14	106-25	113-31+	4-16
12.63	May 1995		123-10	113-24	120-03+	3-26
8.88	Jul 1995	p	105-24	96-05	103-30+	5-23
10.50	Aug 1995	p	113-12	103-18	111-03+	5-00
8.63	Oct 1995	p	104-21	94-29	102-23+	5-17
9.50	Nov 1995	p	108-29	99-03	106-22+	5-11
11.50	Nov 1995		118-19	108-25	115-27+	4-14
9.25	Jan 1996	p	108-01	98-03	105-21	......
8.88	Feb 1996	p	106-06	96-01	103-29+	5-25
9.38	Apr 1996	p	108-30	100-19	106-14	......
7.38	May 1996	p	98-15	88-08	96-24+	6-19
7.88	Jul 1996	p	101-12	97-10	99-05	......
8.00	Oct 1996	p	101-09	99-21	100-02	......
7.25	Nov 1996	p	97-19	87-03	95-30+	6-29
8.50	May 1997	p	104-14	93-21	102-15+	6-20
8.63	Aug 1997	p	105-11	94-08	103-09+	6-26
8.88	Nov 1997	p	106-27	95-18	104-22+	6-23
8.13	Feb 1998	p	102-12	91-03	100-15+	6-31
9.00	May 1998	p	107-25	96-18	105-23+	6-27
9.25	Aug 1998	p	109-14	98	107-09+	6-27
7.00	May 1993-98		95-21	84-08	93-05+	6-06
3.50	Nov 1998		99-24	90-17	92-26-	1-25
8.88	Nov 1998	p	107-07	95-20	105-05+	6-30
8.88	Feb 1999	p	107-11	95-23	105-08	......
8.50	May 1994-99		103-21	92-21	101-18+	6-07
9.13	May 1999	p	109-10	102	107-04	......
8.00	Aug 1999	p	101-07	97-24	100	......
7.88	Nov 1999	p	100-23	99-17	99-17	......
7.88	Feb 1995-00		99-31	88-14	98-09+	7-14
8.38	Feb 1995-00		102-19	91-18	101-07+	7-02
11.75	Feb 2001		128-14	115-20	126-05+	7-13
13.13	May 2001		139-21	125-11	136-19+	7-25
8.00	Aug 1996-01		101-10	89-04	99-02+	6-25
13.38	Aug 2001		142-07	127-12	139-02+	6-06
15.75	Nov 2001		160-29	147-05	157-17+	7-01
14.25	Feb 2002		149-27	135-07	146-27+	7-21
11.63	Nov 2002		129-29	115-17	127-12+	8-10

122

Government Notes and Bonds

		High	Low	Last	Net Chg.
10.75Feb	2003	123-04	109-02	120-21+	8-09
10.75May	2003	123-13	109-07	120-29+	8-19
11.13Aug	2003	126-26	112-08	124-04+	8-22
11.88Nov	2003	133-08	118-08	130-17+	8-28
12.38May	2004	138	122-15	135-10+	9-11
13.75Aug	2004	150-09	133-28	147-12+	9-17
11.63Nov	2004 k	131-29	116-28	129-17+	9-04
8.25 May	2000-05	102-24	89-17	100-25+	8-17
12.00May	2005 k	135-25	120-13	133-12+	9-10
10.75Aug	2005 k	125-05	110-04	122-21+	9-04
9.38 Feb	2006 k	113-24	99-13	111-14+	8-29
7.63 Feb	2002-07	97-17	84-07	95-22+	8-30
7.88 Nov	2002-07	99-17	86-03	98 +	9-10
8.38 Aug	2003-08	103-30	90-08	101-30+	9-04
8.75 Nov	2003-08	106-31	93-14	104-31+	8-26
9.13 May	2004-09	110-11	96-18	108-01+	8-14
10.38Nov	2004-09	120-28	106-07	118-18+	8-30
11.75Feb	2005-10	133-03	117-11	130-20+	9-22
10.00May	2005-10	118-01	103-10	115-26+	9-03
12.75Nov	2005-10	142-31	126	140-05+	10-07
13.88May	2006-11	153-28	135-19	150-27+	10-27
14.00Nov	2006-11	155-26	137-03	152-23+	11-05
10.38Nov	2007-12	122-24	106-26	120-17+	10-06
12.00Aug	2008-13	138-31	121	136-07+	11-04
13.25May	2009-14	151-29	132-10	149-02+	12-02
12.50Aug	2009-14k	144-25	125-28	141-31+	11-24
11.75Nov	2009-14k	137-20	119-28	135 +	10-29
11.25Feb	2015 k	136-15	117-19	133-20+	11-27
10.63Aug	2015 k	129-28	111-25	127-05+	11-12
9.88 Nov	2015 k	121-23	104-16	119-11+	11-04
9.25 Feb	2016 k	114-30	98-18	112-22+	10-22
7.25 May	2016 k	93-05	79-03	91-12+	9-11
7.50 Nov	2016 k	95-28	81-15	94-01+	9-15
8.75 May	2017 k	109-29	93-24	107-22+	10-16
8.88 Aug	2017 k	111-11	95-01	109-01+	10-19
9.13 May	2018 k	114-11	97-21	112-06+	11-09
9.00 Nov	2018 k	113-04	96-16	110-31+	11-01
8.88 Feb	2019 k	111-26	95-11	109-21	......
8.13 Aug	2019 k	103-09	98-03	101-19	......

STRIPPED TREASURIES

		High	Low	Last	Net Chg.
Feb	1990 a	98-30	94-11	98-30	......
May	1990 a	97-06	92-12	97-06	......
Aug	1990 a	95-09	90-13	95-09	......
Nov	1990 a	93-13	88-18	93-13	......
Feb	1991	91-18	86-23	91-18	......
May	1991 a	89-26	84-30	89-25	......
Aug	1991	88-03	83-05	88-03	......
Nov	1991 a	86-13	81-15	86-13	......
Feb	1992 a	84-23	79-27	84-22	......
May	1992 a	83-03	78-06	83	......
Aug	1992 a	81-16	76-18	81-12	......
Nov	1992 a	80	74-31	79-26	......
Feb	1993 a	78-16	73-14	78-07	......
May	1993 a	77	71-31	76-24	......
Aug	1993 a	75-23	70-16	75-12	......
Nov	1993 a	74-12	69-01	73-31	......
Feb	1994 a	72-24	67-19	72-15	......
May	1994 a	71-12	66-08	71-04	......
Aug	1994 a	70-06	64-28	69-29	......
Nov	1994 a	68-31	63-18	68-13	......
Feb	1995 a	67-06	62-05	66-22	......
May	1995 a	65-27	60-28	65-12	......
Aug	1995 a	64-17	59-17	64-02	......
Nov	1995 a	63-09	58-11	62-28	......
Feb	1996 a	62	57-03	61-18	......
May	1996 a	60-24	55-30	60-12	......
Aug	1996 a	59-19	54-23	59-06	......
Nov	1996 a	58-15	53-19	58-03	......
Feb	1997 a	57-05	52-11	56-22	......
May	1997 a	56-02	51-09	55-19	......
Aug	1997 a	54-29	50-06	54-14	......
Nov	1997 a	53-28	49-05	53-12	......
Feb	1998 a	52-23	48-04	52-06	......
May	1998 a	51-23	47-05	51-05	......
Aug	1998 a	50-22	46-05	50-05	......
Nov	1998 a	49-23	45-07	49-05	......
Feb	1999 a	48-24	44-08	48-04	......
May	1999 a	47-23	43-11	47-09	......
Aug	1999 a	46-28	42-14	46-11	......
Nov	1999 a	45-31	41-18	45-15	......
Feb	2000 a	44-30	40-20	44-15	......
May	2000 a	44-01	39-26	43-19	......
Aug	2000 a	43-05	38-31	42-22	......
Nov	2000 a	42-10	38-05	41-27	......
Feb	2001 a	41-12	37-10	40-29	......
May	2001 a	40-18	36-18	40-04	......

		High	Low	Last	Net Chg.
Aug	2001 a	39-25	35-25	39-10	.....
Nov	2001 a	39	35-01	38-17	.....
Feb	2002 a	38-08	34-10	37-24	.....
May	2002 a	37-16	33-19	37	.....
Aug	2002 a	36-24	32-28	36-09	.....
Nov	2002 a	36-01	32-07	35-18	.....
Feb	2003 a	35-10	31-17	34-27	.....
May	2003 a	34-20	30-28	34-05	.....
Aug	2003 a	33-31	30-07	33-15	.....
Nov	2003 a	33-12	29-19	32-27	.....
Feb	2004 a	32-21	28-31	32-05	.....
May	2004 a	32	28-12	31-17	.....
Aug	2004 a	31-12	27-25	30-28	.....
Nov	2004 a	30-26	27-07	30-10	.....
Feb	2005 a	30-06	27	29-21	.....
May	2005 a	29-19	26-14	29-03	.....
Aug	2005 a	29-01	25-29	28-16	.....
Nov	2005 a	28-15	25-12	27-30	.....
Feb	2006 a	27-30	24-28	27-12	.....
May	2006 a	27-13	24-12	26-27	.....
Aug	2006 a	26-27	23-28	26-13	.....
Nov	2006 a	26-11	23-12	25-26	.....
Feb	2007 a	25-27	22-30	25-10	.....
May	2007 a	25-10	22-15	24-26	.....
Aug	2007 a	24-28	22	24-10	.....
Nov	2007 a	24-12	21-17	23-27	.....
Feb	2008 a	23-30	21-04	23-13	.....
May	2008 a	23-15	20-23	22-30	.....
Aug	2008 a	23-01	20-09	22-16	.....
Nov	2008 a	22-19	19-28	22-04	.....
Feb	2009 a	22-06	19-15	21-24	.....
May	2009 a	21-25	19-03	21-10	.....
Aug	2009 a	21-12	18-22	20-29	.....
Nov	2009 a	21-03	18-10	20-23	.....
Feb	2010 a	20-19	18-01	20-03	.....
May	2010 a	20-06	17-22	19-22	.....
Aug	2010 a	19-25	17-10	19-10	.....
Nov	2010 a	19-16	16-31	19	.....
Feb	2011 a	19-06	16-22	18-21	.....
May	2011 a	18-26	16-11	18-09	.....
Aug	2011 a	18-14	16	17-30	.....
Nov	2011 a	18-04	15-22	17-20	.....
Feb	2012 a	17-25	15-12	17-09	.....
May	2012 a	17-14	15-02	16-30	.....
Aug	2012 a	17-03	14-26	16-19	.....
Nov	2012 a	16-26	14-16	16-10	.....
Feb	2013 a	16-16	14-06	16-01	.....
May	2013 a	16-08	13-30	15-24	.....
Aug	2013 a	15-29	13-22	15-14	.....
Nov	2013 a	15-21	13-13	15-05	.....
Feb	2014 a	15-12	13-05	14-28	.....
May	2014 a	15-03	12-29	14-20	.....
Aug	2014 a	14-27	12-21	14-10	.....
Nov	2014 a	14-19	12-12	14-03	.....
Feb	2015 a	14-08	12-06	13-27	.....
May	2015 a	14	11-30	13-18	.....
Aug	2015 a	13-23	11-23	13-11	.....
Nov	2015 a	13-19	11-15	13-05	.....
Feb	2016 a	13-11	11-08	12-31	.....
May	2016 a	13-05	11-02	12-25	.....
Aug	2016 a	12-29	10-29	12-17	.....
Nov	2016 a	12-23	10-23	12-11	.....
Feb	2017 a	12-18	10-17	12-05	.....
May	2017 a	12-10	10-11	11-31	.....
Aug	2017 a	12-04	10-05	11-24	.....
Nov	2017 a	11-31	9-31	11-20	.....
Feb	2018 a	11-25	9-27	11-14	.....
May	2018 a	11-19	9-22	11-09	.....
Aug	2018 a	11-14	9-18	11-03	.....
Nov	2018 a	11-11	9-14	10-29	.....
Feb	2019 a	11-05	9-10	10-26	.....
Aug	2019 a	11-12	10	10-27	.....
Nov	2004 b	30-26	27-11	30-09	.....
May	2005 b	29-21	26-11	29-03	.....
Aug	2005 b	29-04	25-25	28-19	.....
Feb	2006 b	29-07	24-28	27-20	.....
Feb	2015 b	14-10	12-02	13-28	.....
Aug	2015 b	13-26	11-21	13-13	.....
Nov	2015 b	13-18	11-14	13-06	.....
Feb	2016 b	13-14	11-07	13-01	.....
May	2016 b	13-12	11	12-30	.....
Nov	2016 b	12-27	10-20	12-14	.....
May	2017 b	12-12	10-09	11-31	.....
Aug	2017 b	12-08	10-04	11-26	.....
May	2018 b	11-22	9-20	11-09	.....
Nov	2018 b	11-11	9-08	10-31	.....

Government Notes and Bonds

		High	Low	Last	Net Chg.
Feb	2019 b	11-09	9-08	10-28	......
Aug	2019 b	11-04	10-20	10-22	......
Nov	1994 c	68-21	63-07	68-02	......
Feb	1995 c	67-05	61-28	66-21	......
May	1995 c	65-28	60-21	65-12	......
Aug	1995 c	64-19	59-13	64-01	......
Nov	1995 c	63-10	58-07	62-25	......
Feb	1996 c	62-02	56-30	61-18	......
May	1996 c	60-29	55-25	60-14	......
Nov	1996 c	58-20	55-12	58-04	......
May	1997 c	56-13	51-13	55-28	......
Aug	1997 c	55-10	50-13	54-26	......

		High	Low	Last	Net Chg.
Nov	1997 c	54-09	49-14	53-24	......
Feb	1998 c	53-09	48-09	52-23	......
May	1998 c	52-08	47-10	51-21	......
Aug	1998 c	51-08	46-10	50-21	......
Nov	1998 c	50-09	45-12	49-21	......
May	1999 c	48-15	47-29	47-31	......
Aug	1999 c	47-06	46-20	46-22	......
Nov	1999 c	46-09	45-23	45-25	......

k—Non U. S. citizen exempt from withholding taxes. n—Treasury note. p—Treasury note and non U.S. citizen exempt from withholding taxes.

MUTUAL FUNDS

The following table shows the closing net asset value for 1988, the dividends paid in 1989, and the closing NAV for the year.

	NAV 12-30-88	Divs 1989	Cap. Dist	NAV 12-29-89
AAL Mutual:				
CapGro p	8.88	.24	....	11.26
Income p	9.38	.81	....	9.67
MunBd p	9.76	.60	....	9.96
AARP Invst:				
CapGr n	24.72	.19	1.93	30.83
GinieM n	14.82	1.30	....	15.18
GenBd n	14.68	1.22	....	15.20
GrwInc n	20.90	1.06	....	25.36
TxFBd n	16.31	1.07	.25	16.70
TxFSh n	15.21	.89	....	15.23
ABT Funds:				
Emerg p	7.99	....	1.63	8.96
GwthIn p	9.76	.42	1.16	9.64
SecInc p	9.62	.47	....	10.81
UtilInc p	13.37	.90	.39	13.60
AddisnCa p	14.50	.33	....	18.13
ADTEK n	9.19	.36	....	9.67
AIM Funds:				
Chart p	5.21	.25	.42	6.51
Constl p	7.01	.01	1.57	8.06
ConvYd p	9.27	.41	....	10.22
HiYld p	8.29	1.09	....	6.93
LimMtTr p	9.74	.83	....	9.81
Sumit n	6.57	.16	.64	7.79
WeingEq p	9.19	.06	.63	11.79
A M A Funds:				
ClassGt pn	8.89	.39	1.06	9.10
GlbGth pn	19.84	.95	.30	22.83
GlbInc np	19.61	1.38	....	19.80
GlbST np	9.80	.39	....	9.80
GrwPl pn	18.34	.51	....	21.55
USGvPl np	8.53	.65	....	8.60
AMEV Funds:				
AstAll	9.86	.41	....	11.68
Capitl	11.90	.21	.61	15.61
CapAp	11.00	.03	.71	15.16
Fiducr	18.67	.18	.03	25.96
Grwth	15.04	.04	.48	20.92
HiYld	9.78	1.21	.06	8.06
TF MN	9.65	.68	....	9.73
TF Nat	9.85	.71	....	9.98
US Gvt	9.51	.92	....	9.72
AcrnFd n	36.36	.57	1.80	42.92
AfutureFd n	9.15	.09	....	10.38
Advest Advant:				
Govt np	8.26	.72	....	8.47
Gwth np	11.96	.20	.75	13.85
HY Bd p	10.00	.59	....	8.55
Inco np	9.71	.68	....	10.71
Spcl np	9.55	....	....	11.67
AlgersSCp t	11.23	....	3.79	14.58
AlgrGP t	10.30	....	....	13.91
Alliance Cap:				
Aliance p	5.60	.04	....	6.87
Balan p	12.25	.40	1.63	11.91
Canada p	7.39	.02	1.59	7.38
Conv p	9.06	.51	.16	9.44
Countpt p	14.50	.21	1.08	18.12
Govt p	8.27	.86	....	8.39
GroInc p	2.52	.09	.43	2.62
HiYld p	8.21	1.05	....	6.21
Intl p	15.74	.03	2.11	18.20
InsCalTx p	12.03	.80	....	12.30
InsMuni	9.33	.62	.07	9.52
MonInc p	11.64	1.13	....	11.96
Mortg p	8.81	.96	....	8.76
MuniCA	9.47	.69	.04	9.68
MuniNY	8.80	.64	....	9.05
NtlMuni	9.41	.70	.01	9.61
Quasar p	18.12	....	2.02	21.18
ST Mult p	9.70	.74	....	9.77
Surveyor p	11.65	....	3.11	11.33
Tech p	20.35	....	....	21.57
AlpnCA	....	....	....	9.98
AlpnNat	9.73	....	....	9.81
Altura Funds:				
Grwth	10.54	.31	.40	12.43
Income f	9.98	.87	....	10.03
Amer Capital:				
Comstk	13.08	.54	1.22	15.29
CorpBd p	7.02	.70	....	6.59
Enterp p	10.33	.29	1.70	11.52
ExchFd	66.39	1.84	.56	82.32
FdMtg p	12.38	1.13	....	12.88
FundAm p	10.39	.22	.64	11.12
GovSec p	9.98	1.02	....	10.37
Harbor p	12.39	.84	....	14.06
HiYldInv p	8.77	1.12	....	6.70
MuniBd p	18.41	1.33	....	19.04
OTC p	6.32	.09	....	8.49
PaceFnd p	21.83	.73	2.65	24.63
Providnt	3.94	.29	....	4.48
TxE HY p	10.72	.90	....	10.89
TaxEx p	10.79	.76	....	10.96
Venture p	11.70	.25	....	14.84
AExpEV	12.03	.51	.56	13.35
American Funds:				
AmBal p	10.46	.67	.58	11.41
AmcapF p	9.99	.27	.98	11.39
AmMutl p	17.59	.98	.79	20.20
BondFd p	13.24	1.30	....	13.21
CapInBl p	22.56	1.25	....	25.72
CapWld p	14.87	1.14	....	14.38
Eupac p	25.61	.56	1.83	29.23
FundInv p	14.60	.62	1.66	16.43
Govt p	13.34	1.30	....	13.53
GwthFd p	17.51	.61	1.99	20.17
HI Trst p	14.09	1.58	....	13.29
IncoFd p	11.48	.88	.37	12.80
IntBd p	13.70	1.23	....	13.80
InvCoA p	12.94	.59	.85	15.24
NwEcon p	20.08	.58	2.26	23.60
NewPer p	9.95	.29	1.01	11.18
TaxExpt p	10.88	.73	....	11.14
TxExCA p	13.92	.82	....	14.42
TxExMD p	13.69	.83	....	14.23
TxExVA p	14.16	.86	....	14.53
WshMut p	12.62	.62	.68	14.89
AmGwth	6.51	.03	1.08	7.82
AHrtge n	1.07	....	....	1.04
AmInv	6.39	....	....	7.42
AInvl n	7.83	.78	...	6.13
Amer Natl Funds:				
Growth	4.11	.12	.72	4.25
Income	17.66	.79	1.64	20.11
Triflex	14.46	.84	.93	14.62
API Tr n	11.28	.08	2.25	10.74
AmwyMut	6.49	.16	1.16	7.26
Analytic n	12.06	.50	.66	13.01
Armstng n	6.94	.24	.54	7.14
Aquila Funds:				
AZ TF	9.60	.66	....	9.88
CO TF	9.66	.65	....	9.80
HI TF	10.65	.73	....	10.93
KY TF	9.53	.68	....	10.05
OR TF	9.64	.64	....	9.91
AscPlStk	13.54	.27	1.92	16.48
AvonG n	9.63	.76	....	9.95
Axe Houghton:				
Fund B np	7.93	.41	....	8.95
IncoFd np	5.00	.47	....	5.04
Stock np	5.47	....	....	6.50
BB&K n	10.35	.45	....	11.20
Babson Group:				
Bond n	1.51	.13	....	1.56
Entrp n	11.39	.19	.69	13.06
Gwth n	10.97	.28	1.45	11.61

	NAV 12-30-88	Divs 1989	Cap. Dist	NAV 12-29-89
Shadow n	8.60	.16	.26	9.14
TaxFree n	8.60	.60	....	8.73
UMB St n	12.62	.58	.52	13.87
UMB B n	10.19	.82	....	10.50
Value n	16.27	.50	.03	18.68
BairdBlCh p	11.38	.26	....	14.20
BairdCa p	14.65	.10	....	18.11
BaronAst r	14.00	.15	1.25	14.67
Bartlett Funds:				
BascVl n	12.18	1.02	.18	12.58
FixedI n	9.46	.84	....	9.76
BascomBal	20.76	1.17	.45	21.61
BeaconHill n	26.21	...	1.88	29.66
Benham Capital:				
CalTFL n	10.51	.72	....	10.76
CaTFIn n	8.98	.59	....	9.28
CalTFH n	8.57	.65	....	8.71
CaTFI n	10.08	.62	....	10.22
GNMA n	9.69	.90	....	10.10
GoldIn n	9.05	.04	....	11.75
NITFI n	9.92	.61	....	10.09
NITFL n	10.78	.73	.04	10.98
Tar1990 n	85.70	....	....	94.00
Tar1995 n	56.33	....	....	64.96
Tar2000 n	37.16	....	....	44.52
Tar2005 n	24.36	....	....	30.18
Tar2010 n	17.31	....	....	22.16
Tar2015 n	12.63	....	....	16.86
T Note	9.74	.77	....	10.09
Berger Group:				
100 n	5.99	.01	.89	7.98
101 n	6.1/	.44	...	7.16
Bernstein Fds:				
GvShDu n	12.50	.95	.08	u12.60
ShtDur n	....	1.00	.10	u12.56
IntDur n	12.50	.93	.20	u12.77
DivMun n	12.50	.70	.04	u12.67
NYMun n	12.50	.71	.04	u12.72
BigEGv p	9.72	1.02	.19	10.06
BlanPrcMtl p	7.37	.03	.10	7.83
BlnStGr np	9.69	.37	.50	10.28
Boston Co:				
CapApr np	28.67	.55	7.60	27.49
GNMA np	11.66	....	....	12.05
MgdIn np	11.43	.93	....	11.18
SpGth np	14.33	.24	2.36	14.28
Brndywn n	12.87	.19	.51	16.40
Bruce	85.66	....	....	96.18
Bull & Bear Gp:				
CapGrth np	8.49	....	2.65	u8.28
EqInc np	11.02	.42	.28	u11.94
FNCI p	20.54	.56	....	20.29
GoldInv np	13.26	.13	....	u15.61
HiYield np	10.43	1.20	....	8.93
SpecEqt np	18.17	....	4.05	21.68
TaxFree np	17.44	1.13	.52	17.29
USGvt np	13.65	1.14	....	13.87
Burnham	20.89	1.75	.50	23.62
CJL Trust	9.96	.85	....	10.41
Calmos nf	10.08	....	.67	10.98
CalMun np	8.87	.53	.21	8.82
CalTrst n	11.25	.79	....	11.54
CalUGv n	9.29	.85	....	9.64
Calvert Group:				
Ariel	22.55	.38	.12	27.68
Equity p	17.49	.27	.11	22.40
GvLtd	14.49	1.13	....	14.55
Inco	15.67	1.40	....	16.54
Social p	24.33	.86	.45	27.49
SocBd	15.24	1.30	.05	15.87
SocEq	14.37	.23	.05	18.02
TxFLtd n	10.55	.67	....	10.61
TxFLng	15.20	1.00	....	15.64
USGov	14.11	1.22	....	14.76
WshArea t	17.72	....	1.80	17.24
Capstone Group:				
EqGuard	9.01	.28	1.61	7.66
Fund SW	10.60	.23	....	13.84
Income	5.17	.48	....	5.05
PBHG	10.51	.04	2.81	10.71
Trend	11.71	.40	1.37	13.48
Carnegie Funds:				
CapGth p	15.41	.27	2.38	17.54
CapTotR	10.14	.59	.02	12.94
Govt p	9.27	.72	.16	9.45
TxEOhG	9.17	.57	....	9.21
TxE NHY	9.41	.67	....	9.67
Cardinal	14.81	.63	.73	16.67
CardnlGvt	8.62	.84	....	8.80
CntryShr n	14.62	.50	.71	19.42
ChampHY p	11.84	1.43	....	11.23
ChestnutS n	76.62	2.21	.27	95.96
CIGNA Funds:				
Agresv p	11.07	.03	.04	13.30
GovSec p	9.70	.84	....	9.91
Growth p	11.93	.27	1.15	13.92
HiYld p	10.01	1.21	....	8.94
Income p	7.53	.71	....	7.80
MuniBd p	7.64	.54	....	7.81
Util p	10.99	.69	.40	13.73
Value p	12.79	.43	1.81	14.53
Citibank IRA-CIT:				
Balan nf	1.75	....	....	2.17
Equity nf	1.92	....	....	2.44
Income nf	1.72	....	....	1.93
ShtTr nf	1.49	....	....	1.62
Clipper n	37.74	....	....	43.45
Colonial Funds:				
AdvGld p	20.17	.17	....	22.61
CalTE	6.90	.48	....	7.03
CorpCsh p	42.70	3.73	.17	46.14
CrpCsII p	42.75	3.88	....	43.27
DvsdIn	7.27	.66	.06	7.25
Fund p	18.25	.66	.45	20.53
GvtSec p	11.03	1.02	.25	11.24
GrwthSh p	11.45	.22	2.09	12.41
HighYld p	7.21	.89	....	6.34
Income p	6.61	.66	....	6.45
IncPls	8.94	.76	.24	9.07
IntEqt p	18.21	....	1.04	19.41
MA TF	7.10	.47	....	7.16
MI TE	6.61	.38	....	6.60
mn te	6.78	.39	....	6.88
NY TE	6.62	.38	....	6.69
OhTE	6.75	.40	....	6.84
SmIndx p	12.00	.06	....	13.35
TXIns p	7.53	.51	....	7.69
TxExpt p	13.03	.99	....	13.05
US Gov p	7.10	.70	....	7.11
US Idx p	13.57	.29	....	17.22
Colonial VIP:				
AggGr t	10.78	.06	.40	11.79
DivRet t	10.38	.22	.44	11.43
FedSec t	9.71	.82	....	10.00
Hilnc t	9.93	1.12	....	9.21
HYMun t	10.03	.74	....	9.96
Co DTE	9.74	....	....	10.00
Columbia Funds:				
Fixed n	12.75	....	....	12.75
Grth n	21.21	.54	3.40	23.40
Muni n	11.42	....	.01	u11.61
Specl n	33.96	.03	3.16	41.56
Common Sense:				
Govt	10.93	....	.22	11.17
Growth	10.68	.20	.64	12.82
GroInc	10.49	.32	....	13.00
MunB	12.30	.77	....	12.47
CmwlthBal	2.06	.02	.03	2.02
Compass Capital:				
EqtyInco	10.00	.23	....	10.34
Growth	10.00	.19	....	10.93
ShrtInt	10.00	.42	....	10.08
Composite Group:				
BdStk p	9.99	.59	.10	10.51
Growth p	10.90	.47	.65	11.08
IncoFd p	8.67	....	....	8.36
NW 50 p	14.93	.14	....	20.42
TaxEx p	7.20	....	.09	7.17

	NAV 12-30-88	Divs 1989	Cap. Dist	NAV 12-29-89
USGov p	9.72	....	....	10.07
ConcrdCnv	9.51	.64	....	9.55
Conn Mutual:				
Govt	10.06	.84	....	10.58
Grwth	11.00	.50	1.24	13.04
TotRet	11.51	.75	.63	12.68
ConstEl p	9.69	.26	.10	10.31
Copley n	12.12	....	....	14.28
Counsellors Fd:				
CapApp n	9.39	.35	.23	11.31
EmGth n	11.42	.38	.15	13.37
FixdInc n	9.75	.92	....	9.69
IntEqu	10.00	.12	....	12.31
IntGvt n	10.04	.82	....	10.33
NY Muni	9.63	.58	....	9.68
CntryCaG r	14.75	1.03	.91	16.59
CowenlGr t	9.96	.48	.47	11.32
CowenOp p	9.36	....	.24	10.65
Critrn Transam:				
GvInc p	8.55	.85	....	8.58
GvSec p	8.38	.94	....	8.25
GrIn p	8.80	.49	.07	10.16
InvQual fp	8.88	.90	....	8.96
Lowry p	8.40	.26	.03	9.57
Sunblt p	16.24	.94	.03	19.67
TF In p	10.00	.61	....	10.29
Technol p	17.99	.13	.28	21.29
CritTrans Spcl:				
BlChip t	8.04	.05	.43	9.34
CvSecs t	9.23	.52	....	9.76
EmgGr t	10.28	....	.22	13.02
Global t	10.84	....	....	12.60
GvInc t	9.98	.99	....	9.98
HiYld t	9.58	1.26	....	7.88
HYTF t	9.27	.68	....	9.30
CumbrldG n	9.90	....	....	10.14
DR Bal	10.00	.18	.02	9.92
DR Eqty	10.50	.43	.65	11.30
Dean Witter:				
AmVal t	13.19	.32	1.38	14.81
CalTxFr t	11.68	.71	....	12.05
Convt t	8.68	.56	....	9.22
DvGth t	9.43	.05	....	10.79
DivGth t	19.24	.76	.64	23.74
GPlus t	8.72	.70	.15	9.25
HiYld	11.63	1.67	....	8.56
Intmd t	10.00	.57	.01	9.86
NYTxF t	10.94	.68	....	11.25
NtRs t	9.41	.31	.37	11.67
Optn t	7.59	.20	.50	9.03
SearsTE np	11.07	.67	....	11.41
TaxAd np	8.93	.99	....	8.27
Managed t	9.97	.72	.11	10.06
Strat t	9.46	.43	.20	10.96
TaxEx	10.96	.81	....	11.27
US Gvt t	9.42	.90	....	9.51
Util n	10.41	.67	....	12.22
ValAd t	12.05	.24	.26	14.35
WWInc	10.00	.65	....	9.61
WldWd t	14.62	.23	.83	15.91
Delaware Group:				
Dectrl	16.55	1.05	1.49	17.51
Dectrll p	11.39	.60	.47	13.30
Delawre	14.81	.81	....	17.74
Delcap p	13.80	.16	.29	18.03
Delchl	7.59	.92	....	6.76
Delchll p	7.59	.90	....	6.76
GvtInc p	8.51	.77	....	8.67
Inves np	9.72	.84	....	9.72
TxFrPa	7.76	.55	....	7.94
TFUSIns	10.51	.72	....	10.76
TxFrUS	11.34	.83	....	11.65
Trend	8.06	.05	2.22	9.68
Value	10.90	.14	.72	13.50
Destinyl n	11.91	.38	1.05	13.54
Destll n	17.69	.36	2.00	19.99
Dimensional Fds:				
US Small n	6.93	.70	.62	6.94

	NAV 12-30-88	Divs 1989	Cap. Dist	NAV 12-29-89
Japan n	28.80	....	1.29	38.57
UK n	25.14	1.72	.97	21.81
Cont n	12.05	.20	.26	16.94
Fixd n	100.45	8.74	....	100.98
Govt n	99.75	8.52	....	100.51
DG Div n	22.45	.75	1.74	23.32
Dodge&Cox:				
Balan n	32.09	1.76	.71	36.85
Income	10.00	.69	.01	10.68
Stock n	35.26	1.23	.82	42.57
Dreyfus Grp:				
A Bond n	13.34	1.18	....	13.98
CalTx n	14.42	1.03	....	14.58
CapVl p	24.54	1.68	....	28.89
CvSec n	8.96	.37	.56	9.34
Dreyfus	10.55	.58	.35	12.06
GNMA np	14.21	1.29	....	14.49
GwthOp n	9.94	.46	.80	10.12
InsTx np	17.30	1.16	....	17.60
Interm n	13.37	.95	....	13.54
Levge	13.55	.70	....	15.61
MA Tax n	15.54	1.07	....	15.62
NJ Tax np	12.16	.83	.04	12.36
NwLdrs np	23.40	.38	1.08	29.27
NY Tax n	14.73	1.06	....	14.94
NYTEIn n	16.32	1.10	....	16.68
NYITx np	10.56	.70	....	10.75
ShtIntTE n	12.54	.78	....	12.55
ShInGv n	11.03	1.02	....	11.20
StrAgg n	25.71	....	....	29.37
StrtInc p	12.77	1.20	....	13.26
StrtInv p	14.70	.21	.44	18.78
StrWld p	19.98	....	....	24.18
TxExpt n	12.27	.90	....	12.48
ThdCntr n	5.82	.18	.19	6.45
USGv Bd	12.74	1.16	....	13.56
USGvIn n	12.22	1.13	....	12.59
Eaton Vance:				
EV Stk	12.69	.50	1.04	14.71
GvOblg p	11.22	1.11	....	11.52
Growth	6.76	.08	.52	8.19
IncBos	9.37	1.11	....	8.65
Invest	7.01	.42	.46	7.52
MunBd	8.99	.66	....	9.25
Nautilus	10.35	....	....	11.81
SpecEqt	18.25	....	1.35	21.14
TotRet p	7.92	.55	....	9.94
VS Specl	10.59	.09	....	12.83
Eaton V Marathon:				
CalMn t	9.80	....	....	9.99
HiInc t	9.36	....	....	8.34
HiMun t	9.56	....	....	9.59
EclipEq n	10.12	.27	.63	10.86
Emblem Fund:				
EarnEq	10.00	.03	....	10.28
OH Reg	10.00	.04	....	9.74
RelEq	10.00	.05	....	10.33
SI Fxd	10.00	.15	....	10.01
EmpBld	16.81	....	.08	16.93
Enterprise Group:				
AgrGr p	13.01	....	.52	16.91
GvSec p	11.70	.91	....	11.92
GrInc p	13.77	.38	.10	15.24
Growth np	6.69	.01	.43	7.24
HYBd p	12.49	1.34	....	10.98
IntlGr p	12.91	....	.64	14.48
PrecM p	11.27	.27	.68	12.95
EquitB t	11.08	.24	.67	13.19
EquitG t	12.31	....	1.01	14.73
Equitec Siebel:				
AgGth t	11.91	.07	....	13.68
HiYld t	8.73	....	....	8.18
TotRet t	12.94	.51	....	14.79
USGvt t	9.17	....	....	9.00
EqtySt n	19.48	1.09	....	21.49
EurpEm p	10.00	.03	.05	12.58
Evergreen Funds:				
Evrgrn n	11.49	.97	.61	12.21

	NAV 12-30-88	Divs 1989	Cap. Dist	NAV 12-29-89
TotRt n	17.01	1.08	....	18.76
ValTm n	10.62	1.28	.75	12.03
LtdMkt	17.79	4.03	3.67	17.37
ExcelMidas	2.56	....	....	3.12
ExcelVal	6.80	.66	.47	7.36
ExInvHi p	9.00	1.20	....	7.74
FBL Gth t	10.01	.62	....	10.76
FPA Funds:				
Capit	12.46	.22	1.21	13.89
NewInc	9.61	.76	.05	9.92
Parmnt	13.91	.45	1.47	14.73
Peren	19.28	.72	.59	22.60
Fairmt n	45.56	.63	....	48.05
Federated Funds:				
FCCT n	8.99	.77	....	8.34
ExchFd n	50.04	1.32	2.48	54.94
FBF n	8.78	.70	....	9.24
FIGT n	9.41	.79	....	9.71
FFRT n	9.45	.98	....	9.32
GNMA n	10.61	1.00	....	11.14
FGRO n	17.13	.60	1.48	19.99
FHYT n	9.96	1.29	....	8.59
FIT n	10.02	.93	....	10.28
FIMT n	9.78	.64	....	9.98
FVRM n	9.89	.87	....	10.00
FSIMT n	10.10	.58	....	10.15
FSIGT n	9.86	.83	....	10.00
FSBF n	14.93	.94	.70	15.11
FST n	22.62	.75	2.13	22.64
FGVT n	8.98	.71	....	9.64
Fenimore	10.39	.10	....	13.57
Fidelity Invest:				
AgrTF nr	11.33	.88	....	11.49
AMgr	10.05	.38	.24	10.94
Balanc	10.57	1.00	.22	11.37
BlueCh	10.56	.12	.17	14.09
CA TF n	10.99	.76	....	11.26
CA Ins n	9.49	.62	....	9.68
Canada r	12.59	.01	.68	15.29
CapApp r	14.29	.24	1.22	16.63
CongrSt n	90.14	3.35	.05	116.48
ConnTF n	10.39	.70	.02	10.72
Contra n	12.64	.25	1.07	16.78
CnvSec n	9.83	.77	....	11.60
DisEq	10.15	.13	.13	13.52
EqutInc	25.20	1.75	1.16	26.91
EqutIndx n	10.71	.42	.14	13.48
Europe r	12.85	.19	....	16.81
ExchFd n	69.85	2.30	7.12	80.21
FidelFd n	15.43	.68	1.17	17.93
FlexBd n	6.65	.89	....	6.88
Freedm n	12.31	.38	....	15.66
GloBd n r	10.72	.49	....	11.08
GNM n	9.91	.85	....	10.38
GvtSec n	9.27	.78	....	9.61
GroInc	14.85	.75	1.27	17.17
GroCo	15.00	.14	2.00	18.92
HiIncm n	8.56	1.07	....	7.27
HighYield n	12.36	.89	.39	12.44
InsMun n	10.78	.71	....	11.05
IntBd n	9.87	.89	....	10.10
IntlGrl r	11.79	.16	....	13.88
Ltd Mun n	9.23	.61	....	9.31
Magellan	48.32	1.24	3.82	59.85
MI TF n	10.79	.76	....	11.10
MA TF n	10.98	.80	....	11.16
MN TF n	10.31	.71	....	10.52
MtgeSec n	9.77	.84	....	10.21
Muncpl n	7.95	.55	....	8.13
Oh TF n	10.50	.72	....	10.79
NJ HY n	10.31	.70	.08	10.56
NYHY n	11.55	.80	....	11.78
NYIns n	10.65	.69	....	10.89
OTC	17.68	.51	2.41	20.14
Ovrsea	25.30	.28	1.06	28.20
PacBas r	14.82	.01	.63	15.87
Pa TF n	9.66	.67	....	9.90
Puritan	12.76	.99	.54	13.70
Real Est	8.92	.54	....	9.59
ShtTBd n	9.21	.80	....	9.34
ShtTGov	9.80	.81	....	9.96
Sht TF n	9.45	.53	....	9.49
SprtGv	10.00	.93	.03	10.54
Specl Sit	15.49	.71	....	19.88
TexaTF n	10.01	.70	....	10.40
Trend	37.43	.63	4.22	44.22
UtilInc n	10.93	.76	.31	12.60
Value n	26.14	.30	2.85	28.99
Fidl Inv Instit:				
CT ARP nr	9.12	.85	....	8.61
EqP G n	12.31	.08	2.04	15.58
EqP I n	11.08	.78	.18	12.13
IP LTD n	10.11	.93	....	10.35
IP SG n	9.39	.87	....	9.49
TEP Ltd n	10.53	.67	....	10.65
QualDv n	11.65	.90	....	11.87
Fidelity Selects:				
SelAir r	9.68	....	.57	11.66
SelAGld r	14.34	....	....	17.50
SelBio r	10.10	....	.24	14.30
SelBrd r	12.98	....	2.57	14.61
SelBrk r	7.52	.16	....	8.42
SelCh r	21.70	.16	1.13	24.14
SelCom r	10.53	....	....	11.25
SelDef r	11.35	....	....	12.35
SelElec r	6.70	....	....	7.75
SelEUtl r	9.20	.22	....	11.56
SelEgy r	12.44	.07	.22	17.47
SelEnSv r	7.52	....	....	11.99
slEnv r	10.00	.01	..,.	11.71
SelFinS r	26.73	.33	.19	31.39
SelFood r	18.42	.04	2.17	23.29
SelHlth r	34.13	.13	.84	47.58
SelIndl r	13.27	....	....	13.86
SelLesr r	24.13	.07	2.03	29.52
SelMD r	7.85	.05	.26	12.09
SelMetl r	11.06	.18	....	14.44
SelPapr r	12.13	.15	....	12.47
SelProp r	11.05	.15	....	15.08
SelReg r	9.45	.11	.65	11.21
SelRtl r	12.74	.16	2.57	13.70
SelSL r	9.30	.04	.49	9.65
SelSoft r	14.34	....	.86	15.19
SelTech r	16.60	....	....	19.42
SelTele r	18.73	.12	.98	27.11
SelUtil r	25.90	.81	....	35.05
Fidl Plymth:				
GovSec t	9.26	.82	....	9.30
GrwOpp p	13.54	.05	1.17	15.55
HiYield p	9.77	1.27	....	8.88
incGth p	10.93	1.06	.52	11.99
ST Bd p	9.80	.82	....	9.94
SpecSit p	15.36	.55	....	19.81
FiduCap n	15.04	.19	....	17.54
Financial Prog:				
Dynamc	6.61	.11	.28	7.70
FSB Gv n	6.87	.55	....	7.18
FSP Eng	9.32	.24	....	13.10
FSP Eu	9.11	.13	....	11.17
FSP Fn	7.38	.09	.80	9.19
FSP U n	8.47	.37	.71	9.96
FnclTx n	14.42	1.00	....	15.05
Gold n	4.94	.02	....	5.97
HiSci	14.39	.10	1.94	20.76
HiYld n	7.82	.95	....	7.16
Industrl	3.55	.10	....	4.55
Income	7.98	.41	.73	9.26
Leisr	11.94	.20	1.99	14.34
Pacific	12.91	.02	....	15.49
Select n	6.39	.63	....	6.26
Tech	10.45	....	....	12.69
FstEagl nr	11.56	.11	1.40	13.11
Fst Investors:				
BlChip p	11.13	.40	....	12.41
Globl p	4.46	....	.76	5.38
Govt p	10.75	.98	....	11.01
HighYd p	6.52	.78	....	5.26
Income p	5.19	.66	....	4.16

	NAV 12-30-88	Divs 1989	Cap. Dist	NAV 12-29-89
NYTxFr p	13.52	.88	....	13.87
SpecBd	13.17	1.56	....	11.46
TaxExpt p	9.91	.71	....	10.04
First Trust:				
TF Incm p	13.42	....	....	13.95
TF Insur p	15.11	....	....	15.67
US Gov p	9.92	....	....	10.31
Flag Investors:				
EmGwth p	11.64	1.04	.82	13.48
IntTr p	12.18	.57	.61	u13.97
QualGr p	10.00	.08	....	10.28
TelIncSh p	8.24	.55	.64	10.98
TotRTsy p	9.96	.85	....	10.41
Flagship Group:				
AA TE p	9.80	.73	.01	9.90
AZ TE p	9.48	.64	....	9.75
CpCsh np	34.29	3.02	....	33.03
CT TE p	9.54	.63	....	9.82
GA TE p	9.62	.64	....	9.78
KY TE p	9.69	.66	.05	9.99
MI TE p	10.44	.70	....	10.77
NC TE p	9.30	.61	....	9.60
OH TE p	10.32	.69	....	10.60
PA TE p	9.34	.62	....	9.57
TnTE p	10.00	.66	.02	10.26
VA TE p	9.58	.64	....	9.80
Flex Funds:				
Bond np	18.25	....	....	18.24
Growth np	9.67	.32	....	10.33
IncGrth np	18.83	1.48	....	19.08
Muirfd fpn	5.31	.07	.10	5.82
Fortress Invst:				
GISI r	9.05	.87	....	9.35
HiQual t	12.03	.40	....	13.33
HY Muni t	9.96	.74	....	10.25
TP US r	9.86	.75	.38	10.07
Util r	9.13	.59	....	10.85
44 Wall Eq	4.42	....	....	5.46
44Wall	2.41	....	....	2.55
Founders Group:				
BlueChp np	6.31	.30	.89	7.32
Frntr np	13.45	.87	.02	18.49
Grwth np	7.61	.72	.61	9.41
Incom np	6.89	.45	.18	7.97
Specl n	5.47	.57	.38	6.64
France	11.45	1.66	3.39	9.47
Franklin Group:				
AGE Fund	3.30	.43	....	2.78
AdjMtg	10.07	.97	....	10.09
AF TF	10.38	.76	....	10.59
CalIns	10.86	.72	....	11.20
CalTFr	6.90	.51	....	6.96
CO TF	10.50	.75	....	10.75
CvtSec	9.23	.69	....	9.59
DNTC	11.91	.19	1.21	13.94
Equity	6.45	.21	.25	7.04
FedTxFr	11.32	.86	....	11.44
FL TF	10.62	.81	....	10.81
GlOpl	10.23	1.02	....	9.75
Gold	10.94	.43	....	14.88
Growth	19.23	.41	.40	22.87
HY TF	10.51	.90	....	10.60
IncoStk	2.06	.22	.01	2.06
InsTF	11.10	.81	....	11.36
MassTF	10.60	.70	....	10.83
MichTxF	10.89	.73	....	11.16
MNIns	11.26	.79	....	11.50
NJTF	10.59	.78	....	10.77
NY Tax	10.82	.79	....	11.02
OhioITF	11.02	.73	....	11.27
ORTF	10.43	.70	....	10.67
PATF	9.53	.72	....	9.76
OptionFd	5.12	.15	.52	5.16
PuerTF	10.56	.72	....	10.83
SI Gov	10.11	.82	....	10.22
TA Gov	9.89	.96	....	10.17
TxAdHY	9.26	1.17	....	8.52
Utilities	7.44	.58	.01	8.66
USGov Sc	6.82	.69	...	6.97
VA TF	10.44	.75	....	10.70
Franklin Mgd Tr:				
CorpCsh p	21.11	1.78	....	20.67
InvGrade p	8.66	.78	....	8.57
RisDiv p	10.01	.36	....	11.58
Freedom Funds:				
Envrn p	9.57	....	....	9.80
EqVl t	10.01	.42	.27	11.14
Globl t	10.84	2.49	2.49	11.78
GlblP t	10.78	1.32	.37	10.15
Gold t	14.45	1.16	.14	15.71
GvPlus t	9.48	.78	....	10.07
MgdTE t	10.65	.77	.03	10.91
RgBk t	10.78	1.05	.89	11.62
FremntMA	10.06	.48	.14	11.02
FundTrust:				
Aggres fp	12.13	.06	1.01	13.53
Gwth fp	12.93	.27	1.59	13.30
GroIn fp	12.71	.51	....	14.52
Inco f	9.69	.77	....	9.64
Gabelli Funds:				
Asset nt	14.69	.55	.72	17.41
ConvSc n	10.00	.11	....	10.51
Growth np	12.65	.17	.48	17.07
Value p	9.45	.05	.01	9.58
GeicoQD fpn	21.10	3.20	....	17.95
GIT Invst:				
EqSpc n	15.38	....	....	18.40
HiYld n	10.71	....	....	10.75
IncMax n	8.24	....	....	7.59
InARt n	9.94	....	....	10.21
TxFrVA n	10.92	....	....	11.07
GNA Inv p	9.41	.86	.02	9.70
GatewyGr n	9.67	1.40	1.11	11.76
GatewyOp n	13.67	.56	.43	15.49
GT Global:				
Amer p	8.76	.10	.57	12.84
Bond p	10.98	.82	....	11.23
Europe p	7.77	....	....	10.94
GovInc p	10.70	1.17	....	10.60
HlthCr p	11.43	.03	....	12.41
Intl p	6.77	.02	.11	9.25
Japan p	10.57	.12	.44	16.39
Pacific p	8.74	.06	.27	12.61
Wldw p	10.18	.03	.33	13.63
GW Sierra Tr:				
CalBd	10.00	.27	....	10.04
GvSec	10.00	.36	....	10.01
GrInc	10.00	.09	....	10.05
Galaxy Funds:				
Bond	9.90	.84	....	10.17
Equity	10.33	.37	.70	10.98
GenAgr np	20.55	.33	1.38	24.40
Gen Elec Inv:				
ElfDiv	10.33	55.5	12.5	11.86
ElfGl	10.73	2.6	.88	12.45
Elfuninc n	10.57	.91	....	11.11
ElfunTr n	25.99	1.04	2.80	31.29
ElfunTxE	11.04	.77	.10	11.14
S&S n	29.63	1.38	1.71	35.33
S&S Lng n	10.83	.99	.08	11.26
GnNYTx np	18.31	1.05	....	18.43
GnSec n	11.25	1.89	1.50	11.62
GnTxEB np	13.48	1.01	....	13.97
Gintel Group:				
CapAp np	13.56	1.35	1.03	13.80
Erisa np	36.34	4.34	4.24	32.31
GintlFd n	66.55	5.88	....	74.35
Gradison Funds:				
EstGr pn	16.64	.72	.50	18.07
GovInc p	12.65	1.05	.11	13.03
OppGr pn	12.40	.33	.26	14.67
Greensprng	12.43	.78	.18	12.83
GwthWash p	12.22	.28	.48	13.34
GwthInd n	7.81	.25	2.02	7.84
Guardian Funds:				
Bond n	11.16	1.01	....	11.67
ParkAv	20.47	.98	2.71	21.59
Stock n	19.18	.90	1.33	21.41

	NAV 12-30-88	Divs 1989	Cap. Dist	NAV 12-29-89
HTInsEq p	10.58	2.28	1.83	11.22
HanifnColo	9.53	.75	....	9.56
Harbor Funds:				
Growth n	10.91	.59	.48	12.81
Intl n	12.90	.89	.72	16.74
US Eqt n	11.05	1.38	1.18	12.31
Hartwell Fds:				
EmgGwth	11.32	....	.09	15.60
Gwth	14.82	....	....	19.98
HarvestGr p	9.32	.59	.09	9.51
HeartGv p	9.04	.77	....	9.25
Heartland p	14.35	.35	1.11	13.82
Helmsman Fds:				
DiscEq	10.00	.40	.34	11.09
GrEq	10.00	.20	.54	11.29
Income	9.68	.77	.23	9.73
IncEq	9.52	.60	.02	11.32
Heritage p	11.43	.19	1.13	12.44
HrtgCnv p	9.13	.49	.23	9.63
HiMark	10.08	.51	1.04	11.12
Home Group:				
GovSecs	9.43	.96	....	9.42
GroInc	10.26	.43	.21	11.54
HY Bond	9.70	1.17	....	8.43
NatTF p	6.99	.18	....	7.01
HoracMn n	17.30	.62	2.94	18.90
Hummer n	13.74	.23	.36	16.41
IAI Funds:				
Apollo n	12.08	.17	1.97	12.60
Bond n	9.39	.71	.02	10.10
IntFd n	10.80	.29	.62	11.85
Region n	17.99	.50	3.97	18.98
Resrv n	10.04	.78	....	10.11
Stock n	14.70	.42	2.76	15.79
IDS Group:				
Bond p	4.61	.42	....	4.66
CA TE p	4.82	.32	....	4.97
Discov p	6.29	.14	.05	8.04
EquitPl p	8.20	.34	.63	9.58
Extrinc p	4.63	.53	....	3.95
FedInc p	4.96	.42	....	5.04
GlobBd	5.00	.21	.02	5.34
Growth p	17.45	.27	2.15	21.39
HiYdTE p	4.42	.33	....	4.57
InsrTE p	4.86	.31	....	5.03
Intl p	8.78	.10	.86	9.38
MgdRtmt p	7.64	.27	.67	9.31
MN TE p	4.86	.33	....	5.04
Mutual p	11.56	.75	.74	12.18
NY TE p	4.73	.31	....	4.87
NewD p	8.06	.18	.53	9.88
PrecMt p	6.56	.10	....	7.61
Progress p	6.43	.34	.77	5.99
Select p	8.40	.73	....	8.65
Stock p	17.35	.85	2.61	18.93
TE Bond p	3.96	.27	.15	3.98
StrAgg t	9.19	....	....	12.20
StrEq t	7.57	.31	.70	8.13
StrInc t	5.62	.42	....	5.73
StrST t	1.00	.08	....	1.01
UtilInc	5.06	.35	.06	6.07
StrPan t	4.33	.03	....	4.83
IDEX Group:				
Idex	12.20	.09	2.02	15.29
Idex II	11.56	.10	1.57	14.97
Idex 3	10.24	.08	.42	14.11
TotInc	9.86	.95	....	9.27
IMGBd Acc	10.33	.80	....	10.56
IMGStk Ac	12.54	.39	1.83	15.29
Integrated Resc:				
AggGth p	14.21	....	.53	16.95
CapAp t	12.75	.16	1.35	12.95
CnvSec p	9.65	.70	....	u9.68
Growth p	13.18	.12	1.09	16.73
HiYld p	10.70	1.42	....	u8.99
Home t	9.83	.87	....	10.15
IncPl t	8.87	1.14	....	7.28
Stripes p	12.19	.87	....	12.34

	NAV 12-30-88	Divs 1989	Cap. Dist	NAV 12-29-89
TotRet p	14.13	.37	.37	16.27
GvtPlus p	10.51	1.21	....	10.18
ICP Glbl	14.28	.91	....	13.82
ICP Hard	12.50	....	....	13.45
Invst Portfolio:				
DivInc t	5.86	.77	....	5.50
Equit t	11.14	.14	.05	14.44
GvtPlus t	7.39	.71	....	7.48
HiYld t	9.24	1.05	....	7.91
InPTR t	9.28	.47	....	10.65
ShtInt t	8.50	.61	....	8.52
InvPfrInc p	9.68	....	....	10.08
Inv Tr Bost:				
GrOpp p	9.55	.33	.95	10.88
HiInco p	11.08	1.39	....	10.08
MassTxFr p	16.16	1.06	.08	16.27
InvResh	4.71	....	....	5.63
IstelFd np	12.33	.33	.37	13.99
Ivy Funds:				
Gwth n	13.59	.81	.80	15.57
Inst n	11.04	.65	.46	8.13
Intl n	16.73	.27	.84	20.30
JP Growth	12.31	.40	.87	14.81
JP Income	9.21	.84	....	9.48
JW Gant	1.79	.05	.03	1.86
Janus Fund:				
FlxInc n	....	.98	.07	9.35
Fund n	11.55	.19	2.50	14.21
Twen n	10.01	.01	.42	14.66
Ventr n	27.85	.44	2.35	35.85
JapanFd n	16.24	.08	3.59	14.27
John Hancock:				
AstAll	10.00	.46	.03	10.92
Bond	14.51	1.44	....	14.76
Globl	15.31	.15	.01	17.84
Growth	13.33	.28	1.95	15.18
HighIn p	9.22	1.11	....	8.08
FedPl p	9.21	.88	....	9.22
PacBas p	10.90	....	.82	12.14
SpclEq	5.05	.01	....	6.44
TaxEx p	10.49	.73	....	10.68
USGvSc	8.56	.79	....	8.72
GtdMtg	9.70	.90	....	10.04
Kaufman nr	1.11	....	....	1.63
Kemper Funds:				
BlueChp p	8.16	.20	....	10.17
DivInco	7.87	1.22	....	7.28
EnhGv p	8.52	.88	....	8.15
Calif	6.97	.49	.09	7.16
Gold p	7.70	.04	....	8.86
Growth	7.47	.18	....	9.58
HiYield	10.83	1.34	....	9.41
Income	8.35	.87	....	8.16
IntlFund	9.32	.58	.24	10.14
MuniBd	9.43	.69	....	9.77
NYTF	9.78	.72	.02	10.17
Summit	3.60	.11	....	4.43
Technol	8.63	.29	.30	10.15
TotRetrn	7.17	.38	....	8.20
US Gvt	8.78	.90	....	9.05
KyTxFr n	6.58	.47	....	6.80
Keystone:				
CusB1 t	15.45	1.32	....	15.90
CusB2 t	18.16	1.84	....	17.22
CusB4 t	6.58	.87	....	5.42
CusK1 t	8.37	.54	.18	9.27
CusK2 t	6.43	.18	.25	7.54
CusS1 t	20.04	.72	.04	24.80
CusS3 t	7.31	.25	....	8.87
CusS4 t	4.62	.05	....	5.66
Intl t	7.48	....	.35	7.42
KPM t	15.92	....	....	19.83
TxETr t	10.70	.72	....	10.90
TaxFr t	8.18	.59	.24	8.06
Keystone America:				
EqInc t	9.54	.42	.53	11.09
GlobInc t	10.04	.50	....	9.88
GovSc t	9.71	.74	....	10.1e
GroStk t	11.16	.10	1.21	12.98

	NAV 12-30-88	Divs 1989	Cap. Dist	NAV 12-29-89
HiYld †	9.21	1.12	.02	8.13
InvGrd †	9.03	.73	....	8.85
Omega †	13.66	.20	1.90	16.05
TaxFree †	10.12	.63	.23	10.11
Kidder Group:				
Gvt †	14.12	1.16	....	14.70
KPE †	16.35	.55	....	20.49
MktGrd	14.18	.82	1.90	14.00
Natl	15.49	1.14	....	15.71
NY Ser	14.93	1.05	....	15.18
SpGth nt	15.01	....	....	19.41
KBGblIn p	10.62	....	.03	10.55
KBIntEq p	14.66	.22	2.15	15.58
Landmark Funds:				
CapGth n	9.06	.10	....	11.20
GthInc n	10.52	.45	.17	11.10
NYTF np	9.65	.58	....	9.98
USGv n	8.93	.72	....	9.23
LMH n	19.20	.71	2.35	18.44
Legg Mason:				
GvtInd np	9.79	.79	....	10.20
InvGr p	9.88	.82	....	10.29
SpInv np	10.38	.08	....	13.63
TotRet np	9.40	.21	.18	10.54
ValTr np	26.28	.66	1.47	29.38
LehOpport n	22.40	.82	.89	25.35
Lexington Grp:				
CrpLead	12.32	1.92	....	13.68
GNMA n	7.45	.68	....	7.88
Global	10.89	.59	.20	12.83
Goldfd n	5.21	.05	....	6.40
Growth n	8.72	.21	.17	10.79
Resch n	14.39	.93	1.21	16.19
TE Bd n	10.03	.63	....	10.12
TechStr	9.64	.40	.95	11.70
LibAdG	9.07	.90	....	9.15
LibAdT	9.49	.64	....	9.64
Liberty Family:				
AmLdr	12.59	.60	1.18	12.26
CnvInc	10.37	.87	.93	9.44
FTIT n	15.73	.20	2.14	16.20
HiIncSe	11.06	1.39	....	9.68
ProgInEq	9.07	.75	.06	10.31
TxFree	10.34	.71	....	10.67
USGvSec	8.12	.75	....	8.41
LtdMun p	12.72	.85	....	12.82
LtdGvt p	11.85	1.03	....	12.04
LindDv n	22.67	2.20	....	23.11
Lindnr n	17.31	1.75	.64	19.21
Loomis Sayles:				
Capital n	15.87	.31	....	18.37
Mutual n	19.94	.93	.95	22.34
Lord Abbett:				
Affiliated	9.20	.47	.36	10.49
BondDeb	9.59	1.04	....	9.03
Devel Gth	6.89	.03	.19	7.64
FdValu p	9.90	.22	.31	12.23
GlEq p	9.61	.12	.11	11.09
GlInc p	9.37	.99	.02	9.27
GovtSec p	2.87	.30	....	2.91
TaxFr	10.79	.77	....	11.01
TxFrCal p	10.14	.70	....	10.40
TaxNY	10.88	.78	.10	10.97
TFTX	9.27	.68	....	9.53
ValuApp	9.53	.32	.48	10.59
Lutheran Bro:				
BroHiYd	9.62	1.15	....	8.27
Fund	14.93	.31	1.49	17.07
Income	8.44	.80	....	8.65
Municipal	8.11	.58	....	8.30
MFS:				
MIT	11.22	....	....	u14.83
FinlDev	10.08	....	....	u11.36
GrthStk	7.94	.09	1.20	9.47
CapDev	10.96	....	....	u13.78
Special	9.02	....	....	u10.20
Sectors p	10.16	....	....	u14.14
EmgGth	13.52	....	.15	16.85
TotlRet	10.23	....	....	u11.73
GovGuar p	9.10	.82	....	9.33
GovInPls p	7.77	.52	.42	7.80
IntBnd	12.32	....	....	u11.92
FinlBnd	12.75	1.07	....	13.24
GovPrem p	9.52	.74	.30	9.52
HiIncBnd	5.93	.75	....	5.09
HiIncII	8.89	1.00	....	7.69
MuniBnd	10.41	.71	.27	10.39
TaxFrCA p	5.08	.32	....	5.24
MuniMA p	10.59	.71	....	10.69
MuniMD p	10.70	.68	....	10.94
MuniNC p	11.07	.72	....	11.32
MuniSC p	11.20	.72	....	11.46
MunTE p	....	.66	....	9.90
MuniVA p	10.86	.73	....	11.11
MuniWV p	10.62	.71	....	10.85
MuniHiY	9.52	.81	.04	9.63
MFS Lifetime:				
CapGr †	9.46	.17	....	12.05
Global †	11.16	....	.29	13.53
Sectr †	7.99	....	....	11.20
EmgG †	6.21	....	....	u7.79
DivPl †	8.50	....	....	u9.43
GovPl †	7.70	.47	....	7.72
HiInc †	6.80	.74	....	5.76
IntrInc †	9.58	.83	.03	9.47
MunBd †	8.18	.49	....	8.41
MIM Funds:				
BdInc	9.68	.69	....	9.28
SCO Inc	10.12	.45	....	10.46
SCO Gr	9.44	.34	....	9.89
StkAp	7.63	.17	....	8.69
MIMLIC Funds:				
AsstAll	10.48	.72	.14	11.61
Invl	10.72	.27	.39	12.69
MtgSecs	9.82	.85	....	10.26
MSB Fd n p	16.40	.25	2.86	17.81
Mackenzie Grp:				
AmerFd	11.75	.40	.37	12.98
Canada	10.15	.24	.02	10.89
FixInc	10.00	.99	....	10.45
GvtSc p	7.52	.60	....	7.86
NA TR	6.55	.51	....	6.87
MainStay Funds:				
CaAp †	9.66	.02	.68	11.47
Conv †	8.77	.53	....	8.82
CrpBd †	8.79	.99	....	7.41
Globl †	9.93	....	.34	10.43
Gold †	8.74	....	....	10.50
GovPl †	8.85	.80	....	9.08
TxFB †	9.68	.58	....	9.79
TotRt †	10.42	.39	.45	11.13
Val †	9.99	.14	.72	11.25
MassMutl Fds:				
Balance p	10.08	.51	.12	11.32
CapApp p	11.85	.31	.38	13.09
InvGr p	10.12	.94	....	10.29
TF Bd p	10.13	.64	.16	10.24
US Gov p	9.53	.75	....	9.98
ValStk p	10.47	.40	.25	12.08
Mathers n	15.60	.97	1.73	14.52
McDnldInt	....	....	....	10.01
Meschrt	23.71	....	....	21.74
Merrill Lynch:				
BasVlA	17.90	.87	.22	19.94
CalMnA	10.99	.75	....	11.31
CapFdA	21.39	1.09	.72	24.43
CpHiA	7.80	.96	....	7.17
CpHQA	10.90	.99	....	11.33
CpIT	10.83	.98	....	11.13
CpDiv	9.59	.95	....	9.24
DevCap	10.00	.13	....	10.13
EqBdI r	11.34	.44	1.21	11.32
EuroA	8.83	.08	....	10.99
FedSec p	9.07	.86	....	9.39
FdFTA	14.08	.40	1.03	16.85
GlAlA	10.00	.48	.19	10.76
GlCvA f	9.76	.48	.43	9.50

MUTUAL FUNDS

	NAV 12-30-88	Divs 1989	Cap. Dist	NAV 12-29-89
InstIn p	9.27	.82	....	9.39
IntHdA	11.01	.21	1.49	11.77
MnHYA	10.11	.74	....	10.25
MnInsA	7.79	.56	....	7.94
MnLtd	9.68	.59	....	9.74
MnIA	9.29	.60	....	9.41
NtResA	12.00	.37	....	14.89
NYMnA	10.76	.74	....	11.00
PacA f	18.88	.06	1.04	20.74
PhnxA	11.78	.61	.31	12.49
RtBnA	10.78	.76	....	11.93
RtEqA	9.44	.21	....	12.33
RtGIA	10.24	1.13	....	9.77
SciTA	9.56	.06	1.42	9.09
SpVIA	11.83	.23	....	11.65
StrDvA f	10.56	.61	....	12.50
BasVIB †	17.89	.75	.22	19.83
CalMnB †	10.99	.70	....	11.32
CapFdB †	21.38	.96	.72	24.29
CpHIB †	7.80	.90	....	7.17
CpHQB †	10.90	.91	....	11.33
EuroB †	8.80	.07	....	10.85
FdFTB †	14.07	.22	1.03	16.85
GlAIB †	10.00	.39	.19	10.75
GlCvB †f	9.77	.37	.43	9.51
IntHdB †	11.00	.13	1.49	11.71
MnHYB †	10.11	.67	....	10.25
MnInsB †	7.78	.50	....	7.94
MnIB †	9.29	.57	....	9.41
NtResB †	12.00	.23	....	14.89
NYMnB †	10.76	.68	....	11.00
PacB †f	18.87	....	1.04	20.58
PhnxB †	11.77	.51	.31	12.45
RtBnB †	10.78	.63	....	11.95
RtEqB †	9.45	.08	....	12.35
RtGIB †	10.24	1.05	....	9.77
RtInc †	9.13	.80	....	9.47
SciTB †	9.55	....	1.42	9.07
SpVIB †	11.82	.13	....	11.61
StrDvB †f	10.56	.50	....	12.49
MeriAstAl	10.00	.08	....	10.57
MetLife StateSt:				
CapApr p	10.90	.05	1.60	12.65
EqInc p	8.93	.04	.61	10.00
EqInvst p	9.57	.30	.15	11.51
GovSec p	6.65	....	....	6.87
GvInc np	11.31	....	....	11.63
HiInc p	7.19	.03	....	6.44
MgdAsts p	7.39	.45	.14	8.03
TaxEx p	7.24	....	....	7.42
MidAmerica Fds:				
MidAmer	5.24	.53	.29	5.61
MidAHGr	3.88	.58	.40	3.90
MidAHYld	9.89	1.03	....	10.01
Midwest:				
Fl Gwth p	11.85	.39	....	13.79
Fl Govt p	9.95	.84	....	10.09
Fl Treas p	8.78	.64	....	9.37
IntGv p	9.95	.77	....	10.19
TFLtd p	10.06	.65	....	10.13
Monitrnd p	15.09	.33	....	15.31
Monitor Funds:				
Bond p	20.11	.60	....	20.02
IncGr p	19.79	.42	....	20.25
IntBd p	20.17	.66	....	20.11
OhTF p	20.22	1.15	....	20.23
MrgKgSo p	10.71	.47	....	11.75
Morison	5.09	.24	....	5.57
MutlBnft	14.28	.41	.44	17.46
Mutual of Omaha:				
Americ n	9.78	.85	....	10.30
Growth	7.36	.83	.81	8.95
Income	8.90	.76	....	9.53
Tax Free	11.16	.79	....	11.47
Mutual Series:				
Beacon n	22.85	1.17	1.55	24.08
Qualfd n	22.71	1.36	2.39	22.21
Shares n	67.77	4.09	6.55	67.15
NtAvTec	10.31	....	....	11.67

	NAV 12-30-88	Divs 1989	Cap. Dist	NAV 12-29-89
NtlInd	11.41	.20	1.47	12.53
National Funds:				
Bond	2.41	.28	....	1.87
CalTxE	12.65	.90	....	12.96
Fairfld	7.36	.08	....	7.93
FedScTr	8.93	.83	....	9.22
Income	7.72	.49	.16	8.50
PremIn p	10.74	.30	.50	10.23
RealEst	8.30	.52	....	7.86
RE Inc	9.53	1.00	....	7.90
Stock	7.44	.27	1.06	8.05
StrAll p	10.91	.39	....	11.99
TxExmpt	9.84	.72	....	10.03
TotRet	6.97	.34	1.08	7.42
NatTele	15.31	....	....	16.94
Nationwide Fds:				
NtBond	9.11	.87	....	9.18
NatnFd	11.94	.47	1.31	14.15
NtGwth	8.43	.28	.33	9.07
TxFre r	9.28	.61	....	9.58
Neuberger Berm:				
Genesis	5.16	.02	.12	5.91
Guardn n	36.50	1.07	3.56	39.67
LtdMat n	9.74	.82	....	9.96
Manhat n	9.04	.18	1.05	10.44
MMPlu n	9.83	.91	....	9.80
Partnrs n	16.72	.76	1.68	18.06
SelSect	16.96	.47	2.57	18.93
NewAlter f	45.10	....	....	56.37
NewCntCap nfp	10.00	.39	.24	11.07
NewEngland Fds:				
BdIncp p	10.89	.90	....	11.23
Equity p	9.50	.41	.61	9.47
GlobGv p	12.13	.51	....	12.12
GvtSec p	11.85	.94	.32	11.99
Growth p	7.46	.11	.51	8.50
RetirEq p	6.07	.12	.81	6.51
TaxExmpt p	7.10	.47	....	7.29
NY Mun np	1.09	.07	....	1.12
NewtnGth n	20.37	.90	.12	23.19
NewtnIn n	7.88	.64	....	8.13
Nicholas Group:				
Nichol n	32.63	.92	1.05	38.61
Nch II n	17.98	.31	.66	20.16
NichInc n	3.68	.38	....	3.44
NchLd n	11.29	.14	.61	12.49
NodCnvS n	8.07	.63	....	7.92
NeInvGr n	18.27	.28	.29	23.70
NeInvTr n	11.89	1.49	....	10.43
Nomura nf	19.39	.10	3.97	19.24
North Am Sec Tr:				
AggAA p	7.27	.11	.06	u6.73
ConsvAA p	9.56	.41	.04	u9.08
Growth p	12.25	.37	.21	10.70
ModAA p	8.25	.16	.02	u7.85
North Am Sec Tr:				
US Gvt p	9.73	.30	....	u9.74
Nuveen Funds:				
CA Spcl	9.42	.64	....	9.85
CA Ins Bd	9.26	.60	....	9.59
InsNat	9.37	.63	.08	9.61
MuniBd	8.59	.59	.02	8.87
NY ITFB	9.07	.59	....	9.34
OhTF	9.11	.62	.02	9.56
TF MA	8.64	.58	....	8.90
TFNY	9.23	.63	....	9.57
Oberweis	9.70	....	....	12.06
OlyEqInc	11.75	.59	.25	13.65
OldDomin	20.14	1.15	1.08	21.17
Olympus Funds:				
Equity †	8.82	.08	....	10.39
PremInc †	8.10	.11	.92	7.84
TE CA	7.63	....	.11	7.58
TE NY	7.86	....	.04	7.78
TE HY r	8.02	....	.13	7.78
USGovt †	8.91	.76	.02	9.10
Oppenheimer Fd:				
AssetA p	9.78	.48	.29	10.67

	NAV 12-30-88	Divs 1989	Cap. Dist	NAV 12-29-89
BlueChp p	12.92	.41	....	15.83
CA TE	9.58	.69	.01	9.94
Direct	20.07	.61	1.22	22.24
EqInc	8.44	.50	.24	9.24
GNMA p	13.14	1.22	....	13.43
Global	23.82	.11	3.00	28.98
Gold	11.52	.27	1.34	13.93
HighYld	15.56	1.92	....	14.25
NYTax p	11.88	.84	.01	12.02
90-10	13.53	1.16	....	12.99
OTC Fd p	17.94	.30	1.56	22.13
OpenhFd	7.94	.24	.41	9.15
Premum	21.56	1.01	1.39	20.60
Rgncy	12.34	.34	1.15	13.47
Special	16.60	.70	....	19.42
StrInc	5.00	.12	.01	5.03
Target	16.04	.62	.08	18.27
TaxFree p	9.27	.66	....	9.45
Time	14.50	.51	1.32	16.68
TotRt p	6.35	.27	.59	6.68
USGvt p	9.35	.89	....	9.52
OstrandHi	....	1.24	....	7.77
OverCountS p	14.14	.12	.48	16.23
OverCA TF	10.03	.72	....	10.35
PNC Cap p	10.00	.06	....	10.76
PNC Mgdl p	10.00	.12	....	9.98
Pacific Horizon:				
AgGr p	13.32	....	....	18.28
CATF p	13.51	.94	....	13.79
HYBd	14.14	1.72	....	11.78
Pacific Inv:				
LowDur n	9.80	.88	.01	9.99
ShortT	10.00	.89	....	10.01
TotRet n	9.73	.87	.05	10.13
Paine Webber:				
AstAl t	9.79	.67	.12	10.03
Atlas p	14.46	.11	1.66	15.50
CalTx	10.74	.73	....	10.95
ClGrIn p	13.67	.51	.16	16.32
ClHiYd p	9.90	.74	....	10.09
CGwth p	11.87	....	.11	14.79
CWorld p	9.55	.36	.01	10.23
GNMA	9.18	.79	....	9.49
HiYld	8.44	1.06	....	7.26
InvGrd	9.51	.83	....	9.77
MstEU r	10.41	.21	.72	12.59
MastGl t	10.64	.91	....	10.25
MastG nt	10.91	....	....	14.23
MastI np	8.97	....	....	9.05
TxExpt	11.06	.80	....	11.23
Parkstone Fds:				
Bond	9.83	.38	....	10.07
Equity	10.00	.24	.98	12.19
HYIEq	10.21	.50	.22	12.21
IntGvt	9.83	.79	.02	9.93
LtdMat	9.93	.89	.04	9.87
MunBd	10.01	.61	.02	10.07
SmCpVl	9.95	.02	....	13.15
Parnassus	20.06	.34	.06	20.62
PasadenG	16.81	1.11	.93	21.06
PatrtCC	48.17	....	....	47.22
PaxWorld n	11.93	.62	.24	13.98
Pelican	10.11	.23	.04	10.08
PennSqre p	8.74	.36	.58	10.00
PennMtl nr	6.41	.22	.41	6.85
PermPrt n	14.96	....	....	15.91
PermTBill n	54.53	....	....	58.96
PeritCG	10.50	.17	....	10.54
Phila Fund	5.57	.14	.89	6.34
Phoenix Series:				
BalanFd	11.99	.73	.03	14.15
CvFdSer	15.43	.92	....	17.53
Growth	15.82	.67	.27	19.15
HiQual	8.86	.71	....	9.18
HiYield	8.80	1.00	....	7.74
StockFd	10.89	.47	....	12.74
TotRet p	12.55	.55	.38	13.90
Pilgrim Grp:				
CorpInv p	17.12	1.84	....	14.79
FGvSec	9.31	.80	....	9.54
FgnHiInc p	8.86	1.06	....	7.82
GNMA	13.73	1.32	....	14.07
HiYld p	7.16	.89	....	6.40
MagCap	9.41	.15	.94	10.40
Prefd p	19.30	2.87	....	14.07
Pioneer Fund:				
Pionr Bd	8.91	.81	....	9.09
PionMuBd	9.40	.63	....	9.66
PionrFd	20.34	.68	1.08	23.28
Pionr II	17.41	.64	1.91	18.70
Pionr III	14.72	.46	1.23	16.03
Piper Jaffray:				
Balanc p	8.96	.49	....	9.96
Govt n	9.28	.82	....	9.33
InstGv	9.81	.90	.02	10.13
MNTE	9.92	.67	....	10.23
NatlTE	10.01	.69	....	10.17
Sector p	8.26	.42	....	10.11
Value p	9.41	.17	....	12.90
Premier Group:				
CA TE	11.89	.89	....	12.18
CT TE	11.01	.80	.02	11.22
FL TE	13.35	1.02	.02	13.84
GNMA p	14.01	1.36	.03	14.28
MDTE	11.69	.86	.02	11.93
MI TE	13.98	1.06	.02	14.31
MA TE	10.89	.82	....	11.05
MN TE	13.75	1.05	.05	14.12
OH TE	11.59	.88	.04	11.91
PA TE	14.66	1.12	.01	15.02
TE Bd	12.87	.99	....	13.11
Price Funds:				
CalTx n	9.30	.59	....	9.48
CapApr n	10.42	.45	1.36	10.82
EquIn n	13.39	.76	.39	14.06
FEF	10.00	.04	....	10.62
GNM n	9.01	.85	....	9.37
Growth n	14.55	.34	1.58	16.27
GwthIn n	12.32	.64	.79	13.25
HiYld n	10.25	1.26	....	8.88
Income n	8.37	.76	....	8.59
IntlBd n	10.25	.68	....	9.15
IntlDis f	10.00	.13	.10	13.94
IntStk n	8.97	.16	.67	10.24
MdTxFr n	9.29	.60	.03	9.53
NwAm n	12.38	....	.23	16.90
NewEra n	18.79	.56	1.05	21.73
NwHrzn n	10.74	.07	1.01	12.43
NYTxF n	9.65	.62	....	9.52
SciTch n	8.57	.06	1.39	10.52
ST Bond n	4.92	.42	....	4.97
SmCapVal	8.98	.14	.90	9.53
TxFree n	8.62	.60	....	8.79
TxFrHY n	11.21	.84	.06	11.45
TxFrSI n	5.06	.30	....	5.10
PrimryT n	11.19	.41	.20	11.60
Prncipl Presv:				
DivAch	10.00	.28	....	11.65
GovtPrt	8.94	.74	....	9.11
InsTEx	9.50	.57	....	9.82
SP 100 Pl	10.11	.26	....	12.27
TEPrt	8.06	.54	....	8.23
Princor Funds:				
AggGwth	11.83	.26	.09	13.89
CapAcc	17.14	.55	.94	18.17
Govt	10.08	.84	....	10.69
Growth	17.12	.30	.89	18.99
Managed	10.77	.58	.54	10.78
TE Bd	10.65	.66	....	11.15
PrudSpc np	7.35	....	....	7.16
Prudential Bache:				
CalMu t	10.65	.65	....	10.88
Equity nt	9.18	.19	.08	11.83
EqInc nt	9.52	.29	....	11.15
FlxAg nt	9.50	.37	.35	10.55
FlxCn n t	9.35	.54	.10	10.13
GNMA nt	14.29	1.21	....	14.86
Globl t	9.93	.26	....	10.85

133

MUTUAL FUNDS

	NAV 12-30-88	Divs 1989	Cap. Dist	NAV 12-29-89
GlbGA nt	10.51	....	.86	12.70
GlbRs nt	9.32	.05	.60	10.76
GovPl nt	9.20	.70	.24	9.32
GvtSc np	9.75	.87	....	9.90
GthOp t	11.32	.10	....	13.36
HiYld nt	9.70	1.09	....	8.52
IncVer nt	10.08	.74	.09	11.35
MunArz t	10.86	.67	....	11.10
MuGa t	11.11	.66	....	11.37
MunHY t	10.45	.80	.05	10.68
MunIn t	10.43	.69	.07	10.62
MuMd t	10.32	.64	....	10.53
MunMA t	10.65	.67	....	10.78
MuMn t	10.95	.64	....	11.26
MunMI t	10.82	.67	....	11.13
MuniMod t	10.11	.65	.02	10.27
MuNC t	10.52	.64	....	10.74
MunNJ t	10.18	.72	.02	10.44
MUNY t	10.77	.67	....	10.93
MuOr t	10.93	.61	....	11.20
MunOh t	10.72	.67	....	10.98
MuPa t	9.70	.64	....	9.92
NtMun t	15.04	.97	....	15.15
OptG nt	8.14	.24	.44	9.23
Resch nt	12.82	.40	....	15.34
Struct	11.61	.35	.01	11.63
US Gvt nt	8.85	.63	....	9.52
Util t	14.61	.72	.88	18.34
Putnam Funds:				
CCsArp	38.68	3.93	....	35.63
CCsDsp	40.62	4.07	....	41.01
CalTax	7.77	.97	.03	7.94
CaPres p	11.51	1.05	....	11.57
Convert	14.28	.96	....	15.65
DvrInc	12.53	1.15	.18	11.80
EngyRes	13.83	.53	.20	17.85
GNMA p	9.72	.84	....	10.22
George	12.32	.81	.88	13.46
Global p	15.89	1.56	....	15.43
Gro&Inc	11.21	.62	.75	12.12
Health	16.63	.30	1.81	21.48
HighInc p	10.08	.85	....	10.17
HighYld	14.46	1.88	.02	12.20
HiYdll p	11.14	1.41	.06	9.26
Income	6.74	.67	.01	6.84
InfoSc	15.85	.10	1.90	19.82
Intl Equ	6.50	.13	.07	7.88
Invest	6.93	.27	.54	8.44
MaTx t	11.97	.77	....	12.15
MiTx t	12.18	.71	....	12.54
MnTx t	12.07	.76	....	12.37
NY TaxEx	8.43	1.04	.04	8.57
OhTx t	12.04	.76	....	12.36
OTC Emg p	6.52	....	.46	7.95
Option	8.32	.34	.26	8.30
Option II	8.83	.45	.20	9.24
PA TE	8.50	.25	....	8.40
TaxExpt	8.45	1.57	.04	8.71
TFHY t	13.88	.97	....	14.08
TF Hi	8.50	.39	....	8.53
TF In t	14.23	.83	.47	14.27
US Gt	13.57	1.36	....	13.85
Vista	5.91	.53	.59	6.57
Voyage	6.63	.09	.80	8.00
QuestGov	11.22	.94	.08	11.48
QuestFd	25.22	.77	1.64	27.85
RNC Group:				
CvSec p	9.01	.42	.11	9.17
Regency p	12.03	.15	.07	14.85
Westwind p	9.41	.24	....	10.96
Rainbow n	5.36	.45	.17	5.27
ReaGra	13.67	.96	.01	13.78
RchTang n	14.11	.45	1.93	14.24
ResEq n	13.62	....	....	13.41
Rightime Group:				
BlueCh p	24.00	.46	1.31	26.91
RT Fd nfp	29.62	.35	....	32.55
GovSec p	13.84	.75	....	14.32
Growth p	22.67	.18	1.94	24.93

	NAV 12-30-88	Divs 1989	Cap. Dist	NAV 12-29-89
Rochester Fds:				
ConvGr p	9.03	.59	....	9.16
CnvInc p	6.38	....	....	u5.47
Growth p	6.86	.13	....	6.43
Muni p	16.14	1.20	....	16.29
Tax p	7.82	....	....	8.63
Rodney Square:				
BnchUS p	8.50	.62	....	8.22
Growth p	10.05	.15	....	12.62
IntlEq p	11.14	.07	.33	12.68
Royce Funds:				
Inco t	8.32	.91	....	7.44
Value t	7.99	.18	.60	8.48
TotRet t	4.79	.22	....	4.67
Rushmore Group:				
AmGas	10.00	.24	.06	12.14
SMP Idx n	12.23	.43	....	14.60
OTC Idx n	12.12	.11	1.63	12.22
GovLT n	9.24	.73	....	10.33
US Int n	9.58	.77	.22	9.95
TFLT n	10.34	.68	....	10.33
TxFrInt n	10.12	.59	....	10.31
SBSF Cv n	9.73	.82	.19	10.52
SBSF Gr n	12.97	.51	.58	16.26
SEI Funds:				
Bond np	9.80	.81	.29	10.34
LtdVBd np	9.78	.81	.03	10.02
ShtGv np	9.53	.74	....	9.71
IntGvt np	9.30	.76	....	9.59
EqInc p	10.53	.45	.27	12.40
EqIndx np	10.24	.36	.05	13.00
PA Muni p	10.00	.18	....	10.10
Value np	9.92	.31	.23	11.27
CapA np	10.22	.31	1.02	12.45
SFT Group:				
AstAll	10.01	.06	1.56	9.09
Envir p	11.12	.22	....	13.93
Equity p	11.55	.85	....	11.80
OddLot	16.92	.36	.28	23.41
US Gov p	6.63	.72	....	6.62
SP IFG Fds:				
DEAF f	11.26	.54	....	12.54
IntMu f	10.06	.60	....	10.18
TIF f	11.04	.12	1.87	11.41
Safeco Secur:				
CalTFr n	11.11	.72	.18	11.26
Equity n	8.55	.39	.63	10.48
Growth n	15.04	.42	.90	16.61
Incom n	14.23	.81	.08	16.23
Munic n	13.05	.89	.44	12.97
USGov n	9.03	.77	....	9.37
SalemFi t	9.70	.75	....	9.93
SalemGr np	13.91	.55	1.31	15.66
SchieldV p	10.58	.22	....	11.31
Schroder	7.05	.17	.42	8.06
SchrodIn fpn	16.04	.44	.08	19.10
Scudder Funds:				
CalTx n	10.31	.65	.18	10.50
CapGt n	16.13	.16	1.45	19.91
Develop n	20.32	....	2.28	22.69
EqtInc n	10.95	.65	....	12.45
Globl n	14.74	.11	.64	19.48
GNMA n	14.09	1.72	....	14.56
Gold n	11.04	.06	.04	12.12
GrwInc n	13.18	.47	1.77	14.14
Income n	12.41	1.06	....	12.89
IntlBd n	12.21	1.04	....	u11.99
Internatl n	33.10	.43	3.15	38.20
MgdMun n	8.60	.58	.39	8.54
MA Tx n	12.24	.83	.10	12.46
NY Tx n	10.64	.70	.09	10.88
ST Bond n	11.19	.82	.08	11.71
TxFHY n	11.06	.07	.06	11.35
TxF90 n	10.02	.56	....	10.04
TxFr93 n	10.54	.06	....	10.63
TxFr96 n	10.70	.66	....	10.87
Zer1995 n	10.67	.68	.04	11.62
Zer2000 n	10.92	.52	.02	12.61
SeagInGv n	9.92	.84	....	10.36

MUTUAL FUNDS

	NAV 12-30-88	Divs 1989	Cap. Dist	NAV 12-29-89
Security Funds:				
Action n	8.74	1.34	.15	8.88
Bond p	7.48	.73	....	7.45
Equity	4.79	.37	.36	5.50
Invest	8.00	.51	.64	8.44
OmniFd	2.79	....	....	2.61
Ultra	6.53	.06	.37	6.84
Selected Funds:				
AmShs np	13.67	.45	2.10	13.78
GovTR	9.34	.72	....	9.20
SplShs np	17.04	.37	1.65	19.87
Seligman Group:				
CapitFd	10.41	....	1.36	12.38
ColoTax	6.96	.45	....	7.18
ComStk	11.30	.43	1.59	12.24
Comun	10.07	....	2.91	10.10
FlaTax	6.87	.45	....	7.17
GrowthFd	4.38	.07	.67	5.10
Income	12.04	1.03	.34	12.43
LaTx	7.77	.53	.06	7.94
MassTx	7.59	.51	.08	7.63
MdTx	7.45	.48	....	7.73
MichTx	7.98	.53	.09	8.18
MinnTx	7.55	.49	.05	7.72
MO Tx	7.21	.46	....	7.41
NatlTx	7.70	.52	.09	7.81
NJ TE p	7.07	.47	.06	7.26
NYTax	7.63	.51	.04	7.76
OhioTx	7.74	.53	.10	7.85
OrTE	6.92	.44	....	7.18
PaTxEx p	7.41	.48	....	7.66
CaTxHy	6.31	.43	.10	6.34
CalTxQ	6.41	.41	.11	6.48
SCTE	7.29	.47	....	7.56
GovGtd p	7.06	.64	....	7.04
HiYBd p	7.02	.89	....	6.40
MtgSec p	6.68	.63	....	6.63
Sentinel Group:				
Balanced	12.09	....	....	13.21
Bond	6.00	....	....	6.17
ComStk	21.93	....	....	25.68
GvSecs f	9.25	....	....	9.55
Growth	11.60	....	....	14.54
Sequoia n	38.81	1.28	1.43	46.86
Sentry Fund	11.33	.23	.79	12.93
Shearson Funds:				
AggrGr	14.05	.02	2.03	17.81
Apprec	7.04	.24	.22	8.66
ATTGr	49.58	.16	.82	8.78
ATTInc	99.10	5.85	2.81	140.92
CalMun	15.44	....	....	15.79
CnvFd	9.39	.60	.11	9.35
FundVal	5.84	.18	.56	6.17
GlobOpp	24.07	.63	....	27.86
HighYld	17.44	1.65	....	14.42
LehCap	15.58	....	5.13	16.75
LehInv	15.55	.63	1.59	16.65
MgdGv	12.05	....	....	12.11
MgMun	14.86	....	....	15.23
MAMuni	11.96	....	.02	12.09
NJMun	11.86	....	.03	12.07
NYMun	15.97	....	....	16.26
PrecMM	15.61	.32	....	17.71
PrnRet	9.50	.63	.22	10.60
SmCap	13.46	....	1.28	14.03
Shearson Ports:				
BasVal t	12.55	.32	2.25	12.85
Convert t	12.77	.87	.10	13.03
GlbBd t	16.37	1.30	....	16.11
GlobEq t	11.16	.11	.69	12.04
GovSec t	8.75	....	....	9.25
GrOpr t	14.72	.47	.01	16.85
Gwth t	11.61	.82	....	13.79
INVG Bd t	10.33	.87	....	11.01
HiInc t	13.71	2.32	....	11.52
IntGov t	11.08	....	....	11.28
Intrnt t	16.69	.59	....	18.94
MtgSc t	10.79	....	....	10.92
MOPS t	48.11	....	....	59.04

	NAV 12-30-88	Divs 1989	Cap. Dist	NAV 12-29-89
OptInc t	12.61	1.12	....	13.53
PrecMt t	13.50	.05	....	15.79
Sector t	9.95	.45	....	11.73
SplEq t	12.04	.51	....	13.76
Strateg t	14.34	.71	.38	16.25
TxExmt t	16.77	....	.03	17.10
Util t	12.26	.94	.21	13.54
ShrDean np	6.60	....	....	9.72
Sigma Funds:				
Capital p	8.14	.26	.99	7.88
ISIGrth	6.52	.30	....	7.00
ISITrShs	10.32	.62	.36	11.98
Income p	8.16	.68	....	8.26
Invest p	9.83	.44	1.83	10.34
PaTax p	12.06	.72	....	12.35
Specl p	8.43	.26	1.76	7.90
TxFrB p	8.91	.53	.07	9.11
TrustSh p	13.03	.79	1.85	13.28
USGvt p	11.75	.98	....	11.84
ValShrs p	9.11	.42	.54	10.41
VenturSh p	8.22	....	1.56	8.36
WorldFd p	13.90	.09	.47	14.70
SitNBG n	25.33	.34	1.44	32.43
skylineBal p	9.42	.47	.15	10.22
SkyInSpEq p	10.32	.93	.35	11.49
Smith Barney:				
Equity p	12.56	.42	.75	15.24
IncGro	11.00	.70	.31	12.69
IncRet	9.12	.75	....	9.31
MoGovt	11.74	1.11	....	12.36
MuniCal	11.32	.84	....	11.63
MuniNt	12.23	.92	....	12.47
MunNY	11.69	.86	....	11.94
USGvt	12.56	1.21	....	13.16
SoGenIn p	16.68	.94	.78	17.83
SoundSh n	12.67	.34	1.41	13.73
SAM SC	11.02	.14	.36	12.87
SAM Val n	11.60	.15	1.53	12.62
SthestGth t	12.80	.17	.40	14.44
SovgnInv	11.19	.60	.58	12.60
SpPtStk	18.67	.03	1.70	24.57
State Bond Grp:				
Commn Stk	6.23	.15	.59	8.10
Diversifd	7.39	.36	.22	8.84
Progress	9.37	.13	.32	11.53
TaxEx	10.27	.73	.05	10.51
US Gov p	4.75	.40	....	4.96
St FarmFds:				
Balan n	18.43	.93	.42	u21.69
Gwth n	13.37	.44	.45	u16.60
Muni n	7.99	.58	....	u7.98
StStreet Resh:				
ExchFd n	133.20	3.90	.72	173.79
Growth n	74.71	2.35	3.23	98.80
Invst r	72.35	2.56	6.40	86.48
Steadman Funds:				
AmInd n	2.08	....	....	2.20
Assoc n	.58	....	....	.76
Invest n	1.22	....	....	1.33
Oceang n	3.04	....	....	3.95
Stein Roe Fds:				
CapOpp n	20.20	.11	5.06	22.20
GvtPlu n	9.42	.78	....	9.84
HyMun n	11.61	.86	.20	11.82
Income n	9.47	.95	....	9.17
IntMun n	10.39	.62	.03	10.55
MgdBd n	8.35	.73	....	8.63
MgdMu n	8.76	.60	.25	8.80
PrimeEq n	8.89	.23	....	11.39
Specl n	15.14	.39	2.08	18.31
Stock n	14.43	.36	....	19.14
TotlRet n	22.15	1.40	.73	24.41
Strategic Funds:				
GoldMn	4.62	.04	....	3.76
Invst⁻	2.81	.14	....	4.36
Silvr	3.86	....	....	4.48
StratD n	23.63	2.05	....	25.88
StrattnGth n	19.06	.71	2.49	20.24

MUTUAL FUNDS

	NAV 12-30-88	Divs 1989	Cap. Dist	NAV 12-29-89
Strong Funds:				
Advtg n	10.00	1.02	....	9.87
Discov	11.44	.27	.71	13.18
GovSc n	9.98	.79	.05	10.08
Inco n	11.88	1.40	....	10.57
Invst	17.57	.96	.13	18.41
MuniBd n	9.35	.52	....	9.47
Opptnty	16.90	.67	.15	19.21
STBond n	10.09	.98	.04	9.86
Total	18.96	1.31	.50	17.72
Templeton Group:				
Foregn	19.28	.75	1.00	23.32
Global	7.29	.21	.38	8.01
Growth	13.75	.62	.47	15.76
Incom	10.08	.93	.03	9.94
World	14.16	.56	.53	16.28
Thomson McKinn:				
CvSecs t	10.18	.53	.68	10.09
Global t	10.57	....	1.17	12.39
Grwth t	14.03	.13	1.12	18.04
Income t	9.59	.93	....	9.16
Opor t	11.71	....	1.70	13.58
PrecMet	9.45	....	....	10.98
TaxEx t	10.91	.65	....	11.38
USGov t	9.21	.83	....	9.46
TowerCap	10.10	.32	.23	12.73
TowerGv	10.03	.87	.01	10.26
TreasFst n	9.31	.78	....	8.89
20th Century:				
BalInv n	10.10	....	....	11.83
Gift n	6.97	....	....	9.52
Growth n	12.31	....	....	16.95
HerInv	6.22	....	....	7.64
LTBond n	90.66	....	....	94.59
Select n	26.98	....	....	36.51
TxEInt n	96.68	....	....	97.31
TxELT n	97.01	....	....	98.83
Ultra	7.06	....	....	8.53
USGv n	92.36	....	....	92.94
Vista	5.97	....	....	8.39
TyndNwGl	11.11	.05	....	12.24
USAA Group:				
AgsvGth n	16.34	.19	2.62	16.28
Balanced	10.00	.40	.02	11.18
Cornst n	16.54	.71	....	19.44
CA Bd	10.00	.27	....	9.86
Gold n	8.21	.15	....	9.55
Grwth n	11.72	.46	....	14.45
Income n	10.96	1.03	.03	11.62
IncStk n	10.28	.57	.58	11.85
Intl	10.51	.02	.45	11.82
TxEHY n	12.84	.95	....	13.21
TxEIT n	11.76	.83	....	11.98
TxESh n	10.35	.67	....	10.42
UST Master:				
IntTE	8.65	....	....	8.80
LT TE	8.91	....	.34	9.06
MgdIn	8.56	....	.10	9.11
Unified Mgmnt:				
General n	8.92	.63	.04	8.61
Gwth n	19.57	.47	1.98	20.41
Inco n	10.92	.85	....	11.07
Indiana n	9.14	.67	....	8.92
Mutl n	14.67	.66	.56	15.94
United Funds:				
Accumultiv	6.43	.29	.76	7.12
Bond	6.03	.55	.01	6.07
ContInc	14.85	.97	....	17.33
GoldGvt	7.47	.17	....	8.66
GvtSec	4.81	.41	....	4.92
IntlGth	6.41	.14	.26	6.85
HighInc	11.83	1.50	....	9.50
HiIncII	4.57	.52	....	3.92
Income	16.76	.65	1.96	18.69
Municpl	6.98	.49	.23	7.00
MunHi	4.87	.40	....	4.97
NwCcpt	4.96	.18	....	5.20
Retire	5.41	.26	.12	6.26

	NAV 12-30-88	Divs 1989	Cap. Dist	NAV 12-29-89
SciEngy	9.91	.19	.70	11.72
Vanguard	5.74	.23	.72	5.84
Utd Services:				
GBT n	15.41	.56	....	17.42
GNMA n	9.16	.79	....	9.47
GldSh n	3.34	.17	....	5.31
Growth n	6.36	.06	.28	7.32
Inco n	9.98	.45	....	13.25
LoCap nr	6.13	....	....	6.03
NwPro nr	1.21	.01	....	1.40
Prspct nr	.68	.05	.04	.74
RealEst n	9.11	.37	.27	9.15
US TxFr n	10.97	.61	....	11.24
USBosF	12.32	.04	.77	12.15
USBosG	11.87	.16	1.32	14.79
ValForg n	9.57	1.21	....	9.60
Value Line Fd:				
Aggrln n	7.95	.88	....	7.26
ConvFd n	10.70	.72	....	11.12
Fund n	13.15	.34	1.80	15.06
Income n	5.84	.46	....	6.66
Levrge Gth n	18.87	.38	1.45	23.10
MunB n	10.26	.78	....	10.30
NY TE n	9.78	.70	.06	9.79
SpclSit n	11.27	.22	....	13.49
USGvt n	11.57	1.10	....	11.80
Van Eck:				
GoldRes p	4.49	....	....	5.33
IntlInv	11.30	.31	.32	16.38
WrldInc p	9.46	.92	....	9.54
WrldTrn p	13.27	.20	....	14.83
VanKampen Mer:				
CA TF p	15.23	.98	....	15.61
Growth p	15.20	.58	.17	17.31
HiYld p	13.42	1.68	....	10.73
InsTxF p	17.39	1.16	....	17.80
PA TF	15.20	1.07	.01	15.70
TxFrHi p	16.18	1.31	....	16.38
US Gvt p	14.70	1.37	....	15.28
Vance Exchange:				
CapExch n	96.60	2.45	....	114.84
DepBst n	55.73	1.28	3.70	64.89
Divers n	104.92	2.31	....	127.48
ExchFd n	148.93	3.55	3.58	184.73
ExchBst n	133.45	3.07	1.05	156.01
FiducEx n	81.70	1.90	....	103.94
SecFidu n	81.97	1.87	.76	97.82
Vanguard Group:				
AssetA n	10.27	.51	.15	12.01
BdMkt n	9.05	.79	....	9.44
Convt n	8.72	.56	....	9.52
EqInc n	10.77	.70	.03	12.86
Explorer n	27.85	.37	1.01	29.06
ExpllI n	19.55	.21	2.46	20.25
Morgan n	10.27	.28	.59	11.72
Prmcp n	44.74	.63	2.45	51.26
Sm Cap n	35.91	.39	6.50	33.21
VHYSk n	14.38	1.25	.84	12.73
V Pref n	7.89	.74	....	8.56
V ARP n	19.41	1.66	....	18.62
Quant n	11.08	.47	....	14.14
STAR n	11.12	.77	.38	12.04
TCEF In n	28.27	.79	2.08	32.43
TCES US n	26.35	.88	3.81	26.15
GNMA n	9.27	.88	....	9.70
HiY Bd n	8.39	1.00	....	7.55
IG Bond n	7.83	.73	....	8.24
ShrtTrm n	10.20	.89	....	10.43
STGvt n	9.76	.84	....	9.98
US Tr n	9.16	.78	....	9.96
IndxExt n	11.60	.23	.23	13.89
Idx500 n	27.18	1.20	.75	33.64
MuHiYd n	10.05	.75	.11	10.26
MuniInt n	11.88	.84	.06	12.12
MunLtd n	10.09	.64	.01	10.22
MunLng n	10.31	.75	.16	10.53
MuInsLg n	11.45	.83	.15	11.64
MunSht n	15.21	.89	....	15.35
Cal Ins n	9.85	.67	....	10.18

MUTUAL FUNDS

	NAV 12-30-88	Divs 1989	Cap. Dist	NAV 12-29-89
NJ Ins n	10.12	.70	.01	10.42
NYIns n	9.41	.63	....	9.72
Penni n	9.83	.68	....	10.15
VSPE n r	11.39	.36	.57	15.40
VSPGd n r	9.27	.34	....	11.73
VSPH n r	18.43	.49	.72	23.21
VSPS n r	15.04	.41	.84	18.49
VSPT n r	10.75	.15	....	12.12
Wellesly n	15.26	1.31	.24	16.81
Welingtn n	16.01	1.02	.60	17.78
Windsor n	13.07	.75	.85	13.41
WindII n	12.81	.74	.61	14.96
WldInt n	10.30	.15	.28	12.42
WldUS n	7.51	.13	....	10.21
Venture Advisers:				
IncPl	8.11	1.15	....	6.63
Muni t	9.50	.67	....	9.72
NYVen	7.64	.40	.70	9.15
RPF B t	6.90	.57	....	6.86
RPF E t	17.47	.75	1.76	21.88
VikEqIdx n	14.45	.36	.39	17.66
Voyageur Fds:				
DblExCC	10.21	....	....	10.26
DblTax	11.48	....	....	11.68
GrnGv p	....	....	....	10.31
GrnGs p	16.78	....	....	19.59
WealthM p	6.46	....	....	6.99
Weiss Peck Greer:				
Tudor n	21.65	.16	.74	25.97
WPG n	20.47	.23	1.35	25.27
WPG Govt n	9.74	.86	....	10.18
WPG Gth n	93.78	.20	....	116.96
WallSt	6.57	.07	.82	7.09
Wells IRA-401K				
AssetAI n	12.00	....	....	13.41
Bond n f	11.03	....	....	12.48

	NAV 12-30-88	Divs 1989	Cap. Dist	NAV 12-29-89
CrpStk n	19.04	....	....	24.57
SmallCo n f	13.87	....	....	14.60
Westcore:				
STBd f	9.76	.78	....	9.84
IntBd	9.88	.83	....	10.11
BdsPl f	14.71	1.24	....	15.42
BasVl	18.15	2.57	.68	20.58
ModVal	9.90	.53	.16	11.21
MIDCO Gr	9.94	.26	1.93	10.55
SITE f	15.00	.50	....	15.08
Westwd	11.85	.56	.42	14.23
Wood Struthers:				
Neuwrth n	12.64	.06	2.70	11.90
PineStr n	11.29	.48	.90	12.67
WinGr t	9.78	.24	1.16	10.91
Wright Funds:				
GvOb	11.44	....	....	12.30
JrBlCh	12.45	.15	1.18	13.02
NearBd	10.16	....	....	10.33
QualCore	10.59	.22	1.45	11.29
SelBlCh	13.76	.31	1.37	15.37
TotRet	11.43	....	....	12.01
YamGlob	9.76	.96	.28	9.95
Zweig Funds:				
ZST BC p	12.23	.18	.32	14.12
Bond np	10.63	.66	....	10.78
ZS Cv p	8.48	.35	....	9.29
ZST E p	10.17	....	....	11.00
ZS Gv p	9.29	.66	....	9.75
ZST L np	9.51	.60	....	9.80
ZST Op	9.56	.14	....	11.41
Strat	11.34	....	....	u....
ZST P p	10.59	.09	.24	14.11
TxFrLtd	10.42	....	....	u10.33
TFLng p	9.33	....	....	9.45

f-Previous day quotation. (NL) n-No front end load or contingent deferred sales load. p-Fund assets are used to pay for distribution costs-12B1 plan. r-Redemption fee or contingent deferred sales load may apply. t-Combination of p and r. u-Unquoted on last day.

OVER-THE-COUNTER
National Market Issues

Over-the-counter quotations from the National Association of Securities Dealers through NASDAQ, its automated communications system. The quotes for the National Market Issues are for actual trades. The quotes for the remaining issues are the best bid and best offers. Prices don't include retail markup, markdown or commission. Volume represents shares that changed hands. These figures include only transactions effected by NASDAQ market makers but may include some duplications where NASDAQ market makers traded with each other.

The following tabulation gives volume, high, low, close and net change, which is based on the closing bid for 1989.

-A-

Stock	Symbol	Div	Yld	Sales 100s	Hi	Lo	Last	Net Chg
A&W Brands	SODA		28	171540	30	17	29¼	+ 10¾
ABS Ind	ABSI	.32	14	12883	9	6	7⅛	+ ⅞
ACC	ACCC	.16	23	33533	9¾	3¾	8⅝	+ 4⅛
ADC Tel	ADCT		15	80313	18¾	11¼	18⅜	+ 6¼
ADT	ADTLY		10	609200	33¼	21	32	+ 10¾
AEL Ind A	AELNA		...	18910	9	5¾	7	− ¾
AEP Ind	AEPI		13	21435	16	8⅜	14⅞	+ 6⅜
AircoaHosp	AIRC		5	1430	5¼	¾	1⅜	− 2⅜
ALC Comm	ALCCC		...	183110	5 1/16	1⅜	1 7/16	− 7/16
ASK Cptr	ASKI		9	404374	18⅛	6⅝	8¾	− 5⅞
AST Rsrch	ASTA		...	279968	11⅜	6⅝	10⅜	+ 2½
AaronRents	ARON	.10		18295	15¼	9⅛	10½	+ ⅜
AbingtnSvg	ABBK	.32	11	11891	10	6¼	6¾	− ⅞
AbeLincSvg	ALFB	.20e	...	7163	22½	11¼	12¾	− 2
AbramsInd	ABRI	.20	11	1362	5⅝	3 15/16	5⅜	+ 1¼
AcadInsur	ACIG		28	308528	1⅞	15/16	1⅛	− 9/16
AccelInt	ACLE	†	7	15791	8⅝	5⅞	7¼	+ ½
AcceptIns	ACPT		9	9107	21¾	11¾	21¾	+ 9¾
AcclmEntn	AKLM		...	201369	10	5½	6¼	− 2¼
AcclmEntn wtB			...	43633	2½	⅝	1⅛	...
Aceto	ACET	.14b	12	15092	15¾	13½	14¾	− ¾
Acmat	ACMT		23	4141	13¼	7¼	12⅜	+ 3⅝
AcmeSteel	ACME		5	58551	26½	16½	18	− 5¼
ActnAutRnt	AXXN	†	13	173371	22¼	6½	8½	− 8¼
ActionSvg	ANSL	.32b	4	14025	12¾	10	10¼	− ¾
ActnAutStr	AAST		17	10127	6⅛	3⅞	3⅞	− ¾
Acxiom	ACXM		22	51062	23½	11¾	21	+ 9
AdacLabs	ADAC	.16	16	702593	6¼	4	6⅛	+ 1⅜
Adage	ADGE		...	56271	1¾	1	1 3/16	− 7/32
Adaptec	ADPT		24	228693	20¼	4½	17¾	+ 13⅛
AddintnRes	ADDR		22	179316	23	10⅝	16¾	+ 6
AdiaSvcs	ADIA	.14	14	93806	28⅞	21¼	24½	+ 2
AdobeSys	ADBE	.14e	15	940095	30	14	20¼	− 4¼
Adtec	JAIL		29	18109	4⅜	1¼	1¾	− 2¾
AdvCircuit	ADVC		7	110269	11	3½	10⅝	+ 7 1/16
AdvRoss	AROS		145	21322	15½	8⅞	10⅛	+ ⅝
AdvMagnet	ADMG		49	12771	16½	7½	16½	+ 8½
AdvMktg	ADMS		18	96657	18	10	14¼	− 2½
AdvPolymer	APOS		...	133646	9¼	4⅝	5¾	− ⅜
AdvSemi	ASMIF		...	34009	12	6¼	7	− ⅜
AdvTelecom	ATEL		16	181159	26	12¼	16¾	+ ⅞
Advanta	ADVN	.10e	198	119284	12¼	4⅛	9⅞	+ 5 9/16
AdvoSys	ADVO		27	186462	11⅛	4¾	9⅛	+ 4⅜
Aequitron	AQTN		19	45844	4½	1½	1⅞	− 1⅛
Aegon	AEGNY	1.39e	11	8531	60⅝	42¼	60⅝	+ 15⅛
AeroSysInc	AESM		...	33789	1 7/16	⅝	11/16	− ⅝
AfflBcCp	ABCV	.32	7	53493	10⅛	3½	4¼	− 4⅜
AfflBkshCO	AFBK		32	49931	14¼	8⅝	12	+ 2⅜
AgncyRent	AGNC	†	16	510450	23½	10	11⅝	− 3
AgnicoEgl g	AEAGF	.20	...	58518	11	7	8⅜	− 1⅝
AgouronPhrm	AGPH		...	18042	17½	9⅜	9½	− 7½
AirMdwst	AMWI		15	87593	9¼	3⅜	4¼	+ ⅞
AirWisc	ARWS	†	30	172027	15	8¾	9¼	− 3⅝
AirshipInd	AIRSY		...	1361	3⅝	1⅛	1⅛	− 1⅜
AirtranCp	ATCC	.16	17	46391	12⅛	5⅝	11¾	+ 6
Akorn	AKRN	.07e	16	26218	2 3/32	1 7/16	1 31/32	+ 5/32
Akzo	AKZOY	1.46e	...	60735	36⅞	29½	36⅞	...
AlamedaBcp	ALBC	.60a	23	1045	24½	16¾	24½	...
AlatennRes	ATNG	1.10	23	10835	18½	9¼	11⅜	− 3⅞
Aldus	ALDC		13	302013	24½	12¼	15½	− 5½
AlexBrown	ABSB	.22	34	102406	14½	9½	10¾	+ ⅜
Alex&Bldwn	ALEX	.80	8	265020	39½	31¼	37½	+ 6
AlfaCp	ALFA	.36	9	13692	12¼	9¾	11¼	+ 1¼
Alico	ALCO	.20	25	13395	39	22½	30½	+ 8
AllAmSemi	SEMI		7	19246	3¾	1¾	2	− ⅝
AllCityIns	ALCI		6	5780	5⅜	4⅛	5⅛	+ 1
AllghnyWest	ALGH		10	63590	9¼	6½	8½	+ 1⅞
AllenOrgn	AORGB	.40	11	2446	39	27	37¼	+ 11
AllianPhar	ALLP		...	99444	14½	7⅞	11¾	+ 2¾
AllianPhar wt			...	2845	6¼	2	3	...
AllntCptr	ALNT		...	157612	7	3	5¾	+ 1½
AlliedBksh	ABGA	.30	12	4717	11	7¾	8¼	− 1¼
AlliedCap	ALLC	1.15e	13	17383	20¼	15¾	18¾	+ ¼
AlliedCapII	ALII	.15e	...	11005	15⅜	14½	14½	...
AlliedGp	ALGR	.44	8	7077	13½	9⅝	13½	+ 3½
AlliedRsrch	ARAI		...	12210	3⅜	1½	2	− ½
AlloyCptr	ALOY		...	14487	2¾	1	1¼	− 1⅜
AllstFnl	ASFN		...	13073	7½	6⅛	7	...
Allwaste	ALWS		27	407644	12¾	7 5/16	10¾	+ 3 5/16
AloetteCosm	ALET	.32	13	16493	15¾	6½	15¼	+ 8¾
Alpharel	AREL		...	40846	1 13/16	¼	⅝	− ¾
AlphaMicSys	ALMI		7	24306	8¼	4	4⅝	− 1⅜
AltaGold	ALTA	.06e	...	154566	7⅛	2⅝	5¾	+ 2½
Altai	ALTI		6	4062	3¾	2 15/16	3	− ¼
AlteraCp	ALTR		13	246980	9½	4¾	6⅞	+ 1½
AltusBk	ALTS		...	36332	5¾	⅞	1	− 3⅜
AltosCptr	ALTO		...	96609	8⅜	5⅞	7⅜	− 1
Altron	ALRN		19	14650	5¾	2⅝	5½	+ 2
AmbasdrFn	AFGI		...	7486	1⅞	7/32	7/32	− 1 11/32
AmcoreFnl	AMFI	.50	9	8163	19¼	15½	16½	+ ½
AmerianaSvg	ASBI	.40	12	12392	13¼	8¾	12⅝	+ 3⅜
AmeribcInv	AINVS	.22	5	24723	14½	7¼	8¼	− 3
AmFstMtg	AFMBZ	2.31e	...	42766	9¼	7¾	8¼	− ½
AmFstFnlFd	AFFFZ		...	38419	25	17¼	19¼	...
AmFstPfFd	AFPFZ	1.60	...	19704	16½	11¼	12¼	− 3½
AmFstTxEx	AFTXZ	1.70	...	47514	17¾	8½	9¼	− 7¼
AmFstTxEx2	ATAXZ	1.28	...	17986	16	9½	11¼	− 3½
AmWestAir	AWAL		13	445628	12⅞	6½	10⅛	+ 3⅝
AmBkrsIns	ABIG	.50	11	81370	13¼	10⅛	11⅞	− ⅝
AmCapRsrch	ACRCA		...	18835	8¾	8½	8⅝	...
AmCtyBsJnl	AMBJ		288	48378	22¼	14	17¼	− 4¾
AmColloid	ACOL	.44	14	4087	15½	9½	13	− 1
AmConsumr	ACPI		9	8104	11	7	7	− 4
AmEcology	ECOL		...	15691	11¼	5¾	6¼	− 3½
AmSvBkFla	AMJX		14	7747	13⅝	5¼	5⅜	− 7⅜
AmFiltrona	AFIL	.86	13	2897	27½	22¼	26	− 1½
AmGreetgs	AGREA	.66	17	454385	37⅛	20⅜	35¼	+ 14½
AmHlthSvc	AHTS		...	45964	5	2	2⅝	− ⅜
AmIndemFnl	AIFC	.56	...	3965	13	7½	7½	− 3
AmIntegrity	AIIC		8	120569	6½	1 3/16	6¼	+ 5 1/16
AmLocker	ALGI		15	2141	6	4½	5¼	+ ¾
AmMagnet	AMMG		29	21106	7	3¾	5¼	+ 1½
AmMgtSys	AMSY		20	139181	18½	10½	11¼	− 4¼
AmMedElec	AMEI		50	13769	9¼	6	6½	− ⅝
AmMidland	AMCO		2	16941	¾	7/32	¼	− 9/32
AmNatlIns	ANAT	1.60	10	25152	39¼	29¾	34½	+ 4¾
AmNuclear	ANUC		...	8734	⅞	½	9/16	− 3/16
AmNrsyPdts	ANSY		3	20400	3⅛	1⅛	1½	− 11/16
AmPacCorp	APFC		44	69400	14⅞	4¾	10⅞	+ 5¾
AmPhysnSvc	AMPH		13	17045	4⅛	2	2 5/16	− 1 11/16
AmPionSvgs	APIO		2	4768	5½	½	1 7/32	− 2 9/32
AmPwrConv	APCC		12	89610	25¼	7¼	17¼	+ 9¾
AmReInce	ARIG	.32	5	13945	14¾	7½	14	+ 6¼
AmRepBcp	ARBC	.05r	...	5547	10½	7¼	8¾	+ 1⅜

OVER-THE-COUNTER

Stock	Symbol	Div	Yld	Sales 100s	Hi	Lo	Last	Net Chg
AmRice	RICE		...	26036	3	1 1/8	1 1/4	-5/8
AmS&LFla pf		2.19	...	13576	17 1/2	15	16 1/2	-1/4
AmSftwr A	AMSWA	.32	21	179646	22 7/8	10 3/4	22 1/2	+11 5/8
AmSteel&Wr	RODS		12	71119	10 3/8	6 5/8	7 3/4	-7/8
AmTVComm	ATCMA		56	428828	55 1/4	30 3/8	44 3/4	+13 1/4
AmTrvlrs	ATVC		13	52990	20 1/4	4 1/4	19 7/8	+15 1/8
AmVngrd	AMGD	.09i	13	2713	8	6	7	+7/8
AmWestrn	AWST	.10r	30	92329	12 3/4	8 1/8	11 7/8	+7/8
AmWoodmk	AMWD		10	14159	13 3/4	6 1/4	6 3/4	-2 3/4
AmerfstBk	AMRI		...	364339	18 1/2	1 7/8	2 1/4	-16 1/8
Ameritrust	AMTR	1.28	8	181727	29	20 1/2	25	+4 1/8
Amrtek	ATEKF		...	3996	2 7/16	1 1/8	1 1/2	+1/4
Amgen	AMGN		...	796558	60 1/4	31	49	+15 1/4
Amistar	AMTA		...	2753	4 1/4	7/8	1 1/4	-1 1/2
AmtyBcp	AMTY	.20b	5	2383	11	8 1/2	8 3/4	-1 1/4
AmskgBksh	AMKG	.30j	...	186593	14 1/2	3 3/4	4 1/4	-7 5/8
Amoskg	AMOS	.60a	...	3678	30	19 1/2	24 1/2	+4
Amplicn	AMPI		13	25821	19 3/4	10	10 3/4	-7
Amserv	AMSR		14	22898	7 5/8	3	6 1/8	+2 7/8
AmtechCp	AMTC		...	22455	15	11 1/4	13 1/2	...
AmvstrFnl	AVFC	.20	14	116400	8 1/8	5 3/16	6	+5/8
Analogic	ALOG		13	59824	11 1/8	8 3/8	9 5/8	+1 1/8
Anly&Tech	AATI	.15	8	6341	15 1/2	12 1/2	12 1/2	-2 1/4
AnlyInt	ANLY	.48	16	71286	20 1/4	8 5/8	17 3/4	+9 1/8
Anangel	ASIPY	1.60e	5	107446	18 3/8	14 5/8	15 1/2	...
Anaren	ANEN		...	18399	6 1/4	2 1/2	2 7/8	-3 1/8
AnchrSvg	ABKR		...	188215	7 5/8	1 5/16	1 3/8	-5 7/8
AndersnGp	ANDR		5	6422	13	6 1/2	8 7/8	+2 7/8
AndovrBcp	ANDB	.80	7	33607	17 1/4	9 3/4	10 1/8	-5
AndovrTog	ATOG		17	9156	7 3/4	3 3/4	4 5/8	+7/8
AndrewCp	ANDW		15	134119	26 1/4	18	24 1/2	+4 1/2
AndrosAnly	ANDY		48	40936	10 3/8	6 3/4	7 3/4	...
ApogeeEnt	APOG	.20	15	93427	18 3/4	11 7/8	15 1/2	+3 3/8
AppleCptr	AAPL	.44	10	f45456	50 3/8	32 1/2	35 1/4	-5
Applebee	APPB		...	53063	16 1/4	11 1/2	13	...
AppldBiosci	APBI		22	61315	33 1/2	17 3/4	31	+12 1/2
AppldBiosys	ABIO		23	342046	38 1/2	21	27 1/2	+1 3/4
AppldMatl	AMAT		9	553868	32 3/4	21 1/2	28 1/2	+6 1/4
AppldPwr	APWRA	.12	15	126693	25 3/4	16	22 1/2	+4 3/8
AppldSolr	SOLR		...	18223	12 1/2	3 3/4	6 1/4	+2 1/2
ArabShld	ARSD		2	4187	4 3/8	1 3/4	1 13/16	-1 13/16
Archive	ACHV		10	299126	13	7 3/8	11 1/2	+3 1/2
ArborDrug	ARBR	.16	21	72551	24 3/4	9 1/4	22 1/2	+13 1/4
ArdenGp	ARDNA		9	3920	73 1/2	44 1/2	63	+16
ArgonautGp	AGII	1.00	5	55291	69 1/2	43 1/2	69 1/4	+25 1/2
Aritech	ARIT		12	18586	17 3/4	13	14 1/2	+1/4
ARIX	ARIX		5	104465	7 7/8	2 3/4	3 1/2	-3 5/8
ArizInstr	AZIC		39	85128	11 7/8	4 7/8	5 1/8	+1/4
ArkFreight	AFWY		17	24587	15 3/4	12 3/4	15	...
ArmorAll	ARMR	.64	17	66963	24	17	20 3/4	+3/4
ArnoldInd	AIND	1.00	11	14478	33 3/4	28	32 1/4	+3 1/4
ArrowBk	AROW	.64b	...	3885	18 3/4	16 1/4	17 1/4	+1/4
ArtelComm	AXXX		...	106225	8 5/8	1 1/2	7 3/8	+5 7/8
ArtsWayMfg	ARTW	.40	7	14912	14	5 7/8	7 3/4	+1 7/8
AshtnTate	TATE		...	f10048	24	8 3/4	12 1/4	-8 3/4
AsiamerEq	ASIAS	†	17	26385	10	7 3/8	9	+1 1/2
AspenRibn	ARIB		9	23910	4 1/8	2 7/8	3 9/16	-7/16
AssixInt	ASIX		51	44281	8 7/8	5	6 5/8	+1 1/4
AssixInt wt			...	15274	3 3/8	1 1/8	1 3/4	-5/16
AssocBcp	ASBC	.72	10	12791	24 1/4	16 3/4	22 1/2	+5 1/2
AsscCom A	ACCMA		...	53231	40 1/2	23 5/8	36 1/2	+12 1/2
AsscCom B	ACCMB		...	46500	40 1/4	23 5/8	36	+12
AstecInd	ASTE		46	16866	17 1/2	8 1/4	8 3/4	-8 1/4
AstroMed	ALOT		17	14108	11 1/8	8 1/8	10	-1
Astrocom	ACOM		...	13284	1 9/16	5/8	25/32	-17/32
Astronic	ATRO		...	6462	3 3/4	1	1 3/16	-1 9/16
Astrosys	ASTR		...	26602	5 3/8	3 3/4	3 3/4	-1 3/8
AtekMetals	ATKM		...	13639	8 1/8	4 1/4	4 3/8	-3 1/4
AtheyPdts	ATPC	.10r	9	9111	11	9	9 1/2	...
AticoFnl	ATFC	.20	...	4023	11 1/4	7 1/2	7 1/2	-2
AtkinsnGuy	ATKN	.48	...	37796	18 3/4	13 1/4	15 3/4	+1
Atlanfed	AFED	.40	9	2792	12	9 1/4	12	+1 3/4
AtlanAm	AAME		...	29706	3 5/8	2 1/4	2 1/2	-7/8
AtlanFnl	ATLF	.07j	...	47719	4 1/2	1/4	11/32	-3 29/32
AtlanFnl pf		.52j	...	44578	7 1/2	5/16	5/16	-6 15/16
AtlanSEAir	ASAI	.40	8	158399	19 3/4	8 5/8	16 7/8	+8 1/8
AttwoodPLC	ATTWY	.73e	19	28166	41 1/8	26 1/4	36	+10
AtwoodOcn	ATWD		62	6724	19 3/4	12	17 1/4	+4 3/4
AutoTrol	ATTC		...	8710	5 1/2	3 3/4	3 3/4	-1 1/8
AutoclvEngr	ACLV	.20b	10	19505	15	8 5/8	13 1/2	+4 3/8
Autodesk	ACAD	1.60e	22	501429	43 1/2	26 1/2	39	+10
Autodie	ADIE		12	6609	15	11 3/4	12 1/4	-2 1/4
AutoInfo	AUTO		41	76655	4 1/8	1 9/16	4 1/16	+2 1/8
AutoSys	ASII		...	11182	4 7/8	1 3/4	1 3/4	-2 1/2
AutotrolCp	AUTR		...	7258	9 3/8	4 1/4	8 3/4	+4 1/8
Avantek	AVAK		...	200593	7	3 1/2	3 3/4	-1 1/8
Avatar	AVTR		31	13219	31 1/4	23 1/2	24 1/4	+1/8
Avondale	AVDL	.92	32	125261	21 3/4	11 1/4	13 1/8	-2 1/4
AztarCp	AZTR		...	35650	9	7	8 1/4	...
AztecMfg	AZTC	.10	47	18117	6 5/8	3 5/8	6 1/8	+1 3/8

-B-

Stock	Symbol	Div	Yld	Sales 100s	Hi	Lo	Last	Net Chg
BB&T Fnl	BBTF	.80	9	50881	24 1/2	16 1/4	20	+3
B&H BulkCr	BULKF	2.51e	1	55184	13 1/2	4 7/8	5	-5 3/8
BEI Elec	BEII	.02e	6	60780	11	7 1/8	8 3/8	...
BEI Hldg	BEIH	.18j	...	44093	5 1/2	2 1/8	2 3/4	-1 3/4
BF Ent	BFEN		...	5545	11	7 1/2	7 1/2	-1 1/4
BFS Bank	BFSI		...	11730	12	8 1/4	9 3/8	+7/8
BGS Sys	BGSS	.40a	13	14728	15 1/2	9 7/8	15 1/2	+5 3/4
BHA Grp	BHAGA		...	49610	23 1/2	8 3/4	19	+9 7/8
BHA Grp B	BHAGB		...	30893	22	8	18	+9 3/4
BKLA Bcp	BKLA		12	1352	9 3/4	6	9 3/4	+3 3/4
BMA Cp	BMAC	1.20	8	46308	39 3/4	30	39 1/2	+7 1/4
BMC Softwr	BMCS		30	159468	30 3/4	13 5/8	30 1/4	+16 1/4
BMJ Fnl	BMJF	.60	8	4305	21	15 1/2	16 1/4	-3 3/4
BMR Fnl	BMRG		9	6864	9 1/4	8 1/8	8 1/4	-1/8
BNH Bcshr	BNHB	.24	8	7937	12 1/4	6 1/8	6 3/4	-5 1/2
BSB Bcp	BSBN	.60	6	28426	20 3/4	15 3/4	16 1/2	-1/4
BT Fnl	BTFC	.76	9	4259	15 1/2	12 3/4	15 1/2	+2
BT Ship	BTBTY		...	17357	12 1/2	11	12 1/4	...
BTR Rlty	BTRI	.08	...	13162	7 1/4	6	6 3/4	-1/8
BTU Int	BTUI		5	78147	11 1/8	3 1/2	4 1/2	...
Babbage	BBGS		22	64035	15 7/8	6 5/8	7 3/8	-7
BadgerPapr	BPMI	.48a	12	3230	31	18	22 1/2	+4 3/4
Bailey	BAIB		5	14417	3 3/8	1 1/2	1 5/8	-1 1/16
BakrJInc.	JBAK	.06	17	171719	22 3/8	9 7/8	20 5/8	+9
Balchm	BLCC	.03	17	2717	5 1/4	2 1/2	3 1/16	-1 5/16
BaldwnLy A	BWINA	.20	8	257	25	16	24 1/2	+8 1/2
BaldwnLy B	BWINB	.20	8	16635	24	14 1/2	21 7/8	+7
BaldwPiano	BPAO		10	21617	14	9 1/2	10	-3 1/4
BallrdMed	BMED		27	58592	20 3/4	13 1/4	20	+6 1/4
Baltek	BTEK	.15	7	26368	19 3/8	8 1/2	9	-5 3/8
Banponce	BDEP	1.60	12	24056	50	23 3/4	47	+22 1/2
BancoPop	BPOP	.80	8	25222	26 1/4	17 3/8	21 1/2	+3 3/4
BcpHawii	BNHI	1.56	9	88824	62 1/2	38 1/2	54 1/4	+15 1/2
BcpMiss	BOMS	.84	8	6352	23 1/2	20 1/4	20 1/2	-1 1/4
BcpNJ	BCNJ	.40	8	13967	14	8 3/8	10 1/2	...
Banctec	BTEC		12	107835	19 5/8	10 1/8	15 1/2	+5
BandoMcG	BMCC	.88	13	9533	8	6 1/2	8	+1/2
BangorHyd	BANG	1.24	8	13465	16 3/4	13 1/2	16 1/4	+2 1/4
BkAtlantic	ASAL		...	5048	10 1/2	6 1/8	6 1/4	-3 1/4
BkGranite	GRAN	.40	14	2867	22	17 1/8	20 3/4	+1 5/8
BkNH	BNHC	.92	5	6438	23 1/2	12 7/8	14 1/2	-5 1/2
BkSouth	BKSO	.48	9	91813	14 1/4	10 1/8	11 7/8	+1 7/8
Bkeast	BENH	.24j	...	79308	7 3/4	1 3/8	2	-4 1/4
BankFst	BNKF	.21e	6	17144	11 1/2	6 1/4	6 1/2	-1 1/4
BankrNote	BKNT		24	15379	4 3/8	2	2 11/16	+5/16
Banknorth	BKNG		...	4588	21 1/2	15 1/2	19	...
BkIowa	BIOW	1.00	12	8497	82	62 1/4	78 1/2	+12 1/2
BkMidAmer	BOMA		...	10605	11	9	10	+3/4
BkWorcstr	BNKW	1.00	13	127183	18 1/4	9 7/8	12 5/8	-3
BankUtd A	BKUNA		...	475	7	5 3/4	6 1/4	+1/8
BantaCp	BNTA	.56	9	96993	25 1/2	21 3/4	23 1/4	-1/2
Barden	BARD	1.00b	12	3282	40	30	35	+3 3/8
BarretRes	BARC		34	11445	7	2 7/8	6 1/8	+3 1/2
BarryJewlr	BARY		10	13105	17	9	12	+2 1/4
BaseTen A	BASEA		8	18649	5 3/4	2 3/4	3 3/8	-1 3/8
BasicAmMd	BAMI		7	5953	5 5/8	3	3 1/4	-1 1/4
BasicPete	BPILF		...	146169	12 1/2	3 1/8	6 7/8	-2 1/2
BassetFurn	BSET	1.00a	16	21568	40	34 3/4	36 1/4	-2 3/4
BayVwCap	BVFS	.30e	8	116457	27	16 1/4	20 1/2	+2 5/8
Baybks	BBNK	1.80	6	191272	46 1/2	25	31 1/4	-12
BeautiCtl	BUTI	.15i	17	74087	20 3/8	6 1/2	16 3/4	+10
BeautyLb	LABB		41	35051	7 1/4	2	3 1/4	-1 3/4
Beebas	BEBA	.20	11	56974	15 7/8	7 1/2	9 3/4	+2 1/8
BelFuse	BELF		...	27774	6 3/4	3 1/2	4 1/8	-1 5/8
Bell W	BLLW		...	7505	5 7/8	3 1/4	4	-1 1/2
BellSvg	BSBX		3	17079	10 7/8	5 1/8	5 3/4	-3 3/8

OVER-THE-COUNTER

Stock	Symbol	Div	Yld	Sales 100s	Hi	Lo	Last	Net Chg
BelmrlMin	BMEEF		...	17557	1¾	7/16	⅝	– ⅜
BenJerry A	BJICA		21	20291	17½	12¼	15¾	+ 1
Benihana	BNHN		10	20746	4	2½	2⅞	– ¼
BenFrkSvg	BENJ		3	103909	6¼	2½	2⅞	– 1½
BerklWR	BKLY	.40	9	113147	46½	29¼	40¼	+ 10¾
BerkshrGas	BGAS	1.28	19	2782	18½	15¾	17½	– ½
BethelBcp	BTHL	.57e	8	1809	15½	11¾	11¾	– 2¼
BetzLab	BETZ	1.88	17	129006	62⅜	47¼	59½	+ 12
BigB	BIGB	.16	18	38646	15¼	10⅝	12¾	+ ⅛
BigOTire	BIGO		17	64590	2½	1 7/16	1 9/16	– 7/16
BndlyWest	BIND		17	35325	10¾	7	10½	+ 3⅜
BingoKng	BNGO		10	5954	3 13/16	2	2 11/16	– 5/16
Biogen wt			...	4120	7¾	2	7	+ 5½
BioLgSys	BLSC		30	8686	6⅝	3⅛	4½	+ ¾
BioMedicus	BMDS		31	139170	19¾	10⅝	15⅝	+ 4¾
Biogen	BGEN		838	484740	18¼	7⅛	16¾	+ 9⅝
Biogen pf		2.12	...	41268	33	24⅜	30⅝	...
Biomet	BMET		30	246124	28	16	27½	+ 11⅜
Biospheric	BINC		238	7429	6¼	3¼	4¾	– ¾
BiotcRes	BTRL		26	29515	7¼	3⅝	4⅛	– 2⅞
Biotchnic	BIOT		...	14058	3¼	2	2¼	– ⅞
BirdInc	BIRD		38	37115	13⅛	7⅞	11¼	+ 1¾
Birtcher	BIRT		18	8953	4½	2¼	3⅞	+ 1
BizMart	BZMT		...	76318	10¼	7¾	9⅝	...
BlackInd	BLAK	.30e	10	2126	11¾	9	9¾	...
BlauBarry	BLAU		6	1653	5	3¼	3¼	– ¾
BlisLaughln	BLIS		8	6870	10¾	5½	5½	– 4¾
BlockDrg	BLOCA	.70b	15	21189	38	31½	38	+ 3½
BluRdg un			39	1240	22½	12	12¾	– 8
BoatBksh	BOAT	2.12	13	308200	39½	29¾	32	+ 1
BobEvFrm	BOBE	.26b	15	179645	16⅛	12⅞	14	+ ⅜
BogrtOil	BOGO		...	7036	11¼	8¼	9	...
Bohemia	BOHM	.20b	7	82570	28	15½	25⅜	+ 6⅞
BnvlPac	BPCO		...	140598	12¾	7⅜	9⅜	+ 1⅛
BooleBg	BOOL		12	27544	20	9½	15½	+ 5¾
BoontnEl	BOON		72	7394	5⅝	2⅝	2⅞	– 2⅜
Borland	Borl		...	20924	10½	9⅝	9⅞	...
BostnAc	BOSA		13	14695	23	10¾	19¾	+ 8⅝
BostnBcp	SBOS	.60	7	66033	19¼	13⅞	16¼	+ ⅞
BostnDig	BOST		9	5528	5 3/16	2¾	2¾	– 2⅜
BostnFvCt	BFCS	.24	...	91835	15¼	4⅝	6⅜	– 6⅛
BostonTech	BSTN		...	f11559	14⅜	2½	8	...
BlvdBcp	BLVD	.48	13	13336	26	20	23¾	+ 3¼
BradyWH	BRCOA	.40	14	17881	31	20½	31	+ 10
BraeCp	BRAE		...	22826	6⅜	2⅛	5 7/16	+ 3 5/16
BrantreeSvg	BTSB	.36	12	8071	16¾	7	7¾	– 6¾
Braidas	BRJS		...	5170	7½	4	5	– 2
BrandCos	BRAN		33	115877	32½	13¾	32	+ 18
BrandnSys	BRDN	.12	14	5071	12½	7¾	9¾	– ¾
BranfdSvg	BSBC	.60	6	11867	14¾	7¼	7½	– 5
BrkwatrR g	BWRLF		...	60398	4⅛	1 11/16	2 1/16	– 1 1/16
Brenco	BREN	.20	17	50175	10⅞	6¾	7⅞	+ ¼
Brendls	BRDL		...	18507	8⅝	5½	7¾	+ 2⅛
BridFood	BRID	.20	24	2941	28½	12	27½	+ 15¼
BriteVoice	BVSI		...	53650	14¼	8⅜	8⅞	...
BroadNtl	BNBC	.58r	10	1670	25⅜	20	21	– ½
BdwyFnl	BFCP	.48	5	3076	14¾	9	10	– 4
BrkfldSvg	BFBS	1.00	11	203	45	26½	44	+ 14½
BklynSvg	BRLN	.40i	2	6909	8¾	1⅝	1⅞	– 4⅝
BrownTom	TMBR		...	23804	7⅛	4⅝	5⅜	– 1
Brunos	BRNO	.14	24	346096	15⅛	10⅛	15	+ 4¾
BrynMwrBk	BMTC	1.52	11	2791	35	26¾	33	+ 6
BuckeyeFnl	BCKY		5	10528	8¼	6	7	– ¾
Buffets	BOCB		28	131818	18¼	9⅛	16½	+ 5⅜
BldrsTrnspt	TRUK		...	42454	13	8¾	10¾	– 1⅛
BullBear	BNBGA		...	12973	6⅛	2¼	2⅝	– 1
BullRnGld	BULL		...	34982	2 3/16	15/16	1	– ⅞
BurnupSm	BSIM		19	221423	24⅝	15⅝	16⅞	– 1⅞
BurrBrown	BBRC		8	55911	14½	7	8¼	– 4
BurritInt	BANQ		...	25024	21¾	9¾	11⅜	– 7⅝
ButlrMfg	BTLR	20.00e	6	26032	25½	16¾	17¼	– ¾
Bytex	BYTX		15	66757	9⅝	6⅝	8⅜	...

-C-

Stock	Symbol	Div	Yld	Sales 100s	Hi	Lo	Last	Net Chg
CB&T Fnl	CBTF	.07	8	2619	18	14¾	17	– ¼
CCA Ind	CCAM		...	33933	1⅞	7/16	1⅝	+ 13/16
CCAIR	CCAR		9	49073	8⅜	3¾	4	...
CCB Fnl	CCBF	1.44	9	7707	43¾	33¼	39¼	+ 3½
C-CorElec	CCBL		11	84587	17½	9¾	12¾	+ 1½
CCNB	CCNC	.76	...	13561	23	17¾	20½	+ 2¾
CEM Cp	CEMX		20	57400	12¾	8⅞	10½	+ ½
CFI&I Stl	CFIP		...	22346	5½	3½	3 15/16	– 13/16
CFS Fnl	CFSC	.40e	10	16616	19½	10⅞	14¼	+ 1¼
CIS Tech	CISI		...	75861	3 1/16	15/16	2 15/16	+ 1 11/16
CK Svgs	CKSB	.40	8	4786	18¾	11	16½	+ 5
CNB Bncshr	CNBE	.88	10	4428	22¾	19¾	20¾	+ ¾
CNL Fnl	CNLF	.24	...	497	5¼	4	4½	+ ¼
CPAC	CPAK		...	21476	9¾	5⅛	6½	+ 1⅛
CPB	CPBI	.48	13	18448	33	15¾	25	...
CPC Rxcel	CPST		...	14772	7¾	3	4	– 2⅞
CPI Cp	CPIC	.48	14	42067	26⅜	19¾	25¾	+ 5⅞
CPT	CPTC		...	78190	1 13/16	3/16	½	– 15/32
CRH	CRHCY	.33e	...	201	20	16¼	19¾	...
CSC Ind	CPSL		...	25382	2⅝	¾	13/16	– 1¼
CSP	CSPI		18	5932	6¾	5⅝	5¾	– ½
C-TEC	CTEX		34	52785	30	15⅛	25	+ 9½
CUC Int	CUCD	5.00r	...	480309	14⅞	9⅝	11¼	– 1¼
CabotMed	CBOT		14	36641	3½	1⅞	2 11/16	+ 7/16
Cache	CACH		31	40281	1¾	1 1/16	1¼	+ ⅛
CaciaInt	CACIA		7	62454	3 1/16	1⅞	2	– ⅝
CadburyS	CADBY	1.70e	13	73921	80¼	52	56⅛	– 5
CadeInd	CADE		...	42499	31/32	17/32	9/16	– ⅜
CadencDsn	CDNC		23	398963	22	11⅛	21¼	+ 10
Cadmus	CDMS	.20	21	22451	13¾	8¾	10	– 3⅛
CaereCp	CAER		...	43011	19½	14	18¼	...
CalRpBcp	CRBI	.40b	13	1515	33¾	17⅝	30¾	+ 12⅝
Calgene	CGNE		...	82140	8⅞	5½	8¾	+ 2⅛
CalgnCarb	CRBN	.24	27	194384	47½	24¼	44	+ 16¾
CalifAmp	CAMP		...	20324	1⅞	½	1⅛	+ ⅜
CalifBiotch	CBIO		...	136128	10	4¾	7⅛	+ 1½
CalifFnl	CFHC	.40	8	17667	13¾	7½	10½	+ 2¾
CalifMicDv	CAMD		...	13401	3⅜	1⅜	2¼	– ¾
CalifMicrw	CMIC		12	104521	10⅝	7⅜	7¾	– ½
CalStBank	CSTB		9	6896	20½	11¾	17	+ 3⅞
CalifWtr	CWTR	1.68	12	10262	28¾	23½	28	+ 2½
CallonConsol	CCLPZ	.80e	11	9797	4	2¼	2⅝	– ⅜
Calumet	CALI		...	23731	8¼	4⅜	5	– ¼
Cambrex	CBAM	.05e	14	51114	17¼	12¼	12¾	– 2
CambrBioS	CBCX		...	404159	15½	5½	6¼	– 8
CambrInstr	CAMBY		...	154	12	7¾	12	+ 2⅞
Campeau h	CMAFC	.20i	...	79801	18⅝	2¾	3	– 10⅜
CanalRand	CANLZ		...	692	4	2¼	2⅛	– 1⅝
CandlaLasr	CLZR		...	38139	8¾	3¾	7¾	+ 1¼
CannonExp	CANX		7	13130	8¼	4⅞	5¼	– 1⅞
Canon	CANNY	.39r	29	12985	69½	48¾	64	+ 9¼
CanonieEnvr	CANO		45	92135	27¾	16	18¾	– 8
CantelInd	CATLB		...	2869	6	3½	4½	– 1¼
CapeCodBk	CCBT	1.52	7	5784	34½	27¾	28½	– 2½
CapitalAssoc	CAII		4	68678	9¼	3⅞	4	– 2⅛
CapitalSW	CSWC	1.44e	...	5668	25¼	17¾	25¼	+ 7½
CapitolBcp	CAPB		...	51870	13¾	2¾	2⅞	– 5
CapTrnsam	CATA	.27	6	3162	19¾	11⅛	19¼	+ 8⅛
CaptCrab	CRAB		...	63892	7/16	3/16	7/32	– 1/32
CardnlDist	CDIC	.08	19	90026	24½	12¾	24½	+ 11½
CardnlFnl	CAFS	.50	19	2500	14½	9½	13	+ 2
CarePlus	CPLS		32	109442	14⅛	4	13⅝	+ 8⅞
CarePlus wtA			...	39679	2 3/16	¼	2 5/32	+ 1 27/32
CarltonCom	CCTVY	.30e	18	257809	32⅛	22¼	25¾	+ 1⅜
Carme	CAME		17	17106	5⅜	2½	5	+ 2¼
CarmikeC	CMIKA		13	40322	13⅞	7¾	13⅞	+ 6
CarolBcp	FFCA	.38	13	15155	18	6¾	14½	+ 6⅝
CaringtnLb	CARN		...	91406	41¼	12½	18	+ 3
Carver	CAVR		...	34593	7⅜	4 3/16	5	+ ½
CascadeCp	CASC	.60a	10	28946	25½	18	20	– 2
CascadeInt	KOSM	†	8	113151	4 1/16	2 9/16	2 13/16	+ 1/16
CaseyGnStr	CASY		20	200192	14¼	7¾	11⅛	– 2⅜
CastleEngy	CECX	.06e	28	9592	9¾	2⅞	9¼	+ 6 9/16
CatalystThr	CETH	.20	9	15863	4½	2¼	2¼	– 1¼
CasualMale	CMLE		...	68572	13⅛	1⅜	2⅝	– 7½
CatoCp A	CACOA	.08	...	56127	5¼	3¼	3⅜	– ½
CayugaSvg	CAYB	.50	4	3058	11¾	6⅞	7¼	– 4
Celgene	CELG		...	64979	11⅞	5⅜	7½	– 1⅝
CellTech	CELL		...	70745	7⅜	2	2¾	– 4⅞
CellTech wt			...	8111	2⅝	¼	⅝	– ⅞
Cellcom wi	CLCM		...	293406	12¼	1½	6¼	+ 4⅝
CellulrCom	COMM		...	760800	43¾	24¾	40⅛	+ 13⅜
CellulrInc	CELS		...	79640	30	14	23½	+ 8
CellrInfo	CALLA		...	33607	11	10	10¾	...

OVER-THE-COUNTER

Stock	Symbol	Div	Yld	Sales 100s	Hi	Lo	Last	Net Chg
Cencor	CNCR		12	25195	2 1/2	1 11/16	1 7/8	– 3/8
CentenlSvg	CNSB	.40	10	274	9 3/8	8	8 1/8	+ 1/8
CentrbkCn	CTBX	.80	...	269721	14 3/4	5 3/4	6 7/8	– 3
CentxTlmgt	CNTX		29	212701	22 7/8	13 3/4	19 5/8	+ 5 5/8
Centocor	CNTO		...	158544	27	15	25	+ 10
CentlSoHldg	CSBC	.36a	...	3546	10 1/2	7	7 1/2	– 2 1/2
CentlBkshSo	CBSS	.77	7	36298	16 1/4	12 1/2	13	– 1 5/8
CentlBkSys	CSYSE		...	50068	15	1 7/8	2	– 9 7/8
CentlCoop	CEBK		32	45675	18 1/8	4 3/4	5 3/8	– 12 1/2
CentlFidlBk	CFBS	1.24	9	38548	34 5/8	26 5/8	30 3/4	+ 2 5/8
CentlHldg	CHOL	.10j	...	9619	4 7/16	2	2 1/2	– 1 1/2
CentlJerBk	CJER	.90	8	28484	27 1/4	18	19 1/8	– 1/8
CentlJerFinl	CJFC	.36	5	5134	18 1/4	9 1/2	10 1/4	– 3 7/8
CentlPaFnl	CPSA	.40b	6	5234	15 1/8	12	12 1/2	– 1/8
CentlRsvLf	CRLC	.26	8	15327	7 1/8	4 1/2	5 1/8	+ 3/8
CentlSprnklr	CNSP		17	47118	26 1/2	15	25	+ 7
Centuri	CENT		9	23514	1 15/16	1 3/16	1 3/8	– 5/16
CenturGold	CEUMF		...	27941	3 1/2	1 5/16	1 3/8	– 1 3/8
CentyBcp	CNBKA	.30	5	13231	6 1/4	3 3/8	3 3/4	– 1
Cenvest	CBCT	.48	15	23951	12 1/8	7	7 1/4	– 2 3/4
Ceradyne	CRDN		...	16573	4 3/4	2 7/8	3 5/8	– 5/8
Cerbco	CERB	.06	...	4676	4 1/2	2 3/8	3 3/16	– 5/16
CernerCp	CERN		16	31012	15 7/8	9 1/2	12 1/2	– 3 1/2
CetusCp	CTUS		...	565082	19	11	14 1/4	+ 2 5/8
Chalone	CHLN		66	8052	15	9 3/4	10 5/8	+ 1/8
ChampParts	CREB		...	19870	8 1/4	3 3/4	4 1/2	– 2 7/8
ChanclrCp	CHCR		...	4481	6	2 7/8	3 3/8	– 2 5/8
ChandlrIns	CHANF		6	60089	13 1/4	7	11 5/8	+ 2 1/4
CharmShop	CHRS	.12	13	818037	18 7/8	9 5/8	10 5/8	– 3 7/8
ChartrSvgVa	CHFD		...	36431	8 7/8	1 1/8	1 1/4	– 7 3/8
ChartrSvg	CFED	.50	...	7536	16 1/4	10 1/2	11 3/4	+ 1 1/4
ChartrOne	COFI	.52	7	111277	22 1/8	9 7/8	17 3/4	+ 7 1/2
Chartwell	CTWL		...	84882	6 3/4	3/16	1/4	– 4 3/4
Chattem	CHTT	.56	14	2429	26	21	22 3/4	+ 1 3/4
CheckptSys	CHEK		40	112652	12 3/8	6 3/8	12 1/4	+ 3 1/8
CheckTech	CTCQ		8	18607	3 1/4	1 5/8	2 3/8	+ 1/2
ChemDesgn	CDCC		21	132642	19 3/4	12 3/4	13 1/4	...
Chemfix	CFIX		129	42604	13 1/2	2 1/2	3 7/8	– 1/4
Chemfix wt			...	1457	11/16	3/16	5/16	...
ChmFabric	CMFB		23	23626	19 1/2	8 1/2	19 1/2	+ 10 3/4
ChmFnl	CHFC	1.00b	10	1536	38 1/8	30 7/8	33	– 2 7/8
ChmLeamn	CLEA		26	839	50 1/2	36 1/2	36 1/2	– 12 1/2
Chempwr	CHEM		17	103566	19 1/2	13 3/8	17 1/4	...
CherryCp	CHER	.12	...	8142	17	6 3/4	8 1/4	– 8 3/4
ChesapkUtil	CHPK	.84	16	5277	16 1/4	12 1/4	12 1/2	– 3 1/8
CheshrFnl	CFNH	1.00	10	18089	15 1/4	11	12 1/4	– 2
CheynSftwr	CHEY		...	326137	9 3/8	5	7 1/8	+ 1 1/4
ChgoDock	DOCKS	.30e	181	12248	26 3/4	23 1/2	23 1/2	– 1 1/4
ChildDiscv	CDCRA		71	11141	6 1/4	4 1/4	4 1/4	– 1 1/8
ChildWld	CWLD		17	17878	19 3/4	11 1/2	12 3/8	– 2 1/8
Chips&Tch	CHPS		7	705858	26 1/4	13 1/4	18	+ 4 3/4
Chiron	CHIR		...	276033	34 1/2	13	28 1/2	+ 14 3/4
Chittnden	CNDN	.68	10	16539	18 3/4	10 5/8	11	– 5 3/8
Chronar	CRNR		...	97057	8	1 5/8	2	– 6
Church&Dwt	CRCH	.28	27	276041	18 7/8	9 3/4	18 3/4	+ 7
Cimco	CIMC		19	26437	16	9 7/8	11 1/4	– 1 3/8
CimflexTek	CMTK	†	...	99876	3 1/4	1 5/8	2 3/8	+ 1/4
CincFnl	CINF	2.16	11	46933	82 3/4	52 3/4	79 1/2	+ 26 3/4
CincMicrw	CNMW		46	107425	10 3/4	2 1/4	7 7/8	+ 5
Cintas	CTAS	.17	27	46877	45	32	44 3/4	+ 11 1/4
CipherData	CIFR		...	315857	11	4	7	– 2 3/8
Ciprico	CPCI		...	9190	7 5/8	3 1/2	3 1/2	– 1 3/4
Circadian	CKDN		...	24359	2 5/8	1 1/4	1 3/8	– 3/8
CirclFinArt	CFNE		11	28406	10 3/4	5 3/4	7 7/8	+ 2 1/8
CircIncoShr	CINS	1.14a	...	7469	12 5/8	11 1/8	11 1/4	– 1
Circon	CCON		...	20577	6 5/8	3 1/2	5 1/4	+ 1 3/8
CirrusLogic	CRUS		...	216797	15 5/8	8 7/8	10 1/2	...
CitzBcp	CIBC	1.04	...	21163	25 3/4	20 3/4	21 1/8	– 2
CitzBkNC	CIBA		...	2415	9 3/4	5	8 3/4	+ 3 5/8
CitzBkg	CBCF	1.20	9	15743	29 1/4	23	23 3/4	– 3/4
CitzGrowth	CITGS	1.00e	...	372	10 3/8	8 5/8	9 5/8	+ 1
CitizensInc	CINNA		...	20375	6	2 1/2	5 7/8	+ 1 1/2
CitzSvgNY	CISA	†	8	36425	14	8	8 1/2	+ 1/2
CitzSvgFnl	CSFCB		3	2455	16 3/4	12	12 1/2	– 1/4
CitzUtil A	CITUA	†	22	46174	48 1/2	39 1/2	42 3/4	– 3/4
CitzUtil B	CITUB	1.54	21	17119	42 3/4	28 1/2	39 1/4	+ 7
CityFedFnl	CTYF	.02j	...	166013	4	1/32	1/8	– 3 3/8
CityFedFnl pfB		1.05j	...	28354	12 1/4	1/4	1/4	– 11
CityFedFinl pfC		.20j	...	71970	2 7/16	1/32	1/32	– 2 7/32
CityHldg	CHCO	.40	...	850	23	14 1/4	15	– 6

Stock	Symbol	Div	Yld	Sales 100s	Hi	Lo	Last	Net Chg
CityNtl	CTYN	.64	12	84571	28	18	23 3/4	+ 4 5/8
CityRes g	CIZCF		...	8040	1 9/16	1/4	5/16	– 1 1/16
ClairsnInt	CLICC		...	51567	8 5/8	2 3/4	8 1/2	+ 1 1/4
CLARCOR	CLRK	1.17	14	57490	42 1/2	26 1/2	32 1/4	+ 1/2
CleanHarb	CLHB		26	159376	22	10	11	– 7 3/4
ClevTrust	CTRIS		...	6419	6 5/8	3 3/4	4 1/4	– 3/8
CliffDrl	CLDR		...	19293	14 1/4	7 1/8	13 1/2	+ 4 3/4
CliffDrl pf			...	4750	29	21	28 1/4	+ 7 1/2
ClinData	CLDA		...	17366	2 15/16	1 1/4	1 7/16	– 1/16
ClintnGas	CGAS		...	5887	3 1/2	2 1/4	2 3/4	– 1/2
Clothtime	CTME		32	440646	15 1/4	4 3/8	6	...
CoopBcp	COBK	.60	6	19511	10 3/8	6 3/4	7 1/8	– 1 3/8
CobbRes	COBB		...	11165	1 3/8	5/16	9/16	– 11/16
CobeLabs	COBE		15	67953	25 1/4	18	22 1/4	+ 2 3/8
CokeBtlg	COKE	.88	...	48551	32 1/2	22	23 1/4	– 2 1/2
CocaMine	COCA		...	29547	3 9/16	1 13/16	3	– 1/4
CocaMine wt			...	4335	15/16	1/32	23/32	...
CodaEngy	CODA		...	53254	3 1/2	1 1/4	3 1/16	+ 1 13/16
CodeAlrm	CODL		28	47113	24 1/8	11 3/8	24 1/8	+ 11 1/2
CodenlTech	CODN		...	12488	8 1/2	5	5 3/4	– 1/4
CodenlTech wt			...	2456	3/4	1/8	1/4	+ 1/8
Cognex	CGNX		24	58554	21 1/4	10 1/8	20 1/4	...
Cognos	COGNF		...	44953	9 1/4	3 7/8	4 7/8	– 2 1/4
CohastSvg	CHTB	.24	14	3981	9 1/2	5 1/2	5 1/2	– 3 1/4
Coherent	COHR		16	123308	19 3/4	9 3/4	14 5/8	+ 4 1/4
CollabResrch	CRIC		...	36495	3 1/8	7/8	1 1/16	– 1 5/16
Collagen	CGEN		48	221749	23 7/8	10 5/8	18 5/8	+ 5 3/8
CollectvS&L	COFD	.20	6	75819	11 7/8	5 7/8	7 1/2	+ 1/8
ColonlGp	COGRA	.40	10	18999	15 1/2	11 1/4	13 1/4	+ 1 1/4
ColonlGas	CGES	1.72	12	21996	23	18	22	+ 2 1/2
ColonlBkgp	CLBGA	.60	10	22363	12 1/8	7 7/8	8 7/8	– 2 1/8
ColonlCos B	CLACB	.56	11	28358	23	15 5/8	23	+ 6 7/8
ColoNtl	COLC	.16e	34	82618	22 1/2	12 1/4	17 3/4	+ 5 1/2
Colorocs	CLRX		...	216138	12 1/4	4 1/2	8 7/8	+ 4 1/4
ColumFstSL	CFFS		400	23463	20	14	14	– 3
Comair	COMR	.32	11	66707	14 7/8	8 1/2	13 3/8	+ 4 5/8
Comarco	CMRO		10	34174	4 1/4	2 3/4	3	– 3/8
ComcstCp	CMCSA	.11	...	545755	19 7/8	10 7/8	16 3/4	+ 5 5/8
Comcst spA	CMCSK	.11	...	548643	18 3/4	10 3/4	16 1/4	+ 5 3/8
Comcoa	CCOA		66	2731	11 1/2	10	10 1/2	– 3/8
Comdata	CMDT		...	17152	9 3/4	3 3/4	6 1/2	+ 2 1/2
Comdial	CMDL		...	52793	1 1/4	1/2	11/16	– 3/16
Comerica	CMCA	2.40	10	103238	58 3/4	45 1/4	48 1/4	+ 2 1/2
Comerica pf		4.32	7	1428	47 1/2	41 3/4	47 1/4	+ 3 1/4
ComrcBcpNJ	COBA	.85e	7	8292	18 1/4	11 1/2	14 1/4	– 2 3/4
ComrcBcp pf			...	1576	19 1/2	16 1/2	16 7/8	– 2 5/8
ComrcBcsh	CBSH	.64	9	17916	29 1/2	19 5/8	26 5/8	+ 5 3/4
ComrcClrg	CCLR	1.40	19	52758	65 1/2	42 1/2	43	– 4 1/2
ComrcBcpCA	CBNB	.10r	9	11899	20 1/2	11	14 3/8	+ 3 3/8
ComrcBcpCO	CBOCA	.36	8	1810	10	6 3/4	7	– 1
ComrclFed	CFCN		3	50532	8 5/8	3 3/8	3 7/8	– 4 1/8
ComrclNtl	CNCL		...	5983	8 1/2	3 1/2	4 1/4	– 4 1/8
ComrclIntech	CTEK	.60	39	131586	27 1/4	17 1/4	22 1/2	+ 5 1/8
CmwlthBsh	CBKS	.84	13	5604	20 3/4	16 1/4	18 1/4	+ 3/4
CommCblNC	CABL	†	13	11618	14 1/4	6 3/8	12 1/4	+ 5
CommSys	CSII	.24	21	28894	9 7/8	6 1/8	9 1/2	+ 3 1/4
CommTrnsm	CTIA		...	24844	9 3/8	3 3/8	3 3/8	– 2
CmuntyBcpPa	CBPA	.15e	10	8208	7 5/8	6	6 7/8	...
CmuntyBcNH	CBNH	.72	...	9191	11 3/4	3 3/4	3 7/8	– 6 1/8
CmuntyBkSys	CBSI	.76	9	7319	19	13 3/4	15	+ 1
CmuntyBkPa	CBKI	.70b	14	1021	23	20 1/2	21 1/4	– 3/4
CmuntyNtlBcp	CNBT		9	59911	8 3/4	4 11/16	8 1/4	+ 3 7/8
Comnet	CNET		...	10270	10 1/2	7 1/2	9 1/2	1/4
ComprsnLab	CLIX		106	177853	11 1/4	3 1/8	9 1/2	+ 6
Comptronix	CMPX		11	78877	5 5/8	2 1/4	2 5/8	...
Compuchem	CCEM		23	119784	16 1/2	9	13 5/8	+ 3
Compucom	BYTE		22	100041	2 5/16	1	1 1/8	– 3/8
Cptr&Com	CCTC		...	94873	3 3/8	5/8	3/4	– 1 3/4
CptrAutomtn	CAUT		...	42281	6 1/4	1 7/8	3 3/8	– 2 1/2
CptrDataSys	CPTD	.12	19	14536	18 3/4	9 1/8	9 3/4	– 8 5/8
CptrHorizn	CHRZ		16	16765	10 1/2	6 3/4	9 1/8	– 1/4
CptrIdnt	CIDN		46	26581	2	3/4	1 3/8	+ 9/16
CptrLang	CLRI	.12	53	8615	6 1/8	3 3/4	4 1/4	– 1 1/2
CptrMemor	CMIN		...	58819	2	1 5/16	1 3/8	– 1/8
CptrPrdts	CPRD		11	219614	3 1/2	2	2 13/16	+ 7/16
Comshare	CSRE		17	25962	41 1/2	20 1/2	35	+ 14 1/4
ComstkRes	CMRE		...	208446	3 5/8	1 1/16	2	+ 1/8
ConceptInc	CCPT		20	200515	14 3/8	10	10 3/4	– 1 3/8
ConcrdCam	LENS		6	63083	9 5/8	3	4	– 5 1/8
ConcCareer	CNCD		9	28662	6 1/8	4 1/4	5 1/4	– 1/4

OVER-THE-COUNTER

Stock	Symbol	Div	Yld	Sales 100s	Hi	Lo	Last	Net Chg
ConcrdCmptg	CEFT		19	27800	20¼	11½	19¼	+ 5½
ConcurCptr	CCUR		...	126245	6½	2⅜	3	− 1½
CondorSvcs	COND		8	34296	8½	3⅝	5¼	...
Cnfertech	CFER		19	24492	2⅝	⅞	1⅞	− 11/16
CngrssStPrp	CSTP		...	3546	7½	4	4¼	− 2⅛
Conmed	CNMD		30	12977	7	4	4¼	...
ConnWtrSvc	CTWS	1.56	14	7747	21½	17¾	20¼	+ 1½
ConrPeriph	CNNR		15	f10110	15½	6½	13⅛	+ 5¼
Consilium	CSIM		26	71093	16⅞	10	15½	...
ConFibr	CFIB		...	3298	7⅞	4¼	4⅜	− 3⅝
ConPaper	CPER	1.20	12	116396	44	34	44	+ 9½
ConPdts	COPI	.16b	9	11081	11¼	7⅜	10⅛	+ 2⅝
ConTomka	CTLC	.34a	186	1641	48	35	41	+ 2½
ConstllBcp	CSTL	1.44	7	68802	37⅝	24	26	− 2¼
ConstnBcpNE	CBNE	.50	7	4176	16¾	8½	8½	− 7¼
ConsulRestr	CNSL		...	128169	2	1⅛	1 5/16	− ⅛
ConsumFnl	CFIN	.12	6	3549	5¾	4⅝	5⅛	+ ⅜
ConsumFnl pf		.85	...	3680	10	7⅝	10	+ 2⅛
ConsumWtr	CONW	1.08	13	17222	20½	14¾	18¼	− 1¾
ContelCellr	CCXLA		263	175896	27¼	11¾	25¼	+ 13¼
ContlGenIns	CGIC	.10	7	4007	9¾	5⅝	8½	+ 2⅞
ContlHlth	CTHL		...	27786	7¾	2¾	2⅞	− 2⅞
ContlHome	CONH		11	16470	9½	3½	8⅜	+ 4⅝
ContlMed	CONT		26	85847	11¾	6¾	11¾	+ 3⅜
ContlMtg	CMETS	.48	...	63629	5¼	2 5/16	3⅛	− 1⅛
ContlSavings	CSAV		...	904	7½	3	4¼	− 2½
CtrlRes	CRIX		...	46821	5⅜	3½	4⅛	− 1⅛
ConvrgSolu	CSOL		15	38950	3 15/16	2⅛	2⅝	− 1 1/16
CookerRestr	COKR		...	117110	5⅛	2½	3¼	...
CooperDev	COOL		...	26828	13¼	2⅛	2⅞	− 8¼
CooperLfSci	ZAPS		...	14610	9⅛	3¼	7¼	− ¼
CoorsAd	ACCOB	.50	21	254762	24⅜	17⅜	19¾	− ¼
Copytele	COPY		...	218190	19½	8¾	13¾	− ⅝
Corcom	CORC		...	18471	5¼	1⅞	2½	− ½
Cordis	CORD		...	247759	17½	10¾	15½	+ 1⅝
CoreStFnl	CSFN	1.92	9	291808	50⅜	38¼	42⅝	+ 2⅛
CornrstnFnl	CSTN	1.00a	21	12957	12¼	8½	10¼	...
CornucpRes	CNPGF		...	33707	2⅜	⅞	1⅝	+ ⅛
CorpCapRes	CCRS		...	813577	2¼	⅛	5/32	− ¾
CorpDataSci	CODS		...	74645	7	4⅛	4¾	− 1¾
CorpSftwr	CSOF		15	91735	16¼	8½	9¾	+ ¼
CorrctnCp	CCAX		92	85452	15¼	7⅜	14¾	+ 7⅛
Cosm&Frag	COSF		21	12996	8⅛	4	6	− ⅝
CosmoCom	CSMO		...	17054	2⅜	1 1/32	1⅛	− 9/16
Costar	CSTR		23	2464	16	13	14½	− ½
CostcoWhol	COST		36	412963	35⅝	15¾	35¼	+ 19⅜
CottnStLf	CSLH	.24	7	4795	9¼	5	7¾	+ 2⅜
CntryLkFd	CLFI		13	23940	14¼	9¼	9¾	− ¼
CntryWdTrn	CWTS		...	18023	3⅜	⅞	⅞	− 2¼
CountyBk	CNBA		...	29523	4⅜	1¾	1⅞	− ⅞
Courier	CRRC	.40	8	5860	22¼	17	19¼	...
CourierDsp	CDGI		16	5666	4⅞	3¼	4½	+ 1¼
CousnProp	COUS	.60a	30	35402	21¼	14¼	16¼	+ ⅞
CovngtnDev	COVT		3	95732	1 11/16	½	15/16	+ 7/16
CrckrBrl	CBRL	.07	22	147636	30	17	28½	+ 11½
Craftmatic	CRCC	.25e	6	24455	6⅜	1⅞	4 13/16	+ 2 11/16
CrayCptr	CRAY		...	93107	8	3⅝	3⅞	...
CrestarFnl	CRFC	1.20	9	189445	34⅛	23½	28¾	+ 4¾
CrestmntS&L	CRES	†	7	80149	14½	6¼	7	− 1⅛
CritcrSys	CXIM		125	34320	3⅞	2	2½	− 1⅜
Critclind	FYBR		15	31786	9⅜	3⅜	3½	− 3⅞
Cronus	CRNS		...	42945	14¾	9	12⅜	+ 2⅞
CropGenInt	CROP		...	23164	10	4½	6½	− 2⅝
CrossTrkr	CTCO		...	200282	16¾	5½	7⅜	− 8⅛
CrwnAndrsn	CRAN		34	8848	7¾	2¾	7½	+ 4¾
CrwnBook	CRWN		10	31527	27¼	14¾	20¾	+ 5
CrwnRes	CRRS		...	99145	8 13/16	2 3/16	7⅜	+ 3¾
CrystlOil pfA	COILP		...	26026	3/32	1/32	1/32	...
CullnFrst	CFBI		32	56582	18⅜	10⅛	11	− 1⅜
Culp	CULP	.08	26	18990	9½	7⅞	8⅞	+ ⅝
CumbrldSv	CMBK	.48	5	36266	20	11⅜	12½	+ ⅝
CupertinoBcp	CUNB		...	186	17	14½	15	...
Cybertek	CKCP		15	19855	5⅞	2¼	4⅜	+ 1⅞
Cytogen	CYTO		...	64694	7⅞	3⅜	5⅞	+ 2½
Cytogen pf			...	912	25½	24¾	25	...

-D-

Stock	Symbol	Div	Yld	Sales 100s	Hi	Lo	Last	Net Chg
D&N Fncl	DNFC	.60	6	36300	15	7¾	8½	− 5¼
DBA Sys	DBAS		27	80961	18¼	6¼	7	− 10
DDI Pharm	DDIX		32	32056	5⅝	2½	3½	+ ½
DEP	DEPC		18	38759	10¼	7¼	8¼	+ ⅛
DF Southeast	DFSE		6	62166	22	10⅛	14⅛	+ 3⅞
DH Tech	DHTK		14	78261	15	5¾	14⅝	+ 9
DNA PltTch	DNAP		...	73708	5½	3¼	5	+ ⅝
DOC Optc	DOCO		22	3778	10¾	5¼	6	− 4¾
DS Bcp	DSBC	1.60a	11	37995	26	18	20¼	− 3
DSC Comm	DIGI		29	995390	17⅛	6¾	14½	+ 6¾
DST Sys	DSTS	.16	29	20523	15	9	11¼	− ½
Dahlberg	DAHL		18	16236	11½	6¾	11	+ 2⅜
DlyJrnl	DJCO		...	1156	15¼	13¾	13¾	− ¼
DairyMrtB	DMCVB	.03j	...	11134	14⅝	7¼	9	...
DairyMrtA	DMCVA	.03j	33	41609	14½	7	8½	− ⅛
DaisySys	DAZX		...	530385	7	7/16	⅝	− 5⅞
DakaInt	DKAI		...	76927	1 1/16	⅜	⅜	− ⅝
DallsSemi	DSMI		15	228512	8⅝	5¾	6⅜	− ⅝
DamonBio	DBIO		...	65581	2 1/16	7/16	¾	− 9/16
DartGp A	DARTA	.13	9	6298	101	85	93	+ 7
DataIO	DAIO	4.15e	12	115064	7¼	3⅛	3½	− 2½
Dataflex	DFLX	†	15	40072	14¼	6	12¾	+ 6⅝
Datakey	DKEY		12	17435	10½	6½	9½	+ 2½
DataMeas	DMCB		...	4495	9⅜	5¾	6½	− 1¼
DataSwtch	DASW		...	149101	6⅛	1⅞	3⅝	− 1⅞
DataTransl	DATX		6	25155	14	4¾	5½	− 3¼
Datamarine	DMAR		25	5613	8¼	6⅛	7	+ ¼
Dataphaz	DPHZ		...	11119	3¾	1⅛	1⅜	− 1 5/16
Datascop	DSCP		18	165130	37¼	25½	33¼	+ ½
Datasouth	DSCC		...	3678	2½	1⅞	2¼	+ ¼
DatrnSys	DTSI		9	10613	13⅛	9½	12¼	+ 1¾
Datum	DATM		11	12999	5⅛	3⅞	4⅝	+ ⅛
DauphnDp	DAPN	1.42	9	35455	37½	28⅜	31½	− ¼
Davox	DAVX		...	27481	5¼	2⅞	4⅞	+ 1
DawsnGeo	DWSN		...	5980	6	4⅝	5¾	+ ¾
DebShop	DEBS	.20	13	107193	17⅝	10⅜	14⅛	+ 2⅞
DecomSys	DSII		6	5068	1⅝	1 1/16	1 1/16	...
DeerfldS&L	DEER	.80a	8	4891	31¼	20½	30	+ 9½
Defiance	DEFI		5	40551	4¼	1⅞	2¼	− ⅜
DeKalbEn B	ENRGB	.20	13	62198	34¼	18¼	31½	+ 12⅛
DeKalbGn B	SEEDB	.45e	18	55431	41	24½	39¼	+ 13¾
DelElec	DELE	†	12	1850	4⅞	3	3¾	− ¼
DelTacoRestr	DETA		...	2363	3¼	1⅜	2⅛	− 1
DelwOstgo	DOCP		21	2418	14	10½	13	+ ¾
Delchmp	DLCH	.40	16	48779	30½	20	27¾	+ 7
DellCptr	DELL		14	208826	10⅝	5	5½	− 4½
DlphiInfo	DLPH		...	34440	8¾	5½	6¾	− 1½
DeltaNG	DGAS	1.08	15	6022	16⅜	13½	14¼	+ ⅛
Deltak	DLTK		9	9890	21	6¾	13¾	+ 6⅜
DentoMed	DTMD		...	52977	2 3/16	13/16	1⅛	+ 5/16
DepostGty	DEPS	1.56	7	12989	33½	25¼	27	− 4½
Designs	DESI		29	32597	6¾	3½	3¾	− 1½
DetectnSys	DETC		10	25380	7	4	6¾	+ 2½
Detrex	DTRX	1.20	12	4887	31	19	20½	− 6⅝
DevcnInt	DEVC		8	22798	27½	10¾	23	+ 11
DevonGrp	DEVN		11	35370	19	11¾	15¼	+ 3
Diagnstek	DXTK		53	229117	15⅜	4 7/16	15¼	+ 9⅝
DialREIT	DEAL	1.68	26	40215	20	15¾	16¼	− 1½
DibrellBros	DBRL	.68	9	25035	28½	16½	22¾	+ 5
DiceonElec	DICN		...	37965	13	4¾	6⅛	− 6⅜
DickClarkP	DCPI		21	15394	8¼	3⅝	6¾	+ 2¾
Digi Int	DGII		10	28339	11¾	9	9¾	...
DigitlMcrw	DMIC		27	382571	34¼	19⅝	30	+ 6
DimeFnl	DIBK	.80	8	35591	14¼	9¾	10½	− 1⅞
Dionex	DNEX		20	105754	27½	17	26¾	+ 1½
DistLogic	DLOG		...	15135	3¼	1⅛	1 7/16	− 15/16
Diversco	DVRS		9	26176	8¾	4¾	5	− 1¼
DiversInv	DING		27	20038	15⅝	9	10¾	− 3⅞
DixieYarn	DXYN	.68	11	52103	22½	14	15¼	− 3⅝
DlrGen	DOLR	.20	18	170684	12¾	8⅝	10⅜	+ 1⅜
DomngzWatr	DOMZ	.92	11	1136	15¼	13¾	15	+ ¼
DominBksh	DMBK	.88	8	246583	26⅛	16¼	19⅛	+ 2⅞
DonegalGp	DGIC	.20	9	2454	9¼	5½	9⅛	+ 2⅜
DorchHugtn	DHULZ	.20	40	31768	12	6⅝	10¾	+ 3⅝
Doskocil	DOSK		...	38265	14⅛	5⅛	6⅝	− ¾
Dotronix	DOTX		...	21689	4½	2	2⅛	− 1⅞
DougLomsn	DOUG	.50j	...	4742	22	11¾	11¾	− 7¾
DressBrn	DBRN		14	299516	17⅜	10¾	11¼	− 4
DrewInd	DREW		...	61032	4¾	1¾	1 13/16	− 1
DrexlrTech	DRXR		22	182198	16¼	3¼	6⅝	+ 3⅛
DreyrlcCrm	DRYR		17	109594	34	18	27¾	+ 4¼

Stock	Symbol	Div	Yld	Sales 100s	Hi	Lo	Last	Net Chg
DrgEmporm	DEMP	.05e	12	175018	16¼	7¾	8¼	+ ⅛
DunkDonut	DUNK	.40	29	242405	48	26½	46⅞	+ 20
DuraknInd	DRKN		16	27377	9¾	6	6½	− ½
DuramedPh	DRMD		22	124623	9	2⅜	3⅞	+ ⅛
Duratek	DRTK		22	8568	3⅛	1¾	2⅜	− ¼
DurhamCp	DUCO	.92	30	12011	34¾	29	31	− 2
Duriron	DURI	.46	11	154663	20½	12⅝	17⅛	+ 2⅛
DurrFilMed	DUFM	.24	15	140038	24⅜	18	23¾	+ 5⅜
DutyFreeInt	DFII		28	73610	32¼	11½	27¼	...
Dyansen	DYAN		11	116967	5¼	1 11/16	2¾	+ 11/16
DycomInd	DYCO		15	107221	25	12	17¾	− 2¾
DynRsearch	DRCO		8	17314	9	4½	5¾	− 1
Dynascan	DYNA		8	66221	11⅝	7⅞	7⅞	− 2
DynatechCp	DYTC		14	106674	20½	16⅜	16¾	− 1¼

-E-

Stock	Symbol	Div	Yld	Sales 100s	Hi	Lo	Last	Net Chg
EA Engrg	EACO		22	17187	11	5¾	10¼	+ 4½
E&B Marine	EBMI		...	21224	4	1⅞	2 1/16	− 3/16
ECI Telcm	ECILF		16	53831	13¾	4½	13¾	+ 8⅞
EFI Elec	EFIC		14	50270	8⅝	4 1/32	5⅝	+ 1 19/32
EIP Micrw	EIPM	.12	13	3879	5½	3¼	4½	− ½
ELXSI Cp	ELXS		...	303539	5/16	1/32	3/16	+ 1/16
EMC Insur	EMCI	.52	8	16331	9½	7	8	+ ¼
EMCON	MCON		16	38249	19⅛	10	13¼	+ 3⅛
Empi	EMPI		22	14547	6	2	5	+ 3
ERCEnvSvc	ERCE		16	65312	12¼	7	10¾	+ 3⅝
ESELCO	EDSE	1.44b	12	404	25¼	22	25	+ 2½
EssefCp	ESSF		...	26696	12¼	7¾	8½	− ¼
ETown	EWAT	2.96	19	3583	43	35¾	40½	+ ½
EZEM Inc	EZEM		12	16773	14	9¾	12½	− ¼
EaglBcp	EBCI	.28	13	2334	18	12	17½	+ 3½
EaglBcshr	EBSI		39	9811	13¾	6¾	7¾	− 5¾
EaglFood	EGLE		...	87124	21	14	17½	...
EarthTech	ETCO		40	31906	7¼	4 3/16	7⅛	+ 2
EascoTool	TOOL		...	65961	9⅞	6⅜	6⅞	− 1⅝
EastchFnl	ECFC	.30e	...	88066	15⅜	10¾	11¼	...
EastcoSafe	ESTO		8	67717	6⅛	1⅝	2¼	− 1½
EastBcp	VFBK	.44	6	21192	14	7¾	8½	− 3¾
EastEnvr	EESI		15	32009	5⅛	3¼	3¾	− 1¼
EastxEngy	ETEX		...	18826	3⅝	1½	2	− ¼
EastldFnl	EAFC	.40e	...	81787	11⅞	4⅜	5¼	− 3¼
EastovrCp	EASTS	1.36	...	2784	15¼	11	12½	− 2½
EatonVance	EAVN	.44	14	8217	28¼	22	27¼	+ 4¾
Ecogen	EECN		...	54071	5¾	3¼	3⅝	− ½
EdisnCtrl	EDCO		...	11641	3	1⅛	2⅝	− ⅛
Egghead	EGGS		...	272328	14¼	9	11¼	− ¼
ElChico	ELCH		56	23795	4½	2⅞	3⅜	+ ½
ElPasoElec	ELPA	.38j	...	388362	15⅜	6½	8½	− 6⅛
ElanCp	ELANY		54	260423	16⅝	9¾	13½	+ 3⅜
ElbitCptr g	ELBTF	.19e	11	12670	9⅞	5⅛	9	+ 3¾
ElcoInd	ELCN	.52	9	11813	17¾	13	15	...
Elcotel	ECTL		...	49083	4⅞	2¼	3⅞	+ 1⅛
Eldec	ELDC	1.00e	5	18403	16¼	9⅜	10¼	+ ⅞
ElectData	EDAT		15	36293	11⅞	7⅛	9⅜	+ ¾
ElectroRent	ELRC		9	22543	20½	13¼	15	+ 1½
ElectroSci	ESIO		5	81467	14½	7	7¼	− 2¼
ElectroSensr	ELSE	.10	9	1680	3⅞	2½	2¾	− ½
Electrolux	ELUXY	1.47e	8	35233	59⅜	36⅞	45¾	− 1½
ElectrmgSc	ELMG		14	80062	8¼	6	6¼	− 1¾
ElectrArts	ERTS		...	46382	9⅜	7	9⅛	...
ElecTelComm	ETCIA	.10	...	3469	6	3½	6	+ 2¼
EliotSvg	EBKC	.24j	...	41989	9¾	1⅛	2	− 7⅛
ElmwdSvg	EFSB	.16e	...	14321	16¼	10¾	15¼	+ 3⅛
ElronElec	ELRNF		...	19323	7¾	3 3/16	7	+ 3⅜
Empire-Orr	EORR		...	13497	⅝	1/16	5/32	− 13/32
EmpireSvgNJ	EMPR		5	1370	10½	6	6	− 1¼
EmplyrCas	ECRC	.60	...	60671	27¾	10½	13⅞	− 12⅝
EmployeBen	EBPI		...	57331	18¾	12½	17¾	...
Emulex	EMLX		7	195218	12⅜	5⅜	6⅜	− 4⅝
EnClean	ENCL		28	32025	11½	6¾	11	...
EncoreCptr	ENCC		...	149636	3⅞	2	2 5/16	+ ¼
EngyNorth	ENNI	1.00	13	8407	19	13⅝	19	+ 4¾
EnexRes	ENEX		...	5289	3⅝	1⅞	2¼	− ½
EngrSupprt	EASI		9	15718	6¼	3⅛	3¾	− ¾
EngrgMeas	EMCO		31	6084	4⅛	1 7/16	1 9/16	− 3/16
EnglChina	ECLAY	1.04e	10	32928	28	17¾	21¾	− 2¾
Engraph	ENGH	.13	18	29881	14¼	8	11	+ 2¼
Enstar	ENST	.08	...	966080	9⅛	2¾	3	− 4½
Entroncs	ENTC		97	36942	5⅝	1⅜	3⅞	+ 1¾
EnvrCtrls	ECGI		60	39088	13¾	5¼	6	− 7¼
EnvrPwr	POWR		...	25616	2½	⅛	⅜	− 1½
EnvrTectncs	ENVT		10	5951	5¼	2¾	2⅞	+ ⅛
Envrosafe	ENVI		21	21462	18⅛	11½	14¼	+ 2½
Envrsource	ENSO		...	82566	14⅛	6¾	11⅝	+ 3⅞
Enzon	ENZN		...	45593	5⅞	3⅛	3¾	− ⅛
EpsilnData	EPSI		...	8487	11½	6¼	7½	− 2¼
EqtblBcp	EBNC	1.04	11	58903	39¼	20	30¾	+ 10¼
EqtblIowa B	EQICB	1.08	9	14346	36¼	22	31¼	+ 9¼
Equitex	EQTX		...	f14572	7/32	1/16	1/16	− 3/32
EqityOil	EQTY	.05e	66	59048	5½	3½	5¼	+ 1
EricsnTel	ERICY	1.33e	...	89637	144	58⅝	143⅝	+ 84½
ErieLkwna	ERIE		9	887	55	43	53	+ 9
ErlyInd	ERLY	†	306	31751	9¾	4 1/16	6⅛	+ 1½
Escalade	ESCA	†	10	16050	13	7½	8⅝	+ ½
EssexCp	ESEX		12	2357	3⅞	2½	3⅛	− ⅛
EssexGas	ECGC	1.32	10	1700	18¾	16¾	18	+ ¼
EvanSuthrld	ESCC		46	94215	25¼	14¾	24⅛	+ 7⅝
EvansInc	EVAN		...	41874	6¼	3⅜	3¾	− 1¾
EvansvlSvg	EVSB		...	1336	8¼	5¼	7¾	+ 2½
EverxSys	EVRX		8	412417	13⅜	5⅞	7¾	+ 1⅝
EvergrnBcp	EVGN	.60	8	5790	21¼	14¼	17	+ 2
Exabyte	EXBT		...	69286	13⅛	10⅛	11⅜	...
ExarCp	EXAR		8	9108	8½	5½	7⅝	+ 2⅛
ExcelBcp	XCEL	.68	8	60954	13	6⅝	7⅝	− 2
ExchBcp	EXCG	.16	14	50434	23¾	13¼	23¾	+ 9¾
EXECUTONE	XTON		63	299982	5⅛	2½	3¾	+ ¾
ExideElec	XUPS		...	8381	12¾	12⅜	12⅝	...
Expeditor	EXPD		17	63089	28½	15⅝	26¼	+ 10½
ExplorLA	XCOL		...	60315	4 7/16	1 17/32	4⅛	+ 2 13/32

-F-

Stock	Symbol	Div	Yld	Sales 100s	Hi	Lo	Last	Net Chg
F&M Fnl	FMFS	.44	11	3419	20½	14¼	19	+ 4⅜
F&M Ntl	FMNT	.50a	11	4965	15¾	13	14½	+ ¾
FBX	FBXC		...	20721	2⅛	½	9/16	− 13/32
FDP	FDPC		59	8046	5½	4⅛	4⅛	− ⅛
FFO Fnl	FFFG		...	24794	10⅛	6⅛	8⅝	+ 2⅛
FHP Int	FHPC		10	313968	26⅜	5⅞	20¾	+ 14¾
FLS Hldg pf			...	11757	45	37¾	38½	− 3½
FMS Fnl	FMCO		...	17991	12¼	7⅞	9	+ ¾
FNB Rochstr	FNBR	.22r	5	3145	8½	6	6½	+ ½
FNW Bcp	FNWB	.40	13	8933	26	18¼	23¾	+ 4¾
FRP Prop	FRPP		45	7445	17½	11½	14½	+ 2
FSI Int	FSII		5	30170	8½	5½	7	...
FabrcInd	FBRC	.16	16	26015	16	9	16	+ 6⅝
FairIsaac	FICI	.10	19	13515	9	5	6½	...
FrfldCntyBcp	FCBK	.40	7	6342	12¼	4	4¾	− 7
FairfldBk	FRBK	†	...	1933	8⅝	5¾	5¾	− 1
FairfldNbl	FARFE		3	10982	4⅞	1	1 13/32	− 2 19/32
FalcnOil	FLOG		12	3168	3⅜	2⅜	2⅞	...
FamilyBcp	FMLY	.50	7	30214	11½	7	7¾	− 1½
FamStkHse	RYFL		18	46360	3⅛	1⅞	2⅛	...
FamousRestr	FAMS		...	36869	2½	1	1⅞	+ ⅞
FaradynElec	FARA		...	27927	10⅛	3½	6¾	+ 3¼
FarmHmFnl	FAHS	.51j	...	56609	20¼	12¼	13	− 5⅞
FarmHmFnl pf	FAHSP	3.25	...	15383	23½	17¼	22½	...
FarmerBros	FARM	1.20	11	1820	93	64	93	+ 29
Farr	FARC	.30	11	5145	14¼	8¾	9½	− ½
Fastenal	FAST		36	39579	31	18½	30	+ 11
FedlSvg	TFSB	†	...	1003	9	5	6½	− 1⅛
FedlScrw	FSCR	.40a	4	4714	19½	9	12	+ 1¼
FedS&LWis	FEDF	.36	...	9373	10¾	8	8	− 2
Ferofluid	FERO		...	121799	21¼	10¾	14	+ 1
Fibronics	FBRX		18	61564	7⅜	3¾	6	+ 2
FidltyS&LTN	FFTN	.60	10	32627	25¾	18¾	19¾	− ¼
FideltySvVa	FFRV		...	619	10	7½	8¾	...
FidltySvgIN	FFMA		...	8085	19½	12	15½	− 1¼
FidltySvg	FSVA	.24	6	3609	9¾	6½	8½	+ 2
FfthThrd	FITB	1.44	13	40220	59¾	44½	55½	+ 10¼
FftyOffStrs	FOFF		9	24567	6⅝	1¾	4½	+ 2½
Figgie B	FIGI	1.20	9	2842	96	75½	80	− 11
Figgie A	FIGIA	1.20	...	36960	82½	62½	65	− 9
Filenet	FILE		138	57029	13¾	7½	11	+ 2¾
FnlNewsNet	FNNI		40	243437	10½	6⅛	6⅞	− 1¼
FnlTrst	FITC	1.36	11	1654	38¾	28	36½	+ 7½
Fingrmtrx	FINX		...	105665	3 11/16	2 1/16	2⅞	+ ⅜
Finnigan	FNNG		156	65744	20⅛	12½	14	− 2
FstAlaBksh	FABC	.84	9	125265	19⅜	15⅛	17⅜	+ 2
FstAlbny	FACT		40	6040	7¼	4¾	4¾	− ⅜
FstAmrilo	FAMA		10	3585	5½	2⅞	4¼	− ½

OVER-THE-COUNTER

Stock	Symbol	Div	Yld	Sales 100s	Hi	Lo	Last	Net Chg
FstAmBkCp	FABK	2.20	7	86946	56	38¼	47	+ 3¼
FstAmBkCp pf		7.20	...	1774	87½	74	75	− 6
FstAmBkCp pfE		1.90	...	4891	21½	19	19¼	− 1¾
FstAmBkFL A	FIAMA		...	86023	4	1/16	3/16	− 3 1/16
FstAmBcp	FAMB	.30j	...	200482	8	1	1 3/16	− 5 11/16
FstAmFed	FAMF	.80	7	7737	16½	11¼	12½	− ¾
FstAmFnl A	FAMRA	.40	20	15317	17½	11½	12½	− 2¼
FstAmFnl B	FAMRB		...	1516	13¼	10½	11½	...
FstAmCp	FATN	1.25	26	113125	26⅛	19⅝	20¾	− 1⅜
FstAmSvOH	FASB		3	16960	6⅞	4⅛	6⅛	+ 2
FstBcpNC	FBNC	.22b	9	3874	15⅞	11½	13½	+ 2
FstBcpOh	FBOH	1.50	9	22744	34⅝	26½	29½	+ 1⅝
FstCapCp	FCAP	1.00	7	7370	24	20	20½	− 2⅞
FstChrtr	FCTR	.36	13	2725	12	9½	10¼	− 1½
FstChatga	FCHT	.32	10	15625	23	17¾	18¾	...
FstCtzBk A	FCNCA	.40	9	2661	30½	26	26	− 4
FstCtzBk B	FCNCB	.40	18	477	53	45	47½	− 2½
FstCtzFnl	FCIT		...	8346	11¾	7¼	8½	− ⅛
FstCityBcpTN	CITY		...	1862	11	9¼	9½	...
FstColonl	FCOLA	.40	13	18158	19	12	18	+ 5¼
FstCmrclBcp	FCOB	.20e	10	37407	12⅛	6¼	10⅛	+ 3⅜
FstComrclBk	FSCB	.64	11	2506	22¾	20¼	20¾	− ¼
FstCmmrc	FCOM	1.20	11	19323	23⅞	17⅝	23¼	+ 5
FstCmmclCp	FCLR	.64	10	8112	21¼	15⅝	19¾	+ 3½
FstCmuntyBcp	FRFD	.56	10	5907	19¼	15⅞	18⅛	+ 1⅜
FstCnstlFnl	FCON	.45	57	132735	21⅞	13½	17	+ 1
FstContlREIT	FCRES		...	14093	1	⅛	¼	− ⅜
FstEastrn	FEBC	1.12	10	24040	36	26¾	30¾	...
FstEsxBcp	FESX	.32	7	76095	9⅛	5½	5⅝	− 1⅝
FstExec	FEXC	†	57	f16796	17⅛	7⅞	9¾	− 4
FstExec pfE		2.20e	...	44453	20½	10⅛	13½	− 4¾
FstExec pfF		2.88	...	38491	25¾	21	22¼	− 1⅝
FstExec pfG		1.56	...	188092	20⅞	11⅞	14½	− 2½
FstExecCp pf			...	283203	16	11¾	13⅜	...
FstExec wt			...	25788	5½	⅜	1	− 1¾
FstExecCp wt wi			...	413891	1 7/16	⅜	9/16	...
FstFamly	FFAM		25	8294	1¾	¾	1	− ½
FstFedCap	FTFC		...	22519	14½	11¾	12⅜	...
FstFedFinl	FFSW	.40	10	5453	18	13⅜	17	+ 2¾
FstFedGA	FSBG		38	2667	12	4¾	6¾	− 4¾
FstFedMich	FFOM	.60	31	144821	22	13⅝	14⅝	− ⅝
FstFedAla	FFAL	.20	...	2461	8¾	4¼	6¾	− 1½
FstFedCharl	FSCC	.28a	...	15434	13⅜	9	12½	+ 2⅜
FstFedHartfd	FFES	.20	9	7628	9¼	5½	6¾	− 1¼
FstFedElz	FFKY	1.00e	12	563	33	21	31½	+ 10½
FstFedFtMyr	FFMY	.60	12	13483	28¼	18½	21½	+ 1¼
FstFedLaGr	FLAG	.56	...	4846	14¾	10½	12	+ 1
FstFedLnwee	LFSA	.44	...	13793	16½	13	14¼	+ ¾
FstFedSvUT	FFUT		...	17551	8	3⅞	7⅛	+ 3¼
FstFedSC	FTSC		9	44442	9⅝	5	5⅞	...
FstFedWPa	FFWP	.30	...	8384	16	7½	15	+ 7½
FstFdltyWVa	FFWV	.48a	...	1884	11	9	9¾	+ ½
FstFedDcatr	FFSD	.50e	10	5834	20	11½	12½	− 5⅛
FstFedMont	FFSM	.32a	7	3400	9	5¼	9	+ 3½
FstFedPerry	FPRY		...	1182	9¾	7¼	9	+ 1½
FstFedPR	FFPR	.52	4	27876	11⅞	8⅜	9½	+ ⅝
FstFnlBcp	FFBC	1.20a	16	2322	50	34½	47	+ 12½
FstFnlCarib	FRCC	.20e	...	10324	14¼	7	7	− 6¼
FstFnlCp	FFHC	.64b	6	36446	20½	12⅝	16	+ 3⅜
FstFnlHldg	FFCH	.48	7	18520	16¾	11	12¼	− ⅝
FstFnlMgt	FFMC	.10b	15	364371	39	24½	32¼	+ 5
FstFnlSvgPA	FIRF	.24	8	6186	15¾	9¾	12¼	+ 2¼
FstFlaBk	FFBK	.96	9	49184	34¼	24¾	28½	+ 1½
FstFrnklin	FFHS	.50	...	1058	14¼	9⅜	13⅛	+ 3⅛
FstGaHldg	FGHC		...	1837	7	4¼	5¾	+ ½
FstGldnBcp	FGBC		...	384	10¾	6	7	− 2¾
FstHarisbrg	FFHP	.32b	...	1931	13¾	8⅝	13⅜	+ 4⅜
FstHawiin	FHWN	1.60	13	31712	53½	29¾	50½	+ 20¼
FstHomFed	FSEB	.24	10	9958	15	9¾	12½	+ 3
FstHomeSvg	FSPG	.28	5	5570	11½	8	9½	+ ⅞
FstIllinois	FTIL	.44	10	195726	11	6¾	10	+ 3⅛
FstIndiana	FISB	.28	8	12579	18¼	11¼	13⅝	− ⅜
FstIntrBcp	FIBI	.40	...	1874	14½	9	9¾	− 3¾
FstIntstWisc	FIWI	.72	94	26594	24	14½	22½	+ 7½
FstIntstIowa	FIIA	.20	5	64467	6 11/16	4 3/16	5¾	+ 1 9/16
FstLibFnl	FLFC		...	12041	12½	5¼	8	− 3¼
FstMerchnt	FRME	1.00	10	1564	25½	23½	24½	...
FstMichBk	FMBC	.72	10	13771	26½	20	25¼	+ 4¼
FstMdwstBcp	FMBI	.48	14	19636	25	16¼	22⅞	+ 6¼
FstMissGld	FRMG		38	68699	12⅝	8½	11½	+ 1¼
FstMutlSvg	FMSB	.20	9	10360	11⅞	9½	10¼	− 1¼
FstNtlBcpGA	FBAC	.64	10	5823	27	21½	22½	− 2
FstNtlBkMI	MTCL	.80b	...	1452	22½	19	20¾	− ¾
FstNtlPA	FNPC	1.00t	...	7010	34½	18	23½	− 2½
FstNYBusn	FNYB		11	11965	13½	7¾	8	− 5
FstNthnSvg	FNGB	.64	8	5234	17¾	14	14⅜	− ⅞
FstOakBrk	FOBBA	.60a	12	2577	26	22½	24	+ 1¼
FstOhioBcsh	FIRO	1.12a	22	8512	39½	24½	38¾	+ 13
FstPeopFnl	FPNJ		10	19307	44¼	28	37½	+ 9
FstSvgBcp	FFNS	.68	7	1437	20½	12¼	17½	+ 4¼
FstSvgBk	FSBC		...	2709	10⅜	6¾	6¾	− ¼
FstSecUT	FSCO	1.28	10	38350	34¼	24¾	32¼	+ 7½
FstSecFnl	FSFC	.32b	...	4186	18	13⅝	18	+ 1
FstSecKY	FSKY	.44	10	6739	19¼	15	18½	+ 3¼
FstSource	SRCE	.48	8	7416	26¼	16¾	23¼	+ 5¾
FstStFnl	FSFI		8	19113	7¾	3¾	3⅞	− 1⅞
FstTennNtl	FTEN	1.60	13	98696	29¾	23⅜	24⅞	+ ⅜
FstUtdBcsh	UNTD	1.00	13	2433	27½	24½	27¼	+ 2¾
FstWstBcp	FWBI	1.00	8	593	27	22½	23⅝	...
FstWestFnl	FWES	.36	5	51386	9¾	4⅞	5¼	− 1
FstWobrnBcp	WOBS	.20j	...	22976	8¾	1⅜	2½	− 4⅞
FstWldChees	FWCH		26	297809	21	8¼	10¾	+ 2⅛
FstbkIll	FBIC	.72	10	5847	20½	17	19½	+ 2¼
FirsTierFnl	FRST	1.20	8	5498	51½	38	43	+ 4¾
Fiserv	FISV		17	63943	24¾	17⅞	21¾	+ 2⅞
FlaglrBk	FLGLA	.31r	10	3682	11½	8⅞	10	+ 1
FlagshpFnl	FLGF	.40	6	35951	20⅛	12	13	+ ¾
Flamemastr	FAME	.08	26	7029	7¼	4⅜	4⅝	− 2⅛
FleetAero	FLAI		...	4050	6½	1⅞	2	...
Flexstl	FLXS	.48	12	22243	15½	11	12½	+ ½
Flextrnic	FLEX		...	71361	3⅞	⅝	⅞	− 2⅝
FlightInt	FLTIE		2	130573	14½	⅞	1¾	− 11¼
FlaEmplIns	FLAEF	.20	7	9568	13	10	12½	+ 2
FlaFedS&L	FLFE		...	69348	2⅞	5/16	7/16	− 1 11/16
FlaFstSvgs	FFPC		...	13852	4¼	1¾	2⅛	− ⅝
FlaNtlBks	FNBF	.52	...	355112	26⅛	15⅞	25⅞	+ 9½
FlaPubUtils	FPUT	.96	14	832	24½	21¼	23½	+ 1½
FlowInt	FLOW		14	88027	4⅜	2¾	3⅝	...
FlowMole	MOLE		26	55648	10⅛	3½	9⅜	+ 5¼
Flurcarbn	FCBN	.20	12	96833	16½	11⅞	14⅛	+ ¾
FoodLion A	FDLNA	.10	27	333183	12½	9	10⅞	+ 1½
FoodLion B	FDLNB	.10	28	204071	13⅝	9⅝	11¼	+ 1¼
FoothillBcp	FOOT	.16	...	5704	11¼	6¼	8⅞	...
FormstAm	FCOA	1.08	16	70885	39	31¾	35	− 1¾
ForestOil	FOIL	†	...	87762	17⅛	10⅜	14⅝	+ 3¾
ForschnrGp	FSNR		17	39363	14½	5	11¼	+ 4⅛
FtWaynNtl	FWNC	.88	10	10954	25¼	20½	23½	+ 2½
FortnFnl	FORF	.30	89	39973	25¾	16¼	17¾	− 8
ForumGp	FOUR	.06	...	177294	3 1/16	1¼	1⅝	− 13/16
FosterLB	FSTRA		11	77894	6⅝	3⅜	4	− 2½
FourthFnl	FRTH	1.08	13	13977	31¼	22	31¼	+ 8½
FramghmSv	FSBX	.30j	...	53181	10⅜	3⅞	4⅛	− 5¼
Frankfrd	FKFD	1.32	9	2930	23½	19¾	20½	− 2½
FklinCptr	FDOS		8	49709	15½	4¾	6	− 5¾
FklinElec	FELE	.64a	2	13676	9¾	7¾	8½	− ⅝
FrnklnFstFbl	FFFC	.52	8	42882	14¾	9	10⅞	+ 1¼
FklinSvgKS	FSAK	.69r	...	3258	11½	5¼	5¾	− 4¼
FranklnSvg	FSVB		27	5034	8¾	6½	6¾	− ¼
FremontGen	FRMT	.80	24	92469	20⅝	12⅛	20½	+ 7⅛
Fretter	FTTR		24	54857	6⅜	2⅞	3⅜	− 1¼
FreymlrTrk	FRML		11	9829	7¼	4⅝	6¼	+ ¾
FrontrIns	FRTR	†	9	20815	21¾	11⅛	18¼	+ 7
FullrHB	FULL	.58	14	97770	34¼	20¾	22¼	− 4¾
FultnSvgGA	FFSB		...	35632	5⅜	⅜	½	− 3¼
FultnFnl	FULT	.80b	10	16965	25	18⅛	22½	+ 3⅞
-G-								
G&KSvc	GKSRA	.10	21	27206	15	10	13½	+ 2½
GBC Bcp	GBCB	.32e	11	24055	24½	12¾	20¾	+ 7¾
GNI Gp	GNUC		309	21878	7½	2½	6 3/16	+ 3 7/16
GNW Fnl	GNWF	.10e	8	23601	18½	8¾	14	+ 5¼
GIIIApparel	GIII		...	15867	14¼	13	14	...
GV Med	GVMI		...	124051	14	5	5½	− 7⅝
GWC Cp	GWCC	1.44	12	13929	20¼	16¾	19¾	+ 2¼
GZAGeoEnvr	GZEA		18	36548	14½	9	13¾	...
GalileoElec	GAEO		22	44519	10⅛	6¼	7¼	− 2¼
GamaBio	GAMA		...	75659	7⅛	2½	2⅝	− 4⅛
Gandalf g	GANDF		14	47047	6⅝	3⅞	5	− ⅜

Stock	Symbol	Div	Yld	Sales 100s	Hi	Lo	Last	Net Chg
GanderMtn	GNDR		19	22109	11¼	6½	8⅜	– 1⅛
Gantos	GTOS		17	77009	32	12¼	24	+ 11¼
GarnetRes	GARN		...	29373	11⅝	3¼	10⅞	+ 7⅜
GatewyBcp	GBAN	.30r	10	4240	19½	14	15½	– ⅛
GatewyCom	GWAY		12	64926	2⅞	1⅝	2⅛	+ ¼
GatewyS&L	GATW		6	7571	14½	10	11¼	– 2
GatewyFnl	GTWY	.64	7	96349	15⅜	7	9¼	– 3½
GehlCo	GEHL		...	23422	14¾	13¼	14	...
Gencor	GCOR		...	9076	7⅜	2⅜	2⅞	– 1⅞
Gendx	XRAY		22	15095	12¼	6⅜	12¼	+ 4½
GenBindg	GBND	.28	20	41830	30¼	17⅝	26¼	+ 7
GenBldgPdt	GBLD		...	7670	5	1¼	1⅝	– 1⅜
GenCptr	GCCC		...	5649	5½	3½	4⅛	...
GenMagna	GMCC	.04	14	6823	8¼	4	6¼	+ 13/16
GenParmetrc	GPAR	.06e	11	50411	5⅜	3¼	4¼	+ ¼
GenetInst	GENI		...	233313	34½	16¾	34⅛	+ 17⅜
GenetInst pf			...	15396	56¼	48	56¼	...
Genex	GNEX		...	105498	9/16	9/32	11/32	– 1/32
Genex pf	GNEXP		...	1245	15½	9½	11	– ½
Genicom	GECM		...	32055	5	⅞	1	– 3⅞
Genlyte	GLYT		12	137290	13¾	8	10½	+ 1¾
Gentex	GNTX		47	119947	14⅝	4½	12¾	+ 7⅝
Genus Inc.	GGNS		10	309557	14	6¼	7⅞	+ 1
Genzyme	GENZ		...	152275	15½	7½	14½	+ 6¼
Geodynamic	GDYN	.25	8	21300	14½	9¾	10	+ ¼
GeodynRes	GEOD		7	37655	4 1/16	2⅛	2 11/16	+ ¼
Geonex	GEOX		17	12130	9	4⅞	6¾	+ 1⅞
GaBndFibr	GBFH	.10e	625	2526	5¾	3¾	5¼	+ 1¼
GeratyMlr	GMGW		33	80564	15¼	9¾	14¼	+ 3½
GeriatrMed	GEMC		...	23160	2 9/16	1¼	1½	+ ⅛
Germania	GMFD		...	9359	4⅛	⅞	1⅜	– 1 9/16
GermtnSvg	GSBK		8	52421	15¼	9⅝	11¼	+ 1½
GiantBay g	GBYLF		...	12202	11/16	5/32	⅜	+ 1/16
GibsnGreet	GIBG	.34	11	295237	28¾	21	25⅞	+ 4½
GiddLewis	GIDL	.16	...	161577	18	14	16⅝	...
GigaTrnc	GIGA		8	10930	9	6½	6¾	– 2¼
GilbtAssc A	GILBA	.80	14	35064	29¾	20	23	+ 2¾
GishBioMed	GISH		13	38917	9	5⅜	7½	+ 1½
GlamisGld	GLGVF		...	65886	2¾	⅞	2 3/16	+ ¼
GlendaleBcp	GNBC		...	1839	8¾	7	7	– 1¾
GlenexInd	GLXIF		2	54293	3⅜	1¼	1½	– 13/16
GoalSys	GOAL		...	94140	15½	9¾	15½	...
GldnCorral	GCRA	1.00	8	5165	9¼	7	7¼	– 1
GoldenEnt	GLDC	.36	25	19878	11⅜	8¾	8⅞	– ¾
GldnPoultry	CHIK	.04	8	48874	12¾	6¾	7½	...
Goldtex	GLTX		18	3925	4⅝	3¾	4	...
GoodGuys	GGUY		13	36105	13⅜	8¼	12⅛	+ 2
GdhrtWlcx	GWOX	.70	...	284	31	27	27⅜	+ ⅜
GdMrkFood	GDMK		17	29831	20	12⅛	16¼	+ 3⅛
GoodyPdt	GOOD	.20	...	22825	19	9¼	9¼	– 7⅜
GouldPmp	GULD	.76	14	243136	24⅝	16½	17⅞	– 1
GradcoSys	GRCO		14	311627	19½	10	11	– 2¼
GranCoopBk	GNTE	.30j	...	1407	11	4¼	4¼	– 5¾
GranStBksh	GSBI	.36	6	9199	8¾	5¼	5¼	– 1¾
GraphInd	GRPH	.07	14	36027	13¼	6⅜	6⅞	– 6⅛
GraphScan	GSCC		...	384672	12	6⅜	10⅜	+ 3⅞
GtAmComm	GACC	.02e	...	328190	13⅜	8¾	9	– ⅛
GtAmRecr	GRAR		...	122709	¼	1/16	1/16	– 3/32
GtBayBksh	GBBS	.56e	7	25685	13	9¼	9¾	...
GtCountryBk	GCBK	.78j	...	24898	19¾	8	8½	– 10½
GtFallsGas	GFGC	.50	8	6362	10¼	6⅛	10⅛	+ 3¾
GtLksBcp	GLBC	.80	5	39170	24½	14¼	17	– 1¼
GtSoBcp	GSBC		...	4562	9¼	8¾	8¾	...
GtrNYSvg	GRTR	.48	6	251308	13¼	7⅞	9	+ ¾
GreenAp	APGI	.40	10	37839	40	25¼	33	+ 6¾
GrnRehab	GRGI		16	94735	11⅜	5¾	10⅞	+ 2¼
GreenwFnl	GFCT	.28	8	16343	9⅞	6½	6⅞	– ⅜
GreenwPhar	GRPI		...	320005	8⅝	3½	4¼	– ⅝
GrenadaSun	GSSC	.60	17	11362	16¼	11	12¼	– 1¼
GreyAdv	GREY	2.80	15	2493	174	112	170	+ 52
GriffnTech	GRIF		22	5714	7	3	6¾	+ 3¼
GristMill	GRST		16	124006	16⅜	6⅝	10⅛	+ 2¼
Grossman	GROS		8	590959	9¾	4¼	5	– ⅝
GroveBk	GROV	.36	7	6863	11½	8¾	8¾	– 2¼
GrndwtrTech	GWTI		17	163752	30¼	18¼	20	– 6¼
GroupI	GSOF		12	4343	9¼	6½	8	– 1
GrubElRlty	GRIT	.72a	14	12445	7⅜	5¾	6½	+ ⅛
Gtech	GTCH		37	192901	16½	9⅝	16¼	+ 6½
GuestSply	GEST		...	69891	10⅜	4	7¼	+ 2¾
GulfAppld	GATS		22	11014	17	6	15¼	+ 9¼
GullLabs	GULL		...	8096	2½	1⅜	1 15/16	– 9/16

-H-

Stock	Symbol	Div	Yld	Sales 100s	Hi	Lo	Last	Net Chg
HHOilTool	HHOT		...	3347	5½	3⅞	5⅜	+ 1¼
HBO&Co	HBOC	.30	17	264232	16½	9⅜	14⅞	+ 3¾
HDR Pwr	HDRP		8	16211	6½	2	3⅛	– 1⅞
HEI Cp	HEIC		13	16927	3½	1	2⅝	+ 1 19/32
HEI Inc	HEII		...	9297	4⅜	1	1⅝	– 2¼
HMO Amer	HMOA		...	233031	10⅝	15/16	7⅝	+ 6 11/16
HPSC	HPSC		...	54798	50	4½	7½	+ 1
Hach	HACH	.20	24	849	33½	14½	31	+ 14
Hadco	HDCO		15	55108	7	3⅜	5⅞	+ 2⅜
HakoMinut	HAKO	.20	13	5993	11	7	10½	+ 2
HallFnl	HALL		...	20934	15/16	⅜	7/16	– ⅜
HallwdEngy	HWEC		...	94016	9/32	⅛	¼	+ 3/32
HamltnOil	HAML	.10	62	53242	35¾	25¼	35¼	+ 8¾
Hammond	THCO	.10e	...	5282	8¼	2½	4¾	+ 1¾
HamptnBksh	HBSI	.44b	14	1875	19	15	15	– 3
HanaBio	HANA		19	56130	6⅛	1⅜	1¾	– 2⅝
HandexEnvr	HAND		25	66240	20⅝	14⅜	19⅜	...
HanvrIns	HINS	.44	7	86047	33	25¾	30½	+ 3¾
HardgAssc	HRDG		23	69779	20	10	18½	+ 8⅜
HarlysvlGp	HGIC	.60	9	14785	28¾	17¾	27½	+ 9½
HarlysvlNtl	HNBC	1.44	...	683	51½	38	49½	+ 10
HarlysvlSvg	HARL	.40	77	629	17¾	13½	17¾	+ 3⅝
HarmonInd	HRMN	.12	28	17508	8⅞	5¾	6⅞	– ⅝
HarmonaBcp	HBCI		...	44162	10¼	7⅞	8	...
HaroldStr	HRLD		19	7593	5⅜	3⅛	3⅜	+ ⅛
HarprGp	HARG	.10e	14	69996	22½	15¼	20½	+ 5
HarrisHarris	HHGP	.04	125	20094	2 13/16	1½	2½	+ ⅞
HartfdStm	HBOL	1.60	14	113936	59¼	34¾	53½	+ 16¾
Hathway	HATH		...	9508	5¼	2¼	2½	– ⅝
Haverfield	HVFD	.32	...	3171	19	7¾	15½	+ 7¾
HavrtyFurn	HAVT	.36	9	11087	13½	9¾	10¼	– 1
HavrtyFurn A	HAVTA	.36	9	1383	13½	9⅞	10⅜	– 1⅞
HawkeyeBc	HWKB		6	63851	9½	3⅞	8¼	+ 4 3/16
HawknChm	HWKN		12	3469	5¾	3⅝	4¾	+ ¾
HawthnFnl	HTHR	1.00	5	9071	35½	21⅝	27½	+ 5½
HlthCompar	HCCC		23	83270	16½	9	10¾	– 3½
HlthcrSvGr	HCSG	.05e	24	40972	19¼	9¼	19¼	+ 9⅜
HlthImg	HIMG	.02e	37	61992	10	5½	10	+ 4¼
HlthInsVT	HIVT	.18e	9	401	9	7¼	8½	...
HlthcoInt	HLCO		16	113530	22½	13¼	16¼	– 4¼
Hlthdyn	HDYN		...	327490	12⅝	4½	11⅛	+ 6¼
Hlthsouth	HSRC		26	158634	17⅝	9¼	17⅜	+ 8
Hlthsrc	HLTH		...	37298	15	13¼	14¼	...
Hlthwatch	HEAL		7	14942	6⅛	3 15/16	5⅞	+ 1 3/16
HeartFed	HFED	.40	8	66853	19½	9½	14	+ 4
HeartIndExp	HTLD		15	9607	18¼	11¼	17	+ 5¾
Hechngr A	HECHA	.16	12	305959	19¾	10¾	12⅝	– 5¼
Hechngr B	HECHB	.06	10	16341	19¾	11	12¼	– 5½
HeeknCan	HEKN		11	34538	40¾	25¾	40½	+ 12⅛
HeistCH	CHHC		8	1363	13½	7	11	+ 2
HelenTroy	HELE		9	255252	23¾	13	19⅞	+ 4¼
HelixTech	HELX	.76	10	8157	19½	12¼	13½	– 3½
Hemodyn	HMDY		...	88386	6½	1	1 7/16	– 4 5/16
HenleyGrp A	HENG		...	234403	74¼	50½	54¼	...
HenryJack	JKHY		26	15051	4	1⅛	1 13/16	– 1 5/16
HeritagBkcp	HEBC	.52	...	29424	14¼	9	10	...
HeritageBcp	HNIS	.23r	...	123790	14	3⅞	5⅜	– 6⅞
HeritagFnlIL	HERS	.40	11	13645	20¾	13⅝	19	+ 5
HerlyMicrw	HRLY		12	12765	2⅜	1⅛	1¼	– ⅞
HiberniaSvg	HSBK	.36	6	6243	15¾	7¼	8	– 7¼
HickamDow	DBHI		28	19269	15¾	9½	10½	+ ⅜
HighldSupr	HIGH		...	121562	7⅞	3¾	4¼	– 2⅞
HighwdRs g	HIWDF		...	7075	2¼	¾	1 1/16	– ⅞
HilbRogl	HRHC	.28	18	36029	25¾	13⅜	23	+ 9¼
HinghamSvg	HIFS	.32	...	20837	8⅞	4⅜	4½	– 4
Hitox	HTXA		10	38131	14⅜	8¼	9¼	+ ⅛
HoganSys	HOGN		9	189872	7¼	3⅞	4⅛	– ⅝
HolidayRV	RVEE		15	12559	4¾	2½	2½	– ⅞
HollywdPk	HTRFZ		27	23804	27¾	20¾	22¼	+ 1¼
HomeCtySvg	HCSB	.96	9	43235	26¼	19¼	22¼	– 3¼
HomBenef	HBENB	1.20	9	10452	37½	29	37½	+ 7¾
HomFedGA	HFGA		20	3996	12	6¾	10¼	+ 1
HomFedIN	HOMF	.30	8	9950	15½	8½	15	+ 6½
HomFedCpMD	HFMD	.28b	7	1274	10½	8¾	9¾	+ 1¼
HomFdXOH	HFOX	.50	3	674	11¼	8½	9	– 1
HomFdRock	HROK		14	1822	13¾	10½	11	– 2¼
HomFedSF	HFSF		16	8954	24¼	16¼	18	+ 1½

Stock	Symbol	Div	Yld	Sales 100s	Hi	Lo	Last	Net Chg
HomFedTenn	HFET	.40a	9	20290	23½	16¼	19¼	+ 2
HomIntsCare	KDNY		4	395830	8¼	1 7/16	1⅞	− 1½
HomeNutrSvc	HNSI		...	51069	16⅞	13¾	15⅜	...
HomePortBcp	HPBC	.27e	7	24240	11	7⅝	7⅞	− ½
HomS&LNC	HSLD	.60	9	8104	23	15	16½	− 3½
HomSvgNY	HMSB	1.50	8	146062	22	13⅞	15½	− 2¼
HomOfcRef	HORL		14	223174	20½	10⅛	17¾	+ 5
HomeOwnrS&L pf		6.12	...	34217	30¼	2¼	2⅝	− 22¾
HomeownrGp	HOMG		14	38018	12¼	5	9	+ 3¼
HomstdSvg	HMSD	.48	...	3306	12	7	10½	+ 1¾
HomstylBuf	HBUF	t	30	49705	10⅛	4½	8¾	+ 2⅛
HomtwnBcp	HTWN	.05e	23	7485	6¾	3⅞	4½	− 1⅛
HonInd	HONI	.48	15	55466	39¾	17½	37¾	+ 19½
HorznGld	HRIZ		...	71886	1 7/16	9/16	25/32	− 21/32
HorznInd	HRZN	.06e	6	115322	13¾	6¼	6⅜	− 2¾
HorznBkWA	HRZB	.24	14	10874	16¾	10⅛	16½	+ 6
HorznFnl	HFIN	.24	25	30180	14¾	6⅜	14¼	+ 7⅞
HsptlStff	HSSI		17	213372	14⅛	3 9/16	8¾	+ 5
HosposPdt	HOSP		8	7334	6⅜	2¾	5½	+ 2½
Hotelcopy	FAXM		...	13881	8¼	4⅞	5¼	...
HowrdBkNJ	HWRD	.60	3	286804	23¼	6	7⅜	− 10⅛
HowrdBcp	HOBC	.96	9	8623	24½	17½	21¼	+ 3
HufmnKoos	HUFK		6	29546	4	1⅜	2	− ¾
HughHomes	HUHOE	.10	...	26534	4⅝	⅜	7/16	− 4 5/16
HughHomes wt			...	3327	1 5/16	1/16	1/16	− 1⅛
HuntJB	JBHT	.24	15	192327	26	17	19¾	− 3
HuntgBcshr	HBAN	.74b	9	121862	22½	14¾	20	+ 5
Hurco	HURC	.10e	11	83044	22¼	9⅜	18½	+ 9
HutchTech	HTCH		...	57920	15¼	5	6⅝	− 2⅜
HycorBio	HYBD		34	59532	5⅛	1 13/16	5 1/16	+ 3¼
HydeAthl	HYDE		...	21467	8⅞	4⅜	4¾	− 4⅛
HytekMicsys	HTEK		...	16391	2⅞	5/16	½	− 2
-I-								
ICO Inc	ICOC		...	49232	2 1/16	¾	1 9/16	+ 13/16
IDB Comm	IDBX		425	62835	14½	4¾	8½	− ¾
IEH Cp	IEHC		...	10995	2¾	1 11/16	1 13/16	− 13/16
IFR Sys	IFRS	.30	12	73775	15¼	10¼	13¾	+ 2¾
II-VI	IIVI		12	10879	9	6⅛	7¼	− ⅜
IISIntell	IISLF	.16	4	16482	5⅝	4 5/16	4 9/16	...
ILC Tech	ILCT		10	12680	9¾	5¾	9½	+ 1⅝
IMCO Recyc	IMRI		10	79181	8½	4¾	6⅜	+ 1⅝
INB Fnl	INBF	1.20	9	61792	33	25¼	29	+ ¾
INVG MtgSec	INVG	1.40a	...	5043	10½	5½	5⅞	− 2⅝
IPL Sys	IPLSA		19	16968	8¾	4½	6	+ 1¼
IWC Res	IWCR	1.38	13	8419	19¼	16¼	17¼	+ ¼
Icot	ICOT		...	121850	3	1	1½	− 1¼
Ilio	ILIO		...	8239	9¼	4½	8 21/32	...
Ilio wt			...	8197	6¼	1¼	5¼	...
ImagnFilm	IFEI		214	46951	16¾	5¾	15	+ 9¼
ImagnFilm wt			...	25614	3	9/16	2	+ 1½
Imatron	IMAT		...	150739	31/32	7/16	15/32	− ⅛
Imatron wt			...	7714	5/16	1/16	5/32	+ 3/32
Imnet	IMGE		...	14495	4⅛	1⅞	2	− 2
ImpactSys	MPAC		...	56838	3⅛	1⅛	1 7/16	− 1 5/16
Imucor	BLUD		26	49592	11⅛	5¼	10	+ 4½
Imunogen	IMGN		...	11134	10	7¾	8	...
Imunex	IMNX		...	127068	21½	10½	19¼	+ 7¼
Imunomed	IMMU		...	56309	5¾	3⅛	4	− ⅞
ImperlBcp	IBAN	.40e	9	34653	27¾	15⅝	20	+ 3¾
Imreg	IMRGA		...	149099	5⅜	1⅛	2	− 2
InacmpCptr	INAC		9	76053	11⅞	7⅛	8⅛	+ ¾
IndepndBcpPA	INBC	1.16	14	61350	27¾	19	20¾	+ ¾
IndepndBkMA	INDB	.36	...	3845	12	7½	7¾	− 3
IndepndBkMI	IBCP	.44	7	6596	9¾	7¾	8⅝	...
IndepndFd	IFSB		...	910	3½	2	2	− ¾
Indepndlns	INDHK	1.60	9	8018	44	31¾	44	+ 12
IndexTech	INDX		14	44813	11¼	7½	9¼	...
IndiS&L	IFSL	.30	10	30394	15¼	9¾	11¼	+ ¼
IndiFnl	IFII		9	908	9¾	5½	7¾	+ 1⅞
IndlAccous	IACI	.25	...	1777	12⅝	9	9¾	+ ⅛
IndusFdg	IFDCA		...	20214	12⅜	9⅞	10¼	...
IndlTrnCp	ITCC		...	294	6	3½	4	− ¼
Infodata	INFD		...	6474	4¾	1⅞	1⅞	− 1
InfoInt	IINT	.22	20	5978	16	12	12½	− 2
Infotech	ITCH		...	74896	11¾	5⅛	7¾	+ 2
InfoSci	INSI		56	9674	1¼	¼	9/16	− 7/16
Informix	IFMX		513	306435	15⅜	7⅝	15⅜	+ 7
InfoRes	IRIC		...	397246	15⅝	8⅞	12⅞	+ 2⅞
InfotrnSys	INFN		11	24766	12¾	8	8	− 2½
InglsMkt	IMKTA	.22	10	62989	11⅛	8	9¼	+ ⅞
Ingres	RELY		38	192192	16⅜	4½	7¼	− 8½
Initio	INTO		...	5110	1⅝	1⅛	1¼	− ⅜
Inmac	INMC	.05i	...	72149	11½	4¾	6⅝	− 4⅞
Innovex	INVX		15	33860	4 13/16	3	3⅝	− ⅜
Inrad	INRD		325	1860	4½	2⅝	3¼	+ ⅝
InsitufmE	INEI	.05e	12	30499	8⅛	4⅞	6⅜	+ ¾
InsitufmGf	IGSI		10	6640	3⅝	2⅜	2⅞	− ⅛
InsitufmMd	INSMA	.05	24	4646	7½	5¼	6¾	+ 1½
InsitufmGp	IGLSF		725	60126	8⅞	6¼	7¼	− ⅛
InsitufmGp wt			...	5016	5⅜	3⅛	3½	− ¼
InsitufmNA	INSUA		15	58219	11½	6⅞	8⅛	− ⅝
InsitufmSE	ISEC		15	13087	6⅝	3⅛	5	+ 1⅞
InstClinPhrm	ICPYY		18	158211	4⅛	1⅞	2	− 2 5/16
Intec	INTE	t	...	3483	1¾	1	1¼	...
Integon	ITGN	.12	...	60901	7⅛	2⅛	4⅝	− 1⅜
IntegraFnl	ITGR	1.16	9	44626	30¾	20	24⅞	+ 3
IntegDvc	IDTI		12	432817	12⅝	7¼	8⅛	− 3¾
Intel	INTC		18	f38433	36	22⅞	34½	+ 10¾
Intel wt			...	206676	17	9⅝	15½	+ 5¼
Intel wt92			...	196653	13⅝	8½	12¼	+ 3¼
Intelli	INAI		43	123311	5¾	2 9/16	4¾	+ 1½
Intelcall	INCL		21	124016	18½	8¾	15¼	+ 5¾
IntelElec	INEL		14	151493	35¼	11½	27¾	+ 15¾
InterFdSv	IFED		7	5295	15	8½	11¼	+ 2¾
InterTel	INTL		...	15917	2¾	1⅛	1⅜	− ⅞
Intrcargo	ICAR		9	13509	10	7¾	9¼	+ 1
IntrchgFnl	ISBJ	.70	7	1175	15½	10¾	10¾	− 4¼
IntrfaceInc	IFSIA	.24	14	165391	19⅜	14⅝	17¾	+ 2⅝
IntrfaceSy	INTF		10	18527	9½	5⅛	6⅝	− ⅞
Intrhome g	IHEIF	2.00	...	1921	42¾	35⅝	37⅞	+ 1⅞
Intrgrph	INGR		12	f10936	22¾	13¾	17¼	− 3¾
Intrgroup	INTGC		...	1959	15½	13⅜	15	+ 1⅜
InterimSys	INSY		10	153744	3¼	1⅝	1⅞	− 13/16
Intrleaf	LEAF		...	234977	9⅞	5⅜	7⅛	− 1¼
IntrmagGen	INMA		34	53409	8½	5⅜	5¾	− ¼
Intermec	INTR		20	211879	34⅛	18⅝	28¾	+ 9¼
IntermetCp	INMT	.20	10	106497	13¼	6⅞	8¼	− ½
Intrmetric	IMET		6	9727	6	4⅛	4⅛	− 1⅜
IntAmHome	HOME		3	91926	3¾	1	1 3/16	− ¼
IntBdcstCp	IBCA		...	63208	16¼	8½	12¾	+ 2¾
IntCapEqp	ICEYF		24	7043	2⅞	1¼	2⅞	+ 1
IntContainr	ICSI		11	17790	8¾	3	4	− 2
IntDairyQ A	INDQA		19	26092	47¼	34¼	44¼	+ 9¾
IntDairyQn B	INDQB		20	837	48	34¼	45	+ 10½
IntGamTech	IGAM		20	192658	32⅝	19⅞	25⅞	+ 3¼
IntHldg	ISLH	.50	250	3413	24¾	12½	22½	+ 9½
IntLease	ILFC	.10	22	439626	29¼	15¾	25	+ 9⅛
IntLease wt			...	10448	11	5⅝	6⅞	...
IntMicroelec	IMPX		...	181678	2½	13/16	1⅜	− 1
IntMoblMach	IMMC		...	276007	11⅜	5⅜	5⅞	− 2⅞
IntMoblMach pf		2.50	...	7711	25¾	15¾	15¾	− 7¼
IntResrch	IRDV	.20	15	67750	14	6½	12⅛	+ 5⅛
IntRemotImag	IRIS		...	60577	23/32	⅛	5/32	− 5/16
IntShiphld	INSH	.20	9	28991	23	16	20	+ 2½
IntTotlztr	ITSI		19	132790	5¼	1 9/32	5 1/16	+ 3 11/16
Interphase	INPH		976	5752	9¾	4¾	6¼	− 1¼
Interpoint	INTP		24	11188	10¾	4½	8	+ 3¼
Interspec	ISPC		...	25307	7¼	3	3¾	− 2⅜
Intertrans	ITRN	.20e	20	65725	18	11⅜	17⅝	+ 5¼
Intervoice	INTV		24	263767	34	9½	26⅝	+ 16
InrexFnl	TREX		...	67514	8⅛	2¾	3½	− 4¼
Invacare	IVCR		15	45327	17⅜	8⅝	11	+ 1⅛
InvestrFnl	INVF	.20i	6	96770	10⅜	3¾	4½	− ⅞
InvestSvgCp	INVS		9	7658	7¼	5	6	+ ¼
InvestTitl	ITIC	.04	12	7420	8¼	5½	5¾	− ¾
Invitron	INVN		...	57774	10	4¾	5¼	− 3⅛
Iomega	IOMG		7	127381	3 15/16	1 13/16	3 1/16	− ½
IowaNtlBksh	INBS	1.28	12	774	47	30⅜	42½	+ 8⅞
IowaSouthern	IUTL	2.16	11	15102	33¾	26	33¾	+ 6
Ironstone	IRON		...	23062	4¼	15/16	1 5/32	− 2 11/32
Isco	ISKO	.20	13	18881	18	9¾	10¼	− 5
Isomedix	ISMX		25	135151	14½	8	14½	+ 5¾
ItoYokado	IYCOY	.51r	...	5889	143½	100	131	+ ⅝
-J-								
J&JSnackFd	JJSF		15	53704	17⅛	10¾	12⅜	+ 1
JB Restr	JBBB		14	72812	7¾	5¾	6½	+ ⅜

Stock	Symbol	Div	Yld	Sales 100s	Hi	Lo	Last	Net Chg
JG Ind	JGIN		...	11458	5½	1⅜	1⅞	− 1
JLG Ind	JLGI	.20	8	54485	23	14⅞	16⅞	+ 1⅝
JMB Rlty	JMBRS	3.80c	...	2701	12½	7½	8¼	− 4⅛
JRM Hldg	JRMX		...	1108	4	1	2	− 2
JacoElec	JACO	t	10	8426	7⅞	3½	4¼	− 1⅝
JacobsnStr	JCBS	.50	14	23306	29¼	18¾	27	+ 8¼
JacorComm	JCOR		...	56859	8	5⅛	5¾	− ⅞
Jaguar	JAGRY	.19e	98	f19667	14	4 23/32	13¾	+ 9 1/32
JMadison	JMLC		...	1488	11½	8¾	9½	...
JasonInc	JASN	t	13	11711	13½	5⅝	12¾	+ 7⅛
JayJacobs	JAYJ		11	30582	9⅝	6	6⅛	− ⅜
JeffriesGp	JEFG	.20	7	18876	15¼	10¾	11½	+ ¼
JeffsnBkPA	JFFN	.20b	8	1692	9⅛	7	7	− 1½
JeffsnBkshVA	JBNK	1.00	8	13189	26½	19½	22¾	+ ½
JeffsnNtl	JNBK	.36b	8	4443	10	6¾	7¼	+ ⅛
Jerrico	JERR	.16	18	587402	25½	14⅛	23	+ 8
JesupGp	JGRP		10	14276	14¼	5½	10¼	− 2¼
JetbornInt	JETS		...	66414	3 29/32	⅝	1	− 2 3/16
JiffyLub	JLUBC		...	427357	8½	1⅜	1⅞	− 3⅞
JAdamsLf	JALC		...	3384	1⅝	1⅛	1⅛	− ⅛
JHansnSvg	JHSL		...	19716	4¼	2¾	2⅞	− ¼
JohnsnElec	JHSN		...	6086	2¾	1⅜	1½	...
JohnsnWld	JWAIA		12	73157	27½	20¼	21¼	− ¾
JohnstnSvg	JSBK		...	4022	7¼	4¾	4¾	− ¾
JonesIntcbl	JOIN		...	21210	20⅞	12½	15½	+ 2⅝
JonesIntcbl A	JOINA		...	106199	20⅞	11⅛	16	+ 4⅝
JonesMed	JMED	.08r	29	28437	10⅞	4¾	10½	+ 5½
JonesSpclk	SPLKA		...	26592	3½	1¾	1⅞	− 1/16
Joslyn	JOSL	1.60	10	19213	30¾	27	28½	+ ¾
JunoLight	JUNO	.20	16	120150	20¼	13	19¼	+ ½
JustinInd	JSTN	.40	18	37718	25¼	14⅛	23½	+ 9⅛
-K-								
KCS Gp	KCSG		16	16472	15	6¾	10½	+ 3½
KLA Instrm	KLAC		14	323406	13¾	7½	8¾	− 3
KLLM Trnspt	KLLM		11	11519	13¼	10½	10½	− 1½
KMS Ind	KMSI	.12	9	12742	8¼	3⅛	3½	+ ¼
KTronInt	KTII		7	15248	13¾	9	9½	− 1¾
Kahler	KHLR		...	5208	21	14	15¾	− 2½
KamanCp	KAMNA	.44	21	158534	14⅞	7⅝	9¼	− 3¾
MKamnstn	MKCO		8	8524	5¼	2¾	4⅞	+ 1⅞
CarlKarchr	CARL	.08	13	139366	17¾	11¼	12½	+ 1¼
Kasler	KASL	.10e	30	79774	11¼	7½	9	− ⅜
Kaydon	KDON	.40	12	67835	38½	26⅞	31¾	+ 4⅞
KeeganMgmt	KMCI		...	20722	11	9	10¼	...
KellySvc A	KELYA	.60	17	78671	42	26¾	39¼	+ 9⅝
KellySvc B	KELYB	.60	18	260	41½	26⅝	37½	+ 8¾
KenanTrnspt	KTCO	.20	12	3085	15½	13	13½	− ½
KyCtlLf	KENCA	.40	18	82869	21⅝	11⅝	19	+ 7¼
KyMedIns	KYMDA		4	29471	35	3⅝	19¼	+ 15⅝
Keptel	KPTL		15	24583	9⅜	5⅞	8	+ 2
KevlinMcrw	KVLM		16	9220	3¼	2	2¼	− ⅝
KewneeSci	KEQU	.16	13	2424	9½	7⅛	7⅜	− ¾
KeyCenturn	KEYC	.60	12	31216	15¾	12	13½	− 1¼
KeyProdctn wi	KPCI	.30	15	47924	3⅜	2¼	3	+ ¾
KeyTronic	KTCC		14	108456	8	4⅞	5⅛	+ ⅛
KeystnFnl	KSTN	1.08	12	24058	26¼	17¾	24	+ 6¼
KeystnHrtg	KHGI	1.04b	13	3289	39½	28⅛	38½	+ 9¼
KimballInt	KBALB	.60	12	28522	23¼	16¼	20¾	+ 4½
KimnEnvr	KEVN	.05e	24	86664	11½	5¼	10¾	+ 5⅝
KindrCrLrn	KIND		...	236291	6¾	3⅞	4½	− 1⅛
KinetCncpt	KNCI	.03e	12	141606	8¾	4¾	6⅜	− 2
KirschMed	KMDC		32	68615	26¼	12¼	14¼	− 5
KnapeVogt	KNAP	.56a	11	10640	20¾	13¾	15½	− ⅞
Komag	KMAG		...	193633	11½	6⅜	9⅛	+ ⅛
KossCp	KOSS		10	16449	5	3	4⅜	+ ½
KrugInt	KRUG	.03	121	9066	6⅛	3⅝	3⅝	− 1⅞
KulckSoffa	KLIC		10	102748	10	6⅜	7¼	− 1⅝
KustmElc	KUST		11	3577	5	4	4⅛	+ 1/16
KwikPdts	KWIKF		...	4408	⅞	⅛	11/32	− 15/32
-L-								
LCS Ind	LCSI		13	4076	4¾	3½	3¾	− ⅜
LDB	LDBC	1.00e	...	4571	15½	7½	7½	− 7½
LDDS Comm A	LDDSA		...	56308	23	7½	15¼	+ 2¼
LDI	LDIC	t	10	46781	19	12½	15½	+ 3
LPLInv	LPLI		12	54130	18¾	7	17	+ 10
LSBBkNC	LXBK	.60	...	2201	19	14⅝	16½	+ ¾
LSI Ind	LYTS	.05	16	24075	15	9	13⅞	+ 4⅞
LTX	LTXX		...	249635	9¼	1¾	2⅝	− 5⅛
LVMH Moet	LVMHY	1.09e	45	1992	192½	111½	190	+ 82⅛
LaPetite	LPAI		26	136605	10	7¼	9⅜	− ⅛
LacldStl	LCLD	.40	7	20476	23	13	16	− 5¾
LaddFurn	LADF	.28a	10	118201	17¾	11	11⅜	− 2⅜
LaidlTrn A	LDMFA	.24	...	6784	23⅜	13¾	22¾	+ 7½
LaidlTrn B	LDMFB	.24	24	f13194	23¾	12⅝	22⅞	+ 8⅜
LkShorBcp	LSNB		21	4233	28½	20¾	28½	+ 7¼
LakeldInd	LAKE		7	48094	11½	2¾	3⅜	− 1¼
LakeldFst	LLSL	1.00e	...	15123	20	12⅝	14½	+ 1¼
LAM Resrch	LRCX		6	185876	9⅞	4⅞	5⅜	− 2⅝
LamaTony	TLAM		256	12461	14¼	8	10¼	+ 2½
LancastrCol	LANC	.76	13	89843	26⅜	16½	25	+ 6¼
Lance	LNCE	.76	19	66031	25	17¼	24	+ 4⅜
LandmkBcp	LMBC		...	399	13¼	11½	12¼	...
LdmarkBk	LDMK	.40	...	7724	14½	4	4½	− 7¼
LdmarkCmnty	LCBI	.12b	...	9086	9¼	4	4¼	− 4¼
LandmkGph	LMRK		24	318909	23⅞	9¼	17¼	+ 7½
LasrPrcsn	LASR		13	87819	8¼	4⅛	4⅜	− 2⅝
LaserCp	LSER		...	8528	1⅞	1	1⅜	− 1/32
Laserscope	LSCP		...	46701	11⅝	7⅝	9½	...
LatticeSemi	LSCC		...	52374	6⅞	5⅛	6⅜	...
LawsnPdts	LAWS	.36	16	107223	26	18½	22½	− 2½
Lechters	LECH		...	73770	24¼	17¼	19¾	...
Lectec	LECT		18	13923	7	3⅞	3⅞	− 1⅜
LeeData	LEDA		...	83666	3¾	13/16	1 7/16	− 1 11/16
Legent	LGNT		23	188923	32	20¾	26¼	+ 4½
LeisCncpt	LCIC		...	46765	5¼	3	3⅜	− ⅛
LEP Gp	LEPGY	.46e	...	36225	15½	9¾	11⅜	− 1⅞
Lesco	LSCO	.05	27	23311	12¼	6¼	10¼	+ 2¾
Lexicon	LEXI		...	41805	1⅛	¼	5/16	− 7/16
LexPrecisn	LEXP		5	7262	2⅜	15/16	1⅝	+ ⅛
LexgtnSvg	LEXB	.40a	20	19601	12¼	5	5¾	− 5⅜
LibrtyHom A	LIBHA	.24	...	4512	8¾	5⅛	6	− 1⅝
LibrtyHom B	LIBHB	.20	...	206	8½	6¼	6½	− ⅛
LibrtyNtlBcp	LNBC	.82	9	14924	30½	23¾	27¼	+ 2¾
LifeInSys	LIFE		...	18393	4⅛	2⅛	3¼	+ ⅜
LifeTech	LTEK		15	54212	18¾	12½	13¾	− 1
LifecorBio	LCBM		...	56851	5¼	2¾	4¼	+ ¼
LillyIndl A	LICIA	.48b	14	42354	19⅛	14	18½	+ ¾
LINBdcst	LINB		65	f13002	130½	68	120¼	+ 48¾
LincBcp	LCNB	t	12	30429	21¾	11½	17	+ 4
LincLogs	LLOG		...	5435	3	15/16	1⅜	− 1½
LincFnl	LFIN	1.00	9	18741	27	19¾	24⅜	+ 4
LincFdsvc	LINN		14	11486	8½	5¾	5¾	− ⅞
LincSvg	LNSB	.48	12	3909	20¾	17⅝	18⅛	− 1⅛
LincTel	LTEC	.74	23	52552	34⅝	17⅛	32½	+ 15¼
LindCdrH	LNDL	t	26	9428	10	5¼	5½	− 2⅜
Lindbrg	LIND	.28	8	8273	8⅜	4⅝	5	− 2¼
LindsayMfg	LINZ		6	164214	29	18¼	22¼	+ 2¾
LinrTech	LLTC		20	173666	10⅝	7⅜	10⅜	+ 2
LiposmeCo	LIPO		...	131940	3½	⅞	1⅜	− 2
LiposomeTech	LTIZ		...	37001	3¾	1⅛	1¼	− 1½
LiqBox	LIQB	.80	15	6072	63½	43½	55½	+ 9½
LIVE Entn	LIVE		6	203164	25	12¾	16½	+ 2¾
LizClabrn	LIZC	.20	14	f15420	27¾	16½	24	+ 6¾
LoanAmFnl	LAFCB		9	2056	6	4½	4¾	...
Lodgstix	LDGX		...	13977	2⅛	25/32	1¼	+ 9/32
LogicDvc	LOGC		11	78131	9¾	4⅝	7⅝	+ 2⅛
LoneStrTech	LSST		...	281683	15¼	2⅝	4	− 11⅛
LglslCtyFnl	LICF		...	29043	21	16⅜	19¾	+ 3⅛
LongLkEngy	LLEC		...	45753	5¼	2⅞	4	+ ⅝
LotusDvl	LOTS		27	f12975	33½	18	31	+ 12¾
LowrncElec	LEIX		41	3208	3⅝	2½	2⅞	...
LoyolaCap	LOYC		8	34498	19⅜	11¾	15	+ 2¾
LundInt	LUND		6	26648	7⅜	3	5⅛	+ 1⅜
Luskins	LUSK		...	6251	2⅞	1¼	1½	− ⅛
-M-								
Marc	MARC		13	26748	13¼	9⅜	12¼	+ 2½
MCI Comm	MCIC		20	f48537	48½	21⅝	44	+ 21⅜
MDT Cp	MDTC		13	161611	14⅛	6¼	7	− 4½
MISchotHm	MIHO		9	8032	7½	4¾	7	+ 1¾
MipsCptr	MIPS		...	58420	21	19	19½	...
MLX	MLXX		14	40943	2¾	15/16	1⅛	− 1¼
MMIMed	MMIM	.12	6	9837	9⅞	4⅞	5	− 3½
MMRHldg	MMRH		...	19275	19¾	8¾	9¼	− 8¾
MNX	MNXI		...	45851	8⅝	4⅜	5½	− 2⅜
MPSI Sys	MPSG		...	6013	4⅛	2¼	3	...
MSCarr	MSCA		14	46127	24	16	21	+ 4½

OVER-THE-COUNTER

Stock	Symbol	Div	Yld	Sales 100s	Hi	Lo	Last	Net Chg
MTS Sys	MTSC	.40	10	20521	23¾	18¾	23½	+ 3¼
MacDermd	MACD	.60	14	3256	28¼	15	17	− 10¾
MackTrk	MACK		...	306317	15¼	5⅛	5¾	− 6⅝
MacmlBl g	MMBLF	.80	6	130859	18⅛	14¼	15⅝	+ ½
MadsnGas	MDSN	2.56	12	21558	37½	29¾	35½	+ 4½
MagmaPwr	MGMA		32	75802	26	14⅞	25	+ 9¼
MagnaInt	MAGAF	.24	11	86843	13⅝	6⅞	7⅛	− 3⅜
MagnaGp	MAGI	.68b	11	23348	18½	14½	17	+ 1¼
MailBoxEtc	MAIL		29	48571	25¼	8¾	20½	+ 10¼
MajRlty	MAJR		...	46067	13½	9¾	11¼	+ 1
MakitaElec	MKTAY	.30e	34	380	100	58¼	100	+ 38¾
MalrdCoach	MALC		6	37371	10	3¾	4¼	− 3
MallonRes	MLRC		...	11014	6¼	3¾	5¾	+ 1¼
MgtSciAm	MSAI		...	324190	18½	7½	18¼	+ 10⅛
Manatrn	MANA		33	2792	3⅛	1⅝	2	− ⅞
Manitowc	MANT	1.00a	13	79062	26¼	17¼	19⅞	+ 2⅜
MfrsNtl	MNTL	2.16	7	106086	60	44¼	52	+ 7½
MarblFnl	MRBL	.48	...	47017	18¾	6	6⅝	− 9¼
MarcorRsrt	MAAR		47	39390	16¼	6⅝	9⅞	+ 2⅝
MarcusCp	MRCS	.28	14	16275	19¾	13½	17½	+ 2½
MargoNrsy	MRGO		12	7432	3¼	1⅝	2 3/16	− 3/16
MariettaCp	MRTA		20	35178	27	10¾	25¾	+ 14½
MarineCp	MCOR	.40	14	10762	20¾	12¾	20¾	+ 7⅞
MarineDrl	MDCO		...	82426	9¼	4¾	8½	...
MarkCtrl	MRCC		10	28457	8¾	4½	6⅜	+ 1⅜
MkTwainB	MTWN	.80	9	9358	20½	17½	18⅛	− 1⅜
MarkelCp	MAKL		9	27889	24	15⅜	22½	+ 7⅛
MktFacts	MFAC	.32	13	3177	8¼	7	7⅜	+ ⅛
MarqstMed	MMPI		158	37520	8¾	5½	7⅞	+ 2¼
MarsmPhr	MSAM		...	22997	20¼	8½	15¾	+ 7¼
MarshSupr	MARS	.36	14	19814	19¾	15	17¾	+ 2¼
MarshIlsly	MRIS	1.08	9	37195	38	28	34½	+ 6¼
MartnTrnpt	MRTN		...	9201	6¾	4	4¼	− 2
MartnLawr	MLLE		9	215183	13¾	7⅞	8⅝	− 1¼
MaryldBcp	MFSL	†	9	29059	15⅞	10⅛	10⅞	...
MascoInd	MASX		11	269665	10⅝	6¾	7⅝	− 3
Massbk	MASB	.44	14	19809	22⅝	17	18⅜	− 1⅞
MasstrSys	MSCO		59	249758	3¾	1⅞	2⅜	− 1⅛
MaurySvgBk	MFED	.40a	9	1483	15	11	14	+ 1¾
MaxErnRestr	MAXE	†	29	26911	8½	3 1/16	8⅜	+ 5¼
Maxco	MAXC		...	6155	2	1⅜	1¾	+ ⅜
MaximInPdt	MXIM		18	68039	9⅛	6⅜	8¼	+ 1¾
Maxtor	MXTR		19	598834	12¼	7½	8¾	...
MaxwlLab	MXWL	.40e	9	26249	17½	11¼	14	+ 1¼
MayflrCpBk	MFLR	.20	8	5612	10½	4½	5	− 4
MayflrFnl	MFFC		10	13550	15¼	8⅜	11⅛	+ 2¾
MaynrdOil	MOIL		80	6317	7⅛	4⅛	6⅜	+ 1⅞
MaysJW	MAYS		...	2526	33½	28	28¼	− 1¼
McCawClr	MCAWA		...	f11693	47¼	25¾	38¼	+ 11¼
McClainInd	MCCL		11	5182	15¼	5¾	6	− 8
McCrmkCo	MCCRK	.88	23	211495	53¾	25½	51½	+ 23½
McFarlEngy	MCFE		...	24384	12⅜	8¼	11½	+ 2⅞
McGillMfg	MGLL	1.60	15	25565	92¼	38	91	+ 51½
McGrthRent	MGRC		12	25135	18	13⅛	17½	+ 4
MechTech	MTIX		...	4143	7¾	3¾	4	− 3¼
MedalistInd	MDIN	.45i	12	17500	16½	8¼	8⅞	− 5⅛
MedarInc	MDXR		...	24142	4⅛	2¼	3½	+ 1⅛
MedcoCSvc	MCCS	.04	63	527281	18⅞	11⅝	18¼	+ 4⅞
Medex	MDEX	.09b	14	21871	13 1/16	7¼	8½	− 3⅜
Mediagenic	MGNC		...	43587	8 7/16	4¼	6½	+ ¼
MedAction	MDCI		166	29890	2½	1	1 21/32	− 13/32
MedCareInt	MEDC		28	392835	25⅜	10⅜	24¼	+ 13½
MedDevices	MDEV		9	5501	4⅜	2½	2⅞	− 1
MedGraphic	MGCC		88	9337	7	3	3½	− 2¾
MedImgCtr	MIKA		21	166189	11⅞	5¼	11¼	+ 6
MedShop	MSII		24	59757	23⅛	14¾	21¼	+ 6½
MedstatSys	MDST		29	13847	16½	9	13	+ 3
Medstone	MSHK		53	217022	32¾	5¼	8½	− 16½
Megadata	MDTA		1	5966	1⅞	¾	¾	− 1
Melamine	MTWO	.18e	10	39700	15	11⅜	12	− 1
MellonPtMtg	MPMTS	.78e	8	38912	7⅝	5½	6⅛	− 1⅜
MentorCp	MNTR	.16	21	191686	14½	9⅜	13⅛	+ 3⅝
MentorGraph	MENT	.20	15	833677	22⅜	13⅜	16¾	+ 2½
MercBcpMO	MTRC	1.40	...	79652	29¼	25	26	+ ½
MercBkshMD	MRBK	1.60	11	50645	55¼	35	50	+ 14¼
MerchBcpCT	NMBC	.40i	...	5579	11⅛	3½	4½	− 5⅞
MerchBkshrVT	MBVT	.80b	8	1079	21	16¼	16¼	− ⅜
MerchBkNY	MBNY	1.60a	16	809	165	94	102	− 59½
MerchCap B	MCBKB		...	3439	8	6½	6½	+ ⅜
MerchCap A	MCBKA	.20i	...	42524	5⅜	13/32	1	− 3¼
MerchNtl	MCHN	1.20	9	44358	32	25½	28¾	+ 2½
MercuryGen	MRCY	.50	12	95758	18	12	14⅞	+ 2⅜
MeretInc	MRET		22	12438	15/16	⅛	7/16	− 1/16
MeridnBcp	MRDN	1.20	8	196232	26½	17½	19¼	− ⅛
MeridnDiagn	KITS		43	9535	3¾	2⅜	3	− ½
MeridnIns	MIGI	.15i	26	11278	5⅝	4 3/16	4½	− ⅛
MeritorSvg	MTOR		...	525169	5⅞	2¼	2¾	− 2
MerrillCp	MRLL		...	28177	11½	6¼	6½	− 1
MermckBcp	MRMK	.30i	...	21360	9½	1¾	2⅛	− 6⅜
MerryGoRd	MGRE	†	18	222337	20	7¾	19⅝	+ 11⅜
MerryLdInv	MERY	.40e	5	41997	7½	4¾	4⅞	− 2⅝
MesaAirl	MESA		25	29190	8⅝	3¼	7⅜	+ 3⅝
MetCoilSys	METS	.12	6	13204	8¼	5	5¼	− ⅝
Metcalf	METC		26	66147	30	16¼	28⅜	+ 11⅜
MethodEl A	METHA	.07	26	59134	5¾	4	5⅝	+ 1⅛
MethodEl B	METHB	.06	20	1955	6	4	5¼	+ 1
MetroAirl	MAIR		41	149181	10½	6½	7⅜	− ¼
MetroBcshr	MTBS	.10e	...	21590	12⅛	7½	8¼	+ ¾
MetrobkFnl	MFGR	.40	...	10210	11	3¼	3¾	− 5
MetroBcp	METB	.60b	14	503	45½	27	38½	+ 7½
MetroSvTN	MFTN		5	56576	14¾	6¾	7½	− 5¾
MetroTel	MTRO		436	4456	2⅛	1	1⅜	+ ¼
MeyerFred	MEYR		15	93164	23	15¾	18½	+ 2⅜
MicAnthJwl	MAJL		13	11523	4¾	2¼	3⅜	+ ⅜
MichlFood	MIKL	.20	13	233507	21⅞	12¼	13⅝	− 2¼
MichNtl	MNCO	2.00	4	123383	57¾	40½	49½	+ 4⅝
MicroAge	MICA		8	53695	10⅝	6⅛	7¼	+ ⅝
MicroAm	MRAC		9	138941	8⅛	4¼	5	− 1⅝
Microdyne	MCDY		49	16124	5⅛	3¼	4⅜	+ 1
MicronTech	MCRN		5	f12243	25¾	9¼	9¾	− 6
Micropolis	MLIS		...	287968	8½	2⅞	3½	− 3⅞
MicrosSys	MCRS		14	37468	5	1⅜	3¾	+ 2¼
Microsemi	MSCC		...	66107	7	1¾	2½	− 4⅜
Microcom	MNPI		15	171624	23	13½	16	+ 1½
Microlog	MLOG		21	64156	14¼	3	9½	+ 6¾
Microsoft	MSFT		27	f13539	89¼	45¾	87	+ 33¾
MicrowvLab	MWAV		...	9945	2	7/32	7/32	− 1 7/32
MidAmBcp	MABC	.60a	10	6622	20¼	14¾	18¼	+ 3
MidAmInc	MIAM	1.00b	12	6200	23¼	15⅞	22¼	+ 6⅛
MidConnBk	MIDC	.72	9	25939	16	9½	10¾	− ¾
MidMaineSv	MMSB	.40	8	5492	10¾	6½	7¼	− 2½
MidSouthIns	MIDS	.24	58	7428	8½	5¼	7½	+ ½
MidStS&L	MSSB	.40	...	14273	23½	13¼	22⅜	+ 7⅜
MidsexWtr	MSEX	1.84	12	2332	28½	22¾	25½	− 1¾
Midlantc	MIDL	1.88	5	295765	47¾	28	31½	− 6⅝
MidwComm	MCOM		13	45400	9¾	4½	4⅞	...
MidSouth	MSRR		...	67399	16½	12	13¼	...
MdwGrnProd	MWGP	.70	12	38142	33¾	19¾	25¼	+ 5⅛
MillerBldg	MTIK	.02e	10	40049	5½	3 1/16	4 15/16	+ 1⅞
MillerHrm	MLHR	.52	12	248265	23½	17¾	19¾	− ⅛
Millicom	MILL		...	246815	26	8	22¼	+ 13⅞
Miltope	MILT		12	27953	11¼	5	5¼	− ¼
MilwIns	MILW		8	5339	11½	7¼	10	+ 2¾
Mindscape	MIND		...	50939	5⅞	⅞	5⅞	+ 3⅞
MineSftyAp	MNES	.76	14	9762	57	42½	56½	+ 14
MinrNtl	MNBC	1.00	...	567	27	24	25½	− ½
Miniscrb	MINYE		1	f16240	8⅝	⅜	⅜	− 7⅜
Minntch	MNTX		24	43016	13¼	3¾	12½	+ 8⅜
MissionVly	MVBC		14	4110	20⅝	10⅝	17½	...
MrGskt	MRGC		15	18541	4	2¼	2⅜	− 1⅜
Mitsui&Co	MITSY	.72e	...	1066	205½	129¼	192¾	+ 35¾
MoblGsSv	MBLE	.80	17	3310	18	14¾	17¾	+ 1¼
MoblTelcm	MTTL		...	732051	12¾	4⅜	8¾	...
ModnCtrls	MOCO	.20	15	25251	16⅛	11¾	14½	+ 1
ModineMfg	MODI	.60	12	62030	22	15⅜	18⅞	+ 3⅜
MolclrBio	MOBI		55	245481	26¼	15⅜	22⅝	+ 7
MolclrGene	MOGN		33	75478	6	2⅞	4¼	+ 1⅛
Molex	MOLX	.03	18	180225	39¾	30¼	39¼	+ ½
MonrchAvl	MAHI		...	1805	2⅜	15/16	1⅜	− ½
Moniterm	MTRM		...	29461	4¼	1⅝	2⅛	− 1⅝
MonmthRE	MNRTS	.70	11	6139	6⅞	5¼	6⅛	+ ⅛
MontclBcp	MSBI	.60	10	28239	26½	13¾	16	− 6½
MooreHndly	MHCO		...	4767	4¾	3¾	4½	+ ⅜
MoorePdts	MORP	.88	14	2012	34½	27	28½	− 2
MorFloInd	MORF	.01	...	3891	7¾	4½	4¾	− ⅜
Morrisn	MORR	.64	14	194861	34	23⅛	26¾	+ 3½
Moscom	MSCM		18	59970	6⅞	3 3/16	4¾	− 7/16
MosinePpr	MOSI	.28	9	40851	24	15⅞	17¾	+ 1⅝
MotoPhoto	MOTO		...	20178	3¼	1⅜	1 9/16	− 1 9/16
MotoPhoto pf		1.20	...	1422	9½	5¼	5¾	− 3½

Stock	Symbol	Div	Yld	Sales 100s	Hi	Lo	Last	Net Chg
MotoPhoto wt			...	646	7/16	1/16	3/16	− 3/16
MotrClbAm	MOTR	.30	12	10463	14	8¾	8⅞	− 1⅝
MtnWestSvg	MWSB	.36b	...	4443	16½	5⅞	15⅞	+ 9⅛
MountrBk	MTNR	.88	14	2061	20¼	19	20	+ ½
MuellrPaul	MUEL	2.00e	4	1547	28½	23½	26¼	+ 1¼
MultiColr	LABL		15	11634	14	8	12½	+ 4
MultibkFnl	MLTF	.80	6	67230	25¾	11½	15½	− 6¼
Multmda	MMEDC		32	43947	108	74	94¼	+ 17¾
MutlS&LNC	MUTU	.20	16	5887	16½	8⅛	12¼	+ 3⅞
Mycogen	MYCO		...	50968	15	5⅛	13¾	+ 7¾

-N-

Stock	Symbol	Div	Yld	Sales 100s	Hi	Lo	Last	Net Chg
NAC Re	NREC	.20	16	119530	41	20⅝	35¾	+ 14⅝
NBSC	NSCB	.44	...	3471	13¾	11¾	12¾	− ¼
NEC	NIPNY	.25e	50	9085	81	59½	65½	− 13
NESB	NESB	.60j	...	102240	12	3½	4⅝	− 5⅜
NFS Fincl	NFSF	.28	8	19529	10½	5¼	6¼	− 3½
NHD Strs	NHDI		13	7489	10½	4¼	5	− 1⅝
NW Grp	NWGI		...	16261	7	3⅜	5⅜	+ 2
NWNL	NWNL	1.20	10	175759	44⅛	26⅞	39	+ 7⅞
NYMAGIC	NYMG	.40	11	94096	26¼	16½	25	+ 6¾
Nalcap	NPHIF		...	685	29	24	24	− ¾
Nanometrc	NANO		15	19505	2½	1	1 25/32	− 7/32
NapaVlyBcp	NVBC	.28b	12	9721	19¼	10¾	15½	+ 3¾
NapcoSec	NSSC		11	30037	14	4¾	5½	− 7
NashFnch	NAFC	.68	22	43265	26	21	24⅞	+ ⅛
NatecRes	NATC		...	136994	9	3¾	6	+ 1¾
NtlBcpAK	NBAK	.50	12	3085	37¼	25¼	36	+ 7¼
NtlBcCmrc	NBCC	.45	8	5980	11⅜	9¼	9⅝	− 1¼
NtlCapMgt	NCMC		...	13613	1⅞	1½	1½	− 1/16
NtlCtyBcp	NCBM	†	...	9256	14½	11¾	11¾	− 1⅛
NtlCmrcBcp	NCBC	.84b	10	10135	27¼	22½	22½	− 2½
NtlCmuntyBk	NCBR	1.40	7	18134	45	29	32	− 4¼
NtlCptrSys	NLCS	.28	21	151185	15⅛	7¾	8⅝	− 5
NtlDataCp	NDTA	.44	16	243101	35⅛	23⅛	33⅝	+ 8½
NtlHMO	NHMO		13	10555	3⅜	25/32	3	+ 2
NtlHlthLab	NHLI		21	34086	13	7⅜	12½	+ 4½
NtlInco	NIRTS	.48	...	73354	6½	2½	3 7/16	− 1 1/16
NtlInsur	NAIG	.20	20	18478	18½	11⅞	16¼	+ 1
NtlLoanBk	NLBK	.75c	...	197178	2 9/16	1¾	1¾	− 7/16
NrlLumbr	NTLB		...	10858	3⅛	⅞	1¼	− ⅞
NtlMedia	NMCO	†	...	130156	3	1 7/16	2 15/16	+ ⅝
NtlMercBcp	MBLA		9	14752	17	10¼	13	+ 4⅝
NtlMicrnt	NMIC		4	43109	2⅜	¼	11/32	− 1 23/32
NtlPennBcp	NPBC	1.08b	14	807	47½	41½	46	+ 3
NtlPizza	PIZA		21	111086	20	9½	18¼	+ 8½
NtlProp	NAPE	.13	15	169	15	12½	14	+ 1½
NtlSanitSply	NSSX	.16	18	8156	15½	9¾	13	...
NtlSvgsAlb	NSBA	.60	10	9435	29	22¼	28	+ 2
NtlSecIns	NSIC	1.04	7	828	30½	22	30½	+ 7½
NtlTechSys	NTSC		11	16903	3¼	1½	2 3/16	+ ⅜
NtlWestLf	NWLIA		20	6792	14½	9⅞	10¾	− 3¼
NatwdCelr	NCEL		...	121363	14¾	7⅛	13⅝	+ 6⅝
NatwdCelr wt			...	12975	7¾	3¼	6¾	...
NatrBnty	NBTY		22	5887	7⅝	3¾	5¼	+ ¾
NatrSunsh	NATR	.24	19	65984	15¼	6	14½	+ 7½
NavgtrGp	NAVG		11	9250	28½	20½	28¼	+ 7½
Neeco	NEEC		9	89381	17¼	10	14¼	+ 2¼
Nellcor	NELL		35	310930	19⅛	8½	18¾	+ 5⅝
NelsonThos	TNEL	.12	16	21446	8⅞	6⅛	7⅜	+ ⅞
NeorxCp	NERX		...	65610	6¾	2⅝	3½	− 2
NetwkGen	NETG		38	170608	21½	8¾	21½	...
NetwSys	NSCO		21	547714	11¼	7⅛	8⅛	− 3
NetwElec	NWRK		...	6303	10½	3⅞	6½	+ 2⅝
Neutrgna	NGNA		29	167208	29¾	20¾	29¼	+ 6⅛
NevGldfld	NGFCF		...	8439	2¼	¾	⅞	− 1
NwBrunsSci	NBSC		58	26957	10	6¾	8¾	+ 1⅜
NwEngCrit	NECC		36	140552	48½	22	44¼	+ 22⅛
NwEngBusn	NEBS	.72	15	144798	23¾	17	19	− 4½
NHSvgBk	NHSB	.24j	...	92036	12	1¾	2½	− 8¼
NH Thrift	NHTB	.20a	8	8391	7⅝	4¼	4¾	− 1¼
NewHorizon	NHSL		...	1	9	7	9	...
NewImage	NIIS		...	59179	15¾	8½	12½	...
NJSteel	NJST	.60	6	43258	24¾	13	14	− 7¾
NewLondon	NLON		53	7574	2⅜	1	2⅛	+ 1⅛
NYBcp	NYBC		11	61920	13¼	7½	11⅛	+ 2⅞
NewbrNetw	NNCXF		25	193756	18½	11	14⅞	...
NewnS&L	NFSL	.52e	...	831	15	10½	12½	+ ½
NwMlfrdSv	NMSB	.60	8	45931	12¾	5¾	7¼	− 4
NwrldBk	NWOR	.50	5	37788	22½	8¾	9	− 8¾
NewptCp	NEWP	.12	12	70014	13⅛	9⅛	9⅝	− 2
NewptElec	NEWE		133	10947	9½	4	4	− 3⅜
NewprtNwSv	NNSL		...	6825	9¼	5	5	− 3½
NewprtPhrm	NWPH		...	280944	6⅝	1¾	2 15/16	+ ¾
NiagExch	NIEX	.32b	...	7531	12¼	6½	7¼	− 3⅛
NichlsRsch	NRES		9	17137	10	5½	7¾	+ 1
NickelRes	NICL		...	84125	¾	1/16	7/16	+ 9/32
Nike B	NIKE	.80	10	995834	69¼	25¼	53¼	+ 26¾
NoblIns	NOBLF		...	59084	5	1½	2	− 2¾
NoblDrll	NDCO		...	85580	9⅜	4½	9¼	+ 4⅜
Noland	NOLD	.44	24	9063	24¾	21	22¼	+ ½
NoonyRlty	NRTI	.32e	...	2686	10½	7½	9⅛	+ ⅜
Nordsn	NDSN	.72	14	25854	59	44	50	+ 2½
Nordstm	NOBE	.28	23	565986	42½	29¾	37¼	+ 7
NormdyOil	NMDY		...	9977	4½	2	2¾	− ⅝
NorskDta B	NORKZ		...	40687	7⅝	4 7/16	4 9/16	− 1 15/16
Norstan	NRRD		10	45170	12	7¼	10	+ 2½
NoAmBiol	NBIO		...	52630	1 3/16	21/32	15/16	+ 3/32
NoAmNtl	NAMC	.02e	7	5148	10	6⅞	8¼	+ 1⅜
NoAmVntr	NAVI		...	185093	1 13/32	15/32	11/16	+ 3/32
NoAtlInd	NATL		10	44937	6⅝	2⅞	3⅜	+ ½
NoCarNG	NCNG	1.20	10	5398	23¾	16¾	23¾	+ 6
NoFrkBcp	NFBC	.80	7	65354	21¼	15	16⅜	− 2
NoHillElec	NOHL		15	11789	2 15/16	1⅜	1⅝	− 9/16
NoStrUniv	NSRU		40	50925	11⅝	5⅜	6⅞	− 1⅝
NowestTel	NOWT	.53	84	41304	44½	22½	42	+ 13
NoeastBcp	NBIC	1.40	13	33328	80	55½	59½	− 4¾
NrthnTrust	NTRS	1.52	9	115150	71¼	43¾	61¾	+ 17¼
NoSideSvg	NSBK	.10e	26	26206	19¾	15¼	16¾	− 1¼
NrthldCrnbr	CBRYA	.11e	113	8841	9¼	6¼	6¾	...
NwstIllBcp	NWIB	.50	...	5465	18	14½	15	+ ½
NowestNG	NWNG	1.64	11	62255	26⅞	18¾	25	+ 3⅞
NowestTel	NWTL	.36	11	2842	8¾	7½	8¼	+ ¼
NowestPS	NWPS	1.46	10	17695	20¼	16½	20	+ 2½
NwPrtCement	NSTS		...	3964	21	8¼	21	+ 12¾
NorwFnl	NSSB	.60	9	47787	13¼	7	7	− 4⅛
NovaPharm	NOVX		...	199184	6¾	3¾	4⅜	− 1
NovaPharm wt93			...	5192	3¾	1½	1 11/16	− 9/16
NovaPharm wt98			...	5362	3⅜	1⅜	1⅝	− ¾
NovaCare	NVCR		...	131214	16½	4⅞	16½	+ 11⅜
Novametrix	NMTX		...	59150	8⅝	1	1⅜	− 4½
NovarElec	NOVR	.01	26	16219	10	2⅞	9	+ 6
Novell	NOVL		24	f10858	38¼	23¾	31	+ 1
NovellusSys	NVLS		9	229084	19¾	8¾	13¾	+ 5
Noxell B	NOXLB	.50	27	357651	36⅛	17¾	35⅛	+ 15⅞
NuWestInd	FERT		...	331741	18½	2⅝	3¼	− 11
NuWestInd pf			...	1501	84	35	35	− 36½
NuclrMtl	NUCM	.10e	10	7172	14	9	9	− 1½
NuclrSpt	NSSI	.05e	31	33416	14	5⅞	10	+ 3⅞
Nucorp	NUCO		...	64204	9⅞	5½	7⅞	+ ½
Nucorp wtB			...	14822	6⅜	1⅞	4	...
NumericaSv	NUME	.14j	...	51658	10⅜	1¾	2	− 7
NutmegInd	NUTM		26	105174	18¼	8¼	11¾	+ 2¼
NuMedInc	NUMS		...	170930	8½	3⅞	5¾	+ ⅝
NuVision	NUVI		...	23630	9	5½	5⅞	− 2¼
Nycor	NYCO	.08	1	99936	4	2⅝	3	+ 5/16
Nycor pf		1.70	...	9177	19½	15¾	17	+ 1

-O-

Stock	Symbol	Div	Yld	Sales 100s	Hi	Lo	Last	Net Chg
O.I. Corp	OICO		14	22264	6⅝	3⅜	4⅛	+ ½
OMI Cp pf			...	6368	25⅛	22	24⅜	+ 2⅜
OakHlSptwr	OHSC		6	29264	12⅝	6⅝	6⅝	− 1⅝
OccuUrgHl	OUCH		59	154252	21½	5½	18⅜	+ 11¼
Oceanrg	OCER		37	413773	11⅜	2½	10¾	+ 8 1/16
OctelCom	OCTL		27	355024	27¾	16½	22	+ 5⅛
OffcClub	OCLB		...	106616	17	8¾	13⅝	+ 4¼
OffcDepot	ODEP		58	321749	27¼	10⅝	18	+ 7⅜
OffshrLogst	OLOG		16	368819	12	3 5/16	11¾	+ 8⅜
OglebayNrtn	OGLE	1.60	15	13797	38	28	37	+ 8
OhioBcp	OHBC	1.28	9	3904	32¼	23	27¼	+ 3¼
OhioCaslty	OCAS	2.08	7	119641	52½	35½	47¼	+ 11½
OilDriAmer	OILC	.20	27	13358	28	18	27½	+ 3
Oilgear	OLGR	.80	10	1416	26½	21¼	22¼	− 3¼
OldFashnFd	OFFI		...	2316	5	3½	3¾	− ½
OldKentFnl	OKEN	1.06	9	133853	29⅝	22⅜	27⅞	+ 4⅝
OldNtlBcp	OLDB	.84b	14	13616	27¾	25½	27¾	+ ¾
OldRepbInt	OLDR	.74b	13	102744	30⅜	23⅜	25⅜	+ 1⅜
OldStone	OSTN	1.56	...	59857	23¾	7	8	− 15½
OldStone pfB		2.40	...	2294	23½	15	16	− 6¾
OlymSvg	OSBW		...	2399	6¾	3¾	4⅛	+ ⅛

OVER-THE-COUNTER

Stock	Symbol	Div	Yld	Sales 100s	Hi	Lo	Last	Net Chg
OlympusCap	OLCC		...	4299	10	5¾	6¼	- 3½
OmniCap	OCGI	.24	8	10674	17¾	9½	13½	+ 3½
Omnicom	OMCM	.98	15	215143	25¾	19⅜	25¾	+ 6⅛
ONBANCp	ONBK	.12e	6	89167	13⅜	9¾	11⅛	- 1½
OncogeneSci	ONCS		...	69268	3 1/16	1¾	1 15/16	- 15/16
OneBcp	TONE	.15i	...	114742	9⅞	1¼	1⅝	- 6½
OnePrcClthg	ONPR		14	80215	19	8½	9	- 1
OneValBcp	OVWV	1.00	9	8923	23½	18	22¼	+ 2¼
OptekTech	OPTX		9	49350	11⅛	4	4½	- 2⅝
OptoMech	OPTO		9	13180	7¼	3⅞	3⅞	- 2¼
OpticCoatg	OCLI		9	34714	8⅛	5¼	6⅞	+ 1⅝
OpticRadn	ORCO		32	96671	30	13	27¼	+ 14
Optrotch	OPTKF		11	50830	10	4½	9⅝	+ 4½
OracleSys	ORCL		36	f18220	26	9⅜	23⅜	+ 13⅝
OrbitInstr	ORBT		...	79039	5½	3	3½	- 1⅝
OregMetal	OREM	1.72e	13	114989	27¾	11¼	18¾	+ 7⅜
OrfaCp	ORFA		...	394307	2¾	3/16	11/32	- 1 21/32
OrientalSvg	OFSB		...	3939	26½	7¾	10	- ¼
Orthomet	OMET		...	15950	9¾	7	8⅛	- ⅞
OsbornComm	OSBN		150	53480	15	6¾	11½	+ 4⅛
OshBG A	GOSHA	.37a	20	228405	44	20	41	+ 18¾
OshBG B	GOSHB	.32a	18	1114	35	20	31	+ 7
OshTrk B	OTRKB	.50	7	86909	15½	8	9¾	- 2
OshmSport	OSHM	.20	27	17852	20	8¼	9½	- 5½
OsicomTech	OSIC		...	26526	3⅜	1⅛	1¼	- 1
Osmonic	OSMO		14	15732	22¾	13¼	15⅜	- ⅝
OtterTlPwr	OTTR	1.52	12	28807	24⅜	18¾	23¾	+ 4½
OutletCom	OCOMA		16	9078	30	23	25	+ 1¼
OxidyneGp	OXID		...	9776	3⅛	⅜	17/32	- 1 31/32

-P-Q-

Stock	Symbol	Div	Yld	Sales 100s	Hi	Lo	Last	Net Chg
P&F Ind	PFINA		8	13144	3 9/16	2	3⅛	+ 1⅛
PHP Hlthcare	PHPH		32	23160	8⅞	3¾	7¾	+ 3½
PAM Transpt	PTSI		...	31204	3⅝	⅝	¾	- 1¾
PCA Int	PCAI		9	22634	7½	4⅜	5⅜	...
PCS Inc	PCSI		27	76430	21½	11½	15¼	- 2½
PDA Engrg	PDAS		11	36191	6¼	3	4⅜	+ ½
Paccar	PCAR	1.00a	8	158623	52½	37¾	42¾	+ 1¾
PacesettrHom	PACE		5	2345	9¼	3½	8½	+ 4
PacifAgHldg	PAGH		...	21805	4 3/16	2½	3	- ⅞
PacificBcp	PABC		...	1393	7¼	5	5	- ½
PacifDunlp	PDLPY	.52r	...	46932	16½	12⅜	16¼	+ 2⅜
PacifIntSvc	PISC		...	19235	1 7/16	½	¾	- ⅛
PacifNuclr	PACN		15	84887	14¾	5¼	5⅞	- 3⅞
PacifTelcm	PTCM	1.04	13	51536	29	14	23	+ 8¾
PacifCare	PHSY		27	68927	30⅜	6⅛	25½	+ 19⅜
PalfedInc	PALM	.05e	9	12585	19½	10½	15¼	+ 2
PanAtlRe	PATL		...	8643	6¾	3¼	6⅛	- ⅛
Panatech	PNTC		13	39572	3¼	1 1/16	1⅞	+ 25/32
PanchoMx	PAMX	.15	12	23146	10	7	7⅜	- 1⅛
ParametTch	PMTC		...	39924	21½	15¾	21	...
ParisBusnFm	PBFI	.18	13	5033	10¾	6½	9¼	+ 2⅝
ParkComm	PARC		23	11973	25	17¼	20⅝	+ 2⅝
ParkOhio	PKOH		65	83516	9¼	5⅝	5⅞	- ⅜
ParkvlFnl	PVSA	.40	7	9394	15¼	9⅛	13	+ 3¾
Parkway	PKWY	.80	...	4779	17	14⅛	14½	- 1½
Parlex	PRLX		...	13245	6¾	3⅜	4	- 2¾
Patlex	PTLX	†	20	43600	13¼	5	5	- 6¾
PatrickInd	PATK		12	9223	10⅛	6½	6½	- 3¾
PaulHrsStr	PHRS		192	46529	8⅞	4⅞	5¾	+ ⅝
PaxtonFrank	PAXTA	.61j	18	7097	22	14½	20	+ 5⅛
Paychex	PAYX	.16	26	99519	27½	17¼	19½	+ 2
PaycoAmer	PAYC		31	24623	23¼	9½	23¼	+ 13½
PeerlsMfg	PMFG	.72	35	1734	15	10	12¾	+ 2
PennTreaty	PTAC		11	20637	19	7¾	18⅞	+ 10⅝
PennVirginia	PVIR	1.80a	26	7641	52	44½	49	+ 3½
PennEnt	PENT	2.20	21	9084	58½	43½	45½	- 9½
PennvwSvg	PSPA	.24	11	2059	23	11	21½	+ 9½
Pentair	PNTA	.80	9	74771	35⅛	25½	27½	- 3¾
Pentair pf		1.50	...	6822	26¼	21½	22¼	- 1¾
Pentech	PNTK		20	192848	6 1/16	2⅝	5 1/16	+ 2 5/16
Penwest	PENW		22	29434	27¾	17½	27½	+ 8½
PeopBkCT	PBCT	.72	7	65643	10¼	7½	7¾	+ ⅛
PeopBkNC	PEBK	.48	...	789	20½	18	20	+ 2
PeopSvgIN	PFDC	.60	...	2290	20	15¼	17½	+ 2¼
PeopHrtgSvg	PHBK	.96	6	173604	22⅛	13⅛	15⅜	- 3⅝
PeopSvBrck	PBKB	.28	9	36040	10⅛	5½	6¼	- ¼
PeopSvgFnl	PBNB	.64	9	11128	13	9	10	- ½
PeopSvgMA	PEBW	1.12	10	38195	24	18½	19¼	- ¼
PeopTel	PTEL		...	5503	7	4¾	6	...
PeopWstchSv	PWSB	.48b	7	53226	28¾	13¾	18¼	- 1¾
PercptnTech	PCEP		21	62049	10½	3½	4¾	- ¾
Perceptrnic	PERC		...	22378	2½	⅞	1 3/16	- ⅞
PerpetFn	PFCP		5	161460	11⅛	6¼	7⅛	- 1
PerpetFn pf		.85	...	20456	10¼	8¼	8⅜	- ⅞
PetrlInd	PTRL		...	4400	1⅞	⅞	1¾	+ ¾
PetrlDev	PETD		...	23031	1 1/16	⅜	¾	+ 3/32
PetrlEqpt	PTCO		...	56099	4⅜	1½	4⅜	+ 2⅞
Petrlite	PLIT	1.12	44	31215	28½	22	27½	+ 5
Petrminls	PTRO		...	8099	1⅛	¾	15/16	+ 3/16
Pettibone	PETTV		...	3097	6½	3¾	4½	...
Phrmactrl	PHAR		...	93259	1⅝	½	11/16	- 1/16
Phrmacia	PHABY	.20e	20	102962	26¼	16¼	23⅛	+ ⅛
Phrmknetic	PKLB		25	206764	9½	3½	5	- 2½
PhnxAm	PHXA		5	10260	4⅝	2⅞	3½	+ ⅛
PhnxMed	PHNX		...	82255	17	4⅜	4½	- 12½
PhnxRe	PXRE	.05e	11	48694	15½	8¾	13¾	+ 4¼
PhnxTech	PTEC		...	243228	18¾	3⅛	3⅞	- 11⅛
PhotoCtrl	PHOC		21	2419	6	3⅞	5⅞	+ 1⅜
PhtronLab	PLAB		...	11578	6⅛	1	4⅞	+ 3 9/16
PhysIns	PICOA		4	8549	5⅞	2½	4	+ 1½
PicSav	PICN		12	579606	18⅞	11¼	13⅛	+ ⅞
PicdlyCafe	PICC	.48	11	36777	17¼	12½	14	+ ⅝
PiedmtBk	PBGI	.64	...	1944	17¾	15½	16½	+ ½
PiedmtSvg	PFSB	†	...	15003	15	10⅝	14⅛	+ 3¼
PiedmMgt	PMAN		5	22931	15	6¾	13½	+ 6¾
PinnaclBcp	MFSBE	.50	...	464	11½	6½	9¼	- 2¼
PinnaclFnl	PNFI	1.40	...	518	40	35½	38¾	...
PionrAmHldg	PAHC	1.20e	...	318	47	39½	45½	+ 4½
PionrFdSvg	PFBK	.34e	...	37635	33¼	21¼	32¾	...
PionrFnlCp	PION	.24a	1	37279	12⅜	8¼	9½	+ ½
PionrFnlSvc	PFSI		8	136777	18¾	9⅞	17¼	+ 6¼
PionrFnlSvc			...	12718	31⅞	25¼	30	...
PionrGp	PIOG	.80	10	33694	25	18	22½	+ 4¼
PionrHiBrd	PHYB	1.16	14	143695	45¼	33½	44¾	+ 11
PionrSvgFL	PSBF		...	37995	3½	1/16	⅛	- 2⅝
PionrBcp	PSBN	.24b	46	10763	14	8	9¾	+ 1½
PionrStdElec	PIOS	.14	8	35174	11¼	7⅛	8	- 1½
PiperJafr	PIPR	.20a	7	873	25	13½	19	+ 5½
PlainsRes	PLNS		59	141726	1 9/16	⅝	1 3/16	+ ½
Planters	PNBT	.58	9	7487	17½	13½	14¼	- ½
PlastiLine	SIGN		10	8306	14¼	9½	10	- ¾
PlayerInt	PLAY		8	49382	4⅝	1 7/16	3⅝	+ 2 3/16
PlazaComrc	PLZA	.10	10	12657	16	9½	12	+ 2⅜
PlenumPub	PLEN	.80	10	10312	29¾	21¼	28½	+ 5¾
PlexusCp	PLXS		17	17810	9⅞	4½	6¾	+ 2¼
PlymFiveCts	THFI		23	16201	8⅞	2¾	3¼	- 4
PolicyMgt	PMSC		22	193921	37½	21¾	34	+ 9¾
PolifyFnl	PFLY	.40	...	32816	12¾	4¾	5¼	- 6
PolkAudio	POLK		10	9082	11	5½	8¾	+ 2¾
PonceBk	PFBS	.33j	...	43697	8¾	5½	6	- ¾
PopRadio	POPX		...	69862	25¾	7⅞	14	+ 6⅛
PortmBk	POBS	.48	7	28487	12½	8⅞	10¾	- ⅜
PosdnPool	POOL		...	23085	3⅜	1½	2	- ⅜
Possis	POSS		...	27584	5⅝	2⅜	2⅝	- 1½
PoughkpSvg	PKPS	.60	...	98273	23⅛	7½	7¾	- 10
PowelInd	POWL		22	99526	6	1⅛	5⅜	+ 4⅛
PrecisnStd	PCSNC		...	78984	4⅜	1⅝	3¼	+ 3/16
PfdSvg	PSLA		2	8742	3½	¾	1 13/32	- 31/32
PremrBcp	PRBC		150	84983	6¾	4⅛	4½	+ ⅜
PremrBksh	PBKC	.40	10	2141	16½	14	14⅜	- ⅛
PremrFnl	PREM	.10r	...	1900	14¾	11¼	13½	+ 2¼
PresidlLf	PLFE	.12	8	90621	19¾	10½	17½	+ 6¾
PrestonCp	PTRK	.50	16	56938	18	10¼	11¾	- 5¾
PriceCo	PCLB	1.50e	20	724608	49½	34¾	46¼	+ 8¾
PriceStrn	PSSP		...	40483	13½	6¾	7¼	- 5
PriceTRowe	TROW	.84	14	26984	58¾	34¼	58½	+ 24
Pricor	PRCO		...	64887	13	3	11	+ 7¾
PridePete	PRDE		106	148017	6⅝	2⅝	6⅜	+ 3⅜
PrimaEngy	PENG		13	3732	4¼	2¼	3⅞	+ 1⅝
PrimeBcsh	PMBS		...	33346	15¾	11	13½	...
PrimeBk	PMBK	.40	11	6347	27	14½	26⅝	+ 11⅞
PrimeBcp	PSAB	.48	6	8358	18½	13⅞	15¼	+ 1
PrimeMed	PMSI		...	21267	1¼	⅝	11/16	- 3/16
Printrnx	PTNX		...	36752	10⅜	6½	9⅞	+ 2
Procyte	PRCY		...	6110	8¼	7¼	8	...
ProdnOper	PROP	.16	26	47140	16⅞	4⅝	16⅞	+ 11½
ProfInvIns	PROF		2	7977	5	⅝	¾	- 4⅛

Stock	Symbol	Div	Yld	Sales 100s	Hi	Lo	Last	Net Chg
Proffitts	PRFT		24	3752	8	6¾	6¾	− ⅛
ProfitSys	PFTS		...	3963	9	6½	8¼	+ 1½
ProgramSys	PSYS		15	9586	22¼	16	21¾	+ 4¼
ProgressFnl	PFNC	.24	56	2662	13½	10¼	11¼	− ¼
ProgresvBk	PSBK	1.10	5	17211	22½	13	13⅝	− 5
Progroup	PRGR	.20	14	18655	17	8	12¼	+ 4
Pronet	PNET		...	40729	8	3¾	6¼	+ 2⅛
ProspctGp	PROS		19	126971	14	8½	13¼	+ 3⅝
ProsptPkFnl	PPSA	.50b	24	16171	12¼	5⅞	6¼	− 3⅞
ProtctvLf	PROT	.70	13	51987	16¼	12⅞	14⅝	+ 1⅜
ProvenaFood	PVNA	.11	26	6267	5	3	4½	+ 1¼
ProvWorRR	PWRR	.10	8	392	15	5½	8½	+ 3
ProvdtBcp	PRBK	.50	9	1131	29½	23½	24	− 2½
ProvdtBksh	PBKS	.40	27	64439	14	9¾	12⅜	+ 1½
ProvdtLf A	PACCA	.80	9	51753	26⅛	17⅛	21⅞	+ 4½
ProvdtLf	PACCB	.80	9	263090	30⅛	19⅛	25⅝	+ 6⅜
PSICOR	PCOR		18	47143	14	7⅞	10¼	+ 1½
PubSvcNC	PSNC	1.04	12	15768	16⅝	14⅛	16⅜	+ 1¼
PubEqpt	PECN		7	21495	6⅝	3¼	3½	− 1⅝
PugetSdBcp	PSNB	.96	14	83685	27¼	18½	23½	+ 4¾
PulaskFurn	PLFC	.48	9	6493	21	16½	19½	+ 2¼
PulskiS&L	PULS	1.00	6	10106	17½	11¾	12¾	− 3½
PultzrPub	PLTZ	.48	15	30301	30½	24	29¾	+ 5⅛
PuritnBen	PBEN	.11	17	140219	26½	15	24¼	+ 8½
PutnamTr	PTNM	.48	12	2926	21	19	19¼	+ ¼
PyramdTech	PYRD		20	252064	19½	9¼	19	+ 2¼
QED Explr	QEDX		...	5998	2¾	1⅜	2⅜	+ 7/16
QVCNetw	QVCN	.30e	35	209568	21¼	8¼	16½	+ 8
QuadraLogic	QLTIF		...	38317	11⅜	3⅜	7⅞	+ 3⅝
Quadrex	QUAD		...	136515	8¼	1	2	− 3⅛
QuakrChm	QCHM	.68	10	17036	23½	18¾	20¼	+ 1
QualFood	QFCI		24	36286	31¾	12	30¼	+ 18⅛
Quantrnix	QUAN		25	25545	6⅞	3⅞	6⅝	+ 2⅜
Quantum	QNTM		9	731098	16½	4¼	10⅞	+ 6½
Quarex	QRXI	†	14	25148	7⅝	3⅞	6⅛	+ 1⅜
QuartzMtn	QZMGF		...	61459	1 3/16	5/16	7/16	− 11/32
QuestMed	QMED		4	60461	45½	1 11/16	2¼	+ 5/16
Questech	QTEC		...	2445	6	3⅛	3⅛	− 2⅛
QuickslvrInc	QUIK		17	237953	25⅝	7½	19⅛	+ 11
Quipp	QUIP		...	2684	16	6	6	− 7
Quixote	QUIX		21	32353	8⅛	5⅝	6	− 1¾
Qume	QUME		6	145409	8¾	4⅝	5⅛	− ¼

-R-

Stock	Symbol	Div	Yld	Sales 100s	Hi	Lo	Last	Net Chg
RAXRestr	RAXR	.01e	...	33164	3⅞	1⅞	2	− ¾
RELM Comm	RGCY	†	6	104972	1 9/16	⅝	1 3/16	...
RPM	RPOW	.68	17	139432	20	15⅜	19	+ 3⅜
RS Fnl	RFBK		9	42810	15¼	9½	9⅞	− 1⅜
RadtnSys	RADS	.10	17	41841	12¾	8½	11⅞	+ 3¼
RailmanS&L	RRMN	†	7	4578	18¾	9¾	15½	+ 5⅛
RainbwTech	RNBO		19	83693	23¼	6⅛	13⅞	+ 7⅝
Rallys	RLLy		...	93248	24⅞	14	14	...
RamapoFnl	RMPO	.65	8	4356	16¼	13¼	14	− 1¼
RamsayHlthCr	RHCI		12	56092	4	2	2¾	+ ⅜
Rangaire	RANG		14	9772	10¾	6¾	7¼	− 2¼
RaritnBcp	RARB	.30	...	4688	14½	9½	9¾	− ¾
RatnersGp	RATNY	.30e	...	6409	13⅞	9⅞	12¼	+ 3
RauchInd	RCHI	†	11	8658	13½	7	12¼	+ 5¼
Raymond	RAYM	.47	24	34894	16¼	7¼	8	− 7
RediCare	REDI		...	19164	2 3/16	1 3/16	2⅛	+ 7/16
Reading A	RDGCA		2	3845	13¼	11⅛	12½	...
Receptech un			...	13614	13	11¼	12	...
Recoton	RCOT		10	8553	6⅜	3¼	3⅜	− 2¼
RedEagl	REDX		50	27844	1⅝	13/16	1	...
ReedJwlr	REED		16	11019	11	4½	8⅛	+ 2
ReevComm	RVCC		...	299156	7⅛	4⅜	6⅞	+ 1¼
RefacTech	REFC	.25e	10	13573	9	5¾	6⅛	− 1¼
Reflctone	RFTN	†	...	5589	9½	4	4¼	− 3⅞
RgencyCru	SHIP		10	262766	2 7/16	1⅝	1 11/16	− ⅜
RgencyEqpt	RGEQ	.02c	...	104137	5/32	1/16	⅛	...
ReglBcpMA	REGB	.56	12	25664	20	13¾	14	− 3½
ReistrSvg	RFSB		6	2843	22	15	21¾	+ 6¾
Reliablty	REAL		8	14033	5	2	2⅞	− 2⅛
RenCp	RENL		...	4367	6⅞	6½	6⅞	...
RepapEnt	RPAPF	.28	...	48469	12	7¼	8⅜	− 1⅛
Repligen	RGEN		...	59383	10½	6¼	10	+ 3
RepubAuto	RAUT		30	23249	7	5	6	+ ½
RepubBcp	RBNC	†	...	11581	8⅛	6	6⅝	− ⅞
RepubCptl	RSLA	1.20	9	11181	21¼	13¼	15½	+ 1¼
RepubPic A	RPICA		108	34729	13	6	9¾	+ 3½
RepubSvg	RSFC		...	3642	4⅛	1¾	2	− 1⅞
Resdel	RSDL		...	18741	1⅝	9/32	9/32	− 1 5/32
ResearchInc	RESR	.44	11	2358	9½	7¼	8	− 1
ResrchInd	REIC		47	64834	9⅞	5¼	8⅞	+ 2⅞
ReservInd	ROIL		16	4041	4⅛	1 15/16	3¼	− 3/16
ResourcAm	REXI	.03e	9	7962	2½	1 11/16	2¼	+ 9/16
Respronic	RESP		21	5409	19	9½	18	+ 6¼
RetailCp'	RCOA		...	2428	3¾	1¼	1¼	− 1⅞
ReutrInc	REUT		...	28463	11½	6¾	9¼	− ¾
ReutrHldg	RTRSY	.55e	26	f12287	53⅝	28⅛	49⅝	+ 21¼
RevereFd	PREV	1.04e	...	13455	11¾	6¼	6¼	− 4¾
RexhallInd	REXL		...	41619	11	5¼	8¼	...
Rexon	REXN		8	129157	8	5½	7¼	+ ¾
Rexwrks	REXW		...	10948	5⅞	3½	3½	− 1⅞
Rheomtrc	RHEM	†	41	6234	8⅜	4½	4½	− 2¼
Ribilmun	RIBI		...	60830	5¼	2¼	2½	− 1 7/16
RichdsnElec	RELL	.16	14	73341	20	8¼	11	− 9
RichfdHldg	RCHFA	.05j	41	127269	11⅞	6	7⅞	...
RiggsNtl	RIGS	1.25	7	32761	28	18⅜	21¼	− 1¾
RightMgt	RMCI		14	8239	5¼	2½	5¼	+ 2¾
RivrForest	RFBC	.24	15	8320	30½	15½	29¾	+ 13¾
RivrsdNtl	RNRC	.22e	...	2863	12⅜	9½	12¼	+ 1
RivrsdGp	RSGI		7	2032	12¾	10	10¼	− 1¼
RoadwyMtr	RDWI		69	14920	6	2¾	2¾	− 2 13/16
RoadwySvc	ROAD	1.10	17	282290	43¼	27¾	42¼	+ 11½
RoanokeElec	RESC	.48a	6	12192	16½	13¾	14¾	+ 1
RobnsMyrs	ROBN	.10e	8	6123	18¼	13½	16¼	+ 2¼
Robec	ROBC		6	14567	10⅝	8½	8¾	...
RobtHalf	RHII		15	62259	19⅞	15¾	17¼	− 1½
RobesnInd	RBSN		...	16899	3⅞	¾	1 7/16	− 1/16
RobsnNugt	RNIC	.08	22	15750	7¾	5	6	− ¾
RobotcVsn	ROBV		...	42658	6⅝	2¾	3⅜	− ½
RochstrSvg	RCSB	.44	9	265666	19⅜	10⅞	12	− 2¼
RockFnl	RFIN	1.40b	...	334	34½	29	34½	+ 4½
RockgHrse	RHCC		...	78119	4	1¾	2	− 1
RockyMtUn	RMUC		24	24613	2¾	1 1/16	1 3/16	− 11/16
Ronson	RONC		...	11858	3⅝	1½	1½	− ⅞
RsvltFnl	RFED	.80	4	52725	17⅜	11⅛	12¼	+ ¼
RopakCp	ROPK	†	16	16779	10 7/32	5¾	6¾	− 2¼
RoseStr	RSTO	.16a	15	18961	10	6	6⅛	− 1⅝
RoseStrB	RSTOB	.16a	15	56025	9¾	5⅞	6⅜	− 1¼
Rospatch	RPCH		12	14259	23	11¼	14	− 6
RossStr	ROST		11	393362	24⅝	3⅝	14¼	+ 3¾
RossCosm	RCDC		112	9679	5⅛	1¾	2¼	− 1 15/16
RotechMed	ROTC		15	19403	3⅜	1¼	2 15/16	+ 7/16
RotoRtr	ROTO	.40	16	14519	23¾	18½	19¼	− 3¼
Rouse	ROUS	.56	115	217919	29¾	23¼	26½	+ 2
RoylBkPa	RBPAA	†	...	8152	9¼	7½	8⅝	+ ⅞
RoylGld	RGLD		23	65915	4⅛	1¼	1⅝	− 1⅛
Roylpar	ROYL		12	37337	3½	1 1/16	1 9/16	+ 1/16
Roylpar wt			...	2516	1⅝	⅜	1¼	+ ⅛
RuleInd	RULE		9	9595	9⅜	6¼	7⅞	+ 1⅝
RyanBeck	RBCO	.24a	21	8696	6½	3	3	− 2⅞
RyanFamStk	RYAN		19	664974	9	5⅛	7⅝	+ 2¼

-S-

Stock	Symbol	Div	Yld	Sales 100s	Hi	Lo	Last	Net Chg
S&KBrands	SKFB		12	8808	17½	11½	12¾	+ 1¼
SBT	SBTC	.05r	...	1714	7½	3¾	4	− 3¼
SCI Sys	SCIS		9	363912	16	7⅝	8⅝	− 6⅜
SCS Cptr	SCOM		...	10857	7½	3¼	4½	− 1¼
SDNB Fnl	SDNB	.20b	13	1946	14	7¾	12¼	+ 4⅛
SEI Cp	SEIC	.10	17	70142	20	15⅞	17¾	+ ¼
SFE Tech	SFEM		...	30195	13/16	3/16	7/32	− 19/32
SanFranS&L	SFFD		...	103478	21¾	12	16¼	+ 4⅛
SHL Sys	SHKIF		...	173052	10½	6½	10	+ 1¼
SKF AB	SKFRY		19	19368	28⅝	15⅞	26⅛	+ 10
S-K-I Ltd.	SKII	.09	19	21626	27½	13	19	+ 2½
SJNB Fnl	SJNB		...	6343	11	5	9¾	+ 4¾
SNL Fnl	SNLFA	†	5	13127	7	3⅜	4	+ ¼
SPI Suspen	SPILF		...	3265	1½	⅜	½	...
STV Engr	STVI		...	4367	9¼	4¾	7½	+ 2¼
Safeco	SAFC	1.20	8	561522	39¾	23⅛	38⅝	+ 15
SafegrdHlth	SFGD		14	48734	12½	4¾	8⅞	+ 3⅜
SageSftwr	SGSI		27	65437	10½	6¾	8⅞	+ 1
SaharaResrt	SHRE		65	8182	38	23	28½	+ 4¾
StIvesLabs	SWIS		17	115226	17¾	8⅜	10	+ 1⅛
StJudeMed	STJM		24	476204	50½	19¼	48¼	+ 28¼
StPaulBcp	SPBC	.40	9	128761	19⅞	10¾	17⅛	+ 6
StPaulCos	STPL	2.20	8	500659	63½	43	59⅛	+ 15⅝
SalemCpt	SLCR	.08	8	46291	9⅞	6⅝	7⅝	+ 1

OVER-THE-COUNTER

Stock	Symbol	Div	Yld	Sales 100s	Hi	Lo	Last	Net Chg
SalickHlth	SHCI		18	24167	12 1/8	9 1/2	10 7/8	- 3/8
SallieM vt		.52	193	78378	47 1/2	30 7/8	42 1/2	+ 11 1/2
Samna	SMNA		...	18037	5 1/2	3	4 3/4	- 3/8
SandFarm	SAFM	.30a	8	69275	23 1/2	11 1/2	13 1/2	+ 1 1/8
SandsRegnt	SNDS		12	26397	16 1/2	11	15 1/2	+ 4 1/4
SandwChef	SHEF		36	5382	9 3/4	6	9 1/4	+ 3 1/4
SandwBk	SWCB	.60	6	8541	14 1/4	7 1/2	8 3/4	- 2 3/4
Sanford	SANF	.16	20	67475	26 1/2	16 5/8	26 1/2	+ 8
SatliteInfo	SATI		...	33461	6 7/8	1 1/2	1 11/16	- 4 13/16
SavanFood	SVAN	.72	19	40477	56 1/4	18	55	+ 36 5/8
ScanOptc	SOCR		...	68666	5 3/8	2	2 3/4	- 1/2
SchulmnA	SHLM	.40	15	70763	36 1/4	26 1/2	35 1/2	+ 7 3/8
SchultHome	SHCO		4	980	2 3/4	1 3/4	2 1/4	+ 1/4
SchltzSavO	SAVO	.12	12	11841	18 3/4	13 1/4	17 1/4	+ 4
Schwartz A	SWARA	.10e	7	6347	3 1/2	2 1/4	3 1/8	+ 1/2
ScimedLf	SMLS		24	177153	27 1/4	6 3/4	24 1/2	+ 17 1/2
SciDynam	SIDY		34	12804	2 1/4	1 1/4	1 3/8	- 1/2
SciSftwr	SSFT		12	17101	5 1/4	2 1/2	3 1/2	+ 1/8
SciTech	STIZ	.14e	...	6300	4 1/2	2 1/2	3 1/4	- 1/2
Scitex	SCIXF		10	113923	17 1/4	7 1/4	17	+ 8 7/8
ScotStrgfllw	SCOT	.24	13	2613	9 1/4	8	8 5/8	+ 1/8
ScrippsEW A	EWSCA	.40	23	104106	27	16 7/8	24	+ 6 7/8
ScrippsH	SCRP	1.00	35	1691	81	57 1/2	68	- 2
SeaGalleyStr	SEAG		...	24334	1 7/8	3/4	13/16	- 11/16
SeabdSvg	SEAB	.15j	12	3609	9	3 1/2	3 3/4	- 3
SeacstBkFl	SBCFA	.20j	10	7599	15 3/4	11 1/4	12 3/4	+ 1 3/8
SeacstSvg	SSBA	.28	...	6747	13	3 1/2	4 1/2	- 5 3/4
SeagateTech	SGAT		10	f19924	16 1/8	8 1/2	15	+ 6 3/8
SeagullEngy pf		2.25	...	8869	36 1/2	26 3/8	35 1/2	+ 8 1/2
Sealright	SRCO	.28	19	24343	25 1/2	14 1/2	24 7/8	+ 7 5/8
SeattleFlm	FOTO		6	28459	6 1/4	3 1/16	6 1/4	+ 3 1/4
SeawayFood	SEWY	.36	14	1923	25	15 1/2	23	+ 7 1/2
SecdNtlSvg	SNFS	.36	5	32107	8 1/2	5 5/8	6 1/2	+ 5/8
SecorBk	SECR	.40	3	24038	11 1/2	5 3/8	5 3/8	- 6 1/8
SecurBcp	SECB	.92	9	19186	24	18 3/4	20 1/2	- 1
SecurS&LClv	SFSL	.28	4	1591	15 3/4	8 5/8	15 3/4	+ 7 1/8
SecurSvMT	SFBM	.24	14	6676	9	4 3/4	7 3/4	+ 2
SecurFnlGp	SFGI		15	3154	14	8 1/2	12	+ 2
SecurInv	SSLN	†	3	21349	7	4 1/4	4 5/8	- 1 5/8
SecurTag	STAG		...	35583	2 7/16	1 1/16	2 5/16	+ 13/16
SeeqTech	SEEQ		38	105319	6 3/4	3 3/8	3 7/16	- 1 15/16
SeiblBruce	SBIG	.80	...	50461	13 5/8	10 1/4	10 1/2	- 7/8
Selecterm	SLTM	.28e	12	7490	9 1/4	4 3/4	6	+ 1 1/4
SelectvIns	SIGI	.96	6	53187	20	14 1/2	19	+ 3 3/4
SelervlS&L	SLRV	.16	...	10311	18 1/2	9	17 3/4	+ 8 1/4
Selfix	SLFX	†	13	16893	11 1/2	6 1/8	8 1/4	+ 1 3/4
SenecaFood	SENE		16	8387	21	17 1/2	20 1/2	+ 2 3/4
SensorCtrl	SNCO		11	14144	3 3/4	2	2 7/8	- 1/4
SensrmatEl	SNSR	.05	14	533232	14	9 1/2	11 7/8	+ 2 1/4
SequentCptr	SQNT		34	238091	21	9 1/8	20	+ 10 3/4
ServTech	STEC		20	57829	20	10 1/2	14 1/4	...
ServcFractr	SERF		...	28541	7 1/8	3 3/4	6 1/2	+ 2 1/2
SevenOak	QPON		...	112096	9	4 5/8	6 1/8	- 2 7/8
Sharebase	SHBS		...	144169	3 1/2	1/8	1/4	- 2 1/4
SharedMed	SMED	.84	16	309530	19 3/8	12	12 7/8	- 3 3/4
SharprImag	SHRP		13	20738	9 3/4	4 7/8	7 3/4	+ 2 1/8
ShelbySvg	SHLB	.40	...	3779	22 3/4	10	22 3/4	+ 12 3/4
Sheldahl	SHEL		...	33680	8 1/8	4 1/2	5 3/8	- 1 3/4
SheltonBcp	SSBC	.40	9	1096	13	9 1/2	11 1/4	- 1 1/2
Shopsmith	SHOP		9	11748	8	3 5/16	5	+ 1 5/8
ShorwdPkg	SHOR		20	134971	28 1/2	16	25	+ 8
ShowbizPizza	SHBZ		...	46338	17	5	16 1/2	...
ShowscnFlm	SHOW		...	30691	13	5 3/4	8 1/2	+ 2 1/8
SierraOnLn	SIER		21	100633	23 1/2	10 5/8	23 1/4	+ 12 1/2
Sierra 83		.25e	...	2962	7 1/2	5 1/4	6	- 1/4
Sierra 84		.23j	...	7734	7 5/8	3	3 3/8	- 2 1/8
SierraTuscn	STSN		...	48353	13 1/8	11 1/4	12	...
SigmaAldr	SIAL	.40	23	113294	59 1/2	43 3/4	57 3/4	+ 10 1/2
SigmaDsgn	SIGM		6	126078	20 1/4	7 1/2	9 3/4	- 5 3/4
SilicnGen	SILN		15	48374	3 1/2	1 5/8	1 3/4	- 1 1/2
SilicnGraph	SGIC		32	436842	29 3/8	14 1/4	29 1/4	+ 10 1/2
SilicnVlyBksh	SIVB	.10r	8	35729	28 3/4	11 5/8	19 3/4	+ 7 1/2
SilicnVlyGp	SVGI		8	92984	9 1/2	5 7/8	7 1/4	+ 1/8
Siliconix	SILI		...	44380	7 1/8	2 3/8	2 5/8	- 4
SilkGrnhse	SGHI		10	434479	24 1/4	6 3/4	8	- 4 3/4
SlvrHartMin	SVMHF		...	618	3/4	3/16	1/4	- 3/8
Simetco	SMET		12	10312	6 1/8	3 1/2	3 11/16	...
SimpsnInd	SMPS	.56	8	59064	14 3/4	9	9 1/4	- 1 1/2
SizzlrRstr	SIZZ		16	101324	23 3/4	17	22 1/4	+ 5 1/4

Stock	Symbol	Div	Yld	Sales 100s	Hi	Lo	Last	Net Chg
SkanSvgBk	SKAN	.30	33	3621	11	7 1/2	8 1/4	- 1 3/4
Skippers	SKIP	.10	157	38640	11 5/8	6 3/8	11	+ 4 5/8
SkyWest	SKYW	.05a	7	22402	9 7/8	5	6 5/8	+ 1 1/2
SmithLab	SMLB		54	102952	2 7/8	1 7/8	2 11/16	...
SmithfldCos	HAMS	.06	13	8094	9 3/4	7	7 1/8	- 1 1/2
SmithfldFd	SFDS		18	60347	18 3/4	11 1/2	12 1/4	- 3 5/8
SocietyCp	SOCI	1.60	7	103355	40 1/2	33	34 1/8	+ 7/8
SocietySvg	SOCS	.60b	5	90888	23 1/2	12 1/4	14 1/2	- 1 1/8
Softech	SOFT		10	15120	5 7/8	4	4	- 3/4
Softsel	SOFS		8	121395	7 7/8	5 1/2	6 1/8	+ 1/8
SftwrPub	SPCO		12	356572	20 3/4	10 1/4	16 1/4	+ 3 1/4
SftwrTool	TWRX		28	155193	15 1/8	4 1/2	14 7/8	+ 9 7/8
SftwrSvc	SSOA		11	72660	7 1/2	7/8	1 1/4	- 5 3/4
SomerstGp	SOMR		23	4406	8 3/4	6	7 1/2	+ 1 1/4
SomerstBsh	SOSA	.28	...	72680	14 1/2	4 1/8	5 1/8	- 8 3/4
SonestaHotl	SNSTA	.24	...	687	16 1/4	12 3/4	13	- 1 1/8
SonocoPdt	SONO	.84	16	174848	39	32 1/2	37	+ 2 3/4
SonoraGld	SONNF		...	27974	2	1 1/8	1 1/2	+ 1/16
SoundAdvc	SUND		9	81879	12 7/8	5 7/8	7	+ 1/8
SoCaroFed	SCFB	.87t	...	8595	17 1/2	9 3/4	9 3/4	- 2 1/2
SoCarolNtl	SCNC	.72	8	69571	27 3/8	20 1/2	22	- 1 3/8
SEMichGas	SMGS	.80b	19	8701	20 1/2	15 1/2	19 1/8	+ 2 1/4
SoeastSvgs	SESL	.12	...	5888	4 7/8	1	1 1/4	- 2 1/4
SoeastSvg	SSIF		...	4782	12 1/2	8 3/4	9 1/2	...
SthnBksh	SOBK	1.40e	...	168	43 3/4	32	32	- 10 1/2
SoCalWatr	SWTR	2.12	15	14402	30 3/4	24 1/4	29 3/4	+ 2 3/4
SoMinls	SMIN	.07	13	7248	4 1/4	3 1/4	3 7/8	+ 3/8
SoNtl	SNAT	.40	11	21517	15 1/2	12	13 1/2	+ 5/8
SouthngSv	SSBB	.64a	7	3231	14 1/2	10 1/2	10 1/2	- 3/4
SouthTrust	SOTR	.96b	8	53988	25 1/4	20 3/8	22 3/4	+ 2 1/8
SouthwlTech	SWTX		...	30469	9	4 1/4	7 3/4	+ 2
SowestNtl	SWPA	.84	12	1852	22	19	19 1/2	- 1 1/4
SowestWtr	SWWC	.88	16	5465	16 3/4	13 3/4	16	- 1/4
SowestElec	SWEL	2.20	9	571	42 1/2	36	38	- 1/2
SovrnBcp	SVRN		7	17520	16 1/8	8 3/4	13	+ 4
SpanAmMed	SPAN		8	19366	3 5/8	2 3/8	2 7/8	+ 1/2
SpartnMtr	SPAR	.05e	18	66640	7 1/2	3 1/2	3 7/8	- 1 1/8
SpearFnl	SFNS		...	36800	3 1/8	1 1/8	2	+ 1/2
SpearhdInd	SPRH		...	14666	2 5/8	1 3/8	1 1/2	- 5/8
SpecMusic	SPEK		23	38010	9 1/8	4 7/8	9 1/8	+ 3 3/8
Spectran	SPTR		...	20839	2 3/8	1	1 9/16	+ 1/4
SpectrmCtrl	SPEC	†	5	36111	5 5/8	2 1/4	2 3/8	- 1 1/8
Spiegel	SPGLA	.20a	16	153108	23 5/8	8 7/8	20 1/4	+ 11 1/8
Spinnaker	SPKR		...	26204	2 1/2	3/4	1 1/8	- 1/2
Spire	SPIR		28	20753	7 1/2	2 5/8	5 1/2	+ 2 5/8
SprouseRtz	STRS		...	5871	23 1/4	14	15 1/4	- 4 1/4
SquareInd	SQAI		18	762	21 1/2	15	19 1/2	+ 4 1/4
StafBldr	SBLI		10	85312	7 1/2	2	2 3/4	- 4 1/2
StamfdCap	CGPS	.02e	...	21575	6 3/8	3 3/8	3 7/8	- 1
StakeTech	STKLF		...	44311	4 3/4	1 1/2	2	- 7/8
StdMicsys	SMSC		21	135469	7 5/8	4 1/2	6 1/4	+ 1
StdRegstr	SREG	.56	12	145526	19 3/4	14 3/4	15 7/8	- 1/4
StanfdTel	STII		14	28615	11 3/4	6	7 3/4	- 3 3/4
StansbyMng	STBY		...	40642	1 1/16	11/32	5/8	- 1/32
Staodyn	SDYN		71	16459	4 3/8	2 1/8	4 1/4	+ 2
Staples	SPLS		48	188653	26	14 1/2	18 1/8	...
StarBanc	STRZ	.88	11	49977	27	18 1/2	22	+ 3 1/8
StarStates	STSS	.40	...	46426	14 1/8	7	7 1/4	- 1 1/4
StarTch	STRR		...	64424	1 3/32	3/8	7/16	- 19/32
StOMaine	SOME		10	25667	17	11	13 3/4	+ 1 3/4
StateStBos	STBK	.64	14	298639	40 7/8	25 1/2	39 1/4	+ 12 3/4
StatesmnGp	STTG	.05b	10	56024	3 5/8	1 13/16	2 7/8	...
StwdBcpNJ	STWB	.80	8	36096	20 3/4	9 1/2	12 1/2	- 4 3/4
SteelTech	STTX	.03	13	39723	17	9	9 1/4	- 4 3/4
SteelWVa	SWVA	5.50e	3	5673	3 3/4	2 3/4	3 1/8	...
StewStevsn	SSSS	.12i	14	217517	32 1/2	13 7/8	27 3/4	+ 13 5/8
StewInfo	SISC	.40	...	24593	21	16 3/4	17	- 7/8
StkhldSys	SSIAA	.18e	10	17667	11 1/2	7 1/8	7 3/4	- 7/8
StokelyUSA	STKY	.16a	10	135711	17 3/4	8	17 5/8	+ 9 5/8
StoltTankr	STLTF	.55e	10	208537	29 5/8	15 1/8	21 1/8	+ 5 5/8
StratgPln	SPAIB		69	17920	14 3/4	6 1/2	12 1/2	+ 5 3/4
StratfdAm	STRC		...	44581	21/32	3/32	3/32	...
StrwbClth	STRWA	1.10b	11	29208	40 1/4	32 1/4	33	+ 1/2
Strober	STRB		28	16539	9 1/2	2 3/4	3 3/8	- 6 1/8
Structfab	STRU		...	3565	4 5/8	7/8	1 3/8	- 3 1/4
StructlDyn	SDRC		24	89012	30	17	29 1/2	+ 10 3/4
Stryker Cp	STRY		32	107964	25	13	24 3/4	+ 11 1/4
StuartStor	STUS		22	33898	4 7/8	1 7/8	2 1/4	- 1 7/8
StuartHall	STUH		16	142777	17 1/4	5 5/8	10 3/4	+ 5
SturmRgr	STRM	1.00a	11	3314	36 1/2	19 1/2	30	+ 10 1/2

Stock	Symbol	Div	Yld	Sales 100s	Hi	Lo	Last	Net Chg
SubaruAm	SBRU		...	451226	8½	5	5⅜	– ⅜
SuburbBcp	SUBBA	.31	12	15315	26	17⅝	25	+ 7¼
Sudbury	SUDS		...	98342	7⅝	4¼	4¼	– 1⅜
SuffldFnl	SFCP	.08e	13	26318	8¼	2⅞	3¼	– 4
SuffkBcp	SUBK	.52	7	6997	15¼	12¾	12¾	– ¼
SumitomoBk	SUMI	1.32	7	28830	34¾	20⅜	28	+ 3¼
SummaMed	SUMA		...	463148	6⅛	1⅝	3⅞	+ 1⅞
Sumagraph	SUGR		8	75478	17	10	13	+ 1⅛
Summcp	SMCR	.64	10	29104	23½	19	19½	– 1¼
SummitBcp	SUBN	.80	8	47870	22	15¾	17	– 2¾
SummitHlth	SUMH		...	58129	2⅞	1	1½	...
SummitHldg	SUHC	.79e	...	1292	19¼	13	14¾	– 3¾
SummitSvg	SMMT		...	11706	6½	2¼	5⅛	+ 2⅞
SunCoastPl	SUNI		...	47277	1⅛	17/32	19/32	– 9/32
SunSptwear	SSPW		...	16938	11½	10	11½	...
SunairElec	SNRU		24	6064	3⅝	1¾	2⅜	– 1
SunGard	SNDT		19	183995	23¾	12½	23¾	+ 8¼
SuncoastSL	SCSL	.19r	6	8963	8⅛	6⅝	6¾	– ⅜
SunMicrsys	SUNW		30	f29584	23	13⅜	17¼	+ ⅝
SunriseBcpCA	SRBC		15	4952	6½	4	6⅜	...
Sunlite	SNLT		6	8601	5⅝	4¼	4¾	+ ¼
SunriseMed	SNMD		11	87890	11⅜	3⅝	9⅝	+ 5⅜
SunstrFood	SUNF		...	5361	5¼	2¾	4½	+ 13/16
SunwestFnl	SFSI	1.12	9	30871	32	20½	21¾	– 2¾
Supertex	SUPX		8	22402	3¼	1⅞	2	– ⅝
SuprmEqpt	SEQP		...	5901	4¼	⅞	1⅜	– 2⅝
SurgCare	SCAF	.02i	36	114307	22½	7⅛	19¼	+ 12
SurgLaser	SLTI		...	99125	18	9	10½	...
SurvlTech	SURV		...	11274	9¾	4½	8¼	+ 3¼
SusqhnBk	SUSQ	1.00	9	12844	22¾	19¼	21½	+ 2
SvenskaCl	SCAPY		...	1847	23¾	15¾	18¾	– ⅞
SymTekSys	SYMK		...	2161	12½	4½	8½	– 3½
Symantec	SYMC		...	76435	18	11	15½	...
Symbion	SYMB	1.60e	4	14260	2¾	1⅜	2⅜	+ 1
Symbolic	SMBX		21	304032	2½	⅞	1¼	+ 5/16
SynOptCom	SNPX		23	169843	25¼	11¾	25¼	+ 10¾
Synbiotc	SBIO		...	30588	7¼	2¾	4⅜	– 2⅜
Syncor	SCOR		88	64097	8¼	4⅜	7⅞	+ 3
Synercom	SYNR		19	63211	6⅛	2¼	4⅝	+ 2⅛
Synergen	SYGN		...	72046	15⅛	4⅛	13	+ 8¼
Syntech	SYNE		...	51451	2⅞	¼	11/32	– 29/32
Synetic	SNTC		27	38953	14⅜	10¾	14⅜	...
Syntrex	STRX		...	57150	1⅞	½	13/16	+ 5/16
Syntro	SYNT		...	40764	2⅛	⅝	¾	– 1 1/16
SyrcusSply	SYRA	.28	35	2390	16	9¼	15¼	+ 6
SysSftwr	SSAX		21	217666	31¼	17¼	29¾	+ 12½
Systmatic	SYST	.48	20	43184	40¼	30	35½	+ 4
SysCptrTech	SCTC		30	127296	8	2⅞	7 5/16	+ 4¼

-T-

Stock	Symbol	Div	Yld	Sales 100s	Hi	Lo	Last	Net Chg
T2 Medical	TSQM		31	2199	25	9⅝	25	+ 14
TBC	TBCC		12	112186	13¼	8½	12⅞	+ 4¼
TCA Cable	TCAT	.24	36	59004	21⅜	15⅝	17¼	+ 1⅝
TCI Int	TCII		14	13721	16½	5⅝	7¼	– 8¼
TCellSci	TCEL		...	63478	7⅛	2	5	+ 3
TGX	XTGX		...	94622	1 7/16	9/16	¾	– 11/16
TJ Int	TJCO	.40	11	34590	36¼	23	24½	– ⅜
TM Comm	TMCI		...	14703	¾	⅛	3/16	– 3/32
TPI Ent	TPIE		...	170793	7¾	3¾	7¼	+ 2¾
TSI	TSII	.16	13	8370	14¼	8¾	11¾	+ 2½
TSR	TSRI		33	14937	4½	2¼	4¼	+ 1 15/16
TVX Bdcst h	TVXGC		...	24252	5	1⅝	3¾	+ 2⅛
TW Hldgs	TWFS		...	56114	4½	3½	4½	...
TalmanS&L	TLMN	.25	4	107566	10½	6⅝	7⅞	– ¾
Tandon	TCOR		...	388248	1 7/16	7/16	13/16	– ¼
TechData	TECD		7	99649	17⅜	7⅜	7¾	– 5¼
Technalys	TECN	.34	16	13434	14	6½	13¼	+ 6¾
TechCom	TCCO		7	35954	19¼	9	11½	+ ¼
TechDevl	TDCX		14	8607	3⅞	2⅜	2⅝	– ⅞
Tecogen	TCGN		110	16754	6½	3⅞	5½	+ ⅜
TecmsehPdt	TECU	3.20a	9	6330	149	133	135	– 7½
TejasGas	TEJS		20	45695	28¼	14½	28¼	+ 12
Tekelec	TKLC		9	40563	15¾	7¾	8½	– 7
TelcoSys	TELC		34	126606	12¼	3¾	11¼	+ 6⅝
TelOptic	TOPT		4	6823	3½	1¼	19/32	– 1 11/32
TeleComm A	TCOMA		...	f18491	21⅝	12⅝	17⅞	+ 4⅞
TeleComm B	TCOMB		...	9356	21½	13	18¼	+ 5⅝
TeleComm rt			...	189160	4½	2⅛	3⅛	...
TelcmNetw	TNII		...	23898	8⅛	2¾	6⅛	+ 3⅜
Telcrdit	TCRD	1.00	17	140963	41½	29	39¾	+ 5¾
Telmatic	TMAX		...	262541	9¾	3	4½	– 5⅜
Telmundo	TLMD		...	27863	8	4½	6¼	– 1¾
TelVideo	TELV		...	120420	23/32	3/16	9/32	– 3/16
Telabs	TLAB		12	110044	14½	8¼	9⅜	– 3¼
Telos	TLOS		21	36334	15¼	6½	15	+ 7¾
Telxon	TLXN	.01e	24	265500	20¼	6⅜	8	– 10½
TempstTech	TTOI	1.00e	30	18858	4⅝	1⅝	2⅛	– 1¾
TemtexInd	TMTX		...	5934	4¼	1¾	2	– 2⅛
Tennant	TANT	1.12	13	28276	36½	25¼	35	+ 8¾
Teradata	TDAT		29	258403	22¾	12	22	+ 5¼
TerexCp	TERX	.05	10	52141	25½	12¾	22	+ 9¼
Termiflex	TFLX		...	4769	3⅛	1¾	1⅞	– ¾
TerminlData	TERM		...	22001	2⅞	1	1¼	– 1
TevaPharm	TEVIY	.14e	11	12979	13½	6¼	11¾	+ 4⅞
Thomstn A	TMSTA	.44	15	5166	19¾	14¾	19½	+ 4¼
Thomstn B	TMSTB	.44	25	651	22	15½	21	+ 3½
ThomsonCSF	TCSFY	.81e	...	5971	40⅛	24½	26⅝	– 11⅜
ThornApVly	TAVI		...	3429	8⅜	6¾	7	– ¾
ThousandTrl	TRLS		6	74207	2¾	13/16	1 11/16	+ 7/16
3ComCp	COMS		16	f11656	28¾	10	13¾	– 8⅛
TiercoGp	TIERC		...	2794	4⅞	½	⅞	– 3⅞
TigeraGp	TYGR		...	127041	1⅜	⅝	21/32	– 7/32
TimbrlnSftwr	TMBS		27	5125	7	5¼	6	+ ⅛
Tocor un			...	40211	16½	11	14⅝	...
Todd-AOCp	TODDA	.10	225	6661	13¼	8¼	12¼	+ 3¼
TokioMarine	TKIOY	.24e	33	8344	95½	66	76¾	– 14⅝
TollandBk	TOBK	.48	8	4981	11¾	6¾	7½	– 2⅞
TompkinTr	TCTC	.54b	16	1121	28½	20	22⅛	– 5½
TomkinsPLC	TOMKY	.48e	9	10531	19	14⅜	17⅞	+ 2¾
ToppsCo	TOPPC	.24	16	167469	18¾	8¼	17¼	+ 8½
ToreadrRoyl	TRGL		...	15461	4¼	2¼	3⅛	+ 9/16
TotlEnrgold	TGDGF		...	6341	3¼	1⅞	2 7/16	...
TradnlInd	TRADE		...	131934	10¼	2⅜	2¾	– 4¾
TrakAuto	TRKA		28	7637	12	7¾	8¼	– 2
TransFnlBcp	TRFI	.60	7	881	19	16	16½	– ⅛
TransInd	TRNI		...	5453	5⅜	1⅞	3¼	+ 1¼
TransLeasg	TLII		9	6386	2⅞	2	2¾	+ ⅛
TrWMusic	TWMC		20	62901	29¼	17¼	25	+ 1
Transmation	TRNS		9	18834	4¼	1⅝	3⅞	+ 2¼
TransNtlInd	TRSL		10	10180	3¼	1	1¼	– ⅛
Transnet	TRNT		...	18592	1 7/16	⅝	1	– 5/16
Transtech	TRTI		...	8891	5¾	3⅛	3⅛	– 2⅜
Transtectr	TTOR		...	19533	1 5/16	7/16	7/16	– 9/16
TranwdBcp	TWBC	†	9	2407	19	11¾	16⅞	+ 5
TrenwickGp	TREN	.30e	12	55137	26⅞	13¾	24½	+ 10
TriadSys	TRSC		5	131408	4 15/16	3⅛	3⅝	...
TricoPdts	TRCO	1.00	...	2474	61	44	44	– 17¾
Trimas	TMAS		...	28537	51½	31½	37⅜	...
Trimedyne	TMED		35	184290	21¾	5¼	6¼	– 13¼
Trion	TRON	.09	12	77255	10	4¾	5¼	– 1⅛
TristateBcp	TRIB	.66e	9	1229	22¾	14	17	+ 2
TrustCoBcp	TCBC	.96	11	6248	44	27½	37½	+ 7
TrustCoBkNY	TRST	1.20	10	3995	33	25⅜	30½	+ 4⅝
TrustBk	TRBK		...	6719	10¾	5	6	– 3¾
Trustcorp	TTCO	.75i	...	167064	31½	20	25⅛	– 1⅛
TsengLabs	TSNG		...	324664	6 11/16	1 13/16	3¾	+ 1 15/16
TuckerDrll	TUCK		...	9959	7¼	4⅛	6⅞	+ 2¾
TudorCp	TDRLF		...	3432	25/32	¼	9/16	...
TuesdyMorn	TUES		13	21701	15½	6¾	13⅝	+ 5⅞
TuscaroraPl	TUSC	.25e	15	6424	25¾	17	23½	+ 6½
20CentInd	TWEN	.48	7	181984	24⅞	16⅛	23	+ 6½
TycoToys	TTOY		9	208200	25⅛	11⅞	22⅛	+ 9⅞
TycoToys wt			...	52865	10⅞	3	9	+ 5⅜
TysonFood	TYSNA	.04	16	392270	26¼	14¾	24⅞	+ 7⅝

-U-

Stock	Symbol	Div	Yld	Sales 100s	Hi	Lo	Last	Net Chg
UNR Ind	UNRI		9	21067	6½	3⅜	4⅞	+ 1 7/16
UNR Ind wt			...	4653	2⅛	1	1¼	...
UNSL Fnl	UNSL	.48	6	3968	15½	10¾	11¼	– 1
USA Bcp	USAB		5	10422	7¼	3½	4	– 1½
USMX	USMX		29	72616	6	1⅜	2 1/16	– 1 3/16
UST Cp	USTB	.63	7	27753	20½	14½	15⅝	– 1⅞
UTL Cp	UTLC		2	34719	7⅛	1½	1⅜	– 2⅝
UniMart	UNMAA	.10	15	13121	8	5⅝	6¾	...
UnicoAm	UNAM		5	20780	6⅛	3⅛	4	– 1⅛
Unifi	UNFI		10	224303	17⅝	10¼	13¼	+ 2⅞
UniforcTemp	UNFR	.10	15	21538	18¾	11½	12¼	– ¼
UnigeneLab	UGNE		...	57584	2 1/16	¾	2	+ 1
UnigeneLab wt			...	32700	11/16	¼	17/32	+ 7/32
Unimed	UMED		...	15928	3¾	1⅞	2¼	– 1

Stock	Symbol	Div	Yld	Sales 100s	Hi	Lo	Last	Net Chg
UnionBk	UBNK	1.32a	6	41016	32 1/4	22 1/2	23 3/8	- 2 1/8
UtdArtistsE A	UAECA		...	239720	23 3/4	17	19	...
UtdArtistsE B	UAECB		...	123287	23 5/8	17	18 7/8	...
UtdBkColo	UBKS	.15e	25	116856	23 7/8	11 5/8	20	+ 7 1/2
UtdBkshrsWV	UBSI	.68	...	9797	15 1/2	12 1/2	13 1/4	- 2 3/8
UtdCarBkshr	UCAR	.60	8	21619	17 3/4	13	14 1/8	+ 5/8
UtdCitiesGas	UCIT	.88	16	38451	15 1/2	12 1/4	14 7/8	+ 2 1/4
UtdCoasts	UCOA		7	31111	4 7/8	2 1/2	4 1/4	+ 1/2
UtdCosFnl	UNCF	.60b	8	6434	22 1/4	15 1/4	19	+ 1/4
UtdDomnRlty	UDRT	1.24	34	64154	19 1/8	16 7/8	18	- 1/8
UtdEdSftwr	UESS		...	107954	3 7/8	1/8	7/32	- 3 13/32
UtdFedBcp	UFBK	.36	...	86850	13 5/8	9 1/8	10 1/8	...
UtdFnlSC	UNSA		9	9433	15 1/2	11 1/4	13	+ 1 3/4
UtdFire	UFCS	1.20	8	4402	34 1/2	29	32 7/8	+ 2 3/8
UtdGaming	UGAM		15	102588	15 1/2	7 1/2	10 1/8	+ 1 3/4
UtdGuardn	UNIR		...	17926	10 1/4	4 5/8	7	+ 1 7/8
UtdHlthcare	UNIH		24	451114	12 5/8	4 1/8	12 1/8	+ 7 5/8
UtdHomeLf	UHLI	.30e	...	5162	5 1/2	3 7/8	5 1/4	+ 1 1/8
UtdInsur	UICI		14	11634	16	8 1/4	15 1/2	+ 7
UtdInvMgt	UTDMK	.30	15	38240	19 3/4	10 3/8	19 1/2	+ 8 5/8
UtdMoBkshr	UMSB	.80a	10	7255	32 1/2	24 3/4	30 1/4	+ 4
UtdNMFnl	BNKS	.25e	9	22498	17 1/2	11	12 1/4	+ 1/2
UtdNewsp	UNEWY	.73e	11	54086	16 7/8	12 1/2	15	+ 1 3/4
UtdSavers	USBI	.36j	...	88436	19 1/4	4	4 1/4	- 9
UtdSvgMont	UBMT	.40	11	12456	11	7 1/4	10 1/2	+ 3 1/4
UtdSvgOr	USBA		...	19407	21 1/4	8 1/2	20	+ 11 5/8
UtdSvgVa	USBK		...	7047	16 3/4	3	3 3/4	- 11 3/4
US BancpOre	USBC	1.00	10	317368	32 7/8	18 3/4	31 1/4	+ 12 1/8
USBancpPa	USBP		9	9836	15 5/8	9 1/2	13 1/4	+ 3 3/4
USBcp pf		2.12	...	1680	23 1/4	19	22 1/2	+ 3 1/4
US Engy	USEG		121	45918	8 3/4	5 1/8	8 1/2	+ 1 3/8
US Facilts	USRE		...	40460	4 7/8	1 1/4	4 1/2	+ 2 1/4
US Gold	USGL		29	198083	1 29/32	1	1 15/32	+ 3/16
US Hlthcr	USHC	.23	32	938684	15 1/2	5 1/4	13 7/8	+ 8 1/16
US Intec	INTK		...	15979	12	4 1/4	4 3/8	- 1 7/8
US PrecMtl g	USPMF		...	39621	1 9/16	7/16	13/16	+ 1/16
US Trust	USTC	1.52	12	48425	43 1/4	36 1/2	37	- 3/4
USWestNw	USWNA		...	273157	46 1/4	24 5/8	42 1/2	+ 17 1/2
UtdStatnrs	USTR	.40	10	205123	25 1/2	13 1/2	16	- 6 3/4
UtdTV	UTVI		53	16412	38 3/4	26 1/2	34 3/4	+ 7 1/2
UtdTote	TOTE		27	7354	14	8	12 3/4	+ 4 3/4
UtdVtBcp	UVTB	.68	8	7035	18 1/2	13 3/4	16 1/2	+ 2 1/8
Unitog	UTOG		30	50274	18 3/4	13 7/8	18 1/8	...
Unitronx	UTRX		...	49705	7 3/4	3 1/8	6 7/8	+ 1 3/4
UnivHlth	UHSIB	.20e	17	136375	11 5/8	6 1/8	9 1/4	+ 3
UnivHldg	UHCO		...	19813	2 1/2	1 3/8	1 5/8	- 3/8
UnivVolt	UVOL		...	9683	1 13/16	7/16	5/8	- 13/16
UnivrstyBkCA	UNNB		11	502	38	20 1/2	30	+ 9 1/2
UpprPenEngy	UPEN	2.22	11	2144	28 1/2	25	27 1/2	+ 1
Urcarco	CARS		...	65502	17 1/8	13 1/2	16 3/8	...
UtahMed	UTMD		34	177057	10 7/8	2 7/16	9 5/8	+ 7
-V-								
VBand	VBAN		...	98955	13 1/4	3 1/4	4 1/2	- 3 1/8
VLSI Tech	VLSI		...	336039	10 1/8	6 3/8	7 3/8	- 1 1/8
VMS Mtg un		1.08	3	25825	8 1/4	2 1/4	3 1/8	- 4 1/4
VMS MtgII	VMTGZ	.07	7	79460	7 1/8	2 1/4	2 7/8	- 3 3/8
VMS MtgIII	VMORZ	.90	5	28634	7 5/8	2 1/4	4	- 2 3/8
VMS Land	VLANS	1.20a	5	45109	8 1/2	3 3/8	5 1/2	- 1 7/8
VMS LndTr II	VSLF	1.20	4	69093	8 1/2	3 3/8	4 3/8	- 3
VMX	VMXI		...	185252	4 3/8	1 13/16	2 1/4	+ 1/2
VSB BnCp	VSBC	.50	...	44637	14 1/2	8 3/4	12 1/4	+ 3
VSE	VSEC	.28	8	1583	12 3/4	8 1/2	8 1/2	- 4 1/2
VWR	VWRX	.80	15	23245	22	16 1/4	16 3/4	- 3 3/4
Valcom	VLCM		8	5311	11 3/4	9 3/8	10 3/4	+ 1
ValidLogc	VLID		13	644303	6 1/2	3 3/8	4 1/8	- 7/8
Vallen	VALN		20	980	54	35	54	+ 19
VallyBcpWI	VYBN	1.04	10	19837	27 1/4	22 1/2	24 3/4	- 1 1/8
VallyCap	VCCN	.80	11	10851	36	20 3/4	33 3/4	+ 12 3/8
VallyS&LCA	VFED		...	106493	14	2 5/8	3 1/8	- 10 1/8
VallyBcpNJ	VNBP	1.36	9	9312	28 1/4	24	24 3/4	- 1 3/4
VallyNtlAZ	VNCP	1.08j	...	943631	31 7/8	11	12 7/8	- 11 5/8
VallyWestBcp	VWBN	t	...	3451	7 1/4	3 7/8	6 3/4	+ 2 7/8
Vallicorp	VALY		...	1967	6 3/4	3 1/2	5 3/8	+ 3/8
Valmont	VALM	.26	11	50281	20	11	18 3/4	+ 7 1/2
ValueLn	VALU	.60	18	9920	25 1/2	20 1/2	24	+ 3
VandbltGld	VAGO		...	47930	3 5/8	1 3/4	2 1/2	- 9/16
VanFedBcp	VANF		...	26581	13 1/4	6 1/4	12 1/4	...
VangrdCelu	VCELA		...	270744	41 3/4	20	35 1/8	+ 14 7/8
VREF I	VREOS		...	2797	10	7 1/2	8 1/2	...

Stock	Symbol	Div	Yld	Sales 100s	Hi	Lo	Last	Net Chg
VariCare	VCRE	.04	16	7025	5 1/8	3 1/8	3 3/4	+ 5/8
Varitrnic	VRSY		8	161274	23 3/4	4 3/4	6 7/8	- 16 1/4
Varlen	VRLN	.60	9	20762	30	17 3/4	18 1/4	- 2 1/4
VeloBind	VBND		600	30020	8 7/8	5	6	- 2 1/2
Vencor	VCOR		...	28247	8 7/8	6 3/4	8 1/4	...
VentrxLab	VTRX		25	65128	1 11/16	13/16	1	- 1/16
Venturian	VENT		...	2973	17 3/4	9	11 1/2	- 1 1/4
VtFnl	VFSC	1.00	7	15866	24 3/4	15 5/8	17 3/4	- 2 1/4
VeronxRes g	VEOXF		...	92162	5 3/4	2 1/2	4 3/8	+ 1 11/16
VersaTech	VRSA	.20	12	26857	17	11 1/2	12 1/2	- 1
VertxComm	VTEX		13	33467	6 1/2	3	6 1/8	+ 3 1/8
Vestar	VSTR		...	26191	7 1/2	3	3 3/4	- 2 1/4
VicorpRstr	VRES		19	121776	18 1/4	10 1/4	17 1/4	+ 6 1/8
VictBksh	VICT		...	12251	10 3/4	6 1/4	10	+ 2 1/2
VictCreatn	VITC		...	28483	5 1/4	4 1/8	5	+ 1/2
VideoDisplay	VIDE		9	16766	8 3/4	5 1/2	5 7/8	- 2 1/2
VieFrance	VDEF		...	23376	3 1/8	1 3/4	1 7/8	- 7/8
Vikonics	VKSI		...	25983	9 7/8	1 3/8	8 5/8	+ 6 3/4
VillageFnl	VIFS		...	15531	11	9 1/4	9 7/8	...
VillSprMkt	VLGEA	.15	10	16610	22	14 3/4	14 3/4	- 7
VinlandTr	VIPTS		...	15791	1 1/4	1/4	7/16	- 11/16
VipontPhrm	VLAB	t	29	163370	17	7 1/4	13 1/2	- 7/8
Viratek	VIRA		...	34734	15 1/4	5 3/4	6	- 6 3/4
VirgBchS&L	VABF		2	77725	10 1/8	3 3/4	4 1/2	- 7/8
VirgFstSvg	VFSB	.05r	...	4655	4 3/4	3 7/8	4 5/8	- 1/8
VistaOrg	VISA		...	49514	5/8	5/16	17/32	+ 3/16
VistaOrgLP	TVOPZ		...	120156	2 1/8	1 1/16	2 1/8	+ 7/16
VistaRes	VIST		7	7045	15 3/4	7 3/8	15 1/2	+ 8 1/8
Vitalink	VITA		16	347729	20 3/8	12	15 7/8	+ 3 1/8
Vivigen	VIVI		35	83799	27 1/2	6	22	+ 16
VoltInfoSci	VOLT		24	25990	18	10 3/4	12 3/4	+ 1/4
Volvo	VOLVY	1.84e	8	45582	81 1/8	60 3/4	72 1/8	+ 9 1/8
-W-								
WCRS Gp	WCRSY	.17e	...	3202	11 7/8	6 3/8	8 5/8	+ 2 1/4
WD40	WDFC	1.72	16	33682	38 1/4	30 1/2	32 3/4	+ 1
WLR Foods	WLRF	.44	9	8786	32 1/4	15	25	+ 7 3/8
WNS	WNSI		...	3451	7	2 3/4	3 3/4	- 3 1/4
WPP Gp	WPPGY	1.19e	9	33103	26 1/8	19 1/8	21 3/8	+ 1 1/8
WSMP	WSMP	.16j	31	7602	9 1/2	6 1/4	6 1/2	- 2 5/8
WTD Ind	WTDI		5	174886	17 1/4	6 1/2	10 1/2	+ 1 1/8
WainwrghtBkTr	WAIN		...	9931	14 1/4	9 1/2	10 1/4	- 3 1/2
Walbro	WALB	.40	53	19608	19	11 3/4	16 1/2	...
WalkrTel	WTEL		...	51934	2	3/8	1	- 5/16
WalltoWall	WTWS		...	3902	4 1/8	2 1/2	2 3/4	- 7/8
Walshire	WALS	.20	7	2838	8 1/2	6 1/8	8	+ 1 7/8
Waltham	WLBK	.48	12	20390	11	5 3/4	6 1/4	- 3 1/4
WarehsClb	WCLB		57	27061	5	1 5/8	2 7/8	+ 1 1/4
WarrnBcp	WRNB		...	26171	7 1/2	3 1/4	3 3/8	- 3 5/8
WarwkIns	WIMI		...	19369	6 1/4	1/2	1	- 4 7/8
WashnBcpNJ	WBNC	.28	...	22657	17 1/4	6	7	- 5 3/4
WashnBcpDC	WWBC	.28	14	15108	19 1/2	14 1/2	16 1/2	- 1/2
WashnEngy	WECO	1.32	15	107571	22 3/8	13 3/4	22 1/8	+ 8 1/4
WashnS&LWA	WFSL	1.32	9	124328	47 1/2	24 1/2	36	+ 10 3/8
WashnSvgOR	WFOR	.30	15	37373	15 3/4	7 1/8	13 1/2	+ 5 1/2
WashnSvgDC	WFSB		...	9826	6	3 3/4	4	- 1
WashnSvgWA	WAMU	.40	10	483012	27 1/8	13 7/8	18 5/8	+ 4 5/8
WashnSvgWA			...	12670	52 3/4	43	44 3/4	...
WashnSvgBk	WSBX		6	3766	3	1 1/2	1 7/8	- 7/8
WashnSci	WSCI	.20	7	24830	10 1/2	7 3/8	9 3/4	+ 1
WatfdWedg	WATFZ		...	6264	14 7/8	6 3/8	8	- 6 1/2
WaterhsInv	WHOO	.12e	10	3142	6	3	4 1/2	+ 1 3/4
WatrInst	WTRS	.08e	...	4012	4 3/4	3 1/4	3 7/8	+ 1/2
WattsInd	WATTA	.16	20	50893	37 1/2	27 1/4	36 7/8	+ 8 3/8
WausauPapr	WSAU	.69b	14	29400	39 3/4	27 5/8	34 1/4	+ 5 7/8
WaverlyPrs	WAVR	.36	60	12576	34 1/4	19 3/4	24 1/2	+ 4 3/4
Wavetek	WVTK		40	29364	6 1/4	3 5/8	4	- 1 7/8
WebstrClth	WEBS		...	13113	4	2	2 1/4	+ 1/4
WebstrFnl	WBST	.52	7	20583	13 3/4	9	9 1/4	- 1 1/2
Wegener	WGNR		18	25775	4 3/4	2 3/8	2 3/4	- 1 1/2
WeighTrnx	WGHT	.40	21	3839	24 3/4	18 1/2	18 1/2	- 3
Weitek	WWTK		22	176767	16 1/4	10 3/8	16 1/4	+ 4
WellgtnLeis	WLPI	.10e	14	13744	16 1/2	9 1/4	16 1/4	+ 6 3/4
WernrEnt	WERN	.12	14	46160	23 1/2	17	21 1/2	+ 2 1/4
Wesbanco	WSBC	1.20	8	1466	31 1/4	26 1/4	29 3/4	+ 1 5/8
WstCstBcp	WCBC		13	12192	4 1/2	1 7/8	3	+ 1/8
WMassBksh	WMBS	.28	11	5215	8	5 1/2	5 3/4	- 1 1/4
WNewtnSvg	WNSB	.28e	...	12651	10 1/2	3	4	- 4 1/8
WestOneBcp	WEST	.88	9	34356	27 1/8	19 1/2	22 3/4	+ 2 1/2
Westrbeke	WTBK		...	4528	2 1/4	1 5/16	1 3/8	- 3/8

OVER-THE-COUNTER

Stock	Symbol	Div	Yld	Sales 100s	Hi	Lo	Last	Net Chg
WestnBkOR	WSBK	t	...	2306	14 1/4	10	14 1/4	+ 4 1/8
WestCpInv	WECA		...	93404	13 7/8	8 1/8	8 3/4	− 7/8
WestFnl	WSTF	.03r	3	5498	6 1/4	3 1/4	3 7/8	− 1 1/8
WestSvgPR	WFPR	.80	5	4580	17 1/4	13 1/2	15 7/8	+ 5/8
WestWaste	WWIN		23	39076	33	14 1/2	32	+ 17 1/8
WestMicrT	WSTM		9	44257	8 1/2	5	5 3/8	− 7/8
WestMicrw	WMIC		...	8214	2 1/4	7/8	1	− 5/8
WestPub	WPGI		17	377903	23 1/2	16 5/8	19 5/8	+ 2 5/8
Westmrc A	WSMCA		...	43648	32 1/4	17	32 1/4	+ 14 1/2
WestmrkInt	WMRK		28	236425	51 1/2	26 1/2	46	+ 19
WestmorCoal	WMOR		14	31169	23 1/2	14 1/4	22 3/4	+ 7 3/4
WestonRoy	WSTNA		296	104027	16	7 3/4	8 7/8	− 6 7/8
WestportBcp	WBAT	.31j	...	4980	11 3/4	7 1/2	9	− 2 3/4
WestwdOne	WONE		...	359821	13 1/4	7 1/2	8 3/4	− 1
Wettrau	WETT	.60	16	102964	31 3/4	22 3/4	30 1/8	+ 6 3/8
WynbergSh	WEYS	1.00	12	795	57	39	57	+ 16 1/4
WharfRes	WFRAF		12	31830	6 3/8	3 7/8	5 1/4	+ 7/8
WholsaleClb	WHLS		26	132325	16 5/8	7 3/8	15 1/2	+ 7 3/4
WicatSys	WCAT		...	145390	2 1/2	1	1 3/4	+ 1/8
WilandSvc	WSVS		9	13169	4 1/2	1	3 1/2	+ 2
WileyJn A	WILLA	1.10	90	19791	69 1/2	40 1/2	53	+ 11 1/2
Willamet	WMTT	1.45	8	116160	55 1/2	41	55	+ 10 7/8
WillmWW	WWWM	.68	7	931	16 1/2	12 1/2	15	+ 1
WillmInd	WMSI		44	7238	13	8 3/4	12 1/4	+ 1/2
WillmSnoma	WSGC		27	24223	29 1/4	12 5/8	28	+ 15 1/8
WilmTr	WILM	1.24	11	71351	46 1/4	26 1/2	37 3/4	+ 10 1/2
Windmere	WDMR		12	86524	27 1/8	17 3/4	26 1/8	+ 8 3/8
WisSoGas	WISC	1.18b	15	708	34 1/2	25 1/4	34 1/2	+ 8 3/4
WisToy	WTOY		20	48294	14 1/2	8	12 1/2	+ 4 1/4
WiserOil	WISE	.40	36	47188	21 5/8	13 3/4	21	+ 7
WolfFnl	WOFG		...	13769	7	5 1/4	6 1/4	+ 1/2
WolhnLmbr	WLHN	.28b	9	51149	25	15	16 1/2	− 1 5/8
WolvExpl	WEXCC		...	215550	13 3/4	5 3/4	13	+ 6 1/2
WolvExpl wt			...	44689	8	1 5/8	7 3/4	+ 4 7/8
WoodhdInd	WDHD	.60	11	18312	16 3/4	12 1/4	15 1/4	+ 3
Wordstar	WDST		...	104181	3 1/4	1 5/16	1 7/16	− 13/16
WkgMenBk	WCBK		...	5625	9 7/8	3 3/4	4	− 5 1/4
WrldWdTech	WOTK		...	9395	5 1/4	2	3	− 1/2
WorthtnInd	WTHG	.56	17	260585	25 1/2	20 5/8	23	+ 1/4
WymnGord	WYMN	.80	...	140064	20	14	14 1/2	...
WyomNtlBcp	WYNB	.20e	8	2737	15 3/4	12	15 1/4	+ 3 1/2
-X-Y-Z-								
XL Data	XLDC		8	188261	27 1/2	7 1/4	10 3/4	− 6 1/2
XOMA	XOMA		...	323160	24 1/2	12 1/2	21 3/4	+ 8 1/2
X-Rite	XRIT	.08	18	19358	12 1/2	8 1/4	11 3/4	+ 2 3/4
Xicor	XICO		8	419025	8 3/8	3 1/4	4 1/4	− 3 5/8
Xplor	XPLR	.15j	...	5344	7	3	6 1/2	+ 2 1/4
Xscribe	XSCR		...	21522	1 3/4	7/16	9/16	− 1 3/16
Xylogics	XLGX		10	24795	11 1/8	7 1/2	7 3/4	+ 1/4
Xyvision	XYVI		...	95339	7	2 1/4	2 1/2	− 1 7/8
YankeeEngy	YESS	.76e	14	40855	23	19 1/4	21 1/2	...
YellowFrght	YELL	.76	12	331817	32 7/8	23 7/8	26 3/4	− 4 7/8
YesClothing	YSCO		...	11123	9 1/8	7 1/2	7 1/2	...
YorkFnl	YFED	.64b	7	11381	18 1/2	12 7/8	16 1/2	+ 7/8
YorkRes	YORK		17	84287	9 1/2	4 3/8	9	+ 3
YorkrdgSvg	YCSL		...	4093	5 1/2	3/8	3/8	− 3 7/8
ZSevenFd	ZSEV	.45e	...	4352	16 1/4	13	13	− 3 1/4
Zentec	ZENT		...	20618	13/16	1/8	5/32	− 1/4
ZeusCmpon	ZEUS		30	15750	3 1/2	2 3/8	3	− 3/8
Ziegler	ZEGL	.52a	14	2615	17 1/2	14 1/4	16 3/4	+ 2 1/4
ZionUtBcp	ZION	1.44	...	16125	33	20 1/2	27 3/4	+ 5 3/4
Zitel	ZITL		5	21797	5	2 5/8	3 1/4	+ 5/8
Zycad	ZCAD		14	123889	4 1/8	2 1/4	3	− 1/4
Zygo	ZIGO		31	3814	5 1/2	3 3/4	3 3/4	− 7/8
Zymos	ZMOS		1	76718	2 5/16	5/8	25/32	+ 3/32

Sales figures are unofficial.

f—Share volume in ten thousands; last four zeros omitted.

g—Dividend or earnings in Canadian money. Stock trades in U.S. dollars. No yield or PE unless stated in U.S. money.

h—Temporary exception to NASDAQ qualifications.

n—New issue in the past year. The range begins with the start of trading in the new issue and does not cover the entire year.

s—Split or stock dividend of 25 percent or more in the past year. The high-low range is adjusted from the old stock. Dividend begins with the date of split or stock dividend. The net change is from an adjusted previous year's closing price.

v—Trading halted on primary market.

Unless otherwise noted, rates of dividends in the foregoing table are annual disbursements based on the last quarterly or semiannual declaration. Special or extra dividends or payments not designated as regular are identified in the following footnotes.

a—Also extra or extras. b—Annual rate plus stock dividend. c—Liquidating dividend. e—Declared or paid in preceding 12 months. i—Declared or paid after stock dividend or split up. j—Paid this year, dividend omitted, deferred or no action taken at last dividend meeting. k—Declared or paid this year, an accumulative issue with dividends in arrears.

n—New issue. r—Declared or paid in preceding 12 months plus stock dividend. t—Paid in stock in preceding 12 months.

pf—Preferred. rt—Rights. un—Units. wd—When distributed. wi—When issued. wt—Warrants. ww—With warrants. xw—Without warrants.

vi—In bankruptcy or receivership or being reorganized under the Bankruptcy Act, or securities assumed by such companies.

OVER-THE-COUNTER

-A-

Stock	Sales 100s	High	Low	Last	Net Chg.
ACSEn	16836	2 11/32	1 9/32	2	+ 1/2
AFP	31815	1 13/16	7/8	1	− 3/16
APA s	9607	8 1/2	3 7/8	7 1/4	+ 3 1/4
ATC	38519	4 11/16	2	2 3/16	− 1/16
ATS Mny	10793	3 3/4	1 5/8	2	...
Abatix	10024	4 1/4	2 3/8	3 7/8	...
Abtx un	10091	9 7/8	5 5/8	8 7/8	...
ActnSt s	527101	1 3/16	17/32	5/8	...
Adelph h	10090	28 1/2	21	27 1/2	+ 6 1/4
AdCpt	15539	3 3/4	15/16	1 3/16	− 1/2
AdNMR	46099	4 3/8	2 1/2	2 1/2	− 1 7/8
A NMR wt	17239	4	3/4	1	− 3
AdvPr	93876	2 9/16	1 1/4	1 9/32	− 23/32
AdPrd un	1529	10 5/8	5 1/2	5 1/2	− 3 3/4
AdvLfe	18119	3 11/16	1 1/2	3 9/16	...
Advatex	15541	4 1/16	2	2 3/4	− 7/16
Aeroson	10505	1 3/4	7/8	1 3/16	− 3/16
AirSen	46460	2 3/8	1	1	− 5/16
AirInt	68210	3 7/8	11/16	2 13/16	+ 2 1/8
Alcide	136734	4 3/4	7/16	5/8	− 2
Alden .10e	4055	5	3 5/8	4 1/8	− 5/8
AlexEn	12664	15/16	1/2	11/16	...
AllATV	6264	3 3/8	2 1/4	2 1/2	− 1/4
Alpha1	30294	4 3/8	3/4	1 9/32	− 1 11/32
AlsFrm	19705	2 1/32	3/4	1 3/8	+ 9/32
Amribc .20	4770	22	17	18 1/4	+ 1/8
AAcft	159418	1 31/32	13/32	1 3/8	− 1/32
AmBcp1.10e	1000	26	22	22	− 3
AmBdy	34842	6 1/4	2 3/4	4 1/8	...
ABsCpt	121463	4 1/16	7/8	4 1/16	+ 3 1/8
ACty pf 1.50	11828	16 1/4	12 3/4	15	− 1 1/4
AClaim	4643	7 7/8	3 1/8	7	+ 3 1/2
AmDrg	47459	1 7/8	5/8	1 11/16	+ 5/16
AmFB	4491	7 1/4	4	4 1/4	...
AmFlm	108139	3 11/16	15/16	2 7/8	+ 1 3/8
AmFl wt	20163	2 9/16	9/16	1 1/2	+ 15/16
AmFl un	2910	6	1 7/8	4 1/8	+ 2 1/8
AFn pfD1.00	2177	10 1/2	10 1/8	10 1/4	+ 1/8
AFn pfE1.00	2087	10 3/8	10	10 1/8	...
AFn pfF1.80	1208	17	15 1/2	15 1/2	− 3/4
AmFran	18308	1 1/8	9/16	9/16	− 1/4
AShd rt	14290	1 1/4	5/8	1 3/16	...
AIM 843.58e	30000	18	13 1/4	13 1/4	− 2 1/8
AIM 851.51e	21027	17	12	12 1/4	− 2 1/2
AmMdTc	30094	3 7/8	1/4	9/32	...
AMetl	5073	2 1/4	1	1 3/8	+ 1/4
AMobl h	20321	4 1/8	1 7/8	2 1/4	− 5/8
ANtPt	9137	2 1/4	1 1/4	1 31/32	+ 5/8
AmNwk	91756	2 1/2	1 1/2	2 1/4	...
ANtwk wt	31701	1 1/2	1/4	1 1/4	...
ANtwk un	15315	8 13/16	5	7 1/2	...
ARecr .13	17405	7 1/2	7	7 1/2	+ 1/8
AScr pf	7588	12 1/2	3/16	1/4	...
AmVacn	14377	9 1/2	5 1/4	5 1/4	− 2
AmVisn	11555	2 5/8	15/16	15/16	− 13/16
AmAll .36e	3691	6	4	4 7/8	− 1 1/8
Amrhst s	158862	5 1/8	1 9/16	2 1/2	− 5/8
Amfx un	6929	5 17/32	4 3/4	5 3/8	...
Ampal pf.32	829	5 5/8	4 1/2	5 5/8	+ 1 1/8
Amtech	9431	4 1/4	1 15/16	4 1/8	+ 1 15/16
AnlySur	26967	4 7/8	2	2 3/4	+ 3/4
AndwGp	50154	7 1/4	3 3/8	3 5/8	+ 1/4
Angecn	83418	5 1/8	2 5/8	3 1/2	+ 1/2
Apco .62e	3533	7 3/8	4 3/4	7 3/8	+ 1 1/8
ApogRb	20565	2 13/16	1 1/4	2 5/16	+ 13/16
ApogeTc	22824	16 1/4	7	10 1/2	+ 1/2
Ap DNA	104490	1 3/4	3/8	15/16	− 3/16
ApdMicr	33708	5 3/8	2 3/8	3 1/8	+ 1/8
Aquant	49698	1 11/32	1/2	15/16	+ 15/32
ArchCm	186468	21	7	19	...
ArdenIn	8693	1 3/4	11/16	1 5/8	+ 15/16
Artagph	59919	4 5/8	3/4	3 3/8	+ 5/8
AtristG	25074	5	1 7/8	4 5/8	+ 2 5/8
ArytOp	3099	1 7/8	1 1/4	1 3/4	+ 1/8
Asar wt91	52357	19 7/8	10 5/8	16	+ 3 3/4
ASEA 1.13e	37070	116 1/2	62 7/8	116 1/2	+ 53
Astec wt	8524	6 1/4	1 1/2	2	− 4 1/4
AtlExp	14810	3 7/8	1 7/8	2 3/4	− 1/8
AtlnGp	1134	5 3/4	3 1/2	3 3/4	− 2
Ault	8756	2 3/4	1 3/4	1 7/8	− 3/8
AuraSy	191706	5 5/8	2 7/8	3 7/8	+ 7/8
Aurora	17463	2 1/4	3/4	1 1/8	+ 5/16
AuthDis	20543	3 7/8	2 1/2	2 1/2	...
AutDs un	35575	7	5 1/4	5 1/2	...
AutLng	18638	5	1 1/2	1 7/8	− 2 5/8
AutProt	48389	1 5/8	3/4	3/4	− 1/2
AutPr un	3817	7	2 3/4	2 13/16	− 3 15/16
vjAutIn	71860	4 1/4	3/8	7/16	− 3 5/16
Avry h	103378	2 1/2	1/2	9/16	− 1 1/16
AvonRnt	15737	8 5/8	3	5 1/4	...
AvnRt wt	2209	4	1/2	2 1/4	...

-B-

Stock	Sales 100s	High	Low	Last	Net Chg.
BI Inc	47681	7 3/8	2 5/8	6	+ 2 3/8
BaliJwl	43307	2 7/8	2 1/16	2 1/2	...
BaliJ un	28308	3 5/8	2 1/2	2 7/8	...
BncOn pf3.00	979	81	53	69	+ 15 1/2
BkMd	1485	23	16	16 1/2	− 5 1/2
Barrie	28843	4 3/8	2 3/16	2 1/2	...
BarLab	764	3 3/4	3 1/2	3 5/8	...
BargRs	21864	2 3/8	7/8	1 5/8	− 7/16
Barton	35234	5 21/32	5/8	4 7/8	+ 4 1/8
BsTnB	772	5 1/2	3	3 1/4	− 1 1/4
Bayly h	9350	4 1/8	1 1/2	1 5/8	− 3/8
Bayou	1437	7	4 3/4	6	− 1
Belmac	46056	7 3/8	3 3/8	5 1/8	− 2
BenhnA	75293	2 1/2	1 5/8	2 1/4	+ 1/4
Benhn wt	15902	5/8	5/16	9/16	+ 3/16
Benhn un	1414	5 1/2	3 3/4	4 3/4	+ 3/4
BntnOG	8552	10 3/4	4 3/4	9 3/4	...
Bntn wt	9396	3 5/8	1/4	2 5/8	...
BrnLei	47914	4 3/16	2 1/4	2 1/4	...
vjBcst pf3.50	5115	28 1/4	5 1/2	10	− 16 1/4
BioAnlg	25837	4 5/8	3/4	7/8	− 2 3/8
BimdDy	19539	3 3/8	1 1/4	3	+ 1 3/4
Bioject	44195	6 1/8	2 7/8	3 1/4	− 3/4
Bioplst	13419	3 1/8	15/16	3 1/8	+ 2 3/16
Biopore	84618	4 7/16	1	2 1/4	...
Biopr wt	63961	2 1/4	1/4	1/2	...
Biopr un	27035	20	5	8 3/16	...
Bioref	66388	3 13/16	2 1/4	2 5/8	− 1
BioMdP	32143	3 1/4	5/8	3/4	− 1/2
BiotcDv	14940	1 3/4	7/8	1 1/8	− 1/4
BiVasc	33536	4 1/16	1 1/4	2 3/8	+ 1/4
BiVas un	3455	5	1 1/2	3	+ 3/4
Birdl pf1.85	1543	16 3/4	14	16 1/2	+ 2 1/4
BlocDv	130370	3 7/8	1 3/8	3 11/16	+ 1 3/8
BobBrk	33109	2 7/8	1 1/4	1 1/2	+ 1/4
Bomed	15840	3 1/8	7/16	1 1/2	+ 13/16
Bons un	1299	5 1/4	4 5/8	5 1/8	...
Bwater .30e	2901	8 1/2	6 1/4	6 7/8	− 3/8
Bralrn g	2153	3/8	3/16	11/32	− 1/32
BrentB .72	2194	31	19 3/4	30 1/2	+ 10 3/4
Brilund	20033	5 3/4	13/16	2 7/8	+ 2 1/16
BristH s	20443	2 13/16	1 5/8	1 7/8	− 15/16
BrstR un	25789	5 3/4	1 5/8	1 5/8	− 3 3/8
BdcstIn	10474	3 7/8	1 5/8	3 9/16	+ 1 1/2
BldrDsg	43166	1 3/8	1/4	7/16	− 15/16
BldDg wt	4397	3/8	3/32	1/8	− 1/16
BldDg un	883	4 1/4	3/4	1 9/32	− 2 31/32

-C-

Stock	Sales 100s	High	Low	Last	Net Chg.
CBL Med	48941	4 9/16	1 15/16	3 11/16	+ 1 1/2
CBL wt	36419	1 11/16	1/4	1 3/8	+ 13/16
CNS	11847	3 7/8	2 3/4	2 3/4	− 1/8
CP Ovrse	3150	1 1/8	1/4	3/8	− 3/4
CTEC B s	6935	31	15	25 1/2	+ 10 1/4
C3 pf	1563	2	1 1/4	1 3/8	...
CblAp un	21443	10 3/8	5 1/2	9 7/8	...
Cadam pf	6044	2 1/8	1 3/8	1 1/2	− 3/8
Cadema	71576	1 3/16	1/2	1/2	− 1/16
CalGrph	1520	11	8 3/8	10 7/8	...
CalBi wt	2130	1/2	1/8	1/4	− 1/4
Calnetcs	4251	4 1/2	2 3/8	3 3/4	+ 1 3/8

	Sales 100s	High	Low	Last	Net Chg.
CamNt g	47700	6 1/4	2 7/8	5 9/16	+ 7/16
Cambex	4947	5 3/8	3 1/2	4 3/4	...
CanTr s	25786	8 1/8	2 5/8	2 3/4	− 4
CndlBk	1153	10 3/4	9	9 1/2	− 1/2
CanyRs	18777	2 5/8	1 5/8	2 5/8	+ 9/16
Caprck	105009	1 21/32	1/2	3/4	− 5/8
CardC un	1003	1 5/8	9/32	9/32	− 1 3/32
CardIn	22231	1 9/16	5/8	5/8	− 5/8
CareGp	26096	6 1/4	2	5 1/2	...
CaroFst †	2592	15 1/2	12	15 1/2	+ 3 1/2
CaroSth	1989	10	8 1/2	9	+ 1/2
CarolB	24642	6 7/8	3/8	3/8	− 5 1/4
Catlgrd	80333	1 9/16	7/8	1 3/8	...
Catlgd un	11421	8 3/4	4 3/4	8 1/2	...
CedrGp	22323	12 3/8	6 3/4	12	...
CedrG wt	6328	8 1/4	2 1/2	7 3/4	...
CedarI .52	1235	6 3/4	3 3/4	3 7/8	− 2 7/8
Celerex	67708	3 5/16	11/16	3/4	− 2 1/4
CellTc un	3044	9 3/4	2	3 1/8	− 5 5/8
Centcre	13252	1 5/16	7/8	1 1/32	− 7/32
CPcMn	40804	2 1/16	15/16	1 5/8	+ 3/8
CenTr pf2.62j	28839	13	3/8	5/8	− 12 3/8
CenT pfB2.67j	15878	13	3/8	1/2	− 12 1/2
CeramPr	7491	3 3/4	2	2 3/8	+ 1/8
Certron	15966	1 15/16	1 7/16	1 11/16	− 3/16
ChnlAm	24757	1 11/16	5/8	5/8	− 7/8
ChnlA un	3846	8 1/4	3 3/4	3 3/4	− 3 1/4
Chantal	177486	5	1 7/16	4	+ 2 1/16
ChkRobt	109865	8 3/8	4 1/4	6 3/8	+ 1 7/8
ChefInt	67232	3/16	3/32	3/32	− 1/32
CkRbt wt	17610	4	1 1/2	1 7/8	− 1/8
CkRbt un	1999	20 1/2	10 3/4	14 1/2	+ 3 3/4
Chemex	121780	4 3/4	7/8	1 1/8	− 1 5/8
Chx wt2	1313	3/4	1/4	5/8	...
Chmx wt94	31271	1 5/8	1/8	3/8	...
Chmx un	2918	7	3	4 1/4	...
Cherne	61045	8 3/4	2 15/16	5 1/2	+ 2 7/16
Chpwch	13627	1 11/16	7/8	1 1/16	− 3/8
ChcDrg	21863	3 7/8	1 1/4	1 5/8	− 1 1/2
Ciattis	1807	4 1/4	2 1/2	4	+ 1 3/4
Ciatti un	3023	6	3	6	+ 3 1/4
Cimm s	37399	6 3/8	1 3/4	5	+ 3 1/8
CircSy	40369	5 5/8	1 1/2	4 3/8	+ 2 1/4
Ciro	4999	3 1/4	1 1/2	3	+ 1
Citdl g	1728	2 1/8	3/16	3/16	− 1 13/16
CtzSec .08	5007	4	3	3 3/4	+ 3/4
CtyLTr	41791	2 1/4	1 3/4	1 13/16	+ 1/16
ClinTc	64928	16	4 3/8	9 1/8	...
ClnTc wt	39953	9 7/8	1/2	5 1/8	...
ColCm pf	9845	1	1/2	19/32	− 3/32
ColEngy .04	2518	7/8	7/16	3/4	− 1/8
CmclPr	23541	3	1 5/8	2 1/2	...
ComGrp	9661	3 1/8	1	1 1/16	− 1 15/16
CmtyBTn.18e	4444	9 1/4	6 3/4	8 3/4	+ 1 1/4
CmpRc s	99972	2 1/2	5/8	1 1/8	+ 11/32
Cpgd wt	41878	1 7/8	1/32	1/16	− 1 7/16
CptrCm	33444	1 9/16	3/4	13/16	− 7/16
CptNwk	108113	3 1/4	1	3 3/16	+ 1 15/16
Comvrse	f18070	21/32	3/32	7/16	+ 11/32
CtBcp	3948	5	3 1/2	4	− 3/4
ConqAr	11695	2 3/8	1 5/8	2 1/4	...
ConAr un	16998	9 3/4	6 5/8	9 3/4	...
ConsSv .50	1899	14 3/4	11 1/2	14	+ 1/2
CnsPrf g	1143	5/8	1/8	5/16	− 5/16
CtlGold	39768	9 1/8	2 1/2	7 3/4	+ 4 1/2
CtlVen	11714	5 1/2	1 7/8	1 7/8	− 2 11/16
Convoy	23263	1 11/16	13/32	13/16	+ 1/16
Copld pf	8243	9	4 1/2	5	...
CoralC s	f19554	1 5/8	1	1 3/32	...
CoralG	13790	5	7/8	1 7/16	− 3 9/16
Corken .16	2201	3 7/8	2	2 1/2	+ 1/8
CrpDt wt	22795	1 3/4	1/16	13/16	− 1/2
CorpIn †	2583	5 1/8	2 3/4	4	+ 1
Cortex	9367	1 5/8	7/8	1 1/32	...
Cortx un	9188	6 1/2	3 1/2	4 1/2	...
CreatL	3469	4	3 1/4	3 1/4	...
CrLr un	10951	9 1/4	6 1/2	7 3/4	...
CreatTc	45697	5 3/4	1 1/4	3 1/2	− 1/2
CredoPt	17513	2 3/16	1 5/16	2	+ 11/16

	Sales 100s	High	Low	Last	Net Chg.
CrwnBd	8007	2 7/8	3/4	1	− 1/4
CrwnA .40	3764	12 3/4	9 1/4	10 1/4	+ 1
Cusac g	14944	1 1/4	5/8	15/16	+ 3/16
Cutco .20	1761	6 7/8	3 1/2	3 1/2	− 1/2
CybrOpt	11542	6 1/4	3 1/4	5 1/2	+ 2 1/8
CytRxC	109186	2 1/32	7/16	1 23/32	+ 15/32
CytrxC wt	46712	31/32	3/32	21/32	+ 1/32
CytrxC un	5596	8 5/8	1 17/32	7	+ 1 1/2

-D-

	Sales 100s	High	Low	Last	Net Chg.
DMI	16996	3 1/2	1 1/2	1 7/8	+ 1/4
DSC	995390	17 1/8	6 3/4	14 1/2	+ 6 3/4
DSP	8708	1 5/16	1/2	1 1/8	+ 1/2
DSP un	6392	2 3/4	3/4	2 3/16	+ 11/16
DTI Md	31302	3 1/2	1	2 13/16	+ 5/16
DVIFn	12251	5 1/2	2	5	+ 2 1/4
DanlFd .20e	887	8	6	6 1/2	+ 1/4
DtSwt wt	1467	2 1/2	3/4	1 3/4	− 1/2
DtTrNw	13712	26 1/2	11 3/4	15 1/2	+ 3
Dtamg	176466	3 1/2	7/8	1 1/16	− 1 15/16
Datvnd	32872	2	1 1/8	2	+ 1/4
Datvd un	2205	7 1/4	5 1/4	6 7/8	− 3/8
DavWht .20	2366	11 1/2	7 1/2	8 3/4	− 1 1/4
DecisSy	13183	2 1/8	3/4	1 7/8	...
DefltPr	37100	2 3/8	15/16	1 5/16	− 11/16
DefltP un	7257	3 1/4	1 1/8	1 5/8	− 1 1/16
DnsePc	12107	2 1/8	5/8	3/4	− 3/16
Depren	17263	15 7/8	10 3/8	15 1/4	...
DigPrd	56393	3 1/16	13/16	3	+ 2 3/16
DigtlSol	43250	2 7/16	5/8	15/16	− 1 1/2
DimVsn	136196	5 3/8	1 7/8	3	+ 1/4
Divcr s	6345	4 3/8	1 1/4	1 7/8	+ 5/16
DivHum †	7383	5	29/32	2 1/2	+ 1 5/8
DixieN s	1961	1 1/4	3/4	1	− 1/4
DrRhb	13947	6 5/8	2	6 1/4	...
Docu un	10249	12	3 1/2	12	...
DblHlx	25320	3 5/8	1 1/2	2 9/32	...
DovrReg.14e	2537	7 7/8	5 7/8	6	− 1/2
DresBk4.53e	2079	258	152 1/2	258	+ 82
Drvfne	16124	1 7/8	7/8	1	...
DrgScr	25167	8 3/8	4	4	− 2 5/8
DynaGp	9567	3 1/8	7/8	2 7/16	...
DyntrL	62447	1 3/8	5/8	1	+ 3/16
Dyncp pf †	7759	17 1/4	11 3/4	15	+ 2 3/4

-E-

	Sales 100s	High	Low	Last	Net Chg.
Estmaq	36753	3 7/8	2	2 13/16	− 11/16
EcoSvg .10e	9100	15 1/2	9 1/2	10 1/2	...
Elctmd	98959	3 11/16	1 3/16	2 1/2	+ 1 5/16
ElcMis	14217	3 1/8	31/32	2 3/4	+ 1 1/4
Elctsrc	39945	6 3/8	1 3/4	2 1/8	− 3 1/2
Emons	1756	4 1/2	2	2 3/4	+ 5/8
EngCn h	84289	10 5/8	4 1/8	6 1/2	+ 5/8
ECnv wt91	3401	1/2	1/8	1/8	...
EngVen	11965	51 1/2	7 3/4	51 1/2	+ 43 1/2
Enscor	10636	2 1/2	1 11/32	1 9/16	+ 7/32
EnMon un	6065	8 1/8	1 1/16	1 7/8	...
Epitope	82591	9 3/4	4 7/8	6	− 1 1/4
Epolin	136395	1 5/32	1/2	13/16	...
EqtlA 1.08	919	34 1/2	22	30 3/4	+ 8 3/4
EqRes wt	13930	2 3/4	1	1 5/8	+ 1/4
EqtyGr	96501	1 5/8	5/8	11/16	− 3/8
EqtG pf	7661	3 5/8	1 5/8	1 3/4	− 5/8
Esprit	5242	5/8	1/16	1/16	− 1/4
EuroCr	141845	2 7/32	1 1/16	1 11/16	...
Excalb	33490	11 3/4	7 1/4	10 1/2	...
ExecBc	1286	9	5 3/4	5 3/4	− 3 1/4
Exovir	18634	7 3/8	2 3/8	2 7/8	− 4 3/8

-F-

	Sales 100s	High	Low	Last	Net Chg.
FB&T .80b	1174	26 1/4	22 1/2	24	− 1
FNB Cp.24b	3022	16	13 1/2	14 3/4	− 1
FahnVin	7662	2 3/16	1 5/16	1 1/2	+ 3/16
FalcnPr	3030	6 1/4	3 7/8	6 1/4	+ 2 3/8
FallFn	9780	14 1/4	12 3/8	13 1/4	...
FamShp	11133	2 1/16	7/8	1	− 9/16
FamSh pf.20	9125	3 1/8	1 1/8	1 1/4	− 3/4
Fibchm	21836	4 1/2	1 5/8	1 13/16	...
FidlMd	126619	3 13/16	3/4	2 1/2	+ 1 5/16
Filmst	47550	4 5/16	11/16	1 1/16	− 7/8

	Sales 100s	High	Low	Last	Net Chg.
FnBenA t	8879	4	2	2 3/4	+ 1/4
Fd SVP s	61309	2 9/16	1 1/4	1 1/4	− 5/8
Firetct	32829	2 1/16	1 1/16	2	...
Firtc un	5934	2 1/2	1 1/4	2 3/8	...
FABc pfg4.05	1266	46 1/2	42	44	+ 1/2
FAmHlt	14148	3 1/2	1 1/2	2 1/8	+ 5/8
FBkPhl	2039	9 1/4	7 3/4	8	+ 1/4
FtFdTn	1532	8 1/2	7 1/4	8	+ 3/4
FFncrp	1269	4 1/2	4	4	− 1/4
FtMed	15828	2 3/8	5/8	5/8	− 1 1/4
FtMd un	2003	7 3/4	2	2	− 4 5/8
FNtOh	2004	3	1 5/8	1 3/4	− 1
FRegBc	2082	4	2 1/8	3 3/4	+ 1 5/8
FtTeam	13096	1 3/8	3/4	1 3/8	+ 1/2
FUtdSv .60e	3528	12 1/4	9 1/4	10 1/2	+ 3/8
FishBu	65306	3 1/8	1 3/8	1 3/4	− 1 3/8
Fisons .74e	106848	23 1/2	16 1/2	22 1/8	+ 5 5/8
Foliage	37159	3 5/8	2 3/8	2 7/16	...
Foreind	40935	4 1/4	1	2 7/8	+ 1 9/16
FrmRe .01e	22357	5/8	1/8	1/8	− 7/16
FndrBk t	322985	11	6 1/2	7	− 3 3/8
4G Dta	11577	7/32	1/32	1/16	− 1/8
Franch	60672	2 3/16	13/32	11/16	− 1/4
Frnchtx	11412	6 1/8	3 3/8	3 3/8	...
FrJuce s	12311	2 3/8	5/8	1 1/16	+ 1/16
FrntDir	54772	2 1/16	9/16	31/32	...
FrntAd .04e	2555	3	1 3/8	2 1/2	+ 1
FrntSvg	3243	1 3/4	1 1/4	1 1/2	+ 1/8
FdAla .14e	1336	9 3/4	6 1/2	6 1/2	− 3 1/4

-G-

GTEC 56pf.90	1497	10 3/8	9 1/8	10 3/8	+ 1
GTEC 5pf1.00	2105	11 1/2	10	11 1/2	+ 1 1/4
Galgph	37711	1 3/4	1	1 5/8	+ 1/8
Galgr un	1426	4	2 3/4	3	− 3/4
GlxyCh	15439	5 1/2	2 7/8	4 7/8	+ 2
Gambro.23e	3507	21 5/8	17 3/8	20 1/8	+ 2
GnCom	53572	3 5/8	1 1/2	2 7/16	+ 13/16
GnNtr pf	14135	5/16	1/8	1/4	...
GenesCp1.20a	2638	51	32	32	− 6 1/2
Gentnr	9482	2 3/16	1	1 5/8	...
GeoTek	11380	3	1 5/8	2	...
GilMed	72239	4	1 5/8	1 3/4	− 1 3/4
GoVide	222074	14 5/8	3	5 1/2	+ 3/16
GoldCo	4870	5 1/2	2 1/8	2 5/8	− 1 1/8
GldStd	25840	4	2 3/8	3 5/16	+ 3/8
GldKngt	1186	10	6 1/4	9 1/2	+ 2 1/2
Goldex	3047	3 1/2	5/8	3 3/16	...
GrayEl	167946	19 1/2	11/16	7 3/4	+ 3 3/4
GtAMg	1369	32 1/2	18	24	+ 5 3/4
GrnstR	191717	1 25/32	15/16	15/16	...
GrnstRs	797	4 7/8	2 5/8	3 3/4	...
GrnwdB	2092	9 3/4	9	9	− 3/4
Grifith	4074	5 3/4	4 1/2	5	− 1/4
Gruene s	98347	10	3/8	3/8	− 4 7/8
Grudge	74038	1 11/16	3/4	1 1/2	...
GuarBn.20a	4042	8 1/2	6	6	− 1 1/2

-H-

HOH	35149	3 17/32	1 1/8	1 9/16	− 1 17/32
HOH wt	23907	1 21/32	1/2	23/32	− 11/32
HOH un	5918	15 3/8	5 1/16	6 13/16	− 5 11/16
HQ OfcS	237700	7	2 7/32	4 3/4	+ 2 9/16
Halador	11239	7/16	1/4	7/16	+ 5/32
HamDig	5394	3 3/8	5/8	5/8	...
HamO pf1.95	1111	19	16 1/2	18	− 1/2
Hrrier s	26836	3 13/16	1 3/8	2 3/8	− 1
HaywdS.25e	1085	14 1/4	11 1/2	14 1/4	+ 2 3/4
HlthCr	29591	3 1/4	1	2 7/8	...
HltCn wt	13730	2 1/4	15/32	1 3/8	+ 11/16
HltCn un	2997	12 3/4	4 7/8	9	+ 3 1/4
HltcrTc	30642	2 1/4	1 1/4	1 3/4	...
Hltcr un	8199	7 1/2	4 1/2	6 1/4	...
Hltplx	48973	2	3/8	1 1/4	+ 7/8
Hecks	24326	24	3 1/4	4 1/4	...
Helian	5030	6 1/4	4 1/2	6 1/4	...
Heln wt	7314	1 3/4	1	1 3/4	...
Heln un	8383	7 3/4	5	7 1/2	...
HemaC	38218	4 7/8	1 9/16	3 11/16	+ 2
Hema un	1292	11 1/2	3 1/4	7 3/4	+ 4 1/4

	Sales 100s	High	Low	Last	Net Chg.
Herblfe	74120	2 11/16	11/32	1 3/4	+ 1 11/32
HeritFn	10963	1 3/16	5/32	1/4	− 3/4
HertF pf .90	4948	6 1/8	3/8	5/8	− 5 3/8
Highldr	1018	2 1/8	17/32	1 31/32	− 1/16
Himed	22817	1 27/32	1/2	3/4	...
Himed un	12152	6 3/8	1 5/8	2 13/16	...
HmFChr	2410	11 1/2	9 1/2	10	− 1 1/2
HmeNtl .33i	7661	9	2 1/4	2 1/2	− 6 1/2
HUSB	11027	4	1 1/4	1 5/8	− 7/8
Hmcall un	20303	2 1/4	1	2 1/4	+ 1/8
Hornbk	41272	7 3/4	1 7/8	7 1/2	+ 4 5/8
HuntEn	128135	7 3/8	4 1/8	4 5/8	− 1
HydrFl	1739	7 1/2	3 3/4	4 1/2	...

-I-

Imre	82564	2 1/2	5/8	1 5/16	− 7/16
Incomnt	56038	3 3/4	1 1/2	2	+ 7/16
IPM s	221995	2 13/32	9/16	21/32	− 3/32
IdanSft	45186	10 3/8	7/8	1 19/32	− 4 13/32
Identix	14669	3 1/16	1 5/16	1 15/16	− 9/16
ImgFl un	3506	19	6 1/4	16 1/2	+ 10 1/4
ImagRtl	9290	1 1/2	3/4	1	...
Imatr 91wt	9549	3/16	1/8	1/8	− 1/16
Imtr un2	2905	1 1/4	5/8	21/32	− 5/32
Imex	27369	3 1/4	5/8	1 11/16	+ 15/16
Imtec	6695	7 1/4	1 1/4	4 1/2	+ 3 1/4
InHome	25300	1 11/16	13/16	1 21/32	+ 27/32
IHme un	16275	2	31/32	2	+ 1 1/32
Inamed	37757	3 1/16	1 3/8	2 1/4	+ 5/8
InBanc s t	727	15 1/2	7 1/4	13 1/2	+ 6 1/4
IndBkgp .72	1940	18	14	16 1/4	+ 2 1/4
IndSqS 1.56	5563	16 1/2	14	16	+ 1/2
IndiBn .48b	811	25	21 1/2	22 3/4	+ 3/4
InfMgt	30756	3 1/8	1 5/8	2 5/16	− 9/16
InfMg wt	19371	2 3/4	1 1/16	1 5/16	− 1 1/16
InfMg un	3836	17 1/2	8 1/2	10 5/8	− 6 1/4
Infrsnc	132016	4 1/16	1 3/4	3 3/8	+ 1 9/16
InldGld	61355	2 1/8	1 1/8	1 3/8	− 1/16
Inovxln	35238	1 1/4	3/16	1 1/8	+ 27/32
InstCp .20e	2693	15 5/8	10 3/4	12 1/8	− 3/4
InMedia	54607	2 29/32	1 1/32	1 1/8	...
Intrcim	21640	3	1 3/4	2 7/8	+ 7/8
IntEnt	117701	7/16	1/16	3/16	− 1/32
IntLfe	6800	34 1/2	9 1/2	33	+ 23 1/2
Intrfd	2802	7 1/2	6	6 1/8	− 5/8
IntmkG	42883	1 11/16	1/4	13/32	− 7/32
Intfrn	10660	6	3 1/8	5 1/4	+ 1 5/8
IntBkcd	41419	1 7/8	3/8	1 1/4	+ 5/8
InBkcd un	5176	10 1/4	3	6 7/8	+ 2 7/8
IntBarr	21082	10 1/2	1 3/8	1 1/2	− 6 1/2
IntBas	9223	3 1/2	3/8	2 1/8	+ 1 11/16
IBS	42173	11 1/2	1 1/2	2	...
IntlBus	88587	1 13/16	7/8	1 5/8	...
InCMOS	19946	2 1/2	1 1/8	1 1/4	...
IntCon	76876	5 3/8	1 7/8	2	− 1 7/8
IntMove	25956	1 15/16	7/8	1 7/16	...
IntPlat	9812	1 1/32	7/16	9/16	...
IntYog	6559	7	3 1/4	4 1/2	+ 1 1/8
Intphrm	2230	3 1/2	2 1/2	3 1/4	+ 3/8
IrwnU s .80	1897	32	22 5/8	27 1/2	+ 4 7/8
Isomet	5965	6 1/4	4 1/2	5	− 1/4
Isramc	86212	2 1/32	25/32	1 1/2	+ 23/32
Isram un	5276	4 7/16	1 7/8	2 13/16	+ 15/16
Isteclm	44168	4	2	3 3/4	+ 1/2

-J-

J2 Com	5626	5	2 1/4	3	+ 1/2
Jayark	14118	1 21/32	1/2	1 3/8	+ 7/8
JnPhilp	28346	1 5/16	7/8	15/16	− 3/16
JPhil un	1622	5 3/8	3 3/4	3 7/8	− 3/4
JeffBcp .50r	5417	14	11 1/2	12 1/2	− 1/2
JenfCv	18439	5 1/4	2	3	− 1 1/4
JifLub wt	1129	3 3/4	1/8	1/4	− 3 3/8
JrnEd un	17614	5	1 1/2	3	...

-K-

KCR	12257	3 3/4	1 3/4	2	− 3/4
KRM	9598	3 1/4	13/16	1 11/16	+ 7/8
KV Ph wt	1882	22 1/2	19 1/4	21	...
KnCtyL 1.04	9234	36	32 3/4	35 1/2	+ 1

	Sales 100s	High	Low	Last	Net Chg.
KaufHW.14e	2161	7 3/4	4 1/2	5 1/4	...
KeithG	10864	2 1/2	3/4	27/32	- 1 5/32
KelerIn	70721	3 13/16	5/16	11/16	...
KelyOil	24314	10 7/8	2 1/4	9 3/8	...
KeyCa un	7507	6 3/4	3 1/4	3 1/2	- 1 1/4
KiddePr	710	51 3/4	25	42	+ 17
KingCty.20j	1142	7 1/2	6 1/2	7 1/4	- 1/4
KirinBr.67e	756	160	123 1/2	140 1/4	- 12 3/4
Kleinrt	783	15 1/2	12 1/2	15 1/2	+ 3
Knwldg	154661	2 3/16	27/32	15/16	+ 3/32
KnwlW	54237	17 1/8	13 1/4	15 3/4	...
Krelitz	3361	3 1/2	1 1/2	3	+ 1 3/8
Krisch	19146	2 9/16	1	1 3/16	- 3/8
KushLk	269410	3 7/16	1 1/4	2 9/16	+ 1 1/16

-L-

	Sales 100s	High	Low	Last	Net Chg.
LJ Sim	17345	3 7/16	5/16	1/2	- 1 1/2
LSB SC .60b	1126	15	13 5/8	14 3/8	- 5/8
LaryIce	47358	1 19/32	1/2	21/32	- 11/32
LarDav	5605	4	1 3/8	1 5/8	- 2
LasVDsc	3107	2 3/4	1 7/8	1 7/8	...
LaserP	33840	3 3/4	2 1/2	2 15/16	- 1/8
Lasrtch	120206	2 5/8	1 1/4	1 1/2	- 3/16
LasT wt88	19170	27/32	5/32	9/32	- 1/8
LaurlSv .24	1675	15 3/4	9 1/2	15 1/2	+ 5 3/4
Leadvle	5940	3 1/2	1 1/8	1 1/8	- 1 1/2
Leak X	91707	2 1/8	1	2 1/8	...
Leeco	15298	3 5/8	1 7/8	2 1/4	- 3/4
LgndCo	51256	1 3/8	3/4	1 1/8	..
LgdCo un	7669	8 1/16	4 1/2	7 3/8	...
LehTH	3026	3 5/8	1 5/8	1 3/4	- 1 7/8
Leroy	15894	5 3/8	2 7/8	3 1/8	- 1 3/4
Lery wt	14216	1/2	1/4	3/8	+ 1/8
Lery un	5117	5 7/8	3 1/8	3 5/8	- 1 3/8
Levon	8279	7/8	1/4	13/32	- 11/32
Lifeway	6430	4 1/16	1 7/8	3	+ 1
LoJack	132384	6 1/16	3 11/16	4 11/16	+ 13/16
Logitek	11700	1 13/16	11/16	1 7/16	- 1/16
LouG 5pf1.25	766	14 3/4	12 3/4	14 1/2	+ 1 1/2
LouG pf1.86	838	22	19 3/4	22	+ 1 3/4

-M-

	Sales 100s	High	Low	Last	Net Chg.
MCM Cp	2073	9 1/2	4 3/4	4 3/4	- 4 1/4
MagelPt t	9577	1 29/32	1	1 1/2	- 7/32
MagnCp	54402	1 7/8	1 1/4	1 3/4	...
MgCp un	15378	2 1/2	1 3/8	2 3/8	...
MagnTc	8424	5 1/2	3/4	3 1/2	+ 2 3/4
MailBCs	58432	3/4	1/4	3/8	- 1/8
MgtCo	240752	4 1/4	2 1/8	3 1/16	+ 13/16
MgtC wt	137266	4 3/16	1 1/32	2 3/16	+ 1 1/8
MgtTc s	49698	9 3/4	2 1/4	4	- 5 1/8
MgtTc wt	10147	12 1/2	1 3/8	3 1/4	- 8 3/4
MarPet1.00e	1552	12 1/4	10 3/4	11 1/2	+ 1/2
MarwTc	147334	4 3/16	1 9/16	3 7/8	+ 1 13/16
Martch	2222	10	9 3/4	9 3/4	...
MtnzM unA	8229	6	1	4 1/4	+ 3
Mascott	36953	2 3/4	1 1/2	1 1/2	...
MassMic	26844	6 7/8	4 3/4	5	...
MeasSp	53454	7 3/8	2 1/8	3	- 7/8
MedcR	252498	16 1/2	5 1/4	14 3/4	+ 8 5/8
Medcros	61416	1 3/4	5/8	5/8	...
MediMal	24274	2 1/4	7/8	1 1/2	- 5/16
MediLg	14502	3 7/8	2 1/2	3	+ 7/16
MedDyn	39798	2 7/16	1 1/8	1 13/16	+ 5/16
MedDy un	7377	3 1/16	1 7/16	2 1/16	...
MedInn	30314	1 3/8	7/8	15/16	...
MedclSt	14616	4	1 3/4	1 3/4	- 1 1/4
MedTch	164540	2 9/16	17/32	1 7/32	+ 21/32
MedT un	9486	23 5/8	4 1/4	10 3/8	+ 5 1/2
Medphn	74488	7 1/2	2 5/8	4 1/2	+ 1 1/2
Megmtn	38192	1 7/8	1 1/8	1 1/2	..
Memtek	63466	2 3/8	5/8	11/16	- 1 3/16
Mercm	11819	15 1/4	12 1/4	12 1/2	...
MrdnNt	10360	1 11/16	1 1/4	1 5/8	+ 5/16
Mrdn un	18721	6 3/4	5	6 1/4	...
Metlcld	25030	4 1/4	1 1/2	1 3/4	- 1
Metlrg s	5418	13	5 1/2	12 1/4	+ 6 3/8
MetrCb s	16018	2 5/16	1 7/16	1 1/2	- 5/16
MicrHlt	7381	8 3/4	5	8 1/8	+ 3/8
MicrBi	26345	1 5/16	3/4	3/4	- 1/4
Microtl	8640	9 1/2	6	7 3/4	...
Mikron s	5303	3 3/4	29/32	2 3/4	+ 1 1/2
Milgray	942	19 3/4	13 1/2	15	+ 1
MingSv	13554	1 3/8	3/4	1 3/8	+ 5/8
Minorc .39e	444671	16 1/2	11	15 7/8	+ 4 1/2
MitekSy	34650	2 1/2	15/16	1 13/16	+ 1/16
MrRotr	22290	1 3/8	7/16	1 1/16	+ 9/16
Mizlou	217064	4 3/32	25/32	1 23/32	...
Mizl wtA	189651	3 5/32	1/8	1 1/32	...
Mizl wtB	157077	2 15/32	1/16	1 5/32	...
Mizlou un	51544	58 1/8	6 1/2	23 1/4	...
Moleculn	41394	2	1	1 1/16	+ 1/16
MonAnt	84306	7 3/8	2 3/4	5 3/8	- 3/8
MonPrM	18482	3 7/8	1/2	3/4	- 3
Moran	33632	5 1/4	2	2 1/8	- 3 1/8
Moran pf	16878	4 3/4	1 3/4	2 1/2	...
Moran wt	6180	5/8	1/4	1/2	...
Muscoch	9711	3 5/16	1 1/2	1 5/8	- 1 5/8
MtlFdl .40t	8577	11 3/4	5 3/4	10 1/2	+ 4 3/4
Mylex	102582	2 5/8	1 1/8	1 9/16	- 5/16

-N-

	Sales 100s	High	Low	Last	Net Chg.
NDL	19526	2 7/8	1 3/16	1 7/16	- 5/16
NMR	23811	5 1/2	2 3/4	3 7/8	+ 1 1/8
NY COM	320721	2 1/16	7/8	1 11/16	+ 13/16
Naham	9397	2 1/2	7/8	1 1/2	+ 3/8
NEnvC	12179	1 5/8	1/2	3/4	- 7/16
NtHer un	6415	3 1/8	5/8	1 7/16	...
NLamp	11008	5 7/16	2 7/8	4 5/8	+ 1/4
NTeam	22110	5 23/32	7/8	1 1/16	- 2 5/16
Neogen	9993	6 1/8	4 3/4	5 3/4	...
Neolens	183291	3 27/32	1 3/32	3 1/32	+ 1 15/32
Neoln un	5060	4 7/16	1 1/8	3 3/16	+ 1 15/32
Nestor	21991	7	3 7/8	4 1/2	- 5/8
Neurogn .20	32049	8 1/2	4 1/2	8 1/2	...
NE Bcp .20	4996	7 3/4	3 1/4	3 1/4	- 4 1/2
NE Rlty .68	2720	7 7/8	5 1/2	6 7/8	+ 1 3/8
NwGnFd	49410	3 1/2	1	1 1/2	...
NwMilfd	1544	14	6	6 1/2	...
NwRetl	46647	6 3/8	2 11/16	3 1/8	...
NobleR	2150	4 1/2	3 3/4	4 1/4	+ 1/2
NonlMnt	210543	1 7/8	1/2	1 3/16	+ 11/16
NoInv wt	63978	2 1/16	3/16	1 1/2	+ 1 5/16
NoInv un	3512	23	5	15 1/2	+ 10 1/2
NAmSv t	1985	5 7/8	4	4	- 1 7/8
NE Ins	22765	2 11/16	1 3/8	2 1/8	+ 5/8
NthLily	88715	3 1/8	1 7/8	2 5/16	- 9/16
NorTr pf3.12	9057	71	49 1/2	64 1/2	+ 14 3/4
NostNk	20067	2 7/8	11/16	2 1/8	+ 1 7/16
Noven	59202	3 3/4	2 1/4	3 1/4	+ 3/4
Nowsc g.12e	54329	14 5/8	10 1/2	13 1/2	+ 2 1/4
Noxso	40335	6 1/4	2 1/8	4 1/4	...
NutrPd	77684	2 7/8	1 1/16	1 13/32	...
Nytest	36048	1 9/16	3/4	15/16	- 7/32

-O-

	Sales 100s	High	Low	Last	Net Chg.
OKC un.40e	779	4 1/4	1 5/8	1 3/4	- 2 1/4
OMNI	11584	7	2 7/8	6 1/2	+ 2 1/2
ORS Cp	107713	3 1/4	11/16	13/16	...
OSHP un	4451	9	1 5/8	8 3/4	...
OccuMd	21348	8 1/2	2	3 1/8	+ 1 1/8
Oce-NY.80e	3327	31	26 1/4	29 3/4	+ 3
Odyssey	38062	1 15/16	13/16	15/16	- 11/16
Oficeld	8054	4 1/2	2	4 1/4	+ 3/4
OfcPrd	25708	1 7/8	1 1/8	1 19/32	...
OfcPd un	13620	7	4 9/16	7	...
OlKnt pf1.82	6277	46	35 1/4	43 1/2	+ 7 1/4
OldRp pf1.00	897	43	33 1/2	41 1/2	+ 8
OlyBdc h	12346	3 1/2	1/4	3/8	- 2 3/8
Oncor-	22953	3 1/32	25/32	2 11/32	+ 19/32
Optcrp s	38722	3 3/16	5/8	1 5/16	- 1 5/16
OptC un	13326	2 1/8	7/8	1	- 1 1/8
OrngSv .16	1039	11 3/4	7	7	- 2 3/4
ORFA pf.50t	1055	26	1 1/2	6	- 14 1/2
Origltl	5305	2 5/8	1	1	- 5/8
Overmy	2839	4 1/2	1 1/2	1 3/4	- 2

	Sales 100s	High	Low	Last	Net Chg.
Ovonic h	14987	3 3/4	1 1/2	3	+ 1 1/2
-P-Q-					
P F pf 1.00	1100	7 1/4	6	6 5/8	+ 1/4
P F wt92	4147	7/8	1/8	3/8	+ 1/4
PC Qut	6914	4 5/8	1 7/8	2 1/8	− 1 1/2
ParadF .35e	1290	10	6 3/4	9 1/2	+ 2 3/4
Parlux	20481	7 7/8	3 1/2	4 3/16	− 9/16
Periphl	188741	6 17/32	1 7/16	2 1/8	− 2 1/8
PerCpt s	15814	5 1/8	3 3/4	3 3/4	− 1 3/8
PerDia	59947	4	1 13/16	2 15/16	+ 1 1/16
PtHel vtg.08	8507	26	10	25 1/4	+ 15 1/4
PtHel nv .08	19191	27	9 3/4	26 1/2	+ 16 3/4
Phrmtc	17207	4 7/8	7/8	1 3/16	− 3 5/16
PhrmInc	13598	3	1 1/2	1 1/2	− 1 3/16
PhnxAd	327028	11/32	1/8	5/32	− 1/8
PhnxG s	4234	3 3/4	5/8	2 1/8	+ 5/8
PhnxLa	56503	3 3/8	1 3/8	2 3/8	...
PhnxL wt	19135	1 13/16	1/8	1 3/8	...
Phontel	22214	4 1/8	2 1/4	4	+ 1
Phontl wt	5753	7 1/2	13/16	7 1/4	+ 6 1/8
Phontl un	1156	26	8 3/4	26	+ 15 1/4
PhotSci	12033	3 3/4	1 3/4	2 3/4	− 1/8
PicktSu 1.10	10877	8 1/2	6	6	− 2 1/2
PicTl wt	98151	2 1/16	11/32	1 1/4	+ 7/8
Piemnt	1423	3	2	2 1/8	− 7/8
PiedMn	17398	1 5/16	9/16	7/8	+ 1/4
Pikevle .94e	1119	27	25	27	+ 1 1/2
PlasmT	37120	1 1/2	19/32	1 1/32	+ 3/32
PlexusR	5583	4 1/8	1 3/8	2 5/8	+ 1 3/16
PoeAsc .40	2879	12 3/4	8	12 3/4	+ 4 1/2
PlrMol	233344	5 7/32	1 1/16	1 3/16	− 2 5/8
PolrM wt	18875	5 15/16	1/2	1/2	− 3 1/4
PolrM un	1014	32 7/8	5	5	− 17 5/8
Polydex	30333	1 9/16	17/32	1 1/8	− 1/8
PolutRs	22585	2 3/8	1 5/16	1 1/2	− 1/8
PolRs un	43120	3 5/16	1 3/4	2	...
Polymrx	26745	5	2 1/4	3 3/8	...
PortsCl	7388	4 1/2	1 3/8	1 7/8	− 2 3/8
PwSpec	26842	5 17/32	3 3/8	5 1/2	...
PrabRbt	5037	5	2 1/4	2 1/4	− 2 1/2
PfdHme	160662	2 1/8	15/16	1 1/2	...
Prestek	15634	8 1/2	4 1/4	7 3/4	...
Prstk wt	17958	2 3/4	1/4	2 5/8	...
Prstk un	24232	11 1/8	5 1/4	10 1/4	...
PrestoT	11833	1/2	1/4	3/8	− 3/32
PrvBrd	33533	1 7/16	9/16	1	+ 5/16
PrvB pf .32	3805	3 3/8	1 3/4	2 3/8	+ 1/4
PrvB un .32	1729	4 3/4	2 1/2	3 3/8	+ 5/8
PrfHlt	7632	3 7/8	2 7/8	3 3/4	...
PrftTc	61976	4 1/8	3	3 1/4	− 7/8
PsycCp	96452	6 1/8	7/16	5 1/16	+ 4 1/2
PubcoC	81787	1	1/2	1/2	...
PurTc un	17174	6 5/16	4 1/2	6	...
Purflw s	21825	5 5/8	1 3/4	4 1/2	+ 3 1/8
PyrmO	3374	3/8	1/4	3/8	...
Q Med	38692	4 3/8	1 1/8	1 3/8	− 2
QSR	29232	4 3/4	3/16	4 1/2	+ 4 5/16
vjQintex	219808	10	1/2	19/32	− 2 29/32
Qdrax	58871	3 1/4	1 7/8	2 5/8	− 5/8
QualSy	10363	2 3/8	1 1/4	1 3/8	+ 1/16
Quartzl	8212	7 3/4	3 1/4	4 1/4	+ 1/2
QuebcSt	6288	1 13/16	3/4	1	− 5/8
QukslE	6077	3 3/4	2 5/8	2 3/4	...
-R-					
RCM	168459	7 7/16	3 1/8	5 1/8	+ 1 3/16
RF&P 1.00	8345	32 3/4	27 1/4	27 3/4	− 4 3/4
RHNB .40	1637	13	10	11	− 1 1/2
R Med s	99776	4 3/8	5/8	13/16	− 2 5/16
RSI Hld	1858	5/8	1/2	5/8	...
RadaEl	50774	2 13/16	1 7/16	2 3/4	+ 1 1/4
RadtnDs	41269	4 1/4	1 1/16	1 5/16	− 2 13/16
RailFn	1102	6	4	4	− 1 3/4
RamHO	14508	10 1/2	9 5/8	10 1/2	...
Ramtr s	29231	7 3/8	3 3/8	5 1/16	+ 1 11/16
RandCa	1627	4	2 3/4	3 1/8	+ 3/8
RndAcc	16179	2 1/8	3/4	1 3/4	...
Raycom	43194	2	1	1 3/4	+ 7/16
ReaGld	6021	3 1/4	1 7/8	2 1/4	− 1/4
RegBc pf	1298	10	7 1/2	8 1/2	...
RegFdl .40	1448	15	11 1/2	14 1/2	+ 3
RelbLfe1.20a	943	26	21	25 1/4	+ 3 1/4
RenGRX	95475	2 15/16	7/8	1 1/16	− 1 5/16
Rntrak	24153	3 1/2	1	2	+ 3/4
RschFt	10143	10 1/4	2	3 3/8	− 1 3/8
RespT pf	3528	4	1/4	1/4	− 2 3/4
Resurg s	46236	5 5/8	1 1/4	3 7/8	+ 1/8
RchCst	14701	1 13/16	5/16	3/8	− 1 1/4
Ritzys	2454	5/8	1/16	1/16	− 9/16
Roadmst	210638	2 5/16	1	1 7/32	− 31/32
RckwdN	16975	1 9/16	7/16	7/16	− 1 1/8
RkMCh	4268	6 1/8	1 5/8	5 1/8	+ 2 3/8
Rodime	33529	2 7/16	1/8	3/16	− 1 1/16
RoosInv	4201	1 13/16	1 1/2	1 5/8	+ 1/8
Ryka	384498	7 1/4	1 1/2	3 3/16	+ 1 11/32
-S-					
SI Hand	7487	6 1/8	2 1/4	4	+ 1 3/4
SOI Ind	70472	2 1/2	1 3/8	1 3/8	− 7/8
SOI wt	12909	1 3/4	3/4	3/4	− 3/4
S2 Golf	12855	2 1/16	5/16	1 3/4	+ 1 5/16
SageAnl	76716	7 1/4	2	6 1/2	+ 3 7/8
SageLb .20e	956	16 1/2	12 1/2	15 1/2	+ 3
SIM wt s	135601	18	4 1/8	14	+ 9 3/4
SndTc s	158705	2 3/8	25/32	1 5/16	− 1/4
Sandata	9654	3 5/16	1 1/4	2	− 1
SMonB s .60	2893	52	38	51	+ 5 1/4
Santos .58e	11676	13 1/4	10 3/8	12 7/8	+ 1 3/4
Sanyo .12e	2482	35 5/8	28 1/2	33 3/8	+ 3 3/4
Sasol .15e	5241	3 5/8	1 15/16	3 1/2	+ 1 9/16
Saztec	18518	5 1/4	1 3/8	4 3/8	+ 3
SchrHl	1788	35 1/2	26	34	+ 8
SciIm un	7601	5	3 3/4	5	...
SciMeas	96800	1 3/4	9/16	3/4	− 1/4
ScreBd s	102155	9 1/2	3 1/16	9 1/4	...
ScotLiq	73483	2 19/32	11/16	1 1/8	+ 7/16
ScrptSy	19882	1 7/8	7/8	7/8	− 1/4
Selvac	191621	3 7/8	1 11/32	2 17/32	+ 1 5/32
Selvc wt	50260	2 29/32	9/16	1 3/4	+ 1
Selvc un	4271	26 7/8	8 1/4	17 1/2	+ 8 3/4
Senetek	145118	4 7/16	1 9/16	3 1/16	+ 1
Sntk wtA	18473	2 1/4	1/2	1 7/16	+ 3/4
Sntk wtB	15122	2	3/8	1 3/8	+ 11/16
SenrSv	41711	5 7/8	2 1/4	2 1/2	− 3 3/8
SevEnv	61690	25 3/4	15 1/4	16 3/4	...
ShrdTc	18782	6 1/2	3 7/8	4 3/4	− 3/8
Shredta	53180	7 3/16	11/16	6 13/16	...
Shilgh un	8207	2 3/8	5/8	1 3/4	− 1/2
ShrtShd	25807	2 3/8	1/2	1 7/8	+ 1 5/32
ShrInFn1.08	911	31	24 1/2	31	+ 5 5/8
Sirco	913	4 1/2	4 1/4	4 1/4	...
SkyChili	9278	4 1/2	2 3/4	3 7/8	+ 1 1/8
Skylink	11156	1 1/2	7/8	1 1/4	+ 1/8
Slatery4.00e	3142	40 3/8	25	25 3/4	− 4 1/4
Smtl wtA	8652	6	3 1/2	5	+ 1 1/2
Smtl wtB	29887	2	1/4	1 1/8	+ 1/8
SnelSnl	1102	8 1/2	6 3/4	8 1/2	+ 2
SftwrDv	11859	5	2 5/8	4 1/8	...
Solctr	24606	7 3/8	6	7 1/4	...
Solitec	36188	2 1/4	1 5/8	2	...
SolvEx	91105	2 15/16	1 7/16	1 9/16	− 5/16
SonexR	58858	3 11/16	1 1/8	1 7/8	+ 1/16
SonoTk s	44213	6 5/8	7/8	5 1/4	+ 4 3/8
SoElct h	922	6 1/4	2	6 1/4	+ 4 1/4
SouEdc	1543	8	4 3/4	4 3/4	− 3 1/4
SoPcPt	126490	31/32	13/32	19/32	+ 1/32
SoScLf s	741	2 1/2	1 15/16	2 1/4	...
SthldC	38052	13 1/2	3 1/2	8 7/8	+ 5 1/8
SthCm pf	3778	44	16 1/2	42	+ 25
Sthld pf h t	62261	12 1/4	1	1 5/8	− 10
SwtAir wt	27937	2 1/4	1/8	1/8	− 1/2
SpecRet	49730	3 11/16	2 1/4	2 3/8	...
SprtTch	11016	5 1/2	4	4	...
StdOil s	23992	9	3 3/4	5	...
StrlMed	32649	5	1/2	1 3/8	− 1 13/16
StevelC	39239	3 1/4	2	2 9/16	+ 9/16
Steve wt	7693	1 3/8	3/8	9/16	− 5/16
Steve un	2662	14 1/2	8 3/4	10 3/4	+ 1 3/4

	Sales 100s	High	Low	Last	Net Chg.
StrtAm s	34587	2 1/2	7/8	1 1/2	+ 1/4
Strings	5591	7 3/8	5 1/2	6 1/4	...
SuburB	872	5 1/8	4	5 1/8	+ 1 1/8
Sulcus	10755	4	3/4	1 3/4	+ 1
SumitTc	302591	15 7/8	2 3/8	8 1/4	+ 5 9/16
SunrFd	953	22	13	19	+ 4
SunPre	13598	2 3/16	13/16	1 5/8	+ 1/4
SunrsPr	8029	2 7/16	13/16	1 7/8	+ 7/16
SunrTc	29164	3 7/8	1 1/8	3 1/2	...
Sunrst	9153	6 1/4	3	5 7/8	+ 2 7/8
SupRt pf1.50	2920	6	3 3/4	5 1/4	...
SuprSol	66908	6 1/2	2	2 1/2	+ 1/2
Swank	17995	3 1/2	1	2 1/8	+ 1
Syntc pf	4073	15	1 1/4	1 1/2	− 13 1/2
-T-					
TEL Off.77e	24008	6	4 1/4	4 1/2	− 1/2
TSL	336699	1 1/8	1/4	25/32	...
Talcon	7773	1 25/32	13/16	13/16	− 13/16
TaroVt	11017	1 7/8	15/16	1 3/8	+ 7/16
Tauntn	19756	27 3/4	8	13 1/2	+ 5 1/4
TchKnit	19616	1 11/16	1/2	5/8	− 7/32
Tcknt un	7150	3 5/8	1	1 1/4	− 9/16
Techne	25858	1 15/16	1 1/4	1 3/8	...
Tchclne	32845	2 15/16	1 13/32	1 1/2	− 3/8
Tecngn	81560	5	1	1 5/16	− 7/16
Tchdy un	7811	2	3/8	3/8	...
TchMkt	11650	2 1/2	5/8	7/8	− 9/16
TchRsh	45994	2 5/16	1/2	1	+ 1/2
TelArt s	501302	9 3/8	7/8	2 1/8	− 7 1/4
Telenet	42162	2	1	1 5/16	− 11/16
Teltmr s	117644	3 3/8	1 1/2	2 3/4	+ 7/8
Teltron	27528	1 1/2	1 1/4	1 1/4	...
Telt un	4632	6 1/2	5 1/2	5 3/4	...
Tenet	9353	3 1/4	2 1/4	2 3/4	...
TeraM g	26386	3/8	3/16	3/16	− 1/8
Terano	10987	2 13/32	1 1/2	2 1/4	+ 1/2
TexAEn	12380	1 7/8	1 1/4	1 3/8	− 5/16
Texcel s t	47127	4 17/32	1	1 1/32	− 2 15/32
Texscn	55562	3 1/16	13/16	1 11/16	+ 3/8
Thrmln .04j	1676	4 3/4	2 3/4	3	− 1 3/4
3D Sys	78228	16 3/4	5	15	+ 9 1/4
TideR h.23e	3552	13	9 3/4	11 1/2	+ 1 1/2
TmeMgt	10193	3 5/8	1/16	1/16	− 1 15/16
Tinsly	1348	14 1/4	8 1/2	10	+ 1
TdyHm	25499	2 1/8	5/8	21/32	− 27/32
TopSnd	161864	4 1/8	13/16	29/32	...
TonToy	38568	4 11/16	3/8	3/8	− 3 13/16
TotlAst	24601	3	3/4	1 1/4	− 1 3/4
TotlHlt	73572	2 1/2	1	2 7/16	+ 1 5/16
TotalRs	75354	1 13/16	1 1/4	1 3/8	+ 1/8
TothAl	116287	23/32	1/8	5/32	− 7/32
TourM g	3103	5/16	1/8	1/8	− 3/16
TracePd	33983	1 7/8	7/8	1 7/16	− 1/4
Trnmed	12098	2 1/8	1 1/4	1 1/4	− 1/16
TrnsgS	35075	2 1/2	1 1/4	2 3/8	..
TrnsS un	6948	9	4 1/2	8 5/8	..
TrnspTc	13730	3	1 3/4	2 5/8	− 3/8
TribSwb	16826	1 1/4	1/2	1/2	− 1/4
Truvel	46293	4 1/4	1 5/8	1 5/8	− 2 5/8
TurfPar	2072	8 1/2	5 3/4	5 3/4	− 2 1/4
-U-					
USA Wste	25134	3 9/32	1 1/2	1 9/16	− 7/8
Ultimap	49788	3 3/8	7/8	2 9/16	+ 1 5/16
Unign un	9297	7 5/8	3 1/4	7 1/8	+ 2 7/8
Unilab	84652	5 3/16	1 7/8	5 3/16	+ 2 9/16
UnitC un	1229	10 1/2	5 1/2	10 1/2	+ 5
UAEn pf	9764	19 3/8	17 1/4	18 1/2	..
UCount 2.20	1020	62	59	59	− 2
UFedS .07	4780	3 7/8	2 1/2	3	− 3/4
UnFncl t	873	12 3/4	9 7/8	12 1/4	+ 2 1/4
UHrtg	14606	2 3/16	15/16	2 3/16	+ 7/16
UMobH	2989	3	2 1/4	2 7/16	+ 1/16
UBcNJ .92b	1037	36	26 1/2	26 1/2	− 7 1/2
US Pw un	1383	11 3/4	4 3/4	8 5/8	...
USRlty1.56e	4165	8	5 1/2	6	− 1 1/2
UnityH s	95659	13 1/4	1 1/2	11 1/8	...
UnvSec	14006	2	1	1 3/16	− 1/2
UranRs	3266	2 7/8	1 3/8	1 5/8	...
Utiltch	80743	2 13/16	1 5/8	2 3/16	+ 1/32
-V-					
VCS	93747	4 3/4	1/2	1 1/16	− 3 11/16
VHC	1442	5 3/4	3	3	− 3/8
VacDry	4808	5 1/4	3 7/8	4 3/4	+ 3/4
VlyFed	9100	9 1/2	4 3/8	9 3/8	+ 4 3/8
Varity wt	36519	11/16	1/8	3/16	− 5/16
Velcro	10722	21 1/4	14 1/8	21 1/4	+ 7
VentEnt	12550	11 3/4	8 1/2	11 1/4	...
Verdix	68642	2 3/8	1 5/16	1 9/16	+ 1/16
VersTc	10602	4 1/8	1 1/4	1 7/8	...
Versu un	34437	8 3/4	2 3/4	3 3/8	...
VidJuke	124665	9 5/8	2 1/2	9 5/8	+ 5 5/16
VidSup	27225	4 1/4	15/16	1 1/4	− 2 1/2
Vintage t	44211	2 7/32	17/32	23/32	− 3/32
VsnSci	19349	2 11/16	1 1/4	1 1/4	− 1 7/16
VisxInc	65889	15 1/8	3 3/4	5 1/4	...
Voicml h	29009	3 1/2	5/8	1 7/16	+ 9/16
Voit	15407	5 1/8	1 7/8	2 5/8	+ 19/32
VolunBc .66	1684	18 3/4	12	12	− 6 1/2
-W-					
WCW Wst	180081	3	5/8	2 7/16	+ 1 7/16
WashTr1.20	2029	28 1/2	22 1/2	23 1/2	− 3 1/2
WellHall	925	3 1/8	3	3 1/8	...
Wstcot	41266	16	8 3/4	10	...
WstwdR.20e	19161	2 13/16	1 11/32	2 1/16	...
WetrPr .50e	1690	12 1/4	7 1/2	11 3/4	+ 2 3/4
WhitPt	20401	1 1/2	5/8	1 7/16	+ 25/32
Wildey	17228	5 1/2	1 3/8	2	...
WilyJ B .98	906	68	51 1/2	52	− 1 1/2
WiscRE	1988	11 1/4	6	10 1/2	+ 4 1/2
WldwdCpt	6164	2 1/4	1 1/4	1 1/2	− 5/8
-X-Y-Z-					
Xeta	10593	3	1/2	5/8	− 1 5/8
Xsirus	2054	17 1/4	14 1/2	17	+ 2 1/2
XsirSup	10571	3 3/8	2	3 3/8	...
XsirS un	9351	15	8 1/4	15	...
XtraM un	7282	5 11/16	2 1/2	2 1/2	− 2 11/16
Xytron	15295	14	2 3/4	9 1/4	+ 5 3/8
Zeos	1791	8 1/2	7 1/4	7 3/4	...
ADRs List					
AngSA .87e	58563	30 1/4	15 3/4	30 1/8	+ 14 3/8
AngAG .42e	83578	10	6 1/16	9 7/8	+ 3 1/8
Blyvoor.01e	69828	3 7/8	2 1/16	3 1/16	− 5/16
Buffels1.68e	51775	21 3/8	10 1/8	18 3/8	+ 7 7/8
Burmah1.38e	10335	44 3/4	34 3/4	44 3/4	+ 10 1/2
DBeer .69e	720264	17 1/8	10 3/8	17 1/8	+ 6 3/8
DriefC s.55e	152986	15 1/8	8 1/8	14	+ 5 11/16
FreSCn .91e	113161	14 7/8	6 1/2	13 5/8	+ 6 1/8
FujiPh .16r	20587	78	42 7/8	62 1/8	+ 10 1/2
GoldFd1.01e	30129	28 1/2	13 3/4	28 3/8	+ 13 5/8
Highvld.28e	94843	5 3/16	2 1/32	3 13/16	+ 1 3/4
JapnAir.58r	1049	277	216	267 1/4	+ 18 1/4
KloofG .37e	159120	12 5/8	7 3/8	12	+ 4
Lydnbg .53e	18463	18 1/4	9 1/8	18 1/8	+ 9 1/16
Nissan .15e	11805	24 1/4	19 1/8	20 3/8	+ 1 1/8
OrangF2.42e	32352	34 1/4	16 3/4	33 1/8	+ 15
RankO .52e	24677	17 1/4	12 1/2	13 7/8	+ 7/8
StHlGd1.04e	26990	12 5/8	5 7/8	12	+ 5 1/2
TelMex	f88476	15/16	1/4	7/8	+ 19/32
Toyota .22r	22023	41 3/8	34 1/4	35 1/4	− 5 1/4
VaalRf .57e	250430	11 3/8	6 7/16	10 7/8	+ 4 3/16
WelkG .60e	29018	8 3/4	4 1/8	8 5/16	+ 3 1/2
WDeep1.70e	36606	51 1/2	25 7/8	51 1/4	+ 24 7/8

Footnotes on Page 155

OVER-THE-COUNTER

ANNUAL NASDAQ INDEXES

1989

	High	Low	Last	% Chg.
Composite	485.73	378.56	454.82	+19.3
Industrials	472.42	374.93	447.99	+18.2
Financial	567.23	457.79	505.64	+10.1
Insurance	561.34	424.74	546.01	+27.2
Utilities	788.51	500.81	737.20	+47.1
Banks	491.16	375.38	391.02	−10.2
Transportation	498.20	394.62	498.20	+25.9

1988

	High	Low	Last	% Chg.
Composite	396.11	331.97	381.38	+15.4
Industrials	413.09	334.85	378.95	+11.8
Financial	477.88	410.75	459.34	+12.9
Insurance	435.80	339.41	429.14	+22.2
Utilities	501.13	349.68	501.13	+41.0
Banks	460.78	396.44	435.31	+11.4
Transportation	403.68	320.91	395.81	+24.0

1987

	High	Low	Last	% Chg.
Composite	455.26	291.88	330.47	− 5.3
Industrials	488.92	288.30	338.94	− 3.0
Financial	542.04	382.43	406.96	−11.7
Insurance	475.78	333.66	351.06	−13.1
Utilities	441.61	301.51	355.30	+12.4
Banks	526.64	366.75	390.66	− 5.3
Transportation	436.53	276.03	319.21	− 8.5

1986

	High	Low	Last	% Chg.
Composite	411.16	323.01	348.83	+ 7.36
Industrials	414.45	326.56	349.33	+ 5.80
Financial	553.42	424.52	460.64	+ 8.77
Insurance	467.05	381.59	404.14	+ 5.78
Utilities	362.86	295.97	316.09	+ 4.81
Banks	457.59	346.35	412.53	+18.08
Transportation	365.81	288.13	348.84	+19.63

1985

	High	Low	Last	% Chg.
Composite	325.16	345.91	324.93	+31.4
Industrials	330.17	258.85	330.17	+26.6
Financial	423.52	298.20	423.49	+35.0
Insurance	385.45	276.33	382.07	+41.8
Utilities	303.84	234.87	301.57	+26.4
Banks	350.08	230.23	350.08	+52.0
Transportation	296.91	236.20	291.59	+21.9

1984

	High	Low	Last	% Chg.
Composite	287.90	231.93	247.35	−11.2
Industrials	336.16	250.18	260.73	−19.4
Financial	298.62	252.34	298.62	+ 7.6
Insurance	283.91	226.87	283.11	+ 9.9
Utilities	280.54	194.33	238.66	−11.4
Banks	229.77	192.99	229.77	+12.8
Transportation	290.70	194.33	239.29	−14.8

Annual Market Statistics

NYSE LEADERS

Of the total volume of 41,698,538,270 shares traded during 1989 on the New York Stock Exchange, the 25 most active securities accounted for 6,602,011,700 shares, or 15.8% of the aggregate sales. Individual volume, and closing prices, with the net change for the year of the 25 leaders are shown in the following table.

Issue	Sales(hds)	Last	Chg
AT&T	4620651	45½	+ 16¾
IBM	4023326	94⅛	− 27¾
General Electric	3576287	64½	+ 19¾
Exxon	3361985	50	+ 6
Union Carbide	3168541	23¼	− 2⅜
Texaco	2972602	58⅞	+ 7¾
USX	2866437	35¾	+ 6½
Eastman Kodak	2818632	41⅛	− 4
Philip Morris	2803425	41⅝	+ 16¼
Ford Motor	2638824	43⅝	− 6⅞
Warner Comm.	2561217	63¾	+ 27⅛
General Motors	2522732	42¼	+ ½
Citicorp	2388232	28⅞	+ 3
Amer. Express	2366779	34⅞	+ 8¼
Texas Utilities	2307984	35⅛	+ 7
Bank America	2257983	26¾	+ 9⅛
BristlMyrSquibb	2245272	56	+ 10¾
Phillips Pete	2139117	25¼	+ 5¾
McDonald's	2122531	34½	+ 10½
Navistar	2095026	3⅞	− 1½
Upjohn	2048366	38½	+ 9¾
PanAm	2042926	2⅝	+ ⅜
Unisys	2033333	14¾	+ 13⅜
Chevron	2030646	67¾	+ 22
AMR	2007353	58	+ 4⅜

WHAT NYSE STOCKS DID

	1989	1988	1987	1986
Advances	1565	1534	810	1597
Declines	694	679	1444	699
Unchanged	20	50	25	22
Total issues	2279	2263	2279	2318

NYSE BOND SALES

Total 1989	$8,836,374,000
Total 1988	$7,594,664,000
Total 1987	$9,726,244,000
Total 1986	$10,475,399,000
Total 1985	$9,046,452,000
Total 1984	$6,982,291,000

NYSE STOCK SALES

Total 1989	41,698,538,270 shares.
Total 1988	40,438,346,358 shares.
Total 1987	47,801,308,660 shares.
Total 1986	35,680,016,341 shares.
Total 1985	27,510,706,353 shares.
Total 1984	23,071,031,447 shares.
Total 1983	21,589,576,997 shares.

Annual Market Statistics

AMERICAN LEADERS

Sales, closing price and the net change for the 10 most active American Exchange stocks for the year 1989

Issue	Sales(hds)	Last	Chg
BAT Industries	1736816	13 5/16	+ 5¼
Wang Labs B	1236279	5⅛	− 3⅝
Texas Air	1191205	11½	− ⅜
Amdahl	989666	14⅜	− 5⅞
Echo Bay Mines	844343	18⅜	+ 4⅜
Fruit of Loom	823193	14⅞	+ 8½
DWG	644282	12	+ 5
Energy Servcs	569146	4⅜	+ 2⅜
Diasonic	503066	4 1/16	+ 1 13/16
Bolar Pharmact.	435436	18¼	− 3¼

AMERICAN EXCHANGE

STOCK VOLUME	
Total 1989	3,125,030,000 shares.
Total 1988	2,515,210,000 shares.
Total 1987	3,505,950,000 shares.
Total 1986	2,978,540,000 shares.
Total 1985	2,100,860,000 shares.
Total 1984	1,545,010,000 shares.
BOND VOLUME	
Total 1989	$709,010,000
Total 1988	$604,950,000
Total 1987	$684,965,000
Total 1986	$810,264,000
Total 1985	$645,182,000
Total 1984	$371,990,000

ISSUES TRADED

	1989	1988	1987
N Y Stocks	2279	2263	2279
N Y Bonds	2150	2226	2465
Amer. Stocks	1059	1095	1072
Amer. Bonds	239	257	277
Over-the-Counter	4872	5054	5441

NASDAQ LEADERS

Sales, closing price and the net change for the 20 most active NASDAQ stocks for the year 1989

Issue	Sales(hds)	Last	Chg
MCI Comm	4853772	44	+21⅜
Apple Computer	4545602	35¼	− 5
Intel	3843374	34½	+10¾
Sun Microsyst	2958495	17¼	+ ⅝
Seagate Tech	1992470	15	+ 6⅜
Jaguar	1966783	13¾	+ 9 1/32
Coral Cos	1955445	1 3/32	....
TeleComm A	1849148	17⅞	+ 4⅞
Oracle Systems	1822017	23⅜	+13⅝
First Executive	1679654	9¾	− 4
Liz Claiborne	1542000	24	+ 6¾
Microsoft	1353900	87	+33¾
Laidlaw Trans B	1319400	22⅞	+ 8⅜
LIN Broadcstg	1300200	120¼	+48¾
Lotus Devel	1297500	31	+12¾
Reuter Hldg	1228700	49⅝	+21¼
Micron Tech	1224300	9¾	− 6
McCaw Cellular	1169300	38¼	+11¼
3Com	1165600	13¾	− 8⅛
Boston Tech	1155900	8	....

Foreign Markets
Closing Prices of Selected Issues

	1989 Close	1988 Close

TOKYO
(in yen)

	1989 Close	1988 Close
Ajinomoto	2,840	3,000
Asahi Chem	1,260	1,060
Bk of Tokyo	1,960	1,700
BridgestnTire	1,690	1,360
C. Itoh	1,300	989
Canon Inc	1,830	1,490
Dai Nippon Print	2,390	2,710
Dai-ichi Kangyo	3,160	3,380
Daiwa House	2,770	1,980
Daiwa Secur	2,350	2,440
Eisai	2,140	2,090
Fuji Bank	3,630	3,690
Fuji Photo	4,470	3,570
Fujitsu	1,510	1,510
Hitachi Ltd	1,520	1,570
Honda	1,830	2,030
IHI	1,530	1,100
Isuzu Mot Ltd	975	881
Kajima Corp	2,210	1,850
Kansai Elec	5,020	4,800
Komatsu Ltd	1,380	924
MaruiDeptStr	3,640	3,050
Marubeni	1,170	836
Mazda	1,010	745
Matsushita Com	3,080	3,020
Matsushita Elec	2,320	2,540
Mitsubishi Corp	2,010	1,330
MitsubishiEst	2,490	2,650
Mitsui & Co	1,390	979
MitsuiRealE	2,940	2,900
NEC	1,870	1,960
NTT	1,470,000	181,000
Nikko Secur	1,920	1,870
Nintendo	15,000	9,500
NipponSteel	793	870
NomuraSecur	3,440	3,730
Ricoh	1,280	1,220
Sekisui House	2,440	1,900
Sharp El	1,860	1,120
SumitomoBk	3,730	3,960
SumitomoCh	920	946
Taisei Corp	1,620	1,260
Takeda Chem	2,320	2,650
Teijin	958	798
Tokyo Elec	6,190	7,050
Toshiba	1,270	1,010
Toyota Motor	2,540	2,540
Yamaha	2,080	1,860
YamaichiSec	1,930	1,860
Yasuda F&M	1,710	1,310

FRANKFURT
(in marks)

	1989 Close	1988 Close
AEG-Tele	306.00	196.80
Allianz Vers	2,440.00	1,869.50
BASF	300.00	279.60
Bayer AG	315.50	306.50
BMW	567.00	523.00
Cont'l Gummi	322.00	271.50
Commerzbnk	300.00	233.80
Daimler-Benz	830.00	738.00
Degussa	500.00	382.50
Deutsche Bk	843.00	563.30
Dresdner Bk	436.00	314.50
Hoechst AG	295.50	305.50
Lufthansa	200.00	147.50
Nixdorf	319.00	295.40
Porsche	850.00	633.00
RWE	434.00	227.00
Schering AG	833.00	565.00
Siemens	725.00	540.00
Thyssen-Hut	272.00	191.00
Veba	382.00	268.10
Volkswagen	543.00	348.00

LONDON
(in pence)

	1989 Close	1988 Close
Allied Lyons	496	438
Barclays Bk	571	406
Bass Ltd	1,053	797
BOC Group	559	427
British GE	237	158
BTR PLC	465	295
Cable&Wi	554	377
Cadbury Sch	346	338
Charter Con	436	455
Coats Viyella	143	146
Consol Gold	....	1,289
Dalgety	405	....
Glaxo	785	1,068
Grand Metro	628	430
Guest Keen	441	297
Guinness	686	334
HansonTrust	225½	154¾
Johnson Mat	338	339
Legal Gen	423	291
Lonrho	322	343
Lucas Indust	645	518
Nat'l WestBk	347	513
Nrthrn Food	256	282
Racal Elect	244	280
Redland	574	423
Reed Int'l	444	370
STC	245	269
Tate&Lyle	287	816
Thorn EMI	777	625
Trust House	311	251
T I Group	426	370
Ultramar	373	292½
Utd Biscuit	364	....
Vickers	211	286½
Wellcome	778	409

SOUTH AFRICAN MINES
(in U.S. currency)

	1989 Close	1988 Close
Bracken	1.03	.40
Deelkraal	4.73	2.25
Doornfontein	2.33	1.10
DurbanDeep	9.00	2.75
East Rand Gold	5.19	2.88
East Rand	5.25	3.87
Elandsrand	9.12	4.50
Elsburg	1.73	.90
General Mng	2.95	c14.50
Grootvlei	2.80	0.87
Harmony	8.30	5.62
Hartebeest	9.10	5.90
Impala	c18.25	9.00
Kinross	19.25	9.25
Leslie	1.93	3.00
Libanon	2.43	1.70
Loraine	3.58	1.50
Randfontein	8.75	6.12
Rustnbg Plat	23.25	11.88
Southvaal	46.25	28.00
Stilfontein	4.38	3.00
Unisel	7.06	3.37
West Areas	2.45	1.50
Winkelhaak	28.00	13.25

c-In British pounds.

SWITZERLAND
(in Swiss francs)
Zurich

	1989 Close	1988 Close
Brown Bov	5,130	2,750
Ciba-Geigy	3,740	2,645
Credit Suisse	2,665	2,700
Nestle	8,820	7,240
Sandoz	11,525	9,575
Sulzer	570	420
Swissair	1,215	1,080
Swiss Bancp	349	339
Union Bank	4,100	3,200
Zurich Insurance	5,220	

Foreign Markets
Closing Prices of Selected Issues

	1989 Close	1988 Close
BRUSSELS *(in Belgian francs)*		
Arbed	5,470	3,815
Gevaert	8,100	8,050
Gb-Inno-Bm	1,328	1,346
Metal Hobokn	22,300	11,900
Petrofina	12,100	13,600
SocGenerale	3,410	4,995
Solvay	14,900	13,200
MILAN *(in Lire)*		
Benetton	8,750	10,515
Ciga	5,090	4,335
Fiat	11,131	9,813
Generali	42,140	43,960
Mont Ed	2,080	2,093
Olivetti	7,415	9,000
Pirelli	8,940	7,350
Snia Visc	2,860	2,800
PARIS *(in French francs)*		
AirLiq	688	595
Aquitaine	510	384.5
BSNGrD	774	6,450
Club Med	700	535
Imetal	311	306.90
L'Oreal	4,965	4,400
Hachette	410	270
Lafar Coppee	1,591	1,414
MachBull	78.05	87.50
Michelin	168	196.10
PeugtCtn	825	1,392
Source Perrier	1,875	1,465
Total CFP	575	362.50
STOCKHOLM *(in Swedish Krona)*		
AGA b	236	219
Alfa Laval b	220	470
Electrolux b	280	293
Kone oy	800	415
Saab Scania	252	214
Skanska	557	425
Volvo	445	385

	1989 Close	1988 Close
AMSTERDAM *(in guilders)*		
AKZO	141.50	154.00
Ahold	135.70	89.70
Elsevier-NDU	80.80	62.90
Fokker	39.30	28.30
Heineken's	127	142.50
Holec	....	14.60
Hoogovens	87.80	75.00
Nation Neder	74.20	67.50
Nedlloyd	89	278.50
Robeco	107.60	97.40
Rolinco	106.50	92.80
Rorento	59.60	60.70
Wessanen	61.50	81.00
HONG KONG *(in Hong Kong dollars)*		
Bk of East Asia	17.70	19.80
Cheung Kong	9.65	8.05
Hang Seng Bk	24.20	28.80
Hong Kong El	7.75	7.05
Hong Kong Lnd	8.30	9.20
HongkongShBk	7.40	6.40
Hutchsn Whmp	8.80	8.60
Jardine Mathsn	24.40	14.60
SunHungKaiP	12.50	12.70
Swire Pacific	15.70	19.00
World Intl	3.55	4.37
SYDNEY *(in Australian dollars)*		
ANZ Bk	6.02	5.48
Central Norse	0.67	0.72
Coles Myer	8.40	8.62
CRA	11.75	7.84
CSR	5.30	4.40
Leighton Hld	0.80	0.60
Natl Aust Bk	6.56	6.20
News Corp	13.95	9.80
Pacific Dunlop	5.20	4.58
RensGldFlds	8.76	6.30
Santos	4.08	3.37
SouthrnPacPet	0.40	0.35
Westrn Mining	6.68	4.94
Westpac	5.40	5.28
Woodside Pete	3.13	1.88
Woolworth	....	3.61

Foreign Bonds

	Sales $1000	High	Low	Last	Chg
AfrDB 9½95	94	104⅞	97¾	104⅞	...
Asian 7¾96	1	94	94	94	...
AsiaDv 11⅛98	3	108	108	108	− 6
Asian zr92s	884	80½	70	80½	+ 9
Asian 10¾97	9	109½	101⅞	109½	...
Asian 8s01	10	88	82	88	...
Austla 9⅛96	594	103½	95¾	103½	+ 5⅜
Austla 9s96	136	100	94¾	99⅛	+ 2⅞
Austla 12¾92	231	110¾	107⅛	110¾	+ 1¾
Austla 13⅜07	296	110	106	110	+ 4
Austla 11⅜93	278	108½	102	108½	...
Austla 12⅛08	291	109	102	109	− ½
Austla 9¼96	141	104	101	103½	+ 4
Austria 11¼90	706	102½	100	100 9/32	− 27/32
CaisAut 9⅛97	317	100	94⅛	100	+ 2
Caisse 9.3s96	348	101¾	95	100	+ 1½
Cuba 4½77mf	1344	25	13⅛	23	+ 7
ElFra 9½95	49	101⅛	99	100	...
EurCS 9s96	552	100	97½	98⅝	+ ⅛
EurCS 8⅞96	140	100	96	99⅞	+ 4½
EurCS 9⅛97	551	102	96⅛	99⅜	+ 5⅜
EurCS 9¾99	180	100	96	98¼	− 1¼
EEC 11.6s99	234	105½	101¾	105	− 1
EurIn 8⅞96	268	99½	95½	99⅜	+ 3⅞
EurIn 9s97	453	100¾	94⅝	99¼	+ ¾
EurIn 8⅜92	225	99½	92	99½	+ 4¾
EurIn 9¼98	309	101½	95	100	+ 2
EurIn 9⅛98	388	101	97½	99¾	+ 4¾
EurIn 9⅞99	113	101	98½	101	+ 1
EurIn 10s99	158	101½	99⅜	101½	+ 3½
EurIn 10.15s99	158	102½	99½	102¼	+ 1
EurIn 11⅞00	311	109½	100	106	+ 2½
EurIn 13½00	373	110	105	110	...
EurIn 14⅝91	29	109	103¼	103¼	− 4¾
EurIn 13⅜92	21	109⅜	109	109⅜	− 8¾
EurIn 12⅝99	161	109⅝	106⅛	108	− 3½
EurIn 8¼98	67	98	93	98	+ 5⅞
EurIn 10⅛00	5	105½	105½	105½	− 1⅝
Ekspt 13⅜92	471	103½	101	103½	+ ⅝
Finlnd 8¾92	152	103	95¼	103	+ 4¾
Finlnd 11¾93	28	108	104	108	− 2
Finlnd 7.60s93	70	97	93	97	...
France 96s	20	34 25/32	34 25/32	34 25/32	...
HydroQ 10s08	301	104⅝	97¼	104⅛	+ 5⅛
Japan 9.70s92	7	102½	100	102½	− 2½
Mexco 8⅛97	257	85	77	79½	+ 2½
Mexco 10s90	257	101 1/32	95½	99½	+ 3⅞
NZeal 9⅞11	5	98	98	98	...
NipTT 13.35s94	525	111½	105⅜	110½	+ 1¼
NorgKb 9⅛98	67	98½	94⅞	97	− 2
NorgKb 9⅞99	33	115	99½	102	+ 1½
Oslo 8¾97	105	100	87¾	98⅛	+ 3⅞
OsterBk 11¼90	123	101½	100	101	− 3⅞
SocNC 9s92	236	100	94½	99⅝	+ 2⅛
Swed 9s97	356	101½	93	100	+ 6
Swed 9¼98	176	104	94	99⅝	+ 3⅝
Swed 11⅝99	121	110	102¼	110	+ 7⅞
Swed 11⅜00	72	107	103⅛	106	+ 2¼
Swed 12¾97	230	125	113½	122½	+ 8
Swed 8⅛96	283	98	91⅝	97⅞	+ 5⅜
SwedEx 15½90	47	106	106	106	− 9⅛
Tokyo 7½97	40	98¼	93	93	...
UK 8⅞93	195	101½	95¼	101½	+ 3⅜

Foreign Indexes

**Indexes are based on
local currencies**

FT Ordinary Index
(UK)

1989	
High	Low
2008.60	1447.80
1988	
High	Low
1926.2	1232.0
1987	
High	Low
1369.8	867.65
1986	
High	Low
1425.9	1094.3
1985	
High	Low
1146.9	911.0

Banca Commerciale Italia
Index (Italy)

1989	
High	Low
1237.00	874.00
1988	
High	Low
1229.0	661.0
1987	
High	Low
767.34	476.27
1986	
High	Low
908.2	454.67
1985	
High	Low
460.04	228.56

Swiss Bancorp Index
(Switzerland)

1989	
High	Low
679.00	466.60
1988	
High	Low
639.1	406.5
1987	
High	Low
734.2	453.9
1986	
High	Low
625.5	497.2
1985	
High	Low
587.9	388.7

ANP-CBS Industrial Index
(Holland)

1989	
High	Low
210.5	166.7
1988	
High	Low
327.5	192.2
1987	
High	Low
334.1	192.2
1986	
High	Low
301.0	240.4
1985	
High	Low
255.6	185.6

Foreign Indexes

Agefi (France)

	High	Low
1989	561.60	251.30
1988	393.1	241.1
1987	460.4	270.3
1986	414.3	267.8
1985	265.8	180.9

Commerzbank Index (Germany)

	High	Low
1989	1790.4	1271.7
1988	2061.1	1157.29
1987	2061.1	1221.9
1986	2278.8	1762.4
1985	1951.5	1111.8

Belgian Stock Exchange Index (Belgium)

	High	Low
1989	6805.3	5519.3
1988	5414.5	3508.3
1987	3558.97	2295.84
1986	4131.69	2766.91
1985	2986.36	2090.7

Asia-Pacific Stock Market Indexes

"Asian growth will likely outpace growth in the U.S. and Europe in the coming decade," says Glen Moreno, president of the London-based fund manager Fidelity International Ltd.

Nikkei Average (Japan)

The consensus emerging from 1990 forecasts is that Japan's Stock market won't slow anytime soon. Even cautious predictions call for the Nikkei Index to end 1990 above the 45000-point level, climbing from its 1989 close of 38916.

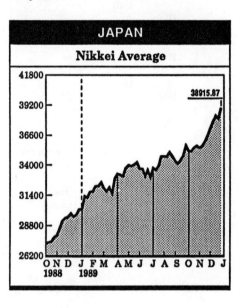

1989

January	High	31,581.30
	Low	30,183.79
	Close	31,581.30
February	High	32,452.49
	Low	31,360.68
	Close	31,985.60
March	High	32,838.68
	Low	31,443.24
	Close	32,838.68
April	High	33,713.35
	Low	32,805.92
	Close	33,713.35
May	High	34,266.75
	Low	33,716.29
	Close	34,266.75
June	High	33,981.35
	Low	32,913.09
	Close	32,948.69
July	High	34,953.87
	Low	33,190.38
	Close	34,953.87
August	High	35,140.83
	Low	34,431.20
	Close	34,431.20
September	High	35,689.98
	Low	34,113.66
	Close	35,636.76
October	High	35,678.49
	Low	34,468.69
	Close	35,549.44
November	High	37,268.79
	Low	35,270.46
	Close	37,268.79
December	High	38,915.87
	Low	37,132.68
	Close	38,915.87

1988

January	High	23,622.32
	Low	21,217.04
	Close	23,622.32
February	High	25,242.81
	Low	23,595.37
	Close	25,242.81
March	High	26,320.07
	Low	25,433.51
	Close	26,260.26
April	High	27,509.54
	Low	26,104.22
	Close	27,509.54
May	High	27,819.98
	Low	26,962.50
	Close	27,416.70

JAPAN

June	High	28,342.46
	Low	27,398.09
	Close	27,769.40
July	High	28,084.08
	Low	27,149.03
	Close	27,911.63
August	High	28,423.38
	Low	27,365.95
	Close	27,365.95
September	High	27,923.67
	Low	26,934.26
	Close	27,923.67
October	High	27,982.54
	Low	27,141.98
	Close	27,982.54
November	High	29,578.90
	Low	27,866.36
	Close	29,578.90
December	High	30,159.00
	Low	29,470.08
	Close	30,159.00

1987

January	High	20,048.35
	Low	18,544.05
	Close	20,023.55
February	High	20,766.66
	Low	19,531.52
	Close	20,766.66
March	High	22,026.66
	Low	20,933.82
	Close	21,566.66
April	High	24,097.79
	Low	22,040.18
	Close	23,274.83
May	High	24,772.39
	Low	23,419.60
	Close	24,772.39
June	High	25,929.42
	Low	24,176.40
	Close	24,176.40
July	High	24,636.46
	Low	22,702.74
	Close	24,488.11
August	High	26,048.17
	Low	24,172.60
	Close	26,029.22

September	High	26,118.42
	Low	24,795.24
	Close	26,010.88
October	High	26,646.43
	Low	21,910.08
	Close	22,765.04
November	High	23,282.18
	Low	21,036.76
	Close	22,686.78
December	High	22,956.84
	Low	21,564.00
	Close	21,564.00

1986

January	High	13,056.42
	Low	12,881.50
	Close	13,024.30
February	High	13,642.14
	Low	13,043.61
	Close	13,640.83
March	High	15,859.75
	Low	13,727.86
	Close	15,859.75
April	High	15,827.28
	Low	15,014.06
	Close	15,825.50
May	High	16,670.77
	Low	15,674.03
	Close	16,629.09
June	High	17,654.19
	Low	16,669.54
	Close	17,654.19
July	High	18,050.59
	Low	17,469.82
	Close	17,509.71
August	High	18,936.24
	Low	17,263.10
	Close	18,787.40
September	High	18,820.75
	Low	17,336.62
	Close	17,852.86
October	High	17,650.23
	Low	15,819.55
	Close	16,910.63
November	High	18,325.50
	Low	16,713.71
	Close	18,325.50
December	High	18,933.07
	Low	18,190.97
	Close	18,701.30

Hang Seng Index (Hong Kong)

Simon Dobson, a fund manager at GT Management (Asia) Ltd. in Hong Kong, says GT is taking different tacks in different markets this year. In the more developed markets— South Korea, Hong Kong, Singapore and Taiwan—the emphasis will be on shares that benefit from domestic demand, such as banks, property concerns and retailers.

1989

January	High	3072.86
	Low	2706.69
	Close	3072.86
February	High	3209.96
	Low	3012.68
	Close	3012.68
March	High	3150.85
	Low	2980.76
	Close	3004.98
April	High	3164.09
	Low	2987.21
	Close	3116.03
May	High	3309.64
	Low	2743.87
	Close	2743.87
June	High	2689.98
	Low	2093.61
	Close	2273.91
July	High	2571.08
	Low	2270.81
	Close	2571.08
August	High	2640.39
	Low	2487.94
	Close	2508.57
September	High	2758.25
	Low	2508.91
	Close	2758.25
October	High	2844.04
	Low	2601.70
	Close	2725.29
November	High	2820.28
	Low	2711.86
	Close	2748.35
December	High	2929.25
	Low	2754.11
	Close	2836.57

1988

January	High	2512.19
	Low	2286.29
	Close	2409.66

HONG KONG

Hang Seng Index

February	High	2418.08
	Low	2223.04
	Close	2418.08
March	High	2607.60
	Low	2454.71
	Close	2543.97
April	High	2684.13
	Low	2551.96
	Close	2602.87
May	High	2641.13
	Low	2488.99
	Close	2496.68
June	High	2719.06
	Low	2516.24
	Close	2671.49
July	High	2772.53
	Low	2647.41
	Close	2678.92
August	High	2703.42
	Low	2439.55
	Close	2443.80

HONG KONG

September	High	2525.14	November	High	2310.86
	Low	2423.23		Low	1960.90
	Close	2441.05		Close	2138.39
October	High	2627.41	December	High	2379.07
	Low	2415.76		Low	1894.94
	Close	2627.41		Close	2302.75
November	High	2666.02	**1986**		
	Low	2566.88	January	High	1826.84
	Close	2659.30		Low	1695.78
December	High	2696.44		Close	1695.78
	Low	2607.97	February	High	1783.08
	Close	2687.44		Low	1695.30
1987				Close	1695.30
January	High	2614.87	March	High	1695.77
	Low	2449.88		Low	1561.72
	Close	2553.25		Close	1625.94
February	High	2879.01	April	High	1848.65
	Low	2585.22		Low	1603.27
	Close	2877.87		Close	1836.99
March	High	2939.05	May	High	1865.65
	Low	2629.28		Low	1765.02
	Close	2713.81		Close	1787.90
April	High	2785.47	June	High	1789.78
	Low	2589.54		Low	1747.37
	Close	2659.85		Close	1754.19
May	High	2950.81	July	High	1855.46
	Low	2685.37		Low	1718.30
	Close	2919.70		Close	1855.46
June	High	3178.98	August	High	1950.12
	Low	2934.19		Low	1874.11
	Close	3178.19		Close	1913.00
July	High	3479.24	September	High	2068.44
	Low	3163.99		Low	1903.02
	Close	3479.24		Close	2068.44
August	High	3611.74	October	High	2355.93
	Low	3391.26		Low	2084.93
	Close	3611.74		Close	2315.63
September	High	3884.65	November	High	2418.75
	Low	3571.36		Low	2203.71
	Close	3943.64		Close	2418.75
October	High	3949.73	December	High	2568.30
	Low	2204.52		Low	2400.72
	Close	2240.13		Close	2568.30

Composite Index
(South Korea)

1989						
January	High	920.28		March	High	656.47
	Low	855.96			Low	603.41
	Close	884.29			Close	656.47
February	High	924.45		April	High	658.66
	Low	878.42			Low	618.73
	Close	917.90			Close	647.15
March	High	1003.31		May	High	717.34
	Low	909.72			Low	634.05
	Close	1003.31			Close	717.34
April	High	1007.77		June	High	737.83
	Low	927.96			Low	684.80
	Close	935.46			Close	702.73
May	High	951.09		July	High	719.05
	Low	924.59			Low	665.79
	Close	932.76			Close	717.08
June	High	994.80		August	High	714.83
	Low	854.61			Low	664.43
	Close	854.61			Close	664.43
July	High	902.38		September	High	683.73
	Low	846.30			Low	662.55
	Close	895.66			Close	677.54
August	High	983.37		October	High	764.85
	Low	889.41			Low	673.78
	Close	975.28			Close	729.79
September	High	984.10				
	Low	923.22				
	Close	942.41				
October	High	934.41				
	Low	891.30				
	Close	894.02				
November	High	932.25				
	Low	872.88				
	Close	872.88				
December	High	936.20				
	Low	844.75				
	Close	909.72				
1988						
January	High	642.11				
	Low	527.89				
	Close	642.11				
February	High	669.83				
	Low	612.35				
	Close	612.35				

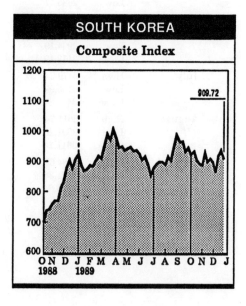

SOUTH KOREA
Composite Index

909.72

SOUTH KOREA

November	High	836.07	**December**	High	517.99
	Low	736.81		Low	465.36
	Close	831.12		Close	517.99
December	High	922.57			
	Low	825.00	**1986**		
	Close	907.19	**January**	High	160.42
				Low	153.85
1987				Close	160.42
January	High	306.02	**February**	High	177.78
	Low	264.82		Low	161.73
	Close	306.02		Close	175.91
February	High	364.16	**March**	High	199.76
	Low	305.53		Low	179.33
	Close	332.58		Close	199.76
March	High	412.15	**April**	High	217.00
	Low	337.85		Low	193.39
	Close	405.13		Close	202.71
April	High	398.72	**May**	High	229.47
	Low	349.49		Low	198.14
	Close	358.64		Close	229.47
May	High	397.62	**June**	High	250.68
	Low	364.55		Low	228.57
	Close	384.20		Close	243.36
June	High	411.76	**July**	High	274.15
	Low	378.21		Low	249.32
	Close	411.76		Close	273.75
July	High	485.48	**August**	High	273.97
	Low	411.11		Low	262.51
	Close	485.48		Close	264.78
August	High	507.07	**September**	High	268.18
	Low	467.32		Low	252.39
	Close	473.96		Close	253.45
September	High	498.17	**October**	High	258.43
	Low	464.89		Low	225.92
	Close	485.35		Close	240.79
October	High	517.15	**November**	High	269.18
	Low	491.60		Low	247.54
	Close	504.96		Close	266.50
November	High	510.28	**December**	High	279.47
	Low	455.77		Low	266.43
	Close	475.59		Close	272.61

Straits Times Index (Singapore)

1989

January	High	1134.81
	Low	1030.69
	Close	1133.32
February	High	1156.39
	Low	1108.31
	Close	1108.31
March	High	1194.63
	Low	1105.47
	Close	1189.78
April	High	1259.41
	Low	1186.66
	Close	1259.41
May	High	1310.02
	Low	1257.72
	Close	1279.24
June	High	1315.29
	Low	1207.11
	Close	1307.67
July	High	1372.29
	Low	1298.06
	Close	1372.29
August	High	1387.01
	Low	1342.54
	Close	1356.01
September	High	1420.52
	Low	1363.73
	Close	1375.25
October	High	1431.85
	Low	1285.04
	Close	1332.41
November	High	1411.28
	Low	1320.84
	Close	1411.28
December	High	1487.76
	Low	1415.92
	Close	1481.33

1988

January	High	924.06
	Low	833.61
	Close	908.90
February	High	901.69
	Low	851.82
	Close	888.84
March	High	969.45
	Low	890.28
	Close	925.82

April	High	965.94
	Low	917.68
	Close	965.94
May	High	999.29
	Low	956.03
	Close	999.29
June	High	1093.24
	Low	1006.44
	Close	1093.24
July	High	1152.50
	Low	1079.42
	Close	1143.41

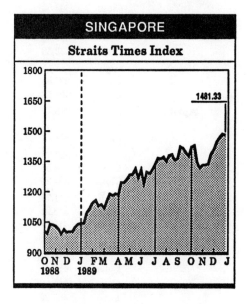

August	High	1177.87
	Low	1020.21
	Close	1036.59
September	High	1070.02
	Low	1022.28
	Close	1034.96
October	High	1044.47
	Low	993.18
	Close	1039.27
November	High	1032.67
	Low	997.83
	Close	1005.49
December	High	1044.20
	Low	993.16
	Close	1038.62

SINGAPORE

1987			1986		
January	High	957.97	January	High	644.89
	Low	882.24		Low	588.41
	Close	949.02		Close	607.32
February	High	1066.02	February	High	640.29
	Low	965.98		Low	611.33
	Close	1066.02		Close	623.27
March	High	1082.89	March	High	626.23
	Low	1011.07		Low	570.29
	Close	1056.77		Close	593.02
April	High	1140.37	April	High	597.41
	Low	1043.94		Low	563.34
	Close	1127.43		Close	570.20
May	High	1220.17	May	High	656.00
	Low	1131.98		Low	573.38
	Close	1220.17		Close	656.00
June	High	1265.70	June	High	776.89
	Low	1216.36		Low	683.30
	Close	1261.04		Close	741.22
July	High	1401.50	July	High	749.75
	Low	1261.18		Low	721.98
	Close	1399.80		Close	741.94
August	High	1505.40	August	High	838.48
	Low	1392.14		Low	741.31
	Close	1453.93		Close	838.48
September	High	1467.67	September	High	853.18
	Low	1358.07		Low	804.26
	Close	1398.28		Close	804.26
October	High	1454.30	October	High	937.37
	Low	778.94		Low	812.34
	Close	818.55		Close	937.37
November	High	878.05	November	High	940.64
	Low	780.83		Low	863.67
	Close	800.01		Close	866.89
December	High	833.15	December	High	901.61
	Low	700.45		Low	871.83
	Close	823.21		Close	891.30

All Ordinaries Index (Australia)

Australian equities aren't drawing much interest because of that country's dismal economic situation.

1989

January	High	1551.8
	Low	1470.6
	Close	1551.8
February	High	1531.3
	Low	1448.1
	Close	1484.6
March	High	1512.8
	Low	1458.7
	Close	1458.7
April	High	1498.8
	Low	1412.7
	Close	1498.8
May	High	1582.7
	Low	1490.7
	Close	1529.1
June	High	1544.6
	Low	1508.5
	Close	1520.8
July	High	1633.5
	Low	1501.5
	Close	1633.5
August	High	1781.6
	Low	1638.3
	Close	1763.2
September	High	1778.5
	Low	1686.6
	Close	1735.7
October	High	1775.6
	Low	1601.5
	Close	1646.2
November	High	1658.4
	Low	1600.5
	Close	1611.6
December	High	1651.8
	Low	1615.2
	Close	1649.0

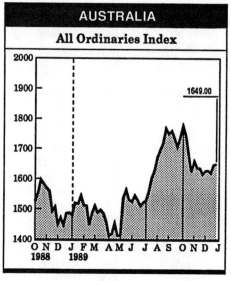

AUSTRALIA

All Ordinaries Index

1649.00

O N D J F M A M J J A S O N D J
1988   1989

1988

January	High	1321.9
	Low	1253.1
	Close	1257.2
February	High	1263.5
	Low	1170.5
	Close	1250.7
March	High	1448.9
	Low	1273.8
	Close	1415.8
April	High	1467.6
	Low	1407.2
	Close	1457.1
May	High	1566.1
	Low	1388.7
	Close	1566.2
June	High	1618.1
	Low	1544.8
	Close	1550.8
July	High	1641.8
	Low	1559.0
	Close	1610.8
August	High	1657.1
	Low	1570.1
	Close	1570.1
September	High	1571.5
	Low	1515.8
	Close	1548.4

AUSTRALIA

October	High	1585.0	**December**	High	1320.0	
	Low	1512.0		Low	1219.4	
	Close	1585.0		Close	1320.0	
November	High	1584.8				
	Low	1470.7				
	Close	1470.7	**1986**			
December	High	1486.6	**January**	High	1075.1	
	Low	1446.2		Low	1010.8	
	Close	1486.4		Close	1075.1	
1987			**February**	High	1075.6	
January	High	1553.6		Low	1039.7	
	Low	1486.8		Close	1050.1	
	Close	1496.4	**March**	High	1168.8	
February	High	1614.1		Low	1053.3	
	Low	1486.7		Close	1136.5	
	Close	1614.1				
March	High	1711.5	**April**	High	1218.7	
	Low	1615.6		Low	1129.7	
	Close	1689.9		Close	1210.6	
April	High	1799.9	**May**	High	1247.0	
	Low	1691.1		Low	1172.3	
	Close	1749.6		Close	1241.0	
May	High	1858.8	**June**	High	1230.2	
	Low	1744.6		Low	1179.8	
	Close	1770.8		Close	1179.8	
June	High	1827.7	**July**	High	1175.5	
	Low	1739.5		Low	1094.7	
	Close	1765.8		Close	1123.5	
July	High	2030.2	**August**	High	1192.3	
	Low	1774.0		Low	1120.2	
	Close	2030.2		Close	1192.3	
August	High	2163.1	**September**	High	1259.0	
	Low	2055.4		Low	1199.2	
	Close	2150.2		Close	1246.9	
September	High	2305.9	**October**	High	1377.2	
	Low	2157.7		Low	1253.6	
	Close	2247.6		Close	1377.2	
October	High	2253.4	**November**	High	1401.8	
	Low	1284.1		Low	1314.7	
	Close	1292.3		Close	1379.6	
November	High	1365.0	**December**	High	1473.1	
	Low	1150.0		Low	1376.8	
	Close	1328.7		Close	1473.1	

Composite Index (Philippines)

Manila's market has fallen from favor, after attracting substantial foreign investment prior to the late-November coup attempt against President Corazon Aquino. Until the government takes decisive steps to confront the country's economic and political problems, investors are expected to remain hesitant.

1989

January	High	863.94
	Low	828.21
	Close	838.02
February	High	870.31
	Low	804.62
	Close	870.31
March	High	933.13
	Low	864.37
	Close	909.39
April	High	1002.35
	Low	922.07
	Close	1002.35
May	High	1102.97
	Low	993.43
	Close	1038.88
June	High	1074.19
	Low	1012.72
	Close	1012.72
July	High	1198.02
	Low	976.30
	Close	1168.20
August	High	1217.44
	Low	1123.14
	Close	1126.51
September	High	1163.01
	Low	1127.46
	Close	1145.90
October	High	1309.37
	Low	1114.74
	Close	1309.37
November	High	1396.26
	Low	1310.44
	Close	1317.86
December	High	1211.82
	Low	985.66
	Close	1104.57

1988

January	High	877.27
	Low	812.28
	Close	815.50
February	High	838.47
	Low	752.23
	Close	752.23
March	High	788.70
	Low	729.42
	Close	744.39
April	High	788.19
	Low	727.42
	Close	788.19
May	High	817.91
	Low	765.49
	Close	795.35
June	High	880.76
	Low	804.59
	Close	847.21
July	High	893.10
	Low	844.38
	Close	870.99
August	High	880.59
	Low	741.81
	Close	786.15

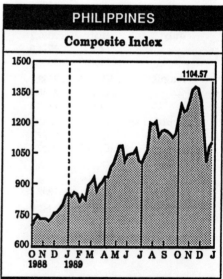

PHILIPPINES

Composite Index

1104.57

THE PHILIPPINES

September	High	774.85	November	High	777.61
	Low	694.85		Low	626.18
	Close	699.98		Close	692.06
October	High	746.30	December	High	813.17
	Low	686.10		Low	642.72
	Close	728.68		Close	813.17
November	High	737.82			
	Low	718.35	**1986**		
	Close	730.73	January	High	169.67
December	High	841.65		Low	160.85
	Low	739.70		Close	168.39
	Close	841.65	Feburary	High	219.22
				Low	164.87
1987				Close	219.22
January	High	527.85	March	High	230.26
	Low	442.27		Low	209.16
	Close	524.89		Close	230.26
February	High	539.85	April	High	236.93
	Low	499.62		Low	227.72
	Close	517.17		Close	232.23
March	High	514.40	May	High	231.69
	Low	449.81		Low	225.05
	Close	514.40		Close	226.71
April	High	575.98	June	High	312.79
	Low	507.70		Low	226.71
	Close	566.65		Close	312.79
May	High	610.59	July	High	391.33
	Low	552.51		Low	324.63
	Close	610.59		Close	351.46
June	High	950.37	August	High	377.78
	Low	613.58		Low	353.08
	Close	930.50		Close	368.42
July	High	1337.59	September	High	482.42
	Low	955.64		Low	386.26
	Close	1150.49		Close	476.83
August	High	1251.77	October	High	587.03
	Low	981.66		Low	465.91
	Close	1049.81		Close	533.80
September	High	1033.37	November	High	567.48
	Low	693.99		Low	486.55
	Close	745.59		Close	567.48
October	High	985.03	December	High	567.99
	Low	732.98		Low	489.90
	Close	743.37		Close	548.03

Bangkok S.E.T. (Thailand)

"In this less developed market, we are looking at the manufacturing sector," says Simon Dobson, a fund manager at GT Management (Asia) Ltd. in Hong Kong.

1989

January	High	435.09
	Low	391.23
	Close	433.68
February	High	447.41
	Low	432.24
	Close	435.78
March	High	444.02
	Low	429.18
	Close	440.88
April	High	502.64
	Low	443.71
	Close	500.21
May	High	540.18
	Low	501.83
	Close	552.54
June	High	606.21
	Low	554.90
	Close	606.21
July	High	628.44
	Low	607.97
	Close	624.13
August	High	682.55
	Low	616.67
	Close	681.92
September	High	724.93
	Low	686.52
	Close	689.51

THAILAND

Bangkok S.E.T. Index

879.19

O N D J F M A M J J A S O N D J
1988 1989

October	High	705.60
	Low	661.45
	Close	695.01
November	High	792.20
	Low	701.52
	Close	769.83
December	High	879.19
	Low	769.14
	Close	879.19

Weighted Price Index (Taiwan)

Analysts are keeping their exposure to the Taiwan market low because they see it as overvalued.

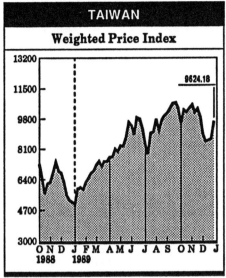

TAIWAN

Weighted Price Index

9624.18

September	High	10773.11
	Low	9910.18
	Close	10180.84
October	High	10602.07
	Low	9317.76
	Close	10602.07
November	High	10639.47
	Low	9040.09
	Close	9402.56
December	High	9624.18
	Low	8123.50
	Close	9624.18
1988		
January	High	2889.26
	Low	2341.06
	Close	2843.87
February	High	3499.01
	Low	2858.76
	Close	3499.01
March	High	3513.63
	Low	3200.34
	Close	3373.86
April	High	4158.44
	Low	3365.38
	Close	4158.44
May	High	4785.03
	Low	4171.08
	Close	4476.26
June	High	5241.08
	Low	4599.68
	Close	4846.03
July	High	6106.15
	Low	4984.73
	Close	6106.15
August	High	8214.46
	Low	6215.85
	Close	7680.48
September	High	8789.78
	Low	7581.59
	Close	8402.93
October	High	8206.43
	Low	5615.33
	Close	6153.49

1989

January	High	6157.12
	Low	4873.18
	Close	6157.12
February	High	7004.44
	Low	6236.72
	Close	7004.44
March	High	7628.91
	Low	7065.59
	Close	7390.15
April	High	8172.48
	Low	7075.74
	Close	7935.95
May	High	9846.15
	Low	8100.06
	Close	9832.38
June	High	10105.81
	Low	9120.54
	Close	9205.56
July	High	9504.20
	Low	7818.11
	Close	9504.20
August	High	10038.35
	Low	9145.46
	Close	9924.30

TAIWAN

November	High	7485.97	**December**	High	2957.01
	Low	6046.03		Low	2297.94
	Close	6814.11		Close	2339.86
December	High	6838.85			
	Low	4980.77	**1986**		
	Close	5119.11	**January**	High	889.41
				Low	839.73
1987				Close	882.95
January	High	1142.33	**February**	High	943.95
	Low	1039.11		Low	885.14
	Close	1142.33		Close	943.95
February	High	1253.76	**March**	High	986.20
	Low	1150.25		Low	926.13
	Close	1253.76		Close	926.13
March	High	1405.51	**April**	High	932.96
	Low	1262.26		Low	890.18
	Close	1405.51		Close	902.87
April	High	1812.99	**May**	High	946.19
	Low	1434.57		Low	885.86
	Close	1812.99		Close	946.19
May	High	1906.13	**June**	High	990.92
	Low	1697.35		Low	954.24
	Close	1857.22		Close	955.21
June	High	1878.61	**July**	High	995.99
	Low	1645.45		Low	935.83
	Close	1648.92		Close	935.83
July	High	2048.21	**August**	High	914.39
	Low	1618.02		Low	877.92
	Close	2048.21		Close	906.22
August	High	3075.23	**September**	High	947.11
	Low	2078.67		Low	906.81
	Close	3075.23		Close	947.11
September	High	4471.62	**October**	High	1017.16
	Low	3024.21		Low	946.17
	Close	4459.01		Close	994.44
October	High	4673.14	**November**	High	1026.78
	Low	2722.32		Low	978.96
	Close	2722.32		Close	996.24
November	High	2979.65	**December**	High	1039.11
	Low	2458.15		Low	995.46
	Close	2952.51		Close	1039.11

Barclays Index (New Zealand)

New Zealand is emerging from a serious recession, and analysts see potential profits there in certain shares.

1989		
January	High	1993.93
	Low	1837.67
	Close	1993.93
February	High	2098.00
	Low	1891.73
	Close	1891.73
March	High	1984.77
	Low	1881.04
	Close	1881.04
April	High	1970.67
	Low	1841.12
	Close	1970.67
May	High	2016.80
	Low	1884.99
	Close	1898.13
June	High	1933.91
	Low	1878.07
	Close	1919.68
July	High	1978.97
	Low	1901.98
	Close	1963.97
August	High	2429.06
	Low	1983.79
	Close	2429.06
September	High	2454.96
	Low	2243.80
	Close	2286.05

October	High	2327.11
	Low	2058.72
	Close	2113.48
November	High	2134.22
	Low	2058.20
	Close	2064.67
December	High	2074.47
	Low	1910.49
	Close	1994.46
1988		
January	High	1993.83
	Low	1832.01
	Close	1832.01
February	High	1827.71
	Low	1625.77
	Close	1625.77
March	High	2028.45
	Low	1646.27
	Close	2000.99
April	High	2032.34
	Low	1961.05
	Close	1997.86
May	High	2006.71
	Low	1919.79
	Close	1995.17
June	High	2035.30
	Low	1982.15
	Close	1989.97
July	High	2085.23
	Low	1933.26
	Close	2024.50
August	High	2071.31
	Low	1995.61
	Close	2026.44
September	High	2027.81
	Low	1944.92
	Close	1951.07
October	High	2045.81
	Low	1951.15
	Close	2020.37
November	High	2016.36
	Low	1846.65
	Close	1859.27
December	High	1842.69
	Low	1750.56
	Close	1839.94

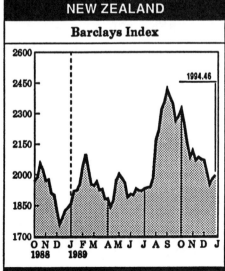

NEW ZEALAND

Barclays Index

1994.46

2600 · 2450 · 2300 · 2150 · 2000 · 1850 · 1700

O N D J F M A M J J A S O N D J
1988   1989